Goebbels

RALF GEORG REUTH

Goebbels

TRANSLATED FROM THE GERMAN

BY KRISHNA WINSTON

Harcourt Brace & Company

NEW YORK   SAN DIEGO   LONDON

HARCOURT
BRACE

© R. Piper GmbH & Co. KG, München 1990
English translation copyright © 1993 by Harcourt Brace & Company

Library of Congress Cataloging-in-Publication Data
Reuth, Ralf Georg, 1952–
[Goebbels. English]
Goebbels/Ralf Georg Reuth; translated from the German by
Krishna Winston.
p.   cm.
Includes bibliographical references and index.
ISBN 0-15-136076-6
1. Goebbels, Joseph, 1897–1945. 2. National socialists—
Biography. 3. Propaganda, German—History—20th century.
4. Germany—Politics and government—1933–1945.   I. Title.
DD247.G6R4913   1993
943.086′092—dc20   93-15900
[B]

Designed by Trina Stahl

Printed in the United States of America

First United States edition

A B C D E

Contents

Goebbels

Preface

Why a book on Joseph Goebbels, of all people? That is a question I have been asked repeatedly over the past few years. Sometimes the question left me at a loss: how to explain that I was motivated by an inner compulsion to confront the puzzling phenomenon of national socialism and its origins, a phenomenon that indelibly marked the face of the twentieth century? Another motive, more concrete if not decisive, for writing this book was the fact that the last book on Goebbels appeared twenty years ago, and the best documented one—that of Helmut Heiber—almost thirty years ago; both books drew on a rather modest body of source material compared to what is available today.[1]

This paucity of sources accounts for the divergent interpretations of Goebbels in the literature. The essays by Rolf Hochhuth and Joachim Fest offer diametrically opposed pictures. Hochhuth calls Goebbels "a man who swept others off their feet because he himself had been swept off his feet," while Fest sees him as "the ultimate Machiavellian."[2] Werner Stephan's book, published only four years after the war, makes Goebbels the "demon of a dictatorship,"[3] and Viktor Reimann portrays him as a thoroughly rational master propagandist.[4] Fraenkel and Manvell see the man with the clubfoot as someone who was cheated by life and finally found compensation in belief in the National Socialist ideology and the Führer.[5] Heiber relativizes Goebbels by locating the true being of the impassioned agitator and the simultaneously pitifully small man in the adolescent fixations he never overcame.

What was Joseph Goebbels really like? At the very beginning of my research, I encountered what seemed to be an insurmountable obstacle. Goebbels's papers from before 1924 were in the Federal Archives in Koblenz, but they were merely photocopies of some of the Goebbels papers stored in a Lausanne bank vault, and access to them was blocked. The Swiss lawyer François Genoud, who makes no secret of his sympathy

1

for Goebbels, not only held the rights to these papers but actually owned them. Only after a great deal of effort and patience did the day come when, in the conference room of the Piper Publishing House in Munich, the old suitcase was first opened for a biographer, revealing several hundred letters, numerous literary attempts, other documents, and several photographs, wrapped in tissue paper, showing the student Goebbels and his girlfriends.

Another important source for the development of Goebbels's personality could be found in his diaries, which are revealing, in spite of the "vain narcissism and autosuggestive mendacity" that their editor Elke Fröhlich sees in them.[6] Because the self-stylization and distortion always follow the same pattern, they can be easily detected. Checking Goebbels's accounts of events against those of other sources serves as an additional corrective. Only a small portion of these diaries had been used by previous biographers; they form one of the three pillars on which this book rests. Since it was known that the diaries from the years 1944–45 and various other fragments were in East Berlin, I tried to gain access to these documents as well. It proved rather easy to establish contact across the Wall, but for actually looking at these papers I was expected to reciprocate in ways I deemed unacceptable. So apart from a few fragments, these sources remained closed to me. In the meantime it was discovered that for many years Goebbels's diaries for the years 1944–45 had been in the hands of the State Security Ministry (Stasi). This secret police organization—which even tried to make capital of historical documents, whether to discredit West German scholarly institutions or to obtain Western currency—no longer exists. In the summer of 1990 the newly located diaries were returned to the Central Archives of the GDR,[7] and photocopies found their way to the Institute for Contemporary History (Institut für Zeitgeschichte) in Munich, where an edition of primary sources has been in preparation for several years. I was thus able to work them into my finished manuscript at the last minute.

The third pillar on which this book rests is the extensive material in the Federal Archives in Koblenz and the Berlin Document Center, along with records of the numerous legal proceedings against Goebbels during the so-called Time of Struggle in Berlin, here used for the first time in a biographical context. These latter documents are housed in the Landesarchiv in Berlin and on dusty shelves in the attic of the State's Attorney's Office at the regional court in Berlin-Moabit. This material was augmented by several smaller collections from archives inside and outside Germany, including the political notes of Horst Wessel, which in the West were previously thought to be lost; when unearthed in the Jagiellonian Library in Cracow, these documents gave valuable insight into

Goebbels's impact as Gauleiter. These sources, together with Goebbels's own fiction writings, essays, and newspaper articles, made it possible not only to revise numerous legends that had persistently cropped up in the literature on Goebbels but also to formulate a new answer to the key question whether he was a true believer or a Machiavellian, and also to the related question as to the nature of his relationship to Hitler and national socialism. New light could be cast on the genesis of Goebbels's anti-Semitism, previously inadequately explained as the result of either opportunism—the desire to ingratiate himself with Hitler—or resentment occasioned by rejections the unemployed Ph.D. received from Jewish newspaper publishers when he applied for a job. Among other things, the sources provided new information on Goebbels's role in the Stennes revolt, the Strasser crises, the Röhm putsch, the response to the 20 July 1944 assassination attempt, and the final days in the bunker in Berlin.

At the same time I am well aware that, in view of the vast amount of source material at my disposal, these questions and many others could merely be touched upon. I could not dwell at length on the organizational structure of Goebbels's propaganda apparatus or the propaganda operations themselves. For thorough treatments of these subjects I refer the reader to the work of Boelcke,[8] Bramsted,[9] and Balfour.[10] It would also have gone beyond the scope of this book to respond in detail to the vast existing literature. The task I set myself was to offer a chronicle, based on primary sources, of the life of Joseph Goebbels, from his birth in Rheydt to his grisly end in the ruins of Berlin, a city that only now, forty-five years later, is finally overcoming the disastrous political legacy of World War II. Perhaps this work, with its extensive documentation, will stimulate a reader here and there to follow up on certain issues more thoroughly.

Before launching into my account of the life of Joseph Goebbels, I should like to acknowledge the help I have received. I wish to thank Dr. Oldenhage and Frau Leonartz of the Federal Archives in Koblenz; Dr. Reichardt, Dr. Wetzel, Dr. Krukowski, and Frau Baumgart of the Berlin Regional Court; Dr. Löhr and Dr. Lamers of the City Archives in Mönchengladbach, and Herr Kunert of the Office for Public Affairs in the same city. They cut through red tape for me, as did Herr Fehlauer of the Berlin Document Center and Frau Perz of the Berlin Internal Administration. I also owe thanks to Professor Herbst at the Institute for Contemporary History in Munich, who, like my colleague from Warsaw, Herr Dietrich, and Herr Striefler of the Free University in Berlin, helped me obtain sources, and to Dr. Blasius and Professor Wollstein, who read the manuscript for factual errors and in addition gave me many valuable suggestions. Dr. Seybold and Herr Schaub helped edit the manuscript and read the galleys, and Herr Wank and Dr. Märtin of the Piper Publishing House proved excellent collaborators. Special gratitude goes to my wife. Without her patience, understanding, and assistance, this book could not have been written.

Berlin, July 1990

CHAPTER 1

Why had God
made him this way?
(1897—1917)

In 1897, the year Paul Joseph Goebbels was born, the second German empire was in full flower. Since its founding after the Prussian victory over France in 1871, the empire had rapidly become a major power. Now it was challenging the great colonial nations for a "place in the sun": "Global politics our calling, global power our goal" was the slogan coined by the military and economic leadership and taken up with alacrity by members of both the grand and the petty bourgeoisie. This slogan brought Germany into obvious conflict with the Franco-Russian entente and the British Empire.

In the year of Goebbels's birth, Kaiser Wilhelm II clearly had global power on his agenda when he directed Secretary of State Alfred von Tirpitz of the Naval Office to build a major German fleet. The kaiser wanted this fleet not only to manifest imperial might but also to guarantee Germany access to new sources of raw materials and new markets overseas. As the century drew to a close, Germany could look back on a phase of breakneck economic development that had brought it into second place in world trade, just behind England; in total industrial output Germany had already overtaken the previous leading economic power. In a period when human mastery over nature seemed to increase daily and the horizons of knowledge were constantly expanding, there appeared to be no limit to growth.

Yet this rapid flowering contained the seeds of a mortality that expressed itself in the contradictions with which the period was fraught. Wilhelm II affected the grand manner of the Great Elector and Frederick the Great, but at a time when organized special interests had long since taken politics into their own hands. And just when middle-class economic, financial, and cultural forces were intent on putting their stamp on the era, critics of the bourgeoisie, from Marx to Nietzsche, from Wagner to Freud, were already predicting the end of the bourgeois order.

Although the impending shift announced itself most noticeably in the metropolitan centers, the basis for it was being prepared throughout the empire, even along the lower Rhine, the region the Goebbels family called home. In this contemplative world, with its old peasant and tradesman traditions and its pervasive Catholicism, the spirit of modern times had already gained a foothold. The long-established weaving and spinning shops had provided the base for a modern textile industry. Work in the towns lured people in from the countryside, for it seemed to offer a better life—prospects that for many soon evaporated in the grinding daily routine of the growing urban proletariat.

One of those who had turned his back on his village to seek his fortune in Rheydt, a bustling industrial town "near Düsseldorf and not too far from Cologne," was Joseph Goebbels's grandfather Konrad, who still spelled his name Göbbels.[1] The farmer from Gevelsdorf near Jülich had married Gertrud Margarete Rosskamp, a tailor's daughter from Beckrath. For the rest of his life he remained a common manual laborer in one of Rheydt's many factories. As a child of the poor, his son Fritz, born on 14 April 1867, had to go to work at an early age. He began as an errand boy in the W. H. Lennartz wick factory. But since the management and administration of the company were growing, ambitious workers had opportunities for advancement. Fritz Goebbels, of whom his son Joseph would later write that he had thrown himself into any assignment, "however humble," seized every opportunity that presented itself.[2] He became a "starched-collar proletarian" with responsibility for paperwork, and eventually advanced during World War I to bookkeeper. In the 1920s the owner of the Lennartz company, now called United Wick Factories, Ltd., actually made him plant manager, authorized to sign for the firm; thus the Goebbels family won admission to the petty bourgeoisie.

In 1892 Fritz Goebbels had married Katharina Odenhausen. Born in Übach on the Dutch side of the Wurm River, which marked the border, she had spent her youth in Rheindahlen. Her father, the blacksmith Johann Michael Odenhausen, had died of heart failure when not yet sixty. His widow, Johanna Maria Katharina, née Coervers, still had several of their six children at home; to support them, she took a job as housekeeper with a distant relative, a pastor whom she reverently called "the Laird." Since every mouth she did not have to feed at the pastor's table eased her difficult circumstances, at an early age her daughter Katharina had to go to work as a dairy maid on a farm, where she stayed until she married Fritz Goebbels.

Fritz Goebbels's family lived very simply and modestly in their little apartment at 186 Odenkirchener Strasse, today no. 202.[3] After Konrad, Hans, and Maria (who died in infancy), her third son, Paul Joseph, was born there on 29 October 1897. Together with his two brothers, who were two and four years older respectively, and the two sisters born later, Elisabeth (1901) and Maria (1910), he grew up in a close-knit family. According to Joseph Goebbels's account, his father, Fritz Goebbels, was a conscientious man of "Prussian integrity"[4] who loved his children "as he understood love. He loved his wife almost more. Therefore he constantly felt the need to torment her with little stratagems and tricks, as people will when they feel they love more than they are loved."[5] If Joseph and his siblings feared their father's "Spartan discipline," they loved the kindness of their artless mother, who tended toward melancholy.[6] Joseph felt a special bond with her, and she in turn had a particular fondness for her fourth-born. Perhaps she "idolized" him precisely because his birth had almost cost her her life, he remarked later; perhaps she lavished on her son the love "she withheld from her husband." His mother, whom he later almost canonized for her "inexplicable unspoiled artlessness,"[7] was his "best and most faithful admirer."[8] All his life she remained his point of reference in the family home, which continued to offer him a place of refuge until he was almost thirty years old.

Joseph Goebbels regarded his relatives with differing degrees of affection. His maternal grandmother died when he was very young, and all he recalled of his grandfather Konrad Göbbels was the large family nose. On the other hand, he had "very dear and pleasant memories" of his paternal grandmother, "a dear little woman." He also very much liked his mother's sister, "godmother Christina," with her friendly disposition. His father's youngest sister, Aunt Elisabeth, he considered cranky, difficult, and spiteful toward him; he remembered her as "following the path of the typical spinster."

Goebbels had particularly vivid memories of Uncle Heinrich, a textile salesman who stopped by twice a year with the newest samples for the coming season. Although he saw him so seldom, Joseph probably had a special affection for this uncle because Heinrich was a convivial, cheerful man. This set him apart from the rest of the Goebbels family, who displayed the gloominess often ascribed to the people of the lower Rhine and sometimes explained as a product of the region's monotonous landscape and deep-seated Catholicism. The simpler folk, to whom the Goebbels family belonged, received from their Catholic faith graphic images of an all-powerful God who chastised and rewarded people in this world, and showed himself all the more favorably disposed, the more often one said the rosary. Fearful of his wrath, they thought they had to show the humblest respect to God and his black-garbed servants on earth. Daily Mass, confession, and devotions at home, in the course of which their mother made the sign of the cross on the children's brows with holy water, formed as important a part of the Goebbels children's lives as the daily bread for which their father toiled at the wick factory.

About two years after Joseph's birth, the family again had reason to thank the Lord: Fritz Goebbels had been made a clerk and now earned 2,100 marks a year, with a one-time holiday bonus of 250 marks.[9] The family could now afford to move into a more comfortable apartment on Dahlener Strasse. When Elisabeth was born, this apartment, too, became cramped. That same year, hard work and thrift enabled the family to purchase one of the little rowhouses typical of the area, again on Dahlener Strasse, but somewhat closer to the center of town. This "unassuming" little house, no. 140 (later 156), which has survived to the present day, was what Joseph Goebbels considered home, for here he "actually awakened to life."[10]

But life did not treat Joseph kindly. As a young child he almost died of pneumonia, accompanied by "terrible fever hallucinations." He survived but remained a "sickly little fellow." Shortly after the turn of the century, Joseph contracted osteomyelitis, one of the "decisive events" of his childhood, as he later called it.[11] He describes in his "Memories" how, after a long walk with the family, the old "foot problem" that they had thought cured manifested itself again, with severe pain. For two years his family doctor and a masseur struggled to rid his right leg of intermittent paralysis. Finally they had to tell the despairing parents that Joseph's foot was "lamed for life," would fail to grow properly, and would eventually develop into a clubfoot. Fritz and Katharina Goebbels refused to accept this prognosis. They even arranged for Joseph to be seen by doctors at the University of Bonn's medical school, a step requiring great courage for people of their humble station. But even these experts merely "shrugged their shoulders." Later, after the boy had hobbled around for some time with an ugly orthopedic appliance that was supposed to hold the paralyzed foot straight and provide support, the surgeons at the Maria-Hilf Hospital in Mönchengladbach agreed to operate on the ten-year-old.[12] The operation proved a failure, putting an end to any hopes that the child might be spared a clubfoot.[13]

Joseph Goebbels's deeply religious parents, especially his mother, viewed his misfortune as a curse on the family. In their world a physical defect was a punishment inflicted by God. Katharina Goebbels would often take her "Jüppchen" by the hand and go to St. Mary's, where she would kneel beside him and pray fervently that the Lord might give the child strength and turn this evil away from him and the family. For fear of the neighbors' gossip, she attributed Joseph's deformity not to an illness but to an accident; she claimed she had picked the child up from a bench without noticing that his foot was caught between the slats. Even so, shortly after the boy fell ill, people had begun to remark that he "didn't take after the rest of the family."[14]

The child himself probably did not understand the religious interpretation that was put on his deformity. The hurt inflicted by adults' pitying looks and his playmates' teasing led him to view his physical defect as a personal abnormality that overshadowed everything.[15] He began to feel inferior, avoided going out, and more and more kept to his little room on the second floor of the house on Dahlener Strasse. Looking back on his childhood, he later wrote that he had always thought his companions were ashamed of him "because he could no longer run and jump like them, and now his loneliness sometimes became a torment to him. . . . The thought that the others did not want him around for their games, that his solitude was not of his own choosing, made him truly lonely. And not only lonely—it also made him bitter. When he saw the others running about and leaping, he grumbled at his God, who had done . . . this to him, he hated the others for not being like him, he mocked his mother for still loving a cripple like him."[16]

The suffering of the scrawny, awkward youth with the outsized head and the increasingly misshapen foot did not diminish when he started school in the spring of 1904. The other children disliked him because he kept his thoughts to himself and remained aloof. The teachers disliked him because he was a self-willed, "precocious lad" whose diligence left something to be desired. Occasionally they would beat him—when he had not done his homework again or when he provoked them. That probably explains why he had mostly bad memories of elementary school, particularly of his teachers. He described one of them as a "villain and a scoundrel who abused us children," another as an "old liar" who "spewed out all kinds of ridiculous nonsense." He liked only one teacher, who "told stories with real gusto" and could thus stimulate the boy's imagination.[17]

When forced to spend three weeks in the hospital for the foot operation, young Goebbels read from morning to night. His godmother Christina had brought him a volume of fairy tales, a present from "rich Herbert Beines" in his class. "My first fairy tales. . . . These books awakened my joy in reading. From then on I devoured everything in print, including newspapers, even politics, without understanding the slightest thing."[18] He worked his way through the out-of-date two-volume version of Meyer's encyclopedia that his father had purchased.[19] He soon realized that his physical disadvantages could be offset by excellence in learning. His sense of inferiority constantly drove him to overcompensate. As he wrote later, he found it unbearable if anyone else knew more than he did, "for he fully expected the others to be cruel enough to exclude him intellectually as well. This thought filled him with diligence and energy." He eventually became one of the best in his class.[20]

Fritz Goebbels and his wife, determined that their children should be better off than they had been, noted with gratification Joseph's passion for learning. They did everything to provide what he might need—no easy task, for the family's social ascent brought with it expenses that gobbled up any surplus. As a salaried employee, Fritz Goebbels had to wear a starched white collar and a proper hat to work. The family owed it to their social position to have a formal parlor, complete with upholstered chairs, a sofa, a display cabinet, gilt-framed family portraits, and a considerable collection of bric-a-brac—all reserved for only the most special occasions.[21]

Although Fritz Goebbels had a little blue ledger in which he kept track of every penny spent,[22] the family had to supplement their earnings with piecework. "We made lamp wicks, a very arduous chore from which our eyes and backs ached. Even Father joined in after he came home from the office in the evening and had read the newspaper. This work of course brought in only pennies. But every penny was needed to climb to the next rung on the social ladder."[23]

The Goebbels parents' chief objective was to see to it that their children had a proper education. It was taken for granted that Joseph, intellectually the most gifted, would attend the municipal Gymnasium on Augustastrasse. His brothers Konrad and Hans had preceded him there. Before he enrolled in the spring of 1908, Fritz Goebbels arranged to have certain changes made in his son's elementary school report card: the number of days missed because of health problems was reduced, and all the grades of "good" were raised to "very good."

Joseph Goebbels was happy to be going to the Gymnasium, chiefly "because now he thought he could triumph over the classmates who had laughed at him and mocked him."[24] If his new schoolmates shunned him because of his deformity, as he talked himself into believing, at least they would also learn to "fear him"; he planned to outstrip them all in academic accomplishments, and with that in mind he worked with grim determination from the very first day. Soon his classmates were asking him for help. He lorded it over them, and "rejoiced . . . deep inside because he saw that the path he had chosen was the right one."[25]

No effort seemed too great to Goebbels. He distinguished himself and rose to the top in everything—Latin, geography, German, mathematics.[26] Even in art and music he manifested an almost pathological ambition, fostered by his father's well-intentioned encouragement. In 1909 the family even decided to buy a piano for the boy. More than thirty years later Goebbels described to his adjutant how his father had called him in and revealed his plan. "We went to look at it. It was going to cost three hundred marks, and was secondhand, of course, and fairly tinny." But at the same time it represented "the essence of cultivation and prosperity, an emblem of the finer things in life, the symbol of the middle class," at whose threshold the Goebbels had arrived by the end of the first decade of the twentieth century.[27] From then on Goebbels practiced the piano under his father's stern supervision.

Joseph Goebbels turned out to have a particular flair for theater. As a child he had already begun writing Gothic tragedies. Now his acting talent attracted attention in the yearly productions at school. Powerful displays of emotion, dramatic facial expressions and gestures were his forte. But he did not confine his acting to the stage; in everyday situations, too, he strove for special effects.[28] On occasion he lied and cheated, for which he afterward suffered pangs of conscience. For spiritual relief he would take his prayer book and go to confession.[29]

Not surprisingly, he showed great interest in the religious instruction provided by Johannes Mollen, the assistant priest of his parish. Young Goebbels was tormented by the questions "Why had God made him this way, so that people laughed at him and mocked him? Why was he not allowed to love himself and life as others did? Why did he have to feel hatred when he wanted and needed to feel love?" He reproached his God with these things. "Often he did not even believe that God was there."[30] And yet he placed all his hopes in him, for only God allowed him to hope that he, too, would some day find recognition and love.

At the beginning of April 1910 Mollen's most assiduous pupil received his first communion from the assistant pastor, whom he worshiped. The program for the ceremony contained a picture of the Blessed Virgin with the Child and a line from the Song of Solomon: "I have found him whom my soul loveth" (3:4).[31] The thirteen-year-old resolved to dedicate his life to that saying, in the hope that justice would come his way. He dreamed of some day celebrating High Mass or marching in splendid vestments at the head of the Corpus Christi procession. His parents encouraged him in his ambition to study theology; they were motivated not only by conviction and thoughts of prestige, but also by the knowledge that the Church would pay for their son's university studies if he chose the priesthood.

Other formative influences on the boy flowed from notions of heroism and national pride that formed the stock in trade of history classes during those years. "We sat there, our fists clenched, and hung on his lips with gleaming eyes," Goebbels wrote later, exalting his history teacher Gerhard Bartels, who guided his pupils through the triumphant campaigns of Alexander the Great.[32] According to Bartels, history was made by the heroic deeds of great men, and the Macedonian embodied the greatness that the kaiser's Germany was just setting out to achieve. The decisive victory over France, for which the battle of Sedan had become emblematic, marked the ascent of Prussian Germany. Historians like Heinrich von Treitschke, Max Lenz, and Erich Marks, as well as German history teachers, now saw the rivalry with England as a continuation of Germany's move toward global power. They buttressed their position with theories derived from Darwin; according to these theories, political expansion would enhance Germany's vitality and at the same time help fulfill the nation's mission by extending the influence of its culture, which they rated higher than that of other peoples.

Convinced though Goebbels was that the Lord must be punishing him, since he made him live as a cripple in a world that worshiped physical beauty and strength, religious faith and the fatherland remained constant reference points in his thinking. The hopes he placed in God merged with daydreams that swept him away from reality. He found his way to these daydreams through books, to which he devoted most of his time.[33] He would identify with the hero, thereby assuming a role he could not play in real life. "Then it did not grieve him so bitterly that he could not gambol around like the others; he was happy that even for him, the cripple, a world of pleasure existed."[34]

He carefully cultivated these sensations, and in 1912 attempted a first poem of his own. The occasion was provided by the death of young Lennartz, son of his father's employer, during an operation. Inspired by the fiction that he had lost a "true friend," Goebbels wrote:

> I stand beside the bier of death
> Stare at your limbs so stiff and cold
> You were my friend with every breath
> The only one my life may hold.
>
> So soon you leave me here alone
> Leaving the life that beckoned you
> Leaving the world with joys untold
> Leaving all hopes for friendship true.[35]

In addition to such "schoolboy melancholy," as he later self-critically described it, Goebbels soon began writing other overblown poems, very much in the spirit of the times, that gave vent to his emotions.[36] He began to think his poetry made him one of those exceptional human beings whom God had equipped with a special gift: "Probably because God had marked his body."[37]

The skill he gradually acquired in handling language, and his interest in literature and poetry, were furthered by his German teacher. This man, Christian Voss, succeeded in breaking through the wall of distrust that Goebbels had built around himself. Voss, too, had had to "struggle in his youth." Probably for that reason—as Goebbels speculated later—Voss tried to reach out to the boy. The teacher invited Goebbels to his home, recommended books to him, and spent many hours talking with him. "Sometimes it almost seemed as though the teacher admired his strange pupil for his idiosyncrasies," Goebbels remarked about this "first friend in his life," who exercised "the greatest influence" over him during his school years.[38]

Voss also helped out when Goebbels's father could no longer afford the tuition and other expenses associated with his son's education. Voss arranged for the young Goebbels to tutor children from wealthy families. "His teacher had recommended him, and as a result he was received everywhere in a very kind and friendly manner." So starved for affection and recognition was the adolescent that when the mother of one of his young charges lavished attention and solicitude on him, he promptly developed a crush on her. For the first time he began to care about his looks and became somewhat less withdrawn, occasionally even high-spirited. "And it made him doubly happy that no one knew about it, not even the object of his love. . . . When he lay awake in bed and his siblings were asleep, he composed verses, repeated them out loud to himself, and imagined she heard him and praised him. That was his greatest joy."[39]

Yet the decisive experience of his youth remained the gap between harsh reality and the fictitious world in which he sought refuge. He was painfully reminded of this gap when he carelessly left poems dedicated to his pupil's mother in his desk at school, and the next day the teacher read them aloud to the entire class, with sarcastic allusions to his defect.[40] The youth's first real attempt to approach a member of the opposite sex proved no less disastrous. Maria Liffers, on whom he set his sights, happened to be his brother's girl. When Joseph made unambiguous proposals to her and penned extravagant love letters, the whole thing came to light. The girl's parents descended on his house, insisting on speaking to his parents, and his brother Hans threatened him with a straight razor. At school he was denied a city scholarship on which his father had certainly been counting. Although Fritz Goebbels would find it extremely difficult to pay for his son's further education, he was determined that in spite of this grave lapse Joseph should finish school and take the final examinations that would qualify him to study theology. His brothers, by contrast, were not being sent to the university.

After the Easter holidays in 1914 Goebbels was promoted to the next-to-last class at the Gymnasium. The adolescent seems to have been little affected by the "grim nightmare" (as Hitler would call it ten years later, writing *Mein Kampf* in Landsberg Fortress) that "lay on the chests of men . . . sultry as the feverish heat of the tropics."[41] But the boy surely registered the debate over whether war would come and relieve the political tensions that plagued Germany. The new mechanized methods of production and the structural changes in society that accompanied them clashed with the prevailing political order in imperial Germany. Glaring contradictions and whirlwind change characterized this era, which many contemporaries saw as excessively rational and "soulless" and therefore threatening. Many looked to the impending war as a breath of fresh air.

On 28 June 1914 in Sarajevo the famous shots were fired at Archduke Franz Ferdinand, heir to the Austrian throne. Soon afterward mobilization began. In the little factory town on the lower Rhine, and everywhere else in Germany, people greeted the outbreak of war with wild enthusiasm. Joseph Goebbels joined in the patriotic chorus. Visions nourished in history class and in Father Mollen's sermons—indeed, the aspirations of the petty bourgeoisie from which Joseph sprang—seemed about to become reality.

The sense of solidarity engendered by the times did not fail to affect him, for the war held out the hope of a better future for the sixteen-year-old. From childhood on he had longed to "belong"; now he could finally feel at one with the crowd that gathered in August 1914 to cheer the mobilized soldiers marching off to war. No one paid any attention to his physical defect. This was as good as going to Mass, except that instead of kneeling he now lifted his voice in "Deutschland, Deutschland über alles."

He would have liked to be among the troops, like his older brother Hans, his classmate Fritz Prang, or his new acquaintance Richard Flisges. He wrote in a school composition: "The soldier who marches forth to offer his fresh young life for wife and child, hearth and home, village and fatherland, serves the fatherland in the most distinguished and honorable way."[42] But once again the physical defect he had so often cursed forced him to remain on the sidelines.

If Goebbels did not follow the war in detail, it was probably because he did not want to be reminded constantly of his own inadequacies. In the first winter of the war he did a few weeks of a sort of alternative service with the Reichsbank. In the school composition just quoted he had written that the "final victory" would be achieved not solely by the brave armies; he saw himself making a contribution by participating in the "diligent horde" of no less essential "noncombatants." Taking to heart the watchword for the civilian population that appeared everywhere on posters, he kept a sharp eye out for suspicious persons. And he proved especially assiduous when the director of his school volunteered the pupils to pack and mail Christmas presents from the people of Rheydt to their sons at the front.[43] Thus he found tasks that gave him a sense of belonging, even though he could not be at the front.

He now opened up more to his classmates, forming friendships with Hubert Hompesch and Willy Zilles. When they joined the army, he wrote to them faithfully, giving news of the home front and especially of school, where the higher classes were rapidly thinning out. His friends in turn reported to him, the "jungle dweller in the distant northwest," giving enthusiastic accounts of their life in the military.[44] Rifleman Willy Zilles, whom Goebbels envied, and who like all those in battlefield gray hoped to return home with the Iron Cross, wrote that his present life appealed to him much more than school.[45]

The nationalistic euphoria that had seized the younger generation in particular also made things easier for Goebbels, the almost-grown-up son of the "starched-collar proletarian," who in peacetime would have seemed more out of place at the Gymnasium among the children of businessmen, civil servants, and doctors. The war enabled the young man to generate a vision of a "true *Volk* community" to which the "common people" would belong as much as the rich (although, to be sure, his own extraordinary achievements in school allowed him to distance himself from the "common people"). "Probably never," he wrote in July 1915 to Willy Zilles, who lay wounded in a military hospital in Silesia, would he be able to echo Horace's *Odi profanum vulgus*—"I hate the lowly people." Instead he would be guided by the nineteenth-century novelist Wilhelm Raabe, who had understood the common people like no other. Raabe's injunction "Take heed of the alleys!" Goebbels interpreted as an admonition to pay attention to the lowly, without forgetting "our exalted duty," the "upward striving" adumbrated in Raabe's words "Look up to the stars!"[46]

Goebbels admired Raabe even more than those other nineteenth-century writers, the Swiss Gottfried Keller and the North German Theodor Storm, whom, along with the classical authors, he valued highly.[47] Raabe he viewed as a "shining example"[48] because of his vision of a German *Volk* community and the way in which he persisted in his creative work, in spite of a hurtful lack of recognition. "He continued to strive, if not for his contemporaries, at least for a later generation. Are we that generation?"[49]

Since the war seemed to promise the young man from the small house on Dahlener Strasse a better world, or at least some of what had previously been denied him, he interpreted the war as an expression of divine will. The emotionally charged compositions he wrote for Voss during the first months of the war reflect this conviction.[50] He quoted old songs from the Napoleonic wars (in Germany called the Wars of Liberation) and invoked ancient Germanic myths. He pronounced death on the battlefield a holy act, a sacrifice like that of Christ at Golgotha. In Goebbels's view of the world, religion and patriotism seemed to merge.

Among his teachers Goebbels thought he detected a "general shirking," with the exception of Voss and Bartels (the latter had just received the Iron Cross). And Father Mollen, of all people, failed to manifest patriotic enthusiasm. Even before August 1914 he had pessimistically painted for his students the horrors of what lay ahead.[51] When the priest continued to swim against the stream, Goebbels grew increasingly skeptical toward him, though still without questioning his authority in any fundamental sense.

But soon the schoolboy was obliged to recognize that Mollen's admonitions had been entirely justified. Reports began to pour into the school on Augustastrasse of the "heroic death" for kaiser and fatherland of former students. In light of the many casualties, the Goebbels family did not rejoice when Konrad received his summons to report for duty on 1 August 1915. They would have reacted very differently the previous year.[52] Although they were proud that he, too, could now wear the kaiser's uniform into battle for Germany, they shuddered at the thought of what might happen to him.

A further sorrow came to the family in the fall of 1915: Elisabeth fell ill. By All Souls' Day consumption, as tuberculosis was then called, had carried her off. Joseph and his father said the Lord's Prayer at her bedside.[53] The boy's teacher Voss, who had been temporarily ordered to Aachen for military service, wrote to his gifted pupil that there was probably no one these days "who does not lose a loved one . . . and thus we must comfort one another and hold up our heads. For we are not yet at the end, and we do not know what we shall have to endure until the great, joyous hour of peace strikes."[54]

Again Goebbels resorted to poetry, this time to express his pain at his sister's death. Then, in early summer of the following year, the family suffered agonies over his brother Hans, who was fighting on the western front and had not been heard from for weeks.[55] To make things worse, daily life became increasingly grim as the war dragged on. At school, where most of the upperclassmen had left, including all the friends with whom Goebbels had shared his thoughts, the composition topics kept reverting to one question: "Why is victory necessary, desirable, and inevitable?" Voss, back in the classroom, now had his students write on the power of hope, which Goebbels called "the force that permits us to endure these times, drenched in blood and tears."[56]

Although the Goebbels family eventually received the reassuring news that Hans was safe in French captivity, for Joseph little of the original euphoria remained. Reports of German victories that never quite led to final victory had made it clear to him that a long, arduous road still lay ahead. The letters from his classmates in the field seemed to confirm this conclusion. Rhetorical flourishes had given way to sober descriptions of hardship, still coupled, however, with an unbending sense of duty to the fatherland. His classmate Hompesch, now a noncommissioned officer, wrote for example that he would "hold out to the last" before he would "let the enemy force his way into our land, threatening our families at home, our worldly possessions."[57]

Gradually the correspondents grew apart, for they were living in different worlds. Another significant factor was Goebbels's first real love affair, with a girl from neighboring Rheindahlen. It began after Easter 1916—around the time of the "hell of Verdun."[58] Lene Krage was "not intelligent" but very beautiful for her years.[59] When they first kissed on Gartenstrasse in Rheydt, Goebbels was, as he later wrote, "the happiest person in the world." He could hardly believe that he, "the poor cripple," had "kissed this most beautiful girl." Lene for her part admired her "dear boy" for his intelligence. "How unworthy I am compared to you," she wrote in one of her many letters. "Yes, you deserve to be worshiped. I could fall into idolatry."[60] But before long he was asking himself how he could possibly love a girl he found stupid. He concluded, "This love, no matter how harmless, had something impure about it."[61] He viewed his "dark" longings, which he ascribed solely to instinct, as despicable; indeed, sexuality altogether must be the work of the devil. He therefore "struggled" against "sex," deciding he must be ill because he saw himself losing the battle. Then he contrived one night to be locked into Kaiser Park in Rheydt with Lene and she became "a loving woman." He had lost the struggle for good, and with it his clear conscience.

In 1917 food was in short supply in Germany. In March of that year Goebbels took the Abitur, the examinations that qualified one for the university. His final report card, like the previous ones at the Gymnasium, was nothing to be ashamed of. "Very good" in religion, German, and Latin; "good" in Greek, French, history, geography, and even physics and mathematics, subjects for which he claimed to have "no talent." Because his written examinations were so good, he was excused from the oral examination. As the student who had written the best German essay, he was the one to deliver the valedictory address for his class. The speech that frail little Joseph Goebbels read on 21 March 1917 before the teachers, school officials, and students assembled in the school auditorium was skillfully structured and carried the patriotic rhetoric of the day to new heights. It contained all the notions that had shaped the worldview of his generation, notions young Goebbels had thoroughly internalized. In a voice quivering with emotion, he told his audience that they were "the limbs of that great Germany upon which the entire world gazes with fear and admiration." He adduced the "global mission" of the people "of poets and thinkers," which now had to prove "that it is more than that, that it bears within it the right to become the political and spiritual leader of the world." In ringing martial tones he spoke of Bismarck, the man "of steel and iron," of "our kaiser," who had boldly drawn his sword "against God and the world." The speech culminated in a vision that melded religion with patriotism: "And Thou, Germany, mighty Fatherland, Thou sacred land of our fathers, stand fast, stand fast in Thy hour of need and death. Thou hast shown Thy heroic strength and shalt go forth victorious from the final struggle. . . . We do not fear for Thee. We trust in the everlasting God, Whose will it is that Right shall prevail, and in Whose hand the future lies. . . . God bless our Fatherland."[62]

After this address the school director is supposed to have patted Goebbels on the shoulder and remarked that unfortunately he was not cut out to be a great orator.[63] But Goebbels did not plan to become an orator, nor did he intend any longer to preach from the pulpit. To his parents' disappointment, he had long since abandoned his plan of studying theology. As early as 1915 Voss had advised him to take up German literature and to learn Dutch as his second Germanic language. Probably with future territorial annexations in mind, Voss argued that in this way Goebbels could get his state teacher's certification "in no time flat" once the war ended. Goebbels had in fact made good progress in learning Dutch during vacations spent near Aachen, where his mother had grown up.[64] Yet he toyed for a while with the idea of studying medicine, until Voss talked him out of it. At his teacher's urging he finally settled on classical philology, German literature, and history.

The "long-awaited hour" that "sets us free" had now arrived. But it certainly bore no resemblance to the picture Goebbels had painted in his speech. The world did not lie before him "in the young, fresh dawn of May Day," nor was there any reason to gaze "with intoxicated eye" "on the beauty and bliss of the world" and to rejoice "in the face of all these wonders": "O world, you lovely world you, in blossoms almost buried."[65] Behind the motto that Goebbels and the others in the graduating class had chosen for their ceremony—"in obstinate optimism"—lurked dreams born of deprivation, the accumulated longings of three years of war that had brought hardship to the civilian population as well as to the troops.

In this difficult time, the only thing that made it possible for Fritz Goebbels to countenance his son's studying anything other than theology was the fact that this year he had been promoted to bookkeeper for the wick factory and would be earning a few more marks. Joseph hoped he would get by with his father's modest support and the money he had saved up from tutoring, until the expected German victory in the war brought a decisive improvement in everyone's fortunes, including his own.

CHAPTER 2

Chaos within me
(1917–1921)

When the dreamy youth with the deep-seated inferiority complex and the powerful yearning for recognition and security left home in April 1917 to enroll at the University of Bonn, he was opening up new horizons for his family. He was proud that he, the son of a lower-level salaried employee, could study with the elite of German youth. Yet at the same time he felt somewhat apprehensive, for he had no idea how his fellow students would receive him, with his small stature and deformed leg. These fears probably explain why the spring day when he said good-bye to his parents' house and his girlfriend Lene Krage seemed "raw and cold."[1]

In Bonn Goebbels found a modest furnished room on Koblenzer Strasse and went out, like every newcomer, to familiarize himself with the city and the university, where, despite the war, student life continued in its traditional form. Social life was dominated by the student fraternities and associations, all of which, no matter what the differences among them, professed veneration for the kaiser and love of the fatherland as their fundamental values. Fascinated by the fraternities' reputation for conviviality, much celebrated in song, Goebbels immediately sought to be admitted to one. On the advice of Father Mollen, he joined a Catholic students' association, Unitas Sigfridia, where his petty-bourgeois origins would prove less of a handicap than in some of the more elite fraternities. He chose the fraternity name "Ulex" because, as he explained, he was very fond of a novel by Wilhelm Raabe with a hero by this name, "an old German idealist, profound and dreamy, as we Germans all are, in spite of industrialization and the materialistic trends of present times."[2]

In the fraternity, whose membership had been considerably reduced by compulsory and voluntary military service, Goebbels found a home of sorts. And in the law student Karl Heinz Kölsch, nicknamed Pille, he found a good friend whom he worshiped from the start. Together with the slightly older Kölsch, the freshman worked tirelessly to strengthen unity within the fraternity. He excelled at organizing events that would inspire greater patriotism and religious faith among Unitas Sigfridia's members. On 24 June 1917 he gave a much-praised speech on Wilhelm Raabe at a fraternity gathering.[3] On another occasion he spoke on church art; a respected professor at the university judged it the best speech by a student he had ever heard.[4] Goebbels invited Father Mollen to Bonn to speak to the "Sigfrids" on church history. Recalling that stimulating evening forty years later, Mollen remarked that he probably had such pleasant memories of it because he had been so happy to observe his former student's lively participation.[5]

Even in wartime, drinking bouts were important in fraternity life. They swallowed up so much money that Goebbels soon realized the funds he had brought from home would not even get him through the semester, in spite of his living very frugally, often skipping meals. He earned a little money tutoring, but by no means enough. When he was called up for alternative military service, it saved him the embarrassment of having to leave the university prematurely for financial reasons.[6] With a pocket full of IOUs and unpaid bills, he returned to Rheydt in June 1917.

Once back under his parents' roof, Goebbels at first took refuge in daydreams, which he began to record under the title of "Those Who Love the Sun," passionate musings on "love, life, and happiness, things that go together like air and water."[7] But then his reveries had to give way to sober service as a desk soldier for the Fatherland Auxiliary. Since his superiors had no idea what to do with this frail young man with the limp who had so little of the soldier about him, they soon sent him home. There he finished the novella he had started and wrote a second one that he entitled "I'm a Wayfaring Scholar, a Wild Fellow . . ."[8] This piece, dedicated to "my dear fraternity brother Karl Heinz Kölsch," dealt with Rhenish student high jinks, love, and death. He soon dismissed both novellas as "dripping with sentimentality" and "hardly palatable," but only after receiving a rejection from the *Kölnische Zeitung*, to which he had submitted them.[9]

Of greater importance at this point was making provision for the winter semester in Bonn. Once more Father Mollen came to the rescue. On Mollen's recommendation, Goebbels applied to the old and respected Albertus Magnus Association in Cologne for a scholarship. In his application he explained that his father had a position as bookkeeper, and with life so much more expensive these days, he, Joseph, could not claim any of the meager funds left over after the household expenses had been paid. Appealing to the patriotism of his readers, he pointed out that any surplus had to be set aside for his two brothers, the elder of whom was serving on the western front, while the younger was languishing in French captivity. Because of a foot injury he himself was exempted from military service. Since he wanted to continue his studies, he was "completely at the mercy of the generosity of my fellow Catholics."[10] Further letters and documents were required of the petitioner, as well as written attestation by Mollen that the young man was the offspring of "good Catholic parents" and deserved the strongest recommendation "for his religious and moral conduct." Finally, at the beginning of October, just in time for the beginning of the semester, the Albertus Magnus Association offered a loan of 180 marks.[11] This sum, and the 780 marks that Goebbels received over the following five semesters, would in all likelihood never have been approved if anyone at the association had suspected that Goebbels was a bad risk. Not until 1930 would the future Gauleiter of Berlin pay back four hundred marks, in installments. Even this partial repayment came only after the association had sued him several times and had his personal property attached.[12]

Back in Bonn, during that late fall when the Bolshevist Revolution aroused hopes that at least in the east the war would soon be over, Goebbels slipped back into the life of a fraternity brother, with Pille Kölsch at his side. In the fraternity minutes that he wrote in the hallowed fraternity jargon, he spoke of "great, masterful drinking fests" they had "thrown," some of which had run a "glorious course." He also mentions "merry excursions into the great expanse of the beautiful German countryside, which the Activitas undertakes almost every Saturday and Sunday."[13] A high point in the life of the Bonn Sigfrid fraternity was participation in the Unitas founders' celebration in Frankfurt. The overzealous Goebbels arrived equipped for dueling, with foils and wax, and showed great disappointment when the Frankfurt brothers explained that, because of the gravity of the times and the many casualties the Unitas had suffered among its members, they were suspending this traditional student practice. But apparently Goebbels soon overcame his dismay; that same evening he wrote in the songbook of one of the Frankfurt alumni the saying attributed to Luther, "He who loves not / wine, women, and song / Remains a fool / his whole life long."[14]

True to the spirit of this venerable motto, Goebbels promptly fell in love with Kölsch's younger sister Agnes, whom he met during a visit to his friend's house in Werl. The gaunt little man with the resonant voice and not unappealing manner received a cordial welcome from the Kölsches. Goebbels was much taken with the family's lavish style of life, with the charm of the mistress of the house, who insisted on being his "Mama No. 2," and especially with the daughter Agnes.[15] During the second half of the semester Goebbels spent almost more time in Werl than at the university. In Bonn he and Pille Kölsch were now rooming together, and when his friend decided to transfer to Freiburg in the spring of 1918, Goebbels followed his idolized friend to the distant university town on the edge of the Black Forest.

Their departure was much regretted, not only by Agnes Kölsch but also by the Sigfrid fraternity. The Unitas logbook notes the stimulus the two of them had provided to fraternity life with "their convivial ways and sunny humor," which attracted many new members.[16]

In May 1918 Joseph Goebbels set out for Freiburg. Meanwhile the last great offensive by the kaiser's army, intended to bring a decision in the west, ground to a halt. "A wonderful trip all through the south. Arrival at 6 o'clock. Kölsch greets me with a hug. I'm living with him. Breisacher Strasse."[17] In addition to plunging into his studies, he immediately joined the local Unitas chapter, again with Kölsch.[18] But their friendship soon came to grief. Kölsch had made friends with Anka Stalherm, a wealthy young woman studying law and economics. During Prof. Hermann Thiersch's lectures on Winckelmann, Goebbels's eye lit on her, and when Kölsch introduced her to him, he was immediately smitten. From then on all his interest focused on the young woman with the "extraordinarily passionate mouth" and the "brown-blond hair" that lay "in a heavy coil on her marvelous neck."[19] They gradually grew closer. Finally the penniless student and the young woman from Recklinghausen became a couple. "Mine was a sense of fulfillment infinite and without measure," he wrote later.[20]

As a result, "terrible scenes" took place between Kölsch and Goebbels, and back in Werl the jilted Agnes Kölsch wrote reproachfully that she had been sorely mistaken in thinking him "so fine, so noble, so mature." Her "farewell, it was not to be" hardly touched Goebbels.[21] Such was his love for Anka Stalherm that the "poor devil," as he styled himself, was oblivious to the end of his friendship with Kölsch, his constant lack of money, and even his clubfoot. Six years later he described that summer semester in Freiburg as probably the happiest time of his life. Only a nighttime attack on the sleepy university town by French bombers reminded him that Germany was still at war.[22]

At the end of the summer semester, Anka Stalherm went home to Recklinghausen, and Goebbels had to pull up stakes in Freiburg, lacking the means to stay on. When he set out for Rheydt on 4 August 1918, he took with him the realization, gained from two semesters and the company of Anka Stalherm, that although his university studies had given him entrée to a higher social class, "within it I was a pariah, an outlaw, one who was merely tolerated, not because I achieved less or was less intelligent than the others, but simply because I lacked the money that flowed to the others so generously from their fathers' pockets."[23]

This perceived injustice inspired Goebbels to write a drama. He had begun it in Freiburg, and at home he withdrew to his little room and worked like one possessed. In his long daily letters to Anka Stalherm he reported on his writing, insisting that it was she who gave him the strength to keep going. By 21 August he announced to her that he had penned the "last stroke" on his "Judas Iscariot," a "Biblical tragedy."[24] This play would tell her "all that passes through my overflowing heart at this moment."[25] Anka received a manuscript of over a hundred pages, written in Goebbels's small, vertical Old German script; in iambic pentameter the play told the story of Judas, the "outsider" and "dreamer" who wants to follow the man he thinks will establish "a new, boundless empire." Once Judas has become Jesus' disciple, he recognizes, to his disappointment, that Jesus' father's kingdom is not of this world. To Judas it is the mark of a "petty mind and spirit" to comfort the people in troubled times with promises of salvation in the hereafter. Finally Judas betrays his master in order to take it upon himself to establish the Kingdom of God on earth. Only afterward does Judas understand that this action, intended simply to bring about a just world, is tragic. "And yet, may the heavens be my witness: Judas / did not turn traitor for the sake of silver." Finally Judas has no choice but to expiate his guilt by committing suicide.[26]

This play, clearly written under the influence of Nietzsche's *Thus Spake Zarathustra*, expressed Goebbels's questioning not so much of the existence of God as of the premise that the Catholic faith would bring about the longed-for just order. Father Mollen had got wind of the play and summoned Goebbels for a discussion. Anticipating unpleasantness, Goebbels built up his courage by writing to Anka Stalherm that he planned to "give Mollen a piece of my mind." But the encounter took a very different course. Such was his respect for the priest that he pulled himself together mightily when Mollen pointed out "the heinousness" of his writing. "Just think, the Church goes so far as to insist that I destroy my own copy within a stipulated period of time," he wrote to Anka, and he indicated that he would have ripped the manuscript into a thousand shreds if he had had it in his possession. Hopes nourished by Voss, his former German teacher, of getting the play published were thus buried, for "under no circumstances" did he want to "break with the faith and religion of my childhood."[27]

Yet Goebbels soon made just such a break, under the impression of events that shattered his entire view of the world. To his (and others') complete surprise, Germany lost the war, and all the expectations he had pinned on victory vanished in thin air. On 11 November 1918, the centrist politician Matthias Erzberger headed a German delegation that signed the armistice in a railroad car in the forest of Compiègne, northeast of Paris; it amounted to total capitulation. A number of factors made this event incomprehensible to many Germans: there had been talk of victory to the very last; no shots had been fired on German soil; and the German armies had proved victorious in the east and penetrated deep into enemy territory in the west.

Subsequent developments inside the Reich seemed even more difficult to grasp. Nothing remained of the sense of national unity invoked by Wilhelm II at the beginning of the war, when he had said he no longer saw political parties, only Germans. The kaiser abdicated the day the armistice was signed. In the days preceding his departure, German sailors had mutinied. Everywhere in Germany—including Goebbels's hometown of Rheydt—soldiers' and workers' councils sprang up. On 9 November the Social Democrat Philipp Scheidemann had declared a republic in Berlin, and shortly thereafter Karl Liebknecht, leader of the Spartacus movement, proclaimed a "free socialist republic."

Goebbels followed these events from Würzburg, where he and Anka Stalherm had enrolled at the university at the end of September and were having "a wonderful fall." In his later "Memories" he noted, "Revolution. Revulsion. Return of the troops. Anka weeps."[28] At first he dismissed the tumult as the ravings of the "blind, coarse masses" who would one day surely require a "guiding spirit." In a letter written on 13 November to his former schoolmate Fritz Prang, he asked:

> Don't you agree that the hour will again come when people will call out for spirit and strength in the lowly, insignificant horde of the masses? Let us await this hour and not cease to arm ourselves for this struggle by determined schooling of the spirit. It is certainly bitter to have to witness these grave hours of our fatherland, yet who knows but that we'll gain from them in the end. I believe Germany lost the war, yet our fatherland won it. When wine ferments, all the impure elements float to the surface, where they are skimmed off, leaving only the precious essence behind.[29]

In fact, Joseph Goebbels could not understand the reasons for the ferment. The war years, the years of national solidarity during which he had grown up, had made it impossible for him to see that the seeds of the present upheaval had been sown long before the turn of the century, with the advent of industrialization. Like the young soldiers in the "hail of steel," as the writer Ernst Jünger called it, this home-front combatant was acquainted only with the bombastic, exaggerated form of solidarity preached by the kaiser. The collapse of this deceptive vision hit him all the harder because he had really believed in a "true *Volk* community."

At the University of Würzburg, Goebbels attended the lectures of Julius Kaerst, professor of ancient history and a confirmed nationalist. He also studied German literature under Hubert Roetteken.[30] Goebbels's reaction to the events of November 1918 resembled that of most of his generation, though it was perhaps more violent, in accord with a destructive streak in his nature; what produced only uneasiness in others filled him with despair. More and more he identified the "German fate" with his own. In a letter he noted that the only thing that mattered was learning from past mistakes, so as to do better next time—this was the lesson of the war. "If I could live, I'd want to live, learn, and be resurrected with Germany, reaching if not political then moral heights," he wrote, searching for the meaning of the war, whose presumed essence he wanted to see preserved.[31]

But increasingly Goebbels had to recognize that his interpretation of the events of November 1918 was inadequate. The self-regulating forces on which he had placed his hopes in his letter to Fritz Prang failed to manifest themselves. Instead, Prang's cynical motto for the future—"*Vive l'anarchie!*"—inspired by the "heroic death" of his brother, seemed to be coming true.[32] Starting on 4 January 1919, members of Liebknecht's and Rosa Luxemburg's Spartacus League declared open season on those who had announced their support for the National Assembly, and thereby for parliamentary democracy. Finally Gustav Noske, a Social Democrat, marched into Berlin at the head of a free corps, which, like most of the paramilitary groups of the time, comprised the flotsam and jetsam of the war. The Spartacus revolt was put down and Liebknecht and Luxemburg were murdered, their bodies thrown into the Landwehr Canal. Although conditions in the capital stabilized, the January street battles in Berlin turned out to be the prelude to revolutionary unrest throughout Germany.

In these troubled times Goebbels's parents worried about their son, studying far from home. His health provided an added reason for concern; he had become mere skin and bones, suffered from constant headaches, and found it harder than usual to walk, because his orthopedic appliance had been damaged and was apparently difficult to repair. At the beginning of October his father had already asked him to "let us hear from you twice a week, if only a few lines." In November Fritz Goebbels wrote that if it became "too dangerous" in Würzburg, "the university will probably shut down, and then you'll simply come home." But in December young Goebbels informed his parents that he would not be spending Christmas at the family hearth, even though his father had written a good dozen letters, sending money as well as solicitous advice on how to get home safely to the Rhineland, now occupied by the French and the Belgians. Fritz Goebbels had long felt that a university closer to home would have been preferable. Time and again he urged his son to be sure to come home as soon as possible when the semester ended, "so your things, like the device, etc., can be put in order and you can finally get fed decently. Staying away longer would also be too expensive."[33]

On 24 January 1919 Joseph Goebbels finally came home to Rheydt. Two days earlier he had properly reported his departure to the residents' registry bureau, and he had written at the end of his notebook "*deo gratias*," underlining it four times. Crossing the Rhine by train at Cologne, he entered occupied territory. "A terribly young Englishman in a battle helmet comes through, very charming, sees that I have a paper in my hand: 'All right!'—all that running around for days beforehand for this!" At the Cologne railroad station, where he had to wait all night in "bitter cold" for his connecting train, the many Englishmen and Frenchmen presented a "strange, colorful picture." But in his hometown the occupation forces seemed far from colorful to him. The Belgians had imposed a curfew and were keeping the town under tight control. Even letters had to be censored and could not be written in the accustomed Old German script. Goebbels "dreaded" having to live under such conditions for three months, he wrote Anka Stalherm. A few days later, when he thought he had borne the daily irritations of the occupation long enough, he wrote that he no longer felt at home here: "In Germany I am no longer in Germany."[34]

Goebbels's return to Rheydt coincided with another event. The elections to the National Assembly had just taken place in the Reich. In Würzburg he had reluctantly carried on the tradition of his Catholic family, voting for the Bavarian branch of the Center Party, the Bavarian People's Party (Bayrische Volkspartei).[35] But when he got together with some of his former classmates, just home from the war, he discovered that they had voted for the German Nationalist Party (Deutschnationale Partei or DNP), as had his brother Konrad. Joseph would have liked to vote for this party, but it had not presented a slate in Bavaria.[36] If he found it painful that not all Germans had been reasonable enough to vote "correctly" for the good of the fatherland, he found it positively unbearable to see the parties embroiled in rivalries when they should have been confronting the country's dire need. When the Social Democratic Party (Sozialdemokratische Partei Deutschlands or SPD), the left-liberal German Democratic Party (Deutsche Demokratische Partei or DDP), and the Catholic Center Party formed a coalition government under the Social Democrat Friedrich Ebert, who made a "wretched impression" on him,[37] Goebbels remarked "how little the people are ready for a republic."[38]

As evidence for this assertion Goebbels cited the centrifugal forces that seemed to threaten the unity of the Reich in this hour of defeat and inner turmoil. He asked Anka Stalherm whether she was hearing much talk at home of "a Rhineland-Westphalian republic" and warned her not to be taken in: "That agitation is all treason to the fatherland, pursued by conscienceless Catholic reactionaries. You know the old expression about the rats leaving the sinking ship. I'm convinced that no group has understood that brave and happy saying as splendidly as our dear old Center. . . . I wouldn't put it past these people to form a South German Reich with Austria and name the pope the first president. One can hardly blame the Catholics for wanting to jettison the Prussians, under whose regime they were in fact second-class citizens." He could weep from rage and frustration, he wrote, "but what can one do? We're a poor people, and anyone who retains a spark of love for his German fatherland has no choice but to clench his fists in his pockets and keep still."[39]

True to form, Goebbels also blamed the republic for the harsh social contrasts he saw when he, a "poor devil" with a chronically empty wallet, contemplated the gulf between himself and Anka Stalherm. In Würzburg he had found it humiliating that the young woman often subsidized him. At one point, when he was physically and emotionally at the end of his rope, she offered to pay for a sorely needed cure at a spa, but his pride would not allow him to accept. To make things worse, Anka Stalherm's family kept warning her not to become too deeply involved with this penniless cripple. Once Anka was back in Recklinghausen, her mother sent her to confession to rid herself of the sins she had committed with him. But she prayed "that the dear Lord may soon let you be well and that everything may turn out as beautifully as you can dream." Although Anka remained loyal, in February the social disparity between them gave rise to a serious altercation, whereupon he wrote to her that she should tell her mother this letter would be his last—"Perhaps she will forgive you then." After they had made up, he complained it hurt his feelings that she had become so obsessed with his poverty, "but you recall you pressed me at one time to let you share my problems and suffer with me."

Although he still styled himself a conservative, Goebbels soon stopped describing those who claimed to be fighting for a more just order as "the blind, coarse masses." In Rheydt he even took part in discussions with organized workers. "In this way one at least comes to understand the stirrings among the workers." Although he could "never ever" approve of them, he wrote cautiously to upper-middle-class Anka Stalherm, these discussions introduced him to "various problems . . . really worth examining closely."[40]

Goebbels had done just that, in his own fashion. In February 1919 he completed a second drama, "Heinrich Kämpfert," in which he again took up issues that troubled him personally. His protagonist is the "silent hero," Heinrich Kämpfert. "Work and keep up the struggle!" is his motto, but "the struggle was harder, for to the spiritual struggle was now added the struggle for his daily bread." Heinrich's hardships and resignation are contrasted with the life of a rich aristocratic family whose daughter the hero loves. She commits herself to him and warns her family, "In wealth resides a great responsibility, a responsibility toward the classes that languish and go hungry. And if one ignores this responsibility, one summons spirits that can never again be harnessed: the social menace." Heinrich Kämpfert suffers from being denied justice, but he cannot bring himself to do wrong to achieve justice. He cannot close the "gaping wound between desire and ability."[41] He remains—like Dostoyevski's Raskolnikov in *Crime and Punishment*, with whom Heinrich Kämpfert debates in the third and final act—a prisoner of his Christian being in a "corrupt world."

To Goebbels the gap between Catholicism's promises and harsh reality seemed unbridgeable. While still in Würzburg he drew the appropriate conclusion and resigned from the Catholic Unitas Association, which he had joined soon after arriving at the university.[42] On Christmas Eve 1918, which he spent with Anka Stalherm in her poorly heated student lodgings, he missed midnight Mass for the first time in his life.[43] From then on he refused to attend church or go to confession. The relatively secure view of the world that he had held until recently now gave way to the admission that he no longer understood what was going on.[44]

In this state of uncertainty, Goebbels leaned on a new friend, his former schoolmate Richard Flisges, a farmer's son from the Rheydt area who, like Goebbels, aspired to study German literature.[45] During long walks they forged plans for their own and the nation's future. This tall man who had come home from the war with an Iron Cross and a shot-up arm—a heroic figure to Goebbels—fascinated him with his views on God and the world. Goebbels persuaded his friend to begin his studies in Freiburg, where he himself was following Anka Stalherm for the 1919 summer semester.

Flisges, whom Goebbels described as "royally free and above all that today passes for 'culture' and is at bottom merely unnatural," advised Goebbels to read Marx and Engels.[46] Goebbels was now thinking more about the social question and sitting up all night discussing God with Flisges; more and more God was becoming synonymous with fraternity, equality, and justice.[47] In God's workings Goebbels now saw the counterforce to the unjust, misanthropic, soullessly materialistic contemporary German reality. Goebbels derived inspiration from Dostoyevski, with his vision of a socialist Russia grounded in mysticism and religion—socialist in the sense that belief in God could serve as the great integrating factor, "the synthetic personality of the entire people."[48]

Again Goebbels drew strength for such self-tormenting explorations from Anka Stalherm. It was she who lightened his gloomy thoughts, flirting with her "dear, sweet rascal" during the lectures they attended together. During that summer in Freiburg he also distracted himself by writing gushing romantic poetry.[49] His poetic ambitions seemed justified when a publishing house in Leipzig offered to publish a collection of his poems. But when the contract arrived in the mail in June 1919, the seventh paragraph put an end to the student's elation: it stipulated that upon signing the contract Herr Joseph Goebbels was to pay the publisher 860 marks in cash.[50] Although he had boasted during the semester break to his old German teacher Voss about the pending publication,[51] Goebbels bitterly rejected Anka Stalherm's offer to pay the required amount; she subsidized him often enough as it was.[52]

In August 1919, in a shabby room in Münster, while Anka Stalherm was spending the vacation with relatives in nearby Anholt, twenty-two-year-old Joseph Goebbels sat down and penned his "own story" in his "heart's blood." In "Michael Voormann's Youth" he reflected for the first and only time honestly and critically on himself; on his way to achieving psychic stability, Goebbels gave expression to "all his suffering," "unvarnished, just as I see it"—his hatred for others, the pathological ambition in school with which he had attempted to compensate for his physical defect, and his tendency to become increasingly "arrogant and tyrannical" as he achieved success.[53] "Thus he was well on his way to becoming a tyrannical eccentric instead of a solid character." Anka Stalherm, who received notebook after notebook from him, could not miss the message: he was prophesying his future as that of a tragic, exceptional being. Addressing his hero, he wrote: "You will become a man, Michael, like the boy you were in your youth, lonely and estranged from the world, always filled with yearning for that which you cannot do, but for which you will strive until your end."[54]

In the winter of 1919–20 Goebbels and Anka Stalherm moved to the university of Munich. In those postwar years the Bavarian capital was seething. In the spring of 1919 a radical minority had proclaimed a soviet republic. Romantic visions had produced grotesque manifestations, as for instance a proclamation to the effect that work, conditions of subordination, and legalistic thinking were abolished, and that the newspapers had to carry poems by Hölderlin or Schiller on their front pages, next to the most recent revolutionary decrees. On the heels of the visionaries had come tough professional revolutionaries. Then troops loyal to the government in Berlin put a bloody end to the brief soviet rule. Now it was hordes of rootless, disoriented, right-wing veterans who constituted a threat to the young Weimar Republic. Organized into fighting squads and free corps, they took their ideology from the numerous nationalistic and anti-Semitic associations, some of which, like the Thule Society, even dabbled in the occult. One of these groups was the German Workers' Party, founded by the engineer Gottfried Feder. Its announced goal was to reconcile nationalism and socialism. This group had attracted a down-and-out former soldier named Adolf Hitler. On 16 October 1919, about three weeks after Goebbels and Anka Stalherm had moved into their separate rented rooms in Munich, Hitler addressed a meeting of the National Socialist German Workers' Party for the first time and "electrified" his audience.

Like all the German universities, now thronged with returnees from the war, Munich offered a microcosm of the political and social shifts taking place throughout Germany. In February 1919 Count Anton Arco-Valley, a student and lieutenant in the reserves, assassinated the Bavarian prime minister, Social Democrat Kurt Eisner. It was in response to this murder that the radicals had proclaimed their Bavarian soviet republic. The count was celebrated by the nationalist students as a "tyrannicide" and "liberator of Bavaria." Goebbels followed his trial and was full of excited sympathy for Arco-Valley. When the judges imposed the death penalty, later commuted to life imprisonment, the student from Rheydt felt shaken, for it seemed to him that Arco-Valley's deed had been motivated by a hatred for social injustice like his own.[55]

Goebbels was living illegally in Munich, since the city council had imposed a ban on "non-Bavarian" students.[56] After only a few days his money ran out. So as not to be entirely dependent on Anka Stalherm, he auctioned off his suits and pawned his cheap wristwatch. When the young woman went to the mountains with well-heeled friends for the Christmas holidays, Goebbels's pride prevented him from going along. He spent Christmas Eve wandering aimlessly through the streets of Munich, agonizing over the "humiliating relationship of dependency" he had fallen into with Anka, "spiritually as well as materially."[57] Complicating matters was the fact that Anka Stalherm's mother was scheming against him again. "Do other people have a right to despise me and to treat me with shame and disgrace just because I love you?" he had brooded in a letter written earlier that year.[58]

Whenever Goebbels suffered intensely from his outsider status, he always came back to the question of a "just God." He puzzled over Ibsen, whose naturalistic plays revealed the fragility of the bourgeois world. He read the works of Strindberg, with their sometimes mystical and magically tinged religiosity. He pored over the plays of the expressionist Georg Kaiser, which dealt with lives twisted by money and technology, and delved into the works of the romantic occultist Gustav Meyrink. Tolstoy's unfinished play *The Light Shines in Darkness* made a deep impression on him; its hero renounces the official church because it not only sanctions unrightfully acquired private property, but also military service and war; yet he remains a prisoner of this "terrible, corrupt" world. In his "Memories" Goebbels later characterized this period with the brief notation "Chaos within me."[59]

As early as the end of October 1919 he had written home about his confusion and begged his father, "Tell me that you don't curse me as a prodigal son who left his parents and went astray!" He received a comforting reply from Fritz Goebbels:

When you write further, "If I lose my faith . . ." I may presume that you haven't yet lost it and that you're merely tormented by doubts. To reassure you, I may say that no one, especially in the early years, is spared such doubts, and that those who suffer them are by far not the worst Christians. Here, too, one attains victory only by way of struggle. To shun the sacraments for this reason is a great mistake, for what adult could claim to approach the table of the Lord with the same childlike purity of heart as at his first communion? Now I must ask you a few questions, for if our relationship is to recover the sense of trust it once had, which no one wishes for more fervently than I, I need answers to these matters. 1. Have you, or do you intend to write books that cannot be reconciled with the Catholic faith? 2. Do you intend to take up a profession unsuitable for a Catholic? If this is not the case, and your doubts are of another sort, let me just say one thing: Pray, and I will pray also, and may our Lord God help you so that all turns out well.[60]

His father's well-meant encouragement did not save Joseph Goebbels from fits of deep depression. The contrast between his vision of a "just, good world" where he would find a suitable position, and the dreary reality of his actual existence seemed almost too painful to bear. As so often before, writing provided relief. Probably under the influence of his friend Richard Flisges, who was still in Freiburg and wrote to him regularly, Goebbels used the Christmas holidays to compose a "fragment of a drama" in a school notebook: "Battle of the Working Class" or, as he later called it in his "Memories," "Work." The play takes place in a factory milieu and denounces social inequities, at times escalating into an outpouring of hatred. Goebbels's hero asks:

Why don't you hate all those who destroyed your youth, who are at it again, destroying the youth of the present generation, and are already greedily reaching out for their children . . . : For they have robbed you of the freedom to hate, to hate with all the ardor of a strong heart, to hate everything that is evil and bad. For they have robbed you of your understanding, have made you an animal that can neither hate nor love. . . . I, however, want to be able to hate . . . and I hate all those who would rob me of what is rightfully mine because God gave it to me. . . . Oh, I can hate, and I don't want to forget how. Oh, how wonderful it is to be able to hate.

Goebbels's protagonist derives strength from his hatred, which he hopes others will acquire. Goebbels concludes, in the nature metaphors typical of his time: "I know it, I feel it. A tempest will sweep over you, smashing all that is rotten and crumbling."[61]

In late January 1920 Goebbels returned to Rheydt, sick in body and spirit. He and Anka had quarreled again. In the circle of his family he hoped to find "peace and clarity." He did in fact gradually recover, thanks to the familiar surroundings, his mother's ministrations, and his good relationship with his brother Hans, whose return from French captivity moved him deeply. He soon patched things up with Anka Stalherm and wrote to her about his brother's return: "I can't begin to describe the scene to you. Tears came to my eyes as I shook his hand. I'll never forget this reunion with him after five years. The first time in so long that the whole family was gathered again around the dear old table. . . . I'll tell you one thing: The so-called Grande Nation deserves to be wiped from the face of the earth. My brother said so." Hans Goebbels was so embittered that the family feared he might attack members of the Belgian occupying forces. Only the plan of going back to school and taking the university entrance examination seemed to distract him. Joseph supported his brother in this project, in the face of his father's and his eldest brother Konrad's opposition; they thought the returnee should look for a job "so he can start earning money."[62]

As usual, Goebbels did tutoring during the semester break, and now he began applying for positions, although the end of his university studies was not yet in sight. He inquired about a job as tutor in East Prussia.[63] An application for a similar job in Holland even drew an expression of interest.[64] He dreamed of staying in Holland if he liked it there.[65]

Goebbels was jolted out of such musings by "sensational news from Berlin" that arrived while he was still home, engrossed in study of Dostoyevski, Tolstoy, and the Russian Revolution. The Erhardt Naval Brigade and other free corps formations that the Reich government had ordered disbanded had marched into the government district and proclaimed their leader, the Pan-German Wolfgang Kapp, chancellor. Goebbels characterized these events in a letter to upper-middle-class Anka Stalherm as a "great success" for the "radical right" and "not unexpected." It was questionable "whether a rightist government is a good thing," he speculated and then asked rhetorically, out of his disdain for the Weimar "system," what was *not* rotten in the state of Denmark?[66]

When the Kapp putsch failed, unrest sprang up in the Reich and the occupied areas. In the Ruhr fifty thousand men formed a German "Red Army" to challenge the Weimar Republic. Goebbels followed these events in the *Kölnische Zeitung*, to which he had a subscription, and commented, "Revolution in the Ruhr. . . . I'm filled with enthusiasm at a distance."[67]

This enthusiasm for the atheist Communists' struggle against the system, a struggle he thought would bring the divine justice for which he yearned, inspired Goebbels to turn his attention again to the struggle of the workers. He produced a bombastic "Happening in Three Acts" entitled "The Seed." Again the theme is a "rotten" and "crumbling" world, to be swept away by a "joyous, bright spring storm" born of the "ardent soul"—in contrast to what he perceived as the prevailing materialistic order. For "the world is good, must be good, and if it is not good now, it must become good once more. A new world will rise out of the old, a gleaming, resplendent one, and all, all shall be happy in this world." For this to come about, a "new human being" would have to appear—this, too, a familiar motif in the literature of the time—who would recognize that "we are all links in one great chain . . . all equally large and equally small." When the workers awakened and rebelled against servitude and oppression, they would plant the seed for the "race that will ripen, a race of strong, beautiful, new human beings."[68]

Richard Flisges, whom Goebbels saw often in Rheydt during the 1920 Easter holidays, responded enthusiastically when he read "The Seed." Probably because he could rely on Anka Stalherm's approbation less and less, Goebbels now considered Flisges his "best friend." When Anka, who reacted indignantly to the play, began to turn away from Goebbels, Flisges stood by him. If the difference in the lovers' backgrounds had often created a tension overcome by the euphoria of love, the gulf created by Goebbels's socialistic views now seemed impossible to bridge. Despite the revolutionary turmoil shaking the Reich to its foundations, Anka Stalherm remained true to her bourgeois origins. The world from which she came offered her every advantage. A lover who showed enthusiasm for the Red revolution and actually seemed happy that her sheltered existence was threatened by political terror could not but appear more and more alien to her.[69]

In mid-April Goebbels wrote Anka Stalherm a letter in which he not only resoundingly condemned the social inequities of which he saw himself a victim, but also named those he considered responsible:

It is rotten and dismal that a world of so many hundred million people should be ruled by a single caste that has the power to lead millions to life or to death, indeed on a whim (for example imperialism in France, capitalism in England and North America, perhaps in Germany as well, etc.). This caste has spun its web over the entire earth; capitalism recognizes no national boundaries (witness the terrible, shameful conditions within German capitalism during the war, whose internationalism created a situation—evidence is available—in which, while battles raged, German prisoners of war in Marseilles were unloading German artillery pieces, marked with the names of German manufacturers, to be used to destroy German lives). Capitalism has learned nothing from recent events and wants to learn nothing, because it places its own interests ahead of those of the other millions. Can one blame those millions for standing up for their own interests, and only for those interests? Can one blame them for striving to forge an international community whose purpose is the struggle against corrupt capitalism? Can one condemn a large segment of the educated *Stürmer* youth for protesting against education's being made a commodity, inaccessible to those with the greatest ability? Is it not an abomination that people with the most brilliant intellectual gifts should sink into poverty and disintegrate, while others dissipate, squander, and waste the money that could help them? . . . You say the old propertied class also worked hard for what it has. Granted, that may be true in many cases. But do you also know about the conditions under which workers were living during the period when capitalism "earned" its fortune?[70]

In the summer of 1920 Anka Stalherm went back to the University of Freiburg, not to Heidelberg with Goebbels. Mentally and materially reinforced by the long vacation at home, Goebbels set to work in a more optimistic frame of mind. "My faith in the future remains unbroken," he wrote her in one of the almost daily letters in which he self-importantly gave her detailed accounts of his studies, which he now planned to wind up. He told her everything he was reading. Now and then he wrote a verse or two, he admitted. "Yes, one can certainly write poetry when one is in Heidelberg and has no cares."[71]

But cares were not long in coming. After Anka Stalherm had visited him at Pentecost, her letters became infrequent. Soon Goebbels heard that a fellow student of hers in Freiburg was courting her, apparently not without success, and in addition a lawyer, one Dr. Georg Mumme, was making advances. Goebbels went on the offensive, proposing that they get engaged. "If you don't feel strong enough to say yes, we must go our separate ways."[72] She did not take him up on the offer. He noted: "Grim days. I shall be alone. I request a final meeting."[73] The meeting took place, but it was not to be the last. Goebbels threatened suicide. Anka Stalherm relented, probably out of pity, after a melodramatic letter from him—"I have suffered enough; how much more shall I have to suffer?"—and promised to be faithful, a promise she did not keep.[74]

On 1 October 1920 Goebbels even drew up a will, in which he named his brother Hans his literary executor, for he apparently still believed firmly in the value of his writings, which now only Flisges appreciated. He meticulously enumerated his few possessions—an alarm clock, a drawing, a few books—bequeathing them to friend and family. In addition he directed that "his wardrobe and other possessions not otherwise assigned" should be sold, and that his debts be paid off from the proceeds. Anka Stalherm should be asked to burn his letters and any other writings. "May she be happy and get over my death. . . . I part gladly from this life, which for me has become a hell."[75]

Goebbels did not die, but suffered a nervous breakdown. With the suicide threat he achieved his objective—getting his family to lavish attention on him. While his mother tried to comfort him, his father promised his chronically impecunious son that he would somehow find the extra money to see him through his studies, although the family finances were already stretched to the limit. Goebbels's brother Hans wrote to Anka Stalherm, trying to bring about a reconciliation. His letter went unanswered.

On long walks Richard Flisges patiently listened to Goebbels's tales of woe; Goebbels wrote gratefully, "Flisges is the only one who understands me . . . he asks no questions, does everything for me, and knows exactly what I'm thinking and feeling."[76]

As the winter semester approached, Flisges accompanied his still shaky friend to Heidelberg for a few days, to help him look for Anka Stalherm. Since she was not to be found there, he went on to Munich at Goebbels's behest and expense. After a few days, at the end of October he wrote to Goebbels that he had seen her "with a money-aristocrat in a cutaway studded with gold buttons and pins."[77] Flisges urged his friend to come at once if he wanted to see her and speak with her. Goebbels hurried to join Flisges in Munich. Together they made their way to the house on Amalienstrasse where she lived. Flisges, who went ahead to the front door, came back after a short time with ill tidings: the young woman had left for Freiburg with "her fiancé." After a long evening at the Café Stadt Wien, Goebbels made his way back to Heidelberg in despair. From there he wrote Anke Stalherm a threatening letter, which he then regretted and followed with a "letter of contrition," which likewise changed nothing. Anka Stalherm married the lawyer Mumme. In her farewell letter to Goebbels she admitted that she was "very unhappy" because "I feel that you were the first and the last man to love me as I wanted to be loved, and as I must be loved to be happy."[78] He responded for the last time that he regretted nothing of what he had said, done, or written. "I had to do it because a demon within me drove me to it."[79]

If he ever amounted to something, Goebbels wrote later, he would like to run into Anka Stalherm again. His wish was granted in 1928. After seeing her again in Weimar, the Gauleiter of Berlin confided to his diary that this reminder of her made all other womanly beauty fade to insignificance. The numerous women with whom he was involved in Berlin became in his eyes "mere playthings." When he asked himself why he toyed with the feelings of other women, he replied that it was "the revenge of the betrayed creature." Thereafter he and Anka arranged to meet now and then during his extended propaganda tours. They loved each other "as if only a day had passed between 1920 and now." A human being could experience a love that fulfilled him completely but once in a lifetime, he wrote in his diary after one of these trysts, for which he yearned greatly. Yet he no longer shared his innermost self with Anka, for he had accepted the chain of events that had altered fundamentally their respective circumstances. The woman who had formerly faced life so confidently was miserable in her marriage, while he, once a penniless wretch, was on his way to the top. "Thus vengeance comes, late but all the more cruelly. But that is good. We were not meant to come together. I had to take the road to action."[80]

When he met Magda Quandt, later to be his wife, Goebbels broke off contact with Anka Mumme. Not until several years later, in 1933, did he hear from her again. Now divorced and in financial distress, she turned to the powerful minister of propaganda for help. He arranged for her to get a job in the editorial offices of the Berlin women's magazine *Die Dame*.

But in the winter of 1920 Goebbels was neither Gauleiter of Berlin nor Reich propaganda minister, but a poor student at Heidelberg, inclined on the basis of experience to view all human beings as *canaille*, beasts. Goebbels tried to master his despair by "drowning his sorrows in drink," as he later confessed, or by burying himself in his books. In this state of mind he came upon Spengler's *Decline of the West*, which dispelled any vision of a "just world" to which he might have clung. In the face of the eternal law of the rise and fall of civilizations, only the strong could prevail. He recorded his impressions as follows: "Pessimism. Despair. I no longer believe in anything."[81]

A sense of hopelessness and general meaninglessness, exacerbated by illness, must have been reflected in Goebbels's letters to his family during this period. Around the beginning of December his father wrote back, advising him not to study too hard and assuring him that his worries about the future were unfounded. "The best thing is to face the future with trust in God. If one does one's duty and lets the Lord's will be done . . . that will get one the furthest."[82] These kindly words from his father and especially the money he wired enabled Goebbels to spend Christmas with his family in Rheydt, which also gave him a more hopeful outlook. In the spring of 1921 he threw himself into his work, determined to finish his studies and free his parents from this financial burden. He had decided to go for the doctorate. Taking the *Staatsexamen*, the state certification exam, would open the door to civil-service jobs, providing security in uncertain times, but it did not enjoy the prestige of the doctorate. Throughout his life—whether as Gauleiter or minister—Goebbels would place particular emphasis on the title of doctor. He always insisted on being addressed as "Herr Doktor" and initialed documents "Dr. G."

During his winter semester in Munich in 1919–20, Goebbels had decided to write his dissertation on pantomime. He wanted the project to be supervised by Artur Kutscher, a professor of literary history and theater, whose distinguished pupils over the course of an illustrious career included Bertolt Brecht.[83] Goebbels went so far as to call on Kutscher during his office hours, but he soon abandoned the topic he had chosen; perhaps it had just been a whim inspired by theater experiences in Munich. He now chose as sponsor the Heidelberg literary historian and Goethe biographer Friedrich Gundolf, a Jew. The professor, whose lecture course on German romanticism Goebbels attended in the 1920 summer semester, was a leading disciple of the poet Stefan George, who proclaimed that the bourgeois era was nearing an end, to be replaced by something entirely new.

Goebbels remarked enthusiastically that Gundolf was an "extraordinarily charming and agreeable man."[84] He sought out the professor and immediately presented his idea for a dissertation. But since Gundolf had just turned down a chair in Berlin, the University of Heidelberg had rewarded him by freeing him of the obligation to give seminars and supervise dissertations. Gundolf referred Goebbels to Prof. Max von Waldberg, who had studied with the famous Germanist Scherer. Waldberg assigned Goebbels a topic: Wilhelm Schütz, a little-known member of the romantic school active as a dramatist in the first half of the nineteenth century. In April 1921 Goebbels assembled a great stack of books and sat down to write his dissertation. His parents had set up his old room as a cozy study.

In exactly four months, working straight through the summer, Goebbels composed a dissertation on this romantic convert to Catholicism.[85] In his preface he quotes, as a sort of declaration of faith, Shatov's famous speech from Dostoyevski's *The Possessed*:

Science and Reason have, from the beginning of time, played a secondary and subordinate part in the life of nations; so it will be till the end of time. Nations are built up and moved by another force that sways and dominates them, the origin of which is unknown and inexplicable: that force is the force of an insatiable desire to go on to the end, though at the same time it denies that end.[86]

Goebbels saw this dominating force at work in romanticism as well as in the present. He wrote in his introduction:

37

Now, as then, there is an almost pathologically intense spirituality, an almost boiling fervor and yearning for something nobler and finer than that for which we now live and strive. A heightening of feeling, not always free of a certain sentimentality, a swirling mass of new thoughts and ideas, often in conflict with one another, yet apparently sprung from the same source; but nowhere does fulfillment, balance, harmony, or peace manifest itself. In both periods, grave, troubled times in the life of the people; one may almost speak of European crises. Everyone senses the tension in the air and breathes with difficulty in this atmosphere. Now, as then, shallow rationalism makes its presence felt everywhere, finding its ultimate goal and purpose in dull, spiritless atheism. But against it struggles the young generation of God-seekers, of mystics, of romantics. They speak of idealism and love, venerate a God who is experienced mystically by the individual, believe in a world that is good.

But nowhere is there "a powerful genius that can lead the way over new billows from the chaos of the times to a new era."[87]

To be sure, Goebbels did not yet see his longed-for "powerful genius" in the obscure Austrian who had just taken control of the small German Workers' Party. What little he had heard of the beer-hall speaker from his former classmate Fritz Prang apparently did not make much of an impression on him. That summer of 1921 Goebbels conceived a "profound affection" for a girl from the neighborhood, Maria Kamerbeek, who typed his dissertation for him.[88] In the fall, when his brother Konrad married Maria's relative Käthe, Goebbels contributed a cartoon to the humorous wedding pamphlet that seemed calculated to offend any Hitler supporters present at the wedding. It showed a child sitting on a chamber pot, with the following couplet as caption:

If I but see a swastika,
I feel the urge to make caca.[89]

A few days after the wedding Goebbels handed in his dissertation, dedicated to his parents, at the office of the dean of the University of Heidelberg. He had received a list of suggested revisions from Waldberg, but he was reluctant to work them into the already typed manuscript. Nor had Goebbels been overly assiduous in tracking down sources; he had missed important assessments of Schütz's works. Although his own evaluation of Schütz followed the conventional judgment, and the low esteem in which he held the Enlightenment echoed current thinking, Waldberg evaluated the 215-page treatise, smoothly written and bristling with loaded concepts like "fate," "*Volk*," "love of fatherland," "enthusiasm," and "spiritual greatness," with *rite superato*—high praise, indeed; the diploma still exists.[90]

On 16 November 1921 Joseph Goebbels received his summons to the oral examination, scheduled for 18 November. "To Heidelberg. . . . Called on the examiners. In top hat. Richard there for support. Crammed all night. A cup of strong mocha. And then to the exam."[91] Although not everything went as well as he had expected, Goebbels satisfied the examiners, Professors Waldberg, Oncken, Paum, and Neumann. He received a provisional doctoral diploma on the spot and felt proud—as he later noted—when Waldberg called him "Herr Doktor" for the first time. After sending his parents a telegram, he spent the night out drinking with Richard Flisges. The next day they set out for Bonn, where some of his friends from Rheydt were studying. For two days Goebbels caroused with them in the same pubs where he had spent many an hour in his fraternity days. Upon his return to Rheydt, he received an unforgettable welcome: "Everyone at the station. At home everything decorated, many flowers."[92]

The family was proud of the youngest son. By late November 1921 Fritz Goebbels could look back on a remarkable rise in status. He himself had started as a lowly assistant laborer and through persistence and purposeful hard work had achieved the rank of plant manager. He and his wife had saved every penny to pay off the modest little house on Dahlener Strasse and provide the children with a good education. Konrad and Hans had achieved the intermediate *Matura*, and now, as their daughter Maria was entering the Gymnasium, Joseph had become a Ph.D. With pride, satisfaction, and many a grateful prayer the parents noted that their ambitions for this problem child had been more than fulfilled. If nature had treated him less than kindly, at least he would be better off as far as prestige and financial opportunities were concerned. Not for a moment did they doubt that all doors would now be open to him.

The successful conclusion of his studies allowed Joseph Goebbels to repress a number of things that had been plaguing him. He relished having the relatives come pay their respects to him, or having neighbors use his title when greeting him. If he held forth at the Remges Café, where he had often sat as a schoolboy, people listened more attentively. Even the heartache of losing Anka Stalherm gave way to the pleasure of a budding relationship with Else Janke, a teacher in Rheydt. In short, his gloomy view of the world seemed to be yielding to hopes for a brighter future.

CHAPTER 3

Away with doubts;
I'm determined to be strong
and have faith
(1921—1923)

Dr. Joseph Goebbels, now intent on escaping from the petty-bourgeois confines of his parents' home, had not given much thought to his future. He aspired to become a writer or a freelance journalist. That such occupations offered little promise of keeping bread on the table hardly affected his musings, which in any case had more in common with daydreams than with real plans. For a while he had flirted with the notion of emigrating to India with Richard Flisges. In Freiburg the two of them had delved into Indian philosophy, fantasizing about spending their lives under southern skies. But when Goebbels returned to Rheydt, everyday reality caught up with him, and the vision of India faded, even though Richard Flisges urged him to keep India in mind, "because things there can't be worse than here."[1] Indeed, as the year 1921 drew to a close, conditions could not have been more unfavorable for a young person trying to become established in a profession. Germany's defeat had brought a grim aftermath of unemployment and poverty. Although the victorious powers had just signed the Treaty of London, reducing the reparations payments imposed at Versailles, the Germans still owed 132 billion marks in gold; there could be no question of economic recovery.

Yet fortune seemed to smile on Joseph Goebbels in early 1922. His penchant for holding forth about God and the world, but especially about his times, found an outlet when the *Westdeutsche Landeszeitung* accepted a series of six articles, to be published between January and March. These pieces attracted a "good deal of attention," as Goebbels proudly claimed in later years.[2] Although the paper's editors did not share Goebbels's views, they presented his articles as "an earnest attempt to interpret the mysterious sphinx-face of our grim times."[3]

Considerably influenced by Spengler, Goebbels identified materialism as the source of "the political, intellectual, and moral confusion of our times." And as a universal curative he proposed, in the spirit of Dosto-yevski, a return to the "German soul," the source of a mystical strength that guided the fate of the *Volk*. He linked this notion to the idea of an "organic body of the *Volk*," which he felt had manifested itself in the solidarity the German people displayed at the beginning of the war. He claimed to love "my Germany from the deepest recesses of my heart," and declared that "love of the fatherland is worship of God," and "To be German today means keeping still, waiting, and working to improve oneself in secret."[4]

In another article Goebbels attacked "those good Germans who believe salvation must come from an external source." He called upon them to reject "everything foreign to our being" and to awaken their "own soul" to new life. Despite the Weimar "system" and the shameful territorial concessions and reparations, they should not let themselves to be per-suaded "that the German soul is dead. It is only sick, indeed very sick, for it has been abused, subjugated, and trampled upon."[5]

Unwilling to accept Spengler's pessimistic prognoses, Goebbels asserted that "the German soul will not fail to react, as always in times of crisis, against all elements foreign to its nature."[6] In the spring of 1922 he thought he could detect the direction from which that soul would draw its strength. Certainly not from the decadent capital of the Reich: "No, no, salvation cannot come from Berlin. . . . Sometimes it looks as though a new sun is about to rise in the south." By this "new sun" Goebbels meant the hotbed of *völkisch* groups in Munich, among which Hitler's National Socialist German Workers' Party (NSDAP) was attracting more and more attention. Although he had laughed at the Nazis only a few months earlier, Goebbels now began to view them as an expression of the rebelling "German soul" and followed their gains with interest.

Goebbels had another reason for feeling confident. The same acquaint-ance who had helped him get the six articles published recommended him for a part-time internship with the *Westdeutsche Landeszeitung*, where he was assigned to the cultural section. But his hopes for a per-manent position were dashed a few weeks later. The editor in chief explained in a letter that the paper was about to launch a morning paper in Dutch; unfortunately he had to ask Goebbels to leave to make room for the new editor.[7]

A period of involuntary idleness ensued, finally broken by a speech on contemporary German literature that Goebbels gave in October at the School for Business and the Trades.[8] Although inflation had driven up the ticket price to thirty marks, the event drew a sizable audience. Goeb-bels welcomed the proceeds from his appearance, a supplement to his earnings from tutoring.[9] The speech, devoted largely to Spengler, also helped repair his frayed self-respect.[10] He recalled later that the evening had been a complete success, and his girlfriend Else Janke had been "ecstatic."

By now Goebbels had established a steady relationship with Else, who taught at the elementary school just down the street from his parents' house. They had met at a party given by the Catholic Businessmen's Association, and he had promptly set about winning her favor. It took many long walks and talks before this practical-minded young woman began to succumb to the "Herr Doktor," who once more concealed his inner turmoil behind charming and urbane chatter. They became intimate when Goebbels visited Else for a few days on the Baltic island of Baltrum, during her vacation. In the letters she wrote after his departure, Else enthused about the "glorious time granted us on Baltrum," and he, too, was quite smitten.[11]

But it was not the love that he had experienced with Anka Stalherm. The relationship with Else Janke was more companionable than passionate. Goebbels could not help noticing that, despite all her compassion and her admiration for his intellect, Else found his clubfoot repulsive and wondered whether he was the right man to father her children. For a long time she went to some lengths to conceal the relationship from their neighbors in Rheydt.[12] The couple often quarreled about this; no doubt the quarrels were particularly painful to Goebbels because they reminded him forcefully of his defect. Bitter confrontations were usually smoothed over with extravagant declarations of love; the two apparently felt that they could withstand life's blows better together than alone.

Eventually "Elslein," as he called her, realized it would be up to her to find a job for her lover. Time and again she had to pull Goebbels back to sober reality when he indulged in euphoric visions of a future as a writer, visions that were almost invariably followed by deep depression. "We must become somewhat more modest and get ourselves to the point where we don't throw everything overboard at the slightest setback," she cajoled him.[13] Her practicality finally bore fruit: a distant relative of hers held out the prospect of a job for Goebbels at a Cologne branch of the Dresden Bank. Goebbels showed not the slightest enthusiasm when the job actually materialized in December 1922. Else had to pressure him to accept: "Let's be happy that things have turned out this way, and I'm convinced that it will be for the best—if it isn't too difficult for you—if you accept the position."[14] His parents likewise urged the reluctant Goebbels to take the job. Feeling obligated to Else and his parents, who were essentially supporting him, Goebbels promised to take this opportunity to earn his own keep, although he did make a few half-hearted and futile attempts to find a position he considered more suitable.

Goebbels saw the bank job as tantamount to betrayal of the vague "ideals" that more and more preoccupied him. He who believed in the rebirth of the "German soul," and had missed no opportunity to proclaim this belief with almost messianic fervor to his friends and acquaintances in Rheydt, now had to take his place in a "temple of materialism." The frustrated writer told Else in a letter written at Christmastime:

> The world has become a madhouse, and even the best people are joining the frenzied dance around the Golden Calf. And worst of all, they don't admit it, but seek to conceal it or even to defend it by claiming that the new times call for a different sort of person, that one must adapt to circumstances. Yes, they'll sing this year with joy and enthusiasm of Christ, bringer of peace. I can't join in, for I see no peace, neither in the world nor in myself. Out there it's without form and void, and inside me the festive altars have been overturned, the images of joy shattered. Worldliness is moving into the mansions where spirit and love once reigned; they call this taking into account the new times. Mighty Fate, how shall I prevail in Thy eyes? I can no longer be Thy faithful servant. All have turned away from Thee; the last and best have abandoned Thy banner and gone forth into the world. Now it's my turn.[15]

On 2 January 1923 Goebbels began work at the Dresden Bank. Every morning at 5:30 he caught the train from Rheydt to Cologne. Around 8:00 in the evening Else would meet him at the station when he returned. After a few days he found a furnished room in Cologne that his "wretched salary" just covered. Since he had no money left for food, he depended on packages and money from home.[16] In spite of his education and his title, he was still a "poor devil." What apparently sustained him in the face of this bitter realization was the encouragement of his fiancée, who begged her "lovie" to stick it out and "simply trust that better times will come."[17] She often visited him in the afternoon after school let out, and they spent the weekends together in Rheydt.

It soon became difficult to maintain this pattern, for political developments in the Rhine-Ruhr region resulted in a collapse of the infrastructure. On the pretext that Germany had failed to pay its reparations, a combined Belgian-French force had crossed the Rhine on 11 January 1923 and occupied the Ruhr. Supported by all the political parties, the German government reacted by halting reparations payments altogether and directing its officials not to obey orders from the occupying powers. Workers went out on strike, bringing mines, factories, and railroads to a standstill. Goebbels found the policy of passive resistance "dreadful," yet another proof of the "decadence" of the "system," which relied on rhetoric rather than deeds. During these weeks he wrote "desperate poems" and looked to the south of Germany all the more expectantly.

There the local agitator Hitler was making incendiary speeches, proclaiming the Führer concept and announcing that he would soon put an end to German impotence. In April 1923 nationalist groups from throughout Bavaria gathered in Munich, planning concerted action for the end of the month. But their attempt to disrupt the leftists' May Day celebration on the Theresienwiese and simultaneously topple the Bavarian government failed wretchedly. The would-be putschists capitulated to the army and the police, thus becoming the laughingstock of the entire nation.

With this hope smashed, Goebbels felt things could only get worse. The French and Belgians had brought in their own technicians and engineers, their railway men and a small army of foreign workers, and had got the mines and railways working again. The Reich, which had been printing money to support the occupied area, now experienced runaway inflation. Unemployment and the resulting poverty took on alarming proportions, especially in the cities. Goebbels wrote accusingly, "Here in Cologne about a hundred children die every month of starvation," while "they sit at the conference table and debate the definition of passive resistance and whether the Ruhr should be evacuated in stages." He inveighed against the Catholic Church, because the Cologne cathedral's holdings included a precious monstrance valued at twelve million gold marks, or 280 trillion at the prevailing rate of inflation. "With that one could send 560,000 starving children to the country or to a sanatorium for two months, thereby saving them for productive lives."[18]

Goebbels, himself in sorry physical and mental condition once again, was outraged at injustices he witnessed daily at the bank. While petty-bourgeois bank customers were losing their life savings, debts secured by land and tangible assets were essentially canceled, making wealthy property owners even wealthier. Speculators were accumulating vast riches by engaging in currency manipulation and acquiring property at rock-bottom prices, while in the streets innocent people suffered dire need. Commented Goebbels: "You speak of capital investments; but behind this fine concept lurks animal greed for more. I say animal, but that's an insult to animals; for animals eat only until they are full."[19]

Some of his fellow bank employees apparently did not hesitate to exploit the galloping devaluation of the mark by taking advantage of insider information. In a letter to Else Janke, Goebbels wrote: "This afternoon I told one of the young louts that I considered his actions a revolting swindle; he responded with nothing but a pitying shrug. And not one person among those who heard us talking spoke up for me. Everyone seemed to agree: a deal's a deal."[20]

He confessed to Else in June 1923 that he felt he did not fit into this world. She, too, was becoming disheartened. She had written at the end of April that it was awful "the way these bleak, grim times unremittingly weigh us down, making you so disconsolate, so miserable."[21] It was probably her sympathy that moved him to write a letter of more than thirty pages, a review of his messed-up life. "I know that at one point my situation was better. Today I'm shipwrecked on a sandbar. . . . I am given no peace to come to myself. Being unfulfilled in one's work is a terrible torment." Extrapolating from his own lot, he speculated that the "intellectual youth" were so anguished because no one let them take their rightful place in society. "The old men of yesteryear" held all the power and insisted on hitching to "their wagon, their world" "us young people, who bear a new world in our hearts and only with shame and disdain tolerate the domination of the old one."[22]

After a phase of deep depression Goebbels typically experienced bursts of fanatical determination. In one such moment he wrote to Else that the new age would be ushered in not by businessmen and bankers but by those who had remained "pure" and had not "dirtied their hands with the lucre of a godless world." And if this new era should come too late for him, that was all right, too; it was grand and fine to smooth the way for an era of greatness. He was not the only one who felt this way, he wrote. He was one of the best, the youth. "We'll be the ferment that brings about the revolution and gives rise to new life. We'll have the right to speak the first word in the new era. And this word will be: truth; death to lies and fraud; love."[23]

Barely ten years would pass before this "great era" dawned for Goebbels. That it dawned at all had much to do with the crisis coming to a head in the early summer of 1923. While the Cuno cabinet groped impotently for a solution, passive resistance in the occupied region threatened to collapse. More and more the initiative passed into the hands of the radicals. Men like Leo Schlageter had long since organized paramilitary groups that carried out raids on the occupying forces and their installations. These raids brought ruthless reprisals, which left people even worse off. In the general confusion, all sorts of irresponsible elements flourished. Goebbels fell victim to them one day while driving from Cologne to Rheydt. Melodramatically stylizing his own experience to make it reflect the chaos of the times, he noted later: "Ambush. Seriously injured. Home in an ambulance. . . . Mother almost had heart attack."[24]

In two weeks the "seriously injured" young man had recovered completely. When he returned to Cologne, he again fell into deep depression. The city revolted him, the work at the bank seemed meaningless, and his earnings were "as good as nothing," even though the number of zeroes on his pay slip kept increasing. He tried to call attention to his despair by threatening suicide. Else Janke again persuaded him to face life: "Away with doubts; I'm determined to be strong and have faith."[25]

Now he took note of the "crazy times" with "secret pleasure," for they seemed to hold the promise of a fresh start. "Yes, chaos must come if things are ever to get better."[26]

In July 1923 Goebbels felt he could no longer stand working at the bank. He decided to take sick leave. He went to two doctors, feigning symptoms, but to no avail. Finally a third doctor certified him as ill for six weeks, for in the meantime he actually had fallen ill. After a few days he was feeling so much better that he could accompany Else to Baltrum, their "El Dorado" of the previous year.[27] But the tranquil days there, which he hoped would bring him inner peace, came to an abrupt end: his friend Richard Flisges, who had left the university and was working as a miner in the Upper Bavarian town of Schliersee, died in a mining accident. Goebbels was "deeply shaken" by the news. "I'm no longer in command of my senses. Alone in the world. . . . So now I have lost everything."[28]

To create a "literary monument" to Flisges, "the brave soldier of labor" who had sustained him so often during his years at the university, Goebbels now decided to write a novel: "Michael Voormann: A Man's Fate in Leaves from a Diary."[29] The name of the hero was borrowed from "Michael Voormann's Youth," written four and a half years earlier. But where that text had been entirely autobiographical, in the 1923 novel the protagonist combined features of Richard Flisges and Goebbels.

The book provides evidence that Goebbels was no longer willing to put up with his and his "poor, lost people" 's wretched lot, which God seemed to tolerate. In the "prelude" he writes: "From mysterious depths the powers of young life surge up in ever-changing forms. Decay and dissolution in these times signify more than that; not destruction but transformation. . . . In the hearts of young people flames the glowing urge for reconstruction, for new life and youthful form. Full of pain, they await their day. In garrets in the great cities, where hunger, cold, and spiritual anguish lurk, grow the hope and symbol of a different era. Faith, work, and yearning are the virtues that unite the new youth in their Faustian creative urge. This brings the young people together: the spirit of resurrection, rejection of materialism, movement toward faith, toward love, toward passionate surrender."[30]

The hastily contrived plot of "Michael" essentially serves one purpose: to present Goebbels's view of the world. By using the diary form, Goebbels got around the necessity of presenting this view in logical order. Instead the novel offers a confused jumble of descriptions of prevailing conditions and theses about a "new era," with bits and pieces from Goebbels's reading thrown in for good measure. The Bible, Goethe's *Faust* and *Wilhelm Meister*, Nietzsche's works, especially *Zarathustra*, and the works of Dostoyevski—all left their traces here.

With the novel, Goebbels finally took leave of his "old world of faith."[31] Michael/Goebbels, who has hoped in vain for the "justice" of the "Christian god," comes to the conclusion that it does not matter what one believes in; the important thing is to believe. He invokes this unspecified faith like a fetish: "O my strong, glowing, mighty faith. O companion on my journey, preparer of the path, my friend and my god!"[32] He asserts that the more forcefully he believes, the more fanatically he worships his fetish, the more vital and strong he will become: "The greater and stronger I make God, the greater and stronger I am myself."[33]

Now that belief itself had become his god, Goebbels thought humanity no longer required Christ's sacrifice for its salvation. "Modern man," who carried within him belief and therefore also God, would save his species through his own sacrifice. Michael/Goebbels, the "Christsocialist," sacrifices himself out of love for humanity.[34] Thus Goebbels gave meaning to Flisges's death in the mine, but also to his own life, that of an unemployed cripple.

Although Goebbels's "modern man" can provide his own salvation, he still seeks the "savior" in human form. In his dissertation Goebbels had already expressed his longing for a "strong genius." Now he has his Michael ask whether there is no one around who knows the way to a better future.[35] Goebbels was still looking for an intermediary, someone who in his new "world of belief" would function as a *vis spiritualis*, like Christ in his former Catholic world.

In focusing on faith, on the longing for an incarnation of faith, and on the notion of self-salvation through sacrifice, Goebbels anticipated the pseudoreligious, bombastic rhetoric of the National Socialist cult that suggested that with its help people could free themselves from the shackles of reality. In 1925 he wrote: "We have learned that politics is no longer the art of the possible. The laws of mechanics would tell us that what we desire is unattainable and unfulfillable. We know that. And yet we act on the basis of our insights, for we believe in miracles, in the impossible and the unattainable. For us politics is the miracle of the impossible."[36] Time and again in the coming years he would pay tribute to belief in the impossible. In 1933, when he had long since found in the Führer Adolf Hitler the incarnation of his belief, he proclaimed the miracle of the impossible become reality. And even ten years later, after the catastrophe of Stalingrad, which he recast as a national sacrifice, the price of the coming victory, Goebbels would invoke the miracle again, though this time it would not come true.

After completing "Michael Voormann," Goebbels devoted an article in the *Rheydter Zeitung* to the memory of his friend Flisges.[37] In "Christmas Salute to a Solitary Grave in Schliersee," he once more celebrated

Flisges's death as a symbolic sacrifice. Olgi Esenwein, his friend's sweetheart, to whom Goebbels sent both the article and later the manuscript of the novel, commented that Goebbels had been the only person who understood Flisges in all his "beauty and grandeur of soul."[38]

After several revisions, "Michael" would eventually be published in 1929 by Eher Verlag, the National Socialist publishing house in Munich.[39] The new title was *A German Life in Leaves from a Diary*, and the protagonist had become a thoroughly Germanic "worker of the mind and hand," the prototype of the new National Socialist human being. Michael's girlfriend, Hertha Holk, represents the bourgeoisie, and, like Anka Stalherm, cannot understand her lover, who denounces the "nigger armies on the Rhine,"[40] and the soulless and corrupt rule of the "fat bellies," the Jews, the "cyst on the body of our languishing German being,"[41] whom he blames for the Germans' misery. In both versions, by some strange coincidence, Goebbels's Michael dies on 30 January, the very day when Hitler would seize power in 1933, fulfilling Goebbels's dream of a "new era."

Heinz Pol, a critic for the left-liberal *Weltbühne*, commented in 1931 that Goebbels's *Michael* was the "full-fledged manifestation" of what the brownshirts called "the German spirit and the German soul." He claimed he had read the book several times without finding a single sentence he could call truly German in spirit or in style. "What I did find—and every third word is evidence for this—was that thoroughly un-German, absolutely pathological shamelessness with which a literary slob continually bares his breast and bellows out 'ultimate truths.' "[42]

But let us go back to 1923. Shortly after Goebbels returned from Baltrum, shaken by Flisges's death, he received a letter dismissing him from the Dresden Bank. He did not tell his parents. To maintain the impression that he was still working, he went back to Cologne, where he in fact joined the army of the unemployed. He had to get by on one gulden a week, for he was not even entitled to unemployment compensation. The only constructive thing he did was to work on a "contemporary drama" that he called "The Wanderer," for he saw himself as a wanderer between the old era and the new.

Goebbels thought the situation so hopeless that he did not go to much trouble to look for a job, although he assured Else he was leaving no stone unturned.[43] His brother Hans had not gone back to school as originally planned, but had found a steady job in Neuss; he gave Joseph the address of a company to which he should apply for work. More he could not do, wrote Hans, for his own job "brought in only enough for my room and board. What more can one expect nowadays, when the rich keep getting richer and the poor poorer? It's truly amazing how these stuffed pigs manage over and over again to pass all our fatherland's sufferings and worries, expenses and debts down to the poorest of the poor in Germany."[44]

By mid-September Fritz Goebbels had heard that his youngest son was looking for a job, but he did not know he was unemployed. Fearing that Joseph might risk his position at the bank, he cautioned him that it was not so easy to find a suitable job in times like these. As a temporary solution he advised that he apply at a bank in Rheydt where his brother Konrad had connections. "Then at least you would have enough to eat and could wait in peace until you find a suitable job," wrote the older Goebbels, who did not know what to make of his son's notions and much preferred a solid profession like banking.[45]

Since even Else Janke's self-sacrificing support could not save him from starvation, Goebbels finally wrote his father a desperate letter, which he hoped would lead to an invitation to come home. He said he had developed a nervous disorder, probably hereditary in origin.[46] He had calculated right. His solicitous father firmly rejected the imputation of a genetic weakness, but urged Joseph to come home at once, in spite of his presumed job at the bank, since only at home could he count on support in this difficult situation. Finally, after his father had sent money for a ticket, Goebbels left Cologne to take refuge, as so often in previous years, in the bosom of his family. It was early October 1923.

From Rheydt he followed the national developments that ensued from the total collapse of passive resistance in the occupied territories. After the fall of the Cuno cabinet, a great coalition government had formed on 13 August, with Gustav Stresemann as chancellor. Of all people, it was this leader of a nationalistic party on the right, the German People's Party (Deutsche Volkspartei, or DVP), who capitulated on foreign policy: on 26 September he called off the failed policy of obstruction. Goebbels noted that the hated "system" parties now all claimed opportunistically to have opposed the policy of passive resistance from the outset.

In the *Kölnische Zeitung*, to which he subscribed, and in other papers as well, Goebbels read accounts of the uprisings staged by rightist and leftist extremists that led Stresemann to declare a state of emergency. He read that in Saxony and Hamburg the Communists' influence was growing rapidly. He read about Hitler's National Socialists, now attracting more and more attention. But on the basis of the events of the past spring, he had little confidence in this group. The "chaos" he had once longed for as the precondition for a new beginning seemed to reign everywhere. He wrote melodramatically of "wild days spent drinking, out of sheer despair," for he now believed he was witnessing the "downfall of the Germanic ideal."[47]

News of the events in Munich on 8 and 9 November jolted him out of his lethargy: Hitler had proclaimed a "national revolution." Had the turning point actually arrived, with the country in dire need, the value of its currency destroyed, industry largely at a standstill, and the Berlin government steadily losing power? But even before 8 November was past, Hitler's presumed conservative allies had backed off. Believing that they might yet force fate to do their bidding, the "betrayed" putschists, led by Hitler and the famous general Ludendorff, organized a march on the following day through the heart of Munich in the direction of the Ministry of War. Then, at the Feldherrnhalle, where the singing marchers found themselves heading straight for a police cordon, a single shot rang out, followed by a brief, heavy exchange of gunfire that left seventeen dead, numerous marchers arrested, and the putsch crushed, to Goebbels's intense disappointment.

Toward the end of 1923 things began to settle down in the Reich. At least for the present, the young republic had withstood attacks from the Right and the Left. By the time Stresemann resigned the chancellorship on 23 November, after one hundred days in office, the inflation was over and German currency had stabilized. As foreign investment resumed, the economy began to recover, and gradually unemployment diminished.

Necessity now impelled Goebbels to look in earnest for work. He applied to the *Vossische Zeitung*[48] and then wrote a long letter to the *Berliner Tageblatt*, a respected liberal newspaper. He asked for a position as editor and named 250 marks per month as an appropriate salary.[49] He also applied to Mosse, a large publishing company that had advertised for an editor. To present himself as a man of broad cultivation, he offered an embellished version of his activities since the end of his university studies. He claimed to have studied the history of modern "theater and journalism" in Bonn and Berlin between November 1921 and August 1922. After a two-month internship at the *Westdeutsche Landeszeitung*, he had undertaken "independent study of national and public-sector economics" from October to the end of 1923. He claimed that during his nine months at the Dresden Bank he had acquired a knowledge of "far-reaching aspects of modern banking." In his "other specialty" he had studied political economy at the University of Cologne and had written intermittently for some of western Germany's major dailies. "Because of a mild nervous disorder brought on by overwork and a accident, I was compelled to terminate my activity in Cologne."[50] Yet the efforts of the "completely recovered" applicant proved in vain.

To help him shed the accumulated bitterness from these repeated disappointments, Else Janke had given him a blank "book for daily use" in October 1923. From 17 October on he wrote in it every evening, dwelling on whatever oppressed his spirit. In the summer of 1924 he added his "Memories," in which he recapitulated in telegram style his life up to that October. He wrote, he explained, "because thinking is at once a torment and a joy to me. Earlier, when it was Saturday and the afternoon wore on, I'd find myself terribly restless. The entire week, with its childish torments, would weigh on my soul. The best solution for me was always to take my prayer book and go to church. I'd think of all the good and the bad the week had brought me, and then I'd go to the priest and purge my soul by confession. Now, when I write, I have a similar feeling. It's like confession. I want to purge every last thing from my soul by confession."[51]

He repeatedly justified himself in his own eyes by saying that he could not be held responsible for his fate. He repeatedly blamed everything on the "degenerate world." Since he refused to be robbed of what was called independence of thought, the courage of his convictions, personality, and character, the entrance to the materialistic world remained blocked to him, he wrote, taking comfort in the notion of being an exceptional person. All the virtues he claimed for himself he found lacking in most of his fellow human beings. To the typical Rheydt philistine, he wrote, any intellectual conversation seemed tedious and awkward. "They are too lazy to play *Skat*, and even, some claim, to make love. No wonder they get so big and fat."

Feeling left out, he hated them all; in spite of, or perhaps precisely because of, his university training and his doctorate, he seemed to have remained an outsider, still living off his parents and his fiancée. "This wretched parasitic condition. I beat my brains out trying to think how I can end this unworthy situation," he wrote in his diary.[52] In another passage he noted, "Nothing awaits me—no joy, no pain, no responsibilities, no task. . . . Oh, what a wretched life that must be directed toward filthy lucre."[53] Money, which he had always lacked, was something he had come to hate above all; he saw it as "the source of all evil. It's as if Mammon were the embodiment of the principle of evil in the world. I hate money from the deepest depths of my soul."[54] He harbored equally hostile feelings toward those with whose finances he had to deal every day—the Jews. The publishers Mosse and Ullstein were Jews, and they—as he saw it—had denied him a chance to earn a living.[55]

The Goebbels family had no more prejudice against Jews than other petty-bourgeois Catholics. The Jews had the reputation of being particularly clever and skillful at handling money, but otherwise they were seen as perfectly normal Germans, especially since they had fought and died for kaiser and fatherland during the war. After Fritz Goebbels had worked his way up, his family became friendly with the family of Josef Joseph, a respected Jewish lawyer.[56] They were rather proud of this contact, which enhanced their own reputation. While at the Gymnasium the boy with the clubfoot had been allowed to call on Dr. Joseph to discuss literature with him, and during his student years he always found in this lover of literature a stimulating conversation partner. To Anka Stalherm he had once remarked in connection with Adolf Bartels's history of German literature, "You know I don't particularly like this extreme anti-Semitism. . . . I wouldn't say the Jews are my best friends, but I think we won't get rid of them with insults or polemical attacks or even pogroms, and if we could, it would be ignoble and unworthy of decent human beings."[57]

At the time Goebbels thought that the best remedy for the Jews' alleged dominance was to do things better than they did. This was the idea behind his studies with the Jewish literary scholar Gundolf, whom he revered. After writing his dissertation under the "half-Jew" Waldberg, whom he also admired, he followed the advice of his friend and neighbor Dr. Joseph, trying to draw the maximum benefit from his studies with the Jewish professor in Heidelberg by becoming a speaker or writer.[58]

Not until 1922 did his attitude toward the Jews begin to change. Around this time his fiancée Else Janke informed him, during a quarrel about his deformed foot, that her mother was Jewish. Goebbels at first reacted with irritation. The "original magic" was gone, he remarked.[59] But he did not alter his behavior toward her, although a "Jewish question" already existed for him. Apparently Spengler's Decline of the West had planted such ideas in his mind. In his October 1922 speech he still had fine things to say about Gundolf, but he described Spengler's ideas on the Jews as "of preeminent importance." It seemed to him, he said, that "here the root of the Jewish question was laid bare. One would assume that this chapter would necessarily bring about an intellectual clarification of the Jewish question."[60]

It was Goebbels's "experiences" and "insights" at the bank that first moved this problem into the forefront of his thinking.[61] The "racial question," whose physiological component the dark-haired man with the clubfoot for obvious reasons always avoided, now began to cloud his relationship with Else. After one of their frequent quarrels, she wrote to him, "That discussion recently about the race question kept ringing in my ears. I could not get it out of my mind, and almost saw in the problem an obstacle to our further life together. I am firmly convinced, you see, that in this respect your thinking goes decidedly too far."[62]

As his "Memories" show, Goebbels now discovered Houston Stewart Chamberlain's Foundations of the Nineteenth Century.[63] This British author had taken the racial theory of the French writer Gobineau, as explicated in his Essay on the Inequality of the Human Races,[64] and developed it further, coming to the conclusion that the Aryan was "the soul of culture," and that only two pure races existed, the Aryan and the Jewish. The former, which carried the legacy of classical antiquity— Greek art and philosophy, Roman jurisprudence and Christianity—had been selected as the "master race" to overcome the prevailing materialistic Zeitgeist and usher in a new era. The prerequisite was "protecting the purity" of the race against corruption by the Semitic dogma of materialism. After meeting Chamberlain in Bayreuth, twenty-six-year-old Goebbels wrote euphorically in his diary that Chamberlain was the "pathbreaker," "the preparer of the way," the "father of our spirit."[65]

Goebbels now began to view the Jews as the embodiment of materialism, of evil, of the "Antichrist," and therefore to blame for all the evil in the world.[66] Weren't Jews the chief proponents of materialistic communism as well as materialistic capitalism and its democratic order? Marx, Trotsky, and Rosa Luxemburg were Jews, as were the former foreign minister Walther Rathenau and the creator of the Weimar constitution, Hugo Preuss. Goebbels concluded that Marxism was "a Jewish plot . . . designed to emasculate the race-conscious peoples and corrupt their morals."[67] Communism and capitalism, or as Goebbels put it later, "Marxism and the stock market," had a common goal: "complete elimination of any national hegemony, subjugation of the economy to one power: investment capital, Juda!"[68] He saw evidence for this theory in the world war and the period dominated by the "system."

The way to a better world, Goebbels now believed, led first into a battle against the power of "international Judaism." The decline of the Western world, which Spengler predicted, could be averted, Goebbels thought, by "elimination" of the Jewish element. It was up to the "new man," Goebbels had said earlier, to overcome fear of the destruction predicted by Spengler.[69]

Even though such "insights" opened up gigantic vistas, Goebbels at first did not dare to articulate them or even to think through the consequences. For the time being he allowed himself only unprovoked outbursts of hatred against the Jews, using his diary as an outlet. His early entries speak of "filthy pigs," "traitors," "vampires." Occasionally scruples still overcame him, as when he added that it was so difficult for a human being to get outside his own skin, and his particular skin was now "one-sidedly anti-Semitic."[70] Not until others who thought as he did stiffened his resolve, not until he had found the leader he could follow, did his scruples succumb to the "compelling logic of that which must be, and which we are determined to do, for it simply must be."[71]

CHAPTER 4

Who is this man?
Half plebeian, half god!
The real Christ, or only John?
(1924—1926)

After returning to his parents' home in October 1923, Goebbels stayed there in near seclusion, avoiding people and railing against his fate, which he identified with that of the nation. He increasingly took refuge in the belief that a "just world" was certain to come, as were those who would pave the way for it. In his "Michael" he had been seeking a personality who would assume leadership.[1] Now, early in 1924, Goebbels began to assign this role to an actual person.

The decisive moment apparently arrived with a trial that took place in Munich in February. The leader of the failed November putsch, Adolf Hitler, stood charged with high treason. Emboldened by the obvious good will of the court, Hitler used the prisoner's dock as a soapbox. He defended the putsch as a patriotic act that had nothing in common with the "shameful betrayal" committed by the revolutionaries of 1918. With every day that the trial continued, Hitler gained new adherents, and by the time the judges announced their markedly light sentence—five years of minimum-security confinement—Hitler had large segments of the German public on his side.

Apparently Goebbels, too, now numbered among his admirers. Hitler had spoken "after my own heart," as Goebbels wrote to him two years later, for the future Führer had lent expression to more than "your own pain and your own struggle. You gave a name to the suffering of an entire generation who were yearning for real men, for meaningful tasks. . . . What you uttered is the catechism of a new political credo amid the desperation of a collapsing, godless world. You did not fall silent. A god gave you the strength to voice our suffering. You formulated our torment in redemptive words, formed statements of confidence in the coming miracle."[2]

By the spring of 1924 Goebbels had become curious to learn more about this man and his party. His former schoolmate Fritz Prang, son of an entrepreneur, had become a supporter of Hitler's National Socialist German Workers Party, or NSDAP, declared illegal in the Rhineland after the attempted putsch; Prang took Goebbels along to some party activities. The ban had forced the NSDAP to improvise. For the May 1924 Reichstag elections it allied itself with the German Nationalist Freedom Party (Deutschvölkische Freiheitspartei), campaigning in the Rhineland on a nationalist-socialist platform.[3] This compromise platform, adopted in March, rested on an explicitly anti-Semitic basis and declared war on parliamentary government, "Mammonism," and Marxism. The "nationalist-socialist bloc" obtained 6.5 percent of the vote throughout the Reich, certainly an achievement.[4] In Rheydt the allied parties attracted 738 votes, which entitled them to representation on the city council.[5]

Now and then Goebbels participated in the alliance's discussion evenings. After one such evening in June 1924 that he attended with Prang, he noted with disappointment in his diary, "So these are the leaders of the *völkisch* movement in the occupied territory. You Jews and you Frenchmen and Belgians have nothing to fear from these fellows. I have seldom attended a meeting at which so much drivel was uttered."[6] If he refrained from voicing criticisms during the meeting in Elberfeld, it was because Friedrich Wiegershaus, a city councilman and the party leader, published a polemical organ, the *Völkische Freiheit*, in which Goebbels hoped to place a few articles. With Prang as intermediary, Wiegershaus agreed to publish them, for he had difficulty finding material for the paper. So Goebbels came home from Elberfeld with an assignment to write five articles, although no fee had been mentioned. He also brought with him the conviction that his place was not among the old-style politicians but among those who wanted first to wipe the slate clean, the "young ones who call for a new kind of human being. . . . It's much more urgent for me to go to Munich than to Berlin."[7]

Only a few miles outside Munich stood Landsberg Fortress, and within its walls the man who would come to occupy a central position in Goebbels's imagination. Hitler had something ghostlike about him, for he had disappeared from the political arena as suddenly as he had appeared. Precisely because Goebbels knew so little about him, because nothing was heard from him during his confinement, because many aspects of his brief public career had already become the stuff of legend—Goebbels began to project onto Hitler his longing for redemption and for a man of deeds. "If only Hitler were free," he wrote in his diary, and a bit farther on commented that it was high time he encountered a *völkisch* leader "to fill me with new courage and new self-confidence. Things can't go on this way."[8]

And a *völkisch* leader, though not Hitler, was soon to cross Goebbels's path. Prang announced his intention of taking Goebbels with him to the August meeting in Weimar of the *völkisch* groups and parties from the entire Reich. An attempt to consolidate the German Nationalist Freedom Party with the successor parties to the banned NSDAP had failed in mid-July, but a new attempt was to be made in Weimar.

When the eagerly awaited day arrived, Prang had to admit to Goebbels on the railway platform that the money he had been expecting for Goebbels's ticket had not arrived. As his friend rode off to Weimar, a disappointed Goebbels comforted himself with the thought that party congresses were "dreadful occasions."[9] But when the money came through after all, he changed his mind just as quickly, and joyfully followed Prang to Weimar. This journey proved a turning point, for it brought Goebbels, who had been hoping in vain to earn his living as a freelance writer or journalist, into politics, and thereby to Hitler.

For the first time Goebbels was traveling to the heart of that Reich whose powerful propaganda minister he would become in less than nine years. Since for a while he had left behind his gray, wretched existence, he saw "a splendid day" dawning as he neared his destination after many hours on the train: "Bebra. Coffee. Continuing on. Eisenach. The Wartburg shrouded in fog. Continuing on. Past roads and villages . . . the train zooms into a basin. A red city glows: Weimar"—the "site of the blessed culture of an era more beautiful than ours."[10] He hurried at once to the National Theater, where the rather modest congress was taking place. With every step he thought of Goethe; "Weimar *is* Goethe," he noted with enthusiasm. When he finally arrived, his heart swelled to see all the "blessed youth" fighting at his side.

In the National Theater, where he caught up with Prang, his blood almost congealed in his veins at the sight of the "great man" who during the war had held the fate of millions in his hands: Gen. Erich Ludendorff. Goebbels felt himself in the presence of history. And soon, among the group of "young German idealists," he actually looked the "great man in the eye" and stood stiffly at attention. "He listens to everyone. . . . I, too, speak. Describe the existing situation. He listens and nods approvingly. Acknowledges that I'm right. Looks me over intently. A soul-searching look. He seems not displeased." Ever responsive to any form of positive attention, Goebbels at once conceived a great admiration for the old general. He asserted that Ludendorff had banished "many skeptical reservations" and imbued him with "firm, unshakable faith." Yet Goebbels did not view the almost-sixty-year-old Ludendorff as the "born leader" of German youth; that title had to be reserved for the man confined in Landsberg Fortress, if for anyone.

In Weimar Goebbels met other men from the "movement," for instance Albert von Graefe, a Reichstag deputy and founder of the German Nationalist Freedom Party. He was "dyed-in-the-wool *völkisch*," a born aristocrat dressed in a black diplomat's cutaway. Also present was Gregor Strasser, "the jolly pharmacist from Bavaria, large, somewhat clumsy, with a deep Hofbräuhaus bass," one of the most important men in the NSDAP. Goebbels likewise met the cofounder of the party, Gottfried Feder, the *völkisch* economist, whom Goebbels characterized as a typical "fraternity brother." Then there was Julius Streicher, creator of the anti-Semitic tabloid *Der Stürmer*. Goebbels described him as "the fanatic with the narrowed mouth. A berserker. Perhaps somewhat pathological. But that's all right. We need people like that as well. . . . Hitler is supposed to have a touch of that, too." The "fine gentlemen" from the Rhineland were also there, Erich Koch and Count Ernst von Reventlow, the "clever, sarcastic count, the movement's expert in world politics," who—if one could believe newspaper accounts—approached leading representatives of the KPD (German Communist Party) in 1923 regarding possible cooperation between the two parties.[11]

Along with the "Hitler guard," the delegates from the occupied Rhine-Ruhr region held center stage in Weimar. "We Rhinelanders are celebrated like heroes," Goebbels wrote. In these circles he no longer played the role of the eccentric outsider. His views, which Ludendorff had lauded, earned him general approbation. He enjoyed the feeling of belonging to the "elite of the honest and true," to which he had promptly promoted those present. "Like in a big house with many children. . . . It is so heartwarming and provides a great sense of security and satisfaction. A sort of grand-scale brotherhood. In the spirit of the *Volk*. . . . Front-line soldiers. Under the sign of the swastika." "Cold shivers" ran up and down his spine as he stood before the National Theater during the closing ceremonies and saw men from all parts of the Reich march with swastika flags past the leaders, heard the songs of the movement ring out, and listened to stirring farewell speeches that were interrupted by resounding cries of "Heil!" whenever Hitler's name was pronounced. After the *völkisch* forces and the National Socialists had joined to form the precarious, ideologically splintered National Socialist Freedom Movement of Greater Germany (NSFB) under the leadership of Graefe, Ludendorff, and Gregor Strasser, Goebbels wrote a sort of summation of his time in Weimar: "For me the *völkisch* question is linked with all questions of the spirit and religion. I'm beginning to think in *völkisch* terms. This has nothing to do with politics; this is a worldview."

Buoyed up by belief in his "higher calling," Goebbels thenceforth placed himself at the service of that worldview, which he depicted in his articles for the *Völkische Freiheit* as "flowing from the social experience of the twentieth century" and the "grandiose attempt to resolve the social question through national means."[12] Together with Prang, on 21 August

1924 he founded a Gladbach chapter of the NSFB.[13] During the first meeting in Rheydt, Prang or Goebbels introduced the small audience to *völkisch* National Socialist thinking. Between meetings the two of them hurried from one discussion session to the next, whether organized by a *völkisch* group, by Social Democrats, or by Communists. Even a run-in with the Belgian occupation officials and a stern interrogation could not deter Goebbels from throwing all his energy into recruiting supporters.[14] "We, the apostles of the new idea, must awaken the people. Germany must rouse itself from its slumber."[15]

At one such meeting Goebbels also made his debut as a speaker. As Prang recounted it in the late 1950s, Goebbels hobbled hesitantly to the podium, where, with his emaciated body in a jacket several sizes too large, he cut a ludicrous figure. When he addressed the assembled Communists as "dear fellow members of the *Volk* community," all hell broke loose. An enraged man in the audience shouted "capitalist exploiter" at him, whereupon Goebbels with great presence of mind invited the man up to the podium to show how much money he had in his wallet. Exclaiming, "We'll soon see which of us has more money," Goebbels pulled out his own shabby wallet and shook a few coins onto the lectern. He thus turned the situation to his own advantage and could continue his speech.[16]

Subsequent appearances also gave Goebbels the feeling that he was a gifted speaker, with or without a script. Ideas came to him as if "of their own accord." He spoke of things that mattered deeply to him, chief among them social injustice. Since his listeners' problems, needs, and worries were his own, and he knew how to articulate their frustrations and longings, he found he had a ready-made audience for his analysis of the "soulless materialistic world," the "madhouse of Bolshevists and Jews." He took pains to make sure that every last person could follow. He knew how to lead his audiences to certain "inescapable conclusions" and then mobilize them. Wherever he spoke—at first only in the immediate neighborhood of Rheydt, but soon throughout the Rhineland— he transformed halls and smoke-filled back rooms of taverns into bedlam. In September 1924 he noted with satisfaction in his diary that his reputation as a speaker was becoming known "in all ranks of the adherents of the National Socialist ideal throughout the entire Rhineland."[17]

Starting on 1 October 1924, Goebbels was managing editor of the *Völkische Freiheit*, now published by Wiegershaus as the regional Saturday organ of, as it said on the masthead, the "National Socialist Freedom Movement for an Ethnically Pure, Socially Just Greater Germany." In this capacity Goebbels now went to Wuppertal-Elberfeld every Thursday and Friday to proofread the copy and supervise the layout.[18] On the other days of the week he wrote articles, when he was not traveling about "preaching." Although terribly overworked, he felt at least somewhat contented for the first time in years, for he had found "a firm goal upon which my eyes remain unwaveringly fixed: freedom for Germany! . . . I'm happy that I must devote my energy to a great task. Our Elberfeld paper may still be just a little smearsheet. But I am young and bold precisely so that I can make something of it. I suppose I'll have to create my own reputation, since no one seems inclined to offer this poor devil anything."[19]

For the *Völkische Freiheit* Goebbels wrote stylistically effective polemics. Almost every number contained a new installment of his "Political Diary," in which he provided biting commentary on every imaginable issue in foreign or domestic politics, for instance the Dawes Plan, with its new disposition of the reparations payments, or alleged abuses by the "corrupt system politicians." In his "Sidelights," which he signed with his old fraternity name "Ulex," he offered news briefs ranging from the ironic to the grotesque to the ridiculous. Under the same heading he attacked prominent Jewish journalists, like the "little Jewish scoundrel Jackie Coogan, alias Jakob Cohn"—his name for Siegfried Jacobsohn, editor of the *Weltbühne*—or "Theodore" Wolff of the respected *Berliner Tageblatt*, to whom he had once unsuccessfully applied for a job and on whom he now took revenge.

In addition to his regular columns, Goebbels provided as much as two-thirds of the copy for some numbers of this little four-to-five-page paper, including grandiloquent articles on fundamental principles. In "The Catastrophe of Liberalism," "The Fiasco of Modern German Literature," "Industry and the Stock Exchange," and "Questions of Racially Pure Culture," among others, he missed no chance to push the theories that underlay all his thinking.[20] In his treatise on the "Führer Problem," he pointed up the weaknesses of the "system"; though overstated, his arguments hit the mark:

The democratic leader is a leader by the grace of the masses. Time and time again he must flatter the lowly instincts of the masses in order to remain alive. He works for the moment, not for times to come. His work is for the party, not for his generation. He is obligated to keep demonstrating to the people successes of the moment; otherwise he will be swept from the scene by the disgruntled voters. . . . Therefore he chooses to lead the nation from momentary success to momentary success, down the path to national destruction. On the other hand, he soon becomes crushingly dependent on the forces of money and business. Indeed, he achieves his ascendance only through these forces—his election is engineered by them, and he degrades himself to a mercenary of the stock exchange and of investment capital. Thus he is hemmed in on both sides in his political activity. On one side he must flatter the fickle favor of the people, on the other pay reverence to the perilous power of money.[21]

Goebbels contrasted this image of the democratic leader with the "heroic leader ideal." He asserted that one of the greatest contributions of the *völkisch* movement was that it had formulated this "heroic leader ideal" so clearly. "It is not the masses who sustain the idea of the future, but the strong individual who has the courage and the will to live and to sacrifice. The masses are dead; how can they generate new life? But the strong man lives. He has life and forms life. He has the power to awaken the dead. It is our duty to believe in this power and to entrust ourselves to it, to serve it willingly and selflessly."[22]

Although Goebbels did not mention Hitler's name in this article, he left no doubt that he saw in Hitler the embodiment of the "heroic leader ideal," for he appended a Hitler quotation to the piece. He devoted the entire issue of 8 November 1924 to Hitler. The front page carried a drawing of Hitler and the demand that he be given back to the German people. In the "Political Diary" of the following issue he celebrated Hitler as the "great German apostle" compelled to suffer for his ideas. Goebbels explained that it was the lot of all great men to be despised and persecuted for their beliefs, then hastened to insist that millions of hearts were beating in unbroken loyalty to "the One and Only." To the dismay of the paper's *völkisch* publisher, Goebbels transformed this Hitler, whom he had not met and whose writings he had not even read, into the mediator of his faith, as his hymnic tone made plain: "He has taught us once more the old Germanic virtue of loyalty; we will remain loyal to him until we achieve victory or suffer utter defeat. Let us thank Fate for giving us this man, our helmsman in need, our apostle of truth, our leader to freedom, our fanatic of love, our voice in battle, our hero of loyalty, our symbol of the German conscience."[23]

Although the leaders of the Rhineland North Gau called on the Bavarian government to release Hitler without delay, and sent the prisoner a telegram saying that they were confident "that our Führer . . . will soon be beating the drum for freedom again,"[24] even here the tensions between the *völkisch* faction and the National Socialists persisted. When the Reichstag election on 7 December 1924 brought a decline of more than a million in the votes for the National Socialist Freedom Movement of Greater Germany, to a total of 907,000, the conflict grew more acute. In the *Völkische Freiheit* Goebbels boldly revealed which side he was on; he blamed the *völkisch* forces for the "lost battle," saying, "We need fighters, not dishrags, not philistines, not party bigwigs, and not yesmen." The movement needed fighters who would develop "the pure National Socialist idea," the "unreserved commitment to socialism, which is our destiny and our world-historical mission," into "new belief within us, unshakable faith in the final victory." He challenged his fellow members of the *Volk* to place the idea "above all else"; "then we shall also find the courage to ride roughshod over things and people in the struggle for this idea, with the somnambulistic confidence of the born revolutionary."[25]

The movement's poor showing in the elections may in fact have led to Hitler's release on 20 December 1924, when he had served not even nine months of his five-year sentence. He had long since announced that he would separate the sheep from the goats among his adherents by asking them one simple question: "Who is to be Führer?"[26] He had no need to ask the managing editor of the *Völkische Freiheit*. Goebbels welcomed Hitler's liberation effusively: "Germany's youth has its leader once more. We await his command."[27]

The command Hitler soon issued called for parting company with the *völkisch* forces, whom he had described in the just finished first part of *Mein Kampf* as "sleepwalkers" whose idle chatter the parties of the left properly greeted only with ridicule.[28] He wanted to see the NSDAP reestablished, the ban on the party having been lifted throughout the Reich in February 1925. On 26 February the *Völkischer Beobachter* resumed publication. In Hitler's editorial, "A New Beginning," in the simultaneously promulgated "Guidelines for the Organization of the Party," and at his carefully orchestrated speech the following day in a Munich beer hall, he asserted his claim to be the sole leader of the party. He rejected any and all conditions and challenged the party members to put aside their differences and engage in political action. Since Goebbels was not alone in worshiping him, Hitler accomplished in one appearance what Ludendorff, Strasser, and others had struggled in vain to achieve during his absence: he unified the movement.

Hitler entrusted the reestablishment of the NSDAP in northwestern Germany exclusively to Gregor Strasser, whose undivided loyalty he possessed. This unpolished, clearheaded man from a Bavarian upper-middle-class family shared Goebbels's notion of a German brand of socialism, although he arrived at this position by an entirely different route. In placing himself at the disposal of national socialism, he became chief organizer of the Hitler movement. Goebbels had spoken with Strasser the previous spring at the Elberfeld celebration of the battle of Tannenberg.[29] Now his path to Hitler had to go by way of Strasser. Toward the end of 1924 the eloquent speaker and propagandist with the clubfoot had already approached Karl Kaufmann, a confidant of Strasser's whom he had met during the 1924 Reichstag election campaign.[30] Goebbels tried to offer this former free corps member and Ruhr resistance fighter his services, for he realized that his days as managing editor of the *Völk-*

ische Freiheit were numbered. And in fact on 20 January 1925 the publisher Wiegershaus wrote Goebbels that he assumed he would relinquish his position as editor now that his friends had parted ways with the *völkisch* forces.[31] With Goebbels's departure the *Völkische Freiheit* ceased publication.

Not until Gregor Strasser officially launched the reorganization of the north German NSDAP on 22 February 1925 did a field of activity open up for Goebbels, who had promptly joined the party. In March, at a meeting of leading National Socialists in Hamburg-Harburg, on Kaufmann's urging he was appointed business manager of the Rhineland North Gau's central office. The German Baltic writer Axel Ripke had been made director.[32] The Wuppertal police had the NSDAP under surveillance because of its declared opposition to the Weimar constitution. According to the police reports, Goebbels, who had taken a small, inexpensive flat in Elberfeld, appeared in his capacity as central-office business manager "as a speaker at all ceremonial occasions . . . ; in addition he presides at the evening discussion meetings instituted by the Elberfeld NSDAP chapter."[33]

Goebbels, by now familiar with the power of the spoken word, made more and more appearances. Between 1 October 1924 and 1 October 1925 he gave 189 inflammatory speeches, primarily in the Rhineland and the rest of the northwestern part of the Reich. He discovered, among other things, that focusing on individual martyrs of the movement stirred up the emotions of his audiences like nothing else.

The National Socialists had targeted not only the impoverished petty bourgeois, but also the workers and the unemployed. Their chief competition was the powerful Communist Party, which, like the NSDAP, proclaimed its intention of replacing the Weimar Republic with a "just social order." If the party was to overcome the factionalism that had marked its beginnings and develop into a battle-ready movement with a fanatically loyal mass membership, the NSDAP's agitation and its speaker Goebbels had to concentrate most of their efforts on undermining the KPD. Some serious clashes with the Communists resulted, for instance in early June 1925 at a flag-dedication ceremony in Remscheid. According to Goebbels's notes, members of the two parties hurled themselves at each other as if berserk. One hundred twenty Communists were arrested, two policemen were wounded with dumdum bullets, and Goebbels stood "in the midst" of the fray, determined to prove to others that he, who had once been declared unfit for military service, did not lack courage.[34]

In his speeches Goebbels took particular aim at Gustav Stresemann's foreign policy as part of the hated "system." Without having studied it in any detail, Goebbels condemned the terms of the Treaty of Locarno, which was then being worked out; Germany was to recognize the existing borders in the west, and in return the French and Belgians would withdraw earlier than scheduled from part of the occupied region. Goebbels likewise condemned the negotiations for a security pact with the Soviet Union. He portrayed Stresemann's successful foreign policy as a "gruesome mixture of deception, baseness, vileness, and philistinism" whose true background was the "international Jewish conspiracy" that exploited both capitalism and Marxism in its campaign for world power.[35]

As Gau business manager Goebbels now threw his efforts into organizing the propaganda campaign. He and his friend Prang had already decided that the working masses could be mobilized only through a "purposefully constructed press and propaganda apparatus," beginning at the local level, and that this task should be in the hands of a "goal-oriented, energetic, and ideologically sound" propagandist or, "in business parlance, advertising director."[36]

Goebbels drew up guidelines for a leaflet campaign that were widely disseminated within the party organization under the heading "Fifteen Models for Posters or Leaflets Announcing NSDAP Speeches."[37] The models were based on "masterful" examples cited by Hitler, who had already studied the importance of propaganda and written at length on the subject in his recently published book. In April Goebbels worked feverishly to bring out the first "Information Letters" for the Rhineland North Gau, circulars with news and directives intended primarily for the lower echelons of the party apparatus.[38]

Among other matters Goebbels addressed the key issue, which had already contributed to the break with the *völkisch* forces and was now arousing controversy in the entire north German NSDAP, namely whether nationalism or socialism should take precedence in the party. This issue had already occasioned a quarrel at the Elberfeld headquarters; while Goebbels and Kaufmann gave top priority to socialism, Ripke, the leader of the Gau, apparently held the opposite view. "He hates . . . my radicalism like the plague," Goebbels wrote in his diary in mid-April. "He's really just a bourgeois in disguise. With these fellows you can't make a revolution. And worst of all, he can cite Hitler in his defense." And a few lines later: "Adolf Hitler, I can't despair of you!"[39] Goebbels persuaded himself that Ripke was not telling the truth about Hitler. Instead, Hitler was "on the way to class struggle."[40]

One thing that made life difficult for Goebbels was the constant conflict with Ripke, who revealed that he had most likely seen through his administrator when he said that Goebbels was dangerous precisely because he actually believed what he said. Another problem was Goebbels's chronic shortage of funds. The few marks he received from the small party treasury as reimbursement for his expenses were not enough to live on. He lived from hand to mouth, constantly having to borrow money.

At the end of April 1925 he reached an impasse—as so often in his life. He noted in his diary that he would probably have to terminate his activity in Elberfeld, since his "damned money" was running out; he added, not without a touch of megalomania, that the German people could hardly hope for salvation, since the best it could do with "the leaders whom Destiny granted it" was hurl filth and calumny at them or let them starve to death.[41]

But Goebbels, who even feared that Ripke wanted to exclude him and Kaufmann from the party, did not give up.[42] He continued to argue with that "radicalized bourgeois" about the true goals of the National Socialists. "Merely break the Treaty of Versailles or go beyond that to launch socialism?" For him it came down to what Hitler thought; to be sure, he assumed that Hitler's view of things coincided with his own. "The second week after Pentecost we will settle these matters."[43] The Gau leaders from northern and northwestern Germany were scheduled to meet then in Weimar; as it turned out, the meeting would not take place until 12 July 1925.[44]

On the morning of that day Goebbels probably first met Hitler.[45] At this encounter, documented only in a brief reference in a report by Hinrich Lohse, Gauführer of Schleswig-Holstein, the Führer once more avoided questions of principle, instead celebrating his own person as an ideology. Gregor Strasser was very impressed by this appearance at Weimar and commented that Hitler alone was the engine that drove the party.[46] Goebbels's reaction has not been recorded, but we may presume that he believed even more fervently in "his Führer" after the Weimar conference.

In the future, whenever Hitler failed to fulfill Goebbels's expectations, he would ascribe the failure categorically to the bad influence of certain elements in Munich. Goebbels saw especially Hermann Esser, who had been with Hitler in the days of the old German Workers' Party, as Hitler's "downfall."[47] In fact some supporters turned their back on the party because of Esser, for this unbridled anti-Semite, propaganda chief of the NSDAP until 1923, had shown himself to be of dubious character. The Führer, determined to appear above the fray, refrained from intervening, concentrating instead on the second volume of *Mein Kampf*. He thereby helped to create a notion that circulated within the party and was later invoked by millions: "If the Führer only knew!" One can see the extent to which Goebbels subscribed to this notion in a conviction he expressed repeatedly: if he could only spend two hours alone with the Führer, he would tear him away from the influence of the "wrong people" and win him over completely to the northwest German socialists.[48]

The more Goebbels, whose radicalism had earned him the nickname Robespierre at the Elberfeld headquarters,[49] formed an emotional attachment to Hitler, the more likely he was to view it as disloyalty to

Hitler when Ripke joined several northwest German Gauleiters who in mid-April 1925 had proposed that "the individual Gau administrations be entrusted with issuing party membership documents," instead of the central office in Munich.[50] Although Munich responded that Herr Hitler placed the greatest importance on having the membership documents issued exclusively by the central office, Ripke did not comply with the directive.[51]

Since Goebbels had long since realized that either he or Ripke would "have to fall,"[52] the question of the membership documents offered him the welcome pretext for overthrowing his Gauleiter. Ripke had a practice of sending the one-mark membership fee, the one-time voluntary contribution, and ten pfennigs of the monthly dues (which amounted to at least fifty pfennigs) to Munich but not submitting the membership lists; this made it relatively easy for Goebbels and Kaufmann to accuse him of embezzlement. They quickly found allies—among them Gregor Strasser, who had always suspected something of the kind.[53] Once they had set the intrigue in motion, the Gauleiter took a leave of absence pending the conclusion of the time-consuming investigation, which ultimately turned up nothing. Goebbels, who with his friend Kaufmann—"almost" a replacement for Richard Flisges—had taken provisional control of the Gau, remarked with satisfaction, "Ripke is finished. Now we can get down to work."[54] Goebbels began by reporting to his Führer the membership statistics for the local party units in the Rhineland North Gau, thereby demonstrating his unconditional loyalty.[55]

Goebbels's attempt to forge ties with Hitler benefited from the plans of Gregor Strasser, who, in order to counter the "dictatorship" of Hermann Esser in the party leadership, decided to centralize the organization of all NSDAP forces in northwest Germany. In addition, Strasser wanted to launch an "intellectual leadership organ" for the party, the *National Socialist Letters*.[56] On 20 August 1925 he came to Elberfeld for an exchange of views with his supporters Kaufmann and Goebbels. They agreed that Goebbels would edit the journal, with Strasser as publisher. Goebbels noted with satisfaction in his diary that the *Letters* would provide a "weapon against the ossified bosses in Munich" that would finally give him and Kaufmann direct access to Hitler.[57] Doubtless some of his satisfaction had to do with the monthly salary of 150 marks he would receive as editor.[58]

At the 10 September meeting in Hagen, attended by the Gauleiters for Pomerania, Schleswig-Holstein, Westphalia, Rhineland South, Hanover, Hanover South, Hesse-Nassau, Lüneburg-Stade, Greater Hamburg, and Greater Berlin, and the provisional leaders of Rhineland North, the position advocated by the Strasser wing prevailed. The group agreed to establish a Working Group Northwest headquartered in Wuppertal-

Elberfeld. Goebbels was to be the business manager, in addition to editing the *National Socialist Letters*. A report on the meeting in Hagen conceded that as a group the party leaders presented an "unedifying spectacle," and that because of their widely divergent programmatic concepts the Gau leaders could hardly function as a cohesive unit to counter the bad influence of the circle around Hitler in Munich, with its politically reactionary views, but Goebbels took a more optimistic view.[59] He dismissed the report as "excessively intellectual" and "at first appearance not entirely trustworthy."[60] Goebbels felt confident that Hitler was on the verge "of coming over to our side entirely. For he is young and understands the meaning of sacrifice."[61]

At a meeting in Düsseldorf on 27 September 1925, Goebbels was elected business manager of the Rhineland North Gau, while Kaufmann became Gauleiter.[62] But Goebbels soon had to recognize that his expectations had been too sanguine, for the Munich functionaries missed no opportunity to intrigue against him and Strasser. He now placed all his hopes in a personal meeting with Hitler that would allow him to set everything straight. Hitler had scheduled a trip to northwestern Germany for the end of October. The intervening time Goebbels devoted to careful study of *Mein Kampf*. He thought he found many of his own views in the book, for instance in the passages on the "Jewish doctrine of Marxism," which denied the significance of "nationalism and race" and thereby robbed "humanity of the premise of its existence and culture,"[63] or in Hitler's reply to the "Jewish-Marxist challenge," which lay in "great . . . popular movements," in "volcanic eruptions of human passions and emotional sentiments, stirred . . . by the cruel Goddess of Distress."[64]

What Goebbels apparently repressed entirely while reading Hitler's book was the recognition that he and the author saw certain issues very differently. For instance, he could not share his "boss's" vision of a "new Germanic march" descending on Russia[65]; his own sympathies for Russian literature and the "Russian soul" expressed in it interfered. On the question of social justice, so crucial to Goebbels, Hitler did not share his view that bolshevism was the heir to Russian nationalism. According to Goebbels, no czar had understood the Russian people's nationalist instincts as well as Lenin, who, in contrast to the German Communists, was not an internationalist Marxist. "Lenin sacrificed Marx and instead gave Russia freedom. Now they want to sacrifice German freedom to Marx."[66] Goebbels attributed this reprehensible goal to the "Jewish leadership" in the German Communist Party. He, who had once described himself as a "German Communist,"[67] accordingly supported bolshevism, so long as it was not internationalist, which to him meant the same as Jewish, while Hitler—indebted to bourgeois thinking—simply rejected bolshevism and saw the Slavs as subhuman. These contradictions apparently did little to affect Goebbels's relationship to Hitler in that fall of 1925. Even so, after reading the book to the end with "gripping tension," he asked himself, "Who is this man? Half plebeian, half god! The real Christ, or only John?"[68]

When Goebbels met Hitler for the second time, on 6 November in Braunschweig, these programmatic questions again played no part. Rather, Goebbels succumbed to the fascination of the "boss." "We drive to Hitler. . . . At once he jumps up, stands there before us. Presses my hand. Like an old friend. And those big blue eyes. Like stars. He's glad to see me. I'm filled with happiness." Goebbels registered only Hitler's appearance, his manner, the way he spoke—"with wit, irony, humor, sarcasm, seriousness, fervor, passion." Now he noted in his diary: "This man has everything it takes to be a king. The born tribune of the people. The coming dictator."[69]

Less than two weeks later, at an NSDAP rally in Plauen, the two men met again. Goebbels made a point of recording in his diary that Hitler greeted him "like an old friend." Apparently Hitler had quickly realized that the little man with the limp was not only the ideological brains of the Strasser wing and a brilliant propagandist; he also outdid everyone else in celebrating the boss as he wished to be understood: as an emissary of a higher power. Hitler accordingly flattered and "nurtured" Goebbels, who promptly responded with glowing affection: "How I love him." Now all Goebbels wanted was to be Hitler's friend.[70] Several months later he wrote of the meeting in Plauen that he had experienced in the "depths of his soul" the "great joy" of standing behind a man who embodied in his entire being the will to freedom. "Until then you were my Führer. There you became my friend. A friend and master with whom I feel bonded to the very end in a shared idea."[71]

With the boss's portrait in his luggage and Hitler's "greetings to the Rhineland" still ringing in his ear, Goebbels made his way to Hanover, where on 22 November 1925 the Working Group Northwest was now officially established "with the express authorization of Hitler."[72] In paragraph 12 of the charter, the members committed themselves "to serve in a spirit of comradeship the idea of national socialism under its leader Adolf Hitler."[73] The north German district of the NSDAP thereby achieved a certain degree of autonomy, without impinging in the slightest on Hitler's claim to sole leadership.

As for the controversial question of the future political course, the Gauleiters and party functionaries assembled in Hanover agreed to prepare a program as quickly as possible. Gregor Strasser had already drafted a lengthy document on the "fundamental questions of national social-ism," to be distributed to the Gauleiters after the Hanover meeting. In addition Kaufmann and Goebbels, who found Strasser's draft "inadequate,"[74] were charged with presenting a detailed draft program by mid-December. On the basis of the various drafts and the responses to them, a mutually acceptable program was to be hammered out at the meeting scheduled for 24 January 1926 in Hanover.

At the beginning of January Goebbels completed the document. He had stayed up many nights working on it in the Elberfeld office. It has not been preserved, but its contents can be reconstructed from the "Little National Socialist's ABC" that Goebbels had written a good two months earlier.[75] According to that document, the goal of the NSDAP's policy should be to fight for and win the rights "of the oppressed portion of the German *Volk*" to "freedom and bread." "To become a nation, one must give the oppressed portion political autonomy, freedom, and property." He called for agrarian reform to restructure and limit private ownership, while in the industrial sector he aimed at the "nationalization" of important firms. He saw the chief enemy of "National Socialist German freedom" in "stock-exchange capitalism." "Stock-exchange capital is not productive but parasitically hoarded capital. It is no longer tied to the soil but rootless and internationalist; it does not produce but has infiltrated the normal production process in order to drain profits from it. It consists of movable assets, i.e., raw cash; its chief carrier is Jewish high finance, whose goal is to put the producing populace to work, then pocket the proceeds from their labor." "Stock-exchange capitalism," having hung out its "shingle," the parliamentary democratic system, worked hand in glove with the leaders of Marxism, because the latter belonged to the same Jewish race. Together they constituted the chief enemy of German freedom. The National Socialists wanted to "fight them to the finish." In his diary Goebbels wrote that he would probably have a "pitched battle" with the working group over the program. "But they won't find any serious flaws. I have already thought through all the possible objections."[76] He felt such preparation was necessary above all because the draft by Strasser, who in many respects thought much as he did, had in the meantime been distributed and had been harshly criticized by some Gauleiters.[77]

Goebbels probably realized that his foreign policy proposals would not gain ready acceptance. He rejected any Western orientation for the future National Socialist Germany. His thinking was reinforced by Arthur Moeller van den Bruck's "prophetic vision," *Das dritte Reich* (The Third Reich), which he had begun reading in December 1925.[78] As a young student Goebbels had already concluded from reading the Russian playwrights that the nature of the Russian people was related to that of the Germans: both mirrored the fundamental issues of human existence. As managing editor of the *Völkische Freiheit* he had written in 1924 that in Russia the same struggle for a "great purification of the people" was taking place as in Germany. He was convinced that Russia would "one day awaken in the spirit of its greatest thinker, in the spirit of Dostoyevski." Goebbels envisioned a Russia "freed from Jewish internationalism" that would win the struggle for a "socialist nation state" as an "eternal rejection of materialism." Russia would serve as Germany's model, for it was "our natural ally against the fiendish temptation and corruption of the West."[79]

When the north German Gauleiters met in January 1926, the business manager of the working group was sharply criticized, as expected, for his ideas on foreign policy. A chief spokesman for these attacks, which Goebbels characterized as "unbridled," was Gottfried Feder, who had come from Munich; Goebbels scornfully called him a mercenary and other unflattering names.[80] After an endless debate Goebbels finally "let them have it from both barrels," as he wrote, not without exaggeration, in his diary: "Russia, Germany, Western capitalism, bolshevism—I speak for half an hour, an hour. Everyone listens in breathless suspense. And then a storm of approbation. We have won. . . . At the end: Strasser shakes my hand. Feder small and ugly."[81]

Yet the meeting was not such a triumph after all, for the draft unanimously adopted in Hanover was later designated as mere raw material to be worked into a planned revision of the twenty-five-point program Feder had submitted. A resolution was also adopted calling for the creation of a newspaper, *Der Nationale Sozialist*, to be issued by a publishing house set up just for this purpose, with Gregor Strasser as editor in chief. Another resolution was passed on the controversial question of compensation for landholders among the nobility. The Social Democrats and Communists in the Reichstag had proposed holding a referendum to see whether members of the royal family and the nobility should be stripped of their lands without reimbursement, with the government taking possession. This proposal aroused great interest not only among leftists but also among middle-class citizens, who were watching in outrage as those large landowners received compensation while the government refused to reimburse the many pensioners who had helped finance the war by buying bonds. In the Hanover resolution the kind of compensation supported by the party in Munich was rejected. An attempt was made, however, not to intensify the conflict; the resolution stated that there was no intention of preempting the central leadership's decision, and furthermore, the issue of compensating the nobility was not "an issue that touches on the fundamental interests of the party."[82]

Thus the Hanover meeting was not a "declaration of war" on Hitler, as Gregor Strasser's brother Otto asserted after World War II. Nor did Goebbels "jump up" during the debate on the compensation policy, which was supported by Munich and rejected by him, and "with biting scorn" demand the exclusion of Herr Hitler from the party, as Otto Strasser claimed.[83] On the contrary: at Christmas Hitler had sent Goebbels a leatherbound copy of his book, which Goebbels described as "the most wonderful Christmas present," especially since it carried a dedication by the author that expressed appreciation for Goebbels's "exemplary struggle." At the beginning of February Hitler had written to him personally, which had given Goebbels, always so receptive to favorable attention, "great joy." Goebbels admitted in his diary to putting up photographs of Hitler "with rapture," as he had earlier put up pictures of Jesus and the Virgin Mary.[84]

Goebbels felt such reverence and enthusiasm for Hitler that he was certainly confident of winning Hitler over to his concept of socialism at the leaders' meeting that Hitler had scheduled for Bamberg "in order to adopt a position on a series of significant unresolved questions."[85] Goebbels found confirmation for his optimism in remarks Gregor Strasser made on a party member who had moved closer to their side. Goebbels noted in his diary: "In Bamberg we'll play the coy beauty and lure Hitler onto our turf. In all the cities I observe to my joy that our spirit, i.e., the socialist spirit, is on the march. No one believes in Munich anymore. Elberfeld will become the mecca of German socialism."[86]

When Goebbels met with Strasser on 13 February 1926 to hammer out a "plan of operation" before the meeting, both men were still "of good cheer," for they did not suspect that Hitler himself would be their adversary.[87] Feder had kept him well informed on the Hanover meetings of the working group.[88] The group's resolution opposing compensation of the nobility ran counter to Hitler's efforts to win over the bourgeoisie and industry. Hitler also had to reject any prolonged discussion of a future party program, since it would restrict him and limit his omnipotence as leader of the movement.

Hitler had called the meeting on short notice and kept the agenda to himself, so as to make it easier to nip in the bud any developments in the NSDAP initiated by the working group. Because of the short notice, some of the most prominent Gauleiters in the working group could not come, which gave the south German Gauleiters, reinforced by Reichstag and Landtag deputies, a majority among the sixty in attendance. Although the north German Gauleiters had representation, the only real spokesmen for the resolutions on compensation and program revision were Gregor Strasser and Goebbels.

Hitler opened the meeting in Bamberg on 14 February with "directives on national socialism's positions on the most important questions of the present," delivered in an emphatic speech lasting several hours.[89] When he finished speaking, drained, having rejected just about everything Goebbels and his friends held dear, Goebbels felt "battered. What Hitler was this? A reactionary? Incredibly awkward and unsure of himself. Russian question: completely off-target. Italy and England natural allies. Gruesome! Our task to smash bolshevism. Bolshevism a Jewish conspiracy! We must inherit from Russia. 180 million! Compensation for nobility! Right must remain right. For the nobility as well. Not rattle the question of private property! (sic!) Gruesome!"[90] Gregor Strasser apparently also felt battered by Hitler's speech. He spoke next, "hesitating, trembling, inept," constantly interrupted by shouts from Hitler's south German followers. Now all were waiting for the rhetorically powerful little Herr Doktor, who had had himself identified at the meeting in Bamberg as the "pioneer of the National Socialist idea in the Rhineland."[91] But he remained silent, to the dismay of Strasser and the other north Germans. Hitler's strategy of maneuvering Goebbels out of the Strasser phalanx achieved a first important success at just the right moment. Goebbels's silence helped sink the working group's attempt to shape the future course of the NSDAP and make Elberfeld a "mecca of socialism." It was a victory for the Führer principle, for Hitler's demand for unconditional loyalty and claim to exclusive power.

Goebbels had remained silent in Bamberg because his belief in Hitler and Hitler's mission in history proved stronger than his socialist views. After all, in "Michael" he had written that it was a matter less of what one believed in than of believing. Since his belief provided him with the key to surviving in a corrupt world, and Hitler had become the incarnation of that belief, he could take leave of his political beliefs but not of his Führer. Goebbels would follow him, even though he stylized the Bamberg experience into "one of the greatest disappointments" of his life; indeed, on the night train back to Elberfeld he even began to sense that he no longer "believed without reservations" in Hitler. But before the sun rose after that "gruesome night," Goebbels had come around once more to seeing Hitler as a victim of his Munich circle. Hitler must not "allow himself to be fettered by that riffraff," he noted in self-protective delusion in his diary. He also recorded the resulting conclusion: he would suggest to Gregor Strasser and Kaufmann that they all go to Hitler "to speak most urgently with him."[92] He did not, however, carry out this resolve, fearing another disappointment.

So for the time being everything remained as before. Goebbels stuck with Strasser, who admitted his defeat to himself and accepted Hitler's unlimited authority as Führer. Strasser's first contribution to the *National Socialist Letters* after Bamberg amounted to a panegyric in which he celebrated "our Führer Adolf Hitler" as the "sower of national socialism" spreading "the power of his idea through all the German lands by the power of his speech and the greatness of his personality."[93] Goebbels commented that the boss really was "quite a fellow."[94] But the rivalry for Hitler's favor between the working group and the Munich circle had not been laid to rest. When the north Germans met again in Hanover on 21 February 1926 to take up "a most important matter," Goebbels summed up the result of their deliberations as follows: "Become strong. Let the Munich crowd have its Pyrrhic victory. Work, become strong, then fight for socialism."[95]

Only a few days had passed since Bamberg, when Strasser and Goebbels resumed the already lost battle. They targeted the editor in chief of the *Völkischer Beobachter*, the Baltic German Alfred Rosenberg, and the party program expert, Feder. Strasser informed Feder that because of Feder's comments on Strasser's draft program he, Strasser, felt compelled to terminate the "previous relationship of trust."[96] At the same time the Elberfeld office, represented by the Herr Doktor, wrote that Feder's speech on "the programmatic foundations of the Nat. Soc. movement" would have to be dropped from the upcoming party rally in Essen, unless Feder "were content with half an hour at the end of the meeting." Feder interpreted this message as it was intended, "as a simple slap in the face." He informed Hitler by telegram and was directed "to go to Essen in any case,"[97] for the controversy between Feder, entrusted with overseeing the party program, and the leaders of the working group suited Hitler's purposes perfectly: it kept Hitler himself out of any disputes over programmatic issues.

Hitler also seized every opportunity to draw Goebbels completely over to his side in matters of substance. He invited Goebbels, along with Kaufmann and Franz von Pfeffer, the joint Gauleiters of the new Ruhr Gau, created in Essen out of the Rhineland North Gau and Westphalia, to come to Munich on 8 April.[98] The planned spectacle began at the railway station, where they were picked up in Hitler's gleaming supercharged Mercedes. As they rode through the city, they noticed on all the kiosks the "enormous posters" announcing Dr. Goebbels's appearance at the Bürgerbräu. The following morning Hitler came to call on them. "In a quarter of an hour he is there," Goebbels wrote in his diary. "Big, healthy, full of life. I like him." The following evening, after hours filled with nostalgic memories of Anka Stalherm, the little man hobbled into the smoke-filled Bürgerbräu cellar, his heart pounding. "And then I speak for 2½ hours. I give all I have to give. The audience screams and shouts. At the end Hitler embraces me. He has tears in his eyes. I am something like happy."

At the end of a meal taken alone with Goebbels, Hitler brought up the question of the strife within the party and presented "a whole batch of accusations." Kaufmann was "reprimanded," and even Goebbels "took a beating," yet Goebbels still saw in Hitler only the "fine fellow." After Goebbels had withstood the master's upbraiding, Hitler spent several hours explaining his programmatic concepts. He spoke of Russia, which wanted to "gobble us up," of England and Italy as Germany's natural allies, and also of the social question, so important to Goebbels; here Hitler seemed to accommodate his guest, though without really meaning it. He advocated a "mixture of collectivism and individualism": "Production, since creative, individualistic. Firms, trusts, finished products, transportation, etc., socialized." Goebbels immediately found Hitler's explanations "brilliant" and "convincing," for he had long since realized that he would have to bow to the "greater man, the political genius."

In the days that followed, Goebbels had several more meetings with Hitler. They ate supper with the Führer's mistress, Geli Raubal, daughter of the stepsister who kept house for him. They spoke again of the question of Germany's future foreign policy. Although Goebbels believed that Hitler had not fully grasped the "Russia problem," he again regarded Hitler's arguments as "compelling." Finally the two of them were driven to Stuttgart for a speaking engagement. Hitler praised Goebbels, embraced him, had apparently "let him into his heart" like no other, Goebbels wrote. He even had the honor of helping Hitler celebrate his thirty-seventh birthday.[99]

Goebbels now resolved to wage at this man's side "the last gigantic struggle" against "Marxism and the stock exchange," a "struggle that will bring us victory or destruction."[100] The propagandist who crisscrossed Germany in 1926, bringing the message, dictated by hatred, of a better future in a Third Reich, now viewed himself as a key player in planning and executing this struggle, as a member of the "General Staff," the title of an article written under the impression of those exciting days in Munich. He wrote: "Around your person stands a closed circle that sees in you the standard-bearer whose thought and being form a bridge to inexpressible ultimate things. The legion of the future, determined to follow the terrible path through despair and torment to its end." And further: "A day may come when everything will shatter. Even then we shall not shatter. A day may come when the mob around you will foam at the mouth and growl and bawl 'Crucify him!' We shall stand with iron determination and shout and sing 'Hosanna!' Then around you will stand the phalanx of the last of the just, who do not despair, even in death. The corps of characters, the iron ones, who no longer want to live if Germany dies."[101]

Hitler's calculated cultivation of Goebbels aroused disfavor and suspicion among Goebbels's adversaries within the boss's inner circle. Feder tried to undermine Hitler's confidence in Goebbels as a propagandist by pointing out Communist tendencies in his speeches and writings.[102]

In the Elberfeld headquarters there was also some dismay, less because of the much-envied favor shown the little Herr Doktor by the boss, than because Goebbels was trying less and less to win Hitler over to socialist views. In early May Goebbels, who continued to contend that Elberfeld would prevail, received a "shameless letter" from Kaufmann, who reproached him for failing to show the necessary firmness. In a discussion, however, they managed to defuse the "explosive issue" between them.[103] In June, when Hitler visited the Greater Ruhr Gau, and the following month, when the party congress took place in Weimar, Goebbels avoided programmatic issues, which merely heightened the tension.[104] Now not only Kaufmann but also Strasser accused him of kowtowing to Munich and Hitler. This accusation, which made the rounds among the north German National Socialists, came to be known as "Joseph Goebbels's Damascus." Goebbels defended himself in personal letters to Strasser and Kaufmann and later in an open reply in the *National Socialist Letters*, which he was still editing. He chastised his fellow party members for getting caught up in theories and not knowing what they really wanted. "Don't try to outguess what lies miles beyond the horizon of the attainable! Don't make promises you can't keep! Don't place your faith in a future paradise, but 'merely' in a task worth living for! Become realists of the revolution so you can someday become realists of politics." "Not under Byzantine compulsion," but "with the ancient manly pride displayed before the king's throne," had he bowed his will to the Führer.[105]

Hitler had played his cards right. The Strasser wing had lost its ideological advantage. It had suffered a grievous defeat in its attempt to give the NSDAP a program more ambitious than the commonplaces in Feder's "Twenty-Five Points," now declared "inviolable" by Hitler. The fateful imposition of the Führer principle had been accomplished. Gregor Strasser continued to believe that the boss was committed to the ideal of a socially just new Germany, even though that ideal had not been formulated; years later he would recognize that he had capitulated to sheer despotism. Goebbels, on the other hand, fanatically embraced that despotism. What Strasser and millions of other Germans eventually saw through, Goebbels venerated to the last, for Hitler to him was an instrument of divine will.

Numerous diary passages written in the summer of 1926 show how far Goebbels's imagination could carry him; he not only transfigured Hitler into the new Messiah but also linked him with miracles and wonderful happenings in nature. At the end of July Goebbels spent time at Hitler's mountain retreat, the Berghof on the Obersalzberg above Berchtesgaden, and accompanied Hitler on several excursions. In his diary he described Hitler as a genius, then continued:

I stand shaken before him. This is how he is: like a child, dear, good, compassionate. Sly like a cat, clever and skillful, magnificently roaring and gigantic like a lion. A fine fellow, a real man. He speaks of the state. In the afternoon of winning the state and of the meaning of political revolution. Thoughts I may already have had myself but not expressed. After supper we sit for a long time in the garden of the seamen's retirement home, and he holds forth on the new state and how we will achieve it. It has the ring of prophecy. Above us in the sky a white cloud forms a swastika. A shimmering light in the sky that can't be a star. A sign from fate? We go home late! Far in the distance Salzburg shimmers. I am something like happy. This life is certainly worth living. "My head won't roll in the dust until my mission is fulfilled." That was his last word. That's how he is! Yes, that's how he is![106]

Goebbels saw himself, too, as an "instrument of divine will," which provided another reason for submitting to Hitler against his own ideological convictions. Since June 1926 there had been public discussion in the Munich inner party circles of sending Goebbels to Berlin as Gauführer. The present Gauführer, Dr. Ernst Schlange, was a Strasser protegé and had thrown up his hands, unable to resolve the conflict between party leadership in Berlin and the SA leadership. Goebbels at first felt little enthusiasm for the idea; he had been in Berlin recently on a speaking assignment and had visited the Reichstag. "They all want me to go to Berlin as a savior. Thanks for the desert of stones," he wrote in his diary, for he felt much more drawn to Munich, to his boss.[107]

Goebbels's task in Berlin would be to reorganize the party, which numbered not even five hundred members. Hitler knew that the strength of the party depended on the competence of his regional "party and SA matadors." If, contrary to his custom, he did not appoint a local man, it was because he knew Goebbels as a powerful orator and dynamic intellectual activist who was unconditionally loyal.[108] In addition, Goebbels would fit in well with "Red Berlin" because of his socialist views. At the same time, as an antagonist of the Strassers who would counteract Strasser's influence in Berlin, Goebbels was the right man to smooth Hitler's path to the capital of the Reich and thereby to power.

When the issue came up again at the Weimar party conference on 3 and 4 July 1926, Goebbels for the first time asked himself seriously whether he should go to Berlin—especially since the atmosphere at the Elberfeld headquarters continued to deteriorate.[109] At the end of August the party leadership formally requested that he "take over provisional direction of the Berlin Gau for four months."[110] Three weeks later he went to Berlin to have a look at the situation. Emulating Hitler's manner, he "received" the deposed Gauleiter Schlange and his deputy Erich

Schmiedicke. "Both want me to come. Should I or shouldn't I?" When he strolled through the streets by night with several party members, he was horrified. "Berlin by night. A sink of iniquity! And I'm supposed to plunge into this?"[111] But the following day saw him reconciled to the idea. In the company of a charming lady he went out to Potsdam. At Sans Souci Palace he experienced "one emotional upheaval after another," as he wrote in his diary. When he lingered in the Garnisonskirche before the tomb of Frederick the Great, it was one of the "great moments" of his life, for once again he thought he felt the "breath of history."

The question of accepting the position of Gauleiter was apparently settled for him when he learned from Hitler's chauffeur, Emil Maurice, how important Hitler considered the Berlin mission. When he spoke at the NSDAP's first Mark Brandenburg Day in Potsdam on 9–10 October, he had already made the decision, but withheld it from the crowd.[112] On 16 October Schmiedicke wrote to Goebbels that he must have sensed how much all the Berlin party members wanted him to come. This desire was grounded in the belief that Goebbels alone could strengthen the organization in Berlin and propel the movement forward.[113]

Before Goebbels left Elberfeld, where his betrayal of the cause of socialism was seen as self-evident, he put his private affairs in order. That included his relationship with Else Janke. The more he had dedicated himself to national socialism, the more he had neglected her, with her half-Jewish parentage; he felt his clubfoot made him vulnerable enough to his enemies as it was. From the beginning he had systematically excluded from his political activity this good-hearted young woman, who had bucked him up time and again and had cherished hopes for a shared future.[114] After his move to Elberfeld, he had at first continued to visit her frequently. He had also acquired a dog named Benno, which, as he said, became "dearer and dearer to him" the better he came to know human beings.[115] Later, when he was constantly on trains traveling from one rally to another, he and Else saw less and less of each other. Sometimes they quarreled over the "racial question," which always ended in bitter humiliation for the woman. But they also spent harmonious hours together, after which Goebbels might note, as he did in June 1925, that he would be so happy to have her as a wife, if she were not a "half-breed."[116]

But in the fall of 1925 he became sure a parting of the ways was inevitable; with bombastic phrases he stylized it into a personal sacrifice that he had to make for the sake of his mission—"My heart bleeds!"[117] When Else finally wrote him a "desperate letter of farewell," he relented once more. But the following year, as he increasingly won Hitler's favor, he became more and more arrogant toward her. He now considered her concerns "small and touching," and saw in the woman "a nice little source of relaxation."[118] In June 1926 she wanted to put an end to this undignified charade. She wrote him another letter of farewell, about which he commented in his diary, "We can't even be friends anymore. We are worlds apart."[119] Yet Else Janke's letter still did not mean the end of the relationship. Not until Goebbels had decided to go to Berlin did he give her her walking papers. In his diary he recorded merely that he had taken leave of her—"in God's name." He promptly turned his attention to that charming woman he had seen again when he visited Berlin in mid-October before moving there for good. His future party comrades in the capital celebrated uproariously, because the "terrible time, the time without an emperor" and the "holy confusion in the Gau" would soon be a thing of the past.[120]

On 28 October 1926, after weeks during which Goebbels was again traveling on a propaganda tour, Hitler, with whom he thought he could conquer the world,[121] officially appointed him Gauleiter of Greater Berlin.[122] He no longer saw the city as an "asphalt desert" or "morass of dying culture," but as a "metropolis" and "hub."[123] Determined to fight and win there for his faith, which meant national socialism and its incarnation, Hitler, Goebbels on 7 November left Elberfeld for the capital.

CHAPTER 5

Berlin... A sink of iniquity!
And I'm supposed to
plunge into this?
(1926—1928)

When the new Gauleiter[1] got off the train on 7 November 1926 at the Anhalt Station in Berlin, he was coming to make his home in the chief metropolis of a country that was just beginning to recover from the war. Thanks to Stresemann's foreign policy, Germany was gradually regaining a position in the play of powers. Under the Dawes Plan, American capital had been flowing into the country for two years, helping the economy to get moving again. All this could be felt in Berlin. Stagnation had given way to a restless, creative ferment. Theatrical premieres, athletic records, and scandals of every variety, whipped into sensations by the press one day and forgotten the next, came hot on each other's heels. In a promotional brochure of the time Berlin was described as the fastest-moving city in the world, the "New York of Europe": "The heart of the Reich, Berlin pulses with life! Four million people in constant motion, a fifteenth of the German population marching in double-quick time!"[2]

Berlin might be dynamic, and seductive in its glitter, but the social contrasts were all the more glaring, in spite of the economic recovery. Nowhere else in the country did ostentatious luxury and bitter poverty clash more drastically. Politically this situation found expression in a strong leftist presence. In the previous year's elections for the city government, the Communists had garnered forty-three seats, more than doubling the seats they had won in 1921. With seventy-four seats the Social Democrats were the strongest party. Together with the Communists they would have held an absolute majority, but cooperation was out of the question because of the ideological disagreements that had already split the working-class movement in 1919. The Communists were fighting for the dictatorship of the proletariat, whereas the Social Democrats supported parliamentary democracy and the republic. As a result, the Social Democrats willy-nilly collaborated, in the city government as in the Prussian Landtag, with part of the bourgeois camp—the German Democratic

Party (DDP), the Catholic Center, and the German People's Party (DVP).

The National Socialists had no representation in the parliament of "Red Berlin," where the Right was principally represented by the German National People's Party (DNVP). In other respects, too, the Berlin National Socialist Party, newly established on 17 February 1925, led the wretched existence of an insignificant splinter group in the *völkisch* movement. Its few hundred members and sympathizers came largely from Spandau. In contrast to the other Berlin working-class districts, Spandau had shown a strong *völkisch* potential as early as 1921, when the German Socialist Union (DSB), with the swastika as its emblem, won 11.9 percent of the vote, becoming Spandau's fourth largest party. In the Reichstag elections in May 1924 this party achieved 8.8 percent of the vote, as much as the German People's Party; only the Social Democrats, the German National People's Party, and the Communists showed greater strength. But even in Spandau the German Socialist Union's share of the vote had shrunk to insignificance in the following years.[3]

In the fall of 1926 things stood no better with the organization of the NSDAP. An ideologically diffuse proletarian activism on the part of the SA, directed chiefly against the KPD and its military apparatus, conflicted increasingly with the circle around the Strasser brothers, who wanted to win adherents through persuasion. When Gauleiter Schlange had to step down in June 1926 and the Berlin party was placed in the hands of his deputy Schmiedicke, likewise a Strasser man, the conflict escalated. At the leaders' meeting on 25 August a fist fight broke out between Otto Strasser and Heinz Oskar Hauenstein, former leader of the SA Schlageter squad; Kurt Daluege and his SA had proposed Hauenstein as future Gauleiter. Such confrontations split the party in half and reduced its effectiveness to nothing.[4]

Although the Strassers had not managed to put an end to the dissension in Berlin, this city, along with Essen, administrative center for the Rhine-Ruhr Gau, played an important part in their influence within the NSDAP. Berlin was the home of the Kampf publishing house, run by Gregor Strasser, just named Reich organizational leader by Hitler, and his brother Otto. The sum total of all their publications amounted to no more than eight thousand copies, and the publishing house was running at a deficit,[5] but the weekly *Der Nationale Sozialist*, which appeared throughout Germany under seven different titles, among them the *Berliner Arbeiterzeitung*, conveyed the Strassers' socialist orientation to party members, rather than Hitler's ideas.

The Strassers took a rather skeptical attitude toward the new leader of the Berlin-Brandenburg Gau, in whom they saw a traitor to socialism sent by Hitler to meddle in their realm of activity. If they kept their resentment to themselves and tried to work things out with the interloper, it was because Goebbels had received special powers from the boss on 5 November 1926.[6] Among other things, the Gauleiter had received authorization to "purge" the Berlin party without the usual statutory consultation with the Munich Investigation and Mediation Committee.

Otto Strasser took these powers into account when he went to meet Goebbels at the station and arranged lodgings for him at an "excellent price" near the Landwehrkanal and the Potsdam Bridge.[7] In the spacious apartment of Hans Steiger, editor of the *Berliner Lokalzeitung* and a friend of Strasser's, whose wife took in carefully selected guests, Goebbels enjoyed special privileges. At his request, Frau Steiger provided a full-length mirror for his large room, so he could practice facial expressions and gestures for his speeches. In addition, he had access to the parlor and other rooms.[8] At the Steigers' Goebbels made the acquaintance of a "circle of intelligent and reliable friends of the party" who smoothed his way in the new city but at the same time kept the Strasser brothers informed of his every move.[9]

It was also Otto Strasser who stood up and introduced Goebbels when he made his first formal appearance as Gauleiter on 9 November 1926 at the memorial service for those who had fallen in Hitler's Munich putsch. Strasser described much later a characteristic "initial skirmish" in connection with this appearance: Goebbels arrived late, in an "especially large and elegant taxi." Strasser felt it was inappropriate for Goebbels to keep them waiting and was annoyed at the "pretentious automobile." He told Goebbels that their followers were all "poor devils" who would take offense. But Goebbels smiled with a superior air: "You are absolutely wrong there, Strasser. . . . You say I shouldn't take a taxi. On the contrary. If I could come in two cars, I would. The people must see that this outfit can make a good showing." Scanning the crowd intently, he finally made his way through the hall to the rostrum.[10] What Otto Strasser fails to mention in his reminiscences is the resounding success Goebbels achieved, precisely because of his manner. The hall apparently erupted like a madhouse when the Doctor hoarsely wrapped up his speech after several hours.

In that 9 November speech Goebbels appealed for party unity. But he had already issued concrete directives. In his first memorandum to the leaders of the local groups and sections, he banned any further discussion of the conflict between the Daluege-Hauenstein and the Strasser-Schmiedicke wings, threatening those who failed to comply with expulsion from the party.[11] At the same time, to the chagrin of the Strassers, he not only left Daluege's position as leader of the Berlin SA intact; he even named him his deputy. Since Goebbels made lively use of his right to "purge" the party, he managed to draw a line through the past and begin anew, for which he soon received unanimous support at a first general membership meeting.[12]

Goebbels took a decisive step forward on the Day of Repentance in 1926 when he founded the National Socialist Freedom Association.[13] In so doing, he was implementing an old plan of his. Back in Elberfeld he had hoped to put the local party's personnel and finances on a sound, if modest, footing by creating a tightly organized cadre, a "circle of pledged donors."[14] In Berlin the Association signed up between two and four hundred party members who committed themselves to monthly donations totaling fifteen hundred marks, which would enable the Gau to finance the first sorties in the struggle for the capital city.[15]

Goebbels emphasized ruthless activism, not the techniques of persuasion favored by the Strasser circle. To Goebbels, who had studied Gustave Le Bon's *Psychology of the Masses* (1911) with care, activism was inseparable from propaganda, which he considered "completely protean," since it had to adapt to existing conditions.[16] In the case of Berlin this meant taking into account Berlin's particular political and social structure, its hectic avant-garde pulse. "Berlin needs sensations as a fish needs water," Goebbels soon realized. "Any political propaganda that fails to recognize that will miss its target."[17]

So it was a matter of attracting attention, whatever the price. That had to happen in public, in the streets. In the age of the masses, Goebbels commented later, "he who can conquer the streets can conquer the masses; and he who conquers the masses conquers the state."[18] To prepare the pledged donors for their future role, training in oratory had to be provided, for "fascism and bolshevism were formed by nothing more nor less than the great orator, the great shaper of words! There's no distinction between the orator and the politician." By 16 November he had already established a school for orators.[19]

To call attention to the presence of the National Socialist Party in Berlin, immediately after his arrival Goebbels scheduled a propaganda march through the Neukölln section. It took place on 14 November, a Sunday. The report in the *Spandauer Volksblatt* ran under the headline "Swastika versus Soviet Star" and described, not without hyperbole, how the march through this heavily Communist part of the city had aroused "an immense stir," with large numbers of people streaming in from all directions, mostly Communists. There had been provocative speeches, soon followed by physical violence, in the course of which "slingshots, blackjacks, sticks, and also pistols" had been used.[20]

The beating his party comrades received at the hands of the Communists made it clear to Goebbels that the time was not yet ripe for such propaganda marches. For the present he had to concentrate on the ideological schooling of his little band of supporters, which would strengthen loyalty in the ranks. Later Goebbels would point to "the idea" as the prerequisite for any propaganda. This idea did not need to be explicated in a thick book; rather, it should contain "a simple and readily grasped theme." "You will never find millions of people who will give their lives for a book. You will never find millions of people who will give their lives for an economic program. But millions of people will one day be prepared to die for a gospel."[21] So not a day passed during Goebbels's first weeks in Berlin when he did not speak to gatherings of like-minded people, hammering belief in this gospel into them by appealing to their emotions. At a "German Christmas Celebration" organized by the local Spandau group, Goebbels proclaimed to his "congregation" that there was a belief that could move mountains, and this belief would create a new Reich in which true Christianity would be at home.[22] Those present greeted the Gauleiter's words with "tumultuous shouts of 'Heil!' "[23]

The fascination that emanated from Goebbels, "irresistible for many," was described by a nineteen-year-old who had just joined the SA—Horst Wessel.[24] The previous year this Protestant minister's son had registered at Berlin's Friedrich Wilhelm University, but he had soon begun neglecting his studies. Already a member of the Bismarck and Viking youth groups, he was attracted to the National Socialists because of their belief in a just world "with the emphasis on socialism," and to the "preacher" of this idea. "The oratorical gifts and organizational talent this man displayed were unique. There was nothing he couldn't handle. The party comrades clung to him with great devotion. The SA would have let itself be cut to pieces for him. Goebbels—he was like Hitler himself. Goebbels—he was *our* Goebbels."[25]

In no time at all Goebbels's frenetic, fanatical activity produced an atmospheric change in the Berlin party, which Wessel described thus: "When one saw the party members' willingness to sacrifice, one found new courage and renewed belief in the future, despite the wretchedness of the times."[26] Every event strengthened solidarity within the party and gained a few new adherents.

At the beginning of 1927 Goebbels moved the party central office, the so-called opium den, from the grubby cellar in a rear building at 109 Potsdamer Strasse to the second floor of the building that fronted on the street at 44 Lützowstrasse, where four rooms "with two telephone hookups" had been rented.[27] Soon he had also created a Gau marching band with forty or fifty members, and had acquired an "emergency vehicle" with which a mobile intervention unit could be transported quickly and inexpensively to the scene of propaganda marches and street clashes. "And so one operation will follow another," wrote Reinhold Muchow, organization leader of the Neukölln section, who was enthusiastic about the new Gauleiter, "until the 'Freedom League'—according to Dr. Goebbels—will undertake its final operation when the order arrives to occupy the Reichstag and seize control of it!"[28]

The way was to be paved by the SA, the counterpart of the Communists' Red Front Combatants' League, the KPD's street-fighting and terrorism organization. The brownshirts could not hold their own against the Red Front, so Goebbels undertook to rebuild the SA. The "groups," previously organized in parallel to the city's administrative districts, were changed to "divisions," each of which belonged to one of the three "standards" assigned to the inner city, the outer districts, and Brandenburg, respectively. Standard I at this time numbered 280 men, with twenty divisions of about fourteen men each.[29] It was difficult, Goebbels wrote in retrospect, to make disciplined "political soldiers" out of these bands of mostly unemployed ruffians who welcomed any fight, including fights among themselves. In fact, the conflict between the party leadership and the SA troops would constitute one of the Gauleiter's chief problems over the next few years.

At the beginning of 1927 Goebbels had to recognize that in spite of all the activities he had organized, the city remained unaware of his party and its new Gauleiter. The leading papers had not even taken notice of the wild clashes with Communists during and after a rally in Spandau at the end of January. Confrontations with the police during a "National Socialist Freedom Day" in Cottbus also went unmentioned.[30]

Impatient and dissatisfied with the results of his propaganda efforts, Goebbels decided to stage a major rally "in the lion's den," in "Red" Wedding. The event was planned as a provocation that would result in an all-out battle with the Communists and finally bring the public attention he hoped for. Goebbels chose the Pharus Hall, located in a rear building on Müllerstrasse, the Communists' traditional meeting place.

Whereas previously the small, cheap NSDAP posters had attracted little or no attention on the city's kiosks, now huge blood-red posters announced the coming event.[31] Goebbels did not invent this form of advertising; he merely introduced it to the capital city, once more following his Führer's stage directions. In *Mein Kampf* Hitler had written, "We chose the red color of our posters after careful and thorough reflection, in order to provoke the Left, to drive them to indignation and lead them to attend our meetings if only to break them up, in order to have some chance to speak to the people."[32]

On 11 February 1927 the "brown" Gauleiter hobbled up to the speaker's platform in "Red" Wedding to speak on "the collapse of the bourgeois class-state." Before he could even open his mouth, a wild brawl broke out in the hall between National Socialists and Communists, both parties armed with brass knuckles and iron rods. Eventually the numerically inferior Communists withdrew, protected by the police, who by then had come on the scene. The spectacle was perfect. The bourgeois newspapers, derogated by Goebbels as "Jewish," gave a large spread to the event. For the first time everyone was talking about the National Socialists and their Gauleiter—though only for a day or so, until the city, with its short attention span, found fresh excitement elsewhere.

Goebbels could call the "battle of Pharus Hall" a "good beginning," not only for the many new members it brought the party, but for other reasons as well. Those who had still had doubts about the scrawny little man with the limp seemed to have learned their lesson. He thought he had shown them that he had courage, that he would stop at nothing. And he had demonstrated his brilliance as a propagandist by coining the idea of the "unknown SA man," supposedly a victim of "Communist terror tactics," who became a symbol of the party's military arm and would later emerge from anonymity in the person of Horst Wessel. Goebbels spoke of this "unknown SA man" as the "aristocrat of the Third Reich" who day in, day out, did his duty "obedient to a law he doesn't know and hardly understands." Goebbels at any rate understood very well how to convey to his audience something of the presumably lofty "idea" of the movement and to make them believers. National socialism should be a matter of the heart; with this assertion Goebbels seemed to set himself apart not only from the other political persuasions but also from the world of the metropolis itself, which he condemned as cold and materialistic.

The propaganda events organized by Goebbels always played on the emotions and instincts of his listeners. This was true of the second Mark Brandenburg Day in March 1927, a celebration of the anniversary of the founding of the Berlin SA. On the evening of 19 March the Gauleiter went to the Anhalt Station to see his Berlin party comrades with their marching band onto the train to Trebbin.[33] When they arrived there, Goebbels and Daluege were already there to meet them. They led the procession in the dark blue Gau automobile, while four hundred people marched by torchlight to the Löwendorf Hills. There, gathered around a bonfire, they remembered the "Victims of the Movement." In the peaceful landscape of the Mark Brandenburg, thirty kilometers from the "Moloch metropolis," the "Judaized center," the "place of terror, of blood, of shame," Goebbels's address to his followers became a "worship service."

A rally in Trebbin's market square had been scheduled for the following morning. The blue Opel Landaulet, a seven-seater, would serve as the speaker's platform.[34] SA men had taken up positions around it with the Gau banner that Hitler had "consecrated" in Weimar in 1925 and sixteen swastika banners. As so often before, Goebbels's topics were nationalism and socialism; "our great Führer Adolf Hitler," the "simple corporal," had united the two principles out of the "realization" that a struggle between them would deliver the German people to destruction. As for the struggle against Jewish Marxism, he shouted, "blood" was "still the best glue that will hold us together in the struggle to come."[35]

And blood was soon to flow. Goebbels and Daluege roared off toward Berlin, as their supporters, shouting "Germany awaken!" formed an aisle of honor. As Goebbels had planned, the National Socialists who got on the train in Trebbin ran into a small shawm band of the Red Front Combatants' League. They were accompanying Paul Hoffmann, the Communist deputy of the Prussian Landtag, from Jüterbog. What began during the train trip escalated at the Lichterfelde East station, where an NSDAP "reception committee" numbering several hundred members and supporters from throughout Berlin had assembled. The train had not yet come to a complete stop when the SA stormed the compartment where the Red Front men were sitting. It was all over in a few minutes. Goebbels, who had kept himself in the background, appeared on the scene and called off his men, while a crowd of hundreds of curious bystanders watched.[36] When the National Socialists set out to march toward the center of town, they left behind, along with the demolished railroad car and smashed shawms, six seriously wounded and ten slightly wounded Communists.[37]

Goebbels drove at the head of the marching columns, to "study" the mood of the passersby, as he later testified to the police.[38] In actual fact he was directing his men and instigating them to further excesses. The victims this time were Jews, whom the SA men attacked with fists and sticks.[39] These first Berlin pogroms of the Weimar Republic were still in progress when the Gauleiter spoke at the closing ceremony for Mark Brandenburg Day, held on Wittenbergplatz, not far from the Kaiser Wilhelm Memorial Church. He shouted, "We came publicly for the first time into Berlin, with peaceful intentions. The Red Front Combatants' League has compelled us to spill our blood. We won't let ourselves be treated like second-class citizens any longer."[40]

The events of 20 March received full treatment in the press; this gave the National Socialists publicity and attracted new members. According to the political surveillance branch of the Berlin police, about four hundred new members joined in March 1927, bringing the total membership to about three thousand, of whom, of course, a considerably smaller number took an active part in rallies and other events.[41]

In another respect, too, the incident at the Lichterfelde East station had consequences for Goebbels. While no actual charges were brought against him, he had to appear for questioning at police headquarters. He had already been a "guest of the Berlin police commissioner" on 11

January 1927. While being questioned, he had learned that a case was pending against him before the state supreme court. He was to be charged with glorifying the murderers of Walther Rathenau, former Reich foreign minister, but the charges were later dropped.[42]

After barely half a year in Berlin, Goebbels began to feel sure that he could provide a sufficiently large following for an appearance by Hitler. Numbers were all the more important because Hitler had been banned from speaking in public in Prussia and would have to address a private gathering. When the man from Munich spoke on 1 May in the Clou, a nightclub on Mauerstrasse, and was frenetically cheered by the audience, Goebbels had the satisfaction of showing Hitler a solidly united little party, evidence of his successful efforts. But the public echo fell far below Goebbels's expectations. Because the Communists ignored Hitler's visit, no excesses occurred, and the press made no mention of Hitler's presence. Only a few regional papers commented—disparagingly—on the event.

Three days later Goebbels took the occasion of a larger party event at the Kriegervereinshaus to express his anger at this neglect, unmistakably baiting the journalists he held responsible, calling them "Jewish swine" and the like. He urged his followers to ferret out the identity of one reporter who wrote under a pseudonym, so they could "pay him a visit and show their gratitude in deeds, not words."

A certain Friedrich Stucke in the audience took exception to Goebbels's racist polemics. He shouted at the speaker, "Yes, yes, you're the perfect Germanic youth yourself!" Goebbels was speechless. After "initial silence" and "collecting his thoughts," he replied, "You must want to be thrown out of this hall," whereupon Stucke snapped back, "That's just like you to say that!" Tumult broke out. Outraged party members demanded that the "dog" be beaten to death. Before Stucke could get out of the hall, they grabbed him and beat him up under the nose of agents from the police political surveillance unit, always present at meetings of the NSDAP and the KPD.[43]

This incident might have remained one among many, had Stucke not been a pastor. Seeing the riot police surrounding the hall, he had become curious and made his way inside.[44] The Berlin papers reacted sharply to the attack on him and helped create a climate of opinion in which the Prussian government found it easy to crack down on the NSDAP. The incidents at the Pharus Hall and the Lichterfelde East station were still fresh in the authorities' minds. The party, wrote Interior Minister Albert Grzesinski, was returning to methods that could be described only as "political rowdyism," creating "an atmosphere like the one that existed in Germany before the Rathenau murder, an atmosphere that had proved so destructive to our people. Anyone who at public meetings more or less openly encourages violence against those who think differently places himself outside the law . . . and will be treated accordingly."[45]

That same day—5 May 1927—Berlin's police commissioner, Karl Zörgiebel, dissolved the NSDAP Berlin-Brandenburg Gau under Article 124 of the Reich constitution. All the party suborganizations—the SA, the Schutzstaffel (SS), the National Socialist Freedom League, the NS Student League of Berlin, and the German Working-Class Youth of Berlin (the Hitler Youth)—were included, because "the aims of these organizations subvert the penal code."[46] Along with the ban on the party, which Goebbels appealed in vain, went a speaking ban for the Gauleiter.[47] With that, there seemed to be no doubt that Goebbels's mission in the capital had failed.

This reversal promptly brought out of the woodwork those who had disagreed from the beginning with Goebbels's methods. The spokesmen came from the circle around the Strasser brothers. They had already attacked Goebbels several times in the *Berliner Arbeiterzeitung*. The high point of these attacks came in an article that appeared late in April 1927 with the title "The Results of Miscegenation."[48] Although signed by the Elberfeld party functionary Erich Koch, later to become Reich commissar for the Ukraine, the article plainly emanated from the Strassers. It ended with an allusion to Goebbels, arguing that "repulsive ugliness" and a particularly shabby character could stem only from racial mixing. The author cited several examples: Voltaire, the "master of malice and falsification," and the clubfooted Talleyrand, who from the French Revolution to the Congress of Vienna had changed his political convictions like his shirt.

At the Ruhr Gau party conference on 23–24 April in Essen, Goebbels cornered Hitler at the edge of a rally and shared with him his supposition that "a little railroad official" like Koch could hardly be clever enough to write such an article; it must be a campaign by the Strassers.[49] Hitler promised to cover Goebbels, but in fact he was concerned as always with keeping out of internal party conflicts. He therefore recommended to Goebbels that he talk things out with the Strassers and lay the matter to rest. With the same goal in mind, Hitler spoke with Kaufmann, the Rhine-Ruhr Gauleiter who was Koch's superior. On 26 April Koch, who swore on his "word of honor" that he was not the author, informed the Berlin Gauleiter that a personal attack had been "the last thing from his mind."[50] His letter, ending with a request that Goebbels "inform Herr Hitler of this," seemed to settle the matter, but that turned out not to be the case.

Goebbels now launched a campaign to counter the influence of the Strassers, which had been increasing since the ban on the party. For this purpose—and not, as he later wrote, to keep the National Socialists together—he went back to a plan already broached in a December 1925 letter to Otto Strasser.[51] He wanted to found a newspaper of his own. Resistance could be expected from his own ranks, for the Strasser brothers published the *Berliner Arbeiterzeitung*, up to then considered the party organ of the Berlin NSDAP. It was already having trouble holding its own and would now have direct competition, in addition to the competition of the other 130-odd political dailies and weeklies published in Berlin in 1927.[52]

The Strassers immediately grasped the significance of the Gauleiter's initiative. They responded to the challenge by telling Hitler that Goebbels was a "liar" and "show-off" who was going around claiming he had been active with Hitler in Munich in 1919 and had hurried to the Ruhr when the resistance against the French and Belgian occupation began, where among other things he claimed to have built up the NSDAP. Goebbels had in fact spread this legend while making speeches for the party. But his enemies did not stop there. At the beginning of June 1927 they launched rumors of a falling-out between Hitler and Goebbels. In that uneventful summer a few newspapers welcomed these rumors. *Welt am Abend* cited "reliable sources" to the effect that Hitler had "thoroughly dressed down" the "black-haired noble Aryan," his "favorite pupil," while the *Berliner Tageblatt* even spoke of "hostile brothers."[53]

So Goebbels was grateful when, on 4 June 1927, a Berlin party member turned up who confirmed his supposition that the Strasser brothers had planted the offensive article to undermine his authority in Berlin.[54] A skillful tactician, Goebbels promptly went on the offensive, turning again to his "very dear and respected Herr Hitler." He assured him of his loyalty, characterized the whole matter as a "cowardly ambush," and announced that for him there was only one "Either-Or": "Do you wish to advise me to keep silent about this most recent villainy and say yea and amen? If so, I'm of course prepared to observe strictest party discipline. . . . But in that case . . . I ask you to relieve me of my post as Gauleiter of Berlin-Brandenburg."[55]

Goebbels felt sure of the rightness of his cause and could therefore play for high stakes. On 10 June 1927 he called in his most loyal followers, but not the Strasser brothers, for an extraordinary meeting of the Berlin party. He opened the meeting by announcing that he wanted a unanimous vote of confidence, such as he expected from Hitler; otherwise he would not remain an hour longer in Berlin. Then he presented the state of affairs from his perspective. He dispelled speculation about the source of his physical defect, explaining, not entirely truthfully, that his "clubfoot was not a congenital defect but the result of an accident," which made the defamatory article "all the more horrendous." His second deputy Gauleiter, Emil Holtz, suggested that the Strasser brothers should have a chance to respond to the charges against them. The suggestion was lost in the storm of general indignation that now broke out. The evening became a tribunal that reached its climax in the suggestion made by Hans Schweitzer, a caricaturist and rabid anti-Semite, that Otto Strasser must "have Jewish blood in his veins," as evidenced by his "reddish, kinky hair, his hooked nose, his puffy, fleshy face."[56]

On that 10 June the creation of the new newspaper was also up for discussion. Someone asked how party members should view the new paper. Daluege responded that the *Völkischer Beobachter* should be considered the central organ and Goebbels's newspaper the Gau organ. Anyone who could afford to was welcome to subscribe to the *Berliner Arbeiterzeitung* as well. Shortly thereafter Emil Holtz, later to become Gauleiter of Brandenburg, wrote to Hitler about the Goebbels-Strasser feud, which was threatening to tear the Berlin movement apart. He conceded that Goebbels deserved credit for spurring the Berlin party members to extraordinary accomplishments. But now Goebbels's new newspaper meant direct competition for the *Berliner Arbeiterzeitung*, an effective organ for the party in Berlin.[57] Little did Holtz suspect that what he was describing as a problem for Hitler to solve dovetailed perfectly with Hitler's desire to see the influence of the Strasser press contained.[58]

The twentieth of June found Goebbels in Munich to clarify the Berlin situation. Wanting to placate his enemies within Hitler's immediate circle, he struck a moderate tone at the NSDAP evening conclave, which Hitler did not attend. To the Strassers' accusation that he had provoked the ban on the party by his methods of agitation, he responded that the ban had been completely arbitrary, and that he himself, as the mounting membership figures showed, had been on the right track.[59]

After meeting with Goebbels, who had probably surprised him with the unexpected defiance expressed in his letter, Hitler published a statement in the *Völkischer Beobachter* on the Berlin conflict.[60] He declared that all the charges against Goebbels had been invented by the "Jewish journalistic riffraff" for obvious reasons. "In my relationship to Dr. Goebbels not the slightest thing has changed. He enjoys as before my fullest confidence."[61] In spite of this statement Goebbels could not be entirely satisfied, even though he had succumbed once more to the fascination emanating from Hitler; Hitler had not damned the Strassers as Goebbels had hoped.

Instead Hitler notified the Gauleiter's opponents by way of the Investigation and Mediation Committee, which had meanwhile been called into the case, that he would "personally, in the largest possible circle of all those involved, bring the matter to a conclusion in Berlin."[62] He announced that Goebbels's newspaper would be issued by the party-controlled Eher publishing house in Munich. Although Goebbels had intended to have sole control over his paper, Hitler's decision signaled that he accepted the general idea of competition for the Strasser publications; he told the Strassers that Goebbels's newspaper would have a "neutral character."[63] Since Hitler's announcement that the paper would be published by Eher amounted only to a declaration of intent, Goebbels forged ahead with preparations for issuing it himself.

Goebbels called his partisan organ *Der Angriff* (The Attack). "This name was propagandistically effective, and in fact it contained everything we intended and aimed for."[64] The first screaming red posters went up on the kiosks 1 July 1927; they bore just the words *Der Angriff* and a large question mark. The next set of posters was intended to heighten the suspense: "*Der Angriff* begins on 4 July." People did not learn that *Der Angriff* was a weekly newspaper until the paper boys began hawking it in the streets of Berlin.

Even with a propagandistically effective design by Hans Schweitzer, the first number of *Der Angriff* could not satisfy Goebbels's ambition to have his paper eventually "take its place among the great press organs of the Reich capital."[65] "Shame, desolation, and despair swept over me as I compared this pale shadow of a paper with what I had really wanted to produce. A wretched provincial rag, printed slops! . . . No lack of good intentions, but very little skill." The layout was crude, the paper and the print of poor quality. Editorially, too, it had weaknesses, largely the result of insufficient journalistic experience on the part of Dagobert Dürr. On short notice Goebbels had had to assign this man, the administrator of the Gau, to stand in for the managing editor, Julius Lippert, later to become mayor of Berlin.[66] Lippert, who had previously been managing editor of the *völkisch* paper *Deutsches Tageblatt*, had to begin serving a six-week prison sentence the day the paper was due to appear.

But even after Lippert's release, things did not go smoothly for *Der Angriff*. The departure of a number of staff members led to a personnel crisis. These difficulties did not prevent Goebbels from using every means to elbow out the Strassers' competing publication. He reserved all party information, such as the times and places of meetings, ticket outlets, and dates of major events for his paper.[67] He even had reliable SA men attack newsboys selling the *Berliner Arbeiterzeitung*, for which he then blamed the Communists. Sales of the Strasser paper stagnated and then declined, while eventually the weekly run of two thousand copies of *Der Angriff* began to sell out. That the paper was actually self-supporting after three months, as Goebbels claimed, seems more than unlikely.

One trademark of *Der Angriff* was the caricatures by Hans Schweitzer. This Goebbels confidant, who also did drawings for the *Völkischer Beobachter* and the *Brennessel*, signed his work with the old Germanic name for Thor's hammer, Mjölnir.[68] As Goebbels's protégé, Schweitzer would be made Reich supervisor of artistic production in October 1935 and then advance to Reich cultural senator, president of the Reich Chamber of the Fine Arts, and SS Sturmbannführer "on the staff of the Reichsführer." He knew just how to translate his boss's verbal aggression into visual form. Even before he founded *Der Angriff*, Goebbels had greatly admired Schweitzer's "artistic genius."[69] Goebbels's editorials and "Political Diary," combined with Schweitzer's caricatures, created a form of "integrated political agitation" that in his eyes set *Der Angriff* apart from all the other papers in Berlin. Goebbels considered its propaganda effect "irresistible," with word and image serving "not to convey information but to spur, incite, drive" the reader to action.[70]

Another characteristic feature of *Der Angriff* was its "dynamic, aggressive, yet simple, folksy style."[71] Especially in his editorials Goebbels sought to convince the reader "that the editorialist is actually a public speaker standing next to him and trying to win him over with simple, compelling arguments."[72] Goebbels had picked up this idea from the Marxist press: "Marxism did not win with editorials, but by making every Marxist editorial a little propaganda speech."[73]

The new paper's position was clear: from the beginning it advocated destroying the Weimar Republic and those supporting it. In accordance with Hitler's dictum in *Mein Kampf* that the masses should never be shown two or more adversaries at once, the paper directed its struggle only against the Jews.[74] "This negative element must be erased from the German reckoning, or it will always spoil that reckoning."[75]

In one of his first editorials Goebbels explained the reason for this focus: "We are opponents of the Jews because we are proponents of the freedom of the German people. The Jew is the cause and beneficiary of our enslavement. He has exploited the social distress of the masses to deepen the fatal split between Right and Left within our people, has rent Germany in two, falsifying the real reasons for the loss of the Great War on the one hand and the betrayal of the revolution on the other."[76] He described "the Jew" as a "parasitic being," the "prototype of the intellectual," the uncreative "demon of decay" and "conscious destroyer of our race," since he "has rotted our morality, undermined our ways, and broken our strength."[77]

As so often in his campaigns, Goebbels borrowed his tactics from the Left. "Just as before the war social democracy fought not only a system that was hostile to it but also its visible, prominent representatives, so we, too, . . . had to adopt such a tactic."[78] Goebbels, whose physical defect had brought him ample acquaintance with the power of stigmatization, found such a visible representative in Bernhard Weiss, who in

March 1927 had been made deputy police commissioner in the "Jewish-Marxist" headquarters on Alexanderplatz, and whose political surveillance unit had played a key role in getting the NSDAP banned.[79]

Weiss, from a prominent Jewish family in Berlin, had been decorated with the Iron Cross First Class in the war. Goebbels happened upon a photograph of him on the front page of the *Völkischer Beobachter* after the banning of the party.[80] Small, with dark hair and horn-rimmed glasses, Weiss matched perfectly Goebbels's image of that Jewish-Marxist adversary who was to be "rubbed out." No matter that Weiss belonged to neither the SPD nor the KPD, but rather to the party of the liberal bourgeoisie, the DDP. All Goebbels needed was a catchy name that would allow him to "cannibalize" Weiss as an object of propaganda. By 15 August 1927 Goebbels had found the name: "Isidor."[81]

Even this name Goebbels had filched from the Communists, who had used it several times with defamatory intent in their newspaper, *Die Rote Fahne*.[82] Although the name was actually Greek, not Hebrew, it was often used along with "Cohn," "Levy," and "Schmul" to degrade Jews. This sort of half-furtive everyday anti-Semitism in German culture provided fertile ground for Goebbels's attack on Weiss.[83]

Goebbels soon transformed *Der Angriff* into an "anti-Isidor campaign organ."[84] Especially the local page, "From the Asphalt Desert," and the material under the heading "Achtung, Truncheons!" bristled with mentions of the derogatory name and with Isidor caricatures by Mjölnir. There one could find a piece on "Isidor's Swastika-Sniffers," a caricature suggesting that Weiss had failed to intervene against illegal actions by the Red Front Combatants' League, and even syllable puzzles whose solution contained the name Isidor: "Just pass around *Der Angriff*, and Isidor will be gone in a jiff," or "With Isidor we'll soon be done, if you donate to the *Angriff* fund."

Goebbels collected the most aggressive caricatures and scurrilous *Der Angriff* articles and published them in 1928 in the *Book of Isidor*, followed the next year by *Bigshot: The New Book of Isidor*, both lauded incessantly in *Der Angriff* and supposedly selling "like hotcakes."[85] The brutal cynicism that characterized Goebbels's campaign against Weiss becomes clear from the motto of the first book: "Isidor is not an individual, not a person in the legal sense. . . . Isidor is the *ponim* of so-called democracy, distorted by cowardice and hypocrisy, which on 9 November 1918 conquered empty thrones and today waves over our heads the nightstick of the freest republic of all."[86]

Goebbels's hatred for Weiss had escalated into sheer frenzy, in part because the deputy police commissioner had been so assiduous in enforcing the ban on the NSDAP. SA men had been hauled daily before the magistrates, Goebbels wrote later, one for wearing the forbidden brown shirt, another for endangering peace and safety by displaying a party badge, a third for giving an "impertinent and arrogant" Jew a box on the ears. He downplayed the seriousness of these provocations, which he himself had instigated in order to let it be known that the party was "banned but not buried."[87]

In fact the ban did little harm to the party because the organization remained in existence, merely changing the names of its units. The headquarters became a deputies' office, the SA units became bowling clubs, swimming clubs, a hiking club, and so on. If the police sniffed out such a club and banned it, the members would simply form another club and meet elsewhere. Furthermore, the members could easily pack their SA uniforms in their rucksacks and for a few pfennigs take the train out to the Mark Brandenburg. There, outside the city limits, they could continue to indulge their "brown" revolutionary romanticism in marches and gatherings.

At the crack of dawn on 5 August 1927, about fifty SA men left Berlin on foot to go to the annual party rally in Nuremberg. Horst Wessel describes how they made their way, hitching rides on railroad flatcars and horse-drawn wagons, and again on foot through the towns and villages of the Mark Brandenburg and Saxony, through the Thuringian and Franconian forests all the way to Nuremberg. On the outskirts of the city they left behind the comrades with the sorest feet, so they could march snappily into the city.[88] There they joined forces with four hundred others from Berlin who had followed their Gauleiter. The city resembled a "brown army camp." "Nuremberg—that won't be so easy to forget," Horst Wessel wrote enthusiastically. "What difference did it make to the Berliners after such a nationwide gathering that they had to return to a city where their activity was prohibited?"[89]

On their return, the 450 participants were arrested for membership in a prohibited organization, and Weiss had them transported in open trucks to police headquarters on Alexanderplatz, where most of them were held overnight. Finally someone was taking notice of them again, Goebbels may have thought. In *Der Angriff* he lamented bombastically, "I ask you: Is this a heroic deed? You blond youth, if you have tears in your eyes, swallow them. Do not weep before these sorry figures of magistrates."[90]

During this time Goebbels became active again as a "writer." He revised his "Michael," originally written in 1923. It was eventually published in 1929 by Eher, the party publishing house in Munich, and gathered dust on the shelves until 1933. But by the beginning of the war it had gone into its fourteenth printing! He also completed "The Wanderer," a "dramatic action with a prologue, eleven tableaux, and an epilogue." In this play, which he dedicated to "The Other Germany," Goebbels took up his timeworn theme of the presumed omnipotence of faith:

> *Faith*
> *is all!*
> *Awaken faith in the world,*
> *And you awaken man.*
> *Man is not dead,*
> *He is but sleeping!*
> *Faith is the power*
> *that awakens him to life.*
> *You have the word.*
> *You have the faith.*
> *You have the power*
>
> . . .
>
> *The new Reich will come.*[91]

Goebbels hired a group of unemployed actors to perform his "Wanderer." The premiere took place on 6 November at the Wallner Theater. While *Der Angriff* praised the play as an example of "the new cultural impulses of a youthful worldview,"[92] other papers tore it apart. That did not prevent the author from sending his National Socialist Experimental Theater on tour in the following years, performing the play in the area around Berlin.[93] After Hitler seized power he even had the play performed in regional and state theaters like Gotha, Würzburg, Göttingen, and Jena.[94]

To propagate the National Socialist idea and hold the party together, at the beginning of October 1927 Goebbels founded his School for Politics.[95] Under the pretext that politics as "study of the facts" should become the common property of as broad a segment of the population as possible, so that people could "convert their historical mission into deed with a minimum of erroneous conclusions and missteps," Goebbels created an opportunity for circumventing the ban on his speaking in public.

He kept the school alive even after the ban was lifted on 29 October 1927. Already on 8 November he appeared publicly at the Orpheum in the southern part of Berlin. The posters announcing this and subsequent appearances now carried the provocative line "With official permission of the police commissioner." In *Der Angriff* the attacks on the police leadership took on new savagery.[96]

Weiss, for his part, continued to subject Goebbels and other leading National Socialists to close surveillance by his political unit. Every number of *Der Angriff* underwent careful analysis as soon as it appeared. On 7 December 1927 Weiss first sued Goebbels for distortion of name and personal insult. Under questioning, Goebbels tried to talk his way out by arguing that as publisher he was not responsible for the paper's content; besides, he had not known what would be in the paper until it appeared, and he did not know the authorship of the incriminating article and caricature.[97] On 28 February 1928 Goebbels first appeared in court, but not to answer the charge of libeling Weiss. The court found him guilty of fomenting violence at the Kriegervereinshaus in May 1927, when Friedrich Stucke was so badly beaten. What gave Goebbels away was an article he had written in the *National Socialist Letters*, describing how those in charge of meetings should deal with hecklers and at what point they should call in their enforcers.[98] This model had been followed to the letter in the manner in which Pastor Stucke was "escorted out of the hall." The court's sentence called for six weeks' imprisonment, against which Goebbels's attorney promptly entered an appeal. This effort met with partial success, for the judges decided that while he had certainly been guilty of inciting to personal injury, he had acted "in good faith and honest conviction."[99] Goebbels wrote: "The judges' panel included a Jew, Löwenstein. Otherwise we would presumably have been cleared. Judgment: instead of the lengthy prison term . . . 600-mark fine for me. I won't pay a single pfennig."[100]

On 31 March 1928 the police commissioner's office lifted the ban on the NSDAP, eleven months after it had been imposed. The reason given was that the party should have the opportunity to prepare for the upcoming elections.[101]

Goebbels commented that it was a "great, solemn moment," a "historic hour" when the party was "newly established" on 13 April.[102] In the short time remaining before the elections on 20 May, Goebbels had to improvise. He focused his political agitation on disrupting the campaign rallies of other parties, trying to undermine the adherents of democratic processes. Aware of the usefulness of modern technology, though he lacked the funds to employ it to any great extent, he had phonograph records made on which "brown" slogans were presented against a background of "spine-chilling military songs." This technique, too, he had borrowed from the Left. The SPD mounted "the heaviest guns of modern propaganda" by equipping automobiles with loudspeakers. Another SPD technique was filmstrips synchronized with the gramophone.[103] Bands of strolling actors performing political skits, and the use of neon advertising signs completed this propaganda inventory. The KPD had its own devices: in Leipzig the Communists put on a "variety show," to which the famous director Erwin Piscator, "fighter for the political in art," contributed.

One of the National Socialists' chief propaganda weapons was the

Gauleiter himself. The best-known speaker in the party after Hitler criss-crossed the Reich during the weeks before the election, preaching the coming of the Third Reich. In addition, he was writing "editorials, leaflets, and posters like a madman!"[104] The Gauleiter's ceaseless activity was impeded only by the Berlin judiciary. On 17 April he received the first two of six summonses to appear on charges of insulting the deputy commissioner of police. "It's high time I received immunity," Goebbels wrote, alluding to his hopes of being elected to the Reichstag as his party's candidate.[105] In the meantime he tried to postpone his court appearance. He claimed he was scheduled to appear at a rally in southern Germany on the day in question and would thus be hindered by the summons from exercising his right to employ propaganda in support of his candidacy for the Reichstag and the Landtag.[106] When his request for a continuance was denied, he threatened the court with "the possible consequences of interfering with the electoral process," but the court was not impressed.[107] Weiss had informed the prosecutor that Goebbels was most likely trying to delay the proceedings in hopes of achieving immunity.[108]

The "Isidor case" came to trial on 28 April 1928. Goebbels had decided to "fight with silence this time."[109] The court certified that the Gauleiter's vicious attacks on Weiss were anti-Semitic insults that evidenced a "complete moral disregard for the adversary . . . and . . . unfounded malice and loss of feeling."[110] As the leading member of the party in Berlin, Goebbels was judged to have a decisive influence on the content and physical appearance of the paper he published.[111] The judges sentenced Goebbels and his codefendant Dürr to three weeks in prison for "joint public defamation of character through the press."

Goebbels's lawyer appealed, on the grounds that the figure of Isidor could not be equated with Weiss personally; the name alluded instead to a "collective concept intended to criticize the prevailing Jewification of leading positions in Prussia." During the appeal the Gauleiter was free to continue his propaganda campaign. Although he was soon "thoroughly fed up" with speaking, his hatred for the "system" kept him going.[112] He played on his listeners' fears of inflation, unemployment, and the victors in the war. During the last week before the election he escalated his involvement still further; on 14 May alone he spoke twelve times in Munich. Though physically exhausted, he rallied his last forces for the capital city and was "in splendid form."[113]

Yet even Goebbels's rather modest hopes for the election outcome were disappointed. Nationwide the NSDAP received only 2.6 percent of the vote, losing 0.4 percent or 100,000 votes as against the results for the Reichstag election in December 1924. This was the poorest showing since the party had sent its first fourteen representatives to the Reichstag in May 1924. Now the party was down to twelve deputies.

By contrast, the SPD with more than nine million votes recorded its greatest success since 1919. The KPD with 3.25 million had gained half a million votes. For the future of the republic the fragmentation of the large parties on the right seemed portentous; along with seventy-three deputies from the DNVP and forty-five from the DVP, fifty-one representatives of various rightist splinter groups with the most diverse agrarian and middle-class platforms would be entering the Reichstag. When the Depression struck in 1929, the millions of voters on the right who had lost their party umbrella would stream into the National Socialist camp.

In the capital of the Reich the National Socialists had themselves constituted no more than a splinter group, capturing only 1.5 percent of the vote in these May 1928 elections.[114] The long ban on the party and the short election campaign waged with limited means certainly contributed to the result. Although Goebbels pretended in his diary that the election had been "a fine success," he was immediately overcome with "depression."[115] He knew perfectly well that during the year and a half he had been fighting for National Socialism in Berlin he had changed next to nothing.

At least the elections brought a degree of personal satisfaction to Goebbels. He, who not even five years earlier had been a "poor devil" forced to live at home with his parents, had won a seat in the fourth postwar Reichstag. This meant a step forward in the direction of the Third Reich. That this Reich would come Goebbels had no doubt, despite all reverses and disappointments. The important thing was that he continue to believe in it.

CHAPTER 6

We want to be—and remain—
revolutionaries
(1928—1930)

On 13 June 1928 Deputy Goebbels hobbled up the steps to the entrance
of the German Reichstag. He was about to participate in its opening
session. He was pleased by the applause he received from a few curious
bystanders, for the twelve National Socialists must have felt lost among
the nearly five hundred members taking their places in the chamber under
the great dome. And among that small contingent Goebbels was essentially an outsider, for Frick, the chairman of the NSDAP delegation, and
the deputies Feder, Gregor Strasser, Franz von Epp (leader of the free
corps), and the "rather bloated" air force captain Hermann Goering[1]
were without exception "veterans" who had been with Hitler in Munich
in 1923. Goering had just returned from abroad, having left Germany
after the November putsch. He was living in Berlin and working for
BMW.

Goebbels's sense of insecurity in this unfamiliar terrain awakened in
him the obsessive notion that he was particularly threatened by the
"temptation of evil." The whole business, he wrote after his first experiences in the plenary session, which he called a "crazy Jewish school,"
was so "sneaky and corrupt," but also so "sweet and seductive" (he now
enjoyed legal immunity, a per diem allowance, and other privileges), "that
very few characters are strong enough to withstand it. I am solemnly
determined to remain strong, and I hope and believe I'll succeed."[2] He
saw himself as equal to the "test," particularly because of his conviction
that parliamentary democracy was "long since ripe for destruction,"[3]
and that the National Socialists were predestined to "eliminate this system
in and for itself and not merely somehow ameliorate its pathological
features."[4]

After the "most blatant liberals" had "pasted together" the government[5] (it was the Great Coalition under the Social Democrat Hermann
Müller), the Gauleiter gave his maiden speech on 10 July, during the first

debate on draft legislation on the national holiday. "When one first participates as a newcomer in this democratic swindle, it makes one's head spin," he began, which earned him not only a rebuke from Reichstag Vice President Thomas Esser but also loud protests from the democrats. Goebbels commented on this first appearance: "I tooted my opinion of these swine so clearly they couldn't believe their ears. And it hit home. The sensation of the Reichstag. How the journalistic riffraff will rave tomorrow!"[6]

The press did Goebbels the favor of covering his speech, although it did not figure as a "sensation," but almost three-quarters of a year would pass before he spoke again. If he kept silent, it was because he understood national socialism as an extraparliamentary revolutionary movement. "What does the Reichstag matter to us?" he wrote scornfully in *Der Angriff*. "We have nothing to do with the parliament. We reject it in our hearts and do not hesitate to express that fact forcefully to others. . . . I am not a member of the Reichstag. I am EtI, EtFT—Entitled to Immunity, Entitled to Free Transportation. One who is EtI curses the 'system' and for that receives the republic's gratitude in the form of 750 marks per month."[7]

But the Reichstag seat not only brought Goebbels the privileges he described so cynically but also improved his standing within the party and thereby his position vis-à-vis the Strassers.[8] In late May and early June 1928 the brothers had indirectly blamed him in the *National Socialist Letters* for the party's disappointing election results in Berlin.[9]

Such attacks provoked boundless hatred in Goebbels. He remarked in his diary that Otto Strasser, "that Satan" of the movement, had to be "exterminated" at "whatever price," but he immediately added that there was no way of getting at Strasser: "That dog is too corrupt and sneaky."[10] Goebbels furthermore claimed to have learned that talks had taken place between Otto Strasser, Reventlow, and Kaufmann "for the purpose of founding a new party in which the socialist line would be more sharply emphasized." He expressed shock and indignation at these men, to whom he actually stood closer politically. But their action went against Hitler. "The gentlemen want to be in charge themselves. I'll keep an eye peeled. I stand with Hitler, come what may. Even if he should slap me in the face."[11]

When his boss did not intervene, despite Goebbels's telling him of his discovery, Goebbels toyed with the notion of submitting his resignation; he was "sick of the mess" in Berlin.[12] He changed his mind, however, when Hitler came to Berlin on 14 July 1928—the same day the Reichstag issued an amnesty for all political crimes committed before 1 January of that year—and in a "long, personal discussion" with the Strassers smoothed the waves. He assured Goebbels that he had taken "stern measures against Dr. Strasser," which led Goebbels to believe that the Kampf publishing house, source of the Strassers' influence in the north German party, would soon be "liquidated." When the skilled tactician Hitler furthermore praised Goebbels highly for his work, all his thoughts of "abdicating" vanished: "I shall stay. The boss is one hundred percent on my side."[13]

Partly to defuse the situation in the Berlin party, Hitler now accelerated his plan of restructuring the NSDAP Gaus so they would correspond to the Reichstag electoral districts. That meant dividing the Berlin-Brandenburg Gau into a Greater Berlin Gau and a Brandenburg Gau. The latter, which Goebbels immediately began referring to as a "sub-Gau,"[14] was headed by the Strassers' friend Emil Holtz.[15] "My Gau is being divided. . . . Thank God! That will rid me of much annoyance," Goebbels wrote.[16] Goebbels's organizational activity was now limited to the capital city itself, but its scope was actually enlarged, for the Strassers in turn were restricted to the "sub-Gau" of Brandenburg.

The Gauleiter of Greater Berlin had something else to worry about that summer: the Berlin storm troopers. Despite all his efforts, he had not succeeded in transforming the SA into a simple arm of the party. If it was still more like a nonideological paramilitary force, that had to do with the directives issued in the course of reorganizing the SA; since November 1926 no party member had been allowed to function as a political leader and belong to the SA at the same time.[17] In the spring of 1928 Franz von Pfeffer, just named SA chief of staff by Hitler, ordered that the Berlin SA divisions also be replaced by a system of storm units, each assigned to one of five standards. Their military leaders, principal among them Walter Stennes, a wartime officer turned free corps member and arms racketeer, demanded independence from the civilians in the Gau leadership. They felt neglected by the leadership because they received such meager funding. Goebbels considered such conduct "lacking in political instinct" and charged that they did not know how to "hate" and had failed to recognize "the Jew" as the enemy.[18] As a result, the paramilitary apparatus now threatened to go its own way.

Goebbels was convinced that if the NSDAP was to survive in Berlin, policy should be left to the politicians, and the SA should be responsible for carrying it out.[19] But even before he could "rap the gentlemen on the knuckles,"[20] the crisis he had long predicted broke out. In mid-August Stennes demanded that the national party leadership come up with 3,500 marks. When Munich did not comply, Stennes summoned the leaders of the Berlin SA to a meeting, railed at Hitler and von Pfeffer, and presented his interpretation of the situation. He then incited some of the leaders to announce their resignation from the party. Their decision was promptly conveyed to the party leadership by telegram.[21]

Goebbels, vacationing in the Bavarian resort of Garmisch-Parten-kirchen, heard of Stennes's action and decided that the problem had to be resolved once and for all: "Party or military, revolutionary or reactionary policy."[22] Discussions with Stennes and other SA leaders after Goebbels's hasty return to Berlin, as well as payment of the 3,500 marks, made an accommodation possible.[23] The Gauleiter felt the crisis was "solved" when Hitler promised to address the Berlin SA twice in the near future. Goebbels was back in his Bavarian resort when Hitler spoke at the end of August in the "jam-packed" Friedrichshain Hall. His appearance was "an unqualified success" according to Horst Wessel, who particularly noticed the many unfamiliar faces in the audience.[24]

Wessel reports that the Gau looked forward to the "fall and winter struggle" with optimism, not only because Goebbels and Stennes had put aside their disagreements and now intended to "cooperate loyally,"[25] but also because of the organizational work initiated in the late summer of 1928. Goebbels had made twenty-three-year-old Reinhold Muchow organization leader for the Greater Berlin Gau.[26] Muchow now developed a plan to replace outdated structures.[27] Following the model of the KPD, he had designed a system consisting of cells, street cells, sections, and districts or regions, leading up to the Gau level, that was now introduced in Berlin and was later taken over by the party leadership for the entire country.[28]

The SA man Horst Wessel was involved in training the cell leaders; he had just been named street cell leader of the Alexanderplatz Storm Section.[29] From January to July 1928 Wessel had been in Vienna, sent there by Goebbels to study the organization and working methods of the Viennese party's National Socialist Youth Group. The Viennese party was highly regarded in the NSDAP for its tight organization, its unity, and its "idealism and sense of sacrifice." Once back in Berlin, Wessel first devoted himself to working with the youth before getting involved in implementing Muchow's cell system, in defiance of SA statutes forbidding actual party involvement.[30]

At the same time Muchow launched another undertaking. With Goebbels's approval he began to build up a system of party cells in factories, to shape more decisively the "struggle for the soul of the worker." During the ban on the party a first National Socialist factory cell had been established in the Knorr brake plant. Then on 30 July 1928 the Berlin Gau headquarters had set up the new Secretariat for Workers' Affairs, with a factory cells division to be established after the city council elections in November 1929.[31] This innovation was later copied by Gregor Strasser for the entire Reich with the establishment on 15 January 1931 of the Reich Factory Cells Division of the NSDAP.[32]

The organizational progress in Berlin found expression in the first major propaganda undertaking of the leadership corps that was developing: the so-called Dawes Week. It was launched at the end of September with a special edition of *Der Angriff*, which sold about fifty thousand copies.[33] After rallies at the Bock Brewery and the Kriegervereinshaus, thousands went out to Teltow for the third Mark Brandenburg Day. The SA paraded and then marched back into the city, singing the Berlin SA "Song of the Storm Columns," which had been published in *Der Angriff*.[34] "Only when Jews are bleeding / Only then shall we be free" rang through the streets. The sidewalks were thronged with people watching, partly in disgust but also partly with enthusiasm, as the storm columns of the Hitler dictatorship, as it said in the song, marched past.

That day Berlin experienced its first National Socialist mass meeting when several thousand people gathered at the Sportpalast to hear the Reichstag deputy Ernst von Reventlow; the Gauleiter of the Ostmark, Richard Paul Wilhelm Kube; and Goebbels.[35] Goebbels was in "the best form." Meanwhile outside the arena those who had not been able to get in because every seat was taken engaged Communists in a bloody street clash that left twenty-three National Socialists injured, three critically. Inside, the crowd became so inflamed that Goebbels had difficulty getting it under control again so that he could repeatedly incite it against the republic, which he described as a "playground for robbers" and a "den of murderers." He promised that the NSDAP would build another state out of the existing one and at the appointed time institute the "new German Reich."[36] When he had concluded his speech and the raging crowd surged toward the exits, while outside the fighting against the Communists flared up again, Goebbels felt in his element: "My heart leaps for joy."[37]

Hitler had read in the papers about the spectacle in Berlin and wrote to congratulate Goebbels. "Full of praise for me. 'Berlin—that is your doing.'"[38] Emotionally overwrought and completely overestimating the importance of the movement in the capital, Goebbels wrote in his diary that "everyone" was looking to Berlin: "We are the hub."[39] When Hitler came to the city on the Spree on 13 October and popped in unexpectedly on Goebbels in the offices of *Der Angriff*, he was again full of praise for the Gauleiter. Goebbels noted that he "spoke very sharply against Dr. Strasser," but waxed enthusiastic about the latest edition of *Der Angriff*, whose circulation was increasing.[40] Goebbels attributed the two hundred new subscribers in November to the "intellectual level" of *Der Angriff*.[41] "Hard-working recruiters" received credit for a record increase in the winter of 1928.[42] In spite of these increases, at this period certainly no more than 7,500 copies were being sold each week.

After the Prussian government had lifted the ban on Hitler's speaking, *Der Angriff* announced an appearance in Berlin for 16 November. When he spoke at the Sportpalast, constantly interrupted by "tumultuous applause," as the *Vossische Zeitung* reported, the hall was "jammed with the curious. In their midst a few thousand supporters of the National Socialists. . . . Up front on the platform several deputies from the party. The little dark-haired Dr. Goebbels with his coal-back fanatical eyes and thin lips."[43] Goebbels recorded the evening as the "greatest success" of his efforts in Berlin.[44]

Hitler's appearance had an epilogue that finally gave Goebbels a first "sacrificial victim" to exploit for propaganda purposes. The body of Hans-Georg Kütemeyer, an SA man who had been sitting in the box office at the Sportpalast, was pulled out of the Landwehr Canal the next morning, a few miles south of the spot where the murdered Rosa Luxemburg had been thrown in January 1919. Goebbels promptly concluded that Kütemeyer had been murdered by Communists. While the "Jewish press," as Goebbels called it, tried to portray the death as a suicide,[45] Goebbels set about transforming the SA man into a mythic figure, the National Socialist ideal type, hard-working, conscientious, full of loyalty to and love for his Führer. When the police investigation turned up concrete evidence for the suicide theory, which the newspapers duly reported, Goebbels had to create contradictory evidence. He claimed to have seen a "taxi crammed with Red ruffians" armed with iron rods that "in a flash crushed" the pale face of the SA man into a "bloody ecce homo."[46]

Deputy Police Commissioner Weiss refused to grant a permit for a funeral procession, so Goebbels had to restrict his propaganda spectacle to the burial. But Goebbels's openly provocative statements induced Weiss to have him questioned. Goebbels wrote in his diary: "The police are looking for material in the Kütemeyer case. Breach of immunity. A terrible mess again. That damned Isidor is pulling out all the stops. Unfortunately they turned up two pistols. A disagreeable business! . . . The persecution is beginning again, no holds barred. But we'll defend ourselves. . . . The whole thing is of course a ploy on the part of the police. They want to silence us before the reparations negotiations."[47] Although the National Socialists arrested in connection with the police search of their headquarters were soon released, and Goebbels remarked that Isidor had "made a total fool of himself" again,[48] the myth of Kütemeyer as a victim of the Reds could not withstand the revelation of the facts of the case, thoroughly covered in the Berlin press.

Even without the Kütemeyer myth, the NSDAP was gaining ground, thanks to political and economic developments. Negotiations got underway in Paris in February 1929 to settle the final amount of Germany's reparations and put an end to the occupation of the Rhineland. The millions of marks being discussed formed a grotesque contrast to the poverty spreading through Germany. The fall of 1928 had seen the economy slacken noticeably, with the poor and the so-called little people the first to feel the effects. Unemployment soared during the bitter-cold winter of 1928–29, reaching 3.2 million by February. It was easy for the NSDAP to seize the propaganda advantage by blaming the economic disaster on the "burden of tribute."

In his speeches and articles Goebbels drummed into his listeners the notion that the negotiations in Paris were part of a gigantic conspiracy by "international Jewry" to enslave the German people and bring about the fall of the West. "The German people has passed the many stations of its Golgotha, and now its executioners are preparing to nail it to the cross, laughing with derision."[49] Goebbels actually believed what he preached, for it all fit his stereotyped view of the situation.

In handwritten notes for a book, begun in 1929, Goebbels commented that it should have been the duty of the German government and public to use radical propaganda to call the world's attention to the widespread poverty in Germany. That way at least some sympathy for the Germans could have been generated in neutral countries while "fateful decisions" were being made. "The German government did not do so, and apparently has no intention of doing so in the coming weeks." Again Goebbels traced this omission to the international Jewish conspiracy.[50]

Goebbels thought he saw confirmation for this theory when an announcement came in February 1929 that Stalin's adversary "Trotsky, alias Bronstein"—a Jew "who probably has more crimes on his conscience than any other human being"—was planning to leave the Soviet Union and possibly seek asylum in Germany. "Stock exchange and bolshevism hand in hand. We ask the oppressed German people: what further evidence do you need?"[51] The extent to which this delusory vision of the gigantic menace of international Jewry had seized hold of Goebbels's imagination can be seen from a dream he jotted down just before Christmas 1929: "I was in a school, and was pursued down the long corridors by several East Galician rabbis. They kept shouting 'Hate!' at me. I was a few steps ahead of them and answered with the same word. This went on for hours. But they couldn't catch me."[52]

It was less this conspiracy theory than sheer desperation that turned many people into supporters of a movement that offered simplistic explanations and promised relief. In the May 1929 elections for the Saxon Landtag, the Nazis increased their percentage of the vote and even achieved a majority in the city council of Coburg. Such successes allowed Hitler to think that coming to power legally was not out of the question. But he needed allies. In addition to the Stahlhelm, the organization of frontline veterans from the war, the most promising group was the German National People's Party. Since the press magnate Alfred Hugenberg had become party chairman in October 1928, the DNVP had made a radical change in its previous line, adopting a principle of opposing the republic and the provisions of the Treaty of Versailles. In 1929 the DNVP was making the Young Plan the chief object of its offensive against the "system." Although the plan offered distinct advantages for the German Reich, including withdrawal of foreign troops from the Rhineland, the fact that paying off the reparations would take generations, and that the payments were still quite high, offered a ready target for attacks from the Right. The campaign was to begin with a petition for a plebiscite and then an actual plebiscite on the Young Plan. In the spring of 1929 Hitler flirted with having his party join forces with the DNVP and the Stahlhelm in the Völkisch Reich Committee created by the DNVP.

To Goebbels any such alliance with the hated reactionary forces seemed a betrayal of the Nazi cause, especially since he thought his party's political agitation against the Young Plan might appeal to the broad masses for the first time. He interpreted the founding of the Völkisch Reich Committee as an attempt by the DNVP to prevent its voters from defecting to the Nazis.[53] Goebbels was determined not to alienate the working class by cooperating with the conservative nationalists.

In his diary Goebbels expressed dismay at his party's rapprochement with the "archreactionary" Stahlhelm and the DNVP, whose platform enshrined nostalgia for the social and political structures of the Wilhelmine era.

We still have too many philistines in the party. Sometimes Munich's course is intolerable. I'm not prepared to go along with a corrupt compromise. I'll stick to the straight and narrow path, even if it should cost me my personal position. Sometimes I have doubts about Hitler. Why does he keep silent? The opportunists want to pluck the fruits before they're ripe. . . . I mull over these things for hours and always come to the same conclusions. . . . Sometimes I could scream with rage at the thought that everything we made such sacrifices to build up may be wrecked.[54]

When Goebbels learned that his boss planned to approach "the reactionaries" in order to "reel them in," he was afraid that Hitler would be reeled in himself. "I'll be on the lookout. And warn him when the moment comes."[55] During a long talk Goebbels had with Hitler at the Sans Souci Hotel in Berlin, all of Goebbels's doubts vanished. He was "completely satisfied," for Hitler decisively rejected the petition for a plebiscite and had even written a memorandum in opposition to it.[56] Hitler's words had given him back "joy and especially certainty," and he was convinced that the "reactionary forces on the march" would be crushed "to a pulp."[57]

Goebbels now wanted to go on the offensive against these "dilet-tantes."[58] He missed no opportunity to attack the conservative right in *Der Angriff* and in speeches, in spite of instructions from Munich that a "unified front" should be preserved.[59] Goebbels was determined to keep the party line straight, for "we want to be—and remain—revolution-aries," he noted in his diary.[60]

The Berlin Gauleiter's position actually fit in nicely with Hitler's cal-culations. It preserved the propaganda distinction between the Nazi Party and the DNVP-Stahlhelm alliance, while Hitler could woo the nation-alists' leadership and cultivate contacts through Franz von Epp. In a conversation with Hitler and his private secretary Rudolf Hess on 28 May, Goebbels was told that Hitler planned not to participate in the Stahlhelm's Frontline Soldiers' Day in Munich. Goebbels was all the more willing to view the compromise as a victory for the "revolutionaries among us," because Hitler had promised him the position of head of propaganda.[61]

The prospect of sweeping the hated Strassers aside allowed Goebbels to continue in his delusion that the boss saw eye to eye with him on collaboration with the DNVP and the Stahlhelm. But after an evening with Hitler in Berlin in early July 1929, he was forced to recognize that this was not the case. In the confrontation with his boss, to whom he felt he owed everything and whom he "loved more than any man," he capitulated completely. Hitler had renewed his promise to put him in charge of propaganda. So Goebbels wrote in his diary, as though he had never held any other opinion, "We'll collaborate on the German Na-tionalist plebiscite petition against Versailles and Young. But we'll force our way to the front and tear the mask from the DNVP. We're strong enough to prevail in any alliance."[62] He viewed it as his own task as "guardian of the revolution" to make sure that the Nazis remained in control of events.[63]

In fact Goebbels was again succumbing to a delusion. Just as in the question of the plebiscite, he would later have little influence over the course the party followed. He had yielded completely to Hitler and now followed him unconditionally, whatever slight doubts he might occa-sionally have. Whenever Hitler succeeded, these doubts quickly dissi-pated. In the present case it turned out that the NSDAP had for the first time found an opportunity to speak out on an important political issue and therefore gained greater credibility with the nationalistically oriented population. This influence would become very important when the Depression caused many people to look in desperation for political al-ternatives.[64]

Hitler's pact with what Goebbels considered the reactionary forces had caused him to fear from the beginning that he would lose the relatively unsuccessful battle for Berlin's workers. The KPD was taking full advantage of the dire conditions brought about by the economic downturn. For the traditional day of labor, the first of May, a ban on outdoor gatherings had been issued. On instructions from Stalin, the KPD sought a confrontation with the Prussian government, the SPD-dominated main pillar of the Weimar Republic.

Die Rote Fahne threatened in innumerable articles to answer the ban with armed actions. On 1 May the Communists issued a call for street rallies in different parts of Berlin. The results were catastrophic. In Neukölln, police officers afraid of snipers fired warning shots, which the Red Front Combatants used as a pretext for firing scattered shots of their own. Soon violent street battles erupted. The police used unusual force, bringing in machine guns and armored vehicles. The battles lasted into the night and flared up again the next morning. This "Bloody May" left 33 dead, 198 civilians wounded, 47 policemen injured, and 1,228 people in custody. The Communist paramilitary organization was banned in Prussia and soon afterward throughout the entire Reich. It continued, however, to work underground.

On orders from its Gauleiter, the Berlin NSDAP had held back on the "worldwide proletarian holiday," for the conflict showed up the weakness of the republic and the threat posed by the Communists, and also destabilized the "system." In *Der Angriff* Goebbels contrasted the meaninglessness of the Communist gunfire with the revolutionary élan of the brownshirts, the only alternative.[65] Apparently, some Red Front Combatants' League members did switch to the SA.[66]

Now Goebbels went on the offensive, sending the SA to march and agitate in proletarian districts so as to demonstrate the attractiveness and superiority of the NSDAP, which was actually very small compared to the KPD. Goebbels put his most competent SA leaders in charge of these missions, among them Horst Wessel.[67]

Wessel's field of activity included the Fischerkiez, an infamous quarter between the Stadtschloss and Alexanderplatz, where the poorest of the poor lived. It was dominated by the KPD. After several light skirmishes, a serious incident occurred at the end of August in front of the Hoppe, a pub where the local KPD had its headquarters. During an attack on the pub, five workers were injured, four seriously, one slightly. *Die Rote Fahne* protested that once more the police had let the murderers get away and had instead arrested four workers. Since the police insisted on protecting the fascists, the proletarians should take matters into their own hands. *Der Angriff* carried an entirely different version, describing how sinister figures had emerged from the shadows and turned the street into a madhouse, while from the vehicle of Storm Unit 5 Horst Wessel was trying to deliver a speech warning against any continuation of Communist terror tactics.[68]

The Communists took the Nazi threat seriously, although they still saw the SPD as the chief enemy. In their eyes, the attack on the Hoppe pub was consistent with other counterrevolutionary measures.[69] Their new slogan, announced in late August in *Die Rote Fahne*, was "Strike the fascists wherever you find them!"[70]

Goebbels accepted the Communists' declaration of war and even seemed to welcome it.[71] But the Communists' fighting units were numerically superior and better organized. More and more often groups of SA men were ambushed, and the brownshirts took revenge in carefully planned attacks. The hatred between the two groups can be seen in the invective they hurled at each other in the pages of *Der Angriff* and *Die Rote Fahne*.[72]

On 22 September Goebbels, who was incessantly agitating at party events and rallies against the "Jewish-Bolshevist world plague" and its "conspiracy," the Young Plan, had a close call with the Communists. They recognized him in "Red" Neukölln, near Görlitz Station. He described the scene as follows: "Before my eyes clubs, daggers, brass knuckles appear. I feel a blow on my shoulder. As I turn to one side, a Communist takes aim at me. A shot rings out. Stones fly. Tonak is already bleeding heavily. A wild volley of shots. Shots crackle from the car. The mob gives ground. I apply pressure to Tonak's wound. He starts up the car and drives off, in full possession of his wits. . . . We're saved."[73]

Goebbels attributed his escape to his higher destiny. He certainly also saw the hand of fate in the events that befell the young republic, starting in October 1929. On 3 October Foreign Minister Stresemann died. Goebbels, who spoke of an "execution by heart failure," noted that a stone had been removed from the path to "German freedom," for with his death the Weimar coalition lost its chief integrating figure. It would soon become clear that in certain questions of social policy the entrepreneurs' wing of the German People's Party and the trade-union wing of the SPD could no longer maintain a workable compromise.

A few days after Stresemann's death, the "Black Friday" Wall Street crash stripped away the basis for the new reparations plan, which was supposed to be linked to the withdrawal of the last Allied troops from the Rhineland in 1930. With the crash, the foreign capital that had flowed so liberally into Germany over the past few years was instantly frozen. A huge depression set in, with unemployment rising to 3.39 million by January 1930. Under the circumstances, paying two billion gold marks in reparations over fifty-eight years, as contemplated by the Young Plan, seemed simply grotesque.

The petition against the Young Plan, which took place from 16 to 29 October, barely squeaked through. Not much more than the required 10 percent of eligible voters supported it. According to the constitution, the draft legislation now had to be introduced in the Reichstag. Since the petition was rejected by a large majority of the deputies, a plebiscite had to be held, with 50 percent of the votes required for it to succeed. When only 13.81 percent supported the referendum, Goebbels felt justified in his original objection to the NSDAP's joining the Reich Committee.[74]

Now only Reich president Hindenburg could prevent acceptance of the Young Plan. Since such a decision was not to be expected, Hindenburg found himself caught in the political agitators' crossfire. Goebbels mocked him in Der Angriff under the title "Is Hindenburg still alive?"[75] The article predicted that on the question of the Young Plan Herr von Hindenburg would do "what his Jewish and Marxist advisors whisper to him," as always. In a caricature the president was portrayed as an unfeeling Germanic god watching coldheartedly as generations of Germans were led off in chains to slavery.

Goebbels attacked the "old man" even more ferociously after the Young Plan was signed in The Hague on 20 January 1930 and was then, on Hindenburg's urging, submitted to the Reichstag on 12 March, where it was ratified by a vote of 270 to 192. In an appearance at the Kriegervereinshaus, the Gauleiter was observed by the police political surveillance unit declaring that now the German people had no more obligations to Hindenburg, since by signing the plan he had made himself "a lackey of the racketeer government and the racketeer republic." Goebbels went on to accuse the Reich president of stealing the younger generation's future.[76]

The political unrest created by agitation against the Young Plan and by the so-called Sklarek scandal, which involved accusations that the mayor of Berlin was guilty of taking bribes and protecting banking irregularities, contributed to the Nazis' gains in the city council elections on 17 November 1929. With 132,097 votes they had 5.8 percent of the total. Goebbels now spoke of "the boldest dreams" that had come true, pointing to alleged "strong growth" in "proletarian areas."[77] In fact, the Communists had received four times more votes than the Nazis. Goebbels simply knew how to manipulate statistics. He pointed out that in "Red" Wedding the NSDAP had increased its share of the vote by 300 percent, but overall the Nazis' votes amounted to only 3.1 percent, as compared with the Communists' 40.6 percent, of the total.[78]

As meager as these results were, they did allow the Nazis to take their place in the city council with thirteen representatives. Goebbels headed the delegation but never spoke, and eventually resigned in 1930, claiming to be "overworked."[79] The other members of the delegation took it upon themselves to make life miserable for their opponents, especially the Communists, who had gained twenty-one seats to become, with fifty-six seats, the second-largest party after the SPD.

While Goebbels was busy establishing an apparatus for communal politics intended to "saturate" Berlin with the party's propaganda and train functionaries for future election campaigns, his confidant Reinhold Muchow set about refining the cell system. The aim was to improve party discipline and strengthen the structure, thereby making it more flexible and effective.[80]

For Goebbels, who was gradually tightening the net of "splendidly trained, determined opponents of the system" around Berlin, the year 1929 ended with a personal blow. On 7 December he received the news that his father had died. His trip to Rheydt became a theatrical excursion into the past. "The sons stand by their father's casket and weep and weep and weep. How often these hands did some kindness for me! How often these lips spoke words of encouragement! Now all silent, cold, motionless." And he drew his mournful conclusion: "Life is hard and inexorable." After two days filled with preparations for the funeral, and two evenings when they sat around and "reminisced about Father," the family laid Fritz Goebbels to rest in the Rheydt cemetery. Soon Goebbels said his farewells to the family, especially to his mother: "I feel with passionate intensity my good fortune in still having this mother. She shall be my dearest comrade."[81]

In the following weeks Goebbels was to lose several of his Berlin comrades. Whether he was really affected or merely played the part, he always found unctuous words and approached their deaths primarily from the propaganda point of view. When Walter Fischer, who had just resigned from the SA, was killed in a confrontation with Communists, Goebbels staged a rally of the SA on Fehrbelliner Platz and claimed the man as a "blood sacrifice" whose death cried out for revenge. He then incited the "huge crowd" against the "Red murder squads." The rally concluded with speeches by Hermann Goering and Sturmführer Horst Wessel.[82]

Horst Wessel's brother Werner, likewise a member of the SA, was buried shortly before New Year's. He had frozen to death while out skiing. Five hundred SA men with torches marched past the Communists' Karl Liebknecht House to the cemetery. "It was gripping and shattering. I could hardly speak," the Gauleiter noted.[83] Two weeks later death would claim one of Goebbels's most faithful followers, Horst Wessel himself.

Since the battle of the Fischerkiez, Horst Wessel had been on the Communists' hit list; they merely needed a pretext to strike. One evening in January 1930 a widow by the name of Salm turned up in a pub on Dragonerstrasse where a Communist street cell held its meetings. The widow asked the members to help her with a Nazi who was giving her trouble about the rent. At first the Communists refused, knowing that the woman had arranged a religious funeral for her husband, an old Communist. But when they heard the name Wessel, they changed their minds.

The men broke up into small groups and then converged on the apartment building on Grosse Frankfurter Strasse where Wessel lived. Two of the Red Combatants went upstairs to his apartment, while the others kept a lookout on the street. Albert Höhler knocked on the door, his pistol drawn. When Wessel opened the door, Höhler pressed the trigger. Wessel collapsed before the eyes of his girlfriend, a former prostitute. The Communists took to their heels.

Late that night, while the doctors at St. Joseph's Hospital struggled to save Wessel's life, the incident was reported to the KPD district headquarters, where plans were immediately made for those implicated to flee. The widow Salm was summoned the next morning to the Karl Liebknecht House, where a functionary instructed her to represent the whole affair to the detectives as a confrontation between pimps.[84]

Three days later Goebbels spent "a heartrending hour" with Wessel's distraught mother. The pastor's widow told him her son's life story— how he had broken off his university studies to join the Nazis and fight for a "better world." She also described her son's missionary zeal: he had fallen in love with a prostitute and rescued her from the streets. "Like a Dostoyevski novel: the idiot, the worker, the tart, the bourgeois family, eternal torment of conscience, eternal agony"—so Goebbels summed up the life of this "idealistic dreamer."

A short time later Goebbels stood at Wessel's bedside. The Sturmführer had survived an operation undertaken to stop the internal bleeding, but the surgeon had not managed to remove the bullet lodged in front of the cerebellum. In his diary Goebbels wrote: "His whole face shot up, distorted. He stares at me rigidly, then his eyes fill with tears, and he mumbles, 'One has to keep going! I'm happy!' I'm close to tears."[85]

Even before Goebbels wrote these lines, he had exploited Wessel's suffering for propaganda purposes with a tear-jerking report in *Der Angriff* that climaxed in the frenzied demand that the murderers be crushed "to a pulp."[86] The Communists replied in *Die Rote Fahne*, claiming that Wessel was a pimp and that Höhler had no connection with the KPD.[87]

While the propaganda war raged, Wessel's condition seemed to stabilize. On 3 February the police arrested Höhler on a tip, and on the following days rounded up others who had been implicated. Since some of them confessed, it was now established that the attack on Wessel had been politically motivated. Goebbels had won. The editors of *Die Rote Fahne* had to disavow Höhler and the other comrades.

But then Wessel began to lose ground. Goebbels wrote in his diary, "May God preserve him," probably because the case was receiving nationwide attention, and a slow death would provoke more sympathy for Wessel and more hatred for a system that could not prevent such violence.[88] When the twenty-three-year-old, who had outdone himself in hundreds of planned brawls and street fights for the movement, died on 23 February, he was promptly transformed into a martyr for the Third Reich. Goebbels met with Goering and Dürr to plan the sequel. They decided that party members would wear mourning until 12 March. During this time they should avoid public amusements. Parents should instruct their children to pray that all German youth might be filled with Wessel's "spirit of sacrifice." Wessel's memory would be invoked at every party gathering until the period of mourning was over. Finally, Wessel's SA storm unit would be named the Horst Wessel Storm Unit 5.[89]

Goebbels planned to make the funeral the occasion of impressive mass demonstrations, with processions and speeches, but the police refused to issue a permit. When Wessel's sister failed to get an audience with Hindenburg to plead the Nazis' cause, the restrictions had to be accepted: only ten vehicles in the funeral cortege.

What helped make the funeral a propaganda success was less Goebbels's emotional obituary in *Der Angriff* than the actions of the KPD. The leadership had called for a counterdemonstration on the day of the funeral. In spite of the increased police presence along the route from Wessel's parents' house to the St. Nicholas cemetery, it was planned that violence would occur. In his supreme cynicism Goebbels calculated that the Communists would appear as impious barbarians, and that the police would demonstrate their inability to guarantee that a funeral could take place in peace.

Goebbels's only disappointment was that Hitler declined to attend the funeral and witness his triumph firsthand.[90] Goebbels blamed Rudolf Hess for keeping Hitler in Berchtesgaden while he, Goebbels, went to Wessel's mother's house in the early afternoon and spoke a few carefully chosen words. Then the Sturmführers of the Fourth Standard hoisted the coffin to their shoulders to bring it to the horse-drawn hearse, followed by mourning relatives, SA men, and party functionaries. "The funeral procession moves past the silently saluting masses, packed in along the sidewalks—probably twenty to thirty thousand people." At Bülowplatz, where the KPD headquarters were located, the Nazis' opponents struck up the "Internationale." At Koblanstrasse Communists broke through the police barriers. Stones flew, the hearse began to sway, shots rang out.

After further dramatic scenes the funeral procession finally reached the walls of the cemetery, on which someone had painted in white, "To Wessel the pimp, a last Heil Hitler!"[91]

Here thousands of people were raging, and equal numbers were inside the cemetery, waiting to pay their Sturmführer the last honors. To the strains of "I Once Had a Comrade," the coffin draped with a swastika flag was lowered into the grave. First the two parish pastors spoke, then representatives of the two student fraternities to which Wessel had belonged in Vienna, and finally the Gauleiter, who celebrated the "last roll call." "Horst Wessel!" called Goebbels. "Here!" shouted the dead man's SA comrades. Then Goebbels spoke of Wessel as a "Christlike socialist," one whose deeds proclaimed, "Come unto me, I will redeem you. . . . One man must be an example and offer himself as a sacrifice. So be it —I am ready." "Through sacrifice to redemption," "through struggle to victory." Just as years before he had stylized the death of his friend Flisges, Goebbels now wanted to turn Wessel into a symbol of the Nazi movement. He proclaimed there in the cemetery of St. Nicholas, "And when the SA assembles for the great roll call, when every man's name is called, the Führer will also call your name, Comrade Wessel! And all, all SA men will answer with one voice, 'Here!' . . . Wherever Germany is, there you are as well, Horst Wessel!"[92]

What helped most to make Horst Wessel a symbol of the movement was a hitherto little-sung song that Wessel had written in March 1929, and that the SA men now sang at his grave:

> Oh, raise the flag and close your ranks up tight!
> SA men march with bold, determined tread.
> Comrades felled by Reds and Ultras in fight
> March at our side, in spirit never dead.

During the funeral, which was followed by wild street battles, Goebbels declared that in ten years' time this song would be sung by children in school, by workers in factories, by soldiers on highways. He was wrong: it would take no more than three years for it to become the de facto German national anthem for the next twelve years.[93]

CHAPTER 7

Now we're strictly legit—
and that's it
(1930—1931)

In a symbolic demonstration of the NSDAP's new standing, on 1 May 1930 Goebbels moved the party headquarters to 10 Hedemannstrasse in Kreuzberg, very close to the Reich Chancellery. The Great Coalition, in disarray since Stresemann's death, had just broken up over the question of raising unemployment insurance contributions by 0.5 percent. With this failure by the democratic parties to achieve even a minimal consensus, the Müller cabinet lost credibility. The cabinet resigned on 27 March, marking the end of the last parliamentary government in the Weimar Republic.

Satisfied though Goebbels felt with the growing strength of the movement, he had reason to fear for his own position of power. At the beginning of the year the latent conflict between him and the Strasser brothers had broken out in force. The opening shot was his adversaries' announcement that their Kampf publishing house would begin issuing a daily newspaper on 1 March. To add insult to injury, the Munich central party leadership was planning to publish a Berlin edition of the *Völkischer Beobachter*. Goebbels, whose *Angriff* appeared only twice a week, saw in these two undertakings an attack on his influence within the north German party.

Goebbels therefore proposed to Hitler that Munich provide the funds for a daily edition of *Der Angriff*.[1] Although Hitler repeatedly assured Goebbels of his "solidarity and affection" and within his immediate circle expressed the "harshest opinions" of the Strassers' "parlor socialism," which he claimed endangered his own policy of remaining open to all sides, especially to major industry, he still refrained from public criticism. Goebbels complained in his diary that the Führer was at fault for not making a decision, not exercising his authority; if Hitler did not remain strong, he and his leadership would lose out to the Strassers. Goebbels let slip no opportunity to besmirch the Strassers in Hitler's eyes. He even decided to organize his own "espionage department." But nothing he did could prevent the Kampf publishing house's daily paper and the Berlin edition of the *Völkischer Beobachter* from coming out on 1 March, the day of Horst Wessel's funeral.[2]

Since it seemed incontrovertible that Hitler had "capitulated," Goebbels felt "ready for anything," though "never for a struggle against Hitler." He did, however, again consider resigning. Not even Hitler's renewed declaration that he intended to make Goebbels head of propaganda could sway him. Hitler had broken his word to him five times. "He conceals his own views, he doesn't make decisions, he's no longer leading but letting things drift."[3] Not until Hitler came to Berlin on 29 March in connection with the Müller cabinet's resignation and told Goebbels that "a curtain had been rung down" between him and Otto Strasser, did Goebbels view the situation more hopefully. Hitler also offered him a ministerial position in Saxony. Goebbels now believed he could persuade Hitler to take action.[4] Hitler, however, intended to do nothing that would reveal dissension in the party, for he was counting on the imminent failure of Brüning, whom Hindenburg had asked to form a cabinet. Hitler did not want to spoil the party's chances in the new elections that would be scheduled if the Reichstag were dissolved.

So the power struggle between Goebbels and the Strasser wing was fought out in their respective newspapers. Goebbels reviled Otto Strasser—using vocabulary dear to Hitler—as a "literary man," an "intellectual." He asserted that Strasser lacked the ability to understand the nature of revolution. "This wretched failure finds it easy to be radical, since his radicalism carries no responsibility to a group of followers. Revolution to him is not a transitional stage on the way to something new, but a thing in itself. He dreams it up at his desk, without considering what is really possible."[5]

When hopes that the Reichstag would soon be dissolved were dashed, Hitler summoned his leading functionaries from throughout the Reich to a meeting in Munich. There, on 26 April, he openly took a position against the Strassers and their followers. He charged that this wing had repeatedly criticized his rapprochement with the German nationalists and his wooing of leading industrialists, and had displayed an obstinate anti-capitalism, arguing for extensive nationalization and an alliance with the Soviet Union. Goebbels rejoiced: "Hitler is leading again. Thank God. Everyone enthusiastically behind him. Strasser and his circle smashed. He sits there like a guilty conscience."[6] Goebbels's gloating at what had really been rather mild criticism of the Strassers probably had more to do with what happened at the end of the meeting: Hitler rose to his feet again and announced Goebbels's appointment as head of propaganda for the Reich.

Goebbels now occupied the position that Gregor Stasser had turned over to Hitler in 1927. Remaining as deputy to the chairman of the Propaganda Committee, the official title of the propaganda chief, was Strasser's former secretary, Heinrich Himmler, who had a degree in agriculture. He had taken this degree in 1922 and spent a long time unemployed, going through a development much like that of his new superior. His character was marked by pedantic narrowness and an increasing fixation on radical anti-Semitism. "Not excessively clever, but hard-working and decent," was Goebbels's first impression of him.[7] It troubled Goebbels somewhat that Himmler still inclined toward Strasser, but Goebbels thought he would "drive that out of him." That proved unnecessary, however, for the man with the wire-rimmed glasses soon left the propaganda directorate to become commander of the SS.

Barely four weeks after his elevation to the top echelon of the party, Goebbels had the further satisfaction of witnessing an open clash between Hitler and Otto Strasser. On 21 May Hitler had proposed to the latter that Max Amann purchase the Kampf publishing house. Hitler was planning quietly to end Strasser's influence within the party. Otto Strasser refused, however, and, in the presence of his brother, who said not a word, began to criticize Hitler's political course. Hitler lost his temper and accused Strasser of being a Bolshevist, then broke off the conversation.[8]

Hitler now promised his propaganda director that he would proceed against Otto Strasser as soon as the elections for the Saxon Landtag were past. Again he did not wish to endanger the sure gains he anticipated for the NSDAP in the elections.[9] Goebbels had to resign himself to keeping the conflict on the back burner.

After the Nazis had almost tripled their share of the vote from the previous May, winning 14.4 percent, Goebbels thought he had reached his goal in the struggle against the Strassers. For Hitler hastily released a directive, supposed to be followed on 30 April by a letter of the same content intended for publication:

Years ago I dispatched you, dear Dr. Goebbels, to the most difficult post in the Reich, in hopes that your energy and vigor would succeed . . . in creating a tight, unified organization. You have fulfilled this task in such a way that you are assured of the movement's gratitude and my own highest recognition. Today I must ask you, in pursuit of this same task, to carry out the most ruthless purge of the party. . . . You have behind you the entire organization of the movement, the entire leadership staff, the entire SA and SS, all representatives of the party . . . and against you a half dozen professional malcontents and literary types![10]

But before Goebbels could remove his adversaries by instituting the necessary proceedings, they seized the initiative. At the Gauleiter conferences for Berlin and Brandenburg, Eugen Mossakowsky, editor of the *Nationalsozialistische Pressekonferenz*, accused Goebbels of lying when he presented himself as a member of the Ruhr resistance movement, thereby cheating "real heroes" like Leo Schlageter of the recognition they deserved. Mossakowsky further charged that Goebbels had falsified a document, backdating his entrance into the party so that he could appear as one of the early members. Mossakowsky demanded an inquiry by the party's Investigation and Mediation Committee. Goebbels was thus in danger of being publicly unmasked.[11]

But Hitler gave instructions that the inquiry should be dragged out and that proceedings should be begun to expel Mossakowsky for "activity harmful to the party." The Strasser man resigned without waiting for the proceedings, citing the Gauleiter as one of the reasons. Goebbels now began his purge. After removing five collaborators of Otto Strasser's, he called a general membership meeting of the Berlin Gau at the Sportpalast on 30 June. It was attended by Maj. Walter Buch, chairman of the Investigation and Mediation Committee, Goering, von Epp, and other leading party members, though not Hitler, who once again left the dirty work to others.[12]

Strasser and some of his followers hoped to use this occasion to present their own viewpoint. But at the entrance to the Sportpalast the SA enforcers blocked their way, on the grounds that they belonged to the Brandenburg Gau, not Greater Berlin. Soon afterward Goebbels let loose a tirade against this "literary clique," threatening to "smash them with the iron hammer of our discipline." As he read a message from Hitler against the "literary crowd," the five thousand spectators in the Sportpalast began to rant and rave. Fanatical cries of "String them up" kept bursting from the crowd. Three people who worked for Strasser's daily paper had the courage to stand up and leave the hall amid catcalls when Goebbels challenged them to do so. The meeting ended with a loyalty oath to the Führer, and by extension to his Gauleiter. The meeting also put an end to the career of Otto Strasser and his followers in the NSDAP. A few days later, after giving Hitler a futile ultimatum to revoke the expulsion of his collaborators within twenty-four hours, Strasser and the other "brown socialists," whose ideology Goebbels still fundamentally shared, left the party.

It was Hitler's tactical skill, not Goebbels's, that prevented these events from doing more than minimal damage to the party. Goebbels was annoyed that only Otto Strasser had been driven from the field of action, not Gregor, who had resigned his position as managing editor of the Kampf publishing house and sworn loyalty to Hitler. Goebbels failed to recognize that having the better-liked Gregor Strasser stay in the party forestalled any residual sympathy within the NSDAP for the mutineer. As it happened, the "literary types" under Otto Stasser did form a new organization called the Black Front, but it never amounted to more than a debating club.

The waves seemed to have been smoothed by the time the Reich president, after consultation with Brüning, dissolved the Reichstag on 18 July and set 14 September as the day for new elections. With the bad economic situation and his party's relatively good showing in the Berlin city council elections the previous year, Goebbels was counting on considerable gains for the NSDAP throughout the Reich. In *Der Angriff* he boasted that the movement was entering the final stages of its rise to power: "It has long since left behind the stage of mere political agitation and is beginning to pursue politics in the grand manner, that is, politics of state."[13]

Under the slogan "Freedom and Bread," the director of propaganda now mounted an election campaign such as the party had never experienced. His schedule called for gradually speeding up the campaign, bringing it to a frenetic pace by mid-August and then "rushing toward 14 September at breakneck speed."[14] He not only organized and coordinated the campaign, which required several trips to Munich, but also designed pamphlets and campaign posters, wrote articles for *Der Angriff*, and traveled throughout the country as a speaker. He meanwhile successfully fought five libel suits, including one brought on behalf of Hindenburg, which Goebbels converted into effective propaganda.[15]

These successes played a considerable part in engendering the optimism with which Goebbels looked forward to the election. Things changed abruptly when he was awakened on the night of 30 August by a telephone call from Berlin to Breslau, where he had just given a speech. Members of the Charlottenburg Storm Unit 31, under orders from Walter Stennes, who had advanced to commander of the East Gau SA, had occupied the NSDAP headquarters on Hedemannstrasse and smashed everything to smithereens. The Berlin SA leaders around Stennes were dissatisfied with Hitler's political course, and anticipated that after the elections the party would push more vigorously to be included in the government, as it had done in Saxony. The SA feared that in such a case its influence in the party would be curtailed even more than it had already been, when the Prussian interior minister issued a ban on wearing the SA uniform. The SA's requests for lower membership dues and for larger subsidies from the party had been turned down; the leaders had then demanded that Reichstag seats in the Nazi delegation be reserved for them. To calm their indignation, Goebbels had promised Stennes some seats, but had then passed over the SA when nominating candidates. When the deception came to light, Stennes promptly revoked his allegiance and decided to take advantage of Goebbels's absence by swinging into action.

When Goebbels received the call, he at first lost his nerve "for a second," for it looked as though now, only two weeks before the election, he would be robbed of the fruits of his efforts.[16] The decision to return to Berlin was quickly made. Before he got into the Gau automobile, which his driver Tonak guided through the Silesian night at a truly "hellish speed," he telephoned Hitler, who was asleep in Bayreuth. After daybreak Hitler immediately flew to Berlin. At the Duke of Coburg, a small hotel next to Anhalt Station, Hitler and Goebbels met with Stennes. The Führer's confidant Ernst Hanfstaengl recalled later that, in an aside during the endless debate, Stennes remarked that the instigator of the entire revolt was none other than Goebbels.[17] Indeed, Goebbels had done much to provoke the SA.

After the first session ended without any resolution, Goebbels, according to his own account, urged Hitler to give in. To what extent Goebbels actually took such a position, we do not know. But after Hitler and Goebbels had discussed the situation all night, the Führer modified his intransigent stance. He had Stennes summoned and promised him that the SA could keep more of the dues it collected. When Stennes agreed to these terms, Hitler is supposed to have confirmed with a handshake that he would not abandon him in the future.[18] This truce was celebrated by the Berlin SA at a gathering in the Kriegervereinshaus. Agents from the police political surveillance unit noted in their report that Hitler in his speech repeatedly asked the SA to trust him, and finally, "his overstrained voice rising to an almost hysterical scream," appealed to the loyalty of those present: "We will vow in this hour that nothing can divide us, as truly as God can help us against all devils! May almighty God bless our struggle." The shouts of "Heil" were hushed, "because Hitler was listening, with folded hands, as if in prayer, to the echo of his own words."[19]

Goebbels rejoiced, and with reason, for the rebellion had been put down so quickly that few details had reached the outside world. The newspapers speculated that followers of Otto Strasser had instigated the revolt, but the scattered reports remained vague and attracted little attention.[20]

In this last phase of the campaign Goebbels worked unceasingly, sometimes to the point of utter exhaustion. In four days he went from Nuremberg to Munich to Königsberg and back to Berlin, where he crisscrossed the city, speaking to all kinds of groups in the most varied settings. During the last week of the campaign he "preached" up to seven times a day, driven by a fanatical belief in success.

The high point of Goebbels's first campaign as director of propaganda was the rally at the Sportpalast on the evening of 10 September. One hundred thousand requests for tickets had supposedly been received. When Hitler stepped onto the platform, the applause and shouts that broke out sounded like a "hurricane."[21] In his hour-long speech Hitler repeated what he had said in his "Manifesto to the German People" that appeared the same day in the *Völkischer Beobachter*: "The slogan for 14 September must be: Strike at those who have bankrupted our old parties! Destroy those who would undermine our national unity! Away with those responsible for our degeneration! Fellow Germans, join forces with the brown front marching at the head of an awakening Germany!"[22] Goebbels was "swept away" by Hitler's speech: "Who would care to speak of all the petty little woes now? We already have victory in our pocket!"[23]

The results exceeded all expectations. The NSDAP won 107 Reichstag seats, almost nine times the previous number. In Berlin 395,000 people voted for the Nazis, where two years earlier it had been 39,000. After the KPD with 27.3 percent and the SPD with 27.2 percent, the NSDAP with 14.7 percent had become the third strongest party in Berlin—a percentage far below what it had achieved on average in the Reich. It became clear that in the economic crisis many members of the middle class had turned to the Nazis, a trend that would continue until 1932. Indeed, the middle of the political spectrum had almost disappeared.[24] Only the SPD, which experienced slight losses, and the Catholic Center Party could hold their own. The other beneficiary of the elections was the NSDAP's bitterest adversary, the KPD, which raised the number of its seats in the Reichstag from fifty-four to seventy-seven.

For a moment it looked to Goebbels as though he would be rewarded for all his efforts. During a discussion in which Goering also took part, Hitler had dangled "power in Prussia" before his Gauleiter.[25] Goebbels's first thought was that he would "do away with" the hated Jews, capitalists, and Bolshevists, in fact with the whole "system." That would be his personal revenge for what the world had done to him. But the prerequisite, Hitler explained, would be that Hindenburg bring the NSDAP, the DNVP, and the Center into a government formed according to the conditions stipulated by the Nazis. He, Hitler, would then take the interior and defense ministries and one more portfolio for his party and furthermore demand that the "Prussian coalition" consisting of the SPD, DDP, and Center be disbanded. Hitler could afford to raise such demands, tantamount to seizing power, because he always had the option of continuing the struggle against the "system" as before, working his way to power in that fashion. Although the latter course coincided more with Goebbels's notion of the NSDAP as a revolutionary party, he found

Hitler's idea of achieving power under the cloak of legitimacy not unappealing—it also opened up attractive prospects for him personally.

Since Goebbels took Hitler's course for a short-term tactical measure, he accepted Hitler's dictum that every opportunity had to be seized to dispel doubts about the legitimacy of the NSDAP; the impression had to be created that the Nazis were fit to participate in the government and a coalition. Such an opportunity presented itself in a case being tried just then before the Leipzig supreme court: three officers of the Ulm garrison were charged with disobeying a decree by the Reich minister of defense that forbade establishing contact with the NSDAP. Hitler's attorney, Hans Frank, managed to get his client called as a witness. In court Hitler declared pithily and self-confidently that he and his party stood "hard as granite" on the foundation of legality.

It must have been irritating to Hitler that the court confronted him with the revolutionary words of the Gauleiter of Berlin. A judge asked him about a pamphlet entitled "Der Nazi-Sozi," in which Goebbels declared that in the struggle for power "heads would roll."[26] Hitler was also asked to explain what Goebbels meant in an "Instructional Letter for Leadership Training Sessions" when he wrote, "Revolutionaries of the word then become revolutionaries of the deed—for this purpose any means are acceptable to us; we do not shirk any revolution."[27] Hitler cleverly got himself out of the potential difficulty by insisting that the path to power chosen by the NSDAP was strictly legal; if this path was followed, the overthrow would come about on its own. "And when we have power, certainly heads will roll!"[28] Goebbels, probably feeling contrite at having put his Führer in such an awkward position, hastened to assure Hitler that he, Hitler, had spoken "cleverly and cautiously." That he still took Hitler's commitment to legality for a ploy he revealed to one of the young officers on trial.[29] "For what can those fellows do to us now? They were just waiting to strike. Now we're strictly legit—and that's it."[30]

Hitler, who like Goebbels saw the parliamentary system as "an institution in which we see one of the gravest symptoms of mankind's decay," managed to sway the judges.[31] The Leipzig trial did much to revise the image of the Führer and his party in the Reichswehr, which was becoming increasingly important as social order collapsed, and in broad segments of the bourgeoisie. Hitler was beginning to be socially acceptable, for it appeared he was shedding his revolutionary past.

Yet the NSDAP was not to participate in the government this time. Chancellor Brüning attempted to win the NSDAP over to the idea of joining a "constructive opposition," but in vain, even though he promised, in a meeting with Hitler, Gregor Strasser, and Frick, to intervene wherever the numbers justified it to make sure that the NSDAP and the

Center formed the government in the individual states.[32] Brüning did not yet face a "negative minority," thanks to a shift in the mood of the SPD. With the growing threat to the republic, the Social Democrats had decided to downplay their conflict with the Brüning regime, and from the fall of 1930 onward adopted a policy of tolerating Brüning, now ruling with emergency powers. Further support for his government came from the Prussian state government, a coalition of the SPD, Center, and DDP under Prime Minister Otto Braun.

So Goebbels was not wrong when he commented in *Der Angriff*, "The key to power over Germany lies in Prussia. Whoever has Prussia has the Reich."[33] And the road to Prussia led through Berlin. While Hitler and Goering were wooing the conservative elite and the captains of industry, Goebbels continued his unrestrained agitation in the capital, adopting any means that would destabilize society and strengthen the movement.

Goebbels's most powerful ally turned out to be the economic misery that was becoming increasingly acute in Germany. In the Reich more than three million people were unemployed, and in Berlin alone in the fall of 1930 every tenth person out of a 2.5 million working-age population was out of work. Barely two-thirds of the unemployed received small amounts from unemployment insurance or emergency funds; the others had to live on the meager alms provided by the city's welfare agency, or languished without any help at all.

Goebbels wanted to mobilize these victims of the economic crisis to overthrow the Prussian government, but he was competing with the powerful Communists. During a metalworkers' strike in Berlin, he activated the cells in the factories and outdid the Communists in the radicalism of his charges. In *Der Angriff* he attacked the Jewish "stock exchange hyenas" who were enriching themselves at the expense of German workers.[34] The *Vossische Zeitung* felt impelled to inquire how this rabid tone fit in with the interviews Hitler had just given the Rothermere and Hearst press to prove to those very "stock exchange hyenas" that national socialism was the only bulwark against social rebellion and the Bolshevization of Germany.[35]

Goebbels's struggle to win over the workers also included "argumentative" confrontations with communism. In mid-October he had approached the Communist leadership and offered safe passage and a specific amount of speaking time to Politburo member Heinz Neumann, Stalin's chief theoretician and editor in chief of *Die Rote Fahne*, if he would come to the Friedrichshain Hall. Neumann agreed and appeared on 28 October with a large entourage. But Goebbels noted with disappointment that the feared "Red czar of Germany" seemed very nervous from the beginning and talked "pure horseshit." He spoke only briefly, "because he has nothing more to say, and then I mop him up mercilessly.

. . . So that's the great Neumann. He sits there, small and ugly, and at the end his own people abandon him. Jubilation without end."[36] What Goebbels did not know was that the man was a Neumann look-alike, one Willi Mielenz, who had had to dye his hair, learn a speech by heart, and stand in for his comrade, who was not willing to face the anticipated mass brawl.

Although that evening ended without violence, brutal clashes between members of the banned Red Front Combatants' League and the SA had become the rule, alarming the Berliners and exacerbating the crisis. The Gauleiter kept pushing his men deeper into working-class areas, where the SA men gave free rein to their hatred for their Communist adversaries, a hatred they also felt for the bourgeoisie.[37]

Meanwhile the Prussian state's attorney and the police were waging a bitter struggle against the enemies of the republic on the right and the left. Deputy Police Commissioner Weiss and two colleagues had prepared a report for the Prussian minister of the interior on the NSDAP and its leaders' attitude toward the constitution. They concluded that the party was a subversive organization and that Hitler, Goebbels, and others could and should be prosecuted on suspicion of grave violations of the penal code and of belonging to and promoting a subversive organization. On 28 August their memorandum was conveyed to the attorney general for the Reich, Karl August Werner, but no charges were brought.[38]

The collaboration between Weiss and the Prussian state's attorney general's office functioned better. The latter used the immunity-free periods between Reichstag sessions to pursue the charges pending against Goebbels. But getting Goebbels to appear in court proved difficult. In one case, when his lawyer's request for a postponement on grounds of Goebbels's ill health was rejected, Goebbels himself wrote to the court, enclosing a doctor's statement. When the court again rejected the appeal, Goebbels simply failed to appear at the appointed time. The judge then issued a subpoena for the day the Reichstag session was to begin. Goebbels sneaked into Berlin huddled on the floor of a limousine with curtained windows, and managed to slip into the Reichstag with the crowd, avoiding detectives waiting at the entry. His delegation, wearing their brown shirts, greeted him with noisy shouts of "Long live the savior of Berlin!" Goebbels exclaimed to his political enemies, "You see, I'm sabotaging your bourgeois judicial system!"[39]

To Goebbels it counted as a more significant success in the struggle against the Prussian government that, starting in the fall of 1930, *Der Angriff* could appear daily. Hitler had pushed him to incorporate the paper, with the Nazi Eher publishing house holding 60 percent and the Gau 40 percent of the shares. At first Goebbels feared a trick, but when he was given sole control over the paper's content, he let himself be persuaded that the party merely wanted to safeguard its influence in case Goebbels should no longer be around.

Goebbels wanted the new *Angriff* to be even more radical than its predecessor. He therefore launched a fresh, ambitious campaign against Deputy Police Commissioner Weiss. Attacking Weiss for alleged misdeeds by his brother, Goebbels hoped to "destroy" his hated adversary,[40] but it turned out rather differently. Police Commissioner Grzesinski countered the attack on his deputy by imposing a one-week suspension on the Gauleiter's paper, starting on 10 November. He based his action on a brief report expressing approval of a Communist who had slapped Grzesinski's predecessor, Zörgiebel; under Paragraph 5, Article 4, of the Law for the Protection of the Republic, such support for subversive political violence was punishable.[41]

Grzesinski's decisive action cost the paper about fifteen thousand marks, a loss that was difficult for the Gau to absorb, since it was chronically short of funds. Goebbels soon took revenge by sabotaging the showing of the German version of the American film *All Quiet on the Western Front*, based on the antiwar novel by Erich Maria Remarque. The Gauleiter had in mind to undermine the prestige of Interior Minister Carl Severing, whose ministry had just cleared the film for distribution.

The campaign began in the Mozartsaal, a large cinema on the west side of Berlin. For this operation Goebbels lined up 150 party members and SA men, and himself. On 4 December 1930, the evening following the film's premiere, just before the film began, this group transformed the cinema into a madhouse. Whistles and shouts of "Jews get out!" were heard. SA men slapped members of the audience whom they took for Jewish, tossed stink bombs from the balcony, and released white mice in the orchestra. In the general confusion, NSDAP Reichstag deputy Ludwig Münchmeyer, a Protestant minister, stood up to make a speech protesting the film. Goebbels interrupted him, shouting that Hitler was at the gates of Berlin. When the police cleared the cinema, quite a few of them refrained from using their nightsticks vigorously, because they themselves felt hostile toward the antiwar film.

Goebbels believed the entire nation was on his side, and the response in some parts of the press seemed to confirm his opinion. The next day he launched street demonstrations. They were held on the evenings of 8–10 December, and he claimed forty thousand people participated, though in fact it was only about six thousand.[42] Especially on 8 December real street battles took place between the demonstrators and the police, who kept trying to break up the demonstrations. To the strains of the "Horst Wessel Song" the crowd finally formed a "huge protest march," which Hitler and a few other functionaries "reviewed" with their arms raised in the Nazi salute. "Over an hour. Six abreast. Fantastic! Berlin West has never seen anything like it."[43]

The *Vossische Zeitung* described these demonstrations as a new variation on Nazi terror tactics. The paper noted that up until now only the leftist radicals had planned demonstrations for public places clearly chosen for purposes of provocation and terrorism, not orderly gatherings. The paper strongly supported the police commissioner's declaration that he would do everything in his power to safeguard the showing of the film and protect the audience "from all provocations and violent acts by rowdy elements."[44]

After the riots had kept the city on edge for days, Grzesinski consulted with the Prussian interior ministry and then moved to ban all outdoor demonstrations, rallies, and processions. The government's decisiveness was undermined, however, when on the following day the Film Board announced that it was rescinding its approval of *All Quiet on the Western Front* as a "threat to Germany's honor." Goebbels spoke of a victory "that could not have been any grander," for the Nazis' actions in the streets seemed to have dictated the government's moves.[45] Even though the protests had merely exploited the frustration and resentment of conservatives from many quarters, the Gauleiter took full credit for the outcome.

With the beginning of 1931 unemployment increased and violence in the streets escalated, for Berlin's glittering façade and the ostentatious luxury enjoyed by the rich contrasted harshly with the spreading destitution. Before the sun had risen on the first day of 1931, before Goebbels left the New Year's celebration at the salon of his patron Viktoria von Dirksen, who was always ready to come to his aid with donations and contacts, the first victims had fallen. In the northeastern part of the city an SA man had shot a member of the Reichsbanner in a fight, and an innocent bystander had also been shot. Both died afterward in the hospital. Goebbels commented cynically, "That creates respect."[46]

On the evening of 22 January 1931 Goebbels found himself in the middle of a massive brawl. He had scheduled a debate in the Friedrichshain Hall with Walter Ulbricht, a KPD Reichstag deputy and chairman of the Berlin-Brandenburg district directorate. After the Communist finished his speech, the Red Front Combatants who had accompanied him struck up the "Internationale" to prevent Goebbels from speaking. The Nazis countered with the "Horst Wessel Song." Then the first chairs began to fly, and a pitched battle ensued. By the time the police arrived and arrested thirty-four rioters, more than one hundred people had been injured, many of them seriously. Concussion was the most common injury.[47]

The next few days brought a stabbing and a shooting that left two Communists dead and two critically injured.[48] The Communists organized mass rallies, and in the Reichstag Walter Ulbricht accused Goebbels of working with industry and the bourgeoisie to destroy the unemployed. He charged that the Prussian police were cooperating with the Nazis and declared that the workers would have to arm themselves in self-defense. Goebbels in turn accused the Social Democratic police commissioner of being a Marxist.[49]

With the support of the Prussian government, Grzesinski banned *Der Angriff* again, this time for two weeks. He also sent a police detachment to occupy NSDAP headquarters to secure material evidence for the pending trials. The residences of leading SA men were searched.[50] The police commissioner ordered increased patrols for areas of the city that had become flashpoints for Communist-Nazi confrontations. He threatened to revoke the licenses of pubs and other meeting places where Nazis or Communists met and violence occurred.[51]

Although the police had an excellent record of solving political crimes, Grzesinski and his deputy could not succeed, in spite of their decisive intervention, in stemming the tide of terror. The means at their disposal proved simply inadequate in the face of the political constellation blocking their way. Brüning felt he had to work toward integrating the Nazis into the government, at least in the long run. That left the Prussian government isolated in its struggle against the brown terror. Meanwhile bitterness over the increasingly desperate economic situation drove more and more people into the arms of the red and brown seducers. Both parties proved adept at channeling people's fears, needs, and hopes into hatred and fanaticism. On 30 January 1931, for example, Goebbels, speaking at the Sportpalast, lashed out at existing conditions and then proclaimed that an eruption was coming, "deliverance from evil" in the form of the Third Reich. He remarked that the mood in the packed arena anticipated the day when the people would rise up and the storm would break out. (Twelve years later he would speak in the same place and use the very same formulation. The storm it unleashed almost swept the entire people away.)

In accord with the revolutionary dynamics escalating in the streets, Goebbels led a walkout of the 107 Nazi deputies in the Reichstag. His delegation had just failed to prevent a change in the rules that placed a limit on possible abuses of parliamentary immunity.[52] The pretext for the walkout was the failure of a no-confidence vote against Brüning's government, spearheaded by the Nazis and supported by the DNVP and the KPD. But Goebbels actually intended to demonstrate that his party dissociated itself from the hapless "Young Parliament" and still understood itself as a revolutionary movement.

This tumultuous beginning to the year gave the party faithful and probably the Gauleiter as well a feeling that they were approaching the final phase of a revolutionary struggle. As a result, the relationship between the SA and the Berlin political leadership improved markedly. The second half of the previous year had brought heightened tensions, a response to Hitler's commitment to legality and the ostentation of the "Munich tycoons," who had just bought the Barlow Palace to serve as the party headquarters. Goebbels, who had always fancied himself on the side of the "proletarian footsoldiers," had intended several times to call Hitler's attention to the growing dissatisfaction in the SA. But each time he spoke with Hitler, the Führer would flatter him, and all his resolutions would evaporate. This happened again in November 1930; Hitler showed him the "fabulous room" in the Barlow Palace that would be Goebbels's whenever he came to Munich, and promised to transform it into a "little jewel."[53]

Back in Berlin Goebbels had chimed in with the chorus of discontented "SA kings" denouncing the "scandalous pigsty in Munich," a denunciation in which he himself did not include Hitler, only the "philistines" around him.[54] He had followed with great interest the SA conference scheduled for the end of November in Munich. Hitler apparently succeeded in eliminating the dissension and presenting his legality concept to SA leaders from the entire country in such a way that it did not clash with their romantic notions of a revolutionary party army.[55]

By February 1931 Goebbels had even improved his relations with Walter Stennes. The SA commander had been his guest several times in his new apartment in Steglitz, and Goebbels decided he had misjudged the man in the past. When the SA man publicly praised Goebbels, the Gauleiter went so far as to declare that the Nazis could win their struggle for power only on the solid foundation of a tightly organized SA filled with revolutionary élan, and never on the spongy layer of general party supporters.

Goebbels and Stennes blamed the "Munich tycoons" for diverting the movement from socialism. The difference between them was that Stennes included Hitler among the tycoons, while Goebbels maintained his political life-lie by seeing Hitler as the victim of Esser, Feder, Rosenberg, and the others who hated him, Goebbels, for being a socialist. On 21 February 1931 he and Stennes formed an alliance that he summarized as follows: "SA plus me. That equals power."[56]

Four days later the newly named supreme commander of the SA, Capt. ret. Ernst Röhm, announced that the storm units were not to participate in street battles and that SA leaders were not to make public speeches. Stennes was angry to see his power thus restricted, and Goebbels decided once again to try to mediate between the SA and Munich. When he arrived in Munich the next day, planning to speak with Hitler alone about the SA and his notion that, instead of returning to the Reichstag, the NSDAP should invoke a rump parliament in Weimar, his resolve soon crumbled.[57] The fascination that emanated from the Führer brought him to the "realization" that Hitler alone saw everything correctly—with the reservation that he was "too soft and ready to compromise."[58]

The conflict between being allied with Stennes and the SA on the one hand and wanting to follow Hitler unconditionally on the other drove Goebbels from one self-deception to another. A sort of climax was reached in March; after elaborate celebrations of the first anniversary of SA man Horst Wessel's death, he decided to further secure the SA's loyalty by staging a bomb attack from which an SA man would save him. The inspiration apparently derived from Hitler's expressions of concern that he might fall victim to assassination.

Goebbels had a package mailed to him, probably by his private secretary, Count Karl-Hubertus Schimmelmann, which arrived on 13 March at party headquarters. It contained a few firecrackers, some loose black powder wrapped in paper, and an ignition mechanism made of matches and a striking surface. Two days earlier the SA man and *Angriff* staffer Eduard Weiss had been directed by Goebbels himself to open all mail addressed to the Gauleiter, explaining that he feared an assassination attempt.[59]

That same day the Gau administrator, Hans Meinshausen, announced during a meeting that "today at one o'clock a ruthless assassination attempt was made against our Goebbels."[60] Before the police were informed, the title page of *Der Angriff* was already printed, featuring the "Assassination Attempt against Dr. Goebbels" in screaming headlines. Page 3 carried a description of the attack, which underlined the bravery of "Ede" Weiss, who had defused the time bomb.[61]

In his diary Goebbels noted: "Yesterday morning an assassination attempt was made against me with a bomb. A package with explosives arrived in the mail at headquarters. . . . Had it exploded, my eyes and face would have been done for."[62] It is worth noting that since January he had been inserting remarks on an expected assassination attempt into his diary entries.

If the staging of the assassination attempt pointed to Goebbels's concern about growing unrest in the SA, he must have been even more concerned when Richard Scheringer, one of the Ulm garrison officers accused in Leipzig of high treason for contact with the NSDAP, went over to the Communists. Scheringer justified his action by charging that the practical policies followed by the Nazi leaders contradicted their radical rhetoric; Hitler and Rosenberg were crawling with the German bourgeoisie toward the "capitalist robber nations," while only Lenin had shown the way to the national and social liberation of the German people.[63]

The KPD of course drew the maximum propaganda benefit from the Scheringer defection. To add to Goebbels's headaches, the "Munich tycoons" issued a draft of an economic plan that seemed to confirm Scheringer's charges. Goebbels could find "not a trace of socialism" in it. Fearing that the party would break apart, he made up his mind to "lay it on the line" to Hitler, who he thought had no inkling of the mood of the masses.[64] At the Munich headquarters he first had a meeting with Röhm, who told him about his problems with Stennes. Stennes was showing less and less restraint in his criticism of the course Hitler had chosen.[65] Goebbels persuaded Röhm, with Hitler's help, not to dismiss Stennes. After that there was not a trace of "laying it on the line." Hitler had been "fabulous" to him. "He alone down there is clever and clear-headed." The conclusion Goebbels drew from his visit to Munich was that in case of any conflict he wanted to be on Hitler's side. He also wanted to bring Stennes back into the fold. He succeeded, probably because he himself had such ambivalent thoughts and feelings that he could persuade the SA commander that he was still his ally.[66]

On 28 March Hindenburg responded to the continuing acts of rightist and leftist terror by issuing an emergency decree that required all political gatherings to be registered, and political pamphlets and posters to be censored. Tensions between the Munich and Berlin branches of the NSDAP increased because the leeway for the operations of the SA, which always had one foot over the line toward illegality, had been narrowed. Indeed, those operations had become almost incompatible with the "obedience to the law" demanded by Hitler. Goebbels gave his anger free rein: "Long live legality! Sickening! Now we must come up with new methods. That will be very difficult."[67]

As a result of the emergency decree, a total ban on the SA was in the air.[68] Stennes now pursued his confrontational course so purposefully that the latent conflict with Munich seemed bound to break into the open. From the Munich vantage point, it looked as though Goebbels and Stennes were working hand in glove, for in his speeches the Gauleiter was reproaching the central leadership with "capital errors" in its treatment of the SA.[69] He accused the leadership of dealing "too much with the enemy," meaning those loyal to the state and the law. He feared that "the revolutionary spirit of the movement" was being sacrificed.[70]

Goebbels considered Goering primarily responsible for this development, when in reality it was Hitler who was setting the course of which his Gauleiter so strongly disapproved. Hitler had made a great point of committing himself to legality, and now he had to fear that increased clashes between the SA and the forces of law and order would undermine his credibility. To make this clear to Goebbels, Hitler summoned him by telephone to the leaders' conference in Weimar on 1 April. He was sure that by giving the Gauleiter increased powers he could make him compliant. The statement Hitler issued referred to "internal enemies" who sought to incite the movement to engage in "illegal activities," thereby giving the "enemies of the German struggle for freedom" a pretext for suppressing the party.[71] Hitler authorized Goebbels to purge the Berlin party of all such elements: "Whatever you choose to do, I'll back you."

By this time Hitler had already initiated the decisive measure himself. He dispatched an order to Röhm to get rid of Stennes. Word of this action leaked out and reached Berlin on 31 March, before the order itself arrived. Goebbels had already left to deliver two speeches in Dresden, and did not learn what had happened until he reached Weimar. Stennes and parts of the SA had mutinied. Goebbels's illusion of mediating between him and Hitler collapsed, and he concluded that he could do nothing now but bow in the face of the facts and commit himself "openly and unreservedly" to Hitler.[72] That same day Hitler received a telegram from Stennes, asking whether his dismissal by Röhm was valid. When Hitler wired back that he was not to ask questions, only to carry out orders, the break was final, and things escalated further. Large groups of SA men chased the functionaries out of the party headquarters on Hedemannstrasse and occupied the editorial offices of *Der Angriff* to publish a call for support that was tantamount to a declaration of war on Munich. Stennes announced that he had "ordered the takeover of leadership of the movement in the provinces of Mecklenburg, Pomerania, Brandenburg-Ostmark, Silesia, and the capital by the SA."[73] The rebels justified their action by asserting that the political leaders of the NSDAP had tainted the "revolutionary élan of the SA" with bourgeois-liberalistic tendencies. That had "severed the vital nerve of a movement that could have been expected to eliminate the social misery of the German people." The statement invoked Horst Wessel and the "thousands of comrades" whose sacrifices should not have been in vain.[74]

As the crisis deepened, it was not only the democratic forces in the republic that hoped this meant the NSDAP had passed its peak. Meanwhile Goebbels did what Hitler often did in such situations: he let things run their course and kept out of the way. Leaving no doubt as to his loyalty, he followed Hitler to Munich. There they jointly organized the necessary countermeasures. These included publishing an editorial in the *Völkischer Beobachter* directed against the mutineers. Hitler denounced the slanderous rumors that reported Goebbels had made common cause with the conspirators and expressed the fullest confidence in his Gauleiter.[75]

At the same time the Führer reprimanded his political commissar for the Upper Eastern Region, Hermann Goering, who was trying to capitalize on the Stennes putsch and Goebbels's absence, angling for the very authorization for a purge that Goebbels had received in Weimar. Hitler's expressions of confidence carried tremendous importance for Goebbels just now.[76] Goering had seemed to be a friend; he had invited Goebbels to his "marvelous house" at Easter the previous year, and had even taken him along to Sweden to visit his wife's family. Now he was becoming his greatest adversary in Berlin. The more Hitler aspired to cultivate contacts with economically powerful and nationalist elements, the more useful Goering could be to him.

When Goebbels finally returned to Berlin on 7 April, resolved to repay Hitler for his loyalty and throw out the traitors, the crisis had already passed its peak.[77] No wildfire had sprung up, as evidenced by the expressions of support that streamed into the Munich headquarters from all the Gaus. In Berlin itself, Hitler's call to party members to close ranks behind Goebbels in unconditional loyalty proved effective. Mutinous SA men returned to the party. Financial concessions that Hitler had made to the SA may have helped.

By 11 April 1931 Goebbels could report in a speech to more than two thousand functionaries that the party apparatus remained "unshaken." He also went out of his way to embrace Hitler's policy of legality.[78] About a week later Stennes's successor, Paul Schulz, presented to Goebbels at the Sportpalast a "purged" and newly constituted SA, loyal to Hitler. Before the four thousand SA men who had reported for their "general roll call," Goebbels did his best to play down any conflict between the political leadership and the SA. Combining revolutionary rhetoric with stress on legality, he succeeded in stirring his audience: "I speak. Many weep. It's a great moment. . . . Parade with rousing music. The Berlin SA stands fast. The flags glow, the troop insignia stand tall. I am immeasurably happy. Now no fiend will ever take these boys from me."[79]

But no matter how impressive such demonstrations were, no matter how rigorously Goebbels and Schulz conducted their purge in the SA and especially in the staff of *Der Angriff*, Stennes did not roll over and play dead. He missed no opportunity to point up in the press the ideological conflicts between Hitler and Goebbels, even charging that Goebbels had secretly cooperated with the rebels. Stennes had also founded a newspaper, *Arbeiter, Bauern, Soldaten* (Workers, Peasants, Soldiers). Goebbels dismissed the paper as "confused, stupid stuff."[80] But the paper did cause one sensation when it printed a retraction by former SA man Eduard Weiss of his testimony in connection with the "assassination attempt" on Goebbels. Weiss swore in an affidavit that Goebbels had instructed him to perjure himself.[81]

Goebbels's supporters dismissed Weiss's retraction as revenge, while the *Vossische Zeitung* commented that the " 'hero' of the assassination, the political magician Goebbels, master of blindworms and white mice," now stood before the public stripped of his magic.[82] *Die Rote Fahne* promptly served up further details. Goebbels of course publicly denied all the charges. Harder to explain is the entry in his diary: he speaks of a "Stenniad of lies and distortions" unleashed against him. Did he really believe he had been the victim of an assassination attempt, or were the "private" diaries actually meant for public consumption?[83]

The Stennes crisis taxed almost to the limit Goebbels's ability to see the situation in a rosy light. The three hundred rebellious SA members were all potential traitors, and Goebbels had to admit that among them were "many decent people." Instead of recognizing that his mistake lay in never having worked things out between Stennes and Hitler, Goebbels chided himself for being "too trusting," believing in people "too readily." True to his earlier pattern, he simply concluded that those around him were bad, a "pile of frozen shit."[84]

In these circumstances Goebbels felt a heightened need for someone to cling to. After numerous superficial affairs—with a Tamara, a Xenia, an Erika, a Jutta—he thought he had found such a person in a young woman whom he had hired in November 1930 to organize his new private archives. But even with this "beautiful woman named Quandt" he proved unable to reveal his innermost feelings.[85] He had written recently in his diary that since the separation from Anka Stalherm, love had been unable to get past the "outer husk of my heart"; the core remained untouched.[86]

Yet Magda Quandt fascinated him. Elegant in appearance and calmly assertive in bearing, she embodied a world that had hitherto remained closed to him. This sort of woman seldom appeared among the Nazis or in Goebbels's inner circle. Johanna Maria Magdalena Friedländer (her stepfather was a Jew) had grown up in very comfortable circumstances and had graduated from a convent school. A short time later she had met the manufacturer Günther Quandt, who married the nineteen-year-old girl in January 1921.[87]

The life she led with Quandt must have brought many extraordinary advantages, but the successful businessman's empire made heavy demands on him. His life had little room for the romantic notions of a young woman who suddenly found herself in charge of a family and a household. The widower Quandt, twenty years older than Magda, had two adolescent sons, Hellmuth and Herbert, and in November 1921 Magda gave birth to Harald. Maternal duties, entertaining, and accompanying her husband on business trips, including one to the United States and Latin America in 1927, at first kept Magda from acknowledging the growing rift between her and her husband. But in 1929 a permanent separation resulted when Magda appeared in public with a young lover.[88]

A settlement was reached: seven-year-old Harald would stay with his mother until he was fourteen, unless she remarried. In that case, or after he reached fourteen, he would return to his father's custody. Quandt provided for Magda so generously that she could look forward to a future without financial cares. She moved into a handsome apartment in Berlin's elegant West End, not far from Quandt's villa.

Looking for something to give her life meaning, Magda wandered into a Nazi rally in the Sportpalast during the 1930 electoral campaign. Hitler and Goebbels were the speakers, and apparently they made such an impression on her that she decided on the spot to join the party.[89] After becoming a member on 1 September, she volunteered with the local NSDAP women's organization before offering her services at party headquarters.[90] There the elegant lady made the closer acquaintance of the frail man with the crippled foot. She saw in him a pure idealist, an untiring fighter for a just world that would come with the Third Reich. That he was prepared to commit any wrong, that his fanatical will was based on boundless misanthropy, cynicism, and hatred, Magda Quandt did not recognize.

Goebbels soon desired the love of the striking young woman.[91] Like the relationship with Anka Stalherm, such an affiliation would do a great deal to compensate for his physical defect and his humble origins. Also important was the fact that Magda, although she had never known poverty and degradation, had seriously committed herself to national socialism. Goebbels raved about her "entrancing beauty," her rationality, her "clever, realistic sense of life," her "generosity in thought and deed."[92] He positively bloomed in her presence. Together they spent "completely contented" evenings, after which he was "almost in a dream. So full of fulfilled happiness."[93]

As the Stennes crisis intensified, Goebbels, who now thought he loved "only one," turned to her more and more.[94] But she could not be his support just now; her attempted breakout from her world had brought a great number of complications. There was her former husband, with whom she was apparently on better terms than before the divorce; they lunched together regularly at the exclusive Horcher restaurant. Günther Quandt and his family, whose name Magda still bore, disapproved of her involvement with the Nazis and criticized most sharply her connection with the Gauleiter. So did her parents. Her mother, Auguste Behrend, despised Goebbels, and her father, Oskar Ritschel, did not want to meet him.[95] From all these quarters Magda was subjected to "horrendous pressure," as she complained to Goebbels.

At the height of the crisis Magda's difficulties reached such a pitch that Goebbels almost thought he had lost her. Her lover, the cause of her divorce from Quandt, brandished a pistol, trying to block her way to the clubfooted revolutionary. All this became a "torment" for Goebbels. He claimed to be driven to "deepest despair" by "insane jealousy" such as he had not known since the days with Anka Stalherm. The apparent inalterability of what he saw as his fate led him to a conclusion that once again mirrored both the role he saw for himself as an exceptional person destined for martyrdom, and his boundless misanthropy: "I must, and am supposed to, and will remain alone. . . . And no longer think of myself. How wretched life is! And this pile of shit known as man!"[96]

In April 1931 Goebbels had not only the Stennes putsch and Magda Quandt to worry about, but also the police and the state's attorney's office. "These trials are killing me. My desk is piled with summonses again. It's sickening. But I mustn't lose my nerve. That's what the enemy wants."[97] The Reichstag vote in February that made it easier to lift parliamentary immunity had allowed the authorities to move against Goebbels again. Although he had previously avoided trial by simply not appearing, he was now charged with slandering "Isidor" Weiss, the Jewish religion, the chief of police, and the previous police commissioner. Eight separate cases against him were heard on 29 April alone. The sentences actually proved quite mild—only 1,500 marks in fines and a month in jail—which his lawyer promptly appealed. On 1 May he was back in court to answer three more charges, for which he was fined 1,000 marks. Goebbels responded with obstruction: "I'm not defending myself anymore. In the face of the Prussian courts the only thing is to keep silent and continue one's work."[98]

To expose the verdicts to ridicule after the fact, Goebbels and his lawyers now began to haggle over the payment schedule for the fines. They wanted to pay in the smallest possible installments, or even postpone payment, in the expectation that the government would soon declare an amnesty to defuse the political conflict. After his appeal of the verdict in the Weiss case failed, Goebbels applied to pay off the 1,804.08 marks in monthly 25-mark installments.[99] The court ordered him instead to come up with 500 marks every month, but from December 1931 to December 1932 he insisted on paying only a hundred a month. These sums were drawn from his private secretary's "discretionary fund." The court had the Gauleiter's financial circumstances investigated and concluded that he could easily manage 250 marks a month.[100] Goebbels ignored the ruling. On 21 December 1931 the anticipated amnesty relieved him of the necessity of further payments. In some of the other cases the discrepancy between what he actually paid and what the amnesty saved him was even more striking, not to mention the prison sentence, of which he served not one day.[101]

The "huge amounts of money" that he owed as a result of the large number of fines soon caused him financial difficulties.[102] To cope with them, he apparently siphoned off monies intended for the SA. Ernst Hanfstaengl, whom Hitler had named foreign press secretary after the September 1930 elections, recalled that a sum of 14,000 marks set aside for the SA had disappeared on its way through the Gauleiter's treasury. In party circles Goebbels was blamed; those in the know connected the money's disappearance with Goebbels's affair with Magda Quandt "and the resulting financial obligations that fell on the ardent suitor."[103]

After Magda had broken definitively with her earlier lover and persuaded the Quandts that she would not alter her decision to follow Goebbels, the two of them began to forge "plans for the future." During the Pentecost holiday, which they spent together on the Quandt estate in Mecklenburg, this strange pair made a "solemn promise": they would not marry until the thing both of them believed in and lived for, the Third Reich, a supposedly better world, became a reality.[104]

Except for further court cases—in mid-May he received a two-month jail sentence for slander of Deputy Police Commissioner Weiss and a fine of 500 marks for inciting to class hatred—that spring Goebbels had reason to feel confident.[105] For in May the third wave of the world economic crisis washed over Germany; it served his purposes by destroying any hope for a general improvement in economic and social conditions. The signing on 24 July of the Hoover Moratorium, which postponed all German reparations payments for a year, did little to change the grim picture.

After the collapse of the Austrian Credit Bank, the Darmstadt National Bank defaulted in mid-July. When people panicked and rushed to withdraw all their savings, the government moved to close all banks, savings banks, and exchanges. In January just over four million people had been unemployed, but by the end of the year this figure had climbed to six million. Hunger, poverty, and hopelessness spread through the land, while public confidence in the Weimar system and its parties rapidly waned.

Although the conditions for a revolutionary struggle against the system continued to improve, Goebbels kept the Stennes revolt in mind and followed his Führer's legality policy, at least on the surface. When the Stahlhelm called for a plebiscite on dissolving the Prussian Landtag before the scheduled time, the Nazis seconded the call. At the end of July the KPD joined the right-wing phalanx on this issue. The Communists had received a warning from Stalin that the German party was lagging behind revolutionary developments, leaving the field open to Nazi nationalist demagoguery. Stalin reminded the KPD's leaders that the spearhead for fascism was the Brüning government, whose chief support came from the Prussian government put in place by the social fascists; it was therefore crucial to topple that government.[106]

Although the stronger coalition served Goebbels's ends, he had difficulty explaining this particular alliance, since he had always spoken of the KPD and the SPD as "Marxist sister parties." Addressing a rally on 6 August, he completely twisted the truth, saying that only pressure from its adherents had forced the KPD to join. The nationalist opposition was concerned chiefly with Prussia and the Reich, he said: "If we succeed in making Prussia Prussian again, we can also make Germany German again."[107]

Fearing that his government could not withstand a joint attack from left and right, Otto Braun, the Social Democratic prime minster of Prussia, citing an emergency decree just issued by Hindenburg, ordered all daily newspapers to print his "Announcement by the Prussian State Government": "Parties of the right, the Stahlhelm, and Communists—implacable enemies united in an unnatural alliance—are calling for a plebiscite for the dissolution of the Prussian Landtag. . . . Upon the successful conclusion of the plebiscite they plan to light the fire that will signal far and wide that the end of democracy, of the people's state, has come in Germany."[108]

To avert another ban on *Der Angriff*, which had just been banned for four weeks in June (subsequently reduced to two) and another week in July, Goebbels complied with the order to print the announcement.[109] But he turned the incident to demagogic purposes, rhetorically asking the whipped-up masses at a rally on 7 August in the Sportpalast how a Nazi felt reading such a thing in his own newspaper. Hatred and anger, he answered, threatened to overwhelm him. And that was good, for "where would we find the courage these days to continue our work, if anger and hatred and rage did not lend us strength?"[110]

The plebiscite failed, probably because many Communists refused to make common cause with the NSDAP. Wild rumors of a Communist coup circulated that evening. In the Prenzlauer Berg section of Berlin the police had to cordon off entire streets, because snipers from the banned military arm of the KPD were shooting at passersby, both military and civilian. Near the Karl Liebknecht House two police captains were shot to death. One of the two young Communists who had received orders from Ulbricht and Neumann to fire the shots was Erich Mielke.[111] Twenty-six years later he would become head of the infamous Stasi, the Ministry for State Security in the German Democratic Republic, a position he held for more than thirty years.

Goebbels converted the failure of the plebiscite into a victory for his party, gloating over the Communists' "total failure" to mobilize their followers. And he whipped up indignation at the treacherous murders, giving a full account in *Der Angriff* and claiming that in the past weeks hardly a day had passed "without a National Socialist, a Stahlhelm member, or a police officer being killed or wounded by Communist criminals."[112] And the Communists had now indeed stepped up the violence against the Nazis. As early as April *Die Rote Fahne* had called for an offensive against the "Nazi barracks," whose locations had been published in *Der Angriff*.[113] Now the pubs where Nazi storm units gathered became the target of attacks, some of them bloody. In all, that year political violence claimed twenty-nine lives in Berlin.[114]

The mounting violence on the part of the Communists did much to turn large segments of the population toward the Nazis. Pious repetition of their commitment to constitutional legality, but especially the Nazi leaders' nationalistic rhetoric, was taking effect. Even leading SPD representatives were beginning to think that the real threat to Germany came from the KPD, steered as it was from Moscow.[115]

An incident that took place on 12 September 1931 on the Kurfürstendamm did little to change the growing support for the Nazis. The political surveillance unit of the Berlin police knew that Goebbels and Count Wolf-Heinrich von Helldorf, leader of the Berlin SA and a deputy in the Prussian Landtag, had discussed a demonstration by "the unemployed" for the Jewish New Year.[116] What they actually had in mind came to light on the evening of 12 September: Helldorf drove up and down the Kurfürstendamm in a green Opel, directing his troops, disguised as ordinary passersby, to abuse, insult, and strike "persons whose appearance allowed one to conclude they were Jewish."[117] The pogrom lasted two hours, during which time the police arrested numerous Nazis, including Count Helldorf.

Goebbels thought he could use such actions to close the widening gap between the leadership in Munich and the revolutionary base of the movement, and to channel aggressions within the SA to suit his own purposes. But now he confronted further difficulties: with the help of several major manufacturers, Hitler, Hugenberg, and other "reactionary" leaders on 11 November formed the Harzburg Front, with the goal of achieving power in the Reich. This step caused consternation, and not only in the Berlin SA, because it seemed to confirm the long-feared "bourgeoisification and tycoonization" of the party.

Goebbels therefore gathered all his energy to explain to the "SA man" at meetings and discussion evenings that the formation of this alliance was a purely "instrumental" move, intended to topple Brüning; for power could be obtained only through a coalition, which in no way compromised what would be done with that power once obtained.[118] Goebbels's tactics did little to convince the SA, and the hope still held by many members that improvement of social conditions could be achieved through the NSDAP gave way to a kind of nervous tension, a paralyzing irritability that might explode at any moment.

That irritability was exacerbated by events that under different circumstances might have been taken less seriously. Among them was the trial of those involved in the pogrom on the Kurfürstendamm. Count Helldorf's lawyer, Roland Freisler, succeeded in getting his conviction as ringleader reduced from a prison sentence to a fine of 100 marks. (As the presiding judge of the dreaded People's Court, this same Freisler would later condemn Helldorf to death after the attempt on Hitler's life of 20 July 1944.) A decisive part in securing the mild sentence was played by Goebbels. On the witness stand he loudly denounced the court, shouting at the state's attorney "so that he completely loses his composure." Goebbels was ordered to pay 500 marks for contempt of court. But he refused to testify on the particulars of the case, which rendered it impossible for the judges to determine Helldorf's responsibility "beyond the shadow of a doubt."[119]

The trial, however, went badly for the accused SA men. For breach of the peace they received prison sentences of one to two years. Although these were reduced on appeal to four to ten months, bitterness over the unequal treatment continued to fester. This bitterness manifested itself in a pamphlet that circulated among SA members in December. The pamphlet said that they had the duty to speak out openly about why they could no longer follow Goebbels and Helldorf, who had betrayed them and sold them out.[120]

In this critical situation Goebbels also had his problems with SA Chief of Staff Ernst Röhm. Partly because of his inactivity and partly because of the rumors circulating about him, Röhm had fallen into discredit with many SA men. In the spring of 1931, as the Stennes crisis was nearing its climax, the Berlin state's attorney's office had received a tip about Röhm. The police searched the office of a Berlin doctor for sexual disorders and turned up several letters from Röhm. In them he openly admitted his homosexuality and complained that he was having trouble finding "playmates."[121]

The state's attorney's office initiated an investigation of Röhm for "unnatural offenses."[122] Before the investigation was terminated for lack of evidence, word had got out, and the sexual inclinations of the corpulent condottiere soon occasioned much talk.

Goebbels, who blamed a good part of the Stennes crisis on the chief of staff, intervened in the matter early on, not only providing incriminating material but also spreading "derogatory expressions and jokes."[123] He maneuvered behind the scenes to get Röhm dismissed, but he failed, and Röhm took revenge by spreading in return all sorts of rumors about Goebbels's relationship with Magda Quandt. He went so far as to suggest that Goebbels was interested less in Magda than in her young son.[124] So along with Röhm's homosexual excesses, people were talking about the "cloven foot's" "impossible (and immoral) relationship."

The distance between the party's leadership and its supporters was growing. When Goebbels addressed an SA audience after a four-week ban on public appearances, he aroused little enthusiasm, although he declared that the party, strengthened by the peaceful weeks just past, was entering the final stage of the struggle, and promised that the decision would come in four to five months. Police observers noted that the applause following this major "impressive" speech was "noticeably sparse."[125] Perhaps, people thought, the heyday of the brown propagandist was nearing its end.

Isn't it a miracle that a mere World War corporal now takes the place of the houses of Hohenzollern and Hapsburg? (1931—1933)

It was a cold day in December 1931 when Goebbels, wearing a dark suit, left the house of the mayor of Goldenbow in Mecklenburg with his newly wedded wife. The civil ceremony had just been performed in the mayor's parlor. As the group set out for the nearby village of Severin, the modestly dressed bride took the arm of her hobbling husband. Beside them walked ten-year-old Harald Quandt in the uniform of the NSDAP youth organization, and behind them their witnesses, Adolf Hitler and Franz von Epp, both in civilian dress, followed by Magda's mother and her former sister-in-law, Ello Quandt, and a few friends. In the church in Severin, decked out with swastika banners, the couple made their vows again before God, on whom at least the bridegroom had long since turned his back. After the Protestant service the wedding was celebrated on the Quandt estate, whose administrator had everything prepared. Seven months later this man, Walter Granzow, would become prime minister of Mecklenburg-Schwerin.[1]

Despite the couple's original pledge, they had not postponed the wedding until the Third Reich became a reality. At Goebbels's express wish, the ceremonies took place quietly and far from Berlin, because of the critical mood among the mostly proletarian party supporters in the metropolis. The important thing was to make the relationship legal and thereby put a stop to the gossip about the Gauleiter. This step seemed all the more urgent now; Magda had just learned she was pregnant.

But things did not work out as Goebbels had hoped. Goebbels's marriage provided a welcome topic both within the movement and among its enemies. Thus one could read in the *AP-Korrespondenz*, a paper close to the SPD:

Herr Goebbels is rightly indignant that certain papers dragged his wife—even before she had become his wife!—through the political mire. He invites everyone who doubts his wife's "purely Aryan ancestry" to "look for himself." We have no such doubts. But we fear that her lord and master must cut a strange figure in this company. Just picture this: a tall, blond woman, blue-eyed and with all the Nordic trimmings, and next to her little Isidor Goebbels. Nordification? We know neither whether Herr Goebbels provides a suitable object, nor whether this process can lead to the desired goal in this case.[2]

Given the growing dissension in the party, Goebbels welcomed the increase in acts of violence that marked the beginning of 1932. With the proper propaganda twist, they could be made to enhance solidarity and self-confidence among the storm troopers. When two Red Front Combatants and one SA man were killed in a severe clash in the Felseneck summer-cottage colony on 19 January, he cranked up his propaganda machine to top speed. In *Der Angriff* he raved about the "murderous Red pestilence" in Moscow that was deliberately provoking violence against the National Socialists, and portrayed the SA involvement in the incident as an act of heroic patriotism.[3]

A few days later, in revenge for Felseneck, Communists stabbed the fifteen-year-old schoolboy Herbert Norkus to death while he was distributing Nazi pamphlets in the working-class district of Moabit. Goebbels called for a final reckoning with these "Red child-murderers," these "subhumans." He indulged in almost unprecedented tastelessness when he dwelled on "the boy's sallow face with half-open broken eyes" staring into the void "in the grim gray dusk," then continued: "The delicate head is trampled to a bloody pulp. Long, deep wounds go into the slender body, and a mortal gash penetrates heart and lungs. . . . Wearily, black night descends. From two glassy eyes stares the emptiness of death."[4]

Goebbels's attempts to hold the Berlin party together were undermined by Hitler's appearance before the Cologne Industry Club on 27 January, taken by many of the party faithful as further evidence of the "bourgeois-ification and tycoonization" of the leadership. Then there was the change in Goebbels's own style of life after his marriage. He moved from his modest flat in Steglitz to his wife's palatial apartment in the West End, which became a gathering place for prominent party members and sympathizers from Berlin's high society. When Hitler was in Berlin, he liked to come over from the elegant Kaiserhof Hotel, where he now stayed. Goebbels and his wife outdid themselves in trying to please Hitler. The lady of the house would bake his favorite pastries, while Goebbels played gramophone records of the Führer's best speeches and hung on Hitler's lips during his long monologues.

On such occasions Goebbels tried to convey to his Führer his tormenting worries about the movement. He stressed that he was sure the tactical alliance with the reactionary forces would be of short duration. To keep the Nazis on track toward their revolutionary goals, it would be a good idea, Goebbels thought, to have Hitler run for Reich president in March 1932.[5] He planned to mount a campaign with "masterpieces of propaganda" and on an "unheard-of scale" that would restore to the movement its lost momentum and shift him, as director of propaganda, into the heart of the action.

For almost a month Hitler vacillated, then on 12 February he finally made up his mind to run.[6] On 22 February, with Hitler's permission to "take the plunge," Goebbels announced Hitler's candidacy during a general membership meeting at the Sportpalast.[7] The "storm of enthusiasm" is supposed to have raged for almost ten minutes. "Wild demonstrations for the Führer. The people stand up and cheer and shout. The roof threatens to cave in. An overwhelming sight. This movement really must prove victorious. . . . Late at night the Führer telephones. I report to him, then he comes over to see us. He's happy that the proclamation of his candidacy had such an impact."[8]

At party headquarters in Munich the Berlin events caused confusion, since Goebbels's announcement was apparently not in accord with agreements Hitler had made before he left for Berlin. The following morning the party leadership sent out telegrams to the press forbidding "publication of this story . . . since Goebbels acted without Hitler's consent." Although Hitler promptly intervened and a few hours later a second telegram rescinded the previous order, the press seized on the notion that the propaganda director had acted without authorization and spread the canard that he had been "carried away by the mood of the gathering." "How badly the journalistic riffraff is informed, or rather, it acts as if it were badly informed. In short, the fight has begun in earnest. . . . The political armies are maneuvering for the decisive battle."[9]

A few hours after noting this in his diary, Goebbels went on the offensive against Hindenburg in the Reichstag. "Tell me who praises you, and I'll tell you who you are!" he exclaimed, and went on to say that Hindenburg was "praised by the Berlin asphalt press, praised by the party of deserters"—he pointed at the Social Democratic benches.[10] Tumultuous scenes ensued, in the course of which Goebbels had the epithet "armchair soldier" hurled at him. The president of the Reichstag suspended the session, and the council of elders voted to exclude Goebbels from further participation because he had insulted the head of state, whereupon he walked out, to the Nazi deputies' shouts of "Heil!" The SPD deputy Kurt Schumacher then bitterly denounced the "moral and intellectual debasement" brought about by national socialism.[11]

Goebbels opened the election campaign with Hitler's appearance in the Sportpalast on 27 February. He called upon the "whole noisy apparatus of sophisticated mass influence": the roll of SA drums, smart military marches, and a parade of flags. "First Goebbels steps onto the podium to soften up the masses," the *Vossische Zeitung* reported; "then the SA receives the command 'Atten-tion!' and in the sudden silence in the vast arena one hears the rising chorus of *Heils* outside. Down the aisle formed by the *Volk* strides Adolf Hitler."[12] He spoke for several hours. The more excitedly he spoke, the more wildly he gesticulated and the more exalted his expression became; he seemed to be intoxicated with his own words. In contrast to Goebbels, he did not attack personally the candidate backed by the majority parties, but merely suggested it was time for him to move on: "At one time we served the field marshal in loyalty and obedience. Today we say to him: 'You are too venerable for us to let those whom we intend to annihilate hide behind you. You must step aside.' "[13]

Hugenberg's DNVP put up Theodor Duesterberg, vice chairman of the Stahlhelm, for Reich president, and the KPD put up Ernst Thälmann, while the SPD willy-nilly had to support Hindenburg. The 27 February edition of the SPD paper *Vorwärts* pointedly summarized the dilemma: "Every vote against Hindenburg is a vote for Hitler. Every vote snatched away from Thälmann . . . and given to Hindenburg is a blow against Hitler."

To gain tighter control over the election campaign, in the spring of 1932 Goebbels moved the Reich propaganda directorate from Munich to Berlin. In his office on Hedemannstrasse he held daily meetings at which he lectured his "leading officials" on the "constantly changing tactics."[14] He coordinated all details with the principal staff members of the party leadership and of *Der Angriff* (banned once again at the end of February); with Karoly Kampmann, appointed propaganda director for the Gau in the previous year; and with the Berlin organization leader Karl Hanke.[15] Hanke, a dedicated foe of the "system" and a party member since 1928, had been dismissed from his senior teaching position at a trade school in Berlin because of his seditious activities for the NSDAP, and now devoted himself entirely to the party.[16]

In addition to Goebbels's numerous speeches, posters formed an important propaganda tool in this campaign. Believing that the quantity of propaganda devices would be reflected in the number of votes cast, at the end of February Goebbels slapped up half a million posters all across the country. In Berlin the kiosks and walls were plastered with huge, colorful ones, some of them designed by the caricaturist Schweitzer. Hanke arranged for SA men to guard the posters, which repeatedly led to clashes, especially with members of the KPD. Since the SA also formed commandos to sabotage the KPD's poster campaign, March saw the beginning of an outright "poster war."[17]

Goebbels also continued his use of technologically advanced propaganda methods, having fifty thousand copies made of a gramophone record small enough to slip into an envelope. He and his assistants also prepared a ten-minute sound film to be played in public squares and cinemas, so as to suggest the omnipresence of the Nazi leaders, especially the Führer.[18]

As never before, Goebbels strove to create the Hitler myth. In the 5 March edition of *Der Angriff* he described him under the headline "We elect Adolf Hitler" as the "representative of Greater Germany," the "Führer," the "Prophet," and the "Fighter." By "representative of Greater Germany," he explained, he meant the born Austrian who had experienced in person the "*völkisch* distress," whose whole life until now had been filled with yearning for the Greater German Reich. He also meant the former construction worker, who knew the workplace and the working class and shared its heavy burden. He meant the frontline soldier as well, who had made it his goal to bring the justified demands of his wartime comrades to political fruition. "Hitler the Führer," Goebbels wrote, had managed to develop a mocked and despised little sect into the most impressive mass movement in Europe.[19]

On election eve Hitler awaited the results in Munich, while Goebbels and his wife gave a party in Berlin. "We listen to the results on the radio. The reports dribble in. . . . By 2:00 A.M. the dream of assuming power is temporarily over. . . . We were mistaken not so much in our estimate of our votes as in our estimate of the other side's chances," Goebbels noted soberly in his diary.[20] Hindenburg had received 49.6 percent to Hitler's 30.1 percent of the vote. But that same night, after a telephone call from Hitler, Goebbels girded himself for the runoff election, necessary because Hindenburg had not received an absolute majority.[21]

In the short time remaining before the runoff on 10 April, Goebbels sent Hitler on a whirlwind tour of Germany by plane, a technique that aroused astonishment even in America.[22] Thinking that it was hopeless to try to lure voters away from the Catholic Center Party and the SPD, Goebbels concentrated on winning over the middle-class elements of the Hindenburg Front. In a circular to all Gau leadership organizations, he described these elements as "primarily the German philistines" whom the enemy was wooing "with emotional ploys and fear of the new," also women, on whom the enemy used "the appeal to the tear ducts and fear of war," as well as "retirees and civil servants," who were being reminded of "inflation, reduction in pensions, and Nat. Soc. hostility to the civil service." Those who had voted for Duesterberg should be told that even if Hitler did not win, every vote for Hitler against the government and the "system" parties would be a warning against continued rule by emergency decree.[23]

When the votes were counted on 10 April, Goebbels had to acknowledge that the Nazis had failed to make inroads into Hindenburg's support. The field marshal had been elected with 53 percent of the vote. Hitler, however, had gained two million votes, having apparently attracted almost all the conservative votes that had earlier gone to Duesterberg, as well as some of those previously cast for Thälmann. Without a moment's pause, Goebbels threw himself into the campaign for the Prussian Landtag elections, to be held in two weeks, at the same time as those for Anhalt, Bavaria, Hamburg, and Württemberg. He gathered the district leaders around him and noted that everyone was in "a fantastic mood."[24]

This mood was dampened that same day when Goebbels learned that Wilhelm Groener, minster of the interior and the Reichswehr, planned to ban the SA and the SS throughout the Reich. Only a short time earlier Groener had characterized Hitler as a modest, orderly, positively idealistic man and had advocated integrating the party into the government. But after subversive instructions from Hitler to the SA were found, he changed his mind. No sooner had Hindenburg issued the emergency decree "To Safeguard the Authority of the State," than the police once more occupied the NSDAP headquarters on Hedemannstrasse, searched them, and sealed off the SA's offices.

Goebbels sensed the far-reaching consequences of this ban, which certainly could no longer destroy the organization but would make it much more difficult to maintain discipline and internal order, since it would now be necessary to go underground. In his diary he noted that Groener, who had acted with Brüning's backing, might be toppled by this action. Indeed, the emergency decree, which Hindenburg had signed reluctantly, aroused passionate disagreement in the conservative camp, which extended into Brüning's cabinet and Hindenburg's inner circle.[25]

Goebbels's analysis, that the ban might mean a "serious defeat" for the Brüning government, seemed on the mark; on 16 April he learned from Helldorf that the Reich president had sent an angry letter to Groener, saying that charges similar to those against the SA could be brought against the Reichsbanner, the SPD organization of frontline veterans. Therefore he had to ask Groener to scrutinize any material available on the Reichsbanner "as closely" as he, Hindenburg, had scrutinized the material for the SA ban.

Goebbels, who found it difficult to conduct an election campaign without the SA, staged another defeat for Brüning during a gathering at the Sportpalast. Because Brüning had refused to come and debate with Goebbels, the Gauleiter played a gramophone record of a speech by Brüning and then proceeded to "refute" his arguments. The eighteen thousand people in the audience went wild with enthusiasm at this charade.

In the regional elections Goebbels again sent Hitler out on an airplane tour and expressed great admiration for his stamina. The outcome of the Landtag elections meant yet another defeat for the forces that sustained the old state. In all five provinces the NSDAP continued its successful march, even becoming the strongest party in Prussia with 36.3 percent of the vote. More consequential, however, was the fact that the Prussian government of Otto Braun, supported by the SPD, the Center, and the DDP, lost its parliamentary majority. The government resigned but continued to function, since the required absolute majority for electing a new prime minster could not be achieved by any candidate.

The results of the elections for the Prussian Landtag left the National Socialists in a quandary. They would have had to join forces with the Center Party to gain the absolute majority. Goebbels commented: "Power with the Center or against the Center against power. Nothing can be done in parliamentary fashion without the Center, neither in Prussia nor in the Reich. That must be carefully thought through."[26]

As Goebbels's diary entries in the period just after the elections indicate, he was plagued with indecision on this question of a coalition.[27] At the end of April, when Hitler visited Goebbels in his apartment on Reichskanzlerplatz, Hitler revealed a plan that still did not seem to offer a way out of the dilemma. While Goebbels had been completely preoccupied with the Prussian elections, Helldorf had apparently gone over his head to arrange with Gen. Kurt von Schleicher, chief of the ministerial bureau in the Reichswehr Ministry, a meeting between Schleicher and Hitler. During this meeting, which took place on 26 April, the devious general was sounding Hitler out: would Hitler take part in a conservative national government, or at least tolerate one, if the SA ban were lifted and new elections scheduled?

Schleicher, who saw the NSDAP as "a healthy reaction on the part of the *Volk*," since the movement was "positively oriented toward the armaments policy . . . in contrast to the KPD," thought that by bringing the NSDAP into the government he could get it to moderate its course, or could even split it into moderate and radical factions. Schleicher wanted to depoliticize the paramilitary forces and transform them into nonpartisan competitive sports organizations. That would prepare the way for converting the Reichswehr from a professional army into a militia. All this required a good deal of tactical skill, which he did not trust Brüning to display. Therefore he exploited the conflict among the rightists over the SA ban, turning it against Groener, and that meant against Brüning. He aimed to topple both of them.[28] Hitler in turn planned to manipulate the "reactionary forces" around Schleicher for his own purposes. The idea was to create the impression that Hitler was entering into a pact with Schleicher. At the right moment, after the dismantling of the Brüning regime, Hitler would jump ship. Goebbels grasped the idea immediately when Hitler reported to him on 27 April on the meeting with Schleicher, which had "gone well."[29] By early May Goebbels could conclude with satisfaction from the newspapers that the intrigues of the "officers' camarilla" against Brüning and Groener were underway.

When Hitler met General Schleicher on 7 May for their "decisive discussion," Goebbels was not included in his entourage. To those he labeled reactionaries, Goebbels was persona non grata. He thus learned only afterward what had taken place. The plan, as Hitler explained it to him, called for the Reich president to withdraw his support from Brüning within the next few days, which would result in Brüning's fall. "A colorless transitional cabinet will open the way for us. As weak as possible, so we can supplant it more easily. The main thing is that we regain our freedom to demonstrate."[30]

By "freedom to demonstrate" Goebbels meant the lifting of all legal restrictions, from the ban on the SA and SS to the prohibition on speeches and marches. Still convinced of the onmipotence of propaganda, he wanted to produce another "masterpiece" after the fall of Brüning and the dissolution of the Reichstag. On 3 May he had already discussed a complete restructuring of the propaganda apparatus with the leaders of the Reich propaganda department, which had recently been moved back to Munich. "The main burden of our work in the coming months rests on propaganda. Our entire technique must be refined down to the last detail. Only the newest and most accurate methods will lead to victory."[31]

For the present, however, Goebbels, intent on maintaining the support of the revolutionary elements in the party, made it his objective to intensify the agitation against Brüning and Groener. On 9 May he therefore published a "sharply critical essay" on Brüning. In the Reichstag Goering then attacked Reichswehr Minister Groener "massively and fiercely." Ill and disheartened, the minister offered an inept defense of his ban on the SA. "We heckle him so persistently that the whole chamber rocks and shakes with laughter. In the end you can only pity him," Goebbels wrote scornfully.[32] Groener's pathetic performance weakened his position in the conservative camp. On 11 May the Gauleiter noted confidently, "The army no longer wants him. Even his own circle is pushing for his fall. That's how it must begin: when one falls, the whole cabinet and the system with it will come tumbling down."[33]

Brüning countered the campaign to undermine his minister of the interior and the Reichswehr by placing the emphasis on foreign policy in his speech to the Reichstag. He pointed to foreign-policy successes and positive developments expected shortly in economic and financial policy. At the same time he pointedly criticized the conservative opposition's politics of destruction, "which gives no consideration to preserving the

German people's strength or to our foreign-policy position," aiming only to "exploit desperation for purposes of agitation."[34] Brüning was convinced he had steered the republic through the crisis. Very soon his negotiations to have the reparations payments canceled would yield the desired result, and then the postponed measures for creating jobs could be put into effect.

During the early summer of 1932, when Brüning believed his goal was just around the corner, Goebbels's old adversary Gregor Strasser took a more moderate approach than before. His speech to the Reichstag on "anticapitalist longings" got an attentive hearing, for in it he came forward with some concrete suggestions for creating jobs. These proposals seemed to express a genuine interest in solving the prevailing economic and social problems, and even Brüning listened with "extraordinary interest." The SPD's *Vorwärts* noted that Strasser's speech in the Reichstag represented a "first attempt to come to grips with real economic problems, though in a very dilettantish manner."[35]

Goebbels, more concerned with revolutionary appearances than with creating jobs, felt only contempt for his old rival, especially because of Strasser's popularity. But he referred in *Der Angriff* to Strasser's speech; "the masters of the collapsing system" should note that, contrary to their contention, the NSDAP did have a program.[36] For another reason, too, Goebbels chose to focus on Strasser's new course, which steered toward reconciliation and preservation of the system: it veiled the conspiracy against the chancellor being pursued by Hitler and the men around Hindenburg. "Amusing to watch the Jewish journalistic riffraff, usually so well informed, staggering around in the dark. They still think we're going to fall in with the Center. Harmless idiots!"[37]

On 12 May 1932 an incident occurred in the Reichstag that suited Goebbels's purposes perfectly. In the lobby Nazi deputies, among them Edmund Heines, leader of the Silesian SA and a friend of Röhm's, beat up the journalist Helmut Klotz, who had published a brochure containing letters in which Röhm described his sexual preferences. The president of the Reichstag summoned the police. When Deputy Police Commissioner Weiss and about fifty officers appeared in the chamber, tumult broke out. "Isidor! Isidor!" roared the Nazi deputies, and from their midst the Gauleiter exclaimed loudly, "Just look at that—the swine has the nerve to come here and stir up trouble!"[38] But Weiss calmly ordered his men to arrest four Nazis. The real high point of this "crazy day" came that evening, however: Reichswehr Minister Groener resigned.

By 23 May Goebbels could note with satisfaction that the crisis was moving along nicely. "Our moles are hard at work nibbling away at Brüning's position."[39] Less than two weeks later Hindenburg refused to sign a new emergency decree that Brüning had prepared. That sealed the chancellor's fate—and that of the Weimar Republic, for it opened the way to a right-wing government headed by Schleicher's close associate Franz von Papen.

Goebbels was just getting ready to dictate a new article against Brüning when word reached him of the chancellor's fall: "The bomb has burst. . . . The system is toppling. . . . I drive out to meet the Führer, who is coming from Mecklenburg. . . . The Reich president wants to speak to him in the course of the afternoon. I join him in his motorcar and orient him on the situation. We're beside ourselves with joy."[40]

A few hours later Goebbels met with Hitler again and heard that his discussion with the Reich president had gone well. Goebbels's joy knew no bounds when he learned that, in return for the NSDAP's provisional acceptance of the Papen government, the SA ban would be lifted. And even more important, the Reichstag would be dissolved.[41] Goebbels anticipated that he would play a pivotal role in the new elections, and that power would shift from those who had been cultivating the "reactionaries" to him, the Reich propaganda director. In the provincial elections in Oldenburg the Nazis had just won an absolute majority, and Goebbels had high hopes for the rest of the country.[42]

One of the objectives of Goebbels's propaganda plan was to "sneak away from the compromising company of these bourgeois adolescents. Otherwise we are lost."[43] Schleicher and Papen, who had formed a "cabinet of national consolidation" on 1 June, were attempting to bring the Nazis into the government in Prussia, so as to "tame" them. In return for lifting the various bans, they demanded that Hitler promise longer-term support for the "barons' cabinet."[44]

After the dissolution of the Reichstag on 4 June, Goebbels turned his guns on the new government. On 6 June he published an attack on the new chancellor, and on 14 June, just before the ban on the SA and SS was lifted, he published his second major polemic against Papen. Papen, meanwhile, in collaboration with Hindenburg, set about fulfilling the promises made to Hitler, without being able to prevent the Nazis' defection. Only Gregor Strasser worked in the opposite direction, signaling readiness for real cooperation. What particularly enraged Goebbels was that Strasser made this move in a radio address, becoming the first member of the party to speak thus to the nation. Aware of the growing importance of this medium, Strasser, who was party organization leader for radio communications, had advised Hitler to insist on free access to the radio as one of his conditions for tolerating the Papen cabinet. On 11 June Papen had directed Reich Interior Minister Wilhelm von Gayl to make the radio generally available.[45]

To make it clear to the revolutionary supporters of the movement that the place of the party was not at the side of the "reactionaries," and to counteract the effect of Strasser's radio address, Goebbels appeared the same day, 14 June, on Potsdamer Platz, the liveliest square in Berlin. In defiance of the ban on the SA, still in effect, he was accompanied by forty-five storm troopers in uniform. Although they did all they could to be provocative, nothing happened. "The policemen stare at us uncomprehendingly, and then sheepishly look away."[46]

Papen's first emergency decree, released on 15 June, provided Goebbels with the ideal pretext for refusing any further toleration of the Papen cabinet. In his diary he remarked that this decree, which focused on economic policy, was "acutely capitalistic" and "would hit the poor the hardest. Our only choice is to fight."[47]

As the campaign heated up in early July, Goebbels attacked the Papen government more and more violently. When the interior minister banned an SA march to the Brandenburg Gate, on the grounds that otherwise he would also have to authorize one for the KPD, Hitler seized the occasion to rescind his support of the Papen regime. Goebbels could then agitate against the government to his heart's content. When Papen returned from Lausanne with a treaty ending reparations payments, Goebbels twisted this success into a failure. His anti-Papen campaign reached a climax on 10 July when he spoke to an audience allegedly numbering one hundred thousand in the Lustgarten, where Karl Liebknecht had proclaimed the socialist republic in 1918. "The declaration of war is received by the masses with unprecedented enthusiasm. With this huge mass rally we have broken the noose. We're free of the toleration policy. Now we can march in our own direction again."[48]

On 18 July Goebbels spoke on the radio for the first time. He had just had an angry confrontation with the Ministry of the Interior, to which he had had to submit his text in advance. The official in charge had noted on the manuscript for the benefit of his minister that the speech "went beyond the bounds of what is usual and permissible on the radio." The manuscript had gone back and forth between him and Goebbels several times, with the result that Goebbels finally rewrote his speech on "Nationalism as a Necessity of State Policy," retitling it "National Character as the Basis of National Culture."[49] He felt that all that remained of his speech was words, "mere words," and that he had not reached his audience. He decided he preferred to speak to real crowds, where he could see them filled with "wild enthusiasm for the struggle."[50]

The schedule Goebbels set for himself demanded every bit of strength he could muster. "You hardly have time to stop and think. You swoop back and forth across Germany by train, motorcar, airplane. You arrive in a city half an hour before the event, sometimes even later, then you mount the podium and speak. . . . But in the meantime you have to contend with the heat, the words, the logic of what you're saying, with a voice that gets hoarser and hoarser, with poor acoustics, with the smell from ten thousand people crammed into one space; . . . When the speech is over, you feel as though you've just been pulled out of a hot bath with all your clothes on. Then you get back in the car and travel another two hours."[51]

The heat of the campaign and the 16 June lifting of the ban on the SA and the SS resulted in a new wave of violence. Paddy wagons rumbled through the streets of Berlin, and politically motivated murders became a daily occurrence. The Prussian government finally banned all outdoor demonstrations, only to be disbanded in turn by Papen on the constitutional grounds that it could not maintain order.

Goebbels was sitting in a pub in Treuenbrietzen in Brandenburg when the news came over the radio. He was delighted to learn that his two nemeses, Police Commissioner Grzesinski and Deputy Police Commissioner Weiss, had also been dismissed. Just a few weeks earlier the courageous Weiss had brought charges against Goebbels for defamation of character—for the seventeenth time. Like a series of other proceedings against Goebbels, these would be dropped in General von Schleicher's Christmas amnesty.[52] (Soon after Hitler took power, Grzesinski and Weiss would flee Germany under dramatic circumstances, having defended democracy for years in the face of overwhelming odds.)[53]

Goebbels would probably have liked to take revenge personally on these two men. He now noticed a "remarkable politeness" in the way their former subordinates, ordinary policemen, behaved toward him.[54] In fact, the police were doing very little. If they intervened at all, it was only against the Communists. As a result, political violence increased. On election day alone, 31 July, nine people were killed.

The outcome of the Reichstag elections must have been another disappointment to the propaganda director. Although the NSDAP came in as the strongest party, with 37.3 percent of the vote, or 230 seats, the party had improved only slightly on its performance in the March and April rounds of the presidential election. The rapid ascent seemed to be at an end.

In Goebbels's own Gau, the NSDAP with 28.6 percent of the vote had outstripped the other parties, clearly doing better in middle-class than in working-class neighborhoods.[55] "So we can't get an absolute majority this way. All right: take the other path," Goebbels commented.[56] The alternatives for the party, as he saw it, were "either bitterest opposition or power," so as to liquidate Marxism at last. The policy of toleration was destroying the revolutionary élan of the movement and threatening to split it.[57] But how was power to be achieved?

Hitler decided to confront Schleicher with the demand that he be made chancellor. He told Goebbels that he would also insist on certain positions for his close associates, including the portfolio for popular education for Goebbels.[58] In fact Hitler must have had no intention of requesting a position for Goebbels, for he knew the "barons" would never stand for it.[59]

When Goebbels joined Hitler on the Obersalzberg on 7 August, the day after Hitler's meeting with Schleicher, the general mood was very cheerful. Hitler seemed to have gained the impression that Schleicher accepted his demands. He indicated to Goebbels that if he took over the government, he would put Goebbels in charge of the Prussian Ministry of Culture, in addition to the post already mentioned.[60] Goebbels rejoiced, sensing that power was within their grasp.

After further conversation with his revered Führer, Goebbels pictured himself occupying a prominent position in the Reich: "Talked through the whole issue of popular education. I'll have schools, universities, film, radio, theater, propaganda under me. A huge area. Enough to fill a lifetime. Historic mission. I'm happy. Agree with Hitler in all essentials. That's the main thing. The patriotic education of the German people is in my hands. I will master it. . . . Talked through question of Berlin Gau with Hanke. I'll keep everything I have now. Gauleiter. Reich Prop. Dir. With deputies for all areas. But I myself will keep direct control."[61]

But on 9 August Goebbels's optimism was dampened. Hitler had just learned from Schleicher, by way of Strasser, that his appointment was more than dubious.[62] Hitler, having decided to wager everything on one card, threatened in the *Völkischer Beobachter* that a "graciously permitted inadequate participation in the government" was out of the question; he had to be appointed "to lead a Reich cabinet of prominent personalities."[63] With Goebbels's encouragement, Hitler underlined his demands by having strong detachments of storm troopers surround Berlin, and by threatening to join forces with the Catholic Center.[64]

Again Strasser provided material for conflict within the party, urging Hitler to accept the position of vice chancellor. The newspapers immediately took note of this difference of opinion, and some of them also reported dissension between Hitler and Goebbels. This latter report had no basis in fact; the reporters were probably drawing erroneous conclusions from the revolutionary tone Goebbels still cultivated in *Der Angriff*, believing as before that he had to speak for the petty-bourgeois and proletarian party supporters if they were to remain in the fold.

Hitler denied these "fictional portrayals of fragmentation within the leadership," asserting that an exemplary unity reigned.[65] He took steps to create such unity by criticizing Strasser at a meeting of party leaders on 11 August and announcing his inalterable decision to stick to his "all or nothing" position.

On the afternoon of 13 August, Goebbels found it "painful and tor-

menting" to wait for Hitler, who had left his apartment on Reichskanzlerplatz with Frick and Röhm for a decisive meeting with Hindenburg.
Upon their return, he learned the outcome. It had taken less than twenty
minutes for Hindenburg—for maybe the last time clearheaded and
firm—to tell Hitler that his conscience would not allow him to make
Hitler chancellor. In accordance with Schleicher's policy of "taming" the
Nazis, he had offered him the vice chancellorship, which Hitler had
rejected.[66]

While rumors of a Nazi putsch spread through the city like wildfire,
and crowds gathered outside Goebbels's apartment calling for the Führer,
the men huddled inside were working feverishly. Röhm and Hitler were
trying to convince the hastily summoned SA leaders that armed insurrection was futile. Goebbels dashed off a biting piece on the "reactionaries" for Der Angriff. Others dictated reports and appeals. A directive
to the SA and SS that was published in the Völkischer Beobachter ordered
a "short intermission in the struggle," during which the members of those
organizations were to "take fullest advantage of their leave" and "refrain
from musters, drills, and military reviews."[67]

Goebbels, too, allowed himself a vacation from the struggle, in Heiligendamm on the Baltic. He felt less downcast than he might have,
because Hitler had once more strengthened him in his belief that national
socialism would prevail. Filled with admiration for Hitler's "calm clarity," Goebbels used a literary allusion to describe his imperturbability:
"like a calm pole in the flurry of phenomena."[68]

After his rest by the ocean, Goebbels was summoned to Berchtesgaden.
Hitler wanted to continue on the old course. He did not believe the
NSDAP could achieve a parliamentary majority. On the other hand, he
feared the party would begin to crumble if he agreed to a coalition
government with the Catholic Center, as Gregor Strasser recommended.
He planned to use the "Center solution" as a means of bringing pressure
to bear on the "barons," to prepare the way for his becoming chancellor
at the head of a presidential cabinet. Goebbels zealously supported his
Führer's strategy, seeing a presidential cabinet as at least having "the
odor of illegality" (as compared to a coalition or opposition), if a revolutionary overthrow à la Mussolini was blocked by Hindenburg and
the Reichswehr.[69]

Goebbels felt it was crucial to emphasize the revolutionary, antireactionary thrust of the party in view of the paralyzing resignation that had
spread through the movement since Hitler's failure to achieve power on
13 August. In the confrontation with the "forces of reaction," he could
give free rein to his own hatred. Unceasingly, with fanatical commitment,
he went around making inflammatory speeches, agitating in Der Angriff,
and pushing forward the reorganization of the propaganda apparatus.

(That Magda gave birth on 1 September to their first child, Helga, seemed an incidental happy event.) The new structure of the propaganda division anticipated that of the ministry Goebbels intended one day to create and direct. Hitler expressed approval of his plans, as well he might; it cost him little to make promises whose fulfillment would not have to be decided on immediately.

On 12 September the National Socialists tried another tack. Instead of aiming for their own breakthrough to power, they now focused on destroying the Papen cabinet and the remains of the presidential system of government. Goering had been elected president of the Reichstag and had allowed a vote of no confidence proposed by the head of the KPD delegation, Ernst Torgler, to go through, ignoring Papen, who had an order in hand to dissolve the Reichstag before the vote was taken. The result showed only 42 of 512 deputies willing to back Papen.

New Reichstag elections were now scheduled for 6 November. Mindful of the impasse into which the party had maneuvered itself since August, Goebbels refrained from optimistic predictions. He could tell that the voters were annoyed at being called to the polls for the fifth time in one year. To make things worse, the coffers of the party were empty, rendering the propaganda director's job all the more difficult.[70]

Goebbels mobilized every means at his disposal. He arranged for *Der Angriff* and the other party papers to appear twice a day. As in the 1930 campaign, he had a stable of about one thousand party speakers available, trained at the "school for orators" he had founded upon coming to Berlin; he judged them the best speakers Germany had ever produced.[71] He and Hitler of course headed the list, with Hitler again undertaking a swing through the country by airplane.

Goebbels drew encouragement from Hitler's directive that Gregor Strasser should hand over to Goebbels responsibility for everything connected with radio. That meant that Goebbels was now in charge of the National German Association of Wireless Participants for Culture, the Professions, and National Concerns, founded in August 1930 by the DNVP and the Stahlhelm and controlled exclusively by Nazis since March 1932.[72] As early as late 1930 the association had put in place a network of radio monitors organized according to Gau, district, and locality, parallel to the party organization; their charge was to spread propaganda against the "Jewish-Marxist radio." NSDAP "company cells" were established at the radio stations, intended to take over the most important transmitting functions and counter any resistance when the party seized power. Goebbels expanded this infrastructure, designed a new Program for the Takeover of the Radio, and drew up new lists of personnel, so as to be well prepared for "Hour X."[73]

Goebbels saw this election campaign as the "last confrontation" the

NSDAP would have to endure before coming to power. Although the SA and the members of the KPD's illegal military arm were fighting each other in bloody street battles throughout the Reich, in Goebbels's view the real target was the "reactionaries." He had launched his campaign at the end of September with a party order forbidding National Socialists to buy the bourgeois newspapers.[74] Goebbels registered a success when he accepted an invitation from the DNVP to speak and swept the crowd away "in one great wave of enthusiasm."[75] The hall was packed with Nazis, who outnumbered the nationalists, and after the speech, as the "spontaneous marches" to the accompaniment of the "Horst Wessel Song" got underway, Goebbels was already hard at work directing his own press coverage in *Der Angriff*, for he sensed the nationalists might use their control over large portions of the press to convert their defeat into a victory.[76]

Goebbels saw it as tantamount to betrayal that Gregor Strasser had drawn the consequences of the 13 August debacle and now professed in his speeches a willingness to cooperate with Hugenberg's German Nationalists. Strasser also stressed that the National Socialist movement was ready to work with anyone who affirmed Germany and wanted to work with the Nazis to save it.[77] Strasser's appearances made Goebbels even angrier, because the bourgeois press covered them thoroughly and thereby brought to the public's attention the growing dissension in the NSDAP's ranks.

When the strike of the Berlin transit workers began on 2 November, Goebbels himself created further confusion. According to an emergency decree, wages for the workers were to be reduced slightly. Although it was a question of only two pfennigs per hour, Goebbels saw in the issue a great opportunity for the party to show "that our antireactionary course really comes from within, that the NSDAP in fact offers a new form of political action, a conscious rejection of the bourgeois methods."[78]

Following his instructions, the organization of Nazi company cells announced its readiness to strike. The Revolutionary Trade Union Opposition did likewise. Since well over half the transport workers voted in favor, the strike was declared that very evening. Goebbels reacted with annoyance to reports in the bourgeois press that he had undertaken this action without Hitler's knowledge, to guide the party "into Bolshevist waters." In fact Hitler, with whom Goebbels claimed to be in hourly contact by telephone, approved of Goebbels's course of action. Goebbels summarized Hitler's opinion thus: "If we hadn't acted in this fashion, we wouldn't be a socialist or a workers' party anymore."[79] And that was what the party remained, in Goebbels's wishful thinking.

While Goebbels and Walter Ulbricht, who had assumed leadership of the strike for the KPD, joined forces to castigate the "oppressors of workers" and "reactionaries" in the pages of *Der Angriff* and the underground edition of the banned *Rote Fahne*, Nazi and Communist strikers paraded in front of the gates to the railyards. They beat up scabs and demolished any buses and streetcars that were still running. On 4 November the violence escalated. In clashes with the police three people were shot dead and almost fifty injured.[80]

The participation of the Nazis in the transit workers' strike aroused deep middle-class fears. The physical appearance of the SA men, their methods, and their socialist slogans made it look as though the socialist wing of the party might be regaining influence; cooperation between extremists on the left and right might be just the beginning.[81] In a speech broadcast throughout Germany two days before the elections, Papen, hoping to exacerbate the distrust of the NSDAP, dwelt on this contradictory state of affairs. He noted that Hitler's battle cry against Marxism and for national renewal had seemed believable, but now the Nazis were trying to destroy the government's economic program by collaborating with "godless bolshevism," the "death of our millennia-old culture."[82]

People reacted with indignation and dismay to the Nazi-KPD collaboration. Goebbels still thought that the party's reputation among the working class had improved "splendidly" in the course of a few days, but he had to concede that the improvement would probably not manifest itself in this election. He preferred to take the long view: "After all, we want to conquer Berlin, and for that it doesn't matter whether one loses a lousy twenty thousand votes or so in a more or less pointless election. Those votes would have no significance anyway in an active, revolutionary struggle."[83]

A "stifling, muggy atmosphere" seemed to Goebbels to hang over Berlin. On election day itself there was no public transportation, because of the strike. The day passed for Goebbels in "incredible tension."[84] It was merely a question of how bad the losses would be. As the results began coming in from the middle-class districts, they showed losses for the NSDAP of 5, 6, 7 percent. The losses were smaller in working-class districts. Over all, the party's share of the vote in Berlin dropped from 28.6 to 26.2 percent. The Communists now had 31.3 percent of the vote, for the first time outdoing the SPD, with its 23.3 percent, to become the strongest party in Berlin.[85]

The NSDAP's losses in Berlin were smaller than in the rest of the Reich. There more than two million voters turned away from the party. With 196 deputies the NSDAP kept the largest delegation in the Reichstag, however, and the Center and the SPD also suffered losses. Sizable gains went to the KPD, the DNVP, and smaller parties like the DVP. The NSDAP could no longer achieve a majority in a coalition with the Center, which meant the DNVP had reached its goal of regaining its key position.

Goebbels knew that the effects of the election had to be serious, for the party had lost its aura of marching ineluctably toward power. He quickly added up the extenuating circumstances. There was the 13 August setback, for which the masses did not yet have the proper understanding. Then there was the "unscrupulous exploitation by the German nationalists' propaganda of our exploratory contacts with the Center."[86] The fact that Goebbels's attempt to win over working-class voters through involvement in the transit workers' strike had been an utter failure he skillfully twisted into the opposite. Drawing on a comparison between the elections of 1919 and 1932, he wrote in *Der Angriff*: "Considering the high voter participation and the constant number of Marxist votes, a decisive breakthrough into the Marxist camp actually occurred."[87]

Since Hitler called for continuing the struggle, Goebbels, too, immediately set his sights on the future. He wanted to give his utmost to a man who was so "fabulous" that he could cheer up his closest associates with tales of seemingly hopeless situations he had experienced during the war.[88]

No matter how energetically Goebbels wanted to resume the struggle, he made the sobering discovery that back in Berlin the "initially defiant mood" in the party had soon given way to "dull depression." Everywhere irritations, conflict, and annoyance surfaced. "As is always the case: after a defeat all the filth comes floating to the top, and you have to labor for weeks to get rid of it." In addition, contributions were dropping off rapidly, leaving the party coffers in an increasingly parlous state. "Nothing but ebbtide, debts, and obligations," Goebbels complained.[89] It was mostly a matter of bills from small creditors—vendors, tailors, carpenters—who, as long as the party's fortunes were improving and a seizure of power seemed imminent, had speculated on getting their money back with interest, and with interest on interest; now they were growing impatient. Even before the election, the *Vossische Zeitung* had commented sarcastically that it was certainly no coincidence that SA men rattling their cans now far outnumbered the beggars in the center of Berlin; they should change their slogan from "For the NSDAP Winter Aid program" to "For the Winter Aid program for the NSDAP."[90]

In view of the crisis in the party, Hitler and Goebbels had agreed to postpone reorganization in favor of "strengthening our propaganda to the utmost."[91] Goebbels ceaselessly spurred on his associates and party comrades. He gave himself the additional task of writing a daily editorial attacking the cabinet, encouraging himself with the observation that constantly dripping water will hollow out a stone.[92]

He needed all the encouragement he could get, for even when Papen dismissed his cabinet in mid-November under pressure from Schleicher, Hitler's chances of being made chancellor looked considerably slimmer than before, less because the NSDAP could no longer muster a majority in the Reichstag in cooperation with the Center Party, than because the party's enemies now felt the NSDAP had passed its zenith.

The party's supporters thought Hindenburg would now appoint Hitler. They gathered outside the Kaiserhof Hotel where he stayed in Berlin and shouted "Heil!" to the putative future chancellor. Meanwhile two meetings between Hitler and the "old man" had already resulted in a deadlock. Hindenburg had set the condition that Hitler put together a parliamentary majority.

With Goebbels egging him on, Hitler refused, on the grounds that the condition contained an inherent contradiction and could therefore not be met. Hindenburg responded that his "oath and his conscience" would not allow him to accept any arrangement that would develop into a party dictatorship.[93]

Neither Goebbels's press releases nor Hitler's appeal to the party could cover up the fact that this second attempt at seizing power had failed. As the press focused more and more on the escalating differences of opinion within the party, Strasser, Goebbels, Frick, Goering, and Röhm got together to issue a statement of unity and loyalty to the Führer in the Völkischer Beobachter.[94] This statement only gave rise to further speculation.

On 3 December Hindenburg named General Schleicher presidential chancellor. The next day Schleicher offered Gregor Strasser the positions of vice chancellor and minister of labor. When Goebbels learned of the meeting, he immediately spoke of "the most terrible betrayal of the Führer and the party." He now hoped to get rid of Strasser once and for all. He thought the break might come on 5 December at a meeting of the party leadership with Hitler at the Kaiserhof. Strasser tried again to persuade Hitler to make peace with Schleicher, who was threatening to call new elections. Strasser pointed out that elections at this point might prove disastrous. Hitler replied that merely participating in the government would surely mean the end of the movement. But the "sharpest clash" Goebbels had dreamed of did not materialize. Thanks to his superiority as an orator, Hitler succeeded in preventing a final break. He proposed a third alternative: he would give Schleicher time, provided Schleicher agreed to an amnesty, economic measures, the Nazis' right to self-defense and freedom to demonstrate, and temporary suspension of the Reichstag.[95]

So success had eluded Strasser yet again. After another confrontation with Hitler, engineered by Goebbels, in which Strasser was forbidden to accept any position in Schleicher's cabinet, Strasser simply gave up. The "sinister fellows" in Hitler's closest circle, the "limping devil" Goebbels, the "swine" Röhm, and Goering, the "brutal egotist" to whom Germany did not matter—that was how the National Socialist patriot Gregor Strasser characterized them—had almost reached their goal.[96]

On the morning of 8 December Strasser sent a letter to Hitler at the Kaiserhof in which he explained that he could no longer support the party's political course—namely, allowing Germany to fall into chaos and only then beginning the National Socialist reconstruction. He therefore wished to give up all his positions within the party, including his seat in the Reichstag, and return to the movement "as a simple soldier."[97]

Goebbels saw this as the moment when Strasser's betrayal came into the open. An article that appeared in the *Tägliche Rundschau* on 9 December seemed to offer confirmation. The paper, which often supported Schleicher, called for a Strasser-led reform of the NSDAP in which all constructive forces in the party would participate. Goebbels found other reasons for suspecting a conspiracy: his old adversary Gottfried Feder unexpectedly asked Hitler for a leave of absence at the same time.[98]

While Hitler feared that Strasser would now go on the offensive against him, Goebbels employed efficient crisis management to propel himself into the foreground with the Führer. With the Führer's approval, he had already declared in *Der Angriff* of 8 December that the leave granted Strasser for reasons of health would never affect the NSDAP's ability to continue on its course, "clear in its goal and without compromise." The Führer would never betray the program he had established from the beginning, neither to "Marxism" nor to the "forces of reaction."[99]

What counted now was the extent to which the party functionaries and especially Strasser's potential supporters could be persuaded to commit themselves to Hitler. Conditions looked favorable, for it was discovered that Strasser had left the country for a vacation in Italy. His departure took the air out of the conspiracy theory that Goebbels was spreading among Hitler's close associates. On 10 December Hitler therefore found it easy to secure the party's loyalty to himself, addressing first a gathering of Gauleiters and inspectors, then the Reichstag delegation, without attacking Strasser.

Goebbels now gloated, convinced that after six years of struggle he had finally "destroyed" Gregor Strasser. On 8 December Hitler had broken up the powerful Political Organization, which had been Strasser's department, giving Goebbels control over "popular education," which became a separate portfolio.[100] But Goebbels soon learned that things were not quite as far along as he had assumed. Hitler had avoided a final break with Strasser. He published a statement in *Der Angriff* declaring that the comments on Strasser's leave had been made without his authorization, since they contained "several tactless observations." Goebbels hastened to assure Hitler in *Der Angriff* of his subservience, stressing as so often before that he did not represent any faction in the party. For him there was "only one direction, and that is the one the Führer determines."[101]

Hitler did succeed in overcoming the crisis, although opinions in the party remained divided. The main thing was that new elections could be avoided; party support was waning rapidly, thanks to the end of the reparations payments, the end of limitations on German military activity, and signs that the worst of the Depression was over. Although the mass of the population had not yet felt any improvement, the major newspapers were stressing that the turning point had come.

In addition to the poor prospects for the party, which Goebbels explained away as the last tests to be endured before the seizure of power, the end of the year saw Goebbels's wife fall ill. When they came home from the Gau Christmas party on 23 December, she suddenly felt very sick. They summoned Prof. Walter Stoeckel, the most noted gynecologist of the day; after visiting the patient, he immediately had her admitted to the private ward of the university's women's hospital. Magda's condition was grave, as Professor Stoeckel informed Goebbels on Christmas Eve.[102] The tremendous strain of the past weeks and months had taken its toll; it was, after all, not long since she had given birth. She was suffering from the same heart spasms for which she had sought treatment several years earlier, during her marriage to Quandt, when his son Hellmuth died suddenly.

When Magda seemed to be feeling better, Goebbels, who had spent Christmas with his stepson Harald, left for Berchtesgaden to celebrate the new year with Hitler and other prominent National Socialists. Just at the moment when word came from Berlin that Magda had taken a turn for the worse, propects seemed to be opening up for Hitler and his party, which had appeared to be in an irrevocable decline. Robert Ley had come to the Obersalzberg in the company of a "gentleman from Cologne" who reported to Hitler that Werner von Alvensleben and Papen wanted to meet with him.

On New Year's Day Goebbels's youngest sister Maria summoned him hastily back to Berlin: Magda's condition had worsened dramatically.[103] Magda was past the crisis by the time he reached her bedside, but Goebbels did not know about the meeting in Cologne on 4 January that had been arranged on the Obersalzberg. At the house of the banker Baron Kurt von Schroeder, director of the exclusive Cologne Men's Club, Papen and Hitler reached an agreement. Hitler told Goebbels in detail about this "sensation" the following day. Goebbels noted in his diary: "Papen sharply against Schleicher. Wants to topple him and eliminate him completely. Still has the Old Man's ear. Lives at his residence. Arrangement with us prepared. Either the chancellorship or the powerful ministries.

Defense and interior. This isn't bad. Schleicher has no authorization to dissolve. Out on a limb."[104]

In December Goebbels had predicted that Schleicher would do himself in with his own intrigues. And in fact, all his attempts to find a broader base for his cabinet proved futile. Although he continued to woo Strasser, he did not succeed in drawing substantial segments of the NSDAP over to his side. The SPD leadership rejected any sort of pact, and the trade unions likewise turned their backs on him. His advances to those interests destroyed any credit he might have had with the Right.

For the NSDAP it was now all-important to convey mightily the impression that the worst had been overcome and that the party had embarked on an unstoppable march to power. Goebbels was planning numerous large rallies and marches for January; the deaths of a Berlin Hitler Youth and an SA man came at just the right moment. These "blood sacrifices" gave Goebbels additional pretexts for mobilizing the Berlin SA, thereby calling public attention to the party. Goebbels, who excelled at staging funeral spectacles, arranged for the two victims to have princely burials with crowds stretching "as far as the eye could see."[105]

Of great psychological importance was the election scheduled for 15 January 1933 in the tiny state of Lippe. Goebbels barely managed to scrape together the money to mount a huge propaganda extravaganza. When almost 40 percent of the voters cast their lot with the NSDAP, even though that was only six thousand more votes than in the November 1932 election, Goebbels gloated in *Der Angriff* with the banner headline "Hitler Victory! The People of Lippe Speak." Beneath the headline he wrote that the electorate was now beginning to understand "that Hitler acted correctly on 13 August and 25 November when he rejected the responsibility, if not linked with corresponding power."[106]

Goebbels also felt gratified by the outcome of the Strasser affair. After his return from Italy on 3 January, Strasser had created all sorts of confusion. The newspapers even claimed he was about to be named vice chancellor. When the outcome of the election in Lippe confirmed the rightness of his course, Hitler no longer saw any need to spare Strasser in the interest of unity. At a Gauleiter conference in Weimar, Hitler spoke for three hours, which Goebbels summarized by remarking that the Strasser case was now "a thing of the past."[107] This time he was not mistaken. The jovial Lower Bavarian, popular far beyond the borders of the party, the man Goebbels had often envied, the man he had feared in competing for the favor of Hitler and the Berlin party comrades, the man he had come to hate because he sensed that he saw through him—Gregor Strasser, one of Schleicher's last trumps in the game for power, was now forced off the political stage.

For another reason, too, Goebbels felt confirmed in his belief that things would go his way if he could only rally his will: Magda's health had taken a turn for the better. In spite of the stress of the election campaign, Hitler had inquired about her almost daily. On 19 January he and Goebbels paid her a visit at the hospital, an occasion Hitler also used for a "political seminar" with the medical faculty.[108] Professor Stoeckel recalled later how Magda Goebbels's fever "dropped suddenly," and he exclaimed spontaneously, "Herr Hitler, if your appearing at Germany's sickbed is as effective as at this sickbed, Germany must soon be healed!"[109]

Papen, Alfred Hugenberg, and Franz Seldte also succumbed to this illusion, when they entered into discussions with Hitler and Goering on the possibility of forming a national government made up of Nazis and German Nationalists. By way of reinforcement, Goebbels cranked up his propaganda machine against Streicher. To make it clear to everyone that nothing would work without the NSDAP, on 22 January he staged a huge demonstration that he hoped would provoke the Communists to violence and let them appear again as a threat to the republic. That same day Hitler was meeting with Papen, Otto Meissner, and Oskar von Hindenburg to "smooth the way."[110]

The demonstration was dedicated to the memory of Horst Wessel. National Socialists from all parts of the city streamed to Bülowplatz, close by the Karl Liebknecht House; there an enormous procession assembled, led by Hitler, Goebbels, Röhm, and other top officials of the NSDAP, and marched to the St. Nicholas cemetery, where they had buried the Sturmführer three years earlier. After drum rolls, chorales, and the old song "I Once Had a Comrade," for which the flags were dipped, Hitler spoke of Wessel's death as a symbolic sacrifice and unveiled a memorial to him. The day concluded, as had so many others, with a rally at the Sportpalast. To Goebbels's disappointment, the massive police presence averted any major incidents.[111]

On 25 January the KPD responded with a march through Berlin. *Die Rote Fahne* called it a "mighty military display against fascism," estimating the participants at 130,000.[112] Even Friedrich Stampfer, editor in chief of the Social Democratic *Vorwärts*, expressed sympathy for these masses of demonstrators, in recognition of their "more than justified hatred for the blatant injustice of existing social conditions," for which he held Schleicher partly responsible.[113] The SPD saw a far greater danger for the republic in the aristocratic general Schleicher than in the demagogue Hitler; it was still assumed by many that the Nazi phenomenon would soon evaporate.

Tension continued to rise as Schleicher tried to dissolve the Reichstag on 28 January but could not secure Hindenburg's assent. Schleicher thereupon announced the resignation of his entire cabinet. Hindenburg commissioned Papen to clear up the political situation. Goebbels, who had heard the evening before from Alvensleben that Schleicher would be resigning, was surprised at the speed with which everything moved. He immediately returned to Berlin from Rostock, where he had been addressing students. But he remained skeptical toward the "gang of traitors," as he called the inner circle of "unpredictable" men around Hindenburg. He saw every reason not to succumb to illusions.[114]

But by this time Hindenburg's resistance to Hitler's chancellorship had already been broken, for reasons that are still not entirely clear. Perhaps the aged field marshal was losing his grip, or perhaps he feared the Nazis might reveal various irregularities that would compromise his reputation for unimpeachable integrity.[115]

In these last days before Hitler gained power, Goebbels remained largely on the sidelines. On the evening of 29 January Alvensleben appeared in Goebbels's apartment and reported that Schleicher and the army chief of staff, Baron Kurt von Hammerstein, were planning a putsch. Goebbels immediately informed Hitler and Goering, who were sitting in the next room.[116] They seized the opportunity to move things along.

On 30 January Goebbels waited at the Kaiserhof with numerous other party members while Papen led the members of the planned cabinet, including Hitler, Goering, and Frick, through the snowy gardens of the ministries to the presidential palace. Demanding a ministry for Goebbels at this point would have been an obstacle to negotiations with the conservatives; Hitler had never stated as much to his propaganda director, but on the previous day he had "solemnly" promised that Goebbels would get his ministry after the new elections. In the meantime a "straw man" would be put in his place.[117]

Goebbels had declared himself satisfied for the time being, although being shunted aside must have been a painful. But then he saw his Führer get out of his motorcar in front of the Kaiserhof and, with a great sense of the theatrical, stride through the crowd into the hotel after Goering, who had bustled on ahead bellowing out the news. As Hitler silently came into the midst of his supporters and his eyes filled with tears, Goebbels's disappointment turned to joy; this man, whom he had begun to believe in years earlier, whom he had come to venerate, had just been named chancellor of the Reich.

The rest of the day passed for Goebbels as in a dream. On this day of the "great decision," this "historic turning point," this "great miracle," he went to the Gau offices and announced there that things were "becoming new." He organized and coordinated, met in between with Hitler, "a very great man," and then went with the foreign press secretary Ernst Hanfstaengl to visit his enthusiastic wife Magda, whose imminent release from the hospital gave further reason for rejoicing. Toward evening Goebbels sat in the Kaiserhof Hotel with a few others and waited for the huge torchlight procession that was to conclude the day. In the flickering torchlight, seemingly endless columns marched by singing the "Horst Wessel Song," many of them believing a better world was dawning. They marched through the Brandenburg Gate and passed the Chancellery. At one of the windows stood the ancient field marshal, staring at the formations as they passed. A few windows farther down stood the man to whom the future seemed to belong, with Goering and Hess at his side. Goebbels appeared now and then behind him, having slipped across from the hotel. He was the chief organizer of the extraordinary spectacle.

Goebbels saw in the parade the triumph of his fanatical faith, a victory of the will, for his belief in the "miracle of the impossible" had been fulfilled, and it was ten years to the day since his friend Flisges had died. Could reason have predicted that the wretched cripple from Rheydt and the stranded World War corporal with the seemingly grotesque sense of mission would have such a future? "Isn't it a miracle," Goebbels would ask later, "that a mere World War corporal now takes the place of the houses of Hohenzollern and Hapsburg?"[118] What seemed a miracle to him was actually the effect of historical and political forces and the particular constellation of protagonists who had emerged from those forces, leading up to that 30 January 1933, but by no means inevitably.

Goebbels had arranged for the event to be broadcast to the entire nation over the radio—only the Stuttgart and Munich stations refused to carry it. A directive from the new interior minister, Wilhelm Frick, enabled him to impose the broadcast on reluctant station chiefs. After an address by Goering, Goebbels continued his propaganda deception by having party members speak on the radio in the guise of "ordinary citizens" from all walks of life. Not one of them was really the person he was announced to be, not even Albert Tonak, the Red Front Combatant who had defected to the SA after the battle in Wedding's Pharus Hall and had become the Gauleiter's driver. Goebbels's concluding words were from the heart:

It is simply moving for me to see how in this city, where we began six years ago with a handful of people, the entire people is now rising up, marching by below me, workers and middle class and peasants and students and soldiers—a great community of the *Volk*, where one no longer asks whether a person is middle-class or proletarian, Catholic or Protestant, in which one asks only: What are you? To what do you belong? To what do you commit yourself in your country? That is the greatest fulfillment of this day for us National Socialists. We are not of the opinion that the struggle is over; no, tomorrow morning we shall begin with the new work and the new struggle. We are firmly convinced that the day will come when in Germany not only the National Socialist movement but an entire *Volk* will rise up, an entire *Volk* will recall its ancient values, and an entire *Volk* will set out marching toward a new future. For work and for bread, for freedom and for honor we must struggle, and we will see this struggle through, for we believe that it will bring blessings and happiness to the German nation. . . . One can rightfully say: Germany is awakening.[119]

In fact, this Germany was split into two camps, as the night of the "great miracle" would make clear. SA Sturmführer Maikowski, leader of the infamous Murder Storm Unit 33, after proudly marching past the Führer, led his men to Wallstrasse in Charlottenburg, a solidly Communist area. There they encountered Red Front Combatants; in the clash that ensued, the Sturmführer was shot to death. That same evening a policeman was killed as well.[120]

Now that the NSDAP was in power, Goebbels viewed the deaths of the SA man and the policeman as justification for the already planned propaganda campaign for the "extermination" of the Communist "blood plague." But his radical project at first encountered opposition. Hitler, with whom he met on 31 January at the Kaiserhof Hotel, wanted to preserve the appearance of legality. "First the Bolshevist attempt at revolution must flare up," he explained to the crestfallen Goebbels.[121]

In the KPD not only strikes and a general strike were being promoted; the rumor even spread that armed insurrection would be the response to Hitler's seizure of power. Neither the majority of German Communists nor many party officials expected the actual outcome, which also took the NSDAP leadership by surprise: the KPD leaders bowed to instructions from the Comintern. They did everything possible to sabotage attempts within the party to forge an antifascist alliance with the SPD, thereby aiding the Nazi takeover, whose thoroughness and rapidity they had perhaps not anticipated.[122]

As clashes between the SA and the Red Front Combatants' League became more frequent, Hitler took "legal" steps to reduce the threat. On 2 February he arranged for Goering, in his new capacity as acting Prussian interior minister, to ban all demonstrations by the KPD and related organizations throughout Prussia. At the same time house searches were conducted at KPD offices. As the *Vossische Zeitung* reported, "illegal literature" was seized at the Karl Liebknecht House.[123]

In the meantime Goebbels focused his efforts on the upcoming elections, which Hitler declared would be the last, one way or the other.[124] Goebbels paid little heed to his rival Goering's measures against the KPD. He was passionately interested, however, in the emergency decree that Hitler managed to get passed on 4 February. Entitled "For the Protection of the German *Volk*," it empowered the government to prohibit strikes in important industries, as well as gatherings and processions when "imminent danger to the public order" could be feared. The decree provided a legal basis for stopping publication of the leftist opposition's newspapers, leaving greater scope for the propaganda of the "national awakening."

Although Goebbels called unceasingly for extermination of Marxism, Hitler's alleged goal continued to be persuading people of the legality of his actions. Speakers for the NSDAP had instructions to point out that the new government owed its appointment to Hindenburg's trust. It went beyond that: election speakers who had referred to the president only a short time before as a "senile, mentally incompetent weakling," as the man who had lost the war, the "tool of the Marxists and Jesuits," now praised him as a "towering heroic figure," the "venerable, untiring trustee of his people." His name was invoked on behalf of a policy "committed to the welfare of the fatherland."[125]

It was now hammered into the Germans that only the National Socialist movement and its Führer could save them from the "Jewish-Marxist world enemy." Goebbels reinforced this message with the sort of thing in which he specialized, an impressive memorial service for those killed on the night of 31 January. It was broadcast to the entire nation.[126]

In this election campaign Goebbels made massive use of the radio, even though the NSDAP had not yet been able to fill all the leading positions with its own people. The Nazis had created the new political position of program director, but for the time being these functionaries were usually second in command. Although Goebbels spoke firmly of kicking out the "old tycoons of the system" by 5 March, he in fact realized that the real "radio reform" would not take place until after the elections.[127]

Hardly an evening passed without an election speech on every station, and those speeches took up the entire evening's programming. Hitler spoke only in cities with radio stations.[128] The broadcasts were designed to give the listeners a vivid image of the rallies, with the bombastic, emotional pseudoreligiosity that apparently stirred the masses so effectively, climaxing in the "Amen" with which Hitler ended his speeches.

Goebbels always set the scene for Hitler's broadcast speeches with a narrative full of escalating superlatives, describing the feverish tension in the crowd, the vastness of the gathering, the loss of individual isolation in the mass of people. When Hitler came on, he would whip up even greater excitement until, as Goebbels noted with satisfaction, the masses fell into an "unthinking delirium."[129]

These radio appearances gave rise to rumors that Goebbels would soon be appointed to the position of political radio commissar.[130] Such rumors intensified his gnawing feeling of having been passed over and increased his notorious distrust. He lamented that the "reactionaries" were dictating his fate, and that they wanted to shove him into a corner; Hitler was doing little to help him. His ambitious wife, who, he said, was "very unhappy" and wept with impatience at this lack of advancement, nourished his fears. When Bernhard Rust was made Prussian minister of education and culture, and Walther Funk, former editor in chief of the *Berliner Börsenzeitung*, became state secretary for press and propaganda, Goebbels fell into a "paralyzing depression." He experienced "bitter hours," felt "abandoned by everyone" and "almost weary of living."[131]

In addition, the party's poor financial situation put a crimp in his propaganda plans. "Not a frigging soul" was concerned about the money question, he complained. In Munich they were much too optimistic about the elections. When Karl Hanke informed him on 13 February that he could not expect any money for the campaign, Goebbels noted with rage in his diary that "fat Goering should go without his caviar for a change."[132]

Goering, whom Goebbels despised as a "reactionary," above all because of his luxury-loving ways, had in the meantime seized the initiative in Prussia, filling the interior ministry with his functionaries, installing SA leaders in all the police headquarters, and creating the Prussian Secret State Police, the beginnings of the Reichssicherheitshauptamt [Central Office for Reich Security]. He declared, "The measures I take will not be sicklied o'er with any legalistic compunctions."[133]

On 24 February Goering had the Karl Liebknecht House seized and closed "until further notice." The Political Police announced that "tons of seditious literature" had been found in the cellars, and that it would take weeks to sift through it all.[134] Meanwhile on 24 February *Der Angriff* devoted only nine lines to Goering's coup, and a single sentence appeared on the following day. There was no mention of printed materials calling for armed overthrow of the government or revolution. Whereas Goering's announcement had described the contents in detail, Goebbels noted merely that "seditious materials" had been seized.

Probably to demonstrate that he did not need Goering, Goebbels concentrated on his preparations for the Day of National Awakening, to be celebrated on 4 March, the day before the elections. By now his depression had lifted. Hitler had informed him that Vice Chancellor Papen had agreed to put Goebbels in charge of a new ministry. His spirits soared when he received a million-mark election contribution from leading industrialists. Now he thought he could show his opponents "what one can do with the state apparatus when one knows how to use it."[135]

On the afternoon of 27 February Goebbels settled the last details for the Day of National Awakening with several colleagues and SA leaders and gave the necessary instructions. That evening Hitler and a few other party leaders were guests of Goebbels and his wife when Ernst Hanfstaengl, who had stayed home because of a cold, telephoned and "breathlessly" demanded to speak to the Führer. When Goebbels said he could pass along any message, Hanfstaengl became impatient: "Tell him the Reichstag is on fire!" Goebbels thought it was a joke. Hanfstaengl replied curtly, "If you think it's a joke, come see for yourself!" and hung up. A few minutes later Goebbels rang back to say the Führer wanted to know what was really going on—"and no more jokes."

Writing about these events after the war, Hanfstaengl said he was at first convinced that the news really took Goebbels by surprise, even though he considered the "little doctor" a consummate liar.[136] Much speaks in favor of this first interpretation (which Hanfstaengl soon revised, after reading the foreign press), for Goebbels was convinced that, with the funds now at his disposal and the power of the state apparatus behind him, he could easily bring about an electoral victory—a success that would be his own personal triumph. Orchestrating the Reichstag fire would have involved Goebbels in close cooperation with Goering, whom he regarded with such distrust; it therefore seems highly unlikely.[137] If the Communists and others quickly identified Goebbels as the mastermind of the Reichstag fire, it was because the nocturnal inferno of 27 February seemed to fit neatly into their cliché of the "clubfooted devil," the embodiment of pure evil.[138]

Hitler and Goebbels were driven at great speed to the Reichstag, which the police had cordoned off. Upon recognizing Hitler's party, the officers let them into the area, where they had to scramble over hoses and pass rows of firemen and police. Inside they found Goering bustling about, who told them that a Communist arsonist had been arrested in the main chamber: a confused, sturdily built man with poor eyesight and a vacant gaze, identified as Marinus van der Lubbe, a Dutch mason's assistant with previous arrests for vagrancy who had been wandering around Berlin for days.[139] It turned out that he had a Communist past. When arrested, the half-naked, sweat-drenched man, who had spent the previous night in a police cell in Henningsdorf, made no attempt to deny having set the fire. He admitted soon thereafter to having decided on the deed spontaneously and having acted on his own. He said he had bought four packets of coal lighter, climbed into the building, and lit fires in several places, using his shirt as tinder. When asked why he had done this, the obviously retarded man replied, "I wanted to make people realize that the worker wants power."[140]

The first press release put out by Goering through the official Prussian Press Service depicted a major Communist conspiracy, an "unprecedented act of terrorism." A police officer had supposedly observed people with torches inside the unlit building and had fired his weapon at once. One of the perpetrators had been seized. The account went on to say that the "seditious literature" found in the Karl Liebknecht House had contained the plans for this terrorist attack, and that other important institutions and factories were next on the list. The discovery of these materials had disrupted the planned implementation of the Bolshevist revolution. "Nevertheless, the burning of the Reichstag was supposed to give the signal for a bloody uprising and civil war."[141]

Certain now of having legitimation for a decisive blow against "Marxism," Goering had the entire police force put on highest alert. While discussing this step with Hitler, he is supposed to have shouted in his excitement that anything that stood in their way should be cut down.[142] That same night about four thousand functionaries, principally from the KPD, as well as leftist intellectuals like the journalists Carl von Ossietzky and Egon Erwin Kisch, were taken into custody. Several Social Democratic party offices and publishing houses were occupied, and those SPD newspapers still in operation were banned.

Goebbels, who had been given a tour of the burning building with Hitler, Papen, and the Berlin city commandant, hurried to the Gau offices to make arrangements, then met with Hitler at the Kaiserhof. From there they went in the middle of the night to the offices of the *Völkischer Beobachter* to grind out articles and proclamations.[143]

The goal of this propaganda was to justify to the public the repressive measures introduced by Goering, to prepare the way for further steps, and again to present the Nazi movement under Hitler as the only force that could save Germany from a Communist revolution. In an article for *Der Angriff* written that night, Goebbels declared that communism had to be destroyed so completely that not even its name would remain: "Now rise up, German nation! Rise up and cast your judgment! On March the fifth let God's punishment smite the Red world plague! Hitler wants to act! Hitler will act! Give him the power to do so!"[144]

On 28 February, while Hitler Youths hawked *Der Angriff* in the streets of Berlin, and Ernst Torgler, head of the KPD Reichstag delegation, turned himself in to the police after having been accused of complicity, the Reich president granted Hitler the power he demanded. After hearing a dramatic account of the previous night's events, Hindenburg signed an emergency decree that suspended all constitutionally guaranteed rights, extended the death penalty, and provided numerous powers that could be used against the states. The emergency decree "For the Protection of the People and the State," followed by a further decree issued that same day, "Against Treason against the German People and Seditious Actions," and by the "Enabling Act" a few weeks later, provided the crucial pseudolegal basis for Nazi rule. Without a doubt it was the most important law passed in the Third Reich, for constitutional rule was now replaced by a permanent state of emergency.

Throughout Germany thousands of Communists and Social Democrats were arrested. In cellars and back courtyards SA men brutally settled old accounts. Red Front Combatants switched over to the brownshirts, out of either fear or fascination. Meanwhile Goebbels's propaganda campaign ran like clockwork. After spectacular mass rallies in Breslau, Hamburg, and Berlin, it approached its culmination on the Day of National Awakening. For Hitler's address to the German people, which would be broadcast on all stations, Goebbels had chosen the ancient Prussian coronation city, Königsberg, in an obvious allusion to the absolute majority expected in the elections of the following day. After Hitler had concluded his speech with an appeal to the German people to carry their heads "high and proud" again, his final words were drowned out in the chords of the "Dutch Prayer of Thanksgiving," whose last stanza was in turn drowned out by the bells of Königsberg cathedral. At that same hour columns of storm troopers were on the march everywhere, and on mountains and along the borders "freedom bonfires" were lit. Intoxicated by his own theatrical effects, Goebbels wrote: "Forty million people . . . become aware of the great turning point. Hundreds of thousands will take the final decision to fall in behind Hitler and fight in his spirit for the resurrection of the nation. . . . All Germany resembles a single great, glowing torch. Indeed this has become, as we wanted it to, the 'Day of National Awakening.' "[145]

But Goebbels's high hopes were not fulfilled. With only 43.9 percent of the vote, the Nazis failed to achieve an absolute majority and remained dependent on their coalition partner, the DNVP, which received 8 percent. The Center and the Social Democrats still received 11.3 and 18.3 percent respectively, and at 12.3 percent the Communists had not lost many votes. It was particularly disappointing to Goebbels that in Berlin the Nazis received only 31.3 percent, making them the second-weakest party.

Goebbels converted these results by way of propaganda into a "fantastic and unbelievable" victory, a "glorious triumph." He could not and would not admit even to himself that, despite the most favorable circumstances, the objective had not been achieved. "But what do numbers mean to us now? We are the masters in the Reich and in Prussia; all the others have sunk to the ground, beaten. . . . Germany has awakened," he told himself, in defiance of the facts.[146]

Goebbels's propaganda had thus not conquered the Reich or its capital for the Nazis—in purely numerical terms. Yet in a decisive fashion it had contributed to the party's ascent to influence and power, for it had lent dynamism to this rather placid South German movement. His propaganda gave breadth to the movement by bridging seemingly unbridgeable differences, by holding together elements that did not belong together. When Goebbels as Gauleiter and later as propaganda director continued to spout his hate-filled propaganda against the bourgeoisie and the "reactionaries," pushing socialism, he bound the proletarian-socialist part of the party's base to himself and ultimately to the "reactionary" Hitler, to whom he had committed himself unconditionally. His actions, which corresponded to his inner conflict, his psychic deformation, deserved credit for keeping the party together when the Bamberg conference, the Stennes putsch, or the Strasser crises might easily have split it in two.

These contradictory elements could not have been united by party programs, but only by personal influence. Goebbels had understood how to make the masses vulnerable to the Austrian corporal and political agitator, to a misfit with a ridiculous sense of mission. Just as this man had become his personal point of reference and support, Goebbels made Hitler the people's point of reference and support by celebrating him in pseudoreligious deification as the bearer of hope, as the guidepost pointing the way out of the despair and deprivation of the times.[147]

Yet even this accomplishment would not have been enough to lead to success, as the last Reichstag elections showed, when the Nazis had the advantages of an incumbent chancellor, an enlarged election apparatus, and an opposition already partially in disarray. It took a major economic crisis, the failure of the democratic parties, a senile president, and finally an arrogant clique of aristocrats who thought themselves omnipotent and who measured Hitler by their own standards. When Hitler found himself in a hopeless situation in the second half of 1932, it was they who actually held the stirrup to power for him. They embodied a "system" in which there had once been no place for an unemployed and physically handicapped young man with a Ph.D. Goebbels despised them all the more because of their weakness. Later he would remark maliciously that it would probably "always remain one of the best jokes of democracy that it provided its own mortal enemies with the means by which it was destroyed."[148]

CHAPTER 9

We want to work on people until they can no longer resist us (1933)

On 14 March 1933 it was reported that President Hindenburg had just sworn in Dr. Joseph Goebbels as Reich minister for popular enlightenment and propaganda. "Well, I guess the trumpeter wants to make something of himself, too," the president is supposed to have said when he signed the appointment document. Six and a half years after moving to Berlin from Elberfeld, Goebbels now found himself in a position to let the "sword of his rage" "whiz down and strike to the ground in their arrogance" those he hated the most—Jews and Marxists. All the others he wanted to unite into a National Socialist *Volk* community, kneading and forming them as if to prove that they were really only a "pile of shit," as he so often described them.[1]

Officially the new ministry was intended to promote "enlightenment and propaganda among the populace as to the policies of the Reich government and the national reconstruction of the German fatherland."[2] The actual purpose was to set in motion a "mental mobilization" of the masses, to work on them "until they can no longer resist us."[3] When the new minister, at thirty-five the youngest member of the cabinet, first spoke at a government press conference on 16 March, he described his goal without mincing words: the people had to begin "to think uniformly, to react uniformly, and to place themselves body and soul at the disposal of the government."[4]

The people as a willing tool in Hitler's hands corresponded to Goebbels's vision of a "united people," a term he borrowed from Schiller's *Wilhelm Tell.* If this government was determined "never to yield, never, in any way, or under any circumstances," he said, it could not be content in the long run to have only 52 percent of the population behind it and to have to terrorize the other 48 percent; rather, it would make winning over that 48 percent its first task.[5]

The National Socialists' partners from the traditional elite had long

172

resisted putting propaganda in the hands of this man, who in the past had missed no opportunity to stir up public opinion against them. Hitler had had to bring considerable pressure to bear on Vice Chancellor Papen before he would assent. Hugenberg, formerly and now again minister for economics and nutrition, held out the longest, but eventually Hitler had the entire cabinet where he wanted it.[6]

On 6 March Goebbels had already discussed the structure of the ministry with Hitler. Like the party's propaganda bureau, it was to unite five departments—for the press, radio, film, theater, and propaganda—in "a single large-scale organization."[7] But responsibility for "popular education," which Hitler had dangled in front of Goebbels in January and August 1932, he turned over instead to the Gauleiter of Hanover, Bernhard Rust, a former teacher and acting minister of education and culture in Prussia, who was to become Reich minister for science, education, and popular development.[8] Goebbels quickly overcame his disappointment, for the areas assigned to him all represented things "that mean a great deal to me personally, to which I will therefore dedicate myself with all zeal and with a deep inner sense of commitment."[9]

Goebbels had not been altogether happy with the name Hitler had chosen for his ministry. The name seemed not to do justice to the extensive responsibilities the ministry would have in the areas of culture and the arts, and the word "propaganda" had "a bitter aftertaste" for Goebbels.[10] But when Hitler objected to the name he preferred—Reich Ministry for Culture and Popular Enlightenment—Goebbels quickly talked himself out of his objections to "propaganda," transforming it into a political art, a creative process, a question of productive imagination—in short, something entirely positive.[11]

There was no debate over the location of the new ministry: the Leopold Palace on Wilhelmplatz, built in 1737 and remodeled one hundred years later by the great Berlin architect Karl Friedrich Schinkel. Goebbels was delighted with the building, but found various things "out of date and obsolete."[12] He brought in a crew of SA men to knock the plaster off the walls and pull down the heavy velvet draperies, dusty and motheaten, because he "could not work" in this gloomy atmosphere.[13] On 22 March Goebbels's headquarters were ready for him.

As he set about creating a ministry that was "National Socialist by birth," Goebbels made sure that positions in Berlin and throughout the country were occupied almost exclusively by party members. The majority of them were hardly more than thirty, which made them on average ten years younger than the party elite.[14] Goebbels was well aware that they would not have the intimate knowledge of bureaucratic practices that the older officials had, but he was looking for qualities that would serve his purposes better—"ardor, enthusiasm, untarnished idealism."[15]

Goebbels succeeded in gathering an ambitious and efficient staff, highly educated (more than half of them had attended the university, and many of those had doctorates), and imbued with a deep resentment against a "system" that despite their education had left many of them unemployed. Like Goebbels, most of them came from the bourgeoisie or petty bourgeoisie and had joined the NSDAP well before 1933.[16] Quite a few of them had already worked with Goebbels in the Reich propaganda directorate, the Gauleiter's office, or on the staff of *Der Angriff*. Almost one hundred of the three hundred fifty officials and staffers with whom Goebbels began wore the golden party badge.[17]

Goebbels named as his special assistant twenty-nine-year-old Karl Hanke, who had earlier worked as organization leader for the Berlin Gau and as bureau chief of the NSDAP propaganda directorate. With this confidant of many years, who had become his personal adjutant in 1932 and had been promoted to the ministerial council in June 1933, Goebbels set current policy.[18]

Hitler had offered one of his most important economic advisors, Walther Funk, responsibility for organization and finances. From 30 January 1933 until the end of 1937 Funk also served as chief government press secretary. Hitler had directed Funk to organize the Propaganda Ministry "so that Goebbels will not have to bother with administrative, financial, and organizational issues."[19] As manager Funk turned out to be perhaps Goebbels's most effective supporter in the interparty struggle over jurisdictions.

Twenty-six-year-old Wilhelm Haegert was put in charge of the propaganda department, which of course enjoyed a privileged position within the ministry.[20] Starting out as an NSDAP deputy leader in Angermünde, in 1931 Haegert had become head of the legal rights protection unit for the Greater Berlin Gau, and had advanced to staff director in the Munich Reich propaganda directorate before Goebbels tapped him for his ministry.

Goebbels appointed Ernst Seeger head of the department responsible for film, and Otto Laubinger was in charge of theater. To head the press department, Goebbels chose Kurt Jahncke, who at the same time worked as Funk's deputy in the government press secretary's office. His assignment was to make sure that the press not only "informed" but also "instructed," as Goebbels formulated it on 16 March. The press had to be "a piano, so to speak, in the hands of the government," on which the government could play. Since monotony and boredom might result if this "ideal state" were achieved, Goebbels developed a theory that the press should be "uniform in principles" but "polyform in the nuances."[21] Goebbels himself saw in the press, as hitherto constituted, a product and instrument of the liberal and enlightening spirit of the French Revolution;

it would therefore try "to do everything possible to resist totalitarian notions and orientation."[22] The influence of "international Judaism" seemed particularly strong. As early as 1926 he had come up with the "analysis" that the newspapers in particular were "messengers of decay," "forces driving toward collapse" that contaminated the "beliefs, customs, and national pride" of "good Germans."[23]

All this was to change. Three press services—the officious Wolff Telegraph Bureau, Hugenberg's Telegraph Union, and the Continental Telegraph Company—were merged to form the German News Service (DNB), which was placed under the supervision of the Propaganda Ministry and became a state monopoly. The crucial process of *Gleichschaltung*, or bringing into line, was overseen by Alfred-Ingemar Berndt, a young man not yet twenty-eight whose competence and ruthlessness so impressed Goebbels that the propaganda minister later gave him important functions in his ministry.[24]

A decisive step toward the *Gleichschaltung* of the press was accomplished by the Editor Statute, which gave to newspaper editors responsibilities that had previously rested only with publishers. Now both were subject to direct intervention by the state. The sanctions Goebbels had at his disposal included removing an editor from the list of those in the profession, issuing a warning, or even "committing" a paper's editor to a concentration camp.

The first wave of newspaper bans on the basis of the decree "For the Protection of the German People" had already had a deterrent effect; after the decree was promulgated on 4 February 1933, several "Jewish organs" succumbed.[25] Then came leftist papers, among them the SPD's *Vorwärts* and the KPD's *Rote Fahne*; Goebbels noted that it "did one's heart good."[26] In July 1933 he had the pleasure of celebrating the end of the huge Mosse publishing enterprise, which had rejected his job application a decade earlier; he rejoiced at the "collapse of a Jewish-liberalistic citadel."[27] In November 1933 the Ullstein publishing house underwent *Gleichschaltung*, and in March 1934 Goebbels stopped publication of its venerable *Vossische Zeitung*. The *Frankfurter Zeitung* remained the exception. This leading paper of the liberal middle class with its large foreign readership was allowed by the Nazis to continue publishing until the end of August 1943, as a token of tolerance.[28] It succeeded better than any other paper in preserving its integrity; occasionally critical points of view peeked out between the lines.

In addition to outright bans, economic pressure, and purges within the editorial ranks of the papers permitted to continue, Goebbels used the "press conference with the Reich government," instituted in 1917 and now renamed "press conference of the Reich government," as his chief instrument for steering the press. He himself participated in the press conference only for the most important matters.[29] Previously the steering committee of the conference had admitted or accredited journalists to the conference. Now the press department of the Propaganda Ministry selected the participants, who were assembled each day at noon to receive the official "directives" and "instructions." Editors also received "confidential information" from the NSDAP press secretary's office. And Goebbels's propaganda directorate ran a magazine service that issued such publications as *Our Will and Way* (from 1936 on) and *Word of the Week* (from 1937 on). These sources contained detailed orders on all imaginable aspects of life—between 1933 and 1945 about seventy-five thousand individual questions were addressed.[30]

Yet control of the press did not rest exclusively in Goebbels's hands. According to his principle of divide-and-conquer, Hitler had given Otto Dietrich, president of the Reich Association of the German Press and vice president of the Reich Press Chamber, responsibility for ideological oversight and direction of editors; furthermore, Dietrich had immediate access to Hitler. Dietrich's desire to issue his own directives to the press representatives soon led to tension and conflict with the Propaganda Ministry.[31]

Another counterweight to Goebbels could be found in Max Amann, president of the Reich Press Chamber and director of the party-owned Eher Publishing House. If in 1933 the NSDAP owned only 2.5 percent of all German newspaper publishing houses, with about 120 dailies and weeklies, accounting for a combined circulation of about one million, by 1939 Amann had bought up about fifteen hundred publishing houses with more than two thousand newspapers. These included the *Frankfurter Zeitung*, purchased in 1939 for Hitler's fiftieth birthday. By 1945 the Nazi publishing trust had swallowed up more than 80 percent of all German publishing companies.[32]

Goebbels took a particular interest in the radio and soon had complete control over it. He considered this medium, now barely ten years old, "by nature authoritarian" and the instrument par excellence—until such a time as televison should be developed—for influencing the masses. He thought it "automatically offers itself to the Total State."[33] To create the technical prerequisites for reaching the entire population, Goebbels had the network of stations expanded, had "Reich loudspeaker columns" erected on streets and squares, and pushed the production of an inexpensive "*Volk* wireless." This radio, available for seventy-six marks, was later nicknamed the "Goebbels blaster" and was the subject of numerous underground jokes.[34]

Even before becoming minister, Goebbels had begun bringing the radio under his organizational control. He cherished the ambition of "creating the first modern broadcasting system in the world."[35] Eleven days after he was made minister of propaganda, Goebbels summoned the general managers and directors of the radio companies to the Berlin Broadcast House. Pounding repeatedly on the lectern, he made it unmistakably clear who now had the say: "We make no bones about it: the radio belongs to us, to no one else! And we will place the radio at the service of our idea, and no other idea shall be expressed through it." In concluding, he ordered a "purge" that would eliminate the "last remnants of Marxism" from broadcasting.[36]

Victims of this purge included the general managers of formerly independent regional broadcasting companies, as well as the directors of many news, lecture, and entertainment departments. Many of the pioneers of early radio—in Goebbels's eyes "literary types, liberalists, technnocrats, money grubbers, and freeloaders"—disappeared from public view, to be replaced by functionaries with the correct political credentials.[37]

A "fantastic wave of political influence, agitation, and propaganda in every form" now flooded over the German listening public.[38] In the early months the broadcasts consisted primarily of speeches delivered by top party functionaries at the many national festivals and mass events. Radio and newsreel came into their own for the first time at the ceremony marking the 1933 opening of the Reichstag. Goebbels intended to shape this 21 March into a "Day of National Uprising," but he did not manage to exclude—as he would have liked to—the Reichswehr, the Stahlhelm, various monarchists' associations, and the churches.[39] The choreography of the event—church services in the Potsdam church of St. Nicholas and in St. Peter and Paul, a ceremony in the Garrison Church (where Frederick the Great was buried), and a concluding parade—did not entirely please him, because it contained too few Nazi elements. He therefore prevailed upon Hitler not to participate in any of the preliminary events, but to appear only at the Garrison Church.[40] Goebbels then organized for Hitler a ceremony "in honor of the fallen." It took place at the Luisenstadt Cemetery, where several SA men who had died in street fighting lay buried.

The subsequent ceremony in the Garrison Church was designed to stress the new regime's continuity with ancient Prussian tradition. Hitler wore a top hat and tails for the occasion, and Goebbels claimed to have seen tears in old Hindenburg's eyes.[41]

This "Day of Potsdam," captured on millions of postcards and posters in the image of the field marshal and the chancellor shaking hands, evoked nationalist emotion and suggested to many, not just to middle-class conservative Germans, a reconciliation between the old and new Germany. The atmosphere of nationalistic fervor still prevailed two days later when the Reichstag convened in the Kroll Opera, draped with swastika flags and cordoned off by the SS, and passed the Enabling Act. Even the Center and the Deutsche Staatspartei [German State Party] assented. Only the SPD delegation, its ranks much thinned by persecution and arrests, refused to vote for granting Hitler complete freedom of action for four years, as the decree stipulated. Before the vote, the head of the SPD delegation, Otto Wels, delivered a courageous speech, in which he explained why his party rejected the decree and appealed to the German people's sense of justice. He concluded with greetings to those who were persecuted and in desperate straits. It was the last oppositional speech in the parliament, which thenceforth provided merely a setting for the Führer's appearances; after all, the Nazis were now "constitutionally the masters in the Reich," as Goebbels noted smugly in his diary.[42]

The day after that portentous session, Goebbels succeeded in having introduced a piece of legislation he had been planning for some time: the first of May would become the national holiday, in fulfillment of an old dream of the German working class.

Thus the new regime tried to offer something to every group in society. But anyone who did not cooperate, who dared to express opposition, was hounded, "reeducated," or, if he did not succumb to reeducation, "snuffed out." Criticism was now permitted only to those "who aren't afraid of landing in a concentration camp," Goebbels warned in *Der Angriff*.[43] Goebbels even enjoyed having some of those about to be shipped off—like the East Prussian writer Ernst Wiechert—"presented" to him, so he could intellectually "stick" them (like pigs) with brutal verbal "philippics," as he phrased it.[44]

Goebbels seemed to derive great satisfaction from such episodes. He gloated over the orgy of revenge that followed the Reichstag fire. Thousands disappeared into concentration camps, men like the Social Democrat Julius Leber, the trade-union official Wilhelm Leuschner, and the anarchist Erich Mühsam. This writer Goebbels called a "Jewish subversive," promising they would make short work of him, and in fact Mühsam died in 1934 from torture in the Oranienburg camp. Many general managers of broadcasting stations also ended up in Oranienburg, on Goebbels's orders.[45] "Ali" Höhler, who had fired the fatal shots at Horst Wessel in 1930, was dragged out of prison under false pretenses by the SA and bestially murdered in a forest outside Berlin.[46]

From his first day in office Goebbels saw it as his "duty" to mobilize his apparatus against those he considered not only responsible for Germany's past misfortunes but also a threat to the nation's future survival—the Jews. Hitler had summoned his propaganda minister to Berchtesgaden so that the two of them and a few others could devise the signal for "eliminating" the Jews from the "body of the German *Volk*."

In "the solitude of the mountains," where according to Hitler he could "think most clearly," the Führer had made the decision to launch a major operation.[47]

Goebbels arrived at the Berghof on 26 March to find several leading party functionaries assembled. Julius Streicher, editor of *Der Stürmer* and a rabid anti-Semite, was put in charge of the newly created Central Committee, which would coordinate planning and organization. Also assigned to this committee were Reinhold Muchow, Goebbels's former collaborator and now deputy director of the Nazi factory cells organization, Heinrich Himmler, and Robert Ley.[48] They agreed that they would need some pretext to justify their operation to the German people and members of the government, something over and above the commonplace that international Jewry was to blame for everything. They lit upon the critical attitude expressed by the English and American newspapers toward the Hitler-Papen government (Goebbels spoke of an "atrocity campaign"), which they ascribed to a plot fomented by "subversive Jewry." The projected boycott of Jews would thus bear the character of a defensive measure decisively carried out to preserve the Reich.[49]

Goebbels prepared a paper calling on all party organizations to boycott Jewish businesses on 1 April 1933.[50] Under Point 11 he wrote: "National Socialists, you performed the miracle of overthrowing the November state in a single attack; you will solve this second assignment in similar fashion. Let international Jewry be put on notice: ... We took care of the Marxist agitators in Germany, and they won't force us to our knees, even if they now carry on from abroad their criminal treachery against the *Volk*. National Socialists! Saturday, at the stroke of ten, the Jews will find out whom they've declared war on!"[51]

On the day of the boycott—also the day on which the Propaganda Ministry officially began operation—Goebbels spoke in the Berlin Lustgarten "against the atrocities of world Jewry." In his speech, broadcast on all German stations, Goebbels announced that if the German Jews asserted that they could not prevent their fellows in England and America from dragging the patriotic forces in Germany through the mire, the National Socialists likewise could not avoid calling the Jews to account, "absolutely constitutionally and legally." A few days later this principle was implemented when the Reichstag passed a law, "For the Restoration of the Professional Civil Service," that excluded "non-Aryans" from civil-service jobs. Goebbels threatened further that the "sins" of the Jews would not be forgotten: "From graves in Flanders and Poland two million German soldiers rise up to charge that in Germany the Jew Toller was allowed to write that the heroic ideal is the most stupid of ideals. Two million rise up to charge that the Jewish *Weltbühne* was allowed to write,

'Soldiers are always murderers,' that the Jewish professor Lessing was allowed to write, 'German soldiers fell for something not worth a damn.' "[52]

Goebbels closed with an appeal to believe in "our proud mission." Throughout Germany that same day, Jews were hauled off, SA patrols surrounded Jewish stores, shopwindows were smeared or smashed. In Leipzig Jewish synagogues and meeting houses were raided.[53] Goebbels, who followed the action closely from Berlin, found it an "impressive spectacle" and noted with satisfaction the "exemplary discipline."[54] But the general population did not receive all this nearly as positively as Goebbels had hoped.

Goebbels wanted the celebration of the Führer's birthday on 20 April to be all the more impressive; it was to become the main event in the Nazi calendar. An evening radio address by Goebbels apostrophizing Hitler as the savior of the nation was followed on the actual birthday by parades, marches, and celebrations throughout the country. This event was hardly past when planning began for May Day, which Goebbels, who had been put in charge, wanted to make a mass event such as the world had never seen, "a masterpiece of organization and mass demonstrations."[55] He worked for days on the nighttime festivities at Tempelhof Field. The planning group Goebbels had assembled was soon joined by a young architect, an assistant at Berlin's Technical University, who had become a member of the SA in 1931 and of the SS the following year. Albert Speer developed a new scheme for the backdrop and the lighting that attracted Goebbels's attention; Speer commented that the original plan would have been more appropriate for a rifle club meet.[56]

Goebbels's work was briefly interrupted by a trip home to Rheydt. The city government, now controlled by the NSDAP, had taken up his friend Fritz Prang's suggestion that Goebbels be made an honorary citizen. Those who had stigmatized the intelligent but eccentric boy because of his physical deformity, those who had mocked him when he had left home and then returned as a party speaker, now fell all over themselves trying to get his attention. Such behavior could only confirm his scorn for "man, that cur." Although he wrote in the published version of his diary that he accepted the honor only for his mother's sake, this was clearly not the case.[57] He could not wait to "show them"—and himself. Here was compensation for all the humiliations of those years. As he drove from Cologne, where he had arrived by special plane on 23 April, the streets were lined with people waving to the limousine of the "Herr Reichsminister." The city was decked out in flags, and Dahlener Strasse, where he had grown up, had been renamed Joseph-Goebbels-Strasse.

The program was elaborate. It began with a production of Max Halbe's *Youth* in the municipal hall, with a well-known actress. The following morning there was a tour of Goebbels's old school, where he "pressed his old teachers' hands for a long time" and, as the *Rheydter Zeitung* put it, could hardly say a word, "so deep was his emotion." He then appeared before the assembled student body in the auditorium, where the principal praised him as an "adornment to the school, a pride to this town, and a glory to our German fatherland." The Herr Reichsminister had laid the foundation for this "high and proud success" in an education "that I can truly call humanistic." By humanistic he meant "the general goal of becoming a *homo humanus*, a true human being, a harmoniously formed personality."[58]

That evening Goebbels received the certificate of honorary citizenship at the festively decorated City Hall, before a crowd that included his mother, his wife, his stepson Harald Quandt, his brothers and sister, and old friends. From the steps of the building he then addressed the crowd outside, announcing to "indescribable rejoicing" that Rheydt would soon be separated from Mönchengladbach to become an independent municipality.[59]

The celebration concluded with a torchlight procession that Goebbels reviewed, arm raised in the Hitler salute, from an open car in front of his parents' house, while his family watched from the narrow windows. After a gathering with old acquaintances and party members, and a night at the Palace Hotel, he set out for Berlin, profoundly satisfied.

Back in Berlin he threw himself into the preparations for the Day of National Labor, which on 1 May brought hundreds of thousands to Tempelhof Field. One of the guests of honor, the French ambassador André François-Poncet, described Hitler's evening speech thus: "After some introductory words by Goebbels, Hitler mounts the speaker's platform. The spotlights go out, except for those that surround the Führer with blazing brightness, so that he seems to float above the waves of the masses like an enchanted ship. It's as quiet as in church. Hitler speaks."[60]

When this first National Day of Labor concluded with spectacular fireworks, culminating in a huge portrait of the Führer in Bengal lights, Goebbels was overwhelmed by what he had achieved. He wrote that the Berliners, who only a few years earlier had been shooting each other with machine guns, had all turned out for the event—with wives and children—workers and middle class, high and low. "A wild intoxication of enthusiasm has seized hold of everyone. Full of strength and conviction, the 'Horst Wessel Song' soars toward the eternal night sky. The airwaves carry the voices . . . across all Germany . . . and everywhere they join the singing. . . . Here none may hold back, here we all belong together, and it's no longer an empty phrase: we have become a united people of brothers."[61]

Although Goebbels was still deluding himself about the "united people," after only a few months of Nazi rule the opposition was indeed crumbling. Workers in large numbers turned their backs on their parties and unions, making it easy for the Nazis to take the next steps. Without encountering resistance, SS and SA units moved in on 2 May to occupy union headquarters and workers' credit unions. Soon thereafter Goering gave orders that all party buildings and the SPD and Reichsbanner financial holdings be seized.

In the process of *Gleichschaltung* the rest of the political parties, organizations, and associations were crushed. The Protestant Church managed to resist, at the price of being split into two parts: the oppositional Confessing Church and the collaborating German Christians. The Catholic Church, which had at first announced its opposition to Hitler, was dragged into the Nazi camp by a concordat negotiated between the Vatican and Hitler; the language of the document, which emphasized "freedom of religious profession and the Catholic religion," did not fail to make an impression on German Catholics.

At German universities, too, few voices of protest were heard. Many university professors saw in national socialism the "*Volk* community" and "organic leadership" about which they had theorized in their courses for years. Noted professors like the philosopher Martin Heidegger, the art historian Wilhelm Pinder, and the surgeon Ferdinand Sauerbruch signed their names to proclamations and declarations of loyalty. The German Student Association, trying to compete with the National Socialist Student League, had elected a Nazi to lead it as early as July 1931. In April 1933 the Association now approached a representative of the Propaganda Ministry, requesting support for a "symbolic" burning of "subversive writings"—by Jewish, Marxist, or other "non-German" authors—planned for early May. Goebbels, whom the students had already listed as the main speaker for the Berlin book burning, had mixed feelings about the event. After all, he himself had studied with Jewish professors like Gundolf and Waldberg. As a non-Aryan the latter, a glowing German patriot, had just been stricken from the list of instructors. In earlier years Goebbels had praised both professors to the skies, and even when he began to see Jewry as the world's downfall, his boundless hatred did not extend to these men personally. Since he now feared that appearing at the book burning might cause his enemies to resurrect his past, he let the German Student Association dangle until the last minute. Finally, a week before the event, he had his adjutant convey his acceptance.

When Goebbels arrived at the Opernplatz in an open car, it was around midnight, and at that hour bonfires were blazing in many German university towns. Goebbels seemed "not particularly enthusiastic." Nonetheless, at the beginning of his address he proclaimed the end of an "era of Jewish hyperintellectualism." In the flames of twenty thousand burning books he saw the "intellectual basis of the November republic" being consumed. But apparently he was not in his usual form during the short address, which was broadcast over the radio. He spoke in a "rather civilized" tone instead of his usual "grating and screeching voice" and tried "rather to act as a brake than to incite," as Golo Mann recalled from observation. Even so, Goebbels was branding some of Germany's greatest intellectual and cultural resources as "intellectual filth" produced by "Jewish asphalt literati."[62]

Goebbels's wife Magda, no less radically committed to national socialism than he, also offered her services to the regime around this time. On 14 May she broadcast the first Mother's Day address—"in perfect form," as her husband noted proudly.[63] In it she stressed that the "German mother instinctively" placed herself at Hitler's side and "after grasping his noble spiritual and moral goals, became his enthusiastic supporter and fanatical warrior."[64] The propaganda minister's blond, blue-eyed spouse made an excellent representative of Nazi Germany, since she corresponded so perfectly to the Nazis' cliché of the "modern German woman." In the National Socialist state, which was supposed to be "masculine" in character, a woman had the duty, as Goebbels once expressed it concisely, "to be pretty and bring children into the world."[65]

Magda, who always had an exceptionally good rapport with Hitler, now proved helpful to the upstart Goebbels in many respects. In contrast to her husband, who was not fluent in any living languages, she knew several well, including Italian, which stood them in good stead when they took their first trip abroad, to Rome, in late May 1933. Elegant and versed in the ways of society, Magda Goebbels handled her public appearances self-assuredly and effectively. Thanks to her, Goebbels's worries about whether he would make a "proper impression" during this state visit quickly dissipated. Time and again he noted in his diary how "wonderfully" Magda carried things off, especially the gala dinner, where she was seated by Mussolini, one of her "great conquests." Mussolini was extravagant in his compliments and said "fabulous" things about Magda.[66]

But Magda not only gave her husband self-confidence; she also watched ambitiously over his political influence. She suffered with him when rivalry with heads of other ministries upset him.[67] The decree establishing Goebbels's ministry had not precisely defined its areas of responsibility, but empowered the chancellor to do so.[68] Since Hitler intentionally left certain areas gray, conflict between the various jurisdictions was inevitable. Goebbels had probably his most serious conflict initially with Reich Interior Minister Frick, whose ministry had previously had primary responsibility for cultural matters.[69] Frick was no mean opponent, but

Goebbels soon succeeded, with the help of the cagey tactician Funk, in outmaneuvering him. Not without pride he recorded in his diary, "The entire cultural division of the interior ministry is now firmly in my bailiwick."[70]

In the "Reich Chancellor's Decree on the Responsibilities of the Reich Minister for Popular Enlightenment and Propaganda," not issued until 30 June 1933 because of the conflict with Frick, Hitler did not give Goebbels everything he wanted. But he did make him responsible for "all areas involving intellectual influence on the nation."[71] From the Interior Ministry he took over "general indoctrination in domestic politics, Institute of Political Science, introduction and festivities for national holidays and state ceremonies in cooperation with the Reich minister of the interior, press (with the School of Journalism), broadcasting, national anthem, German Book Series in Leipzig, art, music cultivation, including the Philharmonic Orchestra, theater matters, cinema," as well as "struggle against foulness and filth."[72]

The Economics Ministry had to turn over to Goebbels commercial promotion, exhibitions, fairs, and advertising. The Ministry of Transportation had to give him transportation advertising. According to the decree, the Foreign Office had to hand over "news dissemination and education abroad," as well as "art, art exhibitions, film, and sports." The press office of the Reich government, previously located within the Foreign Office, was to be moved into the Propaganda Ministry.[73]

On the matter of jurisdictions Goebbels also had a run-in with Goering in the summer of 1933, although their relationship had improved markedly since Goebbels had become a minister himself. Now that he no longer felt overlooked, he had welcomed Goering's appointment as Prussian prime minister, for it meant that "for this largest province a clear, sharp National Socialist course is now guaranteed."[74] But the harmony did not last long. Goebbels, who was master of the Reich theaters, including the Volksbühne, the theater on Nollendorfplatz, and the German Opera in Berlin, as well as theaters elsewhere, constantly harped on the "fat man's" fetish for fancy uniforms.[75] In June, when Goering refused to surrender control of the Prussian state theaters, Goebbels became furious at his "insolent pretensions" and dragged out the old charge that Goering was soft on the "reactionary" nobility.[76] What galled Goebbels was that the theaters under his control could not hold a candle to Goering's, and Goering was not prepared to let this "treasure" out of his hands, though Goebbels tried repeatedly to wrest it from him.

The conflict broke into the open when Goering moved to contest the propaganda minister's monopoly over the radio. In a letter circulated to several ministries and provincial governments, Goering argued that it was unsuitable to have all broadcasting administered by one agency, since different regions had different traditions and interests that should be represented. Close cooperation between the Reich and the individual provinces was necessary for the most effective use of the medium.[77] When Goebbels found out about this letter, he saw it as his "reason to strike." He branded the letter "shameless impudence," was "absolutely furious," and would have liked to "run straight to Hitler" to get him to make a decision. But he decided to "let the matter ripen."[78] He was convinced that Goering would be pulled up short this time because Hitler, like Goebbels, considered "tight organization" the be-all and end-all.[79] "Not preservation but liquidation" was their strategy when it came to the provinces, especially mighty Prussia.[80] Goebbels insinuated that Goering was cultivating "particularism" out of personal hunger for power. Several times he went to see Hitler about the matter, until finally Hitler confirmed Goebbels's undivided control over the broadcasting system.[81]

Goebbels also experienced success in his attempts to secure an official residence. He had identified the perfect building: the former palace of the marshals of the Prussian court, located in the northernmost of the seven so-called ministry gardens, in the shadow of the Brandenburg Gate, and close to the Propaganda Ministry on Wilhelmstrasse. It had been the residence of the Reich minister of nutrition. When Hugenberg resigned from the cabinet, Goebbels informed Walter Darré, even before he was officially appointed as Hugenberg's successor, that Hitler wanted Goebbels "close by." Darré agreed to cede the building to the propaganda minister.[82]

The new master of 20 Hermann-Goering-Strasse (as Friedrich-Ebert-Strasse was called from August 1933 on) caused Darré further difficulties. He prevented him from having needed space added onto the Ministry of Nutrition—on the grounds that the construction would "disturb" Goebbels.[83] Yet Goebbels undertook major remodeling of his own official residence. The project, directed by Albert Speer, included adding on a grand hall for entertaining.[84] On 30 June Goebbels proudly handed his wife the keys. But their joy was immediately mixed with bitterness: the furniture Speer had picked out did not please them, so new furniture had to be procured.[85] Despite all their claims to unpretentiousness, the two were living more and more luxuriously. Goebbels did his best to avoid giving this impression—at Christmas 1933 he reprimanded his brother Hans, by way of his brother Konrad, for driving a fancy automobile.[86] But when it came to their houses and apartments, he completely subordinated himself to Magda, whose "fabulous taste" he always praised. And she, as one might expect in light of her first marriage, gravitated toward expensive things of the highest quality. In contrast to the fondness for kitschy splendor manifested by many other party wives, Magda Goebbels had a refined sense of style, as the work she commissioned from the

Munich Consolidated Workshops showed. And she knew how to create a private setting in which Hitler felt at ease for many years—an additional bond between the Führer and his minister of propaganda.

When she proudly showed Hitler through the house and garden, he expressed "unreserved and honest enthusiasm" and shared her view that it was like a "pleasure palace."[87] But he objected sharply to the watercolors by Emil Nolde that Speer had borrowed from the Berlin National Gallery. Goebbels promptly capitulated to Hitler's taste in art and had the "impossible" paintings removed.[88]

The extent to which Hitler's wish was Goebbels's command can be seen from the role Hitler played in a dispute between Goebbels and his wife. In July 1933 Magda wanted to chair a new German fashion center. Goebbels opposed it categorically, on the grounds that women should concentrate solely on their families and not take an active part in public affairs. "Loud scenes" followed. When Magda then refused to accompany her husband to Bayreuth for the Wagner festival, sacred to the party leadership, the whole thing blew up into a "serious conflict." At seeing Goebbels arrive alone, Hitler was "horrified" and immediately ordered that Magda be flown in from Berlin. Now she did not resist, and appeared during the first act of the *Meistersinger*, "glowing with beauty." The "very grim atmosphere" between her and Goebbels did not change until Hitler had taken both of them aside several times. While still in Bayreuth, Goebbels wrote in childish gratitude in his diary: Hitler "makes peace between Magda and me." He was a "real friend," and Goebbels was "tremendously fond of him."[89]

Such quarrels with his wife may have had their roots in Goebbels's nervousness about a new rival for power. Robert Ley headed the German Labor Front, which had swallowed up the organization and immense financial resources of all the destroyed trade unions and insurance funds.[90] He had come up with a plan to incorporate the artists' professional associations into the Labor Front. This notion sparked "almost panicky" reactions in Goebbels. He promptly went to see Rudolf Hess for a "serious" discussion of Ley's intentions; he let fall the word "Marxism." On 10 July he wrote an essay warning of "Marxist tendencies" within the factory-cell organization.[91] Soon thereafter he submitted to Hitler a draft entitled "Proposals for the Establishment of a Reich Chamber of Culture."[92]

During a "long discussion of basic principles" on 24 August in Berchtesgaden, Hitler gave his approval to Goebbels's concept and expressed his "fullest admiration" for his work.[93] After that, things moved quickly; by 22 September the legal basis had been established for Goebbels to organize all persons "belonging to the areas of activity under his jurisdiction" into a government union.[94] He had successfully outflanked Ley.

Although Hitler announced on 7 July 1933 that the "brown revolution" was over and the most significant *Gleichschaltung* measures had been taken, Goebbels's propaganda apparatus continued to operate at full throttle. The nation had fallen into noticeable lethargy; Goebbels tried to whip up new enthusiasm with celebrations and mass rallies. The Reich Party Rally of Victory was celebrated in Nuremberg that year with unprecedented pomp; hundreds of thousands came to the ancient city just to say they had been there. Radio, newspapers, newsreels, and Leni Riefenstahl's film *Sieg des Glaubens* (Victory of Faith; released that same year) carried the message to those who had stayed at home.

If people did not feel their misery so acutely, at least some of that could be credited to Goebbels's propaganda, which constantly reminded them of improvements in social conditions and of the government's efforts on their behalf. Measures to create employment, like the construction of the autobahn between Frankfurt and Heidelberg, begun in September, and charity initiatives like the Winter Aid campaign—all were reported by radio and press, with extensive coverage of the first shovelful of dirt by the Führer or the opening speech by the minister of propaganda. The dynamics of the events and the constant emphasis on communal experience were intended to convey a sense of new beginnings and consolidation of gains even before material conditions showed actual improvement. In this way more and more people from all classes were gradually brought under the "brown" spell.

To be sure, there were a number of troubling factors, like the excesses against the Jews, the establishment of concentration camps, and the terror tactics practiced against those of different political persuasions, as for instance during the "Köpenick Blood Week," when ninety-one people were slaughtered by the SA.[95] But since things had turned out this way, and as an individual one couldn't do much in any case, many people in Germany simply told themselves it wasn't their fault. And after all, hadn't every revolution had excesses that died down sooner or later?

Among Germany's wartime enemies in the west, Hitler's dictatorship, with its radical exclusion of political opposition, but especially the state-sponsored anti-Semitism, heightened aversion to the Reich. In the fall of 1933 Hitler therefore saw a need to curb his propaganda minister, who after the consolidation of his own power was pouring all his energy into the struggle against citizens of Jewish origin. A speech Goebbels had written for the Nuremberg party rally, "The Race Question and World Propaganda," struck Hitler as too aggressive; to the speaker's chagrin, the treatment of "the Jewish question" had to be moderated.[96]

Goebbels was nonetheless Hitler's first choice when international waves had to be smoothed. As a gesture of Germany's supposed desire for peace (of which Hitler had made so much in his Reichstag speech on

17 May), the Führer dispatched his most skillful dialectician to a League of Nations conference in Geneva in September, along with Foreign Minister Konstantin von Neurath. Goebbels later explained the purpose of this mission in a secret speech to specially invited representatives of the German press: "Just as our political adversaries inside Germany had not even noticed where we were headed before 1932, that our oath to legality was merely a dodge," these professions of commitment to peace were intended to help Germany get through the "danger zone." By that Goebbels meant the phase of "rebuilding military preparedness," which he believed was the prerequisite for Germany's survival in a hostile world and the first step toward a great continental empire.[97] In accordance with this plan, Hitler's and Goebbels's propaganda on the foreign-policy front operated between 1933 and 1936 under the motto "We are not a saber-rattling Germany."[98]

This trip to Geneva was Goebbels's second official visit to a foreign country. For the first time he was encountering representatives of those states whose democratic systems he had vilified without having the slightest acquaintance with them. He accordingly took away a "depressing impression" of the League of Nations session on 25 September. "An assembly of the dead," he called it, mocking the "parliamentarianism of the nations."[99] The German ambassador in Bern, Ernst von Weizsäcker, had hoped that Goebbels would gather "useful impressions."[100] In fact they ran as follows: "Rather interesting to see these people. Sir John Simon: Engl. exterior. Tall and imposing. . . . Dollfuss: a dwarf, a dandy, a sly devil. Otherwise nothing special. . . . How we Germans tower over these people. The whole thing completely without dignity, without style. Stresemann fit in here and felt at home. This is no place for us. . . . I'm annoyed with myself for even being here. The Foreign Office is shitting in its pants with nervousness."[101]

As the "sensation of the plenary session," Goebbels in turn received close scrutiny. According to the report of the chief interpreter for the Foreign Office, Paul Schmidt, Goebbels conducted himself "perfectly calmly" in the Geneva he so despised, "as though he had been a delegate to the League of Nations for years." The "wild man from Germany" actually made a cultivated, quiet impression; he had even exchanged his violent vocabulary of political agitation for the correct language of diplomacy. The mask was perfect. Schmidt heard from the delegates who spoke with Goebbels that "they were almost all as surprised as I to find not a raving tribune of the people but a perfectly normal delegate type, smiling engagingly from time to time, like dozens of others at the September sessions."[102]

Ernst von Weizsäcker confirms this account, saying that the delegates generally decided that this movement must have features deserving closer study.[103] At a dinner given by the Swiss historian Carl Jacob Burckhardt, Goebbels even managed to persuade the skeptical Swiss legislator Giuseppe Motta that he need have no fear of Nazi expansionism.[104]

Goebbels achieved a similar effect in a speech to the foreign press in the crowded dining room of the Carlton Hotel. Speaking on "National Socialist Germany and Its Mission on Behalf of Peace," Goebbels called it "unfair" to conclude that Germany wanted war when the entire reconstruction undertaken by the government was borne "by the spirit of peace." Schmidt reports that Goebbels's description of the new regime as "a nobler sort of democracy, in which the government rules in an authoritarian fashion by mandate of the people," was greeted by many with "disbelieving skepticism" and "ironic smiles."[105] But Goebbels skillfully shifted the focus to the "real" danger of bolshevism, which according to Schmidt brought nods of agreement from the audience, particularly from some of the British and American journalists.[106]

What impressed the journalists more than what Goebbels actually said was the manner in which he said it. Some of them wondered whether this "civilized, agreeable figure" could be the same man who had been making inflammatory speeches for the past seven years.[107] After his speech Goebbels mingled with the audience, answering even the most pointed questions about freedom of the press, the Jewish question, and the concentration camps "spiritedly, quick-wittedly, and smoothly." He could be sure of "their admiration, however grudging."[108]

Before he flew back to Berlin, the propaganda minister complained to Schmidt about the dreadful atmosphere, the disorder, the intrigues, and the dishonesty he had witnessed.[109] In his diary Goebbels recorded his distrust and dislike of those he had met in Geneva. On the question of armaments parity, which Hitler demanded, Goebbels had not succeeded in getting French Foreign Minister Joseph Paul-Boncour or the former head of the reparations commission, Jean-Louis Barthou, to yield an inch, despite two long discussions.[110]

Only Goebbels's meetings with Polish Foreign Minister Josef Beck and the president of the Danzig senate, Hermann Rauschning, had taken a gratifying course. Beck one could "handle"—he was "young and receptive." Besides, Beck wanted "to get free of France and move closer to Berlin," a disposition that on 26 January 1934 resulted in the German-Polish nonaggression and friendship pact.[111] With this treaty Germany took a decisive step out of the isolation into which Hitler had maneuvered it on 14 October 1933, when he pulled out of the disarmament conference and the League of Nations, having been strengthened in his previous intention by Goebbels's negative report from Geneva.

Again Hitler and Goebbels practiced a skillful division of labor in concealing the next phase, that of "rebuilding military preparedness."

While Hitler was announcing his decision on the radio, Goebbels was serving as government spokesman at a press conference, stressing Germany's commitment "to a policy inspired by the most sincere desire for peace and international understanding."[112] He repeated the theme in a speech on 20 October in the Sportpalast: "If we have pulled out of the League of Nations and the disarmament conference, it wasn't so we could prepare for war. Adolf Hitler rightly explained in his radio address that only a madman could want war. We pulled out to clear the air, to show the world that things can't go on this way." And by accusing the other countries of "stamping Germany a scapegoat," he distracted his domestic audience from the other countries' justified fears of Germany.[113]

The indignation felt in Geneva and the isolated calls for military action against Germany soon dissipated, and Goebbels felt confirmed in his judgment of the Western democracies' "decadence." In the Reich, he and Hitler maintained, no one wept a tear for the League of Nations; on the contrary, Germany's withdrawal was welcomed.[114] To demonstrate to the world that the German people stood unified behind him, Hitler decided to submit his policy to a plebiscite, and at the same time to hold new elections for the Reichstag. During the few weeks remaining before 12 November, yet another enormous wave of rallies, marches, speeches, and appeals rolled across the land. Millions of posters called for justice and freedom for the fatherland. As director of the elections Goebbels again took on a superhuman schedule of speaking engagements and interviews.

The result was predictable. Versailles, associated with loss of territory, foreign occupation, reparations, and humiliation, was too fresh in people's minds for them to do anything but vote yes "for Führer and fatherland." So the plebiscite and the election of a new Reichstag with exclusively NSDAP deputies were all of a piece, an early high point in popular approval of Hitler, and therefore also an unqualified success for his propaganda minister.[115]

A few days before, on 8 November, Goebbels had testified at the Reichstag fire trial in Leipzig, trying to limit the damage the trial was doing to the Nazis' reputation abroad. The charges brought against Marinus van der Lubbe, Torgler, and the Bulgarian Communists Dimitroff, Popov, and Tanev had revived discussion of possible Nazi involvement in the crime (although in Germany such ideas had to be whispered). On the witness stand Goebbels called the theory of Nazi involvement "absurd" and, like Goering four days before him, found a whole string of arguments for Communist responsibility for the arson. The judges reached a different conclusion. They convicted van der Lubbe of having "acted alone" and acquitted the other defendants, thereby firmly rejecting the Nazi assertion of a Communist plot.

The judges had not yet announced their decision when Goebbels stepped onto the rostrum in the Berlin Philharmonic. The triumphal success of the Reichstag elections was fresh in his mind as, in the presence of the Führer, he delivered an address to mark the founding of the Reich Chamber of Culture. He spoke of the future of the arts in Germany, which would demonstrate that the "great German awakening of our times" was not only political but also cultural. The "healthy instincts of the *Volk*" would determine the future course for artistic endeavor.[116] What Goebbels meant by this standard a large number of writers, actors, directors, and general managers had already discovered, to their grief, during the first half of the year. It hit the Jewish artists particularly hard, for Goebbels declared openly that a "Jewish contemporary" was in general "unfit" to "administer Germany's cultural heritage."[117] Thus Otto Klemperer, conductor of the Berlin State Opera, received the Goethe Medal in 1933 and was dismissed later that same year "for racial reasons." Anyone who had not emigrated or incurred the displeasure of the regime was forced to join the Reich Chamber of Culture with its seven individual chambers—for literature, journalism, broadcasting, theater, music, film, and the fine arts.[118]

Goebbels, who had just used the Editor Statute to conduct a purge of the newspapers, took great pains in this speech to banish fears and anxieties.[119] He asserted that in Germany "sniffing out ideologies" had no place, and the government merely wanted "to be the good patron of German art and culture." The "heartless and bloodless dilettantism of an army of incompetents" should be stopped in its tracks, and the "philistinism" and "reactionary backwardness" that blocked youth's upward trajectory should finally be consigned to the past. Only "consecrated hands" had "the right to serve at the altar of art."[120] By invoking these high-sounding ideals, Goebbels was trying to appeal to a few noted artists whom the Nazis hoped to keep in Germany for display purposes; a total exodus had to be avoided, if Hitler's claim of a cultural blossoming was to have any justification. And a number of prominent artists were indeed taken in: Wilhelm Furtwängler, one of the most distinguished conductors of the century; the composers Richard Strauss and Paul Hindemith; the poet Gottfried Benn; and the Nobel-prize-winning writer Gerhart Hauptmann.

But Goebbels's cultural policy encountered the bitter opposition of a man to whom he had deliberately assigned a seat in the back rows at the inauguration of the Reich Chamber of Culture: Alfred Rosenberg. This confused ideologue, author of the bitterly anti-Semitic *Myth of the Twentieth Century*, dogmatically guarded the "purity of the idea" of national socialism. To him, the idea meant harking back to the past, to Goethe, Schopenhauer, Nietzsche, Wagner, and the ancient Nordic *thing* (assembly), and radical rejection of anything new.[121] Goering later commented that if Rosenberg had his way, "there would be no more German theater, only cult, *thing*, myth, and that sort of swindle."[122]

In 1925 Rosenberg had attacked Goebbels in the *Völkischer Beobachter*, which he edited, for "probolshevist" deviations, and now he tried to establish that Goebbels had a secret toleration for expressionism and similar modern trends in art.[123] His intriguing against Goebbels can be explained not only by ideological differences but also by greed for power. Rosenberg had wanted to secure greater influence over the arts, the very influence Goebbels possessed through his ministry and the Reich Chamber of Culture, whose memberships now numbered in the hundreds of thousands. Rosenberg's position was further weakened when Goebbels and Ley reached a compromise after the Chamber's founding. Because Ley needed Goebbels's help in developing a program of popular culture for the new Strength through Joy organization, founded on 27 November, he relinquished his claim to the artists he had wanted for his German Labor Front. Goebbels in turn agreed to recognize and support Strength through Joy.[124]

In December 1933 Goebbels could look back on a thoroughly successful year. In addition to heading the Reich propaganda office and the Propaganda Ministry, he had a third pillar of power in the Reich Chamber of Culture, which soon had branches throughout the country. With this power he could "mobilize the spirit" in the people for Hitler's policy of foreign expansion. What made his happiness complete at year's end was a "very warm letter" from the Führer.[125]

CHAPTER 10

Through crises and perils leads
the way to our freedom
(1934–1936)

Goebbels was no longer content with the material blessings that had come with his rise to power—the handsome official residence, the limousine, the custom-made suits. Driven by a deeply ingrained sense of inferiority, he kept searching for fresh self-confirmation, for instance in the glamorous world of film, which now came under his purview. He enjoyed rubbing elbows with "that most remarkable little people in the world," whether at premieres or during his many visits to the Viktoriastrasse club of the Comradeship of German Artists, which he himself had founded.[1] Around him there swarmed stars and starlets whom he had once admired from afar. Later Goebbels rented a weekend house in Kladow on the Havel, to which he would invite favored actors and actresses. Goebbels secretly considered his guests enjoyable to have around but politically "entirely innocuous" and "without a clue."[2] Perhaps it was precisely for this reason that the minister took such pleasure in their company; he spent most of his time combating critical intellectuals, but among these people he could shine with a minimum of effort.

Goebbels's most frequent guest was the actress Jenny Jugo, sometimes with her husband. Goebbels prized her not only for her cheerful ways but also for her expertise in film. A star of silent film, she was one of the few to make the transition to the talkies successfully. With her interpretation of Eliza in Shaw's *Pygmalion*, opposite Gustav Gründgens as Professor Higgins, she established herself in 1935 as an outstanding comic actress.

After Goebbels purchased the snow-white motor yacht *Baldur* at Easter 1934 and received his pilot's license, he organized boating parties on the lakes of the Mark Brandenburg or evening parties on the yacht at its mooring, at which alcohol flowed freely.[3] Another actress always welcome at these events was Luise Ullrich. She had won over the minister with her first film, *Der Rebell* (The Rebel, 1932), which Goebbels soon counted among his favorites, the others being Eisenstein's *Battleship Potemkin* and Fritz Lang's *Nibelungen* (The Nibelungs) and *Anna Karenina*. This latter was filmed in 1935 with "the divine" Greta Garbo, in Goebbels's eyes the greatest of all actresses.[4] He liked to recommend these films to the "gentlemen of the cinema" as models for their own projects.[5]

When Goebbels had guests for the evening, he would arrange to have one or two films shown for them, the newest German—and sometimes American—releases. Privately he had a thoroughly positive opinion of the quality of the American film industry, which, he admitted, was well ahead of the German in some respects.[6] Among the Hollywood films that he castigated in public, the one that entranced him the most was *Gone With the Wind*.

An evening at the Goebbels residence might include the Höpfners, a brother-sister dance team; Irene von Meyendorff; the boxer Max Schmeling and his wife Anny Ondra; Erika Dannhoff; the character actor Emil Jannings; the film director Veit Harlan, at first with his wife Hilde Körber, later with the actress Kristina Söderbaum; Ello Quandt, Magda's former sister-in-law and her closest confidante; Ello's friend Hela Strehl; and the Bouhlers, the von Helldorfs, the von Arents, and the von Schaumburgs. The aristocratic origins of these last-named couples did not seem to disturb Goebbels in the least, although otherwise he expressed nothing but scorn for "high-society rabble."[7] The actress-turned-director Leni Riefenstahl was also a friend of Goebbels and his wife, as she was of Hitler. In Goebbels's opinion she was "the only one of all the stars who understands us."[8]

Actors and filmmakers hovered around the propaganda minister for one simple reason: without his patronage the road to a major career was closed to them. He soon ruled in the film world as absolutely as in broadcasting. He had lists prepared of his favorite actors, as well as of Hitler's. He also kept close track of up-and-coming talent, which he insisted on seeing for himself.[9] Everyone in these circles knew that female aspirants received contracts only if they showed themselves amenable to the minister's erotic proclivities. Géza von Cziffra, a well-known director of entertainment films, reports that the minister's personal assistant, Georg Wilhelm Müller, was responsible for making sure that Goebbels's trysts with actresses, which often took place at the ministry, went unnoticed.[10]

Producers also depended on Goebbels's favor, for he had created a comprehensive apparatus that allowed him to intervene in all phases of film production. The film department in the Propaganda Ministry, whose director Ernst Seeger served simultaneously as head of the office of film standards, oversaw production planning. All screenplays were examined for "appropriate" artistic and intellectual attitudes. For theater, opera, and operetta, analogous supervision and influence were exercised in the corresponding departments.[11] More and more the minister assumed these duties himself. He read film scripts almost every evening, and not infrequently revised them according to his own notions, using a green "minister's pencil" that became infamous among directors. Only after he had approved a project could the Film Credit Bank respond to a request for financing. Goebbels would even intervene in the shooting, often dropping in on a studio, "checking" the rushes, and rating the finished product. From October 1935 on, he alone determined which films would be banned.[12]

In the Weimar Republic censorship and rating had been strictly separate. With both tools in Goebbels's hands, he could not only control the content of German film production but also exert financial pressure on the film companies. Each positive rating point (three being the usual number) carried a tax rebate of 4 percent.[13]

When Goebbels declared himself early on a "passionate fan of cinematic art"—an enthusiasm he shared with Hitler, to whom he one year gave thirty serious films and eighteen Mickey Mouse films as Christmas presents!—it was not without ulterior motives.[14] Goebbels deliberately wooed actors and directors, promoted the star cult, approved payment of princely salaries, helped actors with tax problems, and improved directors' and actors' social standing with honorary titles like "professor" or "state actor." He thereby made these people pliable for the purposes of a regime whose leading functionaries liked to be seen in public with the stars. Amid royal splendor Hermann Goering led "state actress" Emmy Sonnemann to the altar in the Berlin Cathedral.

While Goebbels, whose wife had given birth on 15 April 1934 to another girl, Hilde, was enjoying the chic life of the film world, things had not improved for the working-class masses who had supported the party. The "party soldiers" to whom Goebbels had promised during the Time of Struggle that the Third Reich would bring a social revolution, felt left in the lurch. Every day that passed made it clearer that the economic crisis would not end as quickly as the new leadership pretended.

Among those who constituted the broad base of the party, calls were heard for a continuation of the revolution so that ordinary people could enjoy its blessings as well. In the storm troopers' pubs the slogan "second revolution" gained currency. The SA wanted to recover its former influence. "What I want, Hitler knows precisely," wrote the SA chief of staff Röhm. "I've told him often enough. . . . Are we a revolution or not? . . . If we are, something new must arise out of our élan, like the mass armies of the French Revolution."[15] But it was not Röhm's concept of a people's militia with a leading political role in Germany that Hitler chose to promote in February 1934. With an eye to realizing his plans for territorial conquest, he sided with the Wehrmacht and universal military service, thereby deepening the gulf between himself and the SA leader.

This choice gave comfort to the Nazis' bourgeois nationalist partners in the government. They thought party dictatorship might be transformed into more moderate authoritarian rule, eventually making way for a constitutional monarchy. Such a process could be set in motion through the decision reached on Hindenburg's successor. On 21 May Goebbels learned from Reichswehr Minister Werner von Blomberg that Papen had ambitions to move into Hindenburg's place when the old gentleman died. "Absolutely out of the question. On the contrary, this mess must be cleaned up," Goebbels commented in his diary.[16]

On 17 June Vice Chancellor von Papen gave a speech to the University Association in Marburg that attracted a great deal of attention. Written by his assistant, Edgar Jung, the speech savagely criticized the rule of the NSDAP.[17] It condemned the talk of a second revolution, as well as the regime's suppression of alleged "intellectualism." Papen openly castigated the brown terror tactics as the "outgrowth of a guilty conscience," and denounced the rigid press manipulation practiced by the Propaganda Ministry with statements like "Great men are not made by propaganda; they grow through their deeds," and "No organization and no propaganda, be it ever so good, will suffice in the long run to preserve confidence." Papen even went so far as to characterize single-party rule as a transitional stage, hinting at a restoration of the monarchy.

As early as 11 May Goebbels had gone on the offensive against the reactionary "malcontents and nigglers" with a speech at the Sportpalast, followed by appearances throughout the country. In mid-June he interrupted his tour for an official visit to Poland, where on instructions from Hitler he affirmed the "peaceful" intentions of Germany's policies, which aimed only at "equal rights" and "restoration of honor."

Back in Germany, Goebbels had to step up his propaganda against the bourgeois conservatives in response to Papen's speech. In a speech in Berlin on 21 June he told the crowd that the National Socialists had been forced to take power because no one else had come forward to keep things from "sliding downhill." He finished by referring to the conservative "dignified gentlemen" as "ridiculous twerps," and he appealed to the masses to challenge them—"you will see them beat a cowardly retreat."[18]

At this point Papen threatened to go to Hindenburg and resign, because the Propaganda Ministry had prohibited radio and press dissemination of his speech.[19] Although Hitler managed to persuade his vice chancellor to hold off, Goebbels was convinced that the conflict with the "reactionaries" was approaching the critical stage, and that the Führer would have to act soon.[20]

On the morning of 29 June he thought Hitler had finally made up his mind. Hitler telephoned Goebbels, asking him to join him immediately in Bad Godesberg. Once there, Goebbels learned to his consternation that the Führer planned not to move against the "reactionaries," but rather to decapitate the SA.[21] Although tensions between the party and the SA had noticeably diminished in the weeks just past, and it seemed as though Röhm's ambitions might possibly meet the demands of the Reichswehr halfway, Hitler had apparently decided on this particular course during a three-day stay at the Berghof. He felt he could not at this point risk breaking with the conservative middle-class elements in the Reichswehr, industry, and the civil service. By eliminating Röhm and his friends, thereby rejecting a second "socialist" revolution, Hitler calculated, he could not only avert the crisis that was brewing but also win over his aristocratic partners entirely.[22]

Fixated on the hated "reactionaries," Goebbels had failed to notice, or had not wanted to notice, all the signs pointing to a blow against the unsuspecting leaders of the storm units, which had been dismissed for vacation. On 25 June Hitler's confidant Rudolf Hess had spoken against "provocateurs," meaning the SA, who were trying to incite members of the *Volk* against each other and "cloak this criminal game with the honorable name of a 'second revolution.' "[23] Goebbels did not know that Goering and Himmler, whom Hitler had made head of the Prussian Gestapo in April, and Reinhard Heydrich, the head of the State Security Service, had discussed the operation with the leadership of the Wehrmacht, in particular Werner von Blomberg, and secured pledges of full support. Goebbels likewise did not know why Hitler had left Berlin on 28 June and flown to the wedding of Gauleiter Terboven in Essen; there he had presented the plans to Goering and Himmler, likewise there for the wedding. The SA leadership—Röhm and his immediate circle—was to be ordered to Bad Wiessee, ostensibly for frank discussions, and there arrested.

When Goebbels reached Hitler's hotel in Bad Godesberg and learned of this plan, he had to stare reality in the face for a moment. Again Hitler was turning out to be a "reactionary." And again Goebbels immediately capitulated, even though it meant acting against his own convictions. To dispel even a breath of doubt about his loyalty to Hitler, he is said to have insisted on being allowed to participate. Finally he was, as Rosenberg scornfully described it, "allowed to join a real men's undertaking."[24]

At 2:00 A.M. on 30 June, Hitler set out in a small plane with his adjutants Wilhelm Brückner and Julius Schaub, his drivers Julius Schreck and Erich Kempka, Reich Press Secretary Otto Dietrich, and Goebbels.

It was earlier than they had planned to depart, but reports had come in from Munich and Berlin that the SA leadership seemed to have guessed what was afoot, and a real rebellion was breaking out in Munich. As the propaganda minister melodramatically reported in his subsequent radio address, during this flight the Führer sat silent in the front seat of the large cabin and stared motionlessly into the "cloud-shrouded night sky" ahead.[25]

From the airport, where they landed around 4:30 A.M., the death squad immediately made its way to the Bavarian Interior Ministry. There SS units had collected the alleged instigators of the SA march that had taken place the evening before, during which three thousand rowdy storm troopers had loudly announced their readiness to confront any treachery. Hitler began with Obergruppenführer Schneidhuber, the Munich police commissioner, and Gruppenführer Schmid, head of the Munich SA. He bawled at them and ripped the insignia from their shoulders. Then they were hauled off to the Stadelheim penitentiary.

Goebbels saw it as a particular sign of trust that Hitler took him along to Wiessee for the actual operation. Afterward he boasted that, in addition to the Führer's regular SS escort, only "his most faithful comrades" had been allowed to accompany him. Toward 7:00 A.M. they reached the Hanslbauer Hotel in Bad Wiessee, where Röhm and his people were staying. Without encountering the slightest resistance, they hurried into the building. Hitler with his riding whip took the lead, followed by the others, while Goebbels pushed his way to the front to be right there when Hitler yanked open the door to Röhm's room and shouted at him that he was under arrest. The SA chief of staff just managed to get out a sleepy "Heil, mein Führer" before he grasped the gravity of the situation. Hitler followed the same procedure with the other leaders. Goebbels recalled the "revolting, almost nauseating scenes" that he witnessed when Hitler caught Edmund Heines in bed with another man.[26]

Goebbels described the trip back to Munich as equally dramatic. As he sat very close to Hitler in the back of his supercharged Mercedes, they kept encountering SA leaders going in the opposite direction, on their way to the purported conference in Bad Wiessee.[27] Hitler personally placed them under arrest and turned them over to the SS commando, which brought them, along with Röhm, Heines, and the rest to Stadelheim, where they were executed.

Back in Munich Goebbels was allowed to telephone Goering in Berlin to tell him that "the majority of the criminals are in custody" and he, Goering, should now "carry out his assignment."[28] "Operation Hummingbird" got underway in Berlin and the rest of the Reich. While Goebbels in Munich was receiving instructions from Hitler on the propaganda line to be followed and was issuing the first directives for press and radio coverage, the SS and the police were arresting further "conspirators" among the SA leadership and killing them. In Silesia, Himmler's SS, intoxicated with bloodshed, murdered dozens of unsuspecting SA men.

On the evening of 30 June Goebbels returned to Berlin with Hitler, where they were received by a military honor guard and a large welcoming committee at Tempelhof Field. Goebbels looked "as though he felt sick to his stomach."[29] Hitler, impatient and agitated, immediately asked for the list of those who had been killed, to which Goering had added names on his own.[30]

In a murder squad's hail of bullets, General von Schleicher and his wife had died in the study of their villa in Neubabelsberg. Schleicher's adjutant Ferdinand von Bredow was also killed, as was the leader of Catholic Action, Erich Klausener. One of the murder commandos had killed Papen's private secretary, as well as his closest associate, Edgar Jung, author of the Marburg speech. The vice chancellor himself had been placed under arrest. His life was spared only because Hitler still needed him as a liaison to Hindenburg.

Also listed among the dead was a man who had been Goebbels's comrade, then rival, and finally embittered enemy—Gregor Strasser. After leaving the party he had become deputy director of a pharmaceuticals company, and he had several times assured the party leadership that "since that miserable December 1932" he had "painstakingly refrained from political activity." On 18 June Gregor Strasser, whose brother Otto was conspiring against Hitler from Prague, had written to Rudolf Hess, apparently in a grim premonition of what was to come. He had asked Hess "on the basis of a ten-year self-sacrificing and unflinching involvement in building the party" to provide him with protection and advice as to how he might "vanish from any debate about my person" and above all eliminate the terribly painful sense that he was seen as hostile to the party.[31] The letter did no good. Around 2:30 P.M. on 30 June a squad of ten men took him from his house to the Prinz-Albrecht-Strasse headquarters of the Gestapo. He was liquidated in the cellar early that same evening.[32] That Strasser, Schleicher, and other "reactionaries" were among those killed made it easier for Goebbels to deceive himself as to what had occurred. Against what could this operation have been directed but a conspiracy? Hadn't he long suspected Strasser? Hadn't Strasser collaborated with Schleicher in December 1932? And wasn't this just the sort of thing in which the homosexual Röhm might get involved?[33] Goebbels saw connections where none existed; in accepting them he saved himself from having to recognize that, with the elimination of the SA leadership, Hitler had completed the dismantling of the brown party army, and with it the revolutionary goals it had embodied for Goebbels.

Since Hitler defied all the rules of propaganda and kept silent, making no statement until 13 July, when he delivered an unconvincing speech riddled with contradictions, it was left to Goebbels to deal with the public. As if to explain to himself why he had been left in the dark so long, he announced to his "fellow members of the *Volk*" at the beginning of his broadcast on 1 July that the Führer had, as so often "in serious and difficult situations, acted according to his old principle of saying only what needed to be said to those who needed to know, and only when they needed to know." Through his dramatic account of the events, Goebbels glorified Hitler as the "savior of the fatherland," and harped on the "degenerate life" and the "shameful and repulsive sexual abnormality" of the SA leaders. Hitler and "his faithful followers" had refused to allow "their constructive efforts, undertaken with untold sacrifices by the entire nation" to be jeopardized by "a small guild of criminals," allied with "reactionary forces" and a foreign power. Completely twisting the facts, Goebbels appropriated for Hitler's operation the concept of the "second revolution," which had now arrived, but "differently" from the way the conspirators had conceived it.[34]

The radio and press reports of the following days continued the lies. No exact count of those killed was ever provided—it must have been more than two hundred. The circumstances of Röhm's and Schleicher's deaths were embellished. On 10 July Goebbels broadcast a program entitled "The Thirtieth of June as Seen from Abroad." He thanked the German press for "standing by the government with commendable self-discipline and fair-mindedness," and accused the foreign papers of issuing false reports so as to increase the general confusion in Germany. He branded the speculations in the foreign press a "campaign of lies," comparable in its maliciousness only to the "atrocity-story campaign waged against Germany during the war."[35]

Goebbels's task of presenting the massacre as a political necessity was made considerably easier by the attitude of Hitler's accomplices among the traditional elite. They arranged for the Reich president to send congratulatory telegrams to Hitler and Goering from his estate in Neudeck. In Hindenburg's name the telegrams characterized Hitler as the man who had rescued Germany from "grave danger" and expressed "profound gratitude."[36] Reichswehr Minister Blomberg, who had countenanced the murder of two of his generals, despite outraged protests from army circles emphatically thanked the "statesman and soldier Hitler," whose "courageous and decisive action" had averted civil war.[37]

Goebbels now proceeded to make much of the "legality" of the suppression of the "Röhm revolt," thereby distracting the public from its brutality. Fear of SA terrorism and the threat of a "second revolution" yielded to a collective sigh of relief. And just at that moment, when the public was beginning to relax, despite the uneasiness the events had brought, and when Hitler's conservative partners thought they had got him "on the right track," a team of doctors under Professor Sauerbruch began issuing bulletins from Neudeck that made it clear Hindenburg's end was imminent.

Hitler chose this favorable moment to seize full control. Cavalierly disregarding the legality principle, on 1 August 1934 he presented to the cabinet a law regarding the succession; it combined the office of "Führer and Reich chancellor" with that of president.[38] This change became a reality less than twenty-four hours later, for on the morning of 2 August Paul von Hindenburg died at the age of eighty-six. At 9:25 A.M. all the radio stations interrupted their programs. In a dragging, seemingly grief-stricken voice, the propaganda minister reported the death of the Reich president and field marshal. After half an hour of radio silence Goebbels announced the "first legally required measures and directives."[39] A few hours after the nostalgic old war song "I Once Had a Comrade" had drifted away on the airwaves, Reichswehr Minister Blomberg gave the order that had long since been agreed upon: he had all the soldiers of the German Wehrmacht swear a personal oath of loyalty to the "Führer of the German Reich and *Volk*, Adolf Hitler."

The official mourning observances, which Goebbels immediately took in hand, were staged as a symbol of political continuity, like the Potsdam ceremony of the previous year. In his speech at the monument to the battle of Tannenberg, where Hindenburg had won his most famous victory in 1914, Hitler alluded to Hindenburg's legacy. Yet at the time he spoke, no political testament had been found. Twelve days later it turned up, and Franz von Papen brought it to Hitler in Berchtesgaden. Rumors immediately began to circulate that it was a forgery. For one thing, Goebbels had had it announced right after Hindenburg's death that no testament had been found.[40] For another, the style did not match Hindenburg's. Although the text contained several references to Hitler, there was no mention of the kaiser and the Lord, whom Hindenburg had so greatly venerated.

So as not to be at the mercy of the Reichswehr, Hitler moved for a plebiscite to confirm him in power. Once more Goebbels unleashed one of his massive propaganda campaigns. Once more the question on the ballot gave the voters no leeway, and once more manipulation occurred. Even so, the outcome on 19 August did not fulfill Hitler's and Goebbels's expectations. Although 89.9 percent had supposedly voted for the Führer, Hitler and his propaganda minister received the results with dismay.[41]

Even before the plebiscite Alfred Rosenberg had been mustering his forces for an all-out attack on Goebbels. At the beginning of 1934 Hitler had given in to Rosenberg's pressure and created an agency for him that would supervise all intellectual and ideological training within the NSDAP. Rosenberg now charged that Goebbels's speech justifying the events of 30 June had made "a catastrophic impression" throughout the world, that Goebbels had "confused the position of a Reich minister with that of a small-town rabble-rouser."[42] Early in August, Rosenberg asked Hess "most urgently" to persuade the Führer to give him general authorization to oversee the entire movement's foreign policy.[43]

In cultural matters an interminable struggle between Goebbels and Rosenberg ensued, waged with grim determination by both. Rosenberg wrote to Goebbels in late August that Hitler had authorized him to examine the intellectual and ideological orientation of all organizations that had undergone *Gleichschaltung*.[44] He then began to attack systematically the very personalities in the Reich Chamber of Culture whom Goebbels had enlisted as credible representatives of the regime after the exodus of the leading figures in the arts.

Rosenberg attacked the composer Richard Strauss, probably the most significant figure in German music, a man with an international reputation whom Goebbels himself admired. Rosenberg asserted that having this composer serve as president of the Reich Chamber of Music could result in a "cultural scandal," because Strauss was having the libretto of his opera *Die schweigsame Frau* (The Silent Woman) "written by a Jew" who served as "the artistic advisor to a Jewish emigré theater" in Switzerland.[45] Rosenberg's attack made Goebbels "furious," the more so because Hess sided with Rosenberg.[46] Goebbels took satisfaction in pointing out that Rosenberg had his facts wrong; Strauss's librettist was Stefan Zweig, "an Austrian Jew, not to be confused with the emigré Arnold Zweig."[47]

But the ideological watchdog stuck to Goebbels's trail. His next attack was directed against Paul Hindemith, who had been described in the journal *Die Musik*, published by Rosenberg's Cultural Community, as "not acceptable from the standpoint of cultural policy."[48] Rosenberg now accused Hindemith of spending most of his time in the company of Jews and turning German music into kitsch, which made him unfit to belong to "the highest art institutes of the new Reich."[49] Goebbels himself had praised Hindemith in June as "one of the strongest talents in the younger German generation of composers," although he had to reject "the basic intellectual position that finds expression in most of his works up to this point."[50]

Wilhelm Furtwängler, vice president of the Reich Chamber of Music, whom Goebbels regarded as an inspired conductor,[51] came to Hindemith's defense in the *Deutsche Allgemeine Zeitung*.[52] Demand for Furtwängler's article was so great that the paper had to reprint it. Furtwängler argued that, given the worldwide shortage of truly productive musicians, one could not cast aside a man like Hindemith. He asked a question, implicitly directed at Rosenberg: what would happen "if political denunciation were applied to the fullest extent in the arts?"[53] The evening the article appeared, Goebbels and Goering happened to be at the Staatsoper. Furtwängler received long and pointedly enthusiastic applause. Goering apparently took this incident as the occasion to inform Hitler that a public expression of disapproval of a Reichsleiter had occurred.[54] Goebbels for his part threatened Furtwängler, saying he "would show him which of them was stronger."[55] Furtwängler thereupon resigned as vice president of the Reich Chamber of Music and director of the Staatsoper and decided, with heavy heart, to emigrate to the United States. The "Hindemith case" had thus broadened to become the "Furtwängler case," the case of the Reich Chamber of Music.

Officially it looked as though Rosenberg had won a complete victory in this instance. But then Furtwängler's plan of going to America was thwarted by his rival Arturo Toscanini, who publicly spoke out against him. With Hitler's approval Goebbels then used a combination of offers and threats to persuade Furtwängler to issue a sort of apology for his article.[56] He said he had never intended to meddle in the Reich's cultural policy; such policy should be made "solely by the Führer . . . and by the expert minister appointed by him."[57] Goebbels had killed three birds with one stone: he had enabled Furtwängler to save face, frustrated Rosenberg, and kept this distinguished conductor in Germany. Goebbels probably had the last point in mind when he wrote in his diary, "a great moral success for us." But there remained "the troubling question of how we're going to keep him occupied."[58]

Rosenberg continued to snipe. He demanded that Furtwängler apologize to him as well, for "his political attacks on the NS Cultural Community."[59] Probably at Hess's urging, Furtwängler complied, after which Rosenberg directed his organization, which had no official party status, to "preserve strict neutrality toward Furtwängler."[60] All the prerequisites seemed in place for an official reconciliation between the conductor and Hitler. In the end Furtwängler kept his old positions and in 1936 was made musical director of the Bayreuth Wagner Festival.[61]

In addition to the conflict with Rosenberg, in the fall of 1934 Goebbels had to turn his attention to the upcoming vote on reintegrating the Saar into Germany, for which provision had been made in the Treaty of Versailles. He coined the slogan "Home into the Reich" and attacked as lackeys of "Jewish bolshevism" all those who wanted the area to remain under League of Nations administration.[62] This tactic helped persuade the Catholic bishops to come out in favor of the Saar's return to Germany. Then on 13 January 1935 the overwhelming majority of the Saar inhabitants voted to rejoin the Reich. Goebbels made the most of the victory, pointing out that in spite of all the "international, defeatist, anarchist, and other elements" gathered in the Saar, including "world communism" and "world Marxism," over 90 percent of the population had voted yes, and that meant embracing national socialism as well.[63] Sirens howled throughout Germany on 1 March 1935, the day of the official "homecoming." On 16 March Hitler moved to introduce universal compulsory military service, under the pretext that on 13 March the French government had doubled the term of service in its army. Hitler's step violated the disarmament provisions of the Treaty of Versailles. To avoid alarming the German people, Goebbels's ministry instructed the press not to create "any sort of war psychosis."[64] New assurances were given of Germany's desire for peace.[65] In his diary, however, Goebbels revealed that he knew all about Hitler's plans for expanding to the east to gain *Lebensraum*: "So we must arm, and put a good face on a bad situation. Let us O Lord survive this summer. Through crises and perils leads to the way to our freedom. But it must be traversed bravely."[66]

The reaction abroad gave every reason to hope that this duplicitous game would succeed. The British and French governments merely sent notes of protest. The planned visit to Germany by British Foreign Secretary Sir John Simon and Lord Privy Seal Anthony Eden was not canceled, merely postponed until the end of March. The German-British treaty on fleet strengths, concluded on 18 June, not only sanctioned German rearmament but also seemed to be the first step toward a German-British rapprochement, the prerequisite for Hitler's ambitions on the continent.

These successes in foreign policy gave Goebbels another pretext for celebrating the Führer myth. On the day before Hitler's birthday, Goebbels in a radio address marveled that a man who barely three years earlier had had half of the German people against him "is today in the eyes of the entire people above all doubt and all criticism." This new unity of the people proved that Hitler was the man of fate, a "man with a mission," "to lead the nation upward to the desired freedom from the most terrible cleavages and most shameful humiliation in the sphere of foreign policy."[67]

As happy as Goebbels thought himself as one of the companions of the "apostle" Hitler, his "earthly" tribulations in the area of cultural policy continued. When Rosenberg learned that Hindemith was to be reinstated as an instructor at the Conservatory of Music, he promptly wrote to the Reich minister of education, denouncing Hindemith as a representative of "cultural bolshevism."[68] When Bernhard Rust, Prussian minister of culture and education, gave in to Rosenberg and continued Hindemith's suspension, Goebbels's defeat in this case was sealed. The composer soon afterward left Germany.

Then Rosenberg made the "find" he had been seeking in the Richard Strauss case: the Gestapo intercepted a letter from Strauss to Stefan Zweig in which the composer said he "was going through the motions" of being president of the Chamber of Music, because he wanted to "do good and avoid still greater misfortune."[69] Goebbels expressed tremendous indignation at this letter, which left him no choice but to capitulate to Rosenberg and insist that Strauss resign: "The letter is impertinent and incredibly stupid to boot. Now Strauss must go, too. . . . Strauss 'is going through the motions . . . '—he writes this to a Jew. Damn!" His disappointment and frustration led him to denounce all artists "from Goethe to Strauss" as "politically totally lacking in character."[70]

As Rosenberg had used anti-Semitism against him, so Goebbels now used it to get rid of the Berlin police commissioner, Magnus von Levetzow. This man had drawn the propaganda minister's ire in July 1935 by not proceeding forcefully enough against demonstrators protesting an anti-Semitic film. At the same time Goebbels had the position in mind for his old friend Count Wolf-Heinrich von Helldorf, who was in financial difficulties. Even before Hitler came to power, the newspapers had reported that Helldorf had "squandered his fortune through monomaniacal extravagance." To a great extent he had ruined himself by maintaining a sort of "Wallenstein's Camp" for SA men on his estate.[71] Helldorf's affair with the singer and actress Else Elster was causing a stir in Berlin, and Goebbels sympathized with his attitude toward women—"Isn't every real man like that?" he once asked.[72] But the decisive factor was his knowledge that in Helldorf he would have a radical anti-Semite at his side, with whose help he could proceed more fiercely against the Jewish citizens of Berlin. Hitler agreed to depose Magnus von Levetzow and appoint Helldorf. "Bravo!" Goebbels praised himself, adding, "and we'll clean up Berlin. With united forces."[73]

The great purge, the struggle against the Jews and against bolshevism, which he viewed as originating with the Jews, now moved more and more into the center of Goebbels's political agitation. This emphasis corresponded to Hitler's dual goal of gaining Lebensraum in the east and carrying out a war of racial extermination. Hitler wanted the 1935 party rally at Nuremberg dedicated to the theme of antibolshevism, and Goebbels's speech, "Communism without a Mask," dovetailed perfectly with the remarks of the previous speakers: Hitler, Rosenberg, Darré, and Adolf Wagner.[74] Goebbels began by announcing a German "world mission" against bolshevism; he defined bolshevism as "the declaration of war against culture itself by the international subhuman forces under the leadership of the Jews." He ran down a devastating list of alleged and actual Communist misdeeds, and concluded that bolshevism was "systematic madness" that aimed to "destroy the peoples and their cultures and make barbarity the basis of communal life." The question as to the identity of the "ringleaders of this worldwide contamination" was rhetorical. For Goebbels the "Bolshevist International" was identical with a "Jewish International." To prove his point, he read several pages of names of leading Jewish representatives of communism, starting with "the Jew Karl Mordechai, called Marx, a rabbi's son from Trier." This "sober and dispassionate" listing, Goebbels continued, made it clear that it was Hitler's "great achievement" to have thrown up "a dam in Germany against world bolshevism," "against which the waves of this Asiatic-Jewish tide of filth" had broken. Now Germany was "inoculated against the poison of Red anarchy."[75]

Against the background of this blaring anti-Bolshevist campaign, the Nazi leadership held a special session of the Reichstag in Nuremberg during the party rally. There the hastily drafted anti-Semitic Nuremberg Laws—the Reich Citizenship Law and the Law for the Protection of German Blood and German Honor—were passed. Changes were being made up to the last minute. Goebbels commented in his diary on the beginning of systematic persecution of the Jews: "This is a hard blow against the Jews. We're the first in hundreds of years to have the courage to take the bull by the horns."[76]

In the wrangling over the guidelines for implementing these laws, Goebbels took one of the most radical positions. He fought vehemently for a policy of driving not only "full Jews" but also "half" and "quarter Jews" out of Germany, as well as those married to them. Reluctantly, and only for the sake of peace within the party, he accepted the "compromise" of applying the laws to "half" Jews only under certain circumstances and to "quarter" Jews not at all. All this was to be floated in the press "skillfully and unobtrusively," so as not to create "too much outcry."[77]

In the area he controlled, that of culture, Goebbels with unmitigated zeal set about "purging" Jews.[78] Although he had at first not had any "direct legal basis" for introducing an "Aryan clause" for the Reich Chamber of Culture and its component organizations, he had used the decree of 24 March 1934 as grounds for stiffening the eligibility requirements for "non-Aryans," instructing the chambers not to admit such people in general to the cultural professions.[79]

In the spring of 1935 the systematic "dejewification" of the Reich Chamber of Culture began, pursued by Goebbels in subsequent years with merciless consistency, despite all obstacles. But when he boasted at the chamber's second yearly congress in November 1935 that the organization was now "Jew-free," and that "no Jew is active anymore" in the "cultural life of our people," he was expressing a wish, not a reality.[80]

In the previous fall Goebbels had run into strong objections from economics minister Hjalmar Schacht to measures Goebbels had taken without consultation. Immediately after the adoption of the Nuremberg Laws, Goebbels had directed that Jewish art and antique dealers and Jewish owners of cinemas had to sell their businesses by 10 December 1935 at the latest; otherwise they would be expelled from the chamber. By the end of the year Jewish booksellers had to sell out. Starting on 1 October, newspapers intended principally for Jews could not be offered or sold in public.[81] Several times Schacht had energetically intervened, arguing that the economic interests of the Reich had to be taken into consideration.[82] But Goebbels had ignored Schacht, knowing that he had Hitler behind him. For after Schacht had given a "liberalistic" and "provocative speech à la Papen" in Königsberg in August, Hitler had ordered Goebbels to come up with "material against Schacht," to show the unaffiliated president of the Reichsbank and acting economics minister how "dispensable" he was.[83]

In the second half of 1935 Goebbels's conflict with Rosenberg entered a new phase. To gain an advantage over Rosenberg, Goebbels reverted to a 1933 plan for a Reich Cultural Senate; his idea now was to appoint to this senate persons such as Heinrich Himmler or the Hitler Youth leader Baldur von Schirach, who were critical of Goebbels's cultural policies and could presumably be made more amenable if included.[84] But a memorandum from the National Socialist Cultural Community tipped Goebbels off that Rosenberg had stolen a march on him. On 11 September 1935 Hitler had already authorized Rosenberg to convoke a Reich Cultural Senate "with the goal of selecting and promoting all the creative forces in art and scholarship active in Germany in the spirit of national socialism."[85] Goebbels noted in his diary that the idea was "all copied, and intended as a blow against me," and realized the time had come for "energetic" steps. On 26 September he discussed the "Rosenberg question" with the administrators of the Reich Chamber of Culture. Since Rosenberg was "disloyal," he, Goebbels, had "no choice but to act likewise."[86]

On 2 October Goebbels was on his way to Hohenlychen to talk things out with Rosenberg. But in Gransee his car was flagged down by the police. Back in Berlin Magda had just given birth to their third child. At last it was the son Goebbels had been hoping for: "Indescribable! I dance for joy. . . . Rejoicing without end. Back at 100 km per hour. My hands are shaking with delight. . . . Perfect happiness. I could smash everything for joy. A boy! A boy! . . . My son! O great, eternal life!"[87] Presumably in memory of Günther Quandt's eldest son Hellmuth, who had died young in 1927, the son of the propaganda minister received the name Helmut.

But soon everyday life returned, and with it the Rosenberg problem. Goebbels had to line up allies because Rosenberg, as Reich minister for ideology and culture and as chancellor of the German Order of the NSDAP, claimed the right to issue directives to all organizations concerned with cultural policy. He already had the support of Himmler, Schirach, Lutze, and Darré. Goebbels pursued his own project for a Reich cultural senate and in October managed to enlist Goering. Since Goering spoke "sharply against" Rosenberg, Goebbels this time saw him as representing "thoroughly sound views."[88]

To dislodge Rosenberg, Goebbels went to Hitler and pointed out the difficulties that would arise if two bodies with the same name were created. After a "thorough discussion," he managed to turn Hitler against Rosenberg. Hitler called a halt to Rosenberg's project and gave Goebbels his full approval. On 22 October Goebbels sat down with the managers of the Reich Chamber of Culture and chose the 105 members of the Reich Cultural Senate, an organization that soon existed, although only on paper. But Goebbels was delighted to be able to inform Rosenberg that the Führer had decided against Rosenberg's planned consultative body, while he, Goebbels, would be convoking his senate on 15 November.[89]

Although Goebbels was gradually gaining the upper hand over Rosenberg, in January 1936 he ran into obstacles with his "dejewification" in the Reich Chamber of Culture. Schacht had finally persuaded Hitler that Germany's balance of trade and foreign currency holdings would suffer if Goebbels's radical measures against Jewish businesses dealing in the arts continued. Goebbels had to have an order issued suspending "all measures for dejewification . . . in commercial professions in the arts."[90]

In this situation Goebbels welcomed the murder in Switzerland of Wilhelm Gustloff, local group leader of the NSDAP's organization abroad. At Gustloff's funeral Hitler gave a strong speech, charging the "hate-filled power of our Jewish enemy" with this death as well as "all the misfortune that afflicted us in November 1918 and . . . in the years that followed."[91] Goebbels saw to it that Hitler's speech was broadcast over all German stations and used it as a pretext for taking even more radical measures.

By 6 March Goebbels had already called a meeting of the Jewish affairs officers of the individual chambers, at which guidelines for exclusion of Jews from the Reich Chamber of Culture were adopted.[92] Now all persons were to be eliminated or not admitted who had "25 percent or more Jewish blood." One Jewish grandparent was thus enough to make a person subject to the Aryan clauses. Those who were married to "full" or "three-quarter" Jews were considered "Jewish-related" and therefore came under the ban. In an apparent change from earlier practice, those married to "half" Jews were no longer excluded.

Meanwhile Hitler was weighing a decision to occupy the demilitarized

Rhineland and thereby abrogate the 1925 Locarno Pact. He hinted at this plan over lunch on 20 January 1936. Although he made up his mind on 12 February, his propaganda minister was kept in the dark. He advised Hitler not to act until French ratification of the Franco-Russian mutual assistance pact would justify Germany's breaking the Locarno Pact.[93]

On 27 February the mutual assistance pact passed the French National Assembly, but it had not yet been adopted by the Senate.[94] Hitler did not wait. On the evening of 28 February he telephoned Goebbels, asking him to come to Munich with him, because he wanted to have Goebbels with him "for a difficult decision *re* the Rhineland." During the long train ride Hitler seemed "indecisive" and "serious but calm." Goebbels argued once more for holding off until the "Russian pact" was settled, and gained the impression that that was what would be done.[95] But the next day the Führer informed Goebbels and Papen, likewise present in Munich, that he was "determined." Since Hitler's face expressed "calm and firm resolve," Goebbels was immediately convinced that the moment had come for action, even if it was "a critical time." He tried to talk himself into feeling confident: "Fortune favors the brave! Nothing ventured, nothing gained. . . . History is again being made."[96]

At eleven o'clock the following day Goebbels was at the Chancellery when Hitler revealed his plans to Goering, Blomberg, Ribbentrop, Werner Fritsch, commander in chief of the army, and Erich Raeder, commander in chief of the navy. He noted in his diary: "Saturday Reichstag. There proclamation of the remilitarization of the Rhineland with simultaneous offer to return to League of Nations, nonaggression pact with France. Thus acute danger avoided, our isolation broken, our sovereignty finally restored. Paris can't do much. England will be happy. Italy, which shamelessly abused our trust, can't expect any consideration. At the same time dissolution of Reichstag, new elections with foreign-policy theme."[97]

Goebbels seems to have been still unsure as to the date, but Hitler did not wait until a reconciliation was achieved between Italy and Abyssinia in Geneva, as Goebbels thought he might.[98] On 6 March he presented the plan as a fait accompli to the cabinet. That same afternoon he had Goebbels announce that the Reichstag had been called into session for noon the following day. In the evening the propaganda minister instructed his staff, who were kept in the ministry overnight so as "to prevent any indiscretions." Meanwhile Fritsch's troops, disguised as SA and Labor Front detachments, rolled westward "at breakneck speed."[99]

Goebbels had invited the foreign newspaper correspondents to a Berlin hotel and sequestered them there overnight.[100] Their German colleagues were summoned at the crack of dawn on Saturday morning to the propaganda ministry. From there they were taken "with many precautions" to Tempelhof Field, where they were loaded onto two airplanes that took off for the Rhineland.[101] Not until they were in the air were the journalists informed that they were headed for Cologne, Koblenz, and Frankfurt to see the German Wehrmacht march into the Rhineland. Alfred-Ingemar Berndt, appointed director of the press department in the Propaganda Ministry a few days later, told the reporters what they should write: "Lovely mood pictures from the Rhineland about the arrival of the troops, the enthusiasm of the inhabitants, the feeling among the people that they have been liberated from a nightmare. Of course no quotations from the old song 'Victory over France Will Be Ours,' but there would be no real objection to 'The Watch on the Rhine.' "[102]

On the morning of 7 March 1936, while the Wehrmacht crossed the Rhine amid the rejoicing of the local population, Goebbels worked "in a state of agitation" until Hitler's speech to the Reichstag, the first reports on the success of the highly risky undertaking, and information that other countries had reacted with consternation, blended into a "rapture of enthusiasm." As a "son of the Rhineland" Goebbels in Berlin responded to a radio message from the cathedral square in Cologne and took particular delight in this "rare triumph," for hadn't he "suffered there for a year"? His mother telephoned, "almost beside herself," and his old German teacher Voss, who happened to be visiting Berlin, was "happy and grateful." When Goebbels summed up the day with "Fortune favors the brave," this saying seemed to have been confirmed by events. And when he wrote, "Hitler knows exactly what he wants," that meant more than simply relief; it meant confidence that Hitler would succeed.[103]

Goebbels accordingly focused the "campaign" for the "Reichstag for peace and freedom" on Hitler's "bold step," portraying the Führer as knowing instinctively what course to take. In contrast to the Weimar governments, Hitler had restored to Germany its "freedom and honor" and led the country back into the circle of major powers. With the military seizure of the Rhineland, the battle for equal rights had been concluded, national honor and sovereignty restored. The election posters bore the suggestive slogan "Our gratitude is our vote."[104]

The press was instructed to spread a "confident mood," for "future actions depend on the population's assent. No fear of war can be tolerated."[105] On the evening before the election Hitler broadcast an appeal to the German people. Goebbels was enthralled:

One had the feeling that all of Germany had been transformed into a single, enormous house of God uniting all classes, professions, and religious denominations. And now its intermediary stepped up to the throne of the Almighty to bear witness to will and work, and to pray for his mercy and protection for a future that still lay uncertain and inscrutable before our eyes. . . . That was religion in its most profound and mysterious sense. A nation commended itself to God through its spokesman and placed its fate and its life trustingly in His hands.[106]

This time Goebbels knew what he owed Hitler in the way of election results on 29 March. He lost no time "correcting" a "stupid legalistic nonsense on the part of Frick—'valid' and 'invalid' ballots! How ridiculous!"[107] Thus he could proudly report to Hitler a yes vote of 99 percent.[108] The Nazi press boasted in its headlines, "Adolf Hitler and Germany Are One!"[109]

Goebbels experienced another great satisfaction around this time. On 21 March he and Magda looked at a red-brick "summer house," covered with grapevines, on the island of Schwanenwerder in the Havel. It had access to the lake and a marvelous view of the Klare Lanke. After they had seen the house, it was clear they would buy it. Hitler promised to help. On his instructions Max Amann, director of the party's Eher Publishing House, had to "be generous again."[110] Hitler had given him to understand that he "considered it important that . . . Dr. Goebbels be able to entertain in style in Berlin," and now Goebbels had the opportunity to buy a small estate at a cost of about 350,000 marks. As Amann recalled, "If Hitler had had the money, he would have given it to him, but Goebbels was one of Eher's best authors," which was why he asked Amann to "step in in this case."[111] This source, which would also flow richly for Goebbels in the future, was urgently necessary for him to "be able to breathe freely again," and for "Magda to get some relief." They had "so many other worries" that they couldn't also bear "such worries about money," Goebbels noted in his diary.[112] On the day before they moved in, the financing of Schwanenwerder was settled. Amann had agreed to buy Goebbels's diaries, to be published twenty years after his death, and paid a lump sum of 250,000 marks, with a commitment to subsequent annual payments of 100,000 marks. Magda then discussed with Hitler over the telephone what the promised increase in Goebbels's salary should be, and Hitler did not disappoint her.[113]

After the closing on 2 April, Magda took steps to repay Hitler's favor. Just for the Führer she fixed up the guest cottage on the grounds, hoping to be able to "offer him a little home" on Schwanenwerder. On the day before his birthday Hitler paid the longed-for visit and was again "absolutely enthusiastic."[114] After that he came often, to the delight of the children as well, for "Uncle Adolf" gave them plenty of attention. He always seemed especially taken with the oldest daughter, Helga. Goebbels often gave the Führer photographs of her. Even Helga and her siblings stood in the service of the regime and had to cooperate with their father's vanity. Sometimes they provided charming display objects at official events. Or on Hitler's birthday they would be photographed grouped around him, reinforcing the image of the Führer as very fond of children, which also formed part of the myth.

On Schwanenwerder the children lived like royalty. Goebbels gave them ponies and a pony cart. With the help of Jenny Jugo or the film actor Heinz Rühmann, Magda had little films made of them that were shown for Goebbels's birthday. Magazines were allowed to publish photos of the little band. Whenever time permitted, Goebbels would spend a few hours with them. His particular favorite was also Helga, who was developing into a somewhat precocious girl with whom he liked to "gab seriously" on walks.[115] He was somewhat worried, however, about Helmut, a rather dreamy youth, for which Goebbels blamed the company of his sisters.[116] The children were his greatest treasure, Goebbels remarked again and again in his diary. Years before he became a father for the first time, he had written that children were "God's good thoughts," because only with them could God talk "without the constant feeling of being betrayed."[117]

Not only the children but also Goebbels himself felt "perfectly happy" on Schwanenwerder.[118] In June the propaganda minister authorized for himself a two-seated Mercedes sportscar, in which he had his chauffeur Günther Rach drive him through Berlin "proud as a monarch."[119] In the summer he acquired a little motorboat "for Magda and the children," and a big new boat that was "somewhat expensive."[120] He was living "like the Lord God in France," he thought, while out on the Havel the passing excursion boats carried banners with slogans like "Buying from Jews robs the Volk."[121]

Goebbels's comfortable position and his contentment did nothing to reduce his pathological hatred of Jews. On the contrary, it seemed to him that his own circumstances had begun to improve only when he came to see the Jews as the source of all evil in the world. Convinced that things in the Reich had taken a turn for the better because the Nazi movement had thrown up a dam against Jewish influence, Goebbels at the end of April 1936 intensified the measures for purging the Reich Chamber of Culture.[122] The guidelines were extended to cover "all quarter-Jews" and also "all persons married to half- and quarter-Jews."[123] These measures went far beyond anything stipulated in the Nuremberg Laws.

When athletes from all over the world came to Berlin a few weeks later for the 1936 Olympic Games, few signs of the racial mania of the regime and its propaganda minister were in evidence, for this was an opportunity Germany must not miss to present itself as a peace-loving nation. As recently as the fall of 1935 it had seemed as though an international boycott might keep the Olympic Games out of Germany.[124]

The Olympic statutes asserted the equality of all participants, regardless of religious, racial, or political affiliation. But the International Olympic Committee had fallen under the spell of appeasement and decided not to exacerbate the political situation.

Goebbels had done everything possible to make the illusion perfect. In instructions for the press he explicitly directed that "the racial aspect must not be remarked upon in the reporting."[125] The city was cleared of the signs saying "Jews not welcome" or "Jews enter at their own risk." The anti-Semitic *Stürmer* was not sold on the street during the games, and the Reich athletics leader made a point of including in the German team the world-class German-Jewish fencer Helene Mayer, who had been studying in America.

In June the decision had already been made that the party would lie low during this time, so decisive for Germany's image in the world.[126] Accordingly, Goebbels had to bow to Hitler in the small but significant matter of seating etiquette. Hitler took the "very conservative position" that "the old bourgeois bigwigs" should have precedence over prominent members of the new order because they had "served longer." Goebbels wanted to "do it differently," arguing that those were the people who had fought the Nazis "with every means in 1932–33."[127]

The evening before the games opened, Goebbels inspected the decoration of Berlin one final time. The massive government buildings were draped with red velvet emblazoned with the swastika. Unter den Linden looked like a sea of swastika banners, with the white Olympic flag only now and then in evidence. For the Propaganda Ministry and other buildings on Wilhelmplatz, Albert Speer had designed a decoration of garlands and enormous gold ribbons.[128] Along the six-mile parade route from the Brandenburg Gate to the Reich Sports Field, garlands of little flags were looped from tree to tree, and the flagpoles that lined the road were wound with green, silver, and gold garlands.

After Hitler formally declared the games open, cannon salutes were fired, and innumerable doves were released into the air before the last relay runner carried the Olympic flame into the stadium. Then the Greek marathon winner in 1896, Spyridon Loues, stepped forward from his team. As he handed an olive branch from the sacred grove at Olympia to the man in high boots and uniform who was deliberately leading the German people toward war, probably hardly anyone saw anything wrong.

To Hitler, who like Goebbels spent entire afternoons on the reviewing stand, the athletic competitions clearly bore the character of a racial contest. The French ambassador François-Poncet, seated not far from the two, observed that Hitler, who hated sports, followed the German athletes' performances intently with a strained expression. When the Germans won, he would slap his thighs and turn to Goebbels, laughing. When they were beaten, his face would cloud over.[129]

Germany seemed to be basking in triumph. The Olympics could be thought to symbolize the dawning of a new era, to which the Reich could now look forward, full of self-confidence after the humiliations of the past. It was not only success in the foreign-policy realm that contributed to this mood; in the country itself things were looking up. The huge army of the unemployed had shrunk, in part because of the massive construction projects for the Olympics.

But not all observers allowed themselves to be taken in by the image of a peace-loving, progressive regime. Many foreign newspapers had economized by not sending special reporters to cover the games. Instead they assigned correspondents already living in Europe, who knew the truth.[130] When SA men got drunk and staggered through the streets of Berlin bawling, "When the Olympics are past, the Jews will be gassed," these reporters were not surprised.[131] It actually seemed counterproductive when Goebbels assured the assembled foreign correspondents at the beginning of the games that this was no propaganda display.[132] And when he noted that the daily press accounts abroad were exceedingly positive, he was repressing the results of a secret report prepared in his ministry that showed the opposite to be the case in those quarters from which criticism usually emanated.[133]

One technical and organizational accomplishment certainly made a deep impression. The Reich Broadcasting Company in Berlin succeeded in transmitting to almost all countries in the world that had radio facilities; such coverage had been attempted in Los Angeles in 1932 and had failed.[134] The foreign broadcasters specifically thanked the propaganda minister in a telegram.[135]

The Berlin Olympic Games were also to be filmed. That Leni Riefenstahl, whom Hitler greatly admired, would make the film had been a foregone conclusion. With her films of Nuremberg party rallies, *Triumph des Glaubens* (Victory of Belief) and *Triumph des Willens* (Triumph of the Will), she had demonstrated how perfectly she knew how to combine the regime's propaganda with the medium of the documentary. At first Goebbels was reluctant to give Riefenstahl complete artistic and organizational control of the project, as Hitler wished, because the film department in his own ministry had been preparing for the Olympics for several years, making short sports propaganda films that allowed cameramen and commentators to practice for "the production of two major films on the Olympics in 1936."[136] Even though Hitler's plan put an end to the ministry project, Goebbels's vanity in matters of film still led him to argue strenuously that he should have overall responsibility for Riefenstahl's undertaking. But when Hitler refused to budge, Goebbels as always accepted his Führer's word as his command.[137]

Preliminary discussions between Riefenstahl and Goebbels had already taken place in the fall of 1935.[138] Her contract with the ministry stipulated that she was accountable to it only in financial matters. Goebbels had arranged the finances for her as favorably as possible, though with the ulterior motive of preserving a degree of control. The 1.5 million marks approved by Hitler were paid out of the Reich treasury, so as not to put Riefenstahl under the kind of time pressure that would have accompanied financing through a bank.[139]

The good relationship between Goebbels and Leni Riefenstahl did not suffer from several major confrontations they had during the shooting of the film. Goebbels kept succumbing to doubts as to whether he could trust her, a woman, to accomplish this task. In the past he had often expressed recognition and respect for Riefenstahl, calling her "a clever thing" and "a woman who knows what she wants."[140] Now he recorded in his diary that she was behaving "indescribably badly"—"a hysterical female. Not like a man!"[141] In the fall of 1936, when an audit of Olympia Film Ltd. revealed that Leni Riefenstahl had "turned the company into a complete pigsty," Goebbels ordered immediate "intervention."[142] The filmmaker had the effrontery to submit an entirely different proposal in November 1936, which drove Goebbels into a rage: "Frl. Riefenstahl is pulling hysterical fits on me. It's impossible to work with these wild women. Now she wants another ½ million for her film, and wants to do two. She's made a filthy mess of things. I stay cool to the core. She weeps. That's women's ultimate weapon. But it doesn't work with me anymore. Let her get to work and keep things in order."[143] But here, too, Riefenstahl got her way. The Olympics film became two: *Fest der Völker* (Festival of the Peoples) and *Fest der Schönheit* (Festival of Beauty).

The night before the grand finale of the Olympic Games, Goebbels himself threw the party to end all parties. Although he had concluded during recent weeks that there was "too much celebrating" in the party and in the state, he had invited "everybody who was anybody"—between two and three thousand guests—to the idyllic Pfaueninsel.[144] The setting itself was incomparable, but Reich Stage Designer Benno von Arent had outdone himself with "fairy-tale lighting" and decorations so magnificent that the American ambassador in Berlin, William E. Dodd, kept exclaiming about how much it must have cost.[145]

When the guests had crossed the specially installed pontoon bridge, they passed through an "aisle of honor of young female dancers holding blazing torches" onto the brilliantly illuminated island. "The thousands of lights gleaming from the branches of the ancient trees were shaped like giant butterflies."[146] Three orchestras played dance music. The beaming host in a white suit and Magda in an elegant evening dress received the guests.[147] Champagne flowed like water on this evening, with which neither the garden party the Goerings gave for foreign guests "with cordial German jollity," nor the festive evening at the opera house, decorated with cream-colored silk, could compete.[148]

Among Goebbels's guests that evening were neighbors from Schwanenwerder: the actors Lida Baarova and Gustav Fröhlich. As Fröhlich later recalled, Goebbels "showered" the young actress with "captivating charm."[149] She had already drawn the propaganda minister's attention several times. In December 1934 he had visited the set of the film *Barcarole* with Hitler and been introduced to Baarova and Fröhlich, the stars.[150] Goebbels mentions her in his diary for the first time in 1936, in connection with the film *Stunde der Versuchung* (Time of Temptation): the film was "the usual pap," but Baarova's acting was excellent, he remarked.[151]

The budding relationship between Lida Baarova and Goebbels benefited from the fact that the villa where she lived with Fröhlich on Schwanenwerder was close to the propaganda minister's. Recently divorced from the operetta singer Gitta Alpar, who had had to leave Germany shortly after 30 January 1933 because of her Jewish origins, Fröhlich had bought the splendid twelve-room house with its own dock shortly before the Olympic Games. During the games Goebbels expressed the wish to have a tour of the villa. Several more meetings followed. Small boating parties were arranged.[152] Goebbels showed his interest in the actress more and more obviously, and the ambitious young woman certainly did not object to the attentions of the man who carried the most weight in the German film industry.

Born in Prague in 1914, Lida Baarova had already made nineteen films there, six of them with a subsidiary of Ufa, the leading German film company. She had also played small roles at the National Theater and leading parts at smaller theaters. In 1934 Ufa's foreign director William Carol had brought her to Berlin to audition. A dark-haired Slavic type, more like the femmes fatales officially frowned upon by the regime than like the image of the "German woman" held up as a model, Lida Baarova in looks was the exact opposite of Magda Goebbels. Magda had long since become disheartened, for she suffered from her husband's new style of life, and he had noticed "a certain woebegone quality" in her as early as 1933.[153] He now complained in his diary that Magda was "sometimes very distant."[154] This "very distant" attitude pertained particularly to the question of freedom within marriage. Several times she "explicated" for him in "endless blather" her concept of marriage and the family, which did not match his.[155] She tried to "worm" things out of him about

 is the full-page photograph.

Joseph Goebbels at thirty-two. The photograph bears the dedication "To my dear mother. Christmas 1929. Joseph."

Ich habe gefunden, den meine Seele liebt.
Hoheilied 3, 4.

Andenken

an die erste hl. Kommunion der Schüler der
höheren Lehranstalten:

Aretz Wilhelm	Lennartz Ewald
Backus Peter	Mauß Hubert
Becker Anton	Mauß Wilhelm
Bion Bruno	Meerkamp Ferdinand
Bougartz Wilhelm	Mooßen Wilhelm
Boy Herbert	Prickartz Julius
Brix Karl	Schaefer Rudolf
Finken Franz	Schiffers Joseph
Goebbels Joseph	Schlüter Fritz
Kamerbeek Wilhelm	Schwinges Paul
Kloeters Kurt	Thönnissen Wilhelm
Koerschgen Ernst	Vicus Wilhelm
Krapohl Wilhelm	Wesener Hermann
	Zilles Wilhelm

Halte fest an deinem Bunde und handle darnach.
Sir. 11, 25.

Rheydt, den 3. April 1910.

Oberlehrer Mollen,
Religionslehrer.

ABOVE LEFT: Joseph Goebbels (right) on the day of his First Communion (3 April 1910). ABOVE RIGHT: First Communion Program. BELOW: Goebbels (top row, fourth from left) in the sixth form of the Rheydt Gymnasium, 1908.

Josef Goebbels in der Sexta

ABOVE: Goebbels as a senior in 1916. Standing behind him on his left is Fritz Prang, who introduced him to the nationalists. BELOW LEFT: Agnes Kölsch, the student's first girlfriend, sister of his fraternity brother Karl Heinz ("Pille") Kölsch (1918). BELOW RIGHT: Anka Stalherm, Joseph Goebbels's great love (ca. 1919).

ABOVE: Joseph Goebbels (front row left) at the wedding of Maria Kamerbeek, who had just typed his dissertation. Behind the bride is Goebbels's older brother Konrad (September 1921). BELOW LEFT: The unemployed Ph.D. (1923). BELOW RIGHT: Anka Stalherm.

ABOVE: At a meeting of the Working Group Northwest in 1926: from left to right, Joseph Wagner, Gregor Strasser, Goebbels, and Victor Lutze. BELOW: Always near his Führer: Goebbels at the second party congress in Weimar (July 1926).

Goebbels speaking during the second Mark Brandenburg Day in Bernau.

Ullstein Bildarchiv

ABOVE: Walter Ulbricht, chairman of the KPD regional directorate of Berlin-Brandenburg, at the podium. With him is the Gauleiter of Berlin (front left). The gathering at the Friedrichshain Hall on 22 January 1931 ended in a massive brawl. BELOW: Goebbels as orator: a speech around 1930 at the Sportpalast in Berlin.

Ullstein Bildarchiv

ABOVE: Leaving the polling place, presumably during the second round of the election of the Reich president, 10 April 1932. BELOW: In the living room of the mayor of the village of Goldenbow: Joseph Goebbels and Magda Quandt during their civil wedding on 19 December 1931.

ABOVE LEFT: House of Joseph Goebbels's parents in Rheydt after he was made an honorary citizen of the town. On 23 April 1933 the street was renamed Joseph-Goebbels-Strasse. ABOVE RIGHT: The minister of propaganda arriving in Rheydt. On his left is Karl Hanke. BELOW: Adolf-Hitler-Platz in Rheydt during the address by the new honorary citizen on 24 April 1933.

ABOVE: Afternoon coffee in the garden of the Chancellery: Hitler with Magda and Joseph Goebbels. BELOW: The film actors Lida Baarova and Gustav Fröhlich in conversation with Goebbels during the minister's party given in conjunction with the Olympic Games in Berlin, August 1936.

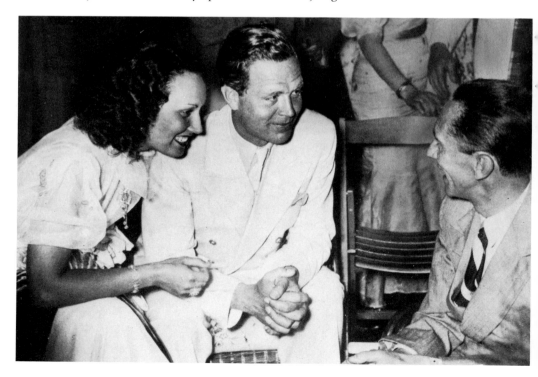

ABOVE: Joseph Goebbels with his daughter Helga during a summer vacation in Heiligendamm on the Mecklenburg coast (1935). BELOW: The Goebbels children. On the back of the photograph Magda Goebbels wrote: "We wish dear Grandma a wonderful Christmas and a happy New Year! Helga, Hilde, Helmut, Holde, Hedda, and little Heide, who is not in the picture!" (1940).

Goebbels as speaker during Mussolini's state visit to Berlin. On the lower left: Mussolini, Ciano, Ribbentrop, and Hitler (28 September 1937).

ABOVE: Hitler congratulates Goebbels on his thirty-ninth birthday (29 October 1936). BELOW: On the balcony of the City Hall in Vienna during the proclamation of the "Day of the Greater German Reich" (9 April 1938).

ABOVE: Goebbels speaking in the Sportpalast. BELOW: Surrounded by (from left to right) Kaltenbrunner, Goering, Dietrich, Himmler, and Bormann.

ABOVE: Conferring with officers of the Berlin Damage Control Station after an Allied air attack (February 1944). BELOW: On 8 March 1945 in the Lower Silesian town of Lauban, Joseph Goebbels shakes the hand of sixteen-year-old Willi Hübner, decorated with the Iron Cross.

ABOVE: Goebbels in October 1943. BELOW: The charred corpse of Hitler's newly appointed successor as Reich chancellor, as found by Soviet Soldiers on the afternoon of 2 May 1945.

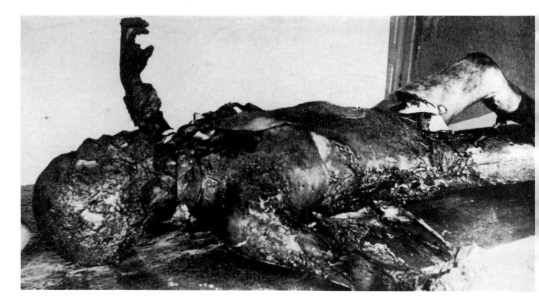

his rumored escapades, and he regretted even "getting involved in a discussion of this unpleasant topic," for Magda would "never change." At times the tension in the household could be "cut with a knife."[156]

Eleonore Quandt, Magda's closest confidante, poured oil on the flames of this continuing conflict. About the same age as Magda, since September 1934 Ello had been divorced from Günther Quandt's brother Werner.[157] She came to see Magda almost daily, bringing her some of the gossip about her husband and his affairs. Goebbels repeatedly tried to placate Magda by accusing Ello of "stirring up trouble" and "fabricating things." He cautioned Magda to be more careful about what she said, especially to Ello.[158] But the loyal Ello continued to drop hints about her suspicions.

So Magda herself occasionally took refuge in affairs. While Berlin was seized with Olympic fever, an "unpleasant business with Lüdecke" cast a pall over both marriages. Goebbels learned about it from Alfred Rosenberg, of all people.[159] Goebbels confronted Magda, but doubted whether she told him the truth. When she confessed "during the night" that "the business about Lüdecke was true," Goebbels was "very depressed." He said he would need a long time to get over this "great loss of trust." In the next few days he was "very curt" with Magda. Then he heard Hitler praise Magda as the best woman Goebbels could possibly have found. Hitler's opinion gave him an incentive he would otherwise probably not have had to patch things up with his wife.[160]

All this emotional upheaval and three pregnancies in quick succession had undermined Magda's delicate health and brought back her latent heart problems. Her stays at the fashionable Dresden sanatorium, the White Stag, became more frequent and prolonged. She had just returned when Goebbels departed for the Reich Party Rally for Honor in Nuremberg. After consultation with Hitler, he arranged for the premiere of the Baarova film *Der Verräter* (The Traitor) to take place in Nuremberg.[161] That gave the propaganda minister a pretext for urging the actress to come to Nuremberg from Franzensbad, the fashionable spa in Bohemia where she was likewise taking the cure; the other two leading actors would also put in an appearance.[162] After the "unprecedentedly successful" premiere, Goebbels again made advances to the actress—apparently not in vain, for he noted in his diary, "Dinner with the Ufa people. Delightful anecdotes. A miracle has occurred."[163]

Goebbels was about to make his big appearance at the party rally. To make an impression and hasten developments with the young Baarova, he called all his oratorical powers into play. He asked her to attend as his guest, and flattered her with all sorts of secret signals from the podium. His two-hour harangue against bolshevism slipped right by her, for she was attending only to the prearranged signals. Mightily impressed with the eloquent minister, she left Nuremberg for Franzensbad, but Goebbels's adjutant intercepted her at the station, bringing her red roses and a photograph of Goebbels with a note saying he hoped to see her again soon.

When Goebbels started a new diary shortly thereafter, he inscribed it with the motto "The wildest life is the most beautiful!"[164] On 20 September he set out for a week-long trip to classical Greece, thereby fulfilling a dream of his youth. But before leaving he received "a visit from Franzensbad."[165] Magda did accompany him on the trip, but the "irritable" and "rotten mood" that had prevailed between them for weeks refused to dissipate, for she bore an "unending grudge" against him.[166]

No sooner was he back in Berlin than Goebbels telephoned Lida Baarova in Franzensbad, where she had been joined by her lover, and asked whether they would come to Berlin for the premiere of their film *Stunde der Versuchung*. She said they would, and after she arrived in Berlin, Goebbels at once urged her insistently to join him on the evening of the film premiere in his box at the Staatsoper, where he was seeing *La Traviata*.[167]

He invited Lida Baarova and Gustav Fröhlich to come the next afternoon to the newly renovated official residence on Hermann-Goering-Strasse, on the pretext that he would be screening Fröhlich's film *Anatol*. After further meetings, secret rendezvous took place. Finally the club-footed propaganda minister and the young beauty became a couple. When interviewed in the late 1980s, Baarova, a robust woman of seventy-three, admitted freely that she had genuinely loved Goebbels.

An added source of happiness for Goebbels in this fall of 1936 was the recognition that his connection with his Führer was growing ever closer. For Goebbels's thirty-ninth birthday Hitler sent him his personal banner and paid him a visit at the Propaganda Ministry. Goebbels's notes reveal his childlike dependence on Hitler: "We go into my room alone. And then he speaks very kindly and confidingly with me. About old times, and how we belong together, how fond he is of me as a person. He is so touching to me. Gives me his pictures with a glorious dedication. . . . A wonderful hour alone with him. He pours out his heart to me. The worries he has, how he trusts me, what great assignments he has in store for me."[168]

The following day, 30 October 1936, Goebbels and the Berlin party celebrated the tenth anniversary of his becoming Gauleiter. For the occasion an exhibition had been arranged in the Red City Hall on Alexanderplatz: "Ten Years of Struggle for Berlin." Next to blown-up photographs of the orator Goebbels inveighing with clenched fists against the "system," certain "trophies" were on display: "Isidor's bell, glasses, and passport." But the propaganda minister also showed himself as a philanthropist: in Friedrichshain he laid the cornerstone for the charitable

Dr. Goebbels Home for "poor and deserving" party members and SA fighters.[169] For actors in need, an old-age fund, the Artists' Gratitude–Dr. Joseph Goebbels Foundation, was established; "full" and "half-Jews" and those "married to Jews," as well as political undesirables, were excluded from its benefits.[170] And in a memorial issue of *Der Angriff*, now the publication of Dr. Robert Ley's German Labor Front, a retrospective noted in a burst of involuntary frankness that "the massed millions of inhabitants" of the city had not taken national socialism "voluntarily upon themselves"; "We forced ourselves on them."[171]

Der Angriff also reported, on 31 October, that the city of Berlin had given "its Gauleiter Dr. Goebbels a special birthday gift." It was a "simple log cabin on one of the quiet lakes in the vicinity of Berlin," where "after the strain of his daily work serving the people and the Reich, he can find peace, relaxation, and a place to collect his thoughts." The city was placing the house "at the lifelong complete disposal of its honorary citizen, as a sign of its profound gratitude for his fruitful activity."[172]

But the high point of the Gauleiter's jubilee was the rally at the Sportpalast on the evening of 30 October, where Hitler began his speech an hour before midnight. He praised Goebbels as a "faithful, unshakable squire of the party" who had begun an almost hopeless struggle in the "outpost" of Berlin, and had "marched on ahead of this Berlin, this awakening Berlin, a fanatic filled with faith." "Therefore I thank you, my dear doctor," Hitler continued, "thank you today especially for taking the flag from my hand ten years ago, which you then planted in the capital of the Reich as the banner of the nation. And your name stands inscribed over this ten-year struggle of the National Socialist movement in Berlin! It is forever linked with this battle, and will never be obliterated from German history." Finally Hitler called upon the crowd to join him in crying "Heil" to Dr. Goebbels.[173] Exhausted, Hitler stepped back from the lectern. Then, in an attempt at a comradely gesture, he thumped Goebbels awkwardly on the shoulders. Goebbels found it difficult to maintain his composure. He admitted to his diary that Hitler had honored him "as never before. This I didn't expect. . . . How happy I am."[174]

CHAPTER 11

Führer, command,
we will follow!
(1936—1939)

When Goebbels remarked in his diary at the end of October 1936 that "the nonpolitical time" was now past, he meant that the "danger zone" had been crossed.[1] The "chains" of Versailles had been "stripped off," and Germany had become "militarily prepared" again. He knew that Hitler would soon set out to implement his program of acquiring *Lebensraum* in the east. To position itself for the eastward thrust, Germany had to annex Austria, and if Czechoslovakia and Poland did not submit to the Reich, they would have to be crushed before Germany could reach out for the huge Soviet empire. That summer Hitler had sent units of all the armed forces to Spain to fight on the side of Francisco Franco, in a rehearsal for the real confrontation to come. At the same time he had intensified negotiations with Japan that would soon result in a pact against the Soviet Union.

The party rally in Nuremberg, held at the beginning of September, focused accordingly on the "decisive world struggle" against bolshevism. The propaganda minister had been charged by Hitler with delivering an address that would provoke the Soviet Union into breaking off diplomatic relations.[2] Goebbels prepared a sixty-four-page paper, "Bolshevism in Theory and Practice," which Hitler considered the best thing his chief propagandist had written in two years; he showered him with compliments.[3] In his paper Goebbels portrayed communism as the "world enemy" that had to be destroyed, if Europe was to "be healed."[4]

In the anti-Bolshevist propaganda generated by his ministry, Goebbels skillfully took account of the hopes and fears of the different groups at which it was aimed.[5] The middle class was to be agitated by reports of the Communists' subversive actions all over the world. Workers were to be stirred up by the specters of hunger, housing shortages, lack of social welfare provisions, unpaid overtime, and total enslavement of labor.

Farmers were to be confronted with the effects of collectivization. The churches were to be given drastic evidence of the godlessness of the Soviet system. And statistics on the enormous numbers of failed marriages, portrayals of women as "free booty," and descriptions of neglected children could not fail to make an impression on German women.

The propaganda campaign was waged not only with words, but also with images.[6] On 17 September the Propaganda Ministry had invited the editors of all the major magazines to a special conference. Each magazine received an anti-Soviet topic for a one- or two-page photo essay. For instance, the *Münchner Illustrierte* was to report on Soviet Jews, and another magazine on the misery of children in the Soviet Union.[7]

On 25 November 1936 the German Reich and imperial Japan concluded the Anti-Comintern Pact.[8] Goebbels set the tenor of the press reaction: as national socialism had "saved Europe from inundation by communism," so the Japanese in the Far East were fulfilling "a similar mission."[9] The concept "anti-Comintern," coined by Goebbels's staffer Eberhard Taubert, was the "moral formula for cloaking a collaboration motivated by considerations of power politics."[10] Furthermore, inconsistencies with the Nazis' racial ideology had to be glossed over, for in the view of National Socialist race theoreticians, the Japanese were not "Aryan."

The counterpart to the struggle against the external enemy, "world bolshevism," was directing the *Volk* community more and more totally toward Hitler's goals. Any form of "deviationism," which was branded "Jewish" and "Marxist," was now to be hunted down even more vigorously. Heinrich Himmler was to guarantee that: on 17 June 1936 he had been placed at the head of the German police, after a power struggle with Frick.[11] Goebbels had welcomed this development because he considered Himmler "energetic and uncompromising."[12]

Within his own area of responsibility Goebbels pushed the hard line first in cultural policy. To do so, he embraced the radical dogmatism of Rosenberg. On 26 November 1936 he prohibited nonideological art criticism, which in his eyes constituted a "cancer on public life."[13] Hitler had just declared that "in a time like today" the "highest duty" was not criticism but "creating a unity of mind and will."[14] Such a goal could not be served by those "arrogant know-it-alls" who reacted to the desired formation of a "German cultural and artistic life" with a "dissonant chorus" of "interminable whining."[15]

The ban on criticism had an anti-Semitic thrust; Goebbels called reviewers the "disguised descendants" of the "Jewish critic-aristocracy," who in the time of "Jewish overrunning of German culture" had been allowed to elevate themselves to the role of "infallible judges of others' accomplishments." Goebbels made the Jews chiefly responsible for "completely twisting the concept of 'criticism' . . . into normative judgment of art."[16]

From now on, any such thing was not to be tolerated in the National Socialist state. Indeed, no leading Nazi saw any reason why he should allow himself to be publicly criticized, Goebbels remarked to himself. Therefore artists, too, should be shielded from critical attacks by the press.[17] A National Socialist orientation and "purity of heart," along with "tact" and "respect for artistic intention," were from now on to form the basis of "art reports" that would supplant art criticism. The purpose of these reports would be not to evaluate but to describe and appreciate works of art.[18]

Goebbels and Hitler also blamed Jewish influence for the negative effect of Christianity on the people. Goebbels asserted that Christianity had "messed up" the German people's morality and attitudes.[19] For Hitler, too, the image of the churches increasingly merged with his image of the enemy, the Jews.[20] Christ, too, had wanted to combat "the Jews' control of the world." Paul, "the Jew in Christianity," had "falsified" Christ's teachings and thereby undermined ancient Rome.[21] Since Nazi Germany did not want to let itself be undermined, Hitler was contemplating the "liquidation of the preachers"; the "final struggle" against the religious denominations was getting underway. It would end in a "cease-fire" when the war started.

Soon repressive measures did not spare the clergy, despite the concordat with the Vatican. At first the Catholic Church had viewed Hitler quite benevolently because of the anticommunist thrust of his propaganda. But soon annoyance arose at the Nazis' constant interference in church affairs through the person of Rosenberg. Thus the notes sent to the Reich government by Cardinal Secretary of State Pacelli, later Pope Pius XII, did not confine themselves to church interests, but commented on the Nazis' use of violence and repression.

On Palm Sunday, 21 March 1937, Pope Pius XI had his encyclical "With Burning Anxiety" read from the pulpit in all German Catholic churches. The point could not have been more clearly formulated. "Anyone who takes race, or a people, or the state, or the form of government, the carriers of state power, or other values fundamental to the shape of human society—which occupy a significant and venerable place within the terrestrial order—and removes them from the terrestrial scale of values and deifies them in an idolatrous cult, distorts and falsifies the order of things created and imposed by God."[22] Such words could not but seem like heresy to Goebbels, who wanted to elevate national socialism to a religion in Christianity's stead, and whose descriptions of

Hitler and his effect on people so often drew on religious vocabulary and imagery.[23]

When Heydrich informed Goebbels late at night on 20 March of the contents of the Pope's pastoral letter, Goebbels reacted "furiously and full of wrath" to this "provocation." But having once believed passionately in the Christian God, he knew the power of the Church over believers and reined himself in. He advised Heydrich, who wanted to "let them have it," to "play dead and ignore it." Instead of making arrests, he could apply economic pressure. Every church newsletter that reprinted the encyclical was to be confiscated and banned. Goebbels ordered himself to "keep calm and wait until the hour comes to shake off these provocateurs."[24]

Goebbels withheld the news from Hitler until the following morning so the Führer would not have to "be angry about it all night." Hitler, who "for tactical reasons" had ordered Goebbels and others not to leave the Church, at first approved of the silent treatment, but then became visibly more radical. On 2 April Goebbels noted that Hitler now wanted to "strike against the Vatican," for the "clerics" did not understand "patience and mildness"; now they should "find out how stern, tough, and merciless we can be."[25]

As the "overture" to the merciless bombardment of the Church in the press, Goebbels found the "gruesome sex-murder of a boy in a Belgian monastery" most opportune, so he promptly sent a "special reporter" from his ministry to Brussels to set in motion the smear campaign against the Catholic clergy. He also dug out press accounts from the previous year of alleged homosexual activity by members of Catholic orders.[26]

Everything Goebbels undertook in this campaign against the "clerics" was done in close consultation with Hitler, the driving force behind it. Goebbels felt "very happy" that Hitler had chosen him, not Rosenberg, to mark the climax of the "hellish concert" against the churches with a speech. In Schwanenwerder, after an afternoon boat ride with Magda and the children, Goebbels and Hitler sat down together to polish the "clerics speech."[27]

Goebbels delivered the speech on 28 May 1937 at a mass rally in the Deutschlandhalle in Berlin; all the radio stations carried it, and the text appeared the following day in the major newspapers, sometimes under the headline "Last Warning!"[28] In the speech Goebbels played the concerned father "whose most precious treasure on earth" was his four children. He lashed out at "these scandals that cry to heaven" created by these "preachers of morality." He worked himself into paroxysms of rage against "bestial and unscrupulous abusers of youth," and declared that this "sexual plague must be extirpated root and branch." One could only be grateful to the Führer that, as "the destined protector of German youth, he is proceeding with iron determination against the corrupters and contaminators of our *Volk* soul!"[29] After "two hours in splendid form" he could be sure of Hitler's gratitude: "He presses my hand. Listened to the entire speech on the radio and, as he told me, could not sit still for a moment."[30]

It is difficult to assess what effect this feigned moral indignation at the alleged homosexual excesses of the "clerics" had on the general population. After all, homosexual tendencies among prominent party leaders were well known in Berlin, while other leaders gave rise to much gossip with their heterosexual affairs. The epidemic of divorces among leading functionaries was just now becoming a "very serious problem" within the NSDAP. It constituted one of the chief topics of conversation between Goebbels and Hitler. In February, when the wife of Press Secretary Otto Dietrich had turned to Hitler for help, Goebbels had seen this as an attempt on her part to have Hitler "order" her husband to continue the marriage. Goebbels dismissed this action as "impossible." Hitler, who viewed the institution of marriage as providing "a certain stability," refused her request on the grounds that he had not married them and therefore could not keep them together. "A thoroughly correct point of view," Goebbels noted; he blamed the women entirely for their marital problems—they were "too stupid and too graceless" to hold their husbands.[31]

As for whether adultery should actually be punished, opinions clashed within the party. Goebbels, who wanted "no den of iniquity" in Berlin but also "no cloister," could certainly not set himself up as an arbiter of morals and preferred to let the reins hang loose, for he saw "eros" as the "most vital life force" after hunger. So he spoke out sharply against a proposal to punish adultery with ten years in jail, and against "chastity commissions" to censor writings harmful to the morals of the young.[32]

Although the Goebbels marriage still appeared intact in the early summer of 1937—their fourth child, Holde, had been born on 19 February—it was actually "near the breaking point."[33] One person who had long been aware of Goebbels's increasingly cynical attitude toward his wife was Ernst (Putzi) Hanfstaengl, who spent a good deal of time with the couple in the early 1930s, when they were still billing and cooing. Goebbels's treatment of Magda can be seen from an incident described by Hanfstaengl. One evening, while the propaganda minister was saying good-night to his guests, he slipped and would have fallen, had not Magda caught him. After a moment of shock, he grabbed her by the neck, forced her down, and hissed at her with an "insane laugh" that no doubt it would have suited her perfectly to appear as his savior.[34]

Around that time not only Magda but Hanfstaengl himself became a victim of the propaganda minister, with his much-feared cruel "jokes." Goebbels always told stories, anecdotes, or jokes—often in installments—at Hitler's lunch table at the Chancellery (he never missed the afternoon meal when the Führer was in Berlin).[35] Speer describes a campaign of harassment directed against Hanfstaengl that began when Goebbels spread rumors about him during these meals, and ended with a cruel practical joke that drove Hanfstaengl into exile in Switzerland and then England.[36] Hanfstaengl eventually found his way to the United States, where he became an advisor to President Roosevelt.

By now Magda Goebbels must have known about the liaison between her husband and Lida Baarova, for in the spring of 1937 the actress was more and more often invited to tea or evening parties at the propaganda minister's house. The affair had long since become the subject of gossip in Berlin. A story made the rounds that during the shooting of the film *Patrioten* (Patriots) there had been an encounter between Goebbels, Lida Baarova, and Gustav Fröhlich that ended in Fröhlich's slapping the minister in the face. What actually happened was that Frölich came upon the two in a compromising situation close to Goebbels's Schwanenwerder villa and, remarking that now he knew the score, slammed the door of his car in the minister's face.[37] Soon afterward Fröhlich and Baarova separated for good, and in the late summer of 1937 Fröhlich—"a little jack-of-all-trades without creative talent," Goebbels disdainfully called him—sold his villa.[38]

In the meantime Lida Baarova's career began a sharp ascent. The propaganda minister personally supervised the production of *Patrioten*, intervening in the casting, directing, and revision of the screenplay. He also undertook last-minute changes to make sure the film had the right "nationalist twist."[39] With the French ambassador François-Poncet and his wife, he visited the Ufa studios during the shooting and reviewed the rushes, which he judged very positively.[40] When he saw the finished film in April, he was "very deeply" moved. It had turned out "wonderfully. Absolutely clear and patriotic in its orientation. . . . an artistic delight." Even Magda was forced to say she was "very satisfied" with the film. When Hitler raved over the film and Baarova's acting, Goebbels's happiness was once again complete.[41]

Goebbels gave the film the highest rating at his disposal, and the critics were obliged to follow. The journal *Filmwoche* wrote that Baarova had been "better than ever before," and the *Licht-Bild-Bühne* even called her performance in this "extremely difficult role" a "masterpiece."[42] Goebbels had the film shown during the German Culture Week at the Paris World Exposition, thereby making a public display of his admiration for his mistress.

During this same year Goebbels managed to gain complete control over the German film industry. By bombarding Ufa's films with damning criticism, he maneuvered Alfred Hugenberg into selling out to the government, although Finance Minister Schwerin von Krosigk was reluctant to undertake the purchase because the industry had been operating at huge losses.[43]

With Universum Film A.G. Goebbels had acquired a company founded in 1917 that counted over five thousand employees, and owned over 120 movie theaters throughout Germany. Soon Goebbels had also swallowed up a number of smaller film companies—Tobis, Terra, and Bavaria— that had survived the Depression. By the beginning of May 1937 Goebbels could boast, "Now we are the masters of German film." He then gave orders for the "dejewification" of the companies' foreign operations.[44] Later in the year he banned the showing of "the last remnants of films from the past" in which Jewish actors could be seen.[45]

Because it was important to achieve financial success with the film industry, Goebbels made an effort to lure back German stars who had emigrated.[46] In some cases he was even willing to offer huge salaries.[47] Thus Heinz Hilpert, general manager of the Deutsches Theater in Berlin, was sent to Paris to approach Marlene Dietrich. She had turned her back on Germany in 1934 after her film *Das hohe Lied* (The Song of Songs) was banned.[48] The star of *Der blaue Engel* (The Blue Angel) turned Hilpert down, saying she could not appear in Berlin until a year later, but she stood solidly behind Germany. The propaganda minister promptly had her rehabilitated in the press.[49] In 1937 Dietrich became an American citizen.

After taking control of the film industry, Goebbels turned his attention to those trends in modern art that Rosenberg and his National Socialist Art Community had been attacking for years as "cultural bolshevism" —expressionism and abstract painting. As recently as June 1934 Goebbels had wanted national socialism, as "the carrier of the most progressive modernity," to evaluate these new directions for their artistic contributions.[50] As a student at the universities of Würzburg and Freiburg, Goebbels had regularly attended lectures in art history.[51] In 1933 he had brooded over the question of whether Emil Nolde was "a Bolshevist or a painter" and had decided this would make a good dissertation topic.[52] And in March 1934 he had even served with Goering as honorary patron of an exhibition on Italian Futurism in Berlin.[53] But now he began to lay plans for a Berlin exhibition of "art of the period of decadence," so "the people can see and learn to recognize it."[54]

The idea of moving the exhibition to Munich grew out of Hitler's annoyance at the choice of art works made by the former *Der Angriff* caricaturist Hans Schweitzer for a pet project of Hitler's, the "Great German Art Exhibition." Schweitzer had selected certain works that did not correspond to Hitler's personal concept of art in the spirit of national socialism, for which, of course, no objective criteria existed. Goebbels saw an opportunity for making amends to Hitler, while gaining more influence over cultural policy in Munich and elbowing out some rivals.[55] He would work together with Adolf Ziegler, the new president of the Reich Chamber of Fine Arts, whose claim to fame was that he had painted a portrait of Hitler's early love, Geli Raubal.[56]

The idea for the exhibition at first encountered opposition from Schweitzer and Speer, among many others.[57] But on 29 June Hitler authorized Goebbels to go ahead, and he passed the authorization on to Ziegler.[58] Not content with seizing the works of post-1910 German painters covered by the authorization, Ziegler went ahead and confiscated works by van Gogh, Cézanne, Munch, Matisse, and others.[59]

The confiscation from public collections of approximately seventeen thousand "cultural Bolshevist botchworks" by artists now vilified as "degenerate" required a "new ordering" of the Prussian Academy of the Arts. This amounted to a total revision of its membership.[60] Artists like Ernst Barlach, Ernst Ludwig Kirchner, Emil Nolde, Max Pechstein, and the architect Mies van der Rohe were urged to resign promptly from the Academy. The artists Max Liebermann, Käthe Kollwitz, Karl Schmidt-Rottluff, and others had already left in 1933–34, and Oskar Kokoschka would be forced out in 1938. While most of the artists complied immediately, Kirchner, Nolde, and Pechstein resisted, claiming that they had a positive attitude toward national socialism.[61]

All their arguments proved in vain, for Hitler and therefore Goebbels as well were bound and determined to conduct "a merciless purge of the last elements of our cultural corruption."[62] So those three artists' works hung alongside works by Eric Heckel, Franz Marc, Max Beckmann, Kokoschka, Schmidt-Rottluff, Lyonel Feininger, Chagall, Klee, Paula Modersohn-Becker, and Barlach in the gallery of the Hofgarten arcades—"degenerate art on display."[63] When Goebbels viewed the exhibition, he noted, "This is the craziest thing I've ever seen," although in 1924 he had expressed great enthusiasm for the work of Nolde and Barlach, which he had seen in the Wallraf-Richartz Museum in Cologne.[64]

In his speech opening the exhibition, Adolf Ziegler described these art works as "the spawn of madness, insolence, and incompetence."[65] After the exhibition was shown in Berlin, Goebbels created a special commission to sell some of the works abroad, to bring in foreign currency. On 20 March 1939 he had the remaining five thousand works burned in the courtyard of Berlin's main fire station.[66]

A constant preoccupation of Goebbels's continued to be the solution of "the Jewish question," on which he kept "undertaking massive initiatives."[67] He was delighted when the Führer gave him the assignment of drafting a law stipulating "that Jews may no longer attend any German theater or cultural function." Instead of a law he chose to formulate a police regulation, since a law would have aroused "too much attention."[68]

Goebbels also ruthlessly pursued the "dejewification" of the Chamber of Culture and took particular pride in the results.[69] Some of his measures had a tragic outcome for those affected. A number of expelled members were driven to suicide long before the actual Holocaust. Goebbels's hatred was not confined to Jews and those married to Jews; he also came down hard on certain Aryans. He systematically subjected Berlin's and later Vienna's cabarets to surveillance, then closed them down and had them "quietly cleaned out."[70] Many of Berlin's cabaret artists, known for their biting wit and political irreverence, spent time in concentration camps.

Hitler also commissioned Goebbels to "aryanize" the financial side of cultural life, which included film export firms, film distributors, music halls, and the record industry. Goebbels's task was made easier by the weakened position of Hjalmar Schacht, Reich minister of economics, who had failed to observe party discipline and was being considered for dismissal by Hitler. Legal objections against the "aryanization" were raised only by a few lawyers; where they did not see a way, Goebbels proceeded "by force." To his mind, lawyers were supposed to play merely "a supporting role," giving "necessary state actions the guise of legality," now that it was established that the Jews were to be driven "out of Germany, indeed out of all Europe."[71]

At the 1937 party rally, dedicated for the third time in a row to the theme of anti-Bolshevism, Goebbels delivered a speech entitled "The Truth about Spain."[72] Hitler criticized it sharply; the propaganda minister had gone too far in asserting that Germany was spearheading the European defense against bolshevism or that Hitler had taken on a "new world mission."[73] Hitler deleted these passages from the published version of the speech. Just now it was important not to hurt the feelings of Mussolini, who did not want to play second fiddle to Hitler in any respect. The Duce was expected shortly for a state visit in Germany, and Hitler had to gain him as an ally if he wanted to annex Austria to the Reich.[74] Goebbels bowed to political necessity, and felt much better after Mussolini praised him extravagantly for the speech when they met in Munich on 25 September. He was even more flattered when the Duce concluded his own address at Berlin's theatrically decorated and illuminated Maifeld with the slogan the propaganda minister had used at the party rally: "Europe, awaken!"[75]

In the talks with Hitler, the Duce had shown himself perfectly willing to give up the South Tyrol, but he had repeatedly dodged the decisive subject—the Austrian question—with references to "wanting to save face."[76] This made Goebbels suspicious, and he remained so even after the Maifeld speech—unlike Hitler, who felt "quite sure" of Italy's support. "I hope he isn't deceiving himself," Goebbels noted.[77]

But on 25 October Italy entered into the German-Italian Axis Treaty, and after a visit from Hitler's special envoy Joachim von Ribbentrop, joined the German-Japanese Anti-Comintern Pact. In December Italy then withdrew from the League of Nations. These steps indirectly manifested an agreement reached between Hitler and Mussolini on the Austrian question.

During the 1937 party rally Hitler had remarked to Goebbels that the Austrian question would be solved some day "by force."[78] Goebbels did not know precisely when Hitler intended to wipe the slate there, but he never doubted Hitler's determination to "go all out." Hitler had told him this state was no state at all; its people belonged to Germany, and it would come over to Germany. His entry into Vienna would be "his proudest triumph."[79]

As eagerly as Goebbels awaited his Führer's decision, he felt overcome with pity for Hitler when Blomberg, Reich minister of war and commander in chief of the Wehrmacht, sparked with his marriage on 12 January 1938 "the worst crisis for the regime since the Röhm affair."[80] A few days after the wedding, at which both Goering and Hitler had been witnesses, police files came to light revealing that "Frau Generalfeldmarshall Blomberg" had been convicted of "purveying obscene pictures of herself."[81] Hitler explained this to himself by noting that Blomberg was "weak and playful," that he came from "a narrow bourgeois background" and had "fallen for the first woman to happen along."[82]

Goebbels saw these events as "a terrible misfortune" that would "not be so easy to get past."[83] But worse was yet to come. Upon Blomberg's unavoidable resignation, the position of commander in chief became vacant. The commander in chief of the army, Colonel General von Fritsch, seemed the obvious man to fill the position. But Goering, enamored of titles and positions, and the uniforms that went with them, also aspired to succeed Blomberg, so together with Himmler he spun an intrigue against Fritsch. Goering showed Hitler a document prepared by Himmler that accused Fritsch of being a homosexual. Hitler fell into the trap. Although Fritsch swore by his honor that he was innocent, the Gestapo produced a man with a criminal record, a "stable boy," as Goebbels called him, who claimed to recognize Fritsch. Fritsch still refused to cave in, even after an all-night interrogation by Heydrich. But when Hitler fired his adjutant, Friedrich Hossbach, for warning Fritsch about the charges against him, thereby allegedly giving him a chance to prepare a defense, it became clear to Fritsch that Hitler trusted the word of the "stable boy" more than that of the commander in chief of his army.[84]

Watching all this unfold, Goebbels finally admitted he did not know himself "what's true and what's false."[85] But he observed Hitler turning "all pallid and gray" as Goering and Himmler fanned the fires of the crisis; this Hitler was the man of whom he had written just a few days earlier that he "loved him like a father."[86] He noted with particular attentiveness how exhausted and shaken Hitler seemed, thought his voice sounded "choked with tears." Not for a moment did he doubt that the Fritsch case had "destroyed all his ideals." Hitler "firmly believes" that Fritsch "has almost been unmasked as a 175-er," and that made Goebbels feel certain as well. (Paragraph 175 of the legal code contained the provisions against homosexuality.) Fritsch was denying it, "but that's what these people always do," Goebbels wrote. He concluded by resolving to share the Führer's feelings "strongly and intensely." "Good that he still has some friends on whom he can rely blindly. I'm determined to be one of them."[87]

On 4 February Hitler dismissed Fritsch, without waiting for the verdict of the court-martial over which Goering was presiding. A short time later the court dismissed the charges on grounds of mistaken identity, even though Fritsch's lawyer's request that Himmler and Heydrich be called as witnesses was denied. On 13 June Hitler made a statement before the assembled generals in which he cleared Fritsch's honor, thus sealing a "terrible defeat" for Himmler, but Fritsch was never fully rehabilitated and died under unclear circumstances during the Polish campaign.[88]

It was decided to stage a "great shake-up" of the military command —for public consumption. Goebbels, along with Hitler, hoped that in the reshuffling the real reasons for Blomberg's and Fritsch's departures would "completely vanish," and the rumors swirling in the world press would be "stopped in their tracks."[89] In the course of the shake-up many of the older, conservative, aristocratic officers were replaced by National Socialists and opportunists; Goebbels noted that the military was being rejuvenated "to an unprecedented degree."[90] Goering, too, benefited; on 4 February Hitler made him a field marshal. Goebbels commented, "He is beaming, and rightly so. He's had a spectacular career."[91] Hitler placed himself at the head of the new, docile Wehrmacht. The shake-up also affected the Foreign Office, with Ribbentrop being named foreign minister over Goebbels's objections.[92] Walther Funk became economics minister, which left the position of undersecretary in the Propaganda Ministry vacant; Goebbels moved his closest confidant, Karl Hanke, into the post.

While the crisis was still brewing, Hitler had been stirring up trouble with Austria. At an "unofficial meeting" between Hitler and the Austrian chancellor Schuschnigg on 12 February, Hitler used every intimidation tactic in the book, including demands that had to be fulfilled immediately.

When Schuschnigg reconstituted his cabinet to include two National Socialists, things seemed to be moving in the direction Hitler wanted. But then Hitler learned on 9 March that Schuschnigg planned to hold a plebiscite for "a free and German, independent and socialist, Christian and united Austria."[93] On 10 March Hitler ordered partial mobilization in Bavaria; Goebbels claimed to see "divine rage and holy indignation" in his face.[94] In the early hours of 11 March, "orders for armed action against Austria" were issued under the code name "Otto."[95]

What followed was a great number of misunderstandings, orders, and retractions by Hitler that showed how unsure of himself the Führer was during this first expansionist operation. But Goebbels painted an entirely different picture in his propaganda: in spite of "nerve-shattering tension," the Führer had been "in every phase of the events at the height of his tactical and strategic mastery of the means and methods appropriate to a political development that had been analyzed and executed according to plan."[96] In fact it was the cold-blooded Goering who finally seized the initiative. After pushing Hitler to be more decisive, he sent an ulti-matum to Vienna on Hitler's behalf, demanding that Schuschnigg resign in favor of the Nazi Artur Seyss-Inquart. He then dictated to Seyss-Inquart a telegram that was to be sent to Hitler: "The Austrian provisional government, which after the resignation of the Schuschnigg government sees as its task the restoration of peace and order in Austria, hereby urgently requests the German government to support this undertaking and help prevent bloodshed. To this end it asks the German government to send German troops as soon as possible."[97]

Late in the evening of 11 March Hitler received word from the German son-in-law of the Italian king, Prince Philipp of Hesse, that Mussolini had agreed to the military operation. At midnight Hitler received his first congratulations from, among others, his propaganda minister and the commander of the Luftwaffe. Coming from a banquet at the Aviators' House, "Goebbels in tails and Goering in parade uniform" hurried to the Chancellery and disappeared into Hitler's study in the upper story, where in this "hour of redemption" they listened with tears in their eyes as the "Horst Wessel Song" was broadcast for the first time from Vienna (or so Goebbels would soon paint the scene for the public, in his radio speech on the occasion of Hitler's birthday).[98]

Barely twenty-four hours later, amid the ringing of church bells, Hitler entered his native land near Braunau, his birthplace. Late in the evening of 13 March 1938, at the Weinzinger Hotel in Linz, he signed the hastily drafted Law on the Reunification of Austria with the German Reich. Before leaving Berlin, he had dictated a long proclamation to the German people, which Goebbels read over the radio at noon.[99]

Back in Berlin, Goebbels followed Hitler's entry into Vienna from the house of Veit Harlan and his second wife, the stage actress Hilde Körber, a close friend of Lida Baarova's. As so often in recent weeks, Goebbels had come to this secret meeting place in late afternoon. The little group sat riveted to the radio.[100]

Goebbels's broadcasting people were on hand again to record the speech Hitler delivered the next day to hundreds of thousands of Viennese gathered on the Heldenplatz.[101] Goebbels went to Tempelhof Field to greet the "victorious general" on his return. The drive to the Chancellery again resembled a triumphal procession, with people lining the route and church bells ringing. The short trip took almost an hour.[102]

Now that Austria belonged to the Reich, Goebbels extended his power base, establishing a Reich propaganda office in Vienna, which Hitler wanted to see stripped of its identity as an independent political center.[103] The building Goebbels had taken over belonged to a Jew who had emigrated, and Goebbels directed that it should be "fumigated again" before his people moved in.[104] He did not have "all the means in hand" to "gain complete control" until the Press and Chamber of Culture Law was adopted on 21 June, but for the time being the important thing was to release a flood of mass indoctrination in preparation for the plebiscite on the annexation.[105] Goebbels used the tried-and-true Hitler tour, this time encompassing the "Greater German Reich." Hitler had directed that his speeches be broadcast only within limited areas. He feared, and probably with reason, that his listeners would become jaded if they heard him speak every day, which would make it difficult to mobilize them for the last enormous rally of the campaign, when he would speak from Vienna.[106]

After this production, which ended with church bells ringing throughout the country and bonfires blazing on the hills, the last plebiscite of the Third Reich yielded a yes vote of 99.08 percent in Germany and 99.75 percent in Austria to the question "Do you assent to the 13 March 1938 reunification of Austria with the German Reich, and do you vote for the list of candidates proposed by our Führer Adolf Hitler?"[107]

In fact the great majority of Germans by now venerated this "Führer." All the attributes of a superman were ascribed to him, for he never let anyone get close to him, least of all women.[108] Accordingly it was women in particular who worshiped him, who fell into ecstasies when they saw him in person, who even set up a "Führer niche" in their living rooms, with flowers and his picture, in place of the little religious shrine they would previously have had. This cult of the Führer found expression in the presents and letters from admirers that arrived by the thousands every day. In the eyes of many Germans, Hitler, as a substitute for God, stood above earthly concerns. Whatever frightened or shocked them about what went on in the Reich, whatever injustice or evil was done, he was too far elevated to be associated with it; others were always to blame. General von Fritsch, who had been stripped of his power in such a humiliating fashion, once commented, "One can speak no ill of the Führer, but what is beneath him—that is horrifying."[109]

On 2 May 1938 Hitler left for Italy with a large entourage that included the minister of propaganda. Goering stayed behind in Berlin as Hitler's deputy. The days in the Eternal City, which was decorated with flags, fasces, and swastikas, were filled with receptions, sightseeing excursions, and consultations that left Hitler with the impression that Italy would give him a free hand in Czechoslovakia. From Rome the party continued on to Naples, where they were introduced to the Italian navy, of which the Duce was inordinately proud. When they returned to shore on the afternoon of 5 May, Goebbels was informed by telegram that his wife Magda had just brought their fifth child, Hedda, into the world.[110]

Around this time Goebbels was giving serious thought to forcing Magda to accept his relationship with Lida Baarova. He no longer took any pains to conceal it, appearing with the actress even at official functions, presenting his conquest with pride. He had even taken her to the premiere of Leni Riefenstahl's *Fest der Völker* (Festival of the Peoples), at which almost all the high-ranking Nazis were present.[111] In December 1937 Goebbels had already moved out of the villa on Schwanenwerder and into the guest house, in order to be "undisturbed." But most of his assignations with Lida Baarova took place in Lanke on the Bogensee. Whenever he would "take a little drive" in the evening to forget his frequent "annoyance" at Magda's "jealous scenes," he and Lida Baarova would go to the idyllic log cabin set in the midst of the woods north of Berlin. The afternoon hours and soon also the nights spent at the side of the young actress, away from the world of high politics, allowed him to drop his constant pose and awakened the last remnants of rationality.

If occasionally questions of morality and ethics arose for him, he would escape from them by throwing himself all the more determinedly into his rabid anti-Semitism. The year 1938 would offer him ample opportunity for that; his Führer had decided, on Goebbels's insistence, that the Jewish population should be reduced through pressure to emigrate, and that Jews should be systematically excluded from German economic life. On 26 April 1936 a decree had been issued requiring all Jewish holdings over five thousand marks to be registered. After looking over the lists, Goebbels concluded that there were "many rich people and quite a few millionaires among them," and that compassion would therefore "be totally out of place."[112] This registration and a decree of 14 June 1938 that required all Jewish businesses to be visually identified and registered as such provided the basis for further plans that Goebbels announced later that month. He was confident that "legal measures would assure" that within the foreseeable future all Jewish influence on economic life would be broken.[113]

At the same time a great wave of arrests and terror spread through the Reich. This operation had been postponed for some time, out of consideration for domestic political events. Now instructions came from Goebbels, which he summarized thus in his diary: "Police act with appearance of legality, party stands by as observer."[114] The operation was aimed at so-called Jewish repeat offenders, who had been classified as "work-shy and asocial." That Jews in general were targeted becomes clear from Goebbels's remarks on 3 June to Count Wolf-Heinrich von Helldorf, with whom he organized the campaign in Berlin. His purpose, Goebbels said, was "to drive the Jews out of Berlin. And without any sentimentality."[115] On 10 June Goebbels galvanized three hundred police officers for the task, practically hammering his hatred into them: "Legality is not the watchword, but harassment." He left the meeting convinced that the police would support him in this undertaking.[116] With deep satisfaction he commented, "Helldorf is now proceeding radically on the Jewish question. The party is helping him. Many arrests. . . . The police understood my instructions. We will free Berlin of Jews. I will not let up. Our path is the right one."[117]

His summer solstice speech on 21 June in the Olympic Stadium pursued the same goal. "Is it not outrageous," he shouted, "and does it not make one's face redden with anger, when one considers that in the last few months no fewer than three thousand Jews have emigrated to Berlin? What do they want here? They should go back where they came from, they should stop provoking us." Goebbels advised them to get out of Berlin as quickly as possible.[118]

The harsh measures evoked protest. The foreign press "ranted and raved" about the pogroms in Berlin. This hardly even irritated Goebbels; he issued a "reassuring explanation" and at the same time ordered that the adopted course be strictly adhered to.[119] He was more upset at internal criticism. His former undersecretary Funk, now economics minister, asked if all this could not be done "legally." "But it takes so long," Goebbels noted, as indignant as disturbed.[120] Foreign Minister von Ribbentrop also expressed concern. To calm his "anxiety," Goebbels promised to be "somewhat gentler," but in principle he did not yield one iota in his determination to "purge" Berlin.[121]

Hitler agreed completely with Goebbels's policy. At the end of July he took Goebbels aside during the Wagner Festival in Bayreuth and assured him of his approval. It did not matter what the foreign press wrote; the "main thing" was to "squeeze the Jews" out of Germany.[122] Now further measures followed in quick succession. In August Jewish doctors lost their license to practice. From the middle of the month on, a measure was implemented to make Jews "more recognizable": all Jews had to adopt the name Sarah or Israel, which was entered in their passports and had to appear on doctors' and lawyers' shingles. As greatly as this pleased Goebbels, he must have been very disappointed to hear Hitler say that "driving out the Jews" should be completed within ten years; for the present Hitler intended to use them "as a pawn."[123]

Goebbels did not hesitate to enrich himself at the Jews' expense. A piece of land next to his villa on Schwanenwerder belonged to Samuel Goldschmidt, director of the Goldschmidt-Rothschild bank. The mayor of Berlin, Julius Lippert, who had been managing editor of *Der Angriff*, forced Goldschmidt to offer the land "to the City of Berlin or to a third party to be named at the closing" for the ridiculous price of 117,500 marks. When the papers were signed, the mayor revealed to the lawyer handling the closing that the "purchaser is Reich Minister Dr. Joseph Goebbels."[124]

During this time Hitler was working on the next stage of his territorial expansion, the destruction of Czechoslovakia. On 2 June 1938 he laid out for Goebbels the plan he had developed. Goebbels was impressed that Hitler had "already solved this problem in his mind" and "established the new Gaus."[125] Goebbels promptly lifted his ban on critical discussion of Czechoslovakia in the press. Instead the Propaganda Ministry issued daily instructions for the papers to report on that country's "anti-German" policies. Bulletins on current incidents and reports on how the Sudeten Germans were oppressed and deprived of their rights were to be sensationalized, so as to intimidate the enemy. Goebbels's staffer Berndt stayed up "entire nights poring over general staff maps, telephone books, and lists of names, fabricating atrocity stories from the Sudetenland."[126] Not only did he magnify small incidents; he also portrayed prior events as if they had just occurred.[127]

While the Czech government reacted with dismay, Goebbels himself seems not to have felt entirely at ease with this method of provoking a crisis. In conversations with his old undersecretary Funk and his confidant Hanke, he sometimes expressed nervousness and concern about the likelihood of war.[128] Goebbels, who studied carefully the analyses of the popular mood prepared by his ministry and the State Security Service (Staatssicherheitsdienst), thought he could detect a "gloomy mood" throughout the Reich, a far cry from the enthusiasm and rejoicing of August 1914.[129] With a sideswipe at Otto Dietrich, he blamed part of the fear of war on the press; one could not keep a crisis simmering for months—that merely produced fatigue in the public.[130] But he banished his uneasiness by persuading himself that Hitler knew exactly what he wanted and had always found "the right moment."[131]

Goebbels derived strength and confidence from a stop he made in

Leonding near Linz while on a trip through what had been Austria. In the village cemetery, at the grave of Hitler's parents, he was overcome by "a sense of awe that here the parents of such a great historical genius lay buried." He lingered for a long time over the graves before he was shown through Hitler's parents' house. As if trying to explain his bond with the Führer, he saw the house as a replica of his own parental home. It was "very small and primitive." "I am led into the room that was his domain. Small and low-ceilinged. Here he forged plans and dreamed of the future." Finally he hobbled through the yard, imagining "little Adolf picking apples and pears here at night." From the tales told by Hitler's old schoolmates, he deduced that Hitler had "always been the leader," had talked to his friends about history, and was a "dear comrade" to them. Like his own, Hitler's mother had also been "dear and kind-hearted," while the father was "curt, taciturn, and stern." He concluded that the sufferings he and Hitler had undergone in their youth had destined them for "something greater." "Happy" to be there, he went through all the rooms once more, and "breathed in deeply the air of this house."[132]

When he returned to Berlin, the trouble between Goebbels and his wife escalated. Before going to Austria, he had enjoyed what he considered the most wonderful vacation in his life with Lida Baarova in Lanke, which he had now made his permanent quarters.[133] Not until early August did he reveal to his wife the full extent of his relationship with the film actress. "Glad that this point has been reached," he still did not talk to her directly, but in typical fashion sent Lida Baarova on ahead. Woman-to-woman she was supposed to prepare Magda for Goebbels's intention of establishing a *ménage à trois*.[134]

Only after his mistress had felt Magda out did husband and wife have a "long exchange" on the following day, after which Goebbels thought "not everything was settled yet, but much clarified."[135] Magda had—apparently—shown willingness to accept her husband's proposals. But during two weekends that the three of them spent together, Goebbels provoked her so blatantly—fondling Lida Baarova on their yacht in front of Magda and their guests, and showing Lida's films in the evenings—that Magda lost patience once and for all.[136] On 15 August she took the very step that Goebbels least expected: she went to Hitler, to put an end to a situation that had become intolerable. Hitler was "deeply shaken," but after the Blomberg scandal in February he was terrified of another such affair and refused to allow a divorce.

Hitler promptly summoned Goebbels, and in a "very long and serious discussion" reminded him of his duty and categorically ordered him to separate from Lida Baarova at once. To put additional pressure on him, he linked Goebbels's political career to the survival of the marriage, leaving it up to Magda to decide whether she would stay with Goebbels. Hitler was playing for time; with the Czech invasion in the offing, he did not want to lose his most skillful propagandist. He ordered a "cease-fire until the end of September" in the couple's marital battle.[137] Goebbels was "shaken to the core" and "thoroughly overcome," but at once reached "very difficult" and "final" decisions: "Duty comes before all else. In the most difficult moments one must obey its call. The rest is all temporary and transitory. So I will bow to my duty. Without complaint." Late at night he had a last "very long and very sad telephone conversation" with Lida Baarova. "But I shall remain strong, even though my heart is breaking. And now a new life begins. A hard, cruel life, devoted only to duty. My youth is ended."[138]

Goebbels spent the next few days "talking things out," alternating between Hitler and Magda.[139] There is no evidence that he seriously tried to effect a separation from Magda.[140] The notes in his diary suggest the opposite. He hoped Magda would reach a positive decision after the agreed-upon cease-fire—to continue the marriage: "By then many things can change, for better and for worse. I hope only for the better. Grass must grow over the whole thing. And time must pass, which, as we know, heals all things."[141] But while Hitler was "like a father" to him, at Magda's hands he experienced "nothing but humiliation."[142] Time and again he lamented how "hard and cruel" Magda was to him.[143] He wrote, full of self-pity, that he was living through the most difficult time of his life. His heart was "wounded unto death," he was sleeping only with the help of "powerful pills," and eating nothing for days on end. Other than from Hitler, he received support only from his mother and his sister Maria, with whom he spent long evenings seeking counsel.[144]

For Lida Baarova the separation from Goebbels meant the end of her career in Germany. She tried to get Goebbels to change his mind, using her friend Hilde Körber as an intermediary, but in vain. Goebbels defended to Hilde Körber the "necessity" of his action and the "irrevocability" of his decision.[145] Lida Baarova promptly lost her lead role in the film *Die Geliebte* (The Mistress) to Viktoria von Balasko, after the Ufa company physician had suddenly diagnosed a "defective heart valve" in Lida. The already finished film *Preussische Liebesgeschichte* (Prussian Love Story), a thinly disguised version of her relationship with Goebbels, was banned, and was not shown in cinemas until 1950 under the title *Liebeslegende* (Legend of Love). But her most bitter moment was yet to come.

"Hitler's thinking is at present entirely preoccupied with military questions," Goebbels noted, even more obsequious than usual because of his guilty conscience.[146] Almost daily he conferred with his Führer. One time they would discuss the Balkans, another time England's likely reaction in case of an attack on Czechoslovakia. Hitler assured his propaganda minister that thorough military preparations had been made in case England did not take the attack lying down. This was not true, but the Führer was counting on England's shrinking from conflict.[147]

Now the Propaganda Ministry "got into high gear for war," for the Nazi leadership and the Wehrmacht had agreed from the outset that the "war of propaganda" should accompany the "war of weapons" on an equal footing.[148] Propaganda had become an official component of the Wehrmacht for the first time during the maneuvers of September 1937, when a staff from Goebbels's ministry was outfitted with the most modern vehicles and communications equipment and allowed to "tag along."[149] In the course of the summer of 1938 Goebbels and Wilhelm Keitel of the Wehrmacht high command reached agreement on how the Wehrmacht and the ministry would divide up the propaganda tasks in case of war.[150] In the "Principles for the Conduct of Propaganda in Wartime," it was determined that "morale-building" among the troops, "active propaganda in the theater of war," and "inciting enemy troops or labor to rebel" came under the organizational purview of the Wehrmacht, but the contents and psychological guidelines would be furnished by Goebbels's ministry. To carry out these assignments, so-called propaganda companies were set up. In August 1938 the order came to integrate them into the Wehrmacht.[151]

In the meantime Hitler was energetically pursuing the "solution" to the Czech "problem." During his concluding speech at the party rally in Nuremberg, he declared that he was not at all inclined to stand idly by and watch with infinite patience "the continued oppression of our fellow Germans in Czechoslovakia." When an uprising engineered by the Germans broke out in the Sudetenland and hectic military activity began in the Reich, the British prime minister Chamberlain took steps. On 15 September he met with Hitler at the Berghof, and a week later in Bad Godesberg. But the discussions achieved nothing, for Hitler did not limit his demands to the Sudetenland; he also demanded territorial concessions from Poland and Hungary.

For 26 September Hitler planned a rally at the Sportpalast that was to whip up enthusiasm for the pending war against Czechoslovakia. In an introductory speech Goebbels expressed to Hitler the people's alleged readiness for war: "You can rely on your *Volk*. . . . It stands as one behind you. No threat and no pressure . . . , as we know, can persuade you to give up your, and our, inalienable claim to these rights. In this attitude and immovable power of conviction the entire German *Volk* stands united with you. Often we have vowed this in the nation's great hours. Now in the hour of gravest decision we repeat it before you with heart full and strong: Führer, command, we will follow!"[152]

Goebbels took refuge in such fanaticism all the more when, as so often in these months of crisis, he was seized with fear of war. Such fear overcame him on 27 September when he saw a division march through Berlin. The next day he voiced his anxiety at lunch in the Chancellery, probably hoping his Führer would help him banish it. Ernst von Weizsäcker, who had become undersecretary in the Foreign Office, describes how Goebbels "bravely and at the right moment" said "loudly to the Führer, ignoring all those present," that "the German public was also . . . very much opposed to war."[153]

Warnings from the army and the navy that they were not ready (General Beck resigned to make that very point), but especially reports from abroad suggesting determination on the part of the Western powers, finally induced Hitler to content himself with the Sudetenland.[154] On 29 September Chamberlain, Daladier, and Hitler, with Mussolini acting as mediator, signed the Munich Agreement, which was then imposed on an unwilling Czechoslovakia. On 1 October German troops marched into the Sudetenland. All Europe breathed a sigh of relief. Many believed that peace was assured. But only three weeks later Gen. Walter von Brauchitsch instructed the Wehrmacht to prepare to smash "Rump Czechoslovakia" and seize the Memel region.

Goebbels's private situation was meanwhile deteriorating, for during the "cease-fire period" Magda had shown no sign of relenting. Assailed by high fever and "incredible pains in my heart," Goebbels took the "firm decision" to put an end to this state of affairs. Since "every road was blocked" for him, he sent his undersecretary Karl Hanke to Magda as an intermediary.[155] Goebbels saw a small ray of hope in Hitler's conversation with Magda at the Berghof on 21 October.[156] Two days later came a further conversation between her, Hitler, and Goebbels.[157] After Hitler had made it clear that he wanted to see the marriage preserved "for political reasons," Magda agreed to a trial period of three months, on condition that her husband show unimpeachable conduct. If they could not work things out, Goebbels would have to offer his resignation.[158]

At the same time, official pressure on Lida Baarova was increased. A convenient pretext was offered by the premiere of her film *Der Spieler* (The Gambler), based on the Dostoyevski novel. When Goebbels had "reviewed" the film in July, he assessed it in the most glowing terms: "Splendid evocation of the milieu, skillful in the psychological portrayal. I'm bowled over."[159] In the film Lida Baarova plays the daughter of a Russian general who is deeply in debt. When a desperately awaited inheritance fails to materialize, she turns to her tutor for emotional support. Her tutor wins one hundred thousand florins by gambling his last gold piece. When the young woman begs her father for money, he turns her away with the words, "Go ask your 'doctor' for the money! He has more than I!" At this point during the premiere, the theater on Kurfürstendamm erupted in whistles and jeers. "Get out, minister's whore!" shouted the paid troublemakers. The tumult did not cease until the showing was stopped. The film's run ended immediately.[160] Lida Baarova suffered a nervous breakdown.[161] Shadowed by the Gestapo wherever she went, she was ordered by Helldorf to stop appearing in public. Her plan to renew old contacts in Hollywood was also thwarted. Fear that the scandal might be revealed abroad led Hitler to send word by way of his adjutant that she could not leave the country. Finally, in the winter of 1938–39, a friend helped her flee to Prague. But even there her troubles were not over.[162]

News arriving on 7 November from Paris distracted people from the Goebbels scandal. A desperate young man named Herszel Grynszpan had shot a diplomat attached to the German embassy. The assassin's family were Polish Jews deported from the Reich. On 9 November in Munich the Nazis always celebrated the anniversary of Hitler's putsch attempt. This time, as Hitler and the party leadership were winding up the ceremony in the Old City Hall, word came that the diplomat had died of his wounds. After a whispered exchange with Goebbels, Hitler left the hall. A short time later Goebbels hobbled up to the lectern, somberly informed the company of the diplomat's death, then launched into a hate-filled tirade against "international Jewry." He noted that the people's rage had already found a way to express itself, and added that while such demonstrations of popular opinion were not to be prepared or executed by the party, nothing would be done to prevent them. Documents found later revealed that the "Night of Broken Glass" that now got underway had been planned down to the last detail by several government agencies working in concert.[163]

In the course of the pogrom, more than twenty thousand Jews were loaded into trucks like cattle and hauled off to Dachau, Buchenwald, or Oranienburg, from where few returned. The following morning Goebbels instructed the press as to what it could report: a few windows had been smashed, some synagogues had somehow caught fire. To foreign correspondents he explained at the regular afternoon press conference in the ministry that all reports of alleged looting and destruction of Jewish property were "filthy lies." "Not a hair" of the Jews' heads had been harmed.[164]

Most of the foreign press representatives were not taken in. The correspondents for the *New York Times* and the London *Daily Telegraph* reported extensively on the pogrom in Berlin, which they had seen with their own eyes. They noted the public reaction: some had shouted "Down with the Jews!" and mobs of looters had gone to work after the SA had finished its destruction, but a majority had been "deeply disturbed by the events." These reports could not be read in Germany, however, because Goebbels had halted distribution of these papers by having them confiscated.[165]

But on the whole, reaction abroad to the biggest and cruelest pogrom to date remained very tentative. President Roosevelt merely called his ambassador back to Washington to report. Four weeks after the event France received the German foreign minister with full diplomatic honors. The situation would become even more menacing for the Jews in February 1939, when England clamped down on Jewish immigration to Palestine. With an eye to securing necessary Arab support for the protection of the Suez Canal, England backed away from its promise to establish a Jewish state, which meant that Jews could emigrate to Palestine only illegally. This development in turn gave impetus to those in Berlin who wanted to proceed radically on the "Jewish question."

The day after the pogrom Goebbels sat at Hitler's table in the Chancellery and explained "convincingly" for many of those present "the significance of the operation."[166] According to Goering, Goebbels, thinking of the wealthy Jews in Berlin, came up with the idea that the Gaus should impose fines on the Jews; Goering, on the other hand, thought the money should go to the Reich government.[167] Hitler instructed Goering to set up a commission of which Goebbels would be a member.

The high-level commission met in the conference room of Goering's aviation ministry on 22 November. A partial transcript of the meeting has been preserved.[168] Goebbels pushed not only for eliminating the Jews completely from economic life, but also for banning them from all forms of entertainment and recreation and for imposing strict separation of Jews from Germans on trains. It was decided that the insurance companies would have to pay the Jews damages from the Night of Broken Glass, but that the government should immediately confiscate the payments. Furthermore, the Jews would have to pay reparations. Jewish holdings were estimated at five billion marks, and the reparations were set at 20 percent—"a nice bloodletting," in Goebbels's eyes.[169]

That same day new measures were announced. They included the "aryanization" of the last businesses in Jewish hands, a ban on Jewish attendance at cultural events, including the circus, and a ban on Jewish children's attendance at school. Recreational facilities were to be closed to Jews. At the beginning of 1939 Goering charged Heydrich with "implementation of Jewish emigration from the entire Reich."[170]

Meanwhile Goebbels's propaganda campaign against the "internationalist enemies of the peoples" continued. Goebbels thought he was now closer to thwarting the "fall of the West" being plotted by what he called *Alljuda*, universal Jewry, with which he was obsessed. The system for stripping Jews of their rights and property was in place. To begin thinking of the physical destruction of the Jews was now only the next, though decisive, step.

But the time for that was not yet ripe. Goebbels complained at the ministry press conference on 24 November that there still existed a "class of whining philistines" who spoke of the "poor Jews" and took their part at every opportunity. It was not acceptable that "only the state and the party be anti-Semitic."[171] No matter how successful Goebbels was at getting the "mass of the people" to swear allegiance to the Führer, he did not succeed in bringing Führer and *Volk* into harmony on the "Jewish question." It was significant that most Germans did not want to think of the pogrom as Hitler's doing. Only a long war, which numbed people and put their own desire for survival uppermost in their minds, would bring them around to Goebbels's point of view.

To get the German people to accept violence as the only solution to certain problems, Goebbels set about building German self-confidence. In addition to the Nazi leadership and the "strength" of the German people, Goebbels now particularly stressed the Wehrmacht as a factor in Germany's new position of strength. This and other forms of consensus-building fell to the press as planning went forward for the seizure of "Rump Czechoslovakia."[172] The press received instructions to avoid any reference to "the horrors of war and the sufferings of the individual."[173] Instead the papers should highlight "the inherently heroic character of war" and the "natural joy in victory."[174] The radio did its part with programs like "Garrisons on the Borders of Greater Germany," which portrayed the "wonderful comradeship" between the soldiers and the surrounding population.[175]

While the nation was being prepared for war, the leading party functionaries were preoccupied with the piquant details of the propaganda minister's marital crisis. Magda Goebbels had supposedly gone to Emmy Goering to pour out her sorrows about the "devil in human form" to whom she was married. Goebbels, for his part, complained to Goering that his wife was "so cold" that he "desperately needed other pleasures."[176] What people had whispered to each other for years now became an open scandal providing general titillation.[177] "Half amused, half revolted," Karl Hanke, Goebbels's undersecretary, told Albert Speer how Goebbels had earlier blackmailed young film actresses.[178] He also knew about the "unanimous rage" in party and artistic circles at Goebbels's improper advances to women.[179] Curiosity as to the newest state of affairs was mixed with often hypocritical indignation at the way Goebbels had abused the Führer's faith in him.

Scorn and mockery poured down on the propaganda minister from all sides. The diary of his archenemy Rosenberg is particularly venomous.

He, like Himmler, saw Goebbels as the "greatest moral burden on the N.S."[180] Open contempt, in Rosenberg's case an outlet for his envy, was expressed toward this minister who for years had subjected not only film actresses but also his female employees to sexual pressure, and was therefore "morally isolated within the party." Rosenberg goes so far as to call Goebbels "the most hated man in Germany." Himmler added fuel to the fire by telling Rosenberg about "dozens" of cases in which women had gone to Frau Goebbels and the Gestapo to describe the abuse they had suffered. Himmler slipped some of the notes on these cases to Hitler. So it was no wonder that Goebbels sensed a "frosty atmosphere" around him. He tried to act "deaf and absentminded" toward the gossip.[181] But with Hanke he frequently had to discuss "the painful aspects of my case," and he concluded almost despairingly, "I can't seem to extricate myself from this." His wish "that the entire past could be forgotten" speaks volumes.[182] Magda's birthday on 11 November was celebrated "very quietly," because at the moment there was no cause for "paroxysms of joy."[183] Yet speculation and rejoicing on the part of his enemies that he had fallen into disfavor with Hitler was unfounded. Hitler made a point of spending two days at the couple's house on Schwanenwerder in mid-November, where he received Keitel, Brauchitsch, and Goering for meetings.[184]

At the end of 1938 Goebbels's frame of mind reached a new low. The moment that would prove decisive for his political career was drawing near, and he was more isolated than ever and close to physical and emotional collapse. In December 1938 he checked into the Charité Hospital, where "serious nervous disturbances, particularly of the stomach," were diagnosed. The pain was so intense that Professor Sauerbruch was summoned from Dresden. He wanted to "operate immediately."[185]

While Goebbels was still in the hospital, Magda had another meeting with Hitler, the content of which remained concealed from her husband. Presumably it had to do with the notes on the testimony of the women to whom Goebbels had made advances, for afterward "a flood of reproaches" rained down on him. So Magda was still not to be moved; she let him suffer for his misdeeds. The mood at their rare encounters was "grim and leaden," which gave him the impression she would not relent.[186] When the propaganda minister had to cancel his previously announced Christmas address, it provided a new "occasion for the craziest rumors."[187]

The family spent Christmas in the villa without Goebbels, who was in the guest house pouring out his misery to his diary. He had brief visits from his children, his mother, his sister Maria and her new husband, and Helldorf. Hitler had sent two books; from the dedications Goebbels inferred that Hitler was still devoted to him. New Year's Eve passed the same way. The only visitor was Helldorf; from Magda he heard not a word. In a despairing mood he summed up the situation: "Horrendous! It's enough to make one want to hang oneself."[188]

Goebbels nevertheless still belonged to that small circle of people to whom Hitler sent a personal New Year's letter. In his reply Goebbels revealed "very honestly" that his situation had not improved. Hitler then invited him to join him at the Berghof. Goebbels arrived there on 5 January 1939. Apparently in their long discussions Hitler urged him to clear up the situation soon, which in light of Magda's intransigence merely made Goebbels's position worse. Magda kept coming out with new "suspicions." Goebbels saw now that he "would have to pay." Whether there was any way out, only the future would tell, he wrote in his diary. "I'm prepared and ready for anything. I tell the Führer this." Hitler promised to do all he could to help him, but Goebbels returned to Berlin on 17 January full of "burning anxiety."[189] He would be obliged to resign, if Magda insisted on a separation.[190]

Since time was running out, Goebbels sent his sister Maria to Magda, who agreed to a meeting. On the afternoon of 18 January a discussion took place in Schwanenwerder that left Goebbels hopeful that perhaps there might still be a "way to a solution." When he and Magda were "halfway in agreement" the following day, he proposed his solution to Hitler. Hitler accepted it and said he would assume part of the responsibility for making it work. On 21 January Goebbels received the draft of a contract that his wife had had the lawyer Rudolf Dix draw up. He accepted it without changes and listened politely to Hitler's "series of good suggestions," even confiding to his diary, "One really has to be fond of him." Still in a "grim mood," husband and wife signed the new nuptial contract on 22 January. Goebbels's summing-up expresses resignation and but little optimism: "So the matter is formally settled. At least this is a new beginning. Where will it lead? At the moment no one can say."[191]

At the end of January 1939 Hitler first revealed his true foreign-policy objectives in public. In a speech to the Reichstag on 30 January he spoke of "extending the *Lebensraum* of our people."[192] Although he had declared the previous September that settling the Sudeten problem was his "last territorial demand," the Czechoslovak crisis continued to fester.[193] Everything possible was being done to make war inevitable.

In a situation like this, those who refused to relinquish their capacity for rational judgment could pose a real threat to the regime, and Goebbels saw it as his task to silence them. Goebbels's rage at the "hothouse intellectuals," whom he and Hitler always mentioned in the same breath with "Jews" and "Marxists," grew out of his awareness that his chief propaganda device did not work with them. He was convinced that one who could reduce problems to the simplest formula and had "the courage to repeat it over and over again in this simplified form will achieve substantial success in influencing public opinion."[194]

This principle was followed by the press in keeping the problem of "Rump Czechoslovakia" before the public eye. Before Pres. Emil Hacha was forced to come to Berlin, the propaganda ministry issued instructions to the press to inflate reports of unrest in Czechoslovakia. On the day he arrived, 14 March, banner headlines proclaimed that Moscow was arming the "Red underworld" in Czechoslovakia. Allegedly a German athletic center had been stormed and other atrocities committed.[195]

While Hacha was reviewing the honor guard lined up to greet him at Anhalt Station, Hitler had given orders for elements of the Eighth Army and the SS's Adolf Hitler Regiment to cross the German-Czech border and occupy the important railway junction of Mährisch-Ostrau. Like Schuschnigg the year before, Hacha had to endure a torrent of abuse from Hitler before he was forced to sign the "agreement" that "placed the fate of the Czech people country trustingly in the hands of the Führer of the German Reich."[196]

On 15 March the Wehrmacht marched into "Rump Czechoslovakia" and for the first time occupied territory not settled by Germans. On the suggestion of his glowing admirer Erwin Rommel, commander of the Führer's headquarters, Hitler made his way to Prague without an escort commando.[197] Only a small minority cheered him along the road. From Hradčany Castle he announced that the country no longer existed. The following day the "Protectorate of Bohemia and Moravia" was proclaimed.

On 18 March Paris and London had their ambassadors deliver notes of protest. Goebbels found he had to agree with the Führer, whose "sovereign calm" had once more dissipated Goebbels's worry and skepticism: the British protest at the breaking of the Munich Agreement could be dismissed as "fake thunder" and "hysterical shouting." "The German press will also treat it with condescension. Contempt is in order."[198]

In his editorials the propaganda minister acknowledged the successful blackmail with mocking arrogance, "reviewing" the "historic week." In one night, he wrote, the "more than bizarre Czecho-Slovak composite state," the "seasonal state," this "monstrosity born of Versailles" that "in reality never was a state," dissolved into thin air.[199] For the day after Hitler's return from Prague, Goebbels ordered a "forceful campaign" to combat the "agitation in the world press," but one can assume that no one in German leadership circles was particularly worried, for Hitler promptly authorized Goebbels's previously planned trip to the eastern Mediterranean.[200]

Since Hitler had not jettisoned him, Goebbels had a more confident air these days as he moved among the leading functionaries. Rosenberg heard that at a party reception in Munich at the end of February, Goebbels had said that "people just had to let him live as he pleased."[201] Since he found "scandals with women" least dangerous because entirely normal, he publicly admitted to them, especially now that he no longer saw why he should kowtow to the hypocritical morality of the Munich philistines.[202] Hitler must have given thought to that in 1924, "otherwise one would have picked a different party," he added for the benefit of his audience, speechless at such insolence.[203]

When Goebbels and his wife set out on separate trips soon after this, it immediately gave rise to more speculation. He left on 30 March for the Balkans, while Magda had been traveling in southern Italy and Sicily for almost three weeks with the Speers and three other couples. Speer reports that Goebbels's undersecretary Hanke would have liked to come along. He had gradually managed to win Magda's confidence, although his relationship with Goebbels had suffered as a result.[204] By the end of 1938 Goebbels had noticed that Hanke's oral reports to him had become a "frosty business."[205] This must have been all the more the case when Hanke's efforts met with success; Speer remarks that while Magda was in Italy, Hanke "bombarded her with love letters." Nevertheless she kept him at a distance; to this mother of five young children, a future with Hanke may have appeared far too uncertain.[206]

Meanwhile Goebbels was trying to distract himself. He visited the Acropolis, the "cradle of Aryan culture," saw the Parthenon, and experienced the old city of Rhodes, whose walls date back to the fourteenth century. He noted that the people who lived in these places should be "used" by the "master races"; otherwise "all the dirt would come to the surface."[207] On 6 April he flew on to Cairo, where he played the tourist, visiting the National Museum, the citadel, and the pyramids of Giza. In Germany, meanwhile, his Führer was setting his sights on Poland. Goebbels reassured himself that Hitler would summon him when he needed him. The last station of his journey was Istanbul, where in addition to the usual sights he visited a German military cemetery and brooded over the quondam greatness of the Ottoman Empire.

The signals were set for war when Goebbels returned in time for the celebration of Hitler's fiftieth birthday. Hitler had sent his foreign minister to approach the Polish government on the question of Danzig, hoping to win Poland over for a joint undertaking against the Soviet Union, but in vain. Poland's own dreams of glory were incompatible with a junior partnership with Greater Germany. If Hitler wanted to achieve his goal of *Lebensraum* in the east, he now had no choice but to "smash" Poland.

In his speech on the evening before the national birthday celebration, Goebbels sounded as though he were not fully informed of what was going on. For he spoke of "the stopping places" that a people fighting for its destiny "now and then seeks amid the tumultuous course of events," so that it might achieve clarity about its situation, path, and goal. Then he went on as usual to praise Hitler as the great statesman and genius of history who had shown himself more than worthy of the blind and unshakable faith of his people. "As if by miracle," he had taken an "issue in Central Europe that one might almost have thought insoluble and brought it to a lasting solution." "Imagination" in his setting of goals, and "realism" about the ways to achieve them, were combined in him in a "unique harmony rarely encountered in history." And so, after the spiritual desperation of the German Austrians and Sudeten Germans had been revealed to him, Adolf Hitler had been able to create, "on the basis of a higher, instinctively sure insight," a "peace of practical reality."[208]

On 20 April 1939 a demonstration of what Goebbels meant by "a peace of practical reality" was offered along the East-West Axis, the first stretch of highway for the project, begun by Albert Speer in 1937, of transforming old Berlin into "Germania," the huge capital of which Hitler dreamed. Against the mighty backdrop of enormous cast-iron eagles grasping the laurels of victory in their talons as they sat atop towering pillars, a five-hour parade of troops and military equipment rolled by. The representatives of foreign countries were shocked and impressed by the splendidly equipped troops. Hitler had given Ribbentrop orders to invite "as many cowardly civilians and democrats as possible," so as to intimidate them.[209] While this fearsome spectacle unfolded, Goebbels's eyes scanned the street from the reviewing stand to the Great Star, where the Victory Column of the Second Reich had been relocated. As the sun reflected off the golden figure of the Goddess of Victory on top, it sent out a glittering ray of light, which the propaganda minister interpreted as a another "miraculous omen" that let him suppress his tormenting worry about what lay ahead.[210]

Goebbels used this military spectacle as the centerpiece of a special Ufa newsreel that he commissioned to commemorate the Führer's birthday. Here the image of Hitler as statesman was to be expanded to include that of the future commander in chief. Twelve carefully chosen photographers shot about twenty-eight thousand feet of film, of which approximately one-twentieth went into the actual newsreel, with solemn classical music on the soundtrack. The whole thing turned out to be a Goebbels masterpiece, which of course received the highest ratings, including one for being "educational," since Goebbels was convinced that film played as important a pedagogical role as schooling.[211] This display of the "strongest armed forces in the world" was intended to create confidence among the Germans about the war with Poland, toward which Hitler was ineluctably moving.

Goebbels now shifted the focus of his propaganda toward England. He hit upon the catchword of "encirclement" as a way of presenting Hitler's offensive strategy as defensive, exploiting the Germans' old complex about their country's unfavorable geopolitical position between powerful blocs.[212] "The ring that England is attempting with intense diplomatic zeal to place around Germany," he wrote, "has no other purpose than to suppress the ascent of the Reich and thereby to restore in Europe that infamous balance of power on which England believes its happiness and security both in the motherland and in its empire depend."[213]

When the German-Italian Pact of Steel was concluded in May 1939, Goebbels portrayed it as a response to the British policy of "encirclement." "A bloc of 150 million people" was rising up in Germany and Italy, prepared to defend their national existence, throwing all their strength and reserves into the struggle.[214] Another motif Goebbels stressed in his propaganda against the British was that of anticapitalism. He posited a struggle of the defenseless, hungry, but happy have-nots against the powerful but decadent haves living in surfeit. The landowning "British plutocracy" dictated the balance-of-power principle to prevent the "proletarian nations" from receiving what was rightly theirs. It was easier to be moral if one had "cobbled together a worldwide empire" as wealthy as the British Empire. A rich man would never dream of stealing bread, but a poor man might have no choice if he was hungry and had no money. Goebbels thus lent the German-British conflict a socioeconomic aspect that reflected the philosophy he had long ago had to subordinate to Hitler's political priorities. England, the "somewhat elderly moralistic auntie of Europe," was masking her real political motives behind "self-righteous phrases" when she charged Hitler's Germany with violating the principles of humanity, civilization, international law, and trust.[215]

Hitler had to restrain Goebbels somewhat; his outpourings of hatred interfered with Hitler's plan to prevent England from intervening when Germany attacked Poland. The plan involved a carefully calculated mix of threats and conciliatory gestures. But on 17 June, at the conclusion of the Danzig Gau Cultural Week, Goebbels was given free rein to be provocative, so as to test London's reaction in a speech just before the projected military action. The press received confidential instructions to play it up.[216]

Hitler knew he could find no man better suited to this task than Goebbels, who translated his own sense of crisis into a display of unbridled passion that swept the audience along. In this "wild speech" from the balcony of the Berlin Staatstheater, Goebbels demanded the return of Danzig, which had "overnight" become "an international problem," to the Reich. He was interrupted by prearranged minute-long chants of "One *Volk*, one Reich, one Führer!"—"Home into the Reich!"—"Deutschland, Deutschland über alles!"—and "The Jews and the Poles think Danzig's theirs!" Then he launched into an attack on the policy of encirclement, concluding: "The National Socialist Reich is not weak, but strong! It is not powerless; rather it possesses the most impressive armed forces in the world! And it is not ruled by cowardly members of the bourgeoisie, but by Adolf Hitler!"[217]

Although the British papers reacted with outrage, Hitler did not allow himself to be distracted from his preparations for war. Now the watchwords for Goebbels's propaganda were "moderation" and "self-control," lest the "awakening of *Volk* passions" overload the situation. Reports of incidents were to be printed as news briefs on the second page, without sensationalism. The "Danzig problem" was to be "pushed into the background." The general motto was "Keep things at a slow boil."[218]

Goebbels found it convenient that the Poles were making loud noises expressing Poland's own dreams of power. When speakers in Poland recalled that Germany had arisen out of Prussia, a former vassal state to Poland, or newpapers pointed out that East Prussia was actually a fief of the Polish republic, Goebbels passed these statements on to his newspaper editors as evidence of Polish "megalomania."[219]

That summer, while Hitler pushed Europe toward war, Goebbels took possession of his splendid new official residence on Hermann-Goering-Strasse. The planning had begun in the summer of 1937. Goebbels had told Finance Minister Schwerin von Krosigk that Hitler wanted the propaganda minister's official residence redone, in line with the reshaping of Berlin being undertaken by Speer. It would be necessary to take over the grounds of that part of the Palais Blücher that was owned by the Americans, as well as the park attached to the Reich Ministry of Nutrition.[220]

The cost of the new building, including demolition of the old one, was estimated by the architect, Prof. Paul Baumgarten, at two million marks. His design for the new Städtische Oper in Berlin had delighted Hitler and Goebbels.[221] Goebbels argued that his steadily increasing obligation to entertain made "a generous scale for the building essential."[222] The finance minister, who "basically" agreed with the plan, found the estimated cost "extraordinarily high, in view of the fact that no costs are attached to acquiring the land, and the interior decorating is not included."[223] Goebbels rejoined that he would not tolerate any substantial modification of the project, and "in particular, only first-class materials should be used."[224]

When it came to the interior, the minister's demands knew no bounds; by the end of February 1939 the cost of the project had reached 2.5 million marks and was still climbing. The reception rooms were done by the Consolidated Workshops of Munich. Among other things, over 14,000 pounds of bronze were worked for the door hardware. There was a marble-topped rosewood dresser in Louis XVI style that cost 30,000 marks, and an eighteenth-century Aubusson carpet costing 283,450 marks. Table settings were ordered for three hundred persons. Finance ministry officials raised "serious objections" to these last items, pointing out that in the previous year's budget extraordinary funds had been requested "for the purchase of silver, table linens, fine china, etc., for 100/500 persons."[225] The ministry urged restraint, suggesting that objects already purchased could be used again in the Herr Minister's new official residence; Goebbels should "for the present agree to the purchase of china for fifty persons."[226]

Eventually the total cost came to 3.2 million marks, and that was still not sufficient. In a tour of the building, Goebbels put together a five-page list of flaws he wanted corrected. Eventually funds had to be drawn from Propaganda Ministry theater or subsidy budgets, for some of the contractors and suppliers were threatening to charge interest or penalties on outstanding bills.[227]

Goebbels's study had been done by the Consolidated Workshops all in red, which left the impression, even on someone as well disposed as Goebbels's future press aide Wilfred von Oven, of "a certain macabre splendor." Almost the entire wall behind the desk was taken up with a huge full-length portrait of Hitler. To the left of the desk hung a portrait of Frederick the Great of Prussia; von Oven counted six different paintings of the king in the residence.[228]

All this luxury, however, could not assuage Goebbels's worries about the future. As at various times in earlier years, he sought solace in his marriage. At the Wagner Festival in Bayreuth at the end of July, word trickled out that he and Magda had had a reconciliation.[229] He had badgered her for days and had brought incredible pressure to bear. When he threatened, not for the first time, to take the children away if she continued to meet Hanke in private, she had no choice but to give in, she confided to Speer.[230]

Magda Goebbels had not yet had time to come to terms with the emotional turmoil she had just undergone, and during the performance of *Tristan and Isolde* she wept incessantly. Hitler, who had no idea what was going on, received an explanation from Speer, then summoned Goebbels the next day and ordered him and Magda to leave Bayreuth at once. As disagreeable as this must have been for Goebbels, at least his marriage was saved once and for all. At the beginning of August Karl Hanke left the Propaganda Ministry and volunteered for the Panzer-Lehr Regiment, with which he took part in the Poland campaign just a few weeks later.

CHAPTER 12

He enjoys the protection
of the Almighty
(1939—1941)

In the summer of 1939 the propaganda minister was frequently overcome with consternation at his Führer's determination to achieve his goal at any cost. Not that he had ceased to worship Hitler; rather it was fear of hubris that now sometimes overcame Goebbels. Too often they had challenged fate, and too often they had triumphed. They no longer suffered the deprivations and pain, the sacrifices that had once inspired Goebbels's unshakable faith. In moments of doubt he would vow to himself that he would talk with Hitler and persuade him to promise to pursue his expansion plans by peaceful means.[1] But whenever Hitler spoke with him, Goebbels would fall under the old spell and talk himself all the more fanatically into believing that "Providence" was guiding Hitler's hand. The magic would last for a while, but then anxiety would rear its head again.

During this period Goebbels was not included in any of the secret meetings at which decisions were being made.[2] Early in the summer of 1939 he began to suspect that Hitler not only wanted war with Poland but also with Great Britain and France, possibly even the Soviet Union. Jealous and full of suspicion, Goebbels kept an eye on his nemesis Ribbentrop; Goebbels considered him Hitler's "evil spirit," who was inciting the Führer to war.[3]

These fears of Goebbels's and his lack of inside information probably explain why he interpreted his instructions from the Chancellery as part of a policy of placating the Soviet Union. On 5 May he received orders from the highest levels of government to instruct the press that it should halt immediately any polemics against the Soviet Union and bolshevism. The justification noted that this had "nothing to do with our fundamental differences in ideology, but is necessary because of the innumerable rumors circulating abroad that merely confuse the situation."[4] It had become known that Paris and London were negotiating in Moscow to revive the League of Nations collective security system. In other words, the Western powers were attempting to enlist the Soviet Union against Hitler's ambitions in Poland. Therefore it was in Germany's best interest to refrain from aggressive propaganda so as not to drive the Soviet Union into the arms of England and France.

Hitler was in fact weighing cooperation with the Soviet Union. Ribbentrop had convinced him that Great Britain would "never, under any circumstances, enter into a treaty with Germany."[5] The Kremlin had already signaled on 10 March that it would like an accommodation with Berlin. On 14 August Hitler instructed the German ambassador in Moscow to convey to Molotov, the new Soviet foreign minister, the Germans' proposal to divide up spheres of influence between the Baltic and the Black Sea. The document pointed to the two countries' shared opposition to the "capitalist Western democracies" and promised rich booty for the Soviet Union. In hopes of increasing that booty, Molotov dragged his feet on the negotiations, knowing full well that Hitler had already set the date for attacking Poland—26 August. Only after Hitler personally intervened with Stalin did the Kremlin agree to move Ribbentrop's visit in Moscow up to 23 August.

Not until this point did the propaganda minister, who remained convinced that the struggle against bolshevism constituted the "great mission" of national socialism in history, learn from Hitler of the plan for a pact with the Soviet Union.[6] At first unnerved, then once more impressed with his Führer's "genius," Goebbels claimed to see in the plan a "brilliant propaganda coup." As late as March 1940 he would note, having completely embraced Hitler's thinking, "What do we really care about the social and cultural standards of Moscow bolshevism? We want to make Germany strong and great, not pursue utopian plans for reforming the world."[7] Even so, this interim solution made Goebbels extremely uneasy, as many later diary entries attest. Unlike Hitler, he did not see the pact with the Soviet Union as a sound basis for going all out in Poland.[8] He still considered the danger of war with England "excessively large," as Speer recalled later, and expressed his deep concern.[9]

In Germany, when word arrived late in the evening of 21 August that the nonaggression pact had been concluded, the news was received with relief by the population. People took it to mean that war had been averted, or at least a risky war. A correspondent for the *Frankfurter Zeitung* described in a letter to his editors the relaxed atmosphere in Berlin; few people were thinking about "the deeper significance of the agreement."[10]

On the morning of 22 August Goebbels issued instructions that the German press should focus on the "sensational turning point" in European politics.[11] In the "confidential information" provided to editors that day, it was noted that the pact built on the "traditional commonality in German and Russian politics." The editors were explicitly forbidden to "discuss the ideological differences between the two nations, in either a positive or negative vein."[12]

"The topic of the Anti-Comintern Pact, which the foreign press will certainly talk to death," was supposed to be glossed over by the German press as much as possible.[13] Soon Goebbels would ostensibly halt the activity of the anti-Comintern unit within the ministry. The "Anti-Comintern" sign on the door was removed and replaced by signs for several new units. Meanwhile the staff continued its old work of gathering intelligence and collecting and recording material, though with sharply reduced staffing.[14]

On 22 August Goebbels had also summoned the foreign correspondents to a press conference at the ministry. Hitler later telephoned from the Berghof to hear about their reactions. Goebbels told him that the news of the pact had caused an indescribable sensation. When nearby church bells rang during the press conference, a British correspondent had remarked that that was "the death knell of the British Empire," a comment that made a strong impression on Hitler, who was in any case euphoric. His eyes "glistened feverishly" as he conveyed to the generals with him at the Berghof what Goebbels had just told him.[15] Firmly believing that he had pulled off a new coup and could now wage a limited war against Poland, he informed the officers that he was determined to act. Most of them sedulously supported him. Hitler said he would provide the pretext for the attack, whether believable or not; afterward, no one would ask the victor whether he had told the truth.[16]

As the German war machinery got into gear, and Ribbentrop returned from Moscow to report that he had felt as if he were among old party comrades there, and that Stalin's personality reminded him of the Führer's, ambassadors shuttled back and forth between the European capitals, and telephone lines hummed in desperate attempts to stop the unstoppable. At a midnight press briefing on 25 August, Hans Fritzsche, who in 1938 had succeeded Berndt as director of the domestic press department in the Propaganda Ministry, instructed the press, under orders from his boss, to ignore the "flood of peace proposals and offers of mediation."[17] They should continue to focus on the Polish situation. This "test of nerves" would continue "for a few days, and become even greater. . . . Germany's iron determination must become increasingly clear," for it was a matter of getting London to blink.[18]

At almost the same time Hitler proposed to the British ambassador, Neville Henderson, that England and Germany divide the world into spheres of influence; the Germans would guarantee the continued existence of the British Empire and accept the Reich's western border in exchange for a free hand in the east. After Henderson had gone to inform his government of Hitler's proposal, Hitler gave the go-ahead for attacking Poland the next day. He hastily postponed the operation when word reached Berlin that Britain planned to ratify an assistance pact with Poland that very evening, and Mussolini's ambassador reported, contrary to previous communications, that the Italian army was not yet ready. On 26 August Goebbels emphasized to the press that the public should on no account receive the impression that things would "start" on a specific date. The Führer could "not have his hands tied."[19]

Goebbels still hoped that Hitler would agree to sit down at the negotiating table after all. He was present at the new Chancellery on the afternoon of 27 August, when Hitler told the assembled Reichstag deputies that the situation was very grave, but he had decided to solve the Eastern Question "one way or another." He had made certain proposals to Henderson and was now awaiting the British reply. That evening at the press conference the Propaganda Ministry announced that, in view of Polish provocations in East Prussia and several other areas, "the power of implementation has passed into the hands of the Wehrmacht"; the Sunday papers received instructions to summarize the week's events "in tough, even intransigent language," while withholding actual bulletins. News of the mobilization in France should also be "mentioned only in passing, on the inside pages."[20]

Late in the evening of 28 August—the day when rationing was introduced for food and other necessities—Henderson brought Hitler his government's response: the government would stand by its treaty obligations, but had obtained Warsaw's firm commitment to negotiate over Danzig and the Corridor. In Hitler's reply on 29 August he welcomed direct negotiations with Warsaw and said he expected a Polish representative to arrive the next day, and would shortly present London with suitable proposals. His answer was to be flanked by the press, which Goebbels instructed on 29 August as follows: "The degree of emphasis on reports of Polish terrorism is the standard by which foreign countries will measure the firmness of the German position."[21]

Toward midnight on 30 August Henderson arrived at the Chancellery. Ribbentrop read him the German proposals, but informed him that they no longer applied because Warsaw had failed to respond. After French and British pressure on Warsaw, the Polish ambassador in Berlin actually asked for an appointment with Hitler or Ribbentrop. Ribbentrop finally agreed to see him, but merely to seek confirmation of what he already knew from monitored telephone calls, namely that the Polish diplomat lacked authorization to negotiate for his government.

Goebbels's propaganda cranked out yet more reports of Polish atrocities against the German minority in the country, lest "this last phase of the war of nerves be lost."[22] Meanwhile the war machine was running full steam ahead. On the afternoon of 31 August Heydrich used the password "Grandmother dead" to signal that the moment had come to create the incident that would provide the pretext for war. SS commandos in Polish uniforms staged an attack on the German radio transmitter in Gleiwitz. At 11:00 that evening Goebbels called a special press conference. He directed that the German News Service reports on the attack should receive great play, with the following points emphasized: "Discipline of the German people hitherto not to be shaken, therefore now this brutal attack. But German *Volk* will not take another attack lying down. Until now terrorist acts only on Polish, but now also on German soil."[23]

Army units had already advanced far into Poland and Warsaw had come under its first aerial attack when, on the morning of 1 September, Hitler drove with Goebbels and other dignitaries to the Kroll Opera, where the Reichstag had met since the fire. He had put on his "favorite" uniform of battlefield gray, which he had not worn since 1920 and now swore he would take off only after victory, or not at all. Aside from the SA and SS men lining the route, the streets seemed abandoned, although the radio and the morning papers had reported that Danzig had now "returned home" to the Reich.[24] The word "war" had been avoided.[25] According to official usage, Germany was merely "retaliating." In his speech to the Reichstag Hitler stressed that his "love of peace" and his "infinite patience" were now at an end; since 5:45 A.M. Germans had been returning fire.[26]

Goebbels had immediately drafted a law on "extraordinary radio regulations" that prohibited the population from listening to foreign broadcasts and spreading news transmitted by them, with violations to be punished by imprisonment and, "in particularly grave cases," death.[27] He was excessively nervous and agitated. How would England react? Would it uphold its treaty obligations toward Poland? He had not failed to notice that Hitler himself was by no means confident, that he was playing Russian roulette. Like Hitler, Goebbels talked himself into believing that there would be no war, and this he repeated frequently to his collaborators; the Western powers were merely bluffing, and "without the military support of the West, Poland would not risk a war either."[28] The negative mood among the German people also worried Goebbels. No trace of the enthusiasm, the patriotic clamor that had marked August 1914, "no joy, no cheering. Everywhere one encountered an oppressive calm, not to say depression. The entire German people seemed seized by a paralyzing horror that made it incapable of expressing approval or disapproval."[29]

This mood would make it all the more difficult for Goebbels's propaganda, if worse came to worst and all-out war broke out. On the evening of 1 September the British ambassador handed Ribbentrop a note saying that Britain would stand by its treaty obligations if German troops did not withdraw. But the British did not issue an ultimatum. The next day passed, full of nervous waiting. On the morning of 3 September Henderson called at the Chancellery in person to deliver a second note. Paul Schmidt, chief interpreter for the Foreign Office, translated it for Hitler, with Ribbentrop present. London was demanding that operations in Poland cease within two hours. In his memoirs Schmidt recalls, "Hitler sat there as if turned to stone and gazed straight ahead. . . . After a pause, which seemed to me like an eternity, he turned to Ribbentrop, who had remained standing by the window as if frozen. 'What now?' Hitler asked his foreign minister. . . . Ribbentrop replied softly, 'I assume the French will send us an identical ultimatum within the hour.' "[30]

Among the many who had gathered in the antechamber to Hitler's study to await the next developments was Goebbels. He stood "in a corner, downcast and pensive, looking literally like the proverbial drenched poodle."[31] His fears had been fulfilled: war would come. The man he had believed to be "the instrument of divine will" had proven fallible. That could not be allowed, and because it could not be allowed, Goebbels would soon take refuge in self-deception. The worse things stood with the Führer and the Reich in the coming years, the more Goebbels would throw himself into his deluded "belief" in Hitler's divine mission to save the West from the "Jewish conspiracy to take over the world."

Goebbels willingly adopted his Führer's notion that *Lebensraum* in the east was an existential necessity for the Reich. So it seemed to him that the "plutocrats" in London and Paris had declared war on the Reich not because of the "relatively insignificant issue" of Danzig, but because they wanted to destroy Germany. For the time being the two-front war Goebbels had dreaded did not materialize, which seemed to him almost a miracle.[32] Alfred Jodl commented at the Nuremberg Trials, "If we didn't collapse in 1939, it was simply because the 110-odd French and English divisions in the west remained completely inactive during the Polish campaign vis-à-vis the twenty-three German divisions."[33]

So Hitler's Wehrmacht, accompanied for the first time in the history of war by propaganda companies, could demonstrate its combat effectiveness and a new form of warfare, the blitzkrieg, with Stuka dive-bombers screaming out of the sky, death-bringing Heinkel bombers, modern Messerschmidt fighter aircraft that could go almost five hundred miles an hour, and sudden surprise attacks spearheaded by massive tank detachments with motorized infantry behind them. The Polish armed forces, which still included cavalry units, were chewed up by that monstrous mechanized Moloch. By 5 September the Polish commander in chief had ordered his forces to withdraw behind the Vistula. Three days later the German Fourth Armored Division reached the outskirts of Warsaw, while to the south the Tenth Army captured Kielce and the Fourteenth Army moved into Sandomierz, at the confluence of the Vistula and the San.

On 8 September, as the Wehrmacht report noted victory after victory, Goebbels suffered a defeat. The Führer issued an order that "the general guidelines and instructions" in the "area of foreign propaganda" would be formulated by the Reich foreign minister; the foreign minister was to make known "to the propaganda minister his wishes and orders" concerning leaflets, radio, film, and press, which were to be "adopted unchanged and implemented" by the Propaganda Ministry.[34] In practice this meant that Ribbentrop had to assign "competent officials as liaisons" to the Propaganda Ministry.[35] This gave Ribbentrop the right to issue instructions on foreign propaganda and implied a complete revision of the assignment of responsibilities dating back to 30 July 1933.[36]

None of this came as a surprise to Goebbels. Shortly after becoming foreign minister, Ribbentrop had begun to show an interest in the work of the foreign division of the Propaganda Ministry and to "nibble away at" the powers Goebbels had managed to pry out of the Foreign Office in 1933.[37] This had only heightened Goebbels's aversion to him. By way of counterattack, he now tried to discredit his adversary by charging him with "faulty and unclear" notions of foreign policy.[38] But this particular summer, after "very ugly confrontations" with Goebbels, Ribbentrop proved successful, primarily because he had played a key role in bringing about the Hitler-Stalin pact and therefore stood high in Hitler's favor. Indeed, Hitler was beginning to view him as a "second Bismarck."[39]

Goebbels tried to circumvent the new directives on foreign propaganda. He particularly resisted the installation of the liaison personnel assigned by the Foreign Office to his ministry, calling them "spies."[40] He also was sickened by the "stupid, intellectual propaganda" of the Foreign Office, as well as its more reserved attitude toward the "Jewish question" when dealing with foreign countries.[41] So the permanent skirmishing between him and Ribbentrop gradually came to extend to the entire spectrum of foreign press and propaganda policy and, like the conflict with Rosenberg, gave rise to a flood of letters—chiefly Ribbentrop's to Goebbels.[42] But for the time being Goebbels simply let coordination with the Foreign Office "rest" and did not even trouble to answer Ribbentrop's "insulting" letters. He took the position that this "megalomaniac" would have to cool his heels a long time before Goebbels answered his whistle.[43]

Reich Press Secretary Otto Dietrich, in Goebbels's eyes a "knucklehead without imagination or insight," also narrowed the propaganda minister's influence. This became possible because, once the war began, Dietrich was usually at the Führer's field headquarters and therefore in direct contact with him.[44] Dietrich decided which daily newspapers and press summaries Hitler would read; after looking them over, Hitler would give Dietrich his daily instructions for the press, sometimes even dictating word for word the official position.[45] Dietrich was in daily telephone contact with Goebbels, which took care of the exchange of information between the front and Berlin.[46] One can see Goebbels's necessarily waning influence in the fact that he simply appended his commentaries to the official announcements coming from the Führer, without offering his "own explanations" to his staff for Germany's conduct of the war.[47]

To avoid being eclipsed altogether, Goebbels reactivated a technique he had used once before, in a difficult situation in 1932.[48] Every day at 11:00 A.M. he called in his leading collaborators and department heads —at first only five or six people, then between 1939 and 1941 about twenty, and from the beginning of the Russian campaign on about fifty—for a "minister's conference." Actually it was less a conference than an occasion for him to personally gave the staff their marching orders.[49] Goebbels's adjutant testified at Nuremberg that no discussion ever occurred; rather, the liaison officer from the Wehrmacht would first summarize the military situation, whereupon Goebbels would give out the propaganda directives, primarily for press, radio, and newsreels.[50]

The Polish campaign concluded at the end of September. The Red Army had entered eastern Poland on 17 September. Nine days later the defenders of encircled Warsaw capitulated. At that very hour Ribbentrop, Molotov, and Stalin were modifying the provisions of the Hitler-Stalin pact in the Soviet Union's favor. The Nazis relinquished Lithuania, and received in return the voivodship of Lublin and the eastern part of the voivodship of Warsaw.

On the day Warsaw fell, the press and radio had begun a great peace offensive. In a speech on 6 October Hitler made a "peace offer" to the Western powers. He declared that it would be utterly meaningless to let millions of human lives be exterminated and billions of marks' worth of property destroyed, merely to reconstitute an entity that had been recognized as misbegotten by all non-Poles from the moment it was created. Goebbels, who secretly hoped "that peace would come," kept asking himself during the nerve-wracking wait for England's response "whether a real world war" would come.[51]

During luncheon at the Chancellery on 10 October, Hitler remarked that he had no idea how London would react. Just a few hours previously he had summoned the commanders in chief of the branches of the Wehrmacht and ordered them to make preparations for an offensive through Luxembourg, Belgium, and Holland that would overwhelm the French forces and establish a base for invading England.

The idea of a rapid victory over the "hereditary enemy" had apparently intoxicated Hitler. Goebbels at any rate was so impressed by his "magnificent certainty of victory" that he wrote in positive euphoria, despite all his doubts and fears: "With the Führer we will always win; he combines in himself all the virtues of the great soldier: courage, cleverness, caution, elasticity, sense of sacrifice, and a sovereign disdain for comfort."[52] Seeing Hitler already dividing up the French provinces in his mind, Goebbels commented reverently: "In all measures he hurries on ahead of developments. Like all true geniuses, I should add."[53]

Nevertheless, the propaganda minister hoped that it would not come to that, that Great Britain would back down; after all, thus far there had been only a few "laughable artillery duels" in the west. Goebbels remarked that this was "the strangest war history has ever witnessed."[54] Chamberlain's speech in the House of Commons threw cold water on his hopes. The prime minister called Hitler's proposals vague and uncertain, since they contained no indication of how the injustice done to Czechoslovakia and Poland could be rectified. Now Hitler "hardly believed in the possibility of peace any more." Goebbels tried to bolster his own confidence with a tautological justification—"We'll win because we must." He ceaselessly told himself, "Our chances are . . . as good as one can imagine. If we don't wreck them ourselves, we'll win. And we will."[55]

Hitler now ordered increased agitation against Great Britain. Part of the campaign included Goebbels's charge that Winston Churchill, First Lord of the Admiralty, had ordered the British passenger liner *Athenia* torpedoed in order to blame it on the Germans. Actually a German U-boat had been responsible—a fact that, even after it became known in Germany, was officially kept secret until after the war. Goebbels himself remained in ignorance, which allowed him to attack Churchill all the more ruthlessly.[56]

In spite of all his fears about the now inevitable war in the west, in spite of the reservations expressed by the military leadership on the basis of experience in World War I, Goebbels kept telling himself that England's "position and power are weaker now than ever."[57] He again expressed relief that Germany did not have to fight on two fronts at once.[58] Astrological predictions, which he denied believing in, "strangely" spoke in favor of Germany, yet life seemed to him "so oppressive that one can lose all one's pleasure in it."[59] He was tormented by terrifying thoughts and images. Yet his relationship to his wife Magda had improved during the first months of the war to such a degree that in November they celebrated her thirty-eighth birthday "all alone" in Lanke. On his birthday, for which the British produced a "loathsome broadcast," he had gazed full of trepidation into the future: "Forty-two years. How many do I have left? I'd rather not know."[60]

On 8 November 1939, when Goebbels accompanied his Führer to Munich for the annual celebration of the anniversary of the Beer Hall Putsch, his mood was no different, especially because he had to acknowledge that his propaganda was "still not universally appreciated." Only the cheering with which Hitler was received at the Bürgerbräu, and his speech, which turned the hall into a madhouse, raised his spirits somewhat. He thought that Hitler's "cutting rejection" of Britain's "rapacious policies," and his announcement that Germany would never capitulate, would become a "worldwide sensation."[61]

But the real sensation was caused by another piece of news that reached Hitler and his propaganda minister when they were already on their way back to Berlin. Just a few minutes after Hitler and his entourage had left the hall, a homemade time bomb had gone off right by the speaker's platform. The massive explosion brought down the ceiling, killed several persons, and injured dozens. Since Hitler had left the gathering much earlier than was his wont, Goebbels was now convinced, despite all the doubts he had harbored recently, that "he enjoys the protection of the Almighty. He will not die until his mission is accomplished."[62]

Part of that "mission" included "pacification" of the conquered areas in the east, which brought new assignments for the propaganda minister. As soon as Hitler returned from Warsaw, after the great victory parade staged on 5 October, he reported his impressions of Poland to Goebbels. The Poles were "more animals than human, completely apathetic and amorphous," and he wanted "no assimilation" with them.[63] What he did want in the newly created Government General under Hans Frank was a people of Polish slaves to be "purged" of intellectuals, Catholic clergy, nobility, and Jews. The "obedience training" of the remaining population would be provided by Goebbels. By way of partial recompense for the drastic inroads into his power, Goebbels would be in charge of all the propaganda in the new territory. To this end he set up departments for popular enlightenment and propaganda in the office of the governor general and each of the district administrative offices in Cracow, Lublin, Radom, and Warsaw, all directly under the propaganda department in his ministry.[64]

At the beginning of November Goebbels went to Poland to see for himself what it was like. The country offered an image of "oppressive hopelessness," which after Hitler's blitzkrieg was not so surprising. To him Warsaw was a "place of horror," and he saw the population, beaten down by war and occupation, scurrying along the streets "like insects," "apathetic and shadowy." His disgust increased when he toured the Jewish ghetto in Lodz: "These aren't human beings anymore; they're animals. So this isn't a humanitarian task, but a surgical one. One must operate here, and radically."[65]

Goebbels, who wondered why Lodz, of all places—that "pile of filth," "inhabited almost exclusively by Polish and Jewish trash"—should be Germanized and transformed into Litzmannstadt, demanded that Hitler authorize the radical operation he had in mind.[66] Goebbels was consciously thinking along the same lines as his Führer, seeing the liquidation of the Polish Jews as a possible first step toward the "eradication" of European Jewry that Hitler had announced at the end of January 1929 as necessary in the event of another world war. Goebbels's account of the "Jewish problem" earned Hitler's "most complete approbation." But as long as Hitler still hoped to work things out with the West, he had no interest in a rapid liquidation of the Jews, since he could use them as pawns, as he argued to Goebbels.

In a first step, for which Himmler had already given the order on 9 October, Jews and Poles not suitable for "Germanification" were to be deported into the Government General, where at the end of the month forced labor was introduced for Jews, who were now obligated to wear the yellow star. In the winter of 1939–40 mass deportations and killings began. The justification for those aspects of the "Polish policy" that could not be entirely concealed from the public was provided by Goebbels's propaganda. For weeks the propaganda hammered away at the atrocities allegedly committed against the German minority in Poland just before and during the German campaign. Goebbels also used film to make Germans accept the deportations and other things that Hitler planned for the Jews. In the Propaganda Ministry the new director of the film department, Reich General Manager for Film Fritz Hippler, worked with Eberhard Taubert, whose anti-Bolshevist activities had suddenly been checked by Hitler's pact with Stalin, to plan and develop the script for the "documentary" *Der ewige Jude* (The Eternal Jew). As a student Hippler had been one of the main organizers of the book burning in Berlin in May 1933.[67] He had brought back from defeated Poland the footage for this "film reportage." It included scenes of a kosher butchering filmed in the Warsaw ghetto. Goebbels lost no time viewing this material, was appalled at "such brutality," and confirmed for himself what was in any case planned: "This Jewry must be destroyed."[68]

After he had shown the scenes to Hitler, Goebbels first decided to have Veit Harlan work them into *Jud Süss* (Jew Süss), the film Harlan was already making, but Harlan refused on the grounds that such cruelty would make the audience sick to their stomachs.[69] Instead the slaughter scenes were transformed into the final sequence of *Der ewige Jude*, with the provision that this part would be shown only under certain circumstances. Women would be allowed to see only the shortened version, which was also recommended for "persons with delicate sensibilities."[70] This crude "documentary" was supposed to inform Germans "calmly and factually" through "pictures, which do not lie," about "World Jewry," specifically about the "original state of the Jews" as preserved in pure form in the Polish ghettos; this image would counter the image of the civilized Western European Jews.[71]

The Jew as "civilized Western European" was the subject of *Jud Süss*, which Goebbels had entrusted to the "leading actor" Harlan. The film was based on a novel of the same title by Lion Feuchtwanger, but the screenplay twisted the novel to fit the Nazis' favorite notions. Harlan described the assignment as "a terrible blow" but ended up contributing "a wealth of new ideas."[72] He also rewrote the screenplay, produced by Eberhard Wolfgang Möller of the Propaganda Ministry's theater department, so "magnificently" that Goebbels was certain Harlan's film would become the classic "anti-Semitic film."[73]

If the negotiations with Harlan went smoothly, it was not so easy to persuade Ferdinand Marian to take on the role of Süss Oppenheimer. The actor turned down the role on the grounds that he normally played bon vivants and romantic leads, and his audience would not want to see him playing this unsympathetic character.[74] Goebbels personally exerted pressure. What he referred to as "giving him a little push" consisted of screaming at Marian that he could make him do anything. He, Joseph Goebbels, did the casting, and it was the Nazis who had made actors socially respectable, allowing them to earn more than the greatest German scientists and scholars, and now, when he asked something of them, they turned it down, with one eye on that "Jewish scum" in Hollywood.[75] After this scene, Marian felt he had no choice. No such pressure was needed with Werner Krauss, whom Goebbels had chosen for the role of Rabbi Löw. Fifty thousand marks sweetened the pot for Krauss, who had been the first deputy president of the Reich Chamber of Theater.[76]

In view of Goebbels's efforts on behalf of anti-Semitic filmmaking, it must have been all the more dismaying to him when, one day over lunch at the Chancellery, Hitler expressed "in the sharpest terms" his displeasure with the films being currently produced. In the presence of his closest enemy, Rosenberg, as well as Rudolf Hess and all the officers and adjutants, Goebbels was told that the films gave no sense that a National Socialist revolution had taken place.[77] Hitler raved that there were only "generally patriotic" but no National Socialist films. He charged that the films had not yet "had the courage to take on the Jewish Bolshevists"— disregarding the fact that the anti-Bolshevist films already made had been put on ice because of his own sudden change of course toward the Soviet Union.[78]

Hitler also criticized the newsreels, of which three thousand prints were distributed weekly to the movie theaters.[79] He said they were put together "without intelligence or any deeper commitment."[80] Goebbels apparently "pieced his footage together without giving the nation the kind of lasting, caring guidance" it wanted. Hitler continued his tirade, putting his finger on the precise problem the propaganda minister had been trying to address for weeks: during the "phony war" there had been a dearth of "proper subjects"; the propaganda units provided only un- imaginative footage, which the civilian Goebbels attributed to their mil- itary training, incompatible with "creative work."[81]

Hitler's torrent of abuse lasted about twenty minutes, according to Rosenberg's gleeful and meticulous account.[82] Goebbels, not usually at a loss for words, after a meek protest—"but we do have good . . . nationalist films"—fell completely silent. Although the position in which his Führer had put him was more than embarrassing, he defended Hitler's behavior to himself, writing in his diary, "He has the right to—he's a genius"; he promised himself to do better from then on.[83]

Perhaps it was the public mood that had irritated Hitler into attacking his propaganda minister. This mood was anything but optimistic. Now that it was clear that war with France and England could not be averted, people had begun to recall the horrors of the seemingly unending trench warfare of 1914–18.

At the end of 1939 Goebbels decided that it was imperative not to make light of the enemy, especially the British, since the "national exis- tence" was at stake. At Christmas he warned against "being overcome with sentimentality," and demanded instead that the people become "tough"; he adopted a similar tone in his New Year's speech.[84] Sure of victory because his Führer exuded "faith and confidence in it," Goebbels proclaimed to the German people, "Victory will not be handed to us. We must earn it. . . . Everyone must do his part and fight for it. . . . We will fight and work and then say, with that old Prussian general, 'Lord, if you can't help us or don't want to, we pray that you at least won't help our accursed enemies either!' "[85]

As the year came to an end, the thermometer measured − 13 degrees Fahrenheit, and there was a coal shortage. Schools, factories, cinemas, and theaters had been closed, and Goebbels had to work at the ministry wrapped in coats and blankets. He thus had all the more reason to raise his glass at his little New Year's party in Lanke with the toast, "God punish England!"[86] Hitler, who was spending the holiday in his mountain retreat, meanwhile brooded over how he could "punish France." Several times he had had to postpone the western campaign because of bad weather. On 10 January he "definitively" scheduled it to begin on 17 January. Four days before the appointed time he had to postpone it again, "in consideration of the weather."

Although Goebbels spent time with Hitler almost every day—on 14 January Hitler visited the Goebbels in Schwanenwerder—he was apparently not kept informed of events. So when he heard that Belgium and Holland had canceled all leaves for members of their armed forces, he thought the governments were "testing the waters." That afternoon he learned from Hitler that he had postponed the campaign because of the weather. Not until ten days later did Goebbels note in his diary that the offensive was being postponed because a Maj. Helmut Reinberger, carrying the secret plans for the campaign, had strayed over Belgium and made an emergency landing.[87]

Instead of telling Goebbels the real reasons for the delay, Hitler spoke to him in "terms of the larger context," using the categories of faith: "We simply cannot allow ourselves to lose the war. And all our thoughts and actions must be guided by that assumption." In analogy to such articles of faith, Hitler announced to his profoundly impressed propaganda minister: "It isn't the dimensions in which the historical genius works that are decisive for his greatness, but the courage and boldness with which he approaches dangers."[88]

After such "pithy statements" Goebbels went back to work "as if reborn." He was focusing as before on propaganda that would drive a wedge between the British people and its leadership. On the one hand there were the "plutocrats," "the Jews among the Aryans," the Chamberlains, Churchills, and a couple of hundred other families who had "everything else, but no moral right to rule the world." The plutocrat's "boundlessly limited arrogance, his mental lethargy, his irritating apathy toward the worries and interests of other people, his hypocritical and slippery morality, his stupidly brazen naiveté in spreading lies and slander" had been developed into a sort of a political art with which he was leading the British people to war and ruin.[89]

In feverish haste Goebbels had undertaken the expansion of the foreign section of the Propaganda Ministry, the number of whose specialists more than doubled between the beginning of the war and April 1941. This section was involved in the broadcasts beamed abroad, which became particularly effective. They were conceived and coordinated to Goebbels's complete satisfaction by Adolf Raskin, who had already gained prominence in the radio component of the "Home into the Reich" campaign for the Saar.[90] In addition to the usual propaganda broadcasts, with translated versions of the Nazi leaders' speeches, secret transmitters also waged the "war of the airwaves."[91] Another assignment of the foreign section was designing pamphlets. Goebbels received particular praise for leaflets that showed English soldiers in unambiguous situations with French women.[92] The propaganda department came up with the idea of slipping biting caricatures of Churchill into packs of cigarette; they were intended for Germans, to whom the Western powers were to be represented as warmongers.[93]

"The most scurrilous propagandist on the opposite side" was Hermann Rauschning, Goebbels thought. Rauschning had been president of the senate in the Free State of Danzig. Goebbels considered his book *Gespräche mit Hitler* (Conversations with Hitler) "extraordinarily skillfully written" and felt it represented a "great threat," for in it the author laid bare Hitler's boundless expansionist and racist ideological goals.[94] Rauschning quoted Hitler as saying that the "decisive battle" against Russia could not be avoided, that he wanted to "land" in England and incite "revolt and unrest" in the United States, and eradicate Christianity and also Judaism "root and branch." On 29 January 1940 the German embassy in Bern protested against the distribution of this book in English and French translations, as well as against the publication of Rauschning's *Revolution des Nihilismus* (Revolution of Nihilism), in which he described the nature of national socialism. Three days later the German ambassador demanded that the *Gespräche* be banned. When Goebbels, who had sent to Danzig for incriminating material on Rauschning, insisted to the neutral countries that he wanted the "concept of neutrality" to extend not only to the military but also to the political sphere, which included publishing, the Swiss parliament gave in and on 16 February banned Rauschning's book.[95]

On 19 February, after it became known that the German auxiliary supply ship *Altmark*, with three hundred captured British seamen on board, had been seized and boarded by a British destroyer in Norwegian territorial waters, Goebbels directed his apparatus to "fire every propaganda gun" and unleash a "hellish choir of indignation." Although the British wire service had already reported the incident, so that most of the world press repeated the British version, Goebbels thought he could "somewhat compensate through clever management for the failure of the German Foreign Office." "All newspapers and broadcasting stations are going full throttle. The rage among the German population is indescribable," he noted in his diary.[96] On 19 February he instructed the press to "concentrate all polemics on this one case" until the sea boiled.[97]

While Goebbels was waging his propaganda war, Hitler was pushing ahead with preparations for "grabbing" Denmark and Norway. The chief aim of the operation was to take possession of the harbors, so as to give German naval forces direct access to the Atlantic and assure the flow of iron ore from neutral Sweden.[98]

After Hitler had met with Mussolini and received assurances that Italy would go to war on Germany's side, preparations for the attack, codenamed "Weser Exercise," were quickly concluded. Hitler had not informed Mussolini of the plan. Goebbels must have been told at the beginning of April, for on 5 April he sent for the editors in chief of the Berlin press and the heads of the foreign press bureaus, and revealed to them that a change would soon occur in the conduct of the war. Even though it was the goal of German propaganda to alienate the population of the Western powers from their governments, that did not make military intervention superfluous.[99]

Simultaneously Goebbels initiated a propaganda blitz intended to present the pending operation in the north as a defensive measure, and not just to the German people. Goebbels's specialists had happened upon a cover photo from the French magazine *L'Illustration* that showed American Undersecretary of State Sumner Welles and French Prime Minister Paul Reynaud looking at a map of Central Europe on which Germany consisted of the area between the Rhine and the Oder, and was divided into a northern and a southern state. Like other propaganda forgeries, this had first been launched abroad. Not until the Italian magazine *Regima Fascista* picked up this map of Europe was the issue highlighted in German propaganda. The press received instructions to present this map as "cynical proof of the Allies' intentions of annihilating us." Together with material about the battle for the Ruhr, this provided a propaganda brew very much to Goebbels's taste.[100]

Two days after Goebbels had instructed the press to disregard a correction that Sumner Welles had issued on the subject of European borders, the war cabinet in London handed the governments in Oslo and Stockholm notes announcing Britain's intention of placing mines just outside Norwegian territorial waters and sending an expeditionary force. The propaganda minister rejoiced. He had found his pretext: "Measures against German navigation, openly revealed as such. That is the jumping-off place we were looking for. O sancta simplicitas! All right, let's go! I'll hold off for a bit in the German press. So as not to reveal our hand too soon."[101]

On the morning of 8 April, during the "countdown" for the Weser Exercise, Goebbels hobbled through the garden of the Chancellery with Hitler. Everything was prepared, "down to the smallest detail," Hitler explained. The operation would involve about 250,000 men. Munitions and artillery pieces had already been smuggled over, mostly in coal barges. He did not fail to note that the war had to be won within a year, since otherwise the enemy's superiority in resources would become too great.[102] That afternoon Goebbels stirred up a whirlwind of activity, working in "breathless suspense." As cover, he had it announced that he would speak for the Winter Aid rally at the Sportpalast; "secretly and unnoticed," he "mobilized the radio"; he met again with Hitler; he instructed the press to make a big fuss over Romania; he spoke with Jodl, who explained in detail this "boldest venture in modern warfare; and he saw Hitler again.

"Now one must have nerves of steel and trust one's lucky stars," he concluded.[103]

Before dawn on 9 April 1940 the Wehrmacht launched the invasion of Denmark and Norway, just a few hours ahead of the British expeditionary force. The propaganda ministry therefore had some basis for declaring the Weser Exercise a defensive measure. Accordingly, the press was told to take this tack: "Instant response to the British attempts to make Scandinavia a theater of war against Germany." During the day London reported heavy German losses, which Goebbels dismissed as "lies." He found confirmation that evening in the Chancellery, when Hitler called the operation "one of the greatest successes of our entire policy and conduct of the war." According to Hitler, London was stunned and the United States had declared itself not interested. For Goebbels that meant "a surfeit of happiness"; he feared "the gods' envy."[104]

Disenchantment did not take long to set in. Unlike Denmark, Norway called on its people to offer military resistance. When the sixteen-vessel German fleet unit under the heavy cruiser *Blücher* sailed into the Oslo Fjord, the *Blücher* came under fire from the shore batteries and was sunk. Soon other units of the German fleet found themselves involved in battles with British naval forces. On 10 April Goebbels heard Hitler say in the Chancellery that Great Britain had suffered an "incredible loss in prestige" in the past two days, but the Führer regretted the German losses and had concluded that this operation was the only major assignment with which he could have entrusted the navy.[105]

At his minister's conference on 11 April Goebbels directed his staff to note that only the success of the Weser Exercise mattered. "Obviously" one had to expect casualties, but that was not the main thing.[106] A day later he spoke of "critical situations" and pointed out that it should be a principle never to keep silent but always to say something.[107] Shortly thereafter he justified the rule with an exception. The press and radio were supposed to preserve silence when more than twenty thousand British, French, and Polish soldiers landed near Narvik, where the iron-ore railroad link ended. While the rest of the German military operations in Norway proceeded according to plan, the German mountaineers under General Dietl found themselves in a hopeless position. On 18 April Hitler therefore informed Dietl that he could not count on any reinforcements and called on him to "act in such a way that the honor of the German Wehrmacht remains untarnished."[108]

In his annual speech on the eve of Hitler's birthday, Goebbels made every attempt to cover up the situation in northern Norway. He abused the British "plutocrats" and their lies, and declared that the entire "flood of lies" hurled against Germany rolled off without doing any damage. "That is because the German *Volk* has in the Führer the incarnation of its *völkisch* power and the most glowing example of its national objectives." Recounting a sequence from the film *Feuertaufe* (Baptism by Fire), about the Luftwaffe in the Polish campaign, Goebbels made Hitler's role as savior more vivid to the radio audience: "Then the camera slowly pans from the group of generals to the Führer, sitting on one side of the room, and with deep emotion the eye of the observer discovers this man to whom we all look, his face filled with sorrows, overcast with the burden of thought, a historical personage, very great and very alone."[109]

At his birthday table Hitler, in whom Goebbels again believed absolutely ever since his miraculous escape from the bomb in Munich, showed himself "inexhaustibly witty and clever." The conversation came around to the question of how long Great Britain would want to go on waging war against Germany. It came as something of a surprise to Goebbels to hear that Hitler did not intend to annihilate England and destroy its empire, but rather wanted "to make peace this very day." The campaign in the west also served this aim, Hitler explained to his propaganda minister on 24 April. France had to be crushed because that would cause London to lose its "thrust on the mainland" and be "powerless." Besides, "smashing" France was an act of "historical justice."[110]

A week later, on 1 May, Hitler ordered Case Yellow, the code name for the attack in the west, to be implemented on 5 May. But again the campaign had to be postponed. Goebbels's nerves were once more at the breaking point. While everyone waited for the great offensive, he tried to distract the world's attention for the time being. He reacted with arrogance to admonitions from the Vatican, whence it had been reported that the pope had spent "the entire Sunday in tearful prayer." "We know this old swindler's routine," he commented.[111]

Over the radio and in the press Goebbels denied that Germany had any intention of attacking neutral Holland and Belgium. He impressed upon the representatives of the media that they should repeat "over and over again" that it was England and France that "declared war on us and now have to pay the price," and that Germany must not "let itself under any circumstances be forced into the role of the aggressor."[112] Meanwhile on 9 May Hitler gave the final order for the attack, to take place the following day. The "sickle swath" strategy first proposed by General von Manstein, which Hitler had adopted as his own, was an offensive plan, though it was portrayed in Hitler's "Proclamation to the Soldiers on the Western Front" as a defensive measure, allegedly designed to prevent France and England from "pushing into the Ruhr territory" by way of Holland and Belgium. The hour had come for the soldiers on the western front. "The struggle now beginning will decide the fate of the German nation for the next thousand years," Hitler announced.[113]

Around 5:00 P.M. on 9 May, Hitler went to the little railroad station in Finkenkrug on the outskirts of Berlin. With his staff he boarded a special train and headed off in a northwesterly direction, to disguise his intentions. While Goebbels, as part of the pretense, sat in the theater watching a performance of Mussolini's play *Cavour*, in his thoughts he followed Hitler, whose train was now heading for his field headquarters, named the "Eagle's Nest," near Bad Münstereifel. Goebbels found Gustav Gründgens's staging of the play not at all convincing. The Duce could "apparently make history better than he could dramatize it," Goebbels decided.[114]

By the first light of day on 10 May the western campaign began. One hundred thirty-seven divisions with almost a million and a half soldiers, nearly 2,500 tanks, and almost 4,000 aircraft swooped down from the North Sea to the southern border. At 8:00 A.M. Goebbels read over the radio memoranda addressed to Belgium, Holland, and Luxembourg, in which he accused their governments of "flagrant violations of the most primitive rules of neutrality." The press and the radio received instructions to report that France and England had been on the verge of occupying Belgium and Holland, and that the Führer had once more stolen a march on them.

The western campaign proved to be a race to victory for the German Wehrmacht. Goebbels followed with enthusiasm the operations in areas that he still recalled from the previous war. More important in his joyous mood than the triumphs of German arms were his almost daily telephone conversations with Hitler, who was directing the operation from his field headquarters. Goebbels noted that the Führer believed firmly in victory, "another reason for it to be assured."[115]

In an essay entitled "Zeit ohne Beispiel" (Time without Precedent) Goebbels wrote emphatically that here, "under the leadership of a historical genius," the National Socialist system, which that genius had conceived and purposefully implemented, would advance to victory. "Fired up" by this man, the old German national virtues had reawakened in the spirit of a new ideal. "The creative German genius has for the first time in its history freed itself from all bureaucratic and dynastic constraints and unfolded in all its glory." Goebbels also tried to convince his readers that the situation in which Germany now found itself bore no resemblance to that of 1914.

This essay, which later lent its title to an edition of his speeches and essays from the years 1939–41, was written for the first number of a new weekly, *Das Reich*. The idea for this publication had been born in November 1939, when the monotony of the German press was being generally deplored, and demand arose for ways to intensify the propaganda directed abroad. Out of discussions with the powerful Rolf Rienhardt, right-hand man of the Nazi press czar Max Amann, came a plan for a weekly aimed primarily at Germans interested in political and cultural matters and at readers in neutral countries abroad.[116] At first there was talk of calling the publication *Die deutsche Rundschau* (The German Review).[117] Rienhardt favored the title *Das Reich*, which Goebbels considered "too officious."[118] But he had to capitulate to the Amann-Rienhardt duo's omnipotence in the publishing realm. Full agreement, however, prevailed as to the basic concept. The planners had in mind a paper like *The Observer*—an intellectual paper that, supported by leading personalities in the German Reich, would employ a cultivated style and be the only paper dispensed from following the daily directives issued by the Reich press secretary.[119]

Goebbels, pleased to be writing in the company of distinguished journalists, was overcome with ambition. From the outset he intended to be "heavily involved," probably because, among other things, he thought he could "accomplish a great deal propagandistically."[120] The German Publishing House (Deutscher Verlag), now under Amann's control, which published the *Frankfurter Zeitung* and the *Deutsche Allgemeine Zeitung*, gave Goebbels a contract stipulating a payment of 2,000 marks for each of his articles. The propaganda minister, who in 1939, after a long hiatus, had begun to write regular editorials again, at first in the *Völkischer Beobachter*, could complete one in an hour or an hour and a half, but when necessary in under fifteen minutes.[121]

From early 1941 on, almost every Monday morning the official courier from the Wilhelmplatz would deliver to the publishing company a carefully crafted manuscript, a "display of energy" that even Goebbels's enemy Rosenberg had to admire.[122] Rosenberg generously conceded that one should therefore "not always assail the articles with petty criticism." But when his "sense of official duty" overcame his resistance, and he read Goebbels's writings more carefully, he found in particular "the polemics against our adversaries of such low caliber" that he several times wrote to Goering complaining, charging that Goebbels was "tied to Churchill's apron strings."[123]

The first number of the new newspaper appeared on Sunday, 26 May, the day on which, with the occupation of Calais, Goebbels thought Germany was "placing its hand on England's throat." Two days later King Leopold III of Belgium followed the Netherlands in capitulating. Although the king belonged to those aristocrats whom Goebbels so hated, Goebbels praised him as a "sober head" because he had followed "the heart of the people." Because he was said to have "strong sympathies" for Germany, Hitler awarded him an allowance of 50 million francs.[124]

From the beginning of the campaign, Goebbels had aimed his propaganda at driving a wedge between the Allies, using official announcements to play them off against each other. Now he took the French prime minister's caustic comments about Belgium's capitulation as an occasion for blasting the "wretched attitude" of the French "warmonger government." First France had won Belgium over to the "criminal plan against Germany," and now, when Leopold had surrendered in view of the hopelessness of further resistance, France had kicked him while he was down and accused him of treason.[125]

While in the Reich the victory fanfare with which the Reich radio introduced the special bulletins sounded repeatedly, and the press had instructions to stress the magnitude of each success, Goebbels's secret transmitters were working overtime, beaming messages to France. He himself wrote bulletins for them, encouraging French soldiers to desert, for example, or recommending that the population flee or withdraw their savings from the bank, since the Germans would confiscate them immediately. Carefully targeted false reports did in fact engender considerable confusion, and when panic broke out at the Gare du Nord in Paris because a false report had announced Goebbels's arrival there, the propaganda minister felt especially flattered.[126]

At the end of May, when a German victory seemed imminent, Goebbels gave orders to intensify further the press and radio attacks on France.[127] The old clichés about the hereditary enemy and the decadence of French culture were dragged out and polished up. France, it was said, could not be the culture-bearer of Europe because "through mixture with inferior races it had debased itself, and after 1918 it had committed the gravest crime against civilization when, during the occupation of the Ruhr, it had placed the racially most highly developed nation under the supervision of Negroes."[128] No opportunity was neglected to recall the French occupation, with all its negative side effects.

The first phase of the western campaign ended with the delayed capture of Dunkirk on 4 June; the delay enabled the British expeditionary force to be evacuated across the English Channel. Two days later Goebbels flew to join Hitler, who had established his headquarters in Brûly-de-Pesche near Namur. Hitler described to Goebbels an excursion to the battlefields where he had fought during World War I; he indulged himself in reminiscences about his unforgettable experiences at the front, of which he had written in *Mein Kampf*. Goebbels was "most deeply affected by these dramatic descriptions." To him, the Führer seemed to "tower above" all others. Once more Goebbels called him a "historical genius," and rejoiced in these "great times" and the happiness of being able to participate in the building of a "new Europe." "Filled with energy and firmness again," Goebbels took leave of Hitler, who had been "very touching" toward him, and set out for the nearby airstrip, where he boarded a Heinkel bomber for the flight back to Berlin.[129]

Hitler had remarked to Goebbels that he expected France to be "overthrown" in six to eight weeks.[130] Italy declared war on France on 10 June, and as it turned out, the campaign lasted only another two weeks. On 14 June German tanks broke through the Maginot Line near Saarbrücken. Verdun, which had been fought over for years during World War I, with seven hundred thousand casualties, fell within a matter of hours. That same day a German combat unit reached the Swiss border in the Jura mountains, thereby cutting off the entire French army in the east, while simultaneously a German infantry division entered Paris. After a telephone conversation with Hitler on the evening of this eventful day, Goebbels thought the Reich had reached the pinnacle of military triumph. He noted in his diary that Hitler would "batter down the French until they plead for peace."[131]

Goebbels was ecstatic when Paul Reynaud's government, which had fled to Bordeaux, resigned instead of holding out, as advised by Churchill, who had recently been named British prime minister. Two days later Marshal Philippe Pétain, the now elderly "victor of Verdun," took over the government and promptly offered the Germans a cease-fire. When Hitler called Goebbels to inform him of this development, Goebbels was so carried away that he could hardly express his congratulations.[132]

After the radio announcement of the cease-fire on 17 June, 1940, crowds gathered beneath Goebbels's window on Wilhelmplatz and struck up "Deutschland, Deutschland, über alles." Hitler had decided to stage the signing of France's capitulation in the very place where representatives of the German army had been obliged to sign a similar document on 11 November 1918. Goebbels was overcome; he described the event taking place on 21 and 22 June in the railroad car in the forest of Compiègne as a "divine judgment that we are carrying out on behalf of a higher historical destiny."[133] The shameful defeat and the subsequent humiliations were now erased, and Goebbels himself, whose grimmest period had begun in that November more than twenty years earlier, now found himself at the center of power of a strong German Reich.

Goebbels kept the nation abreast of the cease-fire negotiations by way of telephone reports from Compiègne, broadcast over the Reich radio. The French negotiator had to agree to Germany's occupying France down to a line extending from near Geneva to the Spanish border by way of Dôle, Tours, and Mont de Marsan. When the guns fell silent at 1:35 A.M. on 25 June, the radio carried a special broadcast that the propaganda minister called, not without vanity, "very effectively put together." He listened to it in Lanke with a small group from his staff. "We have already accomplished so much," he concluded with satisfaction.[134]

The worries and fears that had tormented Goebbels at the prospect of war had dissipated with the Wehrmacht's victorious advance. Firmly believing in the Reich's and the Führer's divine mission, he now even hoped that it would come to a real fight with England. "I hope Churchill doesn't give in at the last moment," he commented.[135] More and more Goebbels hated the British prime minister, who had promised his people nothing but "blood, sweat, and tears." Goebbels hated him for his toughness and persistence, for no propaganda seemed able to touch him. Despite all his attempts to portray Churchill as a "vain monkey in pink panties" or a "vain blabbermouth who aims for the impression of the moment," in the long run Goebbels could not help respecting him. He admired the "scintillating style" of his speeches, and wrote that "the old fox" had neither strength of character nor stature, but was still "a man of great gifts," so dangerous that Germany would not stand where it stood today, "if he had taken the helm in 1933."[136]

During a trip to Belgium, Holland, and France, Goebbels felt confirmed in his notion that England could be conquered. After visiting the battlefield at Ypres and the military cemetery at Langemarck, he talked with German soldiers who told him they were itching to go to England. He heard the same thing from soldiers in Compiègne, "the place of shame and of national resurrection."[137]

On 1 July Goebbels went to Paris for a day, after cranking up his propaganda apparatus for a steady barrage against England. He took in the sights—Les Invalides with the grave of Napoleon, Sacré-Coeur, Notre Dame—and drove out to Versailles, where "Germany was condemned to death." He dreamed of living in Paris for a few weeks. A telephone call from Hitler jolted him out of such dreams. Hitler ordered him to the Eagle's Nest to discuss the present situation and future measures to be taken. Goebbels heard with surprise that, although Hitler claimed he could subdue England in four weeks if he wanted to, he planned to offer England a "last chance" in an address to the Reichstag. Hitler justified this step to the breathlessly admiring Goebbels by explaining that whatever England lost would probably fall not to Germany but to other major powers, by which he meant the United States.

Goebbels doubted that Churchill would take this "last chance." He did not realize the extent to which his Führer was counting on and needed an agreement with England as the basis for realizing his objectives in the east; when Hitler had said weeks earlier that the Norway operation was the only major assignment he could give the German navy, he had implied that a successful landing in England was hardly possible. Goebbels found Hitler's strategy toward Great Britain difficult to justify to the public. During one of the subsequent "minister's conferences," he explained to his staff that it was absolutely essential to "maintain the hatred for England at the previous level, but to avoid the danger of the people's beginning to demand action instead of accusations and threats. So we must tread water, for we mustn't anticipate the Führer's actions."[138]

On the afternoon of 6 July Goebbels drove past huge crowds to the Anhalt Station. He had called upon the Berliners to welcome the Führer back from the field "with unprecedented enthusiasm."[139] At the station, which was decorated with a sea of swastika banners, and where an SA band had taken up its position and newsreel cameras were waiting to roll, he met all the party and Wehrmacht leaders. During a brief "chat," Goering told him he would be glad when the spectacle was over, for he feared British aerial attacks. From the beginning of the war, the British war cabinet had decided to turn the Royal Air Force loose on the German hinterland.

On the stroke of 3:00 Hitler's train pulled in. "Mad enthusiasm fills the station. The Führer is very moved. Tears come to his eyes."[140] To the strains of the "Badenweil March," his favorite, he strode past the leaders of the "Greater German Reich." His motorcade through the city, along streets decked with flowers and lined with cheering masses, became a triumphal procession. As the church bells rang out, the Führer's supercharged Mercedes rolled up to the Reich Chancellery. When he stepped out onto the balcony, hundreds of thousands of arms raised in the Nazi salute stretched toward him from Wilhelmplatz.[141] If ever the propaganda slogan "One *Volk*, one Reich, one Führer" was valid, it was so on 6 July 1940. In the eyes of the Germans, Hitler had become a sublime figure. Yet the pinnacle of power to which he had ascended was shaky. No one knew that better than Hitler himself, for everything depended on whether England would reach an accommodation with Germany, and England had just demonstrated its determination by attacking the French fleet in the Algerian port of Mers el-Kébir.

While Goebbels was again forced to recognize that Hitler still had "a very positive relationship" to England, Hitler had decided, as so often before, to wait. In his foreign propaganda Goebbels continued to snipe at Churchill, but made sure that the English people were not included. In his internal propaganda he did not cease to praise the greatness of the moment, stressing how different this war was from the first, with the alleged betrayal of the homeland. He meant to suggest that this war could not be lost. On 18 July the 218th Infantry Division returned to Berlin and marched through the flag-adorned Brandenburg Gate amid the ringing of all the church bells. People agreed that such a spectacle had not been seen since the founding of the German Reich in 1871.[142] In his address to the troops and spectators assembled on Pariser Platz, Goebbels shouted, "In December 1918, too, you soldiers of the World War armies were received on this spot by a so-called government. But the reception was no better than the government. It was the work of the same political gangsters who had organized the munitions strikes in 1917 and 1918 and who, when the fate of the Reich stood on the razor's edge, knocked the weapons out of the hands of the soldiers at the front through a cowardly internal revolution. Traitors and Jews received you back then. . . . But you, soldiers of our war, find your homeland as you left it. At its head stands the same Führer, from its roofs waves the same flag, its people are filled with the same spirit and the same will. . . . The war is not yet over. Its last stage must still be won. Then let the bells of peace ring out over the land; then we shall build a greater Reich and a better Europe."[143]

Despite all the excitement, Goebbels had not lost sight of the "Jewish question." He kept pushing Hitler to find a solution. Now, when his quasi undersecretary Leopold Gutterer reported that during the parade he had observed on the Kurfürstendamm the same "lack of interest" and the same "strolling riffraff," Goebbels announced that "immediately after the end of the war" he was determined to "have all the sixty-two thousand Jews still living in Berlin removed to Poland within a period of eight weeks at most." For as long as Jews lived in Berlin, the atmosphere in the western part of the city "would always be influenced by them." At the minister's conference, Hans Hinkel, leader of the section in the Propaganda Ministry responsible for the Jewish question, reported on an evacuation plan already worked out with the police. Above all, Goebbels's desire to have "Berlin purged first of all" should be accommodated, since the Kurfürstendamm would "continue to have a Jewish character," even if the Jews were not openly visible, until the city had become "really Jew-free." Only after Berlin would the "other Jew-cities (Breslau, etc.) get their turn."[144]

But things had not yet reached that point; the Reich was still at war with Great Britain, and Hitler was still hoping to work things out with London, although nothing actually pointed in that direction. On 16 July he had halfheartedly given instructions to prepare a landing operation on the British coast. When he addressed the Reichstag three days later, his speech was directed less at the German people than at his wished-for partner.[145] Goebbels's name came up in the speech, though not in a prominent place. Hitler referred to him with approval as the director "of a propaganda whose excellence becomes apparent through a comparison with that of the World War." That was not much, compared with the words of gratitude Hitler found for Ribbentrop. Then, after reading out long lists of promotions and also thanking Goering and conferring on him the newly created title of *Reichsmarshall*, Hitler came to the point. "In this hour," he said, he felt himself obligated "by conscience to appeal once more to reason on the part of England. . . . I see no compelling grounds for continuing this war."[146]

Goebbels, whose hatred forbade him to believe in any British readiness for peace "so long as Churchill is at the helm," turned out to be right.[147]

On the evening of 19 July the BBC broadcast the government's categorical rejection of Hitler's "offer." Hitler did not want to accept this answer at the moment and thought he would "wait a bit longer," since he had "appealed to the British people, not to Churchill."[148] But when the British foreign secretary, Lord Halifax, went on the radio to confirm the rejection, Hitler recognized this as "England's final refusal."[149] Now he weighed various possibilities for forcing England to relent after all. First he considered creating a hostile European alliance that would include the Soviet Union. Then he played with the idea of waging a blitzkrieg against Russia before the year was out. Finally he decided to force England to its knees through a naval blockade and attacks by Goering's Luftwaffe, but the landing operation he had ordered prepared did not play a significant part in these plans.

Goebbels, who felt almost relieved at the stance Great Britain had adopted, remained firmly convinced that Hitler would now launch the great landing operation and saw the aerial offensive as the prerequisite. Assuming that the German public had "been afraid Churchill would grasp the hand of peace proferred by Hitler," Goebbels now wondered only when the offensive would begin.[150] "That only the Führer can decide. He will surely find the right moment" and then act "quickly and unhesitatingly."[151]

While waiting, Goebbels put press and radio "on a war footing."[152] In his conference on 24 July he instructed his staff to intensify the existing warlike mood in the German people. The restraint of the previous weeks should be abandoned; not only the English "plutocracy" but also the English people were to be attacked. In the propaganda intended for the English people it had to be made clear that the "clique of plutocrats" had nothing to do with the people and felt no bond with them. The objective was to sow distrust and fill the people with fear, "laying it on as thick as possible." The same thing went for the official propaganda organs, especially the English-language broadcasts of the Reich Broadcasting Company.[153]

As in the campaign against France, the radio served as Goebbels's major tool. In addition to the official broadcasts in English, there were broadcasts from clandestine transmitters that pretended to be located in England. It was crucial that they not be unmasked as German, Goebbels warned, for which reason each broadcast had to begin with attacks on national socialism.[154] Best known was the New British Broadcasting Station with its Irish announcer Lord Haw Haw, as the listeners called him (actually William Joyce), who belonged to the circle around the British fascist leader Oswald Mosley. The broadcasts called for an England of peace and social welfare, and supported pacifist aspirations on a basis of Christianity. Radio Caledonia played up English-Scottish tensions, while a third station tried to incite the inhabitants of Wales to revolt against alleged English tyranny.[155]

When Operation Day of Eagles finally began in mid-August with a major assault by almost four thousand planes and, as Goebbels put it, "God's chastisement" descended on England, the "war of the airwaves" continued.[156] Goebbels once again felt certain of victory, because his Führer projected "so much optimism and strength of faith."[157] It added to his confidence when reports came in that the German bombing raids were inflicting crushing damage on London. The city was said to be covered by "one great cloud of smoke," Goebbels rejoiced, and when an RAF squadron turned around shortly before reaching Berlin, he wondered whether the enemy was "already so knocked out."[158]

On 10 September Goebbels answered the question as to "whether England will capitulate" with "yes," in agreement with the military, while Hitler remained undecided.[159] Yet nothing of the sort occurred, and a few days later Goebbels had to admit that London was gaining "the upper hand." Goering's Luftwaffe had not succeeded in smashing the British fighter defense. As early as 11 September, after British bombs had fallen on the government quarter in Berlin, Goebbels had instructed the press by Telex to "be more cautious with reports expressing the presumption that London had had enough or the morale of the population had been undermined, or that the British defensive capability had suffered. In the next few weeks an intensification of the air raids on Germany could be expected, but this intensification would be impossible for the people to understand, if the impression were created prematurely that substantial damage had already been inflicted on the enemy."[160]

While the air battle raged over southern England and the Channel, the RAF in fact did intensify its attacks on the Reich. On 25 September the air raid sirens went off twice in Berlin. Shortly before the British Wellingtons and Whitleys reached blacked-out Berlin, before people raced for the air raid shelters and the flak opened fire, the German premiere of *Jud Süss* concluded at the Ufa Palace. It was the second rabidly anti-Semitic film of the summer, after *Die Rothschilds*. Goebbels, who along with Veit Harlan, Ferdinand Marian, and numerous dignitaries of the regime had occupied a place of honor, felt profound satisfaction when the curtain came down and the audience "raved" with enthusiasm.[161] *Jud Süss* had turned out just as he had hoped, a "brilliant piece of work; an anti-Semitic film just as we would wish it."[162] He had sent it to Venice to have its premiere during the German-Italian Film Week in August. Convinced of its impact, he had ordered the press not to characterize the film ahead of time as anti-Semitic.[163] Himmler found the film so convincing that on 30 September he issued an order that "provision be made for the entire SS and police to see the film *Jud Süss* in the course of the winter."[164]

As for the planned deportation of the Jews from Berlin, Goebbels now exerted even more pressure. He had come to hold the opinion, in view of the intensifying war, that Germany would in any case be criticized abroad for its anti-Semitism, so it might as well enjoy the benefits of "putting the Jews out."[165] Hinkel, head of the Jewish section in the Propaganda Ministry, had reported on 6 September "that all preparations are finalized so that—as soon as transportation becomes available at war's end—sixty thousand Jews can be moved to the east from Berlin within four weeks; the remaining twelve thousand will likewise have vanished within another four weeks."[166]

Shortly thereafter the minister was confronted with the so-called Madagascar Plan. The Foreign Office, in collaboration with the Reichssicherheitshauptamt, had been considering deporting the European Jews to Madagascar. On 12 July 1940 Hitler had given the go-ahead to plans for deportation and declared that France had to renounce the island, which numbered among its colonial possessions. He wanted a "forced ghetto" on Madagascar as a "pawn" in Germany's hand, and noted with approval the huge number of deaths that could be expected among the deportees. As tentative as the plans might be, Madagascar from that time on replaced the Government General in the Propaganda Ministry's thinking on a destination for the Jews. Hinkel at any rate used this plan as the basis for his presentation on 17 September.

To "evacuate" 3.5 million European Jews to a German-controlled reservation on Madagascar required the successful completion of the war with Great Britain. Yet that was out of the question at the moment, for the aerial offensive was claiming more and more casualties and even threatening to fail. On 11 October Goebbels noted in his diary that some people still believed "we could force England to her knees in the next few weeks," but he considered this hope "very faint."[167] It therefore seemed to him absolutely essential that Berlin's wholly inadequate air raid shelters be expanded; not one of the hospitals had its own.[168] He realized that without control of the skies Operation Sealion, the landing in England, would be impossible. When Hitler postponed it indefinitely, he spoke evasively to Goebbels of the bad weather and the fear of high casualties.[169] Hitler kept to himself the recognition that Goering's Luftwaffe had failed, and that the navy command had informed him that their preparations could not be completed in the stipulated time. On the other hand, he praised his faithful vassal Goebbels, who still could not believe that the "anti-illusion campaign" he had launched against England at the beginning of October was having no effect.[170] He asked himself almost daily whether "that beast Churchill" was not "buckling at the knees yet," and how long he planned to hold out.[171] Goebbels was absolutely convinced that "precisely now, when a small spiritual crisis is setting in," it was crucial to "stand fast and go one's way without batting an eyelash." Recalling October and November 1932 strengthened him in this conviction, for at that time, too, "it was a matter of the right attitude, and because we had it, we won out in the end."[172]

Thus reassured, in mid-October Goebbels accepted Goering's invitation to visit Occupied France, for which Hitler had given him propaganda assignments in August.[173] In Paris he took tea at the Palais Rothschild, visited an exhibition at the side of the "art connoisseur" Goering, strolled with him through the streets of the metropolis on the Seine, and spent the evening in the Casino de Paris, where "many beautiful women and disarming nudity" allowed him to forget the war for the moment.[174] While Goering "requisitioned" suitable art works for his pretentious country estate, Karinhall, Goebbels occupied himself mostly with film matters, for the propaganda minister intended to extend his control in this area to Occupied France. After his return to Berlin, he discussed with Fritz Hippler, head of the film department of the Propaganda Ministry, how they might set up a "camouflaged system" so that "the Frenchman will hardly notice who's pulling the strings." Goebbels did not mean to stop there; he wanted to have all European filmmaking in his hands.[175] There could be no doubt that film distribution was lucrative. Goebbels's cinematic empire, with almost 3,700 theaters in the Reich and the occupied territories, had receipts of 500 million marks in 1939, when a high point was reached with 111 full-length films produced. In 1940 the clear profit amounted to 70 million marks. To bypass the finance minister, Goebbels promptly set up a special fund "for construction of new movie theaters," but to Hitler's gratification he also siphoned off 5 million marks for Hitler's culture fund and 15 million for the social fund of the wartime Winter Aid.[176]

With such sums coming in, it must have been difficult for the absolute ruler of German film to understand why he was plagued personally "with great difficulties in financing the addition to his property in Lanke."[177] He had begun the work in February 1939, when the log cabin had been found "too small and impractical."[178] To be sure, Goebbels had no authorization to build on the huge, fan-shaped piece of land, which belonged to the Lake Liepnitz nature preserve. The district administrator ordered an immediate halt to construction, "so that the valuable forest land may be preserved in its original beauty for the recreation of the population of the capital and remain open to hiking."[179] Goebbels's rival Rosenberg was only too happy to hear of such things, as he had when he called a meeting of the Gauleiters in mid-May 1939. One of them blurted out that he had thwarted Goebbels's building plans, and "in case he was summoned to the Führer, he would tell the whole story, no matter what happened to him."[180] But Goering, in his capacity as Reich chief forester, at the end of May rendered a decision "that the construction should not be hindered in any fashion."[181]

So on the banks of the Bogensee an estate was being created whose five buildings could well withstand comparison with Karinhall, Goering's pseudofeudal seat. A forest of firs surrounded the one-story sprawling residence, built in farmhouse style but with all the amenities. It had twenty-one rooms, including five baths and of course a cinema. The huge windows could be raised and lowered electrically, as could the bar. The house had air conditioning and forced-air heat. As a wall hanging Goebbels had bought an Aubusson carpet in Paris for 26,000 marks.[182] The service building had twenty-seven rooms decorated in the accustomed luxurious style—the inventory ran to twenty-eight densely written pages.[183] In addition, there was still the original log cabin on the other side of the lake, as well as a guest house and a garage.

Goebbels's worries about the financing of the Lanke project were resolved in November 1940 by Reich Trustee of Funds Max Winkler, who had already performed valuable services when the German film industry was bought out by the Propaganda Ministry. In collaboration with Goering, in the name of the German film industry he assumed the costs of 2.26 million marks for the estate.[184] To the propaganda minister this came as an immense relief, for in addition he had "a whole mountain of taxes to pay." But Goebbels summed up the matter with a slightly different calculation: "If I were to die now, my balance would come out at plus or minus zero. Some reward for twenty years of service to the fatherland!" Thus wrote the owner and user of three residences worth millions in and around Berlin.[185] On 29 October 1940, Goebbels's forty-third birthday, the family moved into the magnificent new official residence at 20 Hermann-Goering-Strasse. They had received the keys the previous year, but there had been a seemingly unending list of "defects" to be taken care of. During these weeks Goebbels was full of dreamy plans for after the war. He toyed with the idea of retiring. He expressed the hope that he would soon be able to write, perhaps in the new diary he was beginning, the "beautiful words" that "we have peace again."[186] Goebbels was glad that the children, who recited poems they had learned by heart, as they did every year for his birthday, liked their new rooms in the splendid palace. And the five children were joined that evening by a sixth, for Magda, who had been in the hospital for several weeks, had given birth to their "reconciliation child," Heide. When mother and child came home and Magda celebrated her birthday on 11 November, the

Führer turned up as a surprise guest and voiced his delight at the infant and the marble palace.[187]

In the months just past, Hitler's visits had become infrequent, for he had been wrapped up in Ribbentrop's suggested political alternative to landing in England. The idea was to isolate the enemy across the Channel by means of a provisional solution, a continental bloc extending "from Madrid to Yokohama," including France and especially the Soviet Union.[188] By this means Hitler expected to prevent the United States, now moving ever closer to Great Britain, from entering the war. He thought London could still be brought around. He had been caught up in a busy program of travel, arranged by his foreign minister, ever since the Tripartite Pact signed on 27 September by Germany, Japan, and Italy had provided a framework into which he could now try to fit the other major European countries.

On 11 November, when Hitler helped celebrate Magda Goebbels's birthday, he was about to receive a visit from Soviet Foreign Minister Molotov. Despite the disappointing outcome of previous discussions and the recognition that "the entire problem of Europe" was the Soviet Union, so that everything had to be done to be ready for the "great reckoning" in the coming year, Hitler still wanted to try to shift Stalin's expansionist ambitions toward India, so as to integrate the Soviet Union into the hostile front against Great Britain.

Goebbels must have been well aware that such cooperation with the Soviet Union could be only an interim solution. Since the relationship between Germany and the Soviet Union was not intended to go beyond "pure political expediency," Goebbels had also opposed the Foreign Office's efforts to establish a cultural exchange between the two countries.[189] Time and again Goebbels had forbidden the press to publish anything favorable to the Soviet Union.[190] When the Moscow correspondent of the *Deutsche Allgemeine Zeitung* reported on the Bolshoi Ballet, an angered Goebbels sent him a coded message saying that he had a week to find a similarly favorable account of German theater in an equally respected Russian newspaper; "otherwise he would be recalled at once for lack of political instinct."[191]

In preparation for the Molotov visit, Goebbels instructed the press to refer to the development of German-Soviet relations since the year before, but not to create the impression "that we're rubbing our hands over the visit." The visit had to be treated simply as a "political point" in German-Russian relations.[192]

Lest the Soviet foreign minister be received too respectfully, Goebbels, who was involved in the preparations for the visit, prevented the SA from forming an aisle of honor and vetoed a "popular demonstration," both suggested by the Foreign Office. On 13 November, when Hitler was having breakfast at the Chancellery with the Russian delegation, Goebbels closely observed the "Bolshevist subhumans." Molotov, with a "face of waxy yellowness," impressed him as "clever and sly" but acted "very buttoned-up." His entourage, on the other hand, struck Goebbels as "more than merely mediocre. Not a single man of any stature. As if they were determined to confirm our theoretical insights into Bolshevist mass ideology. . . . In the faces one can read their fear of each other, and their inferiority complexes."[193] The supposed inferiority of the Soviet visitors did not, however, make them pushovers for Hitler's idea that they should move in on the remains of the British Empire in India. In the course of the visit, Hitler recognized that Soviet interests extended far into central Europe, not into southern Asia, which spelled the collapse of his idea of a continental bloc. As a result, on the day of Molotov's departure he ordered preparations "to settle accounts with Russia when the first fine days arrive."[194] On 18 December he signed Führer's Directive No. 21 for Operation Barbarossa.

Hitler concealed from his propaganda minister the fact that he now wanted to pursue his objectives in the east without having secured the west, which meant risking a war on two fronts. Because Hitler had previously stressed how important it was to have his back protected in the east, and had concluded the pact with the Soviet Union for that very purpose, Goebbels proceeded on the assumption that Hitler would move first to crush Great Britain. Accordingly, he noted in his diary that Moscow's "neutrality" was the most important thing.[195] As he had predicted the collapse of France the previous year, he now predicted England's.[196] Since the invasion could not take place without control of the skies, and Goebbels had detected in Hitler a certain "fear of the water," he placed his hopes in the bombing raids on London, Coventry, and Sheffield, whose psychological impact he far overestimated, and resolved to stand fast and devote all his strength to the work for victory. At the threshold of the second wartime winter, this meant buoying up the population in Germany, informing people that it would not be easy, but that victory was assured if all made the necessary effort. At one of his minister's conferences Goebbels explained that in the long run it would be counterproductive, if the German press constantly tried to create the impression that England would fall the very next day. It was "all right to tell the German people that a world empire like the British does not collapse in a matter of weeks."[197]

At the beginning of November 1940 the propaganda minister suffered a marked reduction in his power. Hitler introduced the "Word of the Day from the Reich press secretary," which gave Otto Dietrich greater direct control of the press.[198] The Word of the Day was formulated in the Führer's headquarters, to be read as the first point during the daily press briefings in the Propaganda Ministry.[199] Goebbels and the representatives of the various departments in his ministry could pass along instructions, information, and bulletins to the press only after they had been submitted in writing to Dietrich or the director of the German press department, who worked under his direction.

Goebbels focused his anger over the Word of the Day exclusively on Dietrich. He tried to compensate for his loss of power over the domestic press by expanding his influence on propaganda abroad.[200] He already controlled propaganda in the Protectorate of Bohemia and Moravia, in the Polish Government General, and in occupied France, Holland, and Norway. Now he hoped that resuming discussions with the Foreign Office would result in having the powers that were conveyed to Ribbentrop in September 1939 formally restored to his ministry. The situation seemed promising, for with the failure of the continental bloc project, Ribbentrop's influence on Hitler had begun to wane. But except for Goebbels's success at keeping the Foreign Office's representatives away from the radio—in one case he even had them physically removed—the negotiations at first accomplished little.

At the same time he experienced increasing difficulty in maintaining morale within the Reich in the face of the continued British bombing raids. On 9 December his hometown of Rheydt was bombed. To make things worse, Italy seemed about to suffer defeat in North Africa and the Balkans. Since only German intervention seemed able to avert a catastrophe on the southern flank, Hitler had decided to "clean up" that situation before the campaign against Russia. In November he dispatched a corps of airmen to southern Italy and Sicily, and at the beginning of 1941 he sent a tank unit to North Africa. In the spring he wanted to stabilize the southeastern flank by launching a campaign across the Balkans toward Greece.

Goebbels, who had been annoyed at Italy's late entry into the war, now accused the Italians of "ruining the whole military prestige of the Axis."[201] Yet Hitler gave him strict instructions to "stress the friendly relations of the Axis powers."[202] Now that England was winning in the Mediterranean, German warfare could not be said to be as effective against the island nation as Goebbels's propaganda was portraying it, so Goebbels directed the press to downplay the German successes. He also eliminated "a whole series of signs of decay in England from our repertoire," so as to accustom the German people "gradually to patience."[203] In other respects he returned his propaganda "to basics," as he had done during the "phony war" and the period of secret diplomacy in the fall of 1940, when it had also been a matter of filling a propaganda void so as to keep the people "occupied."[204] He again zeroed in on his "best point of attack," the British "plutocrats," to whom he devoted a series of editorials in *Das Reich*.[205] When the United States came to England's aid in March 1941 with the Lend-Lease Act, which authorized President Roosevelt to supply war materiel to England without repayment, Goebbels viewed this as London's "saving straw."[206] In *Das Reich* Goebbels commented that what these supplies "cause England to lose in national prestige and international influence is something that American publicists who have preserved their clarity of vision amid this confusion of opinions do not hesitate to express. They say quite frankly that England should go ahead and lose the war; then America will simply step in and liquidate the British Empire."[207]

Goebbels's array of propaganda tools to be used against England also included film. To remove any basis for Rosenberg's accusation that "nothing but pro-English films" was being produced, Goebbels took up an idea proposed by the actor Emil Jannings: he made a film about the "Boer freedom fighter" Paul Krüger, whose resistance to English policies in South Africa resulted in his experiencing "the horrors of the English concentration camps."[208] The historical drama *Ohm Krüger*, with Emil Jannings in the title role, became the "film of the nation."[209]

Even during the war, obvious propaganda films of this sort constituted a small though growing portion of the total film production. Of the 1,094 films made during the Third Reich, 47.8 percent were comedies, 27 percent problem films, 11.2 percent adventure films, and 14 percent propaganda films.[210] Particularly at a time like this, Goebbels saw it as the primary duty of the film industry to create "relaxing entertainment films" so as to keep people in a "good mood," since a war of these dimensions could be won "only with optimism."[211] Since Goebbels saw in film "a national method of education par excellence," apparent distraction or "refreshing of mind and spirit" had an ulterior purpose.[212] Accordingly, the subjects Goebbels authorized for filmmaking were subtly infused with the regime's propaganda intentions. Goebbels saw to it that the war, which became the main theme in films from 1939 on, was linked to the most varied genres, so as to make indoctrination of the audience imperceptible and keep the medium of film attractive.[213] As he expected of all his propaganda ideally, so too in film, one and the same message was to be conveyed over and over again under constantly varied aspects.

Millions saw *Wir tanzen um die Welt* (We Dance around the World), in which music-hall elements mixed with military marches: "Dance and be young, win and be young, laugh and be young—that's us, that's our motto!" was the leitmotif of the film.[214] Twenty-three million people saw the hit *Wunschkonzert* (Request Concert, 1940), which told the story of a German girl who in the confusion of war lost sight of her lover, a stalwart Luftwaffe lieutenant, and located him again through the radio request concert. War scenes were embedded in nostalgic memories of the "great times" of the 1936 Olympic Games and the hits from the most popular radio program of all, the Sunday request concert, which created a sentimental link between the folks at home and the soldiers at the front. Love stories like *Die grosse Liebe* (The Great Love, 1942), starring Zarah Leander, served the Nazis' purposes especially well. (Goebbels at first disliked Leander, but came to appreciate her when he saw what a tremendous following her films had.) The fates of characters in these films were shared by hundreds of thousands; through the characters, messages could thus be delivered and examples given of the desired attitude. Songs like "I Know Someday There'll Be a Miracle" and the melodramatic atmosphere in which Zarah Leander was forced to take leave of her lover, expressing deep gratitude to his Luftwaffe unit as it flew off toward the front, made such "exemplary images" all the more affecting for the audience.

It was the airmen in particular, the Knights of the Iron Cross from Goering's Luftwaffe, whom Goebbels elevated to popular heroes. Names like Werner Mölders, Adolf Galland, and later Hans Joachim Marseille, the "star of Africa," epitomized the new German soldier. Together with men from the submarine fleet, they became the idols of German youth. The army, with its strong ties to tradition, had fewer popular officers to offer. Goebbels focused on Eduard Dietl, who with his mountaineers from "the Führer's homeland" had held out in a hopeless situation in Narvik until the British expeditionary force was withdrawn. Goebbels "heroized" his struggle into a "modern Song of the Nibelungen." He made sure that the "Knights of the Iron Cross from the ranks of the little man" received preferential treatment in his propaganda.[215]

Another member of the armed forces soon won the propaganda minister's particular favor: Erwin Rommel. Rommel's up-'n'-at-'em style of leadership corresponded to the "revolutionary strategy" of the blitzkrieg. Goebbels, who believed that a "modern war" was not meant for "old generals," saw combined in Rommel all the qualities and character traits of the ideal Nazi military leader, for which reason Rommel had already received special propaganda emphasis during the French campaign.[216] In February 1941, when Rommel arrived in Tripoli, where he and the Africa Corps were supposed to halt the British advance and save the Italian colony for the Axis, Goebbels's staff members Wilhelm Haegert and Alfred Berndt were on active duty with the corps.

While Goebbels maintained close contact with his two operatives and coordinated the propaganda war against England from his office on Wilhelmplatz, Hitler remained holed up for weeks at the Berghof. Goebbels did not see him again until 12 March, when the third anniversary of the *Anschluss* was celebrated in Linz.

In the hotel in Linz, or at the latest on 28 March at a dinner Hitler gave for the Japanese foreign minister at the Chancellery, Hitler initiated Goebbels into his plan of attacking the Soviet Union before "taking care of" Great Britain. How Goebbels reacted has not been documented. But everything suggests that Hitler's decision struck him, as so often before, as a work of genius. Early in the morning of 29 March 1941 he wrote in his diary:

The great undertaking will come later, against R. It will be most carefully camouflaged; very few know about it. It will be initiated with large troop transports to the west. We'll steer people's suspicions in all directions except to the east. An apparent operation against England will be prepared, then back we'll go, fast as lightning, and let 'em have it. The Ukraine is a good breadbasket. Once we're established there, we can hold out for a long time. The question of the Balkans and the East will be taken care of for good. Psychologically the whole thing poses a few difficulties. Napoleon parallel, etc. But that we can easily overcome through anti-Bolshevism. . . . We'll produce a masterpiece.[217]

If Goebbels, who was entirely inexperienced in military matters, dropped all his concerns about a war on two fronts, that was due not only to his faith in the Führer's "strategic genius" but also to the news coming in from Libya. There Rommel and the Africa Corps were advancing, contrary to their assigned defensive role. Soon Rommel took Benghazi and Derna from the British troops, encircled Tobruk, and in mid-April reached the Egyptian border near Sollum. The propaganda minister euphorically followed his advance from Berlin, knowing that his men Berndt and Haegert were "right up front."[218] When Rommel took Sollum, Goebbels was almost "shivering and shaking." "And then report after report comes in: Rommel has already pushed past Sidi Barrani. . . . One almost cringes at so much luck in war and would like to throw a ring into the waves to placate the gods, like Polycrates." The "miracle of North Africa" and the campaign against Yugoslavia and Greece, which began very successfully and was to end in a disaster for the British expeditionary force, sent Goebbels into something close to ecstasy: "What an Easter! What a resurrection after the long winter's night."[219]

Although Goebbels's euphoria was somewhat dampened by the difficulties in which Rommel found himself around encircled Tobruk, he still awaited the events to come full of happy anticipation. He took particular satisfaction in the fact that Stalin apparently suspected nothing. The neutrality pact recently signed by the Soviet Union and Japan could not be allowed to distract Germany from its objectives in the east, he noted.[220]

But this resolve was put to the test just a few days after Hitler had summoned the Reichstag to the Kroll Opera House for a triumphant report on the victoriously concluded Balkan campaign. On the evening of 12 May Goebbels was putting the finishing touches on the most recent newsreel when he received "terrible news."[221] Rudolf Hess had taken off from Augsburg two days earlier in a twin-engine ME110 and headed for England, hoping to negotiate an end to the war. Early on the morning after his flight, Hess's adjutant had brought Hitler a letter explaining his intentions. Hitler had decided to wait for the time being, so as not to jeopardize the possible success of the crazy undertaking, however slight.

After another day had passed, with no reaction from the British, these hopes dwindled to nothing. Only now did Hitler pull himself together and order Martin Bormann to take over his former superior's duties, while he dispatched Ribbentrop to Italy to brief Mussolini about the excruciatingly embarrassing affair. He instructed Reich Press Secretary Dietrich to issue a first communiqué, which was read over the Greater German Radio on the evening of 12 May. It informed the German people and the world that in spite of a "worsening illness," "Party Comrade Hess" had managed to gain access to an aircraft and had taken off. A letter he had left behind showed "in its confused ravings traces of mental disintegration" that led one to fear that "Party Comrade Hess had fallen prey to delusions." Unfortunately it had to be expected that Hess "has crashed or had an accident somewhere."[222]

When Goebbels received the news and was summoned to Berchtesgaden at the same time as all the other Reichsleiters and Gauleiters, he admitted that "at the moment I can't grasp the whole thing."[223] He was feeling put out because he had not been consulted on the communiqué.[224] At the Berghof, Hitler, who seemed "broken" to him, showed him Hess's letter. In the meantime Hess's descent by parachute had been confirmed by a brief bulletin from the British. Only the previous October Goebbels had judged Hess very favorably, calling him a "good and reliable man" on whom the Führer could rely "blindly."[225] Now he noted in his diary:

A confused mess—schoolboy dilettantism: he says he wanted to go to England to make clear its hopeless situation, to overthrow the Churchill government with the help of Lord Hamilton in Scotland, and then make peace so as to let London save face. . . . A fool like this was the next man in line after the Führer. Almost too much to contemplate. His letters bristle with undigested occultism. Professor Haushofer and his wife, old lady Hess, were the evil spirits in this case. They artificially pushed their "famous boy" into this role.[226]

Soon thereafter the sixty or seventy persons Hitler had summoned gathered in the great hall of the Berghof. After Bormann, now director of the party chancellery, had read aloud from Hess's letters, Hitler took the floor and condemned Hess's deed in sharp terms. Hess had left him at the very moment when the divisions on Germany's eastern borders were on full alert, and the commanders could expect at any minute to receive orders for the most serious military undertaking yet. How could Hitler expect his generals to follow these orders, if his highest political leader left his "battle post" on his own? Goebbels, once more impressed by Hitler's words, regretted having to depart, after taking "cordial leave" of Hitler, to hurry back to his ministry and direct the propaganda campaign to contain the harm done by Hess's defection.[227]

While still in Berchtesgaden Goebbels had supported the Führer's idea of issuing a second communiqué. The British announcement called for some response, and the German people had to receive some explanation for Hess's presence in England or Scotland. The result was a bulletin that referred again to Hess's alleged delusions.[228] Back in Berlin, Goebbels filled in his staff and gave the cue for how to handle the matter. Internally nothing more was to be said about it, and the most minor military events were to be played up by way of distraction. Externally an allusive description of the incident should be circulated in conjunction with the defense against "lies"—Goebbels's characterization of the wild speculation in the supposedly ill-informed foreign press.[229] Goebbels expected a positive response to professions of faith like this: "We believe in the divinatory gifts of the Führer. We know that everything that seems to work to our disadvantage will in the end redound to our great good fortune."[230]

What would the British do with this propaganda gift, Goebbels wondered; he envied the enemy for the opportunity. Statements could be made in Hess's name of which he knew nothing. His voice could even be imitated in appeals to the German people. As much as the situation stimulated Goebbels's imagination, the possible effects made him shudder. When he failed to discern any "major trend" in the British propaganda, he considered this particularly sly on the part of the enemy, who seemed to be escalating the drama by waiting. When Churchill failed to exploit the incident in the days that followed, Goebbels attributed it to the decadence of the "plutocratic" ruling class, ripe for a fall. Since the guessing soon died down in the foreign press, a relieved Goebbels decided on 18 May, only a week after Hess's flight, that he could "liquidate" the Hess case. "That's how fast things go in these happy-go-lucky times. Hess should have thought of that beforehand. What will become of him now?"[231]

Goebbels considered the Hess crisis over, but the minister was getting more and more nervous, for with every day the "truly great task" of national socialism, the eradication of "Jewish bolshevism," edged closer. Until mid-May he had assumed that Operation Barbarossa would begin on 22 May.[232] The operation was postponed once more when Hitler unexpectedly ordered a landing on Crete, as a sort of wrap-up to the Balkan campaign. The propaganda minister's attention shifted to the eastern Mediterranean, also because his stepson Harald was involved in the military operations "down there," and Magda was worried about him.

Crete became the object of a sort of propaganda poker game. England opened with tough declarations that it had the island firmly in hand and would never relinquish it. The first part was true, for Goering's paratroopers suffered terrible casualties and had a very difficult time establishing a foothold. For days the battles had to go unmentioned in Goebbels's propaganda, while in Great Britain detailed accounts were given. Just when the invaders' situation eased somewhat, London broadcast on 27 May the spectacular news that the battleship *Bismarck*, which had sunk the British battle cruiser *Hood* three days earlier, had been chased by the entire Home Fleet and finally sunk in the Atlantic. The catastrophe cost more than two thousand German seamen their lives. No propaganda could minimize the disaster, although Goebbels pulled out all the stops in praising the heroic courage and the immortal fame of the dead.

Goebbels therefore steered all the news coverage toward the eastern Mediterranean, where the fortunes of war had finally begun to favor the Germans.[233] In early June the British relinquished Crete, which perked up the mood of the German population noticeably. Finally Goebbels had grounds for claiming a serious loss of prestige for Churchill.[234]

Crete, where Harald Quandt had fought bravely, to the gratification of his stepfather and Hitler, inspired Goebbels to undertake a propaganda bluff that would veil the final preparations for Operation Barbarossa.[235] As early as the beginning of May he had spread rumors that the Wehrmacht would soon land in England and bring about a decision in the west; that Stalin was planning a visit to Berlin; and that a military alliance with the Soviet Union was in the works.[236] But these rumors did not quiet speculation at home and abroad about a huge military operation brewing in the east. Although hardly anyone believed Hitler would open a second front before ending the struggle with England, the constant transport movements, as well as the military mail, which came almost exclusively from Poland and East Prussia, pointed to just such an eventuality.

From the American press Goebbels had picked up the notion that the occupation of Crete—if it succeeded—would show that occupation of

Great Britain was also possible.[237] Even though the leadership of the Wehrmacht had tended to draw the opposite conclusion from Operation Mercury, Goebbels saw no reason not to play up the American interpretation for the benefit of foreign opinion. Such a diversion technique, which he himself viewed as "somewhat audacious," was all the more necessary inasmuch as Karl Bömer, head of the foreign press department at the Propaganda Ministry, had had too much to drink at a reception at the Bulgarian Embassy and had blurted out things that led diplomatic circles to conclude that an attack on the Soviet Union was planned. So after obtaining Hitler's approval for the deceptive maneuver, Goebbels "very slyly" wrote an article entitled "The Cretan Example" that let people read between the lines that an assault on the British Isles was imminent. On 12 June a copy of the article, with revisions by the Führer, was submitted with all due ceremony to the *Völkischer Beobachter*, in whose Berlin edition it was supposed to appear the following day. But the paper never reached the newsstands, because the scheme called for the entire Berlin edition to be confiscated in the early morning hours.[238]

The Goebbels article, whose circulation was helped enormously by the incident, landed like a bombshell among the foreign correspondents. Tapped telephone conversations revealed that the conclusion they drew was often the same: "Big Mouth" Goebbels couldn't keep quiet. Correspondents reported that the minister had fallen into disfavor with Hitler for revealing secrets. British radio commentators immediately concluded that the troop concentrations on the eastern borders of Germany were part of a great bluff, concealing preparations for the invasion of Britain.[239] Anyone who referred instead to a deceptive maneuver on the part of the minister and insisted that Hitler would attack the Soviet Union had to confront an official denial from the Kremlin, which asserted that it knew nothing of any German intention of attacking and that the troop movements meant something else entirely.[240] The "total confusion" that prevailed in the Western press strengthened Goebbels in his mistaken belief that he had successfully led the enemy astray.

Except for his closest collaborators, Goebbels tried to put his own ministry staff on a false track. On 5 June, the day before the order came for the Wehrmacht to abrogate the Hague Land Warfare Convention of 1899, Goebbels "informed" his department heads during a confidential meeting that the Führer had realized that the war could not be ended without the invasion of England. The operations planned for the east had been set aside. He couldn't name an exact time, but one thing was certain: in three or perhaps five weeks the invasion of England would begin.[241] To make the deception credible, he commissioned an invasion song, had new fanfares composed for the radio, and selected English-speaking announcers—all at the risk, as he commented in his diary, that "in the end, when it turns out just the opposite, I'll lose prestige."[242]

The public was still trying to puzzle it out, inside and outside Germany, when Goebbels was called to Hitler on the afternoon of 15 June. To give free rein to the rumors that he had fallen into disfavor, he had his chauffeur mount a new license plate on his motorcar and then drive him around to a side entrance of the Chancellery.[243] After Hitler had greeted him "with great warmth," he explained to Goebbels the impending operation in the east. The attack on Russia would begin as soon as all the troops had moved into position, which should take about a week. "It will be a mass attack in the grandest style. Probably the mightiest history has ever seen," Hitler told him. Such a thing was necessary because Stalin planned to wait until Europe bled to death, so he could bolshevize it. But Hitler had no need to provide justification to Goebbels, who in any case saw any cooperation with the Soviet Union as a "blot on our escutcheon." With the extermination of "Jewish bolshevism" this blot would be "washed away," Goebbels thought.[244] That he had succumbed to the fiction that this extermination campaign was a "just war" can be seen from the words he used to describe his departure from the Chancellery: "The Führer is very moved when I take leave of him. This is a very great moment for me. Driving through the grounds, out the gate, and then into the city, where people are walking innocuously in the rain. Happy people who know nothing of all our cares and live only for the day. It's for all of them that we work and struggle and take every risk. So our people may live!"

If Goebbels wrote of a "risk" that the Russian campaign and with it war on two fronts entailed, he did so because he was well aware that Germany's future would depend on whether it could succeed in using a blitzkrieg to knock England's last conceivable "continental weapon" out of its hand. Hitler had said the campaign would last four weeks. Without any expertise in such matters, Goebbels had estimated the duration of the campaign as even shorter, which was his way of talking himself out of the worries that had assailed him since the end of May, according to his personal press aide, Rudolf Semler.[245]

Hitler's mere physical presence always had the ability to banish Goebbels's tormenting uncertainties. In one of his longest diary passages, Goebbels spewed out, in an act of voluntary self-deception, a flood of assertions, some borrowed from Hitler, that would put his reason to sleep and convince him that the example of Napoleon need not be repeated: "Bolshevism will collapse like a house of cards. We're on the verge of an unparalleled march to victory. We must act. . . . Our operation is as well prepared as is humanly possible. So many reserves are built in, that failure is completely out of the question. . . . Japan is in on this with us. . . . Russia would attack us if we were weak, and then we'd have the war on two fronts that we're preventing through this first strike. Only then will we have our back covered. I assess the fighting capability of the Russians as very poor, even poorer than the Führer thinks. If ever an operation was and is safe, it's this one. We also must attack Russia to free up personnel. An unbeaten Russia forces us to maintain a constant strength of 150 divisions, when we need people urgently for our war production. That must be intensified . . . so that even the USA can't be a threat to us."[246]

The last days before the attack, which had been set for the early morning of 22 June 1941, passed in "crazy tension." While in the Reich the muttering became certainty, and the Anglo-Saxon press saw through the propaganda bluff, and news came from the Soviet Union of further troop buildups near its western borders, Goebbels worked tirelessly with the few initiated colleagues in his ministry on last preparations for the propaganda barrage that would begin with the invasion. But toward the outside world he wrapped himself in a cloak of "deepest silence."[247] In absolute secrecy he organized the printing and distribution of one hundred thousand copies of Hitler's appeal to the soldiers of the eastern army, to be handed out on the day of the attack. He put final touches on the fanfares that would introduce special bulletins of the expected victories. And he helped choose the best locations for transmitters that would jam Soviet propaganda broadcasts.

On the evening of 21 June—a Sunday—Goebbels had to excuse himself from the Italian guests he was entertaining in Schwanenwerder, for he had been summoned to the Chancellery.[248] There he found an utterly exhausted Hitler, who, however, became quite intoxicated with excitement as he explained the impending greatest invasion in world history. The Führer felt a nightmare had been lifted from him as the moment of decision drew nearer, Goebbels remarked. It was always that way. As he hobbled back and forth across the great hall in the Chancellery with the Führer, Goebbels noticed that all tiredness left Hitler. Once again Goebbels thought he had been vouchsafed a "deep look" inside the Führer.[249]

It was half past two in the morning when Goebbels finally rode through the night to his ministry, to fill in his staff, who were waiting up. After feverish work he withdrew to his room around 3:30, while along a line about 950 miles in length more than 160 divisions advanced into Soviet Russia. Goebbels remarked in his diary: "Now the guns are thundering. May God bless our weapons! . . . I pace restlessly back and forth in my room. The breath of history is audible. Great, wonderful time in which a new Reich is being born. Amid pain, it's true, but it is mounting up into the light."[250]

CHAPTER 13

Do you want total war?
(1941—1944)

At 5:30 A.M. on 22 June 1941 the new Liszt fanfare sounded from all German broadcasting stations, introducing Goebbels reading Hitler's proclamation. In a sonorous voice the propaganda minister announced that the Führer had decided "to place once again the fate and future of the German Reich and our people in the hands of our soldiers."[1] Everywhere in Germany, but also in the military outposts on the French Atlantic coast, in the officers' casinos in Belgium and Greece, in Denmark and Norway, the proclamation, repeated throughout the day, was received with oppressed silence rather than with rejoicing. Hadn't Hitler said himself that Germany had to learn from the defeat of the World War and avoid a two-front struggle at all costs? Hadn't the pact with the Bolshevist archenemy, so difficult for Germans to understand, been concluded precisely for that reason?

The major challenge Goebbels saw himself confronting was to quiet just such concerns. He therefore resumed the anti-Bolshevist propaganda used before the German-Soviet nonaggression pact. He felt the argument that would prove most persuasive with the German people was that German troops could never have been fully committed in the west so long as an "unknown, treacherous element" remained in the east. As a result of the "treachery of the Bolshevist leaders, discovered by the Führer," national socialism was returning "after an apparent truce" of two years "to the law" governing its existence: the struggle against "plutocracy" and "bolshevism." Convinced that "the Jew, through his demonic system of bolshevism," threatened all Europe, the Führer had launched Operation Barbarossa as a preventive campaign and "world-historical deed" directed against that "sly conspiracy of dogmatic party doctrinaires, sneaky Jews, and greedy state capitalists."[2]

The Germans received their first solid information only after days of skimpy, unrevealing reports. On 29 June the Wehrmacht issued no fewer than twelve special bulletins of victories over the Red Army in places like Brest-Litovsk, Bialystok, Grodno, and Minsk, read at quarter-hour intervals over the radio. Goebbels demanded restraint and disapproved of the method Reich Press Chief Dietrich was following, under instructions from Hitler, because he felt grouping the announcements this way was "laying it on too thick."[3]

But the Red Army seemed to be collapsing in the face of the hard, rapid blows from the smoothly functioning German war machine. Entire armies surrendered, and within a few days the number of prisoners of war exceeded a million. All predictions about the poor fighting capacity of the Red Army and claims of the alleged "racial superiority" of the attackers seemed to have been fulfilled.

But such hasty and arrogant judgments were soon dampened, for with every day that passed, the Red Army's resistance grew. Where optimism had reigned, word of a crisis now made the rounds, and reports of Soviet airmen who committed suicide after being shot down, so as not to fall into German hands, gave even the military layman Goebbels pause.[4] Since it now became clear that the armed forces would not have "a walk" to Moscow, not so much should be promised, he said, criticizing headquarters, where the Wehrmacht reports were written. Excessively optimistic reports always produced great disappointment sooner or later, he commented, noting that in this respect British propaganda offered an excellent model.[5]

The State Security Service, which kept public opinion under constant surveillance, reported that waiting for special bulletins announcing successes on the eastern front was gradually causing a loss of morale.[6] Then, on 6 August, the Wehrmacht high command finally announced the successful end of the battle of Smolensk. Since the Army Group South had pushed through to the Dnieper, and along the northern section of the front the troops had advanced over the Dvina, the propaganda minister noted with relief that the general pessimism was gone, and every German could again look to the immediate future with great confidence.[7]

When Goebbels paid his first visit to Hitler's East Prussian headquarters, the Wolf's Den, in mid-August, the topic of conversation was the crisis in the German leadership of the war, now overcome, and the resistance of the Soviets, which Goebbels attributed to the "primitive toughness" and "animal drive" of the "dull masses."[8] Still shocked and "very irritable" from the events of the previous weeks, the supreme commander admitted to Goebbels that the Soviet thrust and particularly the Red Army's equipment had been drastically underestimated. Goebbels asked whether Hitler might have decided differently about attacking the Soviet Union if he had known these things in advance. Hitler replied that he would "never" have allowed his decision to be influenced, but it would have been "much more difficult." Finally he reassured Goebbels by holding out the prospect that the campaign would be "more or less over" by winter. Perhaps Stalin would sue for peace. He, Hitler, would then be prepared to accept a capitulation, if accompanied by major territorial concessions. Goebbels later talked himself into believing that it had been "perhaps quite good" that they had not been "completely in the picture" when it came to the Bolshevists' potential, and had "had absolutely no conception of a whole series of their weapons, especially their heavy weapons." If "we had been clearly aware of the dimensions of the danger," Hitler would have had to "bear much greater worries" "for months." And "perhaps," he wrote, "we would have shied away after all from confronting the question of the East and of bolshevism, which is due for a solution."[9]

If Goebbels left Hitler's headquarters filled with fresh motivation, it was primarily because Hitler had again shown "clear interest" in propaganda, which had become all the more essential for undermining the Soviet empire, and was now supposed to be brought out of its "Cinderella-like" existence. To make propaganda under happy circumstances, Goebbels noted, was no trick. But "to make propaganda in a crisis and have it lead to success—that is a political art."[10] It pained him, in light of the new challenge, that Hitler had put Rosenberg in charge of propaganda in the east; in July 1941 he had made Rosenberg minister for the occupied territories there. Rosenberg had thus become the beneficiary of the years of strife between Goebbels and Ribbentrop. That relationship had reached its nadir when the Foreign Office had expanded its involvement in propaganda by buying up radio stations during the war in the Balkans, and when Ribbentrop had gone to Hitler to denounce Goebbels's indiscreet staff member Karl Bömer, whom Hitler finally had brought up on charges before the dreaded People's Court (Volksgerichtshof).[11]

Since Ribbentrop had now noticeably lost influence with Hitler, in mid-June Goebbels had allowed himself to inquire of Hans-Heinrich Lammers, head of the Reich Chancellery, whether the Führer's orders of September 1939 still pertained: was propaganda the province of the Reich Ministry for Popular Enlightenment and Propaganda, or of the Foreign Office? And was it wise in wartime to allow a second apparatus to be built up "whose task . . . can only consist in competing with what already exists in my ministry, pointlessly wasting money, personnel, and materials and spoiling my own and my colleagues' enjoyment of our work?"[12] Goebbels soon managed to get formal recognition of the parity of his ministry with the Foreign Ministry in foreign propaganda.[13]

To secure his influence in the realm of eastern and anti-Bolshevist propaganda, Goebbels had expanded considerably the small staff with which he had worked clandestinely since the Hitler-Stalin pact. In July 1941 he created under Eberhard Taubert a special unit for the eastern areas, as an answer to Rosenberg's Ministry for the Occupied Eastern Territories. The duties of the new unit, which reported directly to Undersecretary Leopold Gutterer, included propaganda aimed "at the enemy," which meant propaganda to undermine the Red Army, as well as anti-Bolshevist propaganda directed at all non-Germans under Nazi rule, whether eastern Europeans doing slave labor in the Reich, volunteer units fighting with the Germans, the peoples of eastern Europe, Soviet prisoners of war, or the population in occupied western Europe.[14]

According to Goebbels's diaries, German propaganda had got off to a promising start after the attack on the Soviet Union. To be sure, Goebbels had underestimated the number of planes he would need for transporting 90 million pamphlets to be dropped behind enemy lines.[15] Aside from this literature, Goebbels relied chiefly on the radio for propaganda. At first he had three secret stations working; later this number grew to twenty-two, with thirty-four different programs beamed in eighteen languages toward eastern Europe.[16] Goebbels's impression that the propaganda was effective came from the fact that the subjugated peoples of the Soviet Union at first viewed the advancing Wehrmacht as their liberators; at Lemberg (Lvov) in the Ukraine they greeted the soldiers tumultuously. This attitude toward the Germans quickly changed when the troops were followed not by freedom but by special operations units of the SD, the SS, and the Gestapo. By mid-August Goebbels was forced to recognize that it had not yet been possible to arouse "enthusiasm for the eastern campaign" among the vanquished.[17]

Rosenberg favored limited autonomy for the Baltic states and the Ukraine, thinking the people of these areas could be organized to the economic benefit of the Reich; they should be treated as victims of bolshevism.[18] The Russians, on the other hand, he hated, holding them responsible for bolshevism.[19] While Rosenberg's position differed little from Taubert's, Goebbels categorically rejected any notion of autonomy for the peoples in the east. Nationalist aspirations that took a violent form, especially in the Baltic states, he dismissed as "childish, naive fantasies that do not impress us in the slightest."[20] Apparently these peoples had imagined that "the German Wehrmacht sacrificed its blood to bring new nationalist governments to the helm in these dwarf states." For such a "shortsighted policy" national socialism was too cold-blooded, sober, and realistic. He, Goebbels, did only what benefited his own people, and that no doubt entailed "rigorous imposition of a German order in this area, without regard for . . . the interests of the little nationalities that live there."[21] Goebbels's ideas corresponded to those of Hitler, who was pursuing a war of extermination based on racial ideology and accordingly saw the peoples of the East as "subhumans" and "Bolshevist beasts," and their countries as plunder for the German Reich.[22]

But with the military successes and prospects of September, interest in propaganda declined in Hitler's immediate circle. After successful conclusion of the battle east of Kiev, the Führer immediately ordered Army Group Center to advance toward Moscow, thinking now that the Red Army would be "on the run" within a month, as he told Goebbels during his visit to field headquarters on 23 September.[23]

The double battle of Vjazma and Brjansk that seemed to point to victory led Hitler to proclaim emphatically in a speech at the Sportpalast on 3 October that the enemy was already broken and would never rise to his feet again.[24] Goebbels noted in his diary that his Führer had given mature reflection to all factors, correctly calculating every element of the entire situation, and had come to the "definitive conclusion" that Germany could no longer be deprived of victory. He thus considered the speech a great help for his propaganda.[25]

Yet Goebbels was angry when on 9 October Reich Press Chief Dietrich declared to journalists from the Reich and abroad that, with the destruction of the Army Group Timoshenko, the war in the east had been decided. Goebbels protested to Hitler, for he feared that over the next few days Dietrich's statement might result in a terrible letdown.[26] Hitler replied that Dietrich's statement had been a political chess move, intended to induce Japan to enter the war against the Soviet Union.[27]

Then bad weather set in, turning the roads in the east to seas of mud. Keeping the armies supplied, which depended on deliveries by truck, became increasingly difficult. After the victory at Vjazma and Brjansk, military engagements were infrequent. Toward the end of October Goebbels was not the only one asking himself whether the Soviets were really beaten, as their tremendous losses in men and materiel and the transfer of the Soviet government from Moscow to Kuibyshev on the Volga seemed to suggest. When he met again with Hitler on 27 October, the Führer's extraordinarily positive assessment of the military situation again filled Goebbels with optimism: "We're waiting only for the roads to dry out or freeze. Once our tanks can start their motors again and the roads are free of mud and muck, the Soviet resistance will be broken in a relatively short time," Goebbels now believed.[28]

That October, while the world's gaze was riveted on Russia, columns of Jewish citizens were driven through the streets of Germany's cities. Goebbels had again pressed for an accelerated "evacuation" of the German Jews, for since the beginning of the campaign in the east, he had once again found confirmation for the ideological construct he had first adopted in 1923. Bolshevism, he wrote in an article in *Das Reich*, was the "work of Jewish party doctrinaires" and "sly Jewish capitalists."[29]

According to this view, Stalin, Churchill, and Roosevelt became "principals in the great world conspiracy against Germany."[30] The more this image of the enemy tormented him, the more urgent it seemed to him that the German allies of the "world conspirators" be "erased." He felt that their "elimination" should be pursued "without any sentimentality."[31]

As early as 20 March 1941 Goebbels's deputy, Leopold Gutterer, had reported during a discussion in the Propaganda Ministry that there remained sixty to seventy thousand Jews in Berlin. It was not right "that the capital of the National Socialist Reich should still harbor such a large number of Jews." Gutterer conceded that Hitler himself had not decided that Berlin should be made "Jew-free" immediately, but Goebbels was "convinced that a suitable suggestion for evacuation would certainly meet with the Führer's approval." The general building inspector for the capital, Albert Speer, could certainly use the twenty thousand or so apartments and houses occupied by Jews "as a reserve for those rendered homeless by possible greater bombing damage and later by demolition connected with the revamping of Berlin." The discussion ended with Adolf Eichmann, director of the office for Jewish matters in the Reichssicherheitshauptamt, being "asked" to "work out a proposal for Gauleiter Dr. Goebbels for the evacuation of the Jews from Berlin."[32] This same office under Eichmann would later be in charge of the mass deportations and the "final solution."

In August Goebbels noted again that it was "scandalous" that there could still be 75,000 Jews "roaming around" Berlin, of whom only 23,000 were working; the others were living "as parasites on the work of the host people," waiting for the German defeat. They spoiled "not only the appearance of the streets but also the atmosphere," for which reason they had to be "removed" from the midst of the German people. To be sure, "powerful bureaucratic" and "probably also sentimental resistance" in the Reich agencies stood in the way. But he would not allow himself to be "surprised or dissuaded"; he would not "rest until . . . we have drawn the final consequences as far as Jewry is concerned."[33]

At a meeting with Hitler on 18 August, Goebbels pressed for bringing the "Jewish question" to a quick solution. His notes for the session contained a wealth of suggestions, most of which were soon implemented. In addition to requiring Jews to wear the star for identification purposes and reducing their rations, Goebbels urged his Führer to ban Jews from using public transportation or the services of "German" tradesmen. They should turn in "articles of use and luxury" such as bicycles, typewriters, books, gramophones, refrigerators, electric stoves, tobacco, and hand mirrors. Their monthly support payments should be "rigorously" limited, "so that the Jew cannot buy off Germans weak in character." Furthermore, a "comprehensive survey" of the "lazy, parasitic" Jews should determine which of them could still be used for "work crucial to the war effort." This "thorough combing" would "select out" those Jews who were "ripe" for "transportation to the east."[34]

Goebbels received Hitler's promise that as soon as vehicles became available, he could "remove" the Berlin Jews to the east first. There, "in a harsher climate," they would "get what they deserved."[35] What Goebbels obtained immediately was a police regulation requiring Jews to be identified, and the introduction of the Jewish star; these measures were to go into effect throughout the Reich on 1 and 19 September respectively. Shortly after this Goebbels discussed "various important things" with Heydrich in the Führer's headquarters.[36] At first it had been assumed that the deportations would have to wait until the end of the operations in the east because of a lack of transportation. But on 14 October Goebbels's friend Kurt Daluege, in his capacity as chief of the Berlin Order Police, signed a directive for the first deportation of Berlin Jews.[37]

Goebbels "justified" the transports to the public in an essay unequaled for sheer blind hatred. He wrote that Hitler's prophecy was coming true, that "if the Jews involved in international high finance were to succeed in dragging the peoples of the world into another war, the result would be not the bolshevization of the earth and thereby the victory of Jewry, but rather the extermination of the Jewish race in Europe. We are experiencing now the fulfillment of this prophecy, and for the Jews a fate is being effected that is harsh, but more than deserved. Pity or regret is completely out of place here."[38]

The first "evacuation transport" of Berlin Jews to Lodz was followed by nine others to Lodz, Minsk, Kovno, and Riga. At the end of the month the transports were halted because the Wehrmacht simply did not have the vehicles available. The situation on the eastern front had taken a dramatic turn for the worse since November. The second phase of the battle for Moscow made it clear that the Red Army was far from beaten, but that the Wehrmacht had reached the limits of its capability. Winter had come much earlier than expected, and thousands of German soldiers not adequately equipped for fighting in ice and snow froze to death. Vehicles and automatic weapons failed. At the end of November Gen. Heinz Guderian reported that his troops could do no more. This same general had written home only a few weeks earlier that when he marched into Moscow he did not want a propaganda fuss "à la Rommel" made over him.[39]

Hitler stubbornly rejected his generals' appeals to be allowed to withdraw their armies and establish a front they could defend. Apparently relying on "Providence," which had been so kind to him in the past, he ignored all sober assessments of the situation, taking refuge instead in the notion that Japan would soon enter the war against the Soviet Union, which would greatly improve Germany's position. He outlined this notion to Goebbels on 21 November, whereupon Goebbels noted in his diary that he did not "share the Führer's" hope—his first such expression of doubt in a long time.[40]

On 9 November Goebbels had already written an article for *Das Reich* entitled "When or How?" that expressed none of the high expectations that Hitler and his press chief Dietrich had been disseminating the previous month. Let us not ask when victory will come, Goebbels wrote, "but let us rather make sure that it comes." That would require "a gigantic national effort." Goebbels was thinking of a comprehensive mobilization of the *Volk* community, extending to all realms of life, so that the burdens and deprivations of war would be equally shared by all; in short, he had in mind a "socialistically conducted" war.[41] This was what he meant when he proclaimed "total war" in February 1943.

Since only his propaganda could create the basis for such a mobilization, his early, rather sober assessment of the situation on the eastern front also contained a goodly portion of calculation. Putting his plan into practice became urgent in December, when things rapidly went from bad to worse. The Red Army had begun a counteroffensive with new elite divisions brought out of Siberia. The Kremlin had intelligence that Japan would be striking in the Pacific basin rather than attacking the Soviet Union in the east, which meant that these well-equipped divisions could be moved to the west. Under their assault the front wavered for days. Hitler's strategy of blitzkrieg followed by an all-out effort to subdue or smash the Soviet Union had failed.

In the face of the impending catastrophe for the German armies of the east, Hitler greeted Japan's feelers on 28 November as the "work of Providence." The Japanese were suggesting a military alliance with Germany for a war against the United States and Great Britain. On 4 December Hitler had already decided to go to war against the United States, hoping that by splitting the Anglo-Saxon forces and making them fight two naval wars, he could gain time to realize his objectives in the east.

The news of the 7 December Japanese attack on the American Pacific fleet at Pearl Harbor came as a complete surprise to Hitler, but on 14 December he summoned the American chargé d'affaires Leland Morris to the Foreign Office and had Ribbentrop read him the German declaration of war. In a speech to the Reichstag just before this, Hitler had blamed Roosevelt for provoking war to cover up the failures of the New Deal. Fanatical applause repeatedly interrupted the speech. This dramatic day ended with the signing of a German-Italian-Japanese agreement expressing the three countries' "unshakable decision" not to lay down their arms until the common war against the United States and Great Britain had been brought to a successful conclusion.

Goebbels welcomed the Führer's decision, which Hitler explained to him on 18 December in the Wolf's Den.[42] The propaganda minister had seen war against the United States as inevitable in any case. Now that it had become a reality, Goebbels thought that it clarified the situation and would help him implement his notion of a "socialistically conducted war."

For his propaganda this meant continuing the change of course he had introduced in November, gradually working toward a more sober assessment of how things stood. During a secret minister's conference on 7 December he had announced that the previous propaganda had made the "basic mistake" of keeping any bad news from the Germans, thereby rendering them "oversensitive" to word of any reverses. He called Churchill's "blood, sweat, and tears" propaganda exemplary and said that from now on German propaganda should be kept more realistic— the people wanted this and could tolerate it.[43]

To do justice to his own call for "realistic optimism," Goebbels had to take cognizance of the profound uncertainty that was spreading through the population as bad news trickled in from the front.[44] The United States' entry into the war made it clear that an end was no longer in sight, which dampened the general mood. The propaganda approach on which he had agreed with Hitler involved stressing the military prowess of the Japanese and, so as not to shake people's faith in Germany's military superiority, blaming all the difficulties in the Soviet Union on the weather.[45] Thus was a legend launched that persists to this day. It distracted people from the real reason for the German failure: the German leadership's arrogant underestimation of the strength of the Soviet Union.

Immediately upon his return on 18 December from the Führer's headquarters, Goebbels laid out a propaganda operation that he had coordinated with Hitler: the Winter Aid collection, which would call on people to donate warm clothing for the troops in the east.[46] The goal of this operation was to mobilize the home front, giving people new motivation. In his ringing call for action, Goebbels announced that people at home would not deserve a moment's peace if a single German soldier was exposed to the harshness of winter without the articles of warm clothing of which he read out a long list.[47]

This new indication of how serious the situation was, as well as the description of the "bestial hordes" that had been poised to "inundate" Western Europe, did in fact mobilize the Germans to contribute generously. Well-known actors and athletes carried the message to the country. So many people were eager to donate clothing that the collection had to

301

be extended past Christmas to 11 January 1942. More than 67 million articles of clothing were collected. In a radio speech on 14 January Goebbels described this outpouring of generosity as a "convincing proof of the determination of the German nation to see this war through to victory."[48] But the collection had come much too late and had been too poorly organized to be of much help to the fighting troops.[49]

Goebbels now frequently pointed to the parallels between the present situation and the Time of Struggle. In his editorial commemorating Hitler's accession to power on 30 January 1933, he recalled the major reverses of the year 1932 and concluded that no great goal "can be attained without effort, without sweat, without sacrifice, and without blood." He went on: "Here it becomes clear whether a person has a stout heart or not, and in critical moments that is more valuable than mere cleverness or intellectuality."[50] He himself found his belief strengthened by the increasingly difficult circumstances.

On 29 January Goebbels met in Berlin with the Führer for a "lengthy discussion," which he judged "extraordinarily positive and gratifying." Apparently Hitler agreed with his minister's concept of totalizing the war. Once more completely under the spell of the Führer, Goebbels failed to notice that Hitler was exhausted and on edge. He remarked instead how wonderful it was to see the Führer "looking so well and in such splendid mental and physical form."[51] Since for Goebbels victory was a matter of belief in Hitler, he had to give absolute priority to Hitler's wellbeing, for "so long as he lives and remains in good health among us, so long as he is able to contribute the power of his mind and the power of his manliness to the cause, nothing bad can overtake us."[52]

If the meeting with Hitler impelled the propaganda minister to observe that "the chief psychological difficulties" were overcome, it was not only because of the Führer's effect on him; in addition, bulletins of Japanese victories in the Far East were coming in—just at the right moment—and in North Africa Rommel had mounted a counteroffensive and was preparing to recover lost territory.[53] Goebbels noted triumphantly that the new successes were wonderful; the British would have to admit that the Africa Corps had once more taken them totally by surprise. British propaganda was making Rommel "one of the most popular generals in the entire world."[54] In the military realm Rommel seemed to embody for Goebbels something that he associated closely with national socialism, namely the notion that politics was the "miracle of the impossible." That was one reason why Goebbels considered Rommel "a modern general in the best sense of the word."[55]

The minister now insistently directed the attention of the German public to Rommel, away from the troubling events in the east. Since the end of November he had wanted to use the blazing sands of Africa as a counterpoint to the frozen steppes of Russia, but the British offensive had interfered. Now he seized the opportunity. Whether in the newsreels, on the radio, or in the press, everything revolved around Rommel, whose name gradually became synonymous with the African campaign.

The propaganda commotion about Rommel led to a general overestimation of the war in North Africa and its strategic possibilities. Goebbels therefore found it necessary to direct that "in domestic German propaganda all precautions be taken to assure that no false hopes are aroused."[56]

The fall of Singapore helped greatly to improve the mood in Germany. Goebbels, who had long since stopped promising the imminent fall of the British Empire, kept in this case to his more moderate propaganda. "What was built up over centuries does not fall in a matter of months," was the line he followed, although Hitler seemed optimistic.[57] "He believes that under certain circumstances this could develop into a serious crisis in the English empire. Churchill's position would perhaps suffer extraordinary harm if that happened."[58] Publicly Goebbels explained that the fall of Singapore alone could not bring down the empire, but on the other hand the optimism Churchill was trying to instill in his people was clouding their clear view of the facts, thereby initiating a development that "in the long run has to result in the most serious crisis in the British Empire."[59] He noted with satisfaction that Japan's entering the war was "a real gift of God," for it had fundamentally changed the situation in this "fateful winter."[60]

This "fateful winter" was one of the chief topics he discussed on 19 March when he visited Hitler in his East Prussian headquarters. As had been the case two and a half months earlier, Goebbels failed to recognize Hitler's physical condition, noting instead with gratification that Hitler looked well. Only after the Führer confessed to him that the long winter had had a bad effect on his spirits, did the visitor "notice how gray he has become and how just talking about the worries of the winter made him seem to have aged." Sometimes, Hitler admitted, it had seemed impossible to get through this winter. But then he had always summoned his "last strength of will" to oppose the enemy, and it had always worked.[61]

Once more Goebbels recognized in Hitler's description the "triumph of the will," and from then on presented the winter struggle with its catastrophic loss of human life as a test of mettle destined to lead to victory. In *Das Reich* he wrote: "The great test has been passed. Whether we argued with fate or willingly took it upon us and courageously turned it to our advantage, no matter, it is ours. Never in the future will one be able to speak of German heroism without recalling first this barbarous winter on the Volchow and near Demjansk, near Juchnow and Rshev, on the Donets and by Kerch. Through the centuries will shine the name under which this heroism proved itself: the eastern front."[62]

But on that 19 March 1942 Hitler and Goebbels spoke also of the total mobilization of the home front that Goebbels advocated. Among the many things the two men discussed was the introduction of compulsory work service for women. On many points Hitler agreed with Goebbels, but afterward he undertook no actual steps. In one case, however, Hitler did move: Goebbels's proposal that the legal basis be created to punish with prison, jail, and in very serious cases, execution, anyone who violated the publicly known principles of National Socialist leadership of the *Volk*. Five weeks after Goebbels returned from the meeting, Hitler had the Reichstag grant him full powers to order such penalties.

Goebbels had complained bitterly to the Führer about the Justice Ministry's undersecretary Franz Schlegelberger, who often rejected Goebbels's requests for action against the Jews on the grounds that no legal basis existed. Since Auschwitz was located within the Reich, some legal basis would have to be created for taking Jews there, which had not been necessary for deportation to the ghettos in the Soviet Union.[63]

Obstacles of this sort made Goebbels increasingly impatient. For him the extermination of the Jews was not progressing fast enough. He found a welcome opportunity to move things along when an anonymous attack was made on an anti-Soviet exhibition in the Berlin Lustgarten on 18 May. He immediately blamed the Jews. Soon afterward a chance to "uncover" a conspiracy offered itself. On 29 May Heydrich was driving to his new country estate near Prague when he was ambushed and critically injured. On 30 May Goebbels met with Hitler at the Chancellery and again pushed to have the 40,000 Jews still in Berlin "evacuated" so as to "liquidate the Jewish threat, whatever the cost."[64]

The previous day Goebbels had noted in his diary that he would continue with the planned arrests of five hundred Berlin Jews and would warn the leaders of the Jewish community "that for every Jewish plot and every planned Jewish uprising one hundred to one hundred fifty Jews who are in our hands will be shot." On 5 June, the day Heydrich succumbed to his injuries, the main Berlin office of the Gestapo sent the city comptroller a list of names of Jews "taken into custody in a special operation on 27 May 1942 who have since expired." The "corresponding declarations of financial assets" were attached.[65] Despite this murder operation, as well as further deportations of German Jews to ghettos in the eastern territories, and a series of other measures that prohibited Jews, for instance, from patronizing barbers and beauty salons or purchasing tobacco, Goebbels's anti-Semitic hatred was still far from achieving all its objectives.

Meanwhile military operations in the east had entered a new phase that Hitler hoped would prove decisive. By the end of May the Wehrmacht had captured the Kerch peninsula and annihilated three Soviet armies, encircling them south of Kharkov. At the beginning of June German troops attacked the fortress of Sevastopol in the Crimea, which was taken four weeks later after fierce fighting. For all these operations Goebbels's propaganda refrained from making predictions, focusing instead on the "mendacity" of the Soviet and Anglo-Saxon news reports; Goebbels adopted the technique of denouncing the enemy's optimistic portrayals of events and predictions as "propaganda lies"—*after* developments had shown them to be false.

The main thrust of the German operation along the southern section of the eastern front was to cut off the Soviet Union from its supply of raw materials. To distract attention from this strategy, Goebbels devised several deceptive maneuvers. He placed in the *Frankfurter Zeitung*, which was much read abroad, an article saying that the German attack was aimed at Moscow. Goebbels sent Otto Kriegk, managing editor of the Scherl Publishing House, to the middle section of the eastern front and then to Lisbon, the main listening post in Europe. There Kriegk went to a bar and, pretending to be intoxicated, committed apparent indiscretions. Goebbels hoped that Kriegk's idle talk would quickly come to the ears of journalists from neutral and hostile countries.[66] Although this little operation probably did not sway anyone in the enemy general staffs (if indeed the information even reached them), it at least brought the minister renewed praise from the Führer.[67]

At the beginning of July the actual summer offensive began. The Wehrmacht pressed forward toward the Donets, whereupon the Soviet high command ordered a retreat to Stalingrad, the Volga, and the Caucasus. Disappointed at the dearth of decisive battles, Hitler finally decided in mid-July to divide the attack into two wedge operations. By the beginning of August the foothills of the Caucasus had been reached, while the Sixth Army crossed the Don and approached the Volga. On 23 August Stukas began bombarding Stalingrad, whose southern defenses were broken through soon afterward by German infantry.

In light of the increasing shortages of foodstuffs in the Reich, Goebbels now shifted the propaganda emphasis to the economic goals of the campaign against the Soviet Union. The number of prisoners taken was to be stressed less than the sources of raw materials captured. At the end of May Goebbels had written in *Das Reich* that it was no war for "throne and altar but for grain and bread, for a well-stocked table at breakfast, lunch, and supper. . . . A war for raw materials, for rubber, for iron and ores, in short, a war for an existence worthy of human beings such as we, a humiliated poor nation, were not previously in a position to lead."[68]

The news from North Africa helped to bolster public spirits. At the end of May the "desert fox" had launched an offensive. Barely four weeks later, on 21 June, victory fanfares sounded over the German radio. The fortress of Tobruk, already familiar from the previous year, had fallen, supposedly the last British bastion protecting Cairo and the Suez Canal. The title page of the *Völkischer Beobachter* carried the screaming headline "Rommel's Glorious Victory."[69] Press and radio attributed a greater shock effect to Rommel's victory than to the debacle at Dunkirk or the fall of Singapore. They spoke of a nonplussed British population, of a Churchill at his wits' end. The capture of Tobruk was to be presented as revenge for the British bombing raid on Cologne on 31 May in which one thousand planes had taken part. Goebbels suggested that the press should blame the "dilettante at the head of the English government" for sending out planes against strategically worthless targets in Germany, planes that were then not available for decisive battles.[70] But Goebbels wanted it stressed that the capitulation of 25,000 Empire soldiers in North Africa should not be interpreted as a sign of insufficient resistance on their part. Goebbels's staffer Berndt, who had returned to the North African theater of war and was in the front lines during the storming of Tobruk, had asked Goebbels to emphasize this point, so as not to diminish the victory and the accomplishment of the man responsible for it, Rommel. Not long after this the general became a chief topic of conversation at Hitler's luncheon at the Chancellery. Goebbels praised Rommel as a man who enjoyed the widest public admiration. Hitler, who was promoting Rommel to general field marshal, agreed, and added that the British had made "unheard-of propaganda" about him, hoping that "by stressing Rommel they could more easily explain their defeats to the British people."[71]

But Goebbels soon saw a need to warn his staff not to let their propaganda give the public the impression that Britain was finished. He pointed out that their English counterparts were using the technique of exaggerating the seriousness of the defeat, so as to serve up favorable bulletins that much sooner.[72] But he could not stop the commotion over Rommel's victory from developing a dynamics of its own in which Hitler also got caught up. Berndt, sent home on a secret mission to Hitler, explained why the brand-new general field marshal had advanced in defiance of orders and was continuing the offensive in North Africa, in spite of previous agreements with Italy. So taken was Hitler with Rommel that he decided not to deny the man permission to continue the advance, although he had inadequate fuel supplies and too few tanks at his disposal. Declaring melodramatically that the goddess of luck in battle always tapped field commanders only once, Hitler trampled on the Duce, who was suffering a loss of respect at home because of his lack of military successes.[73]

While the Foreign Office was working on a proclamation assuring Egypt of independence from the British yoke, Rommel's few tanks rumbled toward the Nile and the Suez Canal. By the time the German newsreels were showing the taking of Tobruk, Rommel's troops were stuck in a bottleneck between the impassable Qatarra Depression and the Mediterranean, near a wretched little desert town called El Alamein. The newsreel commentator therefore refrained from mentioning the word "Egypt," speaking only of Rommel's not resting for a moment: "The battle must go on."[74]

During this summer Goebbels managed to establish the "legal basis" for shipping off the Jews not only from the occupied areas but soon also from the Reich. Most of them were sent, crowded together in cattle cars, to Auschwitz, where SS doctors "selected" them either for the gas chambers or for slave labor that usually ended in death. The way had been smoothed by a marginal event: Karl Lasch, governor of the Radom District, had been executed without trial. His friend, Governor General Hans Frank, thereupon used his office as Reich justice commissar to demand in speeches at various German universities that a "National Socialist constitutional state" be established. This demand forced Hitler to act. He not only removed Frank from his post as justice commissar but also fulfilled a wish of Goebbels's, dismissing the more moderate administrative minister of justice Schlegelberger and replacing him with the aggressive and brutal hanging judge from the People's Court, Otto Thierack. Thierack received express authorization to deviate from existing law in order to build up a "strong National Socialist system of law."[75]

Goebbels had favored Thierack as Schlegelberger's successor, and the man seemed to know that he had an advocate in the propaganda minister. On 22 July, a month before his promotion, he had invited Goebbels to give a speech to the members of the People's Court. Goebbels had used the occasion to bemoan the fact that Jews could still turn to the court; he also announced the deportation from Berlin of 40,000 "Jewish enemies of the state." When Thierack became minister, Goebbels suggested to him on 14 September that the Jews be declared "unconditionally exterminable," with "the concept of annihilation through work" remaining "the best."[76]

After Goebbels and Thierack had conferred on the matter, the justice minister arranged with Himmler for the "extradition of asocial elements for execution of their sentences." All Jews, Gypsies, and others displeasing to the regime could be taken to a concentration camp without any need for formal charges. Thierack informed Martin Bormann "that the judicial system can contribute only in a small way to exterminating those who belong to this race." He therefore considered it preferable to turn such people over to the custody of the police, so that "the necessary measures can be implemented without interference from penal regulations bearing on evidentiary requirements."[77] Goebbels had reached his goal. Hitler's notions could become reality. Deportation of Jews from throughout the Reich to Auschwitz now began. The Reich Railways charged four pfennigs a head per rail kilometer; children were transported at half price.

The transports continued, even though the Axis powers' rail capacity did not come close to meeting military needs. On the eastern front supplies were scarce, and transportation of supplies to the Italian harbors was also sporadic. In the south there was the additional factor of British control of the central Mediterranean. Logistics in North Africa had almost collapsed. Rommel's tank troops and their Italian allies, worn out by the fighting around El Alamein, faced far better equipped and better fed British soldiers who were preparing for a major offensive. At home, too, life was growing harsher, with the British air attacks inflicting more and more damage. The summer's high hopes for a rapid end to the war were dwindling. Returning from the yearly film festival in Venice, Goebbels repressed this bitter reality and assessed the latest developments as "a positive thing," since "we'll enter the winter in better spiritual shape than last year."[78]

In mid-September it seemed as though the Wehrmacht had taken a decisive step ahead. On the fifteenth the Word of the Day announced that the struggle for Stalingrad was approaching "a successful conclusion." The German press was instructed to treat the "victorious conclusion of this great battle for Stalin's city in the most effective form"—by issuing special editions, if appropriate.[79] Although victory bulletins failed to arrive, the German newspapers announced the impending victory. Goebbels blamed these premature signals on Dietrich, without considering that Dietrich ultimately did whatever Hitler instructed.[80]

Goebbels now made a particular effort to be consistent in stressing the certainty of victory while not underestimating the sacrifices necessary to achieve it.[81] The chief obstacles to his propaganda were those people who did not close their eyes to reality, who could not bring themselves to believe. Goebbels turned on them in the 30 September speech with which he opened the Winter Aid collection at the Sportpalast: "The dubious political existences who aligned themselves against us during the final phase of our struggle for power in the Reich" still wanted to "bring unrest to the German *Volk* community by spreading stupid and silly rumors and to weaken and undermine our people's belief in final victory."[82]

That evening General Field Marshal Rommel was seated on the podium in the Sportpalast. Although he was home to recuperate from the stresses of the desert war, he was pressed into service as a propaganda weapon, since he embodied, as no one else in the Wehrmacht, optimism and confidence in victory. Goebbels organized an international press conference at which he introduced the "desert fox" to the journalists.

Rommel was still in Germany when the British began their offensive. Two days later he returned to North Africa, resuming command of the German-Italian tank forces. At the beginning of November he started to withdraw, lest his troops be annihilated by the enemy's very considerable superiority. At that moment he received Hitler's order to stand fast: "It would not be the first time in history that the stronger will prevailed over numerically stronger enemy battalions. But you cannot show your battalions any way other than to victory or death."[83] Goebbels's staffer Berndt immediately flew to Hitler's headquarters, where he got Hitler to revoke the order, possibly with Goebbels's help, and thus averted a catastrophe.[84]

During his minister's conferences on 5 and 6 November, Goebbels explained the military situation to his staff and—a victim of his own propaganda—expressed the hope that "General Field Marshal Rommel will gain mastery of the situation, as so often before." He ordered his propaganda apparatus to "tread lightly for the moment." These difficult hours would also pass.[85] Worry—indeed, a sort of panic—had seized him when American warships and troop transports appeared in the Mediterranean, since he had been expecting an invasion of Italy or southern France. When the landings in Morocco and Algeria occurred, he believed once more in the "passivity and ineptitude" of the Americans' conduct of the war; their systematic and cautious way of proceeding was completely foreign to him.[86]

Goebbels's propaganda did not at first take cognizance of the seriousness of the situation on the southern section of the eastern front. On 19 November, almost simultaneously with the arrival of winter, the Soviet counteroffensive had begun. Three days later it resulted in the encirclement of the German Sixth Army, parts of the Fourth Army, and several Romanian brigades—a total of 250,000 soldiers—in the Stalingrad area. Hitler, who had had it announced on 8 November that Stalingrad had already been taken by the Germans, ordered Gen. Friedrich Paulus to hold out and wait for reinforcements.[87] On 16 December Goebbels's press aide Rudolf Semler, just returned from Stalingrad, described the bitter battles taking place around the metropolis on the Volga. When Semler asked whether Stalingrad was to be held at all costs, Goebbels replied that the reputation of the Führer as a strategist was at stake there. "We would not dare destroy his work," he said, trusting in the supreme commander.[88]

Weeks before this, Goebbels had tried again to get Hitler to accept his plan of total mobilization of the home front. Looking around for allies, he had found one in, among others, the new Reich minister for armaments and war production, Albert Speer. Since February 1942 Speer had been busy developing central direction of the economy and successfully reorganizing the armaments industry. Goebbels also enlisted Economics Minister Walther Funk, his former undersecretary, and the Reich organization leader Robert Ley.[89] At Goebbels's Schwanenwerder villa the others agreed to Goebbels's objective of turning Germany into a huge army camp in which war alone would reign and only that which was "essential for the war effort" would be permitted, everything else banned. Anyone not fighting at the front would have to work at home to provide armaments and food. All vestiges of "civilian life," including any appearance of a prewar standard of living, were to be radically eliminated.

At the beginning of October Goebbels and Speer presented the plan to Hitler. Although Hitler promised soon to issue the command for "total war," nothing happened. When Goebbels approached him again at the beginning of December, he again took no action. Goebbels felt it was even more urgent to get moving when on 21 December the Wehrmacht reinforcements for Stalingrad got stuck just forty miles from the city; even a military layman like Goebbels recognized that the collapse of the encircled army could no longer be prevented.

Goebbels spent Christmas in the bosom of his family. Hitler's gift, which signaled his boundless favor, could do little to lift his depression. The gift was an armored Mercedes with bulletproof windows, intended to protect the propaganda minister, who had been assigned four bodyguards, from assassination.[90] At the beginning of the month a certain Dr. Hans Heinrich Kummerow had made an attempt on his life. The engineer, scientist, and section chief at Loewe's in Berlin had composed a report as early as 1939 that was passed to the British naval attaché in Oslo; it gave detailed information on the most advanced German long-range weapons projects.[91] Now Kummerow had disguised himself as a fisherman, planning to place a mine with a remote-controlled fuse under the bridge leading to Schwanenwerder Island. But Kummerow was caught even before he finished installing the mine. The People's Court made short work of condemning him to death.[92]

After the holidays Hitler finally reacted to Goebbels's plans. He sent Martin Bormann to Lammers, head of the Reich Chancellery, and to Goebbels for further discussions.[93] Bormann agreed with Goebbels that cuts in the standard of living and "particular sacrifices on the part of the upper ten thousand" would be unavoidable. He commissioned the propaganda minister to draft as quickly as possible the decree "on the comprehensive deployment of able-bodied men and women for defense of the Reich." The draft was to be ready for review in January. Goebbels, who had been watching jealously as Bormann insinuated himself more and more into Hitler's favor, thought he had at last reached his goal of seeing his ideas put into practice.

On New Year's Eve Goebbels had the sobering experience of hearing from his stepson Harald Quandt that the war would last "at least two more years."[94] In his New Year's greeting to the soldiers at the front he announced that the year just beginning would bring Germany closer to the "definitive victory," the "final victory," even if "its storms rage round about us."[95] On 4 January 1943 he confronted his colleagues at the minister's conference with the ominous situation, but stressed at the same time that he was happy "that gradually his demand for a more total waging of the war was making headway."[96]

On 5 January Goebbels informed his closest collaborators that a three-man committee, most likely consisting of Bormann, Lammers, and himself, would work out a plan of action for total war.[97] Three days later Goebbels, Speer, and Funk conferred with Bormann, Lammers, and Keitel on Goebbels's draft of the decree. On 13 January Hitler signed the document placed before him but did not appoint the projected committee of three.

The decree addressed both civil and military authorities, with the goal of adding at least half a million men, or at best 750,000, to the front within a quarter of a year. To achieve this, they would have to eliminate the designation "essential for the war effort," under which 10 to 15 percent of eligible men were dispensed from military service. On the basis of the statistics of 31 May 1942, this would amount to 5.2 million men. To fill the jobs thus vacated, Goebbels planned a sort of restructuring among those workers remaining in the Reich. He offered figures to show that in the retail sector there were still 2.2 million employees who were frequently "useless." Goebbels felt certain that about a million workers could be shifted to fill places left by those called up for military service.

Goebbels's working paper was based on the layman's notion that half a million men would bring victory in the east closer. On the issue of required troop strength he had been taken in by the Führer's assessment, which was far more optimistic than the actual situation dictated. When it came to armaments capacity, Goebbels was clearly under the influence of Speer. He had conferred extensively with the armaments minister, and the statistical analysis he had prepared, with the help of his collaborator Werner Naumann, struck even Hitler as inadequate.

Probably for that reason Hitler on 18 January nominated Bormann, Lammers, and Keitel as the three-man steering committee, assigning only an advisory function to the initiator of the whole plan. Goebbels, supported by Speer, had certainly counted on being put in charge, and had boasted just the previous day of his influence. He was all the more bitterly disappointed to get the news.[98] "Outraged and most deeply offended," he at once got in touch with the Führer's headquarters to try to bring about a change of assignments, but he was turned down by Lammers.[99]

The atmosphere was predictably bad at the 20 January meeting of Reich ministers, chaired for the first time by Lammers.[100] Seconded by Funk and Speer, Goebbels presented his radical notions. Frick and Lammers offered opposing arguments. For four hours Goebbels had to "fight like a tiger" for his views and even so he did not prevail.[101] Fritz Sauckel, commissioner of work deployment, assured the group that he could provide the needed number of workers from outside the country, including trained workers. This assurance made most of Goebbels's measures for mobilizing additional workers superfluous but did not undermine his determination. Now he had the "calming feeling of having done whatever can be done."[102]

When Goebbels visited the Führer at his headquarters on 22 January, Hitler explained that he had not wanted Goebbels to be personally burdened with administering this large program. "He would like me to take on the role of the moving force behind the whole thing."[103] Hitler's attentions and well-placed flattery, as well as the acknowledgment Goebbels received from Rudolf Schmundt, Hitler's chief Wehrmacht adjutant and head of the army personnel office, and from Gen. Kurt Zeitzler, allowed Goebbels to repress the humiliation he felt at being shunted aside not only by Bormann but also by Hitler.[104] Instead he pretended to himself that his preliminary work had already put down "the deepest roots." With Hitler's assurance in his ears "that in the course of the next three months he would refuse to receive anyone who tried to stir up trouble about him, the minister," Goebbels finally returned to Berlin.[105] Even at the end of January 1943 Goebbels still did not doubt that the "final victory" could be achieved, if only the proper steps were taken; at that time, fifteen hundred miles from his ministry, the final act of the tragedy on the Volga was unfolding. The time when any strategic or tactical objective could be ascribed to the battle in the encircled quarters of Stalingrad had long since past. All that remained was chaotic, painful, meaningless dying. On 24 January 1943 General Paulus had asked his commander in chief for permission to surrender. Hitler's reply was brief: "Surrender out of the question. Troops will fight to the last bullet." So the pointless dying amid the ruins of Stalingrad continued. On 30 January those soldiers who had access to radios crowded around them to hear what the Führer had to say to them from their distant homeland, which most of them would never see again.

Hitler had nothing to say to them. He remained secluded in his headquarters, wrestling with fate. Along with Goering, it was Goebbels who gave the radio address from the Sportpalast for the tenth anniversary of the Nazis' accession to power.[106] He excused Hitler's absence, necessi-tated by the "demands of conducting the war," and in the course of his speech read a "Proclamation from the Führer" that invoked the "heroic struggle of our soldiers on the Volga" and challenged his listeners to "do their utmost for the struggle for Germany's freedom," so as to prevail before "the Almighty," "the righteous judge," the "creator of all worlds."[107] Like Hitler's proclamation, Goebbels's speech announced specific measures for the implementation of total war. "But for us it has always been a fixed and immutable principle that the word capitulation does not exist in our vocabulary! . . . We have faith in victory because we have the Führer! . . . Faith can move mountains! This mountain-moving faith must fill our hearts!"[108]

The echo of Goebbels's profession of faith had not yet died away when General Paulus, whom Hitler had just named general field marshal, in the expectation that this ironic honor would drive him to commit suicide, capitulated with his remaining troops in Stalingrad.[109] It was 1 February 1943. For Goebbels it was absolutely clear what he himself would have done in this situation—"to live fifteen or twenty years longer or to gain eternal life of several thousand years in unfading glory" was the choice, as he saw it.[110] The capitulation was at first not even mentioned in his propaganda. Hitler wanted to skim over the catastrophe as quietly as possible. But he gave Goebbels permission to broach the subject in public, which Goebbels did with a carefully prepared special radio program on the evening of 3 February. The chief component was excerpts from Wag-ner's opera *Rienzi*.[111] With this embellishment, the end of the struggle was portrayed in such a way that the notion of capitulation would hardly occur to the listeners: the Sixth Army, "true to the last breath to its oath to the flag . . . under the exemplary leadership of General Field Marshal Paulus succumbed to the overwhelming superiority of the enemy and unfavorable conditions."[112]

Goebbels now planned to exploit the catastrophe on the Volga, "that image of grandeur truly worthy of classical antiquity," to support his notion of total war. His idea was to stage a massive rally that would forcefully confront the shocked German public with the alternatives of "victory or destruction." Anyone who wanted victory also had to em-brace his concept of total war, with all the consequences. The mighty spectacle would mobilize the population and put an end to previous "half-heartedness," he hoped.

Goebbels began in the Berlin Gau by closing down any businesses not important to the war effort. In his own ministry he had already released three hundred men to the Wehrmacht and the armaments industry, re-placing them with women. He was also thinking about ways to counter the growing defeatism in Berlin's government quarter.[113] He launched an operation to close down the luxury restaurants in Berlin. Up to then people in the upper ranks had eaten there without ration cards at prices ranging from fifty to a hundred marks per person. The best-known gourmet restaurant was Horcher's, whose owner enjoyed the patronage of Reich Marshal Goering. Goebbels simply sent a few SA men to throw rocks through the window several times, because Goering would have opposed any order to close the restaurant. Goebbels feared that ordinary people would feel cheated "unless we finally take the situation seriously," and that included the upper echelons of the party.[114]

At the Gauleiter conference in Posen on 6 February, and following that at the Führer's headquarters in Rastenburg, Goebbels apparently did not succeed in enlarging his influence on the waging of total war. As before, his field of action was restricted to public relations. He received explicit instructions not to let the propaganda treatment of these new measures slide into "class-warfare channels."[115] Nor was Goebbels able to put across his ideas about a change of course in the policy toward the peoples of eastern Europe, a policy that he hoped would improve conditions for the German soldiers in the Soviet Union.

Goebbels had conceived these ideas after reading two memoranda sent to him in January.[116] The first, from the army general staff, painted a more than dismal picture of the mood among the eastern European populace, for which it blamed the ruthless and inhumane treatment inflicted by the German occupation troops. Furthermore, German slogans about the inferiority of the Slavic peoples and the necessity of exterminating them had reached the Russian public, along with reports on manhunts conducted by the Germans. The result had been to stiffen the resistance of the Red Army and win increasingly broad support for Stalin's "patriotic war." The second memorandum, from an early party member named Max Hofweber, coincidentally confirmed the information in the first.

On 10 January Goebbels, before reading these memoranda, had rejected a suggestion from the army general staff that Hitler issue a proclamation promising all Russians equal rights, self-determination, and the reintroduction of private property. Goebbels justified his refusal by noting that the suggestion "was based on a false assessment of the Slavic ethnic character," which exploited political successes as the basis for constantly making new demands.[117] Goebbels now changed his mind. A few days later he wrote that it was incontestable "that a slogan to the effect that we're fighting only bolshevism in the east, not the Russian people, would do much to make our struggle there easier."[118]

Until mid-February Goebbels worked on a draft of a proclamation for Hitler in which, with the support of the generals, he made their suggestions his own. Under the pressure of military developments he had come to believe that "a politically clear-thinking person" could no longer "ignore the logical demand" for providing "psychological relief" in the east, so as to render the military struggle less difficult and at the same time counteract the mounting threat from partisans.[119]

Goebbels's notion was that the population in the occupied territories of the east had to be brought to the realization that Hitler's victory over the "beast Stalin" and the "bestiality of the Bolshevist system" lay in their own best interests. It would not do, therefore, to denigrate them openly and offend their inner sense of worth. Likewise any mention of colonizing or expropriating their lands had to be suppressed.[120] But Hitler rebuffed his propaganda minister's initiative. He wanted to issue a proclamation only when a new offensive got underway in the east. Goebbels blamed his enemy Rosenberg for Hitler's reluctance, because Rosenberg had approached the Führer with a similar notion "at the wrong moment."[121]

In his fanatical desire to produce a "masterpiece of rhetorical skill," Goebbels dictated a speech on 14 February that he revised that same evening and then reworked on the following days, even staying up all night 17 February to finish it. He had softened some passages that were originally "excessively harsh" and had the foreign-policy sections checked over by the Foreign Office. In the end he was convinced that the speech had "turned out very well" and would "almost certainly" be a "great success."[122] On the afternoon of 18 February he rode in his bulletproof Mercedes to the Sportpalast. Shortly before 5:00 P.M. he entered the huge arena, where his wife Magda and, for the first time, his two eldest daughters, Helga and Hilde, were seated. Speer reports in his memoirs that the crowd, which filled the Sportpalast to the last seat, "had been rounded up out of the party organizations; among those present were popular intellectuals and actors like Heinrich George, whose applause was caught by the newsreel cameras for the benefit of the wider public."[123] In addition almost the entire cabinet, numerous Reichsleiters and Gauleiters, as well as almost all the undersecretaries, had seats in the arena. From their balustrade hung a banner proclaiming "Total War—Shortest War."

When Goebbels stepped up to the lectern, his face energetic and intense, he invoked Stalingrad as the "great tocsin of fate" and a symbol for the heroic struggle against "the hordes from the steppe," that "terrifying historical threat" that thrust "all previous threats to the Occident into the shadows." Behind the Soviet divisions bearing down on the troops "we already see the Jewish liquidation commandos," and behind them, "terror, the ghost of famine, and complete European anarchy. Here international Jewry once more reveals itself as the diabolical ferment of decay, which takes a downright cynical satisfaction in hurling the world into deepest disorder, thereby bringing about the destruction of cultures thousands of years old, in which it never shared."

Goebbels unfurled this scenario of terror in every possible variation, and then arrived at the one response he thought fitting, a response infused with hatred: terror had to be answered with counterterror. "Bourgeois squeamishness" had to end, he said pointedly. As the wild applause died away, he moved on to his demand for total war. That was what the moment called for. Here Goebbels resurrected his old socialist views, his vision of a *Volk* community that had never been realized. The party must give no heed to class or profession; rich and poor, high and low had to be called upon to the same degree. This had nothing to do with bolshevism; rather, it was a matter of triumphing over bolshevism.

Goebbels went on to transform the catastrophe of Stalingrad into a positive manifestation of fate, through which the German people had been "profoundly purified." The "heroic sacrifice" of Stalingrad had opened the way to the salvation-bringing recognition that only an unshakable commitment to total war would effect the "final victory." Of Stalingrad he said, "It was not in vain. Why—that the future will show."

Goebbels had used these same images twenty years earlier in his "Michael"—to be sure, on an entirely different scale. Back then the hero of his novel had sacrificed himself in a mine to bring salvation, creating the fetish of belief that gave rise to new strength. This belief, which transcended reason, was now to bring about "the miracle of the impossible." Goebbels recalled Frederick the Great of Prussia, of whom he had so many portraits hanging in his official residence. Just as Frederick had believed, and had snatched victory from the jaws of defeat in the Seven Years' War, so Hitler believed, and would emerge the victor. The Reich's path to victory was "grounded in belief in the Führer."

When he reached the end and asked those assembled in the Sportpalast whether they believed in total war, "more total and radical than we can even imagine today," the Sportpalast exploded in cheering, stomping, shouting, clapping. The propaganda minister, drained but with perfect concentration, intoned, "Now, people, arise, and storm, break loose!" Scenes of mass hysteria broke out, such as the Sportpalast had not seen even during the Time of Struggle. Greater German Radio remained on the air for twenty minutes, broadcasting the sounds to its audience.[124]

Speer reports how Goebbels assessed his own performance: "Back in his home, Goebbels astonished me by analyzing what had seemed to be a purely emotional outburst in terms of its psychological effects—much as an experienced actor might have done. He was also satisfied with his audience that evening. 'Did you notice? They reacted to the smallest nuances and applauded at just the right moments. It was the politically best-trained audience you can find in Germany.' "[125] In the days that followed, Goebbels basked in the praise he received from the press. In view of the detailed instructions issued by his own ministry, his delight in the press's reaction seems downright grotesque.[126]

In fact, the speech did fill many who heard it on the radio with enthusiasm, at least so the reports from the local Reich propaganda offices suggest.[127] The reports may have been doctored, but there was no question that the propaganda minister, with his hatred, illusions, and rhetorical skill, had succeeded in mobilizing at least part of the German population to expend its last reserves of strength. These people now believed they were fighting for their survival; in fact they were only prolonging the war and their own misery.

After the speech a large circle of leading party functionaries gathered in Goebbels's official residence.[128] Here the opinion was expressed that Goebbels had pulled off "a sort of silent coup" against the bureaucracy he so despised. In fact Goebbels saw the bureaucracy as one of the chief obstacles to the realization of his plan. From bottom to top, including Hitler's immediate surroundings, there were no structures that allowed speedy action. Hitler's own principle of "divide and conquer" worked more and more to his disadvantage as he himself, paralyzed by reversals in the war, lost the initiative. Bormann lacked intelligence, Lammers was a cautious "superlawyer and superbureaucrat," and Keitel a simple soldier, a "zero," as Goebbels put it.

To speed implementation of total war, Goebbels and Speer decided to try to recruit Goering as an ally, at which they actually succeeded. But their attempts to outflank the Committee of Three and persuade Hitler to recapture the political initiative eventually failed because of Hitler's anger at the disastrous performance of Goering's Luftwaffe and because of the intrigues of Martin Bormann, whom Hitler had made his secretary.[129] In the end, Goebbels repressed his hostility toward Bormann, judging that he had been "extraordinarily loyal" to the Führer.

Goebbels now turned his attention all the more fanatically toward ridding the capital city of its Jews. On the night of 27 February he staged a major raid in the Berlin munitions factories. He had the factories surrounded by the SS's Adolf Hitler Regiment, which kept the Jewish forced laborers inside until trucks arrived to haul them off to the death camps. Goebbels noted, however, that the raid had not been a complete success; unfortunately it had become clear again "that the better circles, particularly the intellectuals, do not understand our Jewish policy and partly side with the Jews. As a result, our operation was revealed prematurely, so that quite a few Jews slipped through our hands. But we'll catch them yet. At any rate I won't rest until at least the capital has become completely Jew-free."[130]

With the exception of 4,000 Jews who could not be located or who were exempted as partners in "privileged mixed marriages" (actually the number at this time was probably closer to 18,000), Goebbels thought he had reached his goal on 11 March. In a total of sixty-three transports, 35,738 of the 66,000 Jews still living in Berlin in 1941 were deported to Auschwitz and murdered. In addition, by the end of the war 117 so-called old-age transports had taken 14,979 Jews to Theresienstadt. Very few survived.[131] For all these Jews, as for millions of other European Jews, the man who sent them on their way was Joseph Goebbels, whose Gau on 19 May 1943 was declared to be "Jew-free," which he viewed as his "greatest political accomplishment."[132]

No scruples tormented the propaganda minister. The further military success receded into the distance, the more clearly he saw the "extermination" of Jewry as the realizable part of national socialism's great historical assignment to save the West. The alleged threat from the Jews made Goebbels feel justified in murdering even women, children, and the elderly. But his propaganda had not succeeded in spreading such maniacal thinking among the German people, so the genocide had to be kept secret. Wartime stress had reinforced many people's tendency to look the other way, especially since the details about the extermination camps that reached their ears seemed so monstrous as to be incredible.

Germany's enemies, however, drew new impetus for their fight against the Reich from information about the "final solution." Since the end of 1942 the BBC, but also the Soviet information service, broadcast accurate reports on the extent and methods of the mass murders, some in German, and demanded that something be done. In his 1943 New Year's message the Bishop of York summoned the allies to a crusade to free humanity from the barbarity represented by the extermination of the Jews.[133]

To counteract such information, Goebbels's propaganda directed abroad went to particular lengths to unmask the Soviet Union as a "pestilential world enemy" and thereby discredit the country in the eyes of its Western allies. The report from an SS Unterscharführer to the Reichssicherheitshauptamt about a mass grave discovered near Katyn seemed to provide grist for Goebbels's mill. The officer estimated that six thousand corpses of Polish officers and soldiers, bound hand and foot, had been buried in the clay, presumably after being killed by guard detachments of the NKVD. "Numerous identification papers, dogtags, amulets, and diaries" had been recovered. Since there was danger of an epidemic from the corpses and the military forces were not allowed to make propaganda use of this find, the SS officer advised that Berlin act quickly.[134]

The information reached Goebbels after some delay, but he immediately put his propaganda machinery into high gear, with the help of Berndt, recently returned from Africa. At his 11:00 A.M. press conference on 8 April, he emphasized how important it was that the group of journalists leaving for Smolensk the next day should be followed by others, such as Polish reporters, priests, scholars, and delegations from neutral countries and the occupied countries in the west, so they could see the atrocities firsthand. He also wanted to send a writer with a reputation known throughout Europe; he had in mind John Knittel, author of *Via Mala*, who hated England and had earlier expressed a wish to go to Africa with Rommel; "he could then write an open letter, a cry of despair from a European."[135]

What the journalists saw in the forest of Katyn and how they reported it struck Goebbels as so "horrifying" that he speculated the affair would turn into a "huge political issue" that might "cause significant waves."[136] He was not mistaken. Disregarding assertions from Moscow that the atrocities had been committed by the Germans, the Polish exile government in London addressed a communiqué to the public, noting that thousands of Polish soldiers had been captured by the Soviet Union in 1939 and that all inquiries as to their fate had gone unanswered. The Poles knew perfectly well that German propaganda spread lies, but in this case, the statement said, the Polish government had asked the International Red Cross to dispatch a commission to investigate.[137] Since that same day the Germans had likewise asked the Red Cross to look into the matter, *Pravda* simply accused the Poles of working hand in glove with Hitler. On 26 April Stalin, probably already with an eye on the future, had ordered Foreign Minister Molotov to break off diplomatic relations between the Soviet Union and the bourgeois exile government of Poland.[138]

The propaganda minister rejoiced: "All enemy broadcasting companies and enemy papers are unanimous: the break is to be seen as a complete triumph for German propaganda, especially for me personally. People admire the extraordinary cunning and skill with which we linked a highly political issue to the case of Katyn. . . . All of a sudden fissures are appearing within the Allied camp."[139] Goebbels overestimated the significance of these fissures, however, for Churchill and Roosevelt were betting on the stronger power, and that meant the Soviets. How much difference could it make that a few thousand citizens of a Polish state that had not even existed for several years had been murdered?

The propaganda minister's pleasure was clouded by the events in the North African theater of war. On 5 May the British launched a decisive offensive and split in two the Axis troops defending the Tunisian bridgehead. Goebbels found himself facing a dual propaganda problem: how to present this new reversal to the public, but also how to explain the fact that General Field Marshal Rommel, so closely associated with the campaign in Africa, had returned to the Reich weeks earlier. To avoid burdening Rommel's image with a defeat, Goebbels had the Wehrmacht high command announce shortly after the beginning of the English offensive that the "desert fox" had been sent home for two months on sick leave.[140]

Goebbels proceeded to celebrate the defeat in Africa like a victory. Once more he placed Rommel at the center. In May the field marshal conferred several times with Goebbels and Berndt to work out a radio retrospective, "Twenty-Seven Months of Struggle in Africa."[141] But the cult of personality around the "creative strategist" could not change the fact that 240,000 German and Italian soldiers had surrendered in Tunisia. Goebbels suppressed the actual figures.

The defeat in North Africa combined with the increasingly frequent British and American bombing raids on German cities to produce a precipitous drop in morale, as the Security Service's secret reports recorded.[142] "They're costing us a great deal in property and also in moral values," Goebbels conceded.[143] More and more he saw it as his task to contain the psychological effects of the attacks by making personal appearances. As chairman of the new Interministerial Committee for the Relief of Air Raid Damage, he traveled from city to city.[144] Everywhere he was cordially received. These suffering people felt that at least someone cared about their fate, his aide Semler noted.[145] Even when Goebbels visited the old Hanseatic city of Hamburg, where in a seven-day inferno of carpet-bombing thirty thousand people had lost their lives, it was no different.

Goebbels's propaganda did not deny the serious damage inflicted by the bombing attacks, for he felt that by openly addressing the problems he could give the people "more moral fortitude." At the same time an attempt was made to convince the enemy that the attacks were pointless: they merely strengthened German morale. If true at all, this could actually be said only for an almost invisible minority, but Goebbels convinced himself that an "interesting transformation" was occurring within the population. "The positive ones are merely becoming more fanatical in their belief in victory; the negative ones, especially in intellectual circles, fall all over themselves in defeatist utterances."[146]

Once more Goebbels launched an all-out attack on the defeatists. A wave of rallies throughout the Reich was intended to hammer into the *Volk* comrades confidence in victory and absolute faith in Adolf Hitler. At the same time a call went out for people to denounce defeatists. Often a person had only to express skepticism about the outcome of the war to be arrested by the Gestapo and condemned to death by the People's Court. Others were driven to suicide by Goebbels's terror tactics.[147]

In a speech at the University of Heidelberg on 9 July 1943, Goebbels explained how a sober view of the situation, how knowledge of its seriousness, indeed knowledge per se, could be reconciled with faith in "final victory": "We do not belong to those naive, happy natures who derive their inexhaustible strength solely from faith. But we do not seek to reduce knowledge and insight to the opposite of belief; rather, we make them the foundation of belief. Half-knowledge often leads to cowardice; only complete knowledge and the deepest depths of insight endow belief with the victorious strength that remains unshaken even in storms and tempests."[148]

To induce his fellow Germans to abandon reason en masse in favor of blind faith, Goebbels launched an operation that entailed systematically spreading rumors that new wonder weapons would soon bring about the promised retaliation.[149] The operation was probably coordinated by the Schwarz van Berk office in the Propaganda Ministry, which ostensibly existed to prepare news stories about Germany for the foreign press but actually had been set up specifically for spreading rumors and generating new slogans.[150] The success of the undertaking may be gauged from the Security Service report dated 1 July 1943: rumors of the new weapons had been so widespread for several days that almost every German had heard them in some form. Highly detailed discussions of the weapons were taking place not only privately among friends, but also openly in public conveyances, in restaurants, and so on, and everywhere the prospect of these weapons had aroused great hopes for successful retaliation.[151]

Such hopes were all the more needed because the summer brought one military reversal after another. In the east the offensive begun at the beginning of July near Kursk had to be broken off after a huge tank battle because the Red Army had successfully launched a counterthrust. Goebbels recognized the seriousness of the situation; in his diary he admitted that it made him shudder to look at the map and see "what we had in our possession last year at this time, and how far we have been pushed back now."[152] At the end of August he even mentioned to his new press aide, Wilfred von Oven, that Germany might lose the war. For such an eventuality his mind was made up: "A life under the control of these enemies I should be happy to cast off. Either we master this crisis—and I will dedicate all my strength to that end—or I shall make a deep bow once more to the English spirit and put a bullet through my head."[153] From this time on Goebbels kept a .635-caliber pistol in his desk drawer.[154] But he took refuge in faith, which had helped him through the desperate years after World War I and through the party's crisis in 1932.

Once again a visit to Hitler renewed his strength. On 9 September 1943 he set out for Hitler's Rastenburg headquarters. He intended to try to persuade the Führer to speak on the radio for the first time in half a year. Mussolini had been deposed, the situation in Italy was confused, and the mood in Germany had deteriorated. Goebbels succeeded; his revered Führer composed a speech that very day, which Goebbels enthusiastically described as filled with "the spirit of Clausewitz." Hitler condemned the "treachery of the Badoglio clique," swore eternal friendship to the Duce, and sketched out measures for securing the German position in Italy. At the same time he cautioned the German people that such treachery must never be committed in the Reich. He also announced retaliation for the British-American terror bombings and conjured up the image of Germany's "final victory," which would come in spite of the present burdens.

As a result of Hitler's speech and the "heavy blows" against Italy, especially the capture of Rome by the Wehrmacht, Goebbels believed he could detect a change for the better in the general mood. In fact, Germans were simply pleased to see Italy in trouble; Goebbels noted that the hatred felt for the Italians was "indescribable." The propaganda minister did not except himself from this hatred. But after German paratroopers in a spectacular operation rescued Mussolini from his forced confinement on the Gran Sasso in the Apennines, Goebbels noted skeptically: "As long as the Duce wasn't there, we had an opportunity to make a clean slate in Italy. Without any compunctions and on the basis of the grandiose treachery of the Badoglio regime, we could set about solving the problems posed by Italy. I had thought that, quite aside from the South Tyrol, our border could possibly have been extended as far as Venezia."[155]

Now that the smoke had lifted, Goebbels instructed the press and radio to give up their wait-and-see attitude and to treat the events in Italy in Hitler's tenor. After weeks of silence he himself spoke out in an article in *Das Reich*. Although he tried to create the impression that the German government had immediately seen through the "treachery planned by the Badoglio clique" but had kept silent "out of consideration for our national interests," his propaganda did nothing to raise people's confidence in the German conduct of the war.[156] For in the meantime the Allies had landed on the Italian mainland, and the Soviet counteroffensive had begun to make inroads against the midsector of the front in the east; by the end of September Soviet forces would recapture the Donets Basin and Smolensk.

The time-worn propaganda cliché "that the entire nation on its way to definitive freedom and the self-fulfillment of a chosen people cannot avoid suffering its Golgotha" was losing its effectiveness.[157] Apathy was becoming widespread. People suspected that the propaganda promises were empty, though they still followed the Führer and hoped somehow or other to survive. Goebbels felt that among the public and in Hitler's immediate circle people failed to realize that the war at this stage had become a "grim life-or-death confrontation." "The sooner the entire German people and especially our leadership recognizes that, the better for all of us. It would be tragic if at a particular juncture in this war we had to say, 'Too little and too late.' "[158]

To bolster spirits in the country, Goebbels had announced in a speech in Kassel on 5 November that the promises of retaliation meant more than simply striking back: "What we have in mind has become a sort of people's secret; each person knows more than the next. Nevertheless, I believe I may assert that in the not-too-distant future England will receive a response that will probably make the English people break out in a cold sweat."[159]

But for the time being it was the British and their allies who continued to land blows. In mid-November they began systematically bombarding Berlin, something Goebbels and the Berliners had been expecting ever since the terrible raids on Hamburg. During the night of 31 July–1 August, Goebbels had leaflets distributed to all Berlin households calling for the evacuation to safer areas of all old people, children, and non-working women.[160] Hundreds of thousands of people then left the city; four hundred thousand children alone were sent by train under the auspices of the Children's Country Evacuation to Austria or Silesia, which left their mothers free for deployment in the total war. Goebbels's own children had been sent to safety at the Berghof in the spring of 1941 and then to Aussee in the Upper Danube Gau; but now they were back in Berlin, so Goebbels had them move out to Lanke, which was less dangerous. He himself stayed in Berlin. He emphasized that he had been called the Conqueror of Berlin, and now he wanted to earn the name of Defender of Berlin.[161] Air raid shelters had not been provided for all residents, and there was no time to build them, nor were workers or materials available. So Goebbels had to improvise. He refused to listen to the experts, who claimed the subway tunnels should not be used because they were so close to the surface. Goebbels turned out to be right; when the bombing attacks began, thousands fled through the tunnels to escape the conflagrations and survived. Goebbels saw here further evidence that his own improvisations were more reliable than the judgment of cautious "bureaucrats."[162]

During the air raids, which at first came only at night but then by day as well, Goebbels directed civilian operations and the emergency services from the bunker of the Kaiserhof Hotel. He had summarily expropriated the luxurious rooms built under Wilhelmplatz for celebrated hotel guests.[163] After the all-clear sounded, he would hurry through the burning city, the only high party official to do so, directing the fire-fighting operations here, sending emergency help there. People clustered around him, shook his hand, or spoke with him. When cooked food was distributed in "Red" Wedding, working-class people received him with enthusiasm.[164] Even at funerals, like those of the many young flak auxiliaries at which he spoke formulaic words of uplift about sacrifice and salvation before placing the Iron Cross on the coffin, his presence was perceived by the surviving family as a tribute.[165] Now, in these times of trouble, Goebbels's display of being "one of them" made him popular, for people appreciated any word of encouragement, even from the propaganda minister.

The British had hoped to demoralize the people of Berlin, but apparently no such thing occurred.[166] Goebbels had instructed the SA to form special armed units to be deployed in the factories in case of unrest, but they were not needed. In spite of the bombing, workers continued to show up at their plants, and armaments production went full steam ahead. Goebbels took personal credit, probably with justification, for the fact that the workers did not storm the government complex on Wilhelmplatz, demanding an end to the war.[167]

Goebbels finally received his reward for this commitment from Hitler. On 21 December 1943 the Führer put his most loyal follower in charge of the newly founded Reich Inspection of Civilian Air Protection Measures, an outgrowth of the Interministerial Committee for the Relief of Air Raid Damage.[168] The minister thanked his Führer emphatically for this evidence of trust. While spending Christmas in Lanke with his wife, the children, his mother-in-law, and his sister Maria, he wrote to Hitler, saying how happy it made him to be able to assume "a little of the gigantic burden of cares that rests upon you," and offered assurances that in the "Year of Struggle 1944" the Führer could count on him "in any and every situation." He wished him "health and a blessed hand." "The rest, what we all hope for, will be the result of your genius and our hard work."[169]

By the end of 1943 Goebbels had essentially come out on top in his jurisdictional dispute with Rosenberg over propaganda in the east. But by this time propaganda in the occupied territories had little significance. In a report to Hitler dated 23 May 1943, Goebbels had listed 38 million posters, 54 million brochures, political news broadcasts in 18 languages beamed over 32 eastern transmitters, and 7,625 copies of newsreels and propaganda films shown in 650 field cinemas; but all this stood in sharp contrast to the "scorched earth" policy and the indescribable terror visited upon the population by the SS and SD special operations units, the feared Einsatzgruppen. As Taubert wrote, "What good did it do in the long run to put up millions of posters in the cities of the east that described Hitler as 'the liberator,' when under those same posters Russian prisoners were shot or thousands were starving to death, when people were dragged off like cattle to forced labor, when the commissars dealt with the people with riding whips—I mean German commissars, for the Bolshevists were far too canny psychologically to subject the Russian people to beatings." "The fine words of Germany's propaganda were thus increasingly belied by the deeds committed in support of German policy."[170]

Meanwhile the area in question continued to shrink as the Red Army stormed westward. On 4 January 1944 units of the Ukrainian Front crossed the Polish-Soviet border in Volhynia. Ten days later a major attack was launched against the Germans along the northern sector of the front. At the beginning of March the Soviet spring offensive began along the southern sector. Bad news kept streaming in from other quarters as well. In Hungary Prime Minister Miklós von Kállay initiated contact with the Allies, whereupon the Wehrmacht marched in and occupied the country. In Italy, where Badoglio had declared war against the Reich in October, attempts to throw the Allied landing force back into the Mediterranean at Anzio-Nettuno failed. In the Atlantic the German U-boats were making less and less headway, and in the skies above the Reich the woefully inferior German Luftwaffe could do little to stop the British and American planes, which were turning Germany's cities to rubble.

Furthermore, the threat of an Allied invasion, promised more than a year earlier, hung over the continent like the sword of Damocles. In his propaganda Goebbels tried to persuade the Germans, but also himself, that such a venture could never succeed. The generals' optimistic assessment of the military situation lent him encouragement. In mid-February the commander in chief of the western armies, Gen. Gerd von Rundstedt, delivered a "very effective speech" about the Atlantic fortifications, stressing that they constituted an entirely new type of installation that the Allies could not breach.[171] During the great gathering of the party old guard at the Hofbräuhaus in Munich Hitler gave a address that Goebbels considered "extraordinarily vigorous." He announced he was on the "path to victory" and would stay on it "without compromise" until the Jews in the entire world were struck down. When Hitler's words unleashed "huge storms of applause," Goebbels's worries dissolved again —for the time being.[172]

In his written tribute for Hitler's fifty-fifth birthday, Goebbels again described it as his great good fortune that he could help the Führer carry another bit of his burden; Hitler had just made Goebbels president of the city of Berlin, which gave him "absolute authority for leading and directing the capital of the Reich."[173] Although Hitler was by this time looking ashen and had a pronounced tremble, Goebbels did not hesitate to write, "Never have I admired you as much as in moments of crisis, which have always bound me to you even more strongly. That with all these burdens you have remained a great, but also a simple, person is for me the most beautiful confirmation of your personality. That I, like all your closest collaborators, can always come to you with my worries and draw support from your strength gives me ever new energy and faith."[174]

Goebbels needed this faith more than ever, for his propaganda was wearing out its welcome among the German people, even as he was busy building the myth of the impenetrable Atlantic fortifications. The thing most likely to mobilize the population was fear of the Red Army, whose advance Hitler thought he had halted. To explain the steady succession of reversals and defeats, Goebbels now felt he had to have recourse to metaphysical categories. More and more he relied on the notion of "belief in Providence," claiming that history was imbued with a "splendid justice that overshadowed all human deeds and actions" and would eventually reward the "just cause" of national socialism.[175]

At the same time Goebbels's mania gave rise to increasingly powerful aggressive urges. Since he had not yet been able to win Hitler over to totalizing the war effort by mobilizing all forces for the front and the armaments industry, he now advocated radicalizing the fighting itself. In a propaganda campaign he demanded de facto rejection of the Geneva Convention, suggesting that enemy airmen who got shot down should no longer be protected from spontaneous attacks by the civilian population. After all, bombing civilians or residential areas was "naked murder." The enemy had no basis in international law for their actions. Therefore the Germans should "find ways and means to defend ourselves against these criminals."[176]

On 30 May 1944 the Führer's headquarters had already issued a directive, signed by Bormann, to all Reichsleiters and Gauleiters, which called for a halt to legal proceedings against persons who lynched the crews of downed low-flying Anglo-American aircraft.[177] Goebbels wanted this dispensation extended to include bomber pilots.[178] On 5 June he was at the Berghof for a discussion of "rules on lynching." To his disappointment, the existing legal provisions were maintained. But Goebbels's collaborator Berndt, who by now had risen to the rank of SS Brigadeführer, paid no attention to such rules. On 6 June he simply shot dead an American air force lieutenant named Dennis who had ejected by parachute and landed on the street. Berndt's enemies wanted to see him punished, but Keitel and others came to his defense, and finally Himmler also covered for him.[179]

During that 5 June meeting Goebbels again overlooked the outward signs that Hitler's physical and mental health were undermined. They discussed, among other things, the crisis supposedly brewing within the enemy alliance, and foreign-policy issues. Goebbels, who had missed no opportunity to agitate against Goering, learned to his delight that Hitler was "only partly satisfied" with Ribbentrop, and had often toyed with the idea of dismissing him. He had refrained because nowhere did he see a replacement. Goebbels's reaction: "When the Führer mentions Rosenberg as a possible replacement, I'm absolutely appalled. Rosenberg in place of Ribbentrop—out of the frying pan into the fire. . . . He's a bloodless theoretician and hasn't the slightest talent for practical politics." In light of this revelation, Goebbels quickly realized that the Führer was not in a position to do anything against Ribbentrop, and that it was better to "let things slide."

Toward 10:00 P.M. first reports came in "monitored from enemy radio communications that indicate the invasion is supposed to begin tonight," but Goebbels, who had been making jokes for several days about "invasionitis," did not take them seriously.[180] The propaganda minister sat up late with the Führer by the fireplace in the Berghof, while outside a "gruesome storm" thundered over the mountain. Goebbels said goodnight around 2:00 A.M. and looked in on Bormann before having himself driven down to his hotel in Berchtesgaden at 4:00 A.M. There his adjutant Semler presented him with "authentic documents" showing that "the invasion will begin in the early hours of the morning, in the west. That would mean that the decisive day of this war has dawned."[181]

Hours of hectic activity ensued, during which bulletins from the Normandy coast followed hot on each other's heels. What remained unclear was whether or not the landing was a maneuver intended to distract attention from the real invasion elsewhere. Goebbels found it reassuring that the Führer did not show "the slightest sign of weakness." Although the situation remained confused, Goebbels's worries evaporated, for as he boarded his special train for the capital that evening, a "deeply moved" Hitler yet again expressed "his unshakable certainty that we'll succeed in throwing the enemy off European soil in a relatively short time."[182]

To add to Goebbels's confidence, the "wonder weapons," the V-1 rockets, were finally ready after many delays that Goebbels feared had undermined his credibility.[183] Goebbels is reported to have told his press aide, "I think that I, of all Germans, feel the greatest satisfaction now that our means of retaliation is finally a fact. For I promised it to the German people. And they'd have held me responsible if it hadn't come about. You know the hundreds of letters that often contained no more than one sentence: 'Where is our retaliation?' "[184] Now retaliation was there and lent wings to Goebbels's fantasies of victory: "Our stock has risen enormously, not only with our own people but also with the rest of the world."[185]

Yet Goebbels did not want to whip up too much hope with his propaganda. Restraint was advisable, especially now that the promise of the "wonder weapon" propaganda could be tested against reality. To his press aide Wilfred von Oven, Goebbels remarked that the people's mood was a "highly complicated instrument"; one had to know it very well to play on it. A "bumbler" like Dietrich would "never understand" that.[186]

Deployment of the new weapons caused a brief surge in German morale. "The German people is almost feverish with excitement. . . . Some people are even betting that the war will be over in three or four or eight days," Goebbels noted.[187] The SD reports recorded that while battles were raging in Normandy, trust in the Führer was rekindled and people hoped that things would begin to turn around. Even the soldiers at the front drew new confidence and morale from bulletins on the weapons.[188] Goebbels's propaganda attempted to keep morale high by unceasingly stirring up hatred and desire for revenge.[189]

Although the topic of "retaliation" was heavily stressed again in the propaganda around the beginning of July, although further rockets with even more devastating effects were promised, the SD reports soon noted a "fresh decline" in morale, for the remote-controlled rockets seemed to change little in the dramatic development of the military situation. In France the Allies had established a firm bridgehead within just a few days, and in Italy they were pushing vigorously to the north, having ousted the Wehrmacht from Rome on 4 June.

Despite the worsening military situation, favorable assessments continued to flow from the Führer's headquarters. Goebbels did not want to admit that the source of the optimism was not the toadying generals but Hitler himself, who was doing everything possible to conceal his failures.[190] But Goebbels did take steps: he again pulled together a group of high officials to try to identify a course of action. Funk, Speer, Ley, Fritz Sauckel, as well as Herbert Backe, undersecretary in the Ministry of Nutrition and Agriculture, Stuckart from the Interior Ministry, and Naumann from the Propaganda Ministry met with Goebbels regularly on Wednesdays to discuss totalizing the war effort. All those present clung to the propaganda minister with his radical views, feeling that he had the best chance of bringing about the longed-for change of fortunes.

In mid-June Rudolf Schmundt, Hitler's chief Wehrmacht adjutant, was convinced by Goebbels that in view of the extremely critical situation "extraordinary measures" were called for.[191] Schmundt also reported to Hitler on his conversation with Goebbels. Hitler listened in silence for an hour and then summoned Goebbels to come "as quickly as possible" to the Berghof.[192] Goebbels answered the summons, hoping that his Führer would finally agree to totalizing the war.[193]

On 21 June 1944 the two men sat down in the great hall of the Berghof for what Goebbels called this "gravest" and "most important" discussion of the entire war. Goebbels laid out for Hitler "all the considerations against unfounded optimism, not to say illusionism," and complained that total war had become "a mere phrase" and was not actually being waged. After Goebbels had spelled out his ideas in detail, Hitler inundated him with his usual eloquence, to the effect that the moment had not yet come for total war, that the old methods should be given time to work. Goebbels protested that if they waited any longer, it might be too late, but Hitler refused to see the crisis as so critical. The propaganda minister recognized that his efforts had failed yet again. For once Hitler's arguments did not persuade him, but he tried to comfort himself with the thought that in the past the Führer had always instinctively chosen the right moment for action.[194]

But developments on the various battlefronts proved Goebbels's fears correct. On 22 June 1944, three years to the day since Germany's attack on the Soviet Union, the Soviet summer offensive began, resulting in a matter of weeks in the complete collapse of the Army Group Center. At the beginning of July Goebbels had a conversation in Breslau with his former undersecretary Hanke, with whom he had just laid to rest the old conflict over Magda.[195] He noted in his diary afterward: "The situation in the east worries me more and more. There must be some way to stabilize the front. If things continue this way, the Soviets will soon be at the border of East Prussia. I keep asking myself despairingly what the Führer is doing about this."[196] Since the propaganda minister did not know the answer and was hearing reliable reports of "spectacles of wretchedness and horror" from the eastern front—among other things, the rear echelons had already fled—he decided to try to see Hitler again.

He received support in this undertaking from his Wednesday group, especially Albert Speer, who was watching with deep concern the Allies' systematic bombardment of the hydrogenation works, which reduced synthetic fuel production to one-fourth the amount produced in April of that year. Without fuel the entire German war machine would grind to a halt. Goebbels decided to prepare a memorandum for the Führer, and Speer resolved to put together a paper proposing "that Goebbels instead of the incompetent Committee of Three take over the job of rallying all the home front forces behind the war effort."[197]

Goebbels actually considered "absenting" himself if Hitler did not grant him the authority he requested; he had no desire to "be humiliated again" or to see his suggestions "talked to death by bourgeois weaklings."[198] In the memorandum Goebbels started from the premise that the Anglo-American-Soviet coalition was about to break down. But, he said, it alarmed him to think that the Reich might not hold sufficient pawns; therefore all conceivable forces had to be mobilized. That was possible "because internally we still have at our disposal enormous reserves of people and economic strength," and the population actually wanted totalization of the war. Goebbels made a whole series of specific suggestions for procuring manpower, reducing administrative waste, putting civilian life on a true war footing by eliminating frivolities such as "receptions, ceremonies, festivals, and the like." He castigated the bloated bureaucracy, specifically naming Rosenberg's Ministry of the East and Ribbentrop's Foreign Office. He warned against repeating the mistake with the Committee of Three, which had chewed every decision to a pulp. "In the party's great moments, my Führer, you have always gathered around you men, not committees," he wrote, men "who combine imagination, political passion, and deep belief in you and your work with enjoyment—yes, even thirst—for responsibility." He promised that in three or four months fifty new divisions could be put together, and with the "internal war dictatorship" Hitler would have the "battle instrument" necessary for victory. He conceded that his predictions might be overshooting the mark, "but have we ever achieved anything in the history of the party without overshooting the mark?" He closed with assurances: "You know that my life belongs to you"; his family "could never live in a time that is not ours." The memorandum bore the date 18 July 1944.[199]

CHAPTER 14

Revenge our virtue,
hatred our duty!
(1944–1945)

Around noon on 20 July 1944 Goebbels was conferring in his office with Funk and Speer when he was called to the telephone. It was Reich Press Chief Dietrich reporting from the Wolf's Den in Rastenburg that an attempt had just been made on Hitler's life. Goebbels felt as if the ground beneath his feet were quaking.[1] After receiving assurances that the Führer was alive and well, Goebbels asked whether there were any suspects. Dietrich said Hitler thought that one of the eastern European forced laborers working on the Führer's bunker might be responsible.

In his memoirs Albert Speer recalls in detail how events unfolded that afternoon and evening.[2] Goebbels at first thought that one of Speer's forced laborers might indeed be to blame, but he soon realized that a major conspiracy must be underway and concluded that the "aristocratic generals' clique" that he so hated must be involved. As the only high-ranking party functionary in Berlin, he seized control of the situation. His quick action, combined with hesitation on the part of the conspirators, and their fatal error in not cutting telephone lines, doomed the seizure of power they contemplated. By evening Goebbels had broadcast word of the failed assassination attempt and had ordered the arrest of Generaloberst Fritz Fromm, who, to deflect suspicion from himself, had already summarily executed Claus von Stauffenberg, the would-be assassin, and several other conspirators. Not until evening did Heinrich Himmler arrive in Berlin, claiming that he had stayed away for "tactical reasons."[3] At 1:00 A.M. Hitler spoke on the radio, promising to punish the guilty "as we National Socialists are accustomed to do." Around 5:00 A.M. things settled down in Goebbels's official residence, and he summed up the day's events for his confidants Naumann, Schwägermann, and Oven, remarking that probably no one had dared hope that everything would end so quickly and gratifyingly. To be sure, he, Goebbels, was a "calm, clear-thinking person, not given to losing his head." But in this case he had to recognize that "this is a visible expression of divine will. Here even a hard-boiled realist must feel the breath of a supernatural force."[4]

On 22 July the most prominent men in the Reich gathered in Rastenburg to congratulate Hitler on surviving the assassination attempt. Goebbels had set out for Hitler's headquarters, convinced that his well-considered and decisive action in putting down the putsch would have earned him the powers he desired. The preliminary session in Lammers's field quarters seemed to confirm his optimism. Apparently under instructions from Hitler, Lammers suggested reluctantly that the Committee of Three, consisting of himself, Bormann, and Keitel, be dissolved. Himmler would be given "extensive authority" to reform the Wehrmacht, and Goebbels similar authority to reform the state and public life.[5] At first astonished by Lammers's suggestion, Goebbels quickly concluded that the "gentlemen" must be fearing that "their inadequate measures" were "gradually leading to a major crisis in government and the conduct of the war."[6]

Goebbels expressed willingness to assume these new duties, suggesting that he did so only because the fatherland's need called for "major measures" and because Hitler had to be "spared all petty details" so as to devote himself to "his great historical task." To forestall resistance from within the party, especially Bormann's, Goebbels stressed that the party would not be included in his intended measures to free up manpower for the war effort.[7]

Reactions to the new powers for Goebbels varied, with Keitel expressing great enthusiasm for Goebbels's plans, while Undersecretary Stuckart protested that the Reich Railways and Postal Service could not spare any more workers. Goebbels blocked these and other objections by remarking that the present discussion should not deal with particulars. He insisted that the entire group should support the "overall scheme" when they went in to see Hitler. As no one objected, he asked Minister Lammers to propose the plan to Hitler, since "he could not very well nominate himself."[8] In his diary Goebbels noted: "If we get the Führer to accept what we adopted in the meeting with Lammers, we'll have to all intents and purposes established an internal war dictatorship. I feel strong enough to implement this and to use my authority in such a way that the greatest possible benefit will accrue to the war effort." And he resolved to "comb through" the state apparatus "with an iron hand." When the group went to lunch, the man from Rheydt formed the center of attention, telling the dramatic story of how he had blocked the coup in Berlin. Since the others all treated him "as nicely as could be," he hoped that "leading" would prove "extraordinarily easy" in this situation. "It has to do with the fact that there's no one who doesn't fear a great crisis in the war, even a catastrophe," he commented, making an exception of himself and also his "beloved Führer."[9]

When he saw Hitler that afternoon, Goebbels had "the sensation of standing before a person working under the hand of God." The sensation was reinforced when Hitler seemed "much taken" with Goebbels's proposals for crushing the conspiracy. After pouring abuse on the conspirators, Hitler also proved very receptive to the idea of total war. Goebbels came more and more under his spell; the old intimacy of the Time of Struggle returned. That the Führer had grown "very old" and appeared "downright frail" gave Goebbels pause, but he saw Hitler's being as "characterized by extraordinary goodness," and remarked with almost religious fervor that he had "never seen such inner warmth in him as on this day. One simply has to love him. He is the greatest historical genius of our times."[10]

That evening, in the course of further discussions, Hitler directed Goebbels to "set in motion a great wave of meetings throughout the Reich to make the point that the treasonous generals' clique must finally be done away with." The details were later worked out by Goebbels. The speakers had instructions to emphasize that the conspirators came from a small, reactionary group, and that by no means all aristocrats in the armed forces were implicated.[11] The high point of the campaign was to be a radio address by Goebbels on 26 July in which he described his own experience with the assassination attempt and once again glorified Hitler in pseudoreligious terms.[12]

The propagandists fooled themselves about the effect of this campaign. In a report prepared in the ministry from information supplied by the various regional propaganda offices, the rallies were described as "spontaneous demonstrations of loyalty," as an "unconscious referendum" for Hitler—even though they had been organized by the party.[13] In fact, the majority of Germans did see the attempt on Hitler's life as treason to the fatherland, but one could hardly say that his escape from assassination had produced an "upswing in morale."

Goebbels felt his belief in "Providence" confirmed by such reports. As Reich Plenipotentiary for the Total War Effort, his new title, Goebbels now had the authority to issue directives to the entire civilian sector and the heads of the highest Reich agencies. With a staff of twenty he intended to bring about the necessary "structural transformation in the entire state apparatus."[14] Ultimately the whole undertaking aimed to realize the National Socialist utopia of a "government without administration."[15]

In a letter to all the highest Reich agencies, Gauleiters, Reichsstatthalters, and administrative offices, Goebbels suggested that all persons in leading positions should measure the propriety of their actions by asking how they would feel behaving the same way before soldiers on the frontlines and workers in the armament factories.[16] Goebbels's own wife provided an example by working part-time in a Berlin factory.[17]

During the Gauleiter conference on 3 August in Posen Castle, Goebbels offered a detailed description of his measures to totalize the war. He explained the "crisis" in the middle sector of the eastern front, supposedly three times worse than that of Stalingrad, as the result of the 20 July conspiracy. The orders found at the conspirators' Bendlerstrasse headquarters had offered "a classic proof that if the leading minds of this organization had gone to as much trouble to work out orders for holding the eastern front, and had pinned as many hopes and wishes on holding the eastern front as on striking down the National Socialist movement, developments in the east would have taken an entirely different course. . . . This little clique didn't want to win!"[18]

In his speech in Posen Goebbels announced to the Gauleiters that the "traitors" would be dealt with ruthlessly. And indeed, on 4 August, a Wehrmacht court-martial chaired by General Field Marshal von Rundstedt, newly named to head the general staff, and including Heinz Guderian, Keitel, and two other generals, met to expel resistance members from the German armed forces. This action put the conspirators at the mercy of the People's Court. Four days later, after absolutely inhumane proceedings under the fanatical judge Freisler, the first eight defendants were sentenced to death. They were hanged almost immediately at Plötzensee Prison.

These executions and those that followed were filmed by a crew supervised by the Reich cultural administrator and director of the film department in the Propaganda Ministry, Hans Hinkel. Goebbels himself commissioned the film *Verräter vor dem Volksgericht* (Traitors before the People's Court), of which he promised all the Gauleiters a print.[19] But Bormann expressed reservations; he worried that the Gauleiters would show the film to a lot of people, which might result in "a regrettable discussion of the method of trial." To avoid trouble with Bormann, of whom he was "downright afraid," Goebbels informed the Gauleiters that he had decided to show the film at their next meeting, rather than risk having it fall into the wrong hands in the mail.[20]

When Goebbels saw the execution scenes, he is said to have turned away.[21] That may have had to do with the method of execution—the condemned were suspended by steel bands from hooks and slowly strangled. Or it may have been that he recognized among those executed his old comrade-in-arms, Berlin Police Commissioner von Helldorf. This rabid anti-Semite had become increasingly despondent as the war continued and had finally joined the officers' resistance.[22] Shortly before his arrest, Helldorf had given Regierungsrat Hans Bernd Gisevius an unvarnished account of the situation:

He said that everyone was longing for the war to end; that no one would fight for the Nazis on the barricades; the general sense of weariness was overwhelming. Nevertheless there were no signs of revolt. The terror of the bombings forged men together. In rescue work there was no time for men to ask one another who was for and who against the Nazis. In the general hopelessness people clung to the single fanatical will they could see, and unfortunately Goebbels was the personification of that will. It was disgusting to see it . . . but whenever that spiteful dwarf appeared, people still thronged to see him and felt beatified to receive an autograph or a handshake from him.[23]

Once Goebbels discovered that his friend Helldorf had joined the resistance, that "spiteful dwarf" had nothing but contempt for this man who had been deeply in debt and emotionally wrecked by love affairs. Goebbels's hatred for Helldorf was all the greater because that same year he had interceded with Hitler to have Helldorf given the Knight's Cross in addition to the Cross of Merit.[24] Werner Stephan quotes Goebbels as remarking with satisfaction that the "traitor" Helldorf had to watch his fellow conspirators suffering their death torments on the gallows before his own turn came.[25]

Within his own ministry, where fear of him usually induced people to keep up a false optimism, Goebbels had begun accusing close collaborators like Semler or Müller of defeatism.[26] Before the events of 20 July he had even turned on Berndt, head of the propaganda department, who had recently also been put in charge of the Interministerial Committee for the Relief of Air Raid Damage as well as the Reich Inspection. Goebbels charged him with committing "serious indiscretions about the defensive preparations in the west" and about "dissension in the high command of our western troops."[27] Berndt had commented that Rommel, who always seemed so confident of victory when speaking with Hitler, was not really confident at all.[28] To punish Berndt, in June 1944 Goebbels removed him from his position as head of propaganda but refused to release him to go to the front. Finally, after Goebbels and Berndt talked things out and SS Obergruppenführer Maximilian von Herff interceded, Goebbels placed Berndt on leave. In mid-August he joined the Waffen-SS, where he was put in command of a tank division.[29]

Now Goebbels was busy coordinating the last great mobilization of the war, in close cooperation with Speer and Himmler. Caught up in a whirl of activity and blind to the actual effects of the measures he was implementing, Goebbels closed down factories, instituted a sixty-hour work week for civil servants and blue-collar workers, and ruthlessly canceled deferments.[30]

Although the representatives of the state and the party considered these measures absolutely essential, they often tried to win dispensations for their own areas by using personal influence with the Führer. Thus Bormann, jealous of Goebbels as a rival for Hitler's favor, appointed himself a sort of overseer of the fanatical reorganizer. To curb Goebbels's growing power, Bormann tried to persuade Hitler of the senselessness of various measures Goebbels was pushing, so as to undermine his work.[31]

Goebbels hardly took notice of Bormann's criticisms, though as before he studiously avoided any confrontation with the Führer's secretary. Since he really believed that the "treason" of 20 July had been responsible for the disaster on both fronts (he had an utterly false conception of the enemies' armaments), and since Speer spoke of steadily increasing arms production, including remote-controlled airplanes and a new type of U-boat, Goebbels expected the war to take a turn for the better. That would give the Reich time until the enemy coalition broke apart, which he assumed was inevitable. The promised deployment of another "wonder weapon," the V-2 rocket, the world's first ballistic rocket, further encouraged him. Upon seeing a film of the V-2 that Speer had arranged to have shown only to Goebbels and his own closest collaborator, Erhard Milch, Goebbels was so enthusiastic that he hinted in an editorial in *Das Reich* that by deploying "terrible methods" the Führer would very soon put an end to the war.[32]

Such high-sounding words did little to hearten the people, who felt themselves drowning in unfulfilled promises. The flying bomb, the V-1, was already the butt of many jokes; sarcastic names for it proliferated, such as "Vanquished 1" and "Volksfooler 1."[33] As a result, the Führer's headquarters ordered Goebbels not to mention the V-2. Speer himself had warned Hitler of the dangers of creating expectations that could not be fulfilled immediately.[34]

Starting at the beginning of September, the V-2 rockets were launched against England without propaganda accompaniment and actually did considerable damage, although it paled to insignificance in comparison with the Allied bombardment of Germany. The eastern and western fronts continued to move inexorably toward each other. By mid-September the Red Army had marched into the Baltic states and reached the border of Slovakia. In the southeast, where Bulgaria and Romania had declared war on Germany, the Wehrmacht pulled out of Greece. In Italy the troops dug in along the Apennines came under attack, and in the west American and Free French forces under General de Gaulle had already marched into Paris on 25 August, meeting no Wehrmacht resistance, and were pushing vigorously toward the Reich.

On 30 August Goebbels noted in his diary that the reports from the Wehrmacht high command now sounded so drastic "that the people are gradually beginning to lose their nerve."[35] But apparently he was also concerned about the steadfastness of the political leadership; he questioned the wisdom of providing the leaders with daily summaries of enemy radio propaganda, as he had been asked to do. "I myself shall request to see only a fraction of this material, since in these serious and critical times I have no desire to have my nerves ruined by this English-American-Soviet propaganda," he noted in his diary.[36]

Goebbels now admitted to himself that he could not "buck up" the people all by himself on the radio. So he turned to the Führer, who alone had the authority "to give the people strength and courage again in the present situation." He asked him to address the nation. When Hitler refused, Goebbels's concern that he could not maintain German morale grew, particularly because his totalization methods had not yet taken hold, and more "heavy blows" had to be expected in both east and west.[37]

To make things worse, on 9 September he received the "sad news" that his stepson Harald Quandt had been wounded during the fighting on the Adriatic and was missing in action. Goebbels immediately requested that the Red Cross try to trace him; he at first withheld the news from Magda, who had fallen ill again, "so as not to agitate her unnecessarily."[38] Less than twenty-four hours later he learned of a devastating bombing attack on Mönchengladbach and Rheydt. On 12 September a bomb exploded on the grounds of his official residence, knocking off the roof and smashing into the ground floor, so that he had to move out to Lanke, where Hitler had had a bunker built for his family.[39]

Unable to escape the realization that the war on two fronts could no longer be won, Goebbels took refuge in the Führer's prediction that the enemy coalition would come apart. After discussing the situation far into the night with Schwarz van Berk, he noted that the political aspects of the situation were "very promising, if there is any rationality left on the enemy side." But he feared once more that German foreign policy was not in a position to exploit those aspects. "If I were foreign minister, I'd know exactly what had to be done," he wrote.[40]

After speaking with his confidant Naumann, who had just been made undersecretary, Goebbels decided to act. Naumann had told him about a "sensational discussion" he had had with the Japanese ambassador Hiroshi Oshima. The ambassador had argued that the German Reich should make every effort to conclude a separate peace with the Soviet Union. The anti-Bolshevist Oshima insisted that "further bleeding of the German troops in the east was no longer tolerable in view of the danger from the west. Japan would even make concessions that would pave the way to a German-Soviet peace treaty." Naumann continued that the Japanese ambassador saw no prospect of accomplishing anything with the British and Americans, whereas Stalin was a "realist." This analysis corresponded perfectly to Goebbels's own view, so he was all fired up with the idea. He immediately informed Himmler and Bormann and asked them to broach Oshima's idea to the Führer in the most appropriate way.

Goebbels himself went to work at once to put down in a memorandum for Hitler the thoughts on foreign policy that had been gestating within him for a year.[41] He started from the assumption that the Soviet Union and the Western powers were separated by "a mountain of divergent interests." Germany's way out of the present dilemma could be found in the situation the Nazis had faced in 1932. At that time Hitler's clever diplomacy had exploited the differences between the enemies on the left and on the right, "so that on 30 January 1933 we achieved a victory, limited, to be sure, but the prerequisite to gaining total power." What had been done in domestic policy then should be done in foreign policy now.

Goebbels went on to explain that he was no "political adventurer" but was merely fulfilling his obligation to the Führer and his mission. It was crucial to arrive at an understanding with Stalin—better to make peace with "Jewish tricks" than with the even more hated capitalist "stock exchange Jewry" that directed the Western plutocracies. Goebbels took the occasion to castigate Ribbentrop's failures and to accuse the foreign minister of being "largely corrupt and defeatist," or at least lacking in the necessary "glowing fanaticism." He asserted that "hardly anyone in the German leadership of the party, state, and Wehrmacht" disagreed with this assessment. The twenty-seven-page manuscript, which Goebbels typed himself in large type because of Hitler's worsening eyesight, ended with assertions of Goebbels's loyalty and altruism, as well as apologies for his seeming to preach at his Führer. He said that even if this product of "innumerable lonely evenings and sleepless nights of brooding" accomplished no more than allowing him to unburden his heart to his Führer, that was enough.

On 22 September Goebbels sent the memorandum to Hitler. He waited on tenterhooks.[42] He was delighted to hear from Naumann that the Führer had read the document through carefully, then put it in his briefcase to peruse again at night.[43] But then weeks passed and nothing happened. In October Goebbels tried to move the matter along by writing to Hitler that the Foreign Office was "infiltrated to a dangerous degree by traitors and politically unreliable elements."[44] But Hitler had decided to stick to his old concept for conducting the war. Because of the successful defense of Arnheim, he was even planning a counteroffensive in the Ardennes. With this measure and intensified deployment of the V-2, he hoped to soften up England for peace, which would get the Americans off the continent and leave him with his back protected, so he could concentrate on beating the Soviet Union.

Hitler's decision to go on the offensive in the west, which he described as the prerequisite for a separate peace, without stipulating with whom, seemed to dovetail with Goebbels's notion of a conciliation with the east. He saw it as his chief propaganda task to counteract the war weariness of the population in the west, where people now thought that falling into American hands would be the least of evils. The Quebec Conference in September 1944 played into Goebbels's hands. There the Allies accepted the Morgenthau Plan (later abandoned), which called for fragmenting Germany, dismantling its entire industrial base, and transforming Germany into "a country primarily agricultural and pastoral." This plan let Goebbels's propaganda paint an apocalyptic vision of life under American occupation.

At the beginning of October Goebbels visited the "border territories in the west," the scene of fierce fighting. After conferring with the Gauleiters on the total war effort and receiving a briefing on the military situation, he arrived on the afternoon of 3 October in the heavily bombed city of Cologne. There he spoke at a rally organized by the Cologne-Aachen Gau, where he pointed out that occupation by either the Soviets or the Americans would result in "the same gruesome terror regime on German soil." The solution was to "stand fast," and he promised a miracle, suggesting that not only would the enemy siege be broken at Germany's borders, but in the foreseeable future Germany would go on the offensive.[45]

Instead, after weeks of bitter combat, the Americans occupied Aachen. At the beginning of October they took Ubach, the birthplace of Goebbels's mother, though with heavy losses, as he noted with a bit of satisfaction. By now it was unmistakable that the people were longing for the war to be over. Reports prepared for Goebbels by local propaganda offices spoke of "hopelessness" and "general resignation."[46] Even Goebbels now suffered bouts of depression.

It did not help that no word had been received of Harald's fate; Goebbels had had to tell Magda that he was missing. Another depressing factor was the death of Goebbels's friend Rommel. From details that trickled out, Goebbels had to assume that Rommel, too, had been involved in the 20 July conspiracy, although this was not strictly the case.[47] It was ironic that Goebbels's propaganda, which portrayed Rommel's forced suicide by poison as an "accident" and asserted that Rommel's "heart belonged to the Führer," actually came close to the truth; he had, in fact, never broken his oath to Hitler.[48]

The greatest worry for Goebbels was Hitler's illness. The Führer had taken to his bed, shaken by stomach and intestinal cramps, and lay there almost indifferent to what went on around him. Goebbels lamented that it was intolerable that the Führer should be expected to spend five or six hours a day in situation conferences; some new division of labor had to be organized within his staff. Yet the Führer remained capable of nice gestures. Magda Goebbels was depressed, increasingly preoccupied with the end, from which she saw no escape for herself or her family. Upon learning of her depression, Hitler asked to speak to her after telephoning Goebbels at "two minutes past twelve" on 29 October, the evening of his birthday. When Magda rejoined the small gathering of friends in the living room, she had tears of joy in her eyes. The Führer had assured her that he would give the German people a great military victory as a Christmas present.[49]

Hitler wanted this victory to be a reality before he addressed the public, so despite Goebbels's intervention he canceled his yearly address for the anniversary of the November 1923 putsch. Instead he announced that the deployment of the V-2 could be used for propaganda purposes, to give the Germans "something to be happy about" on the anniversary.[50] The Wehrmacht high command thereupon reported on the evening of 8 November that Greater London had been under attack for several weeks by a much more effective rocket than the V-1.[51] To Goebbels this attempt at propaganda must have seemed like pure dilettantism; how could the people derive confidence from a "miracle weapon" that had been in operation for weeks without changing the hopeless situation at all?

Another source of irritation, in addition to Bormann's constant cross-fire, was a letter dated 2 November from Speer in which he asked Goebbels to make sure the press refrained from alluding to "future successes in our armaments production."[52] After a discussion, in the course of which Speer, probably trying to smooth the waves, promised new records in weapons production for the end of the year, Goebbels expressed his anger to Semler: he thought that Speer had been misleading him for months about the status of the country's armaments.[53]

Despite all these reverses, despite all the resistance and the many imperfect solutions, Goebbels managed to mount a frenetic propaganda campaign for final victory. In collaboration with Speer he achieved one more great push for mobilization, though not in the hoped-for dimensions. Once more hundreds of thousands were drafted into the Wehrmacht. They became members of poorly trained and equipped Volks grenadier divisions deployed along the fronts, where they suffered catastrophic losses. Others were reassigned to work in the armaments factories, where Speer was achieving new efficiencies and actually increasing production despite the constant bombing by the Allies.[54]

Goebbels now turned his attention to laying the propaganda foundation for the creation of the Volkssturm. By a decree issued on 25 September but not published until 18 October 1944, Hitler called for drafting all German men between the ages of sixteen and sixty who were capable of bearing arms. Registration centers were set up all over the Reich where old men, adolescents, and those previously declared unfit for service now had to line up. Party functionaries were put in charge of forming the units. These militia-like groups, completely meaningless in any military sense, were led not by soldiers but by the Gauleiters in their capacity as Reich defense commissars.[55] Goebbels had them sworn in en masse on 12 November. As Gauleiter of Berlin, Goebbels enjoyed assuming the role of commander when the "last forces," including the Wilhelmplatz Battalion with staffers from the Propaganda Ministry, reported for duty.[56]

While Goebbels was busy with this desperate mobilization, the day was approaching on which he and his Führer placed such hopes. These hopes were mentioned again on 3 December, when Hitler came to tea at Goebbels's residence, probably for the last time, bringing his own tea in a thermos bottle. The six children were trotted out to greet him, the girls in long dresses.[57] Then Magda and Joseph Goebbels sat for an hour and a half with Hitler, his adjutant Schaub, and Naumann. Although quieter than in the past, Hitler still dominated the conversation, while Goebbels and his wife hung on his every word. It was like old times at the Chancellery. They felt proud after he left, and Magda could not keep to herself the observation that Hitler would probably not have gone to the Goerings'.[58]

Finally, before dawn on 16 December 1944, the Christmas offensive was ready to begin. Between Hohes Venn and the northern part of Luxembourg, the Ardennes offensive was launched against Antwerp, the Allies' supply depot. The Americans were taken by surprise, and the first battles began promisingly. Goebbels seemed transformed, rejoicing at this "miracle" the Führer had pulled off. He told his staff that by the year's end one and a half American armies would have been destroyed or pushed back into the sea. He even believed Hitler had become his old self.[59]

At a press conference on 17 December Goebbels spoke of a "great military success" without mentioning the objectives of the "Rundstedt offensive," as he called it. He presented Hitler's long public silence as a "great coup" intended to lull Washington and London into a false sense of security.[60] Goebbels's hopes in connection with the offensive seemed to be fulfilled when he received a telephone call from the Führer on 19 December. "He is in a splendid mood," Goebbels wrote in his diary, "is in excellent health, and one can tell from his mood that the successes already achieved have brought about a fundamental transformation in his entire mentality."[61] Soon afterward the skies cleared over the Ardennes, and the Allies were able to throw their air superiority into the breach. On 22 December the Americans began a counteroffensive. Goebbels refused to recognize the defeat in the making. In his propaganda he claimed that Operation Watch on the Rhine had been intended to tie up enemy forces and draw them away from endangered sectors of the front, an objective that had been fully achieved.

Despite this self-deception, Christmas 1944, which Goebbels spent with his wife, children, and sister Maria out in Lanke, turned out to be one of the most painful of his life. Outward appearances were preserved: the family sat around the Christmas tree and opened their presents, then listened to the propaganda minister's Christmas address over the radio. But the confidence Goebbels tried to project to the German people could be maintained only artificially in his own household. It was not without deeper meaning that Magda told her secretary on Christmas Eve that the coming year would probably bring peace.[62]

At New Year's the cloud of strain and apprehension that hung over Goebbels's estate was lifted by several visitors.[63] At noon the crack fighter pilot Oberstleutnant Hans Ulrich Rudel stopped by before reporting to Hitler for a promotion and a decoration that had been created just for him, the Knight's Cross with Golden Oak Leaves and Swords and Diamonds. The minister listened to his stories with interest, for Rudel seemed to personify what sheer will could accomplish. Goebbels saw the same attitude embodied in Gauleiter Hanke, who announced with fanatical determination that he would defend Breslau against the Soviets to the last drop of blood. In spite of his earlier relationship with Magda, Hanke enjoyed Goebbels's highest respect. Goebbels had not the slightest doubt on this day that one had to fight to the end for the Führer's cause, whether that meant salvation or utter destruction.

The man to whose health they drank at midnight had again sent Goebbels emphatic best wishes for the New Year. More than ever, Goebbels saw Hitler as his only reason for going on, and he now also began to express the idea that he could not, and would not, contemplate a world without the Führer.[64] Goebbels's health reflected the almost intolerable tension; he was plagued with nervous eczema and colic in the kidneys. In view of the desperate situation—the "merciless struggle for our very existence," as Hitler called it in his New Year's orders to the Wehrmacht—Goebbels sought models of conduct in history.[65] In addition to returning time and again to Carlyle's biography of Frederick the Great, his model for steadfastness, Goebbels now studied the chapters on the Punic War in Theodor Mommsen's *History of Rome*. Ancient Rome had had to fight Carthage for years and years, and at one point Hannibal had even appeared at the city gates, but Rome had never capitulated. It was entirely due to the steadfastness of the Roman state and people that the place where Carthage had once stood was later worked by the Roman plow.[66]

In Zdenko von Kraft's book on Alexander the Great, Goebbels discovered a passage that seemed to him to mirror the situation in Hitler's circle, but also to offer a way out. In this passage Alexander was failing, and no one knew "whether his wide-open eyes still looked into life." Alexander's doctor Philippos had mixed a healing draught for the king, who was stretching out his trembling hand for the chalice when a messenger from Parmenion rushed in with a letter saying that the drink contained poison. As Alexander

> brought the chalice to his lips with his right hand and drank up the contents, he handed the doctor the letter with his left. Philippos read. His face turned pale, but his bearing remained erect. . . . Without a word of reply, Philippos sat down on the edge of the king's bed. It did not occur to him to protest his innocence. Quietly . . . he told of his homeland, rich in forests and meadows, of his childhood and youth, how as a boy he had come to the court of Pella. He praised Macedonia and the deeds of the king, he predicted victories to come and dreamed of the wondrous lands of the east, which he spread so visibly before Alexander's weary eyes that for the first time in a long while a grave smile softened his pale lips. Only then did he rise and gesture to all the others to leave: Alexander had fallen asleep. He was sleeping the sleep of healing.[67]

Goebbels copied out this passage and sent it to his Führer, who returned a few days later from his field headquarters at Bad Nauheim to Berlin, to direct the defense against the Soviets from his bunker under the Reich Chancellery. For the Soviets were advancing along the entire front; by the end of January they had almost reached Königsberg, and soon they had taken East Prussia and farther south had cut off Breslau from the rest of the Reich. In the eastern provinces, where Soviet soldiers were murdering, plundering, and raping the civilian population, panic broke out. Millions of German took to the roads on horseback, in wagons, and on foot in the bitter cold. They were strafed by Soviet planes as they dragged themselves westward. At the end of January forty to fifty thousand refugees reached Berlin, of whom at best 10 percent could be sent on; the rest had to be absorbed. Despite everyone's best efforts, the bombed-out city lacked lodgings, food, heating fuel, indeed almost everything.

Although Goebbels noted that Hitler radiated "incredible certainty and strength of belief" upon his return to Berlin, by 26 January the Führer's optimism struck even his Philippos as excessive.[68] Goebbels doubted "very seriously" that it would prove possible to hold the current lines of defense. But when Hitler, weakened by Parkinson's disease, had difficulty maintaining his show of confidence, his faithful vassal tried to prop him up, recounting analogous situations from history to renew Hitler's sense of his mission. He actually succeeded, for on 28 January he noted: "He wants, as he explains to me, to show himself worthy of the great examples of history. Never will he be found to waver in the face of danger."[69]

If Goebbels lent Hitler strength, Hitler did the same for him. One day Goebbels tried again to persuade Hitler to turn Germany's conduct of foreign affairs over to him, and again he failed. On the way home he thought over everything the Führer had said and concluded, "It's true, after all, that a great man must wait for his great moment, and that one can't give him any advice about this. It's more a matter of instinct than of rational analysis. If the Führer should succeed in turning things around—and I'm firmly convinced that the opportunity to do so will come—he will be not only the man of the century but the man of the millennium."[70] It did not occur to Goebbels that Hitler might not be seeking any political solution because he calculated the chances of achieving one as equivalent to zero. As Reich Plenipotentiary for the Total War Effort, Goebbels finally had the power to check up on the administrative offices of the Wehrmacht, the Waffen-SS, and the police within the "home war zone, with the objective of getting them to free up the maximum number of soldiers for the front."[71] He hoped to mobilize one hundred additional divisions, and had his staff working feverishly to achieve this goal.[72] It was enough to drive him crazy to think that two years had gone by during which laziness, irresponsibility, jealousy, or malice on the part of others had prevented him from implementing total war. Only now could he do what he wanted, "and yet" it was "all too late."[73]

Goebbels had one small success to boast of at the end of January 1945. He had finally persuaded Hitler to speak on the Reich radio again. It was the last time that the "Führer of the Greater German Reich," which no longer existed, invoked the "Almighty" who on 20 July had confirmed his mission; the last time he called upon his would-be ally England to see reason, for England could not combat bolshevism alone; the last time he proclaimed his "inalterable will" "never to waver in this struggle for the salvation of our people, in the face of the most terrible fate of all times."[74]

At the very hour when Hitler broadcast these words to the nation on 30 January, the refugee tragedy in the east reached a first grim climax. The *Wilhelm Gustloff*, a Strength through Joy ship evacuating refugees from the Baltic coast, was sunk by a Soviet submarine. Over five thousand people lost their lives in the icy waters. While the Berliners received the news lethargically, the report the following day that the Soviets had reached the Oder River set off widespread panic. Rumors of further Soviet advances spread like wildfire.[75]

On this same day Goebbels sent his adjutant Schwägermann out to Lanke to bring Magda, the six children, the grandmothers, the servants, and the necessary luggage to safety, which now meant back to the official residence on Hermann-Goering-Strasse. Magda wrote to her son Harald, whom the Red Cross had meanwhile located in a British prisoner-of-war camp: "Despite the air attacks our house is still standing, and we're all well provided for, including Grandmother and the other family members. The children are in good spirits, and are happy not to have to go to school. Thank God they're too young to realize how critical these times are. As for Papa and me, we're full of confidence and do our duty as best we can."[76]

For Goebbels, part of this duty now consisted of working with General von Hauenschild, the new commandant of Berlin, to organize the defense of the city. On 1 February Goebbels declared the city a fortress. Trenches were hastily dug around the outskirts of the city, and in the center barricades and temporary tank traps were thrown up. The Volkssturm occupied the railroad stations, bridges, and public buildings. As Goebbels arranged with Speer, wartime production would not only continue but be accelerated. Now that Upper Silesia had been cut off, Berlin had become the most important armaments production center in the Reich.[77] Goebbels was much impressed by the Soviet film *Leningrad Fights*, which showed how Leningrad had withstood more than a year of siege by the Wehrmacht. He gave instructions that all those responsible for the defense of Berlin should see the film.[78]

At the beginning of February the Soviet offensive ebbed. While hopes rose among the people that the Red Army had been bled dry, Goebbels knew that this was only the calm before the last storm. He told Oven that it was perfectly clear now what would happen: the Allies meeting in Yalta would reach an agreement, and Germany would be attacked from east, west, and south and from the air, leaving it a pile of rubble that the victors would occupy according to plan. All the talk of a world peace organization was just sand thrown in the eyes of war-weary humanity to mask the Allies' ruthless pursuit of power.[79]

Yet the situation provided time, time that Goebbels thought had to be exploited in spite of everything. A miracle might yet occur—the British and Americans might break with the Soviet Union, if one helped the miracle along with faith and deeds. To the deeds belonged the uninterrupted propaganda campaign blasting the alliance between the Western "plutocracies" and bolshevism as a "grave historical crime."[80] As a warning to the German people against laying down their arms, he predicted that the Allies would occupy Germany until the year 2000, and even coined the term and concept of the Iron Curtain.[81]

Goebbels also wanted to stiffen German resistance by means of atrocity propaganda, at the risk of causing still greater panic among the population of the eastern provinces.[82] Goebbels had even hired painting firms to paint slogans on the bombed streets of Berlin: "Hatred our duty— revenge our virtue."[83]

Goebbels now met more frequently with Hitler and Bormann for situation conferences.[84] His boundless hatred still impelled him to seek expansion of his authority to totalize the war and to urge that the conduct of the war be intensified. The carpet-bombing of Dresden on the night of 13–14 February by British and American planes gave him a new opportunity for promoting his radical aims. Dresden, one of Germany's most beautiful cities, had been crammed with refugees from Silesia. At least thirty-five thousand people died in the inferno. With tears in his eyes and trembling with rage, Goebbels demanded Hitler's permission to shoot "ten thousand or more English and American prisoners of war."[85] Although such a step would have meant abrogating the Geneva Convention, Hitler was quite prepared to take it, until others expressed reservations.[86] Finally he appointed a commission to study the advantages and disadvantages of violating the international agreement on the conduct of warfare. The commission advised him to uphold the convention.[87]

Goebbels also used the destruction of Dresden to topple his old adversary Hermann Goering, who in the meantime had become hopelessly addicted to morphine. On 14 February Goebbels spoke in the presence of Naumann and Semler of his outrage at this "parasite," whom he had despised for his bourgeois attitudes ever since the Time of Struggle. He accused this "no-good" of being responsible for the Allied bombing terror and said he would haul him before the People's Court if he could.[88] In his diary he wrote that the Reich marshal was not a National Socialist but a "sybarite." "Fools covered with medals and vain, perfumed dandies have no place in the conduct of a war. Either they change or they must be eliminated."[89]

At the beginning of February Goebbels had asked Hitler again to broaden his authority.[90] To line up support for eliminating his enemies within the party ranks—Goering, Ribbentrop, and Rosenberg, who was refusing to dissolve his Ministry for the East—and for organizing the German defense more efficiently, he met with Himmler on 14 February. Himmler was in the SS hospital in Hohenlychen, twenty-five miles from Berlin, recovering from a bout of angina. Goebbels presented his concept of the new government: he would be Reich chancellor, Himmler would take over the high command of the Wehrmacht, and Bormann would head the party, all with the approval of the Führer. Goebbels argued that it was crucial to lighten Hitler's burden because of his worrisome physical condition. His plan assigned to Hitler the role of a grand historical figure presiding over the rest.[91]

Goebbels and Himmler also discussed political possibilities for saving the Reich. Days later Goebbels noted down the view of the Reichsführer-SS that England would "come to its senses," which Goebbels somewhat doubted. It seemed clear that Himmler was oriented entirely toward the West; he expected nothing from the East. Goebbels on the other hand still felt it was "more likely that something could be accomplished in the East," since Stalin appeared "more realistic" than the "English-American runners amok."[92] Himmler had apparently concealed from Goebbels his contacts with the Swedish count Bernadotte, who came to see him soon thereafter in Hohenlychen. Himmler's companion Hedwig Potthast had urged him to explore the possibility of a separate peace with the Western powers and he did so, obviously with the hope of saving his own skin.

Since Goebbels on 25 February failed to persuade Himmler to make common cause with him, he had to act alone.[93] When he went to see the Führer on 27 February, he confined his comments to the bureaucratic difficulties he kept encountering in his effort to totalize the war. He did ask again for expanded powers and requested that those who stood in the way of his measures be "put on ice." Hitler admitted that he was right "on every point" and "praised him highly." Hitler's flattery induced Goebbels not to insist on Goering's dismissal; instead he now hoped that the Führer would succeed "in making a man out of Goering again."[94] A short while later, however, Goebbels again resolved to eliminate the Reich marshal, and several times brought up the topic with Hitler, who probably remained loyal to Goering because they had marched side by side to the Feldherrnhalle during the 1923 putsch.

On 4 March Goebbels was feeling troubled as he descended the steps into the Führer's bunker. The Soviets in East Pomerania had begun a push toward the Baltic and had broken through the German defenses. But he felt strengthened after the meeting; the Führer had explained that one had to view the situation in the east in relative terms, and it was actually better than four weeks earlier. Goebbels ascribed the improvement to the Führer's decision to come to Berlin and take things in hand.[95] During the discussion, Goebbels finally obtained permission to organize women's battalions in Berlin.[96] Hitler also approved his plan of gathering dispersed soldiers and forming them into new regiments. Goebbels, who was more and more enjoying the role of organizing the people's militia, did not confine himself to planning behind a desk. In a leather trenchcoat and a German officer's cap without insignia of rank, he often inspected the fortifications being built to defend the city or visited units of the

Volkssturm. At the Oder front, where he hobbled past the military positions, he impressed upon the commanders of the odds and ends of troops that they should give their utmost "for Führer and fatherland."[97]

On 8 March Goebbels went to Lower Silesia, where a limited German counteroffensive had recovered the towns of Lauban and Striegau. He was delighted with the commander on the Silesian front, Gen. Ferdinand Schörner, who struck him as a real "fighter," not an armchair general. What particularly impressed Goebbels was the general's treatment of "cowards" in his ranks, which had earned him the nickname "bloodhound." "He handles such characters fairly brutally, has them strung up from the nearest tree," Goebbels wrote approvingly.[98]

In the marketplace of the destroyed town of Lauban, Goebbels addressed the assembled units of paratroopers and child soldiers. He again invoked the image of Frederick the Great, "whose persistence and unbroken heart on this very historic soil saved Prussia, and thereby the future Reich. Like Frederick, the Führer with unbroken heart will lead our generation to victory, if the people in faith and loyalty place themselves at his disposal, as the people once did with the great king of Prussia."[99] Survivors reported after the war that his words, at once realistic and emotionally charged, had made an impression on them.[100] In this and other speeches Goebbels went to great lengths to evoke images of the bestiality and cruelty of the Bolshevist soldiers, who slaughtered babies and raped wives and mothers.[101]

Breslau, encircled since mid-February, along with Königsberg, which was likewise cut off, became in Goebbels's propaganda a "bulwark in the struggle against bolshevism." On 3 March he had the Reich radio broadcast a speech from Breslau by Gauleiter Hanke, and remarked in his diary that if all Gauleiters were like Hanke, Germany would be in much better shape.[102] He was thinking of the Gauleiter of East Prussia, Erich Koch, who had abandoned Königsberg, putting Kreisleiter Wagner in charge of the fortress. Together with Gen. Otto Lasch, the commandant of Königsberg, Wagner not only defended East Prussia's encircled metropolis but also opened an important passage to the port of Pillau. In all the papers Goebbels had a radio message from Wagner to Hanke published whose style bore all the earmarks of Goebbels: "Revenge our virtue, hatred our duty! . . . Brave and true, proud and defiant, we shall turn our fortresses into mass graves for the Soviet hordes. . . . We know, as you do, that the darkest hour is just before the dawn. Think of that when in the midst of battle blood runs into your eyes and darkness falls around you. Come what may, victory is ours. Death to the Bolshevists! Long live the Führer!"[103]

In the face of such emotionally displayed heroism, Goebbels found it "all the more shameful and humiliating" that his hometown of Rheydt capitulated without a struggle to the Americans. He could hardly stand the thought of a white flag over his parents' house, and found it unbearable that the occupying force planned to establish "a so-called free German newspaper" there, as an insult to him. "But the triumph they're staging seems rather premature to me. I'll find ways and means to restore order in Rheydt at least," he threatened. He planned to send commandos to liquidate Mayor Vogelsang, a "perfect National Socialist philistine" who had placed himself at the disposal of the Americans. The assassination would be carried out by "Berlin party members . . . already trained in such acts." Every detail of their equipment, from false passports to K rations, from submachine guns to radios, was thoroughly discussed, for Goebbels wanted to leave nothing to chance.[104] But in the end that assassination did not take place.

Goebbels was even more affected by the destruction of his ministry by a bomb on the evening of 13 March, twelve years to the day since President Hindenburg had administered the oath of office to him. Quite at a loss, he stumbled through the ruins, while staff members who had hurried to the spot tried to save what they could. Hitler was worried about his minister, and summoned him to the bunker under the Chancellery. There Goebbels described the extent of the destruction, blaming the increasingly savage attacks by British Mosquito aircraft that came every night. Goebbels did not miss the opportunity to inveigh against Goering and demand action.[105]

But Hitler did not take up the point. Instead he spoke of divisions that by now existed only on paper; with them he intended to stabilize the eastern front and throw the Americans in the west back over the Rhine. He spoke of U-boat warfare, which he meant to intensify, and placed his hopes on the deployment of the new jet fighters. A trembling, decrepit man, plainly very ill, he still managed to cast his spell over his most faithful follower, so that before Goebbels's eyes shimmered visions of an unending Third Reich. Goebbels resolved that after the war he would "not only build a new, monumental ministry—as the Führer suggests—but also have this old ministry restored to its former glory."[106]

On the one hand Goebbels still managed to intoxicate himself with such visions, but on the other hand reality now always caught up with him sooner or later. Then he would picture his own end, in self-tormenting sarcasm. He spoke of taking poison at the last moment or blowing himself up. In his imagination he saw himself dying on the barricades with a swastika banner in his hand.[107] He avoided speaking of the end with his wife, for the subject drove her to despair. So Magda talked of her misery with his associates, who had been working in the official residence since the destruction of the ministry. To Semler she said that she was afraid of death but had come to terms with facing it for herself. She still could not bear the thought of taking her children's lives. She agonized constantly over how she would manage when the moment came. She could not speak to her husband about it. He would never forgive her if she did anything to weaken his resistance. As long as he could still fight, he said, all was not lost.[108]

Her sister-in-law Maria Kimmich and others who were close to her tried to dissuade her from killing herself and the children in the hour of doom. Even Naumann, who alone remained amazingly "calm," "fresh," and "relaxed" through the last days, and whose fanatical belief helped Goebbels through moments of despair, looked for some way out for Magda and the children.[109] He went to the trouble of having one of the large Havel barges moored near the Goebbels's island estate and equipped with food supplies. He suggested that in the chaos of the collapse Magda and the children should hide in the boat and surrender to the occupying forces when things quieted down.[110] But Magda Goebbels's decision to stay at her husband's side to the end was irrevocable.

Meanwhile Foreign Minister von Ribbentrop was still trying to avert this end. On 4 March Goebbels learned from Ambassador Walther Hewel that Ribbentrop was "throwing out a line to the Western allies." Goebbels saw this as not only a step in the wrong direction but also hopeless "so long as we have no military successes to point to."[111] After Ribbentrop's soundings in Stockholm had failed, Goebbels heaped scorn on him. Without acknowledging that his Führer had authorized Ribbentrop to take this step, Goebbels noted that "one could have predicted with a fair degree of certainty that it would end this way."[112]

While Hitler now set about staging his own end and simultaneously that of his Reich, Goebbels saw in his actions merely further totalization of the war. On 19 March Hitler ordered the destruction of "all installations for military traffic, communications, industrial and food production, as well as objects of value within the Reich territory that the enemy could make use of for continuing the fight, either immediately or in the foreseeable future."[113] When Speer, who had begun to turn away from Hitler, managed with all sorts of arguments to water down and finally completely invalidate this "Nero Order," Goebbels was pleased, for he had not entirely ceased to believe in a turning point when all these things would be needed again.

At the end of March Goebbels was working on plans to launch partisan activity in the occupied territories through the so-called Werewolf operation started by the SS.[114] He planned to establish a newspaper and construct a powerful radio transmitter, both of which would bear the name of this organization and employ decidedly revolutionary language. But the "werewolves," which Goebbels elevated to mythic status, did not get beyond a few terrorist acts like shooting the mayor of Aachen who had been installed by the Americans. The accompanying radio propaganda did have some effect; among the Western Allies it initially created fears that the Germans would mount a tough underground resistance.

Goebbels continued to try to depose his enemies. On 25 March he achieved a small triumph against Goering. After Goebbels sent Hitler a letter in which he argued that the Luftwaffe's entire organization should be simplified, Hitler granted him the powers to undertake the necessary measures.[115] Six days later Goebbels succeeded in getting Dietrich dismissed as Reich press chief, after years of fruitless intriguing against him. Hitler decided to call his replacement "Press Chief to the Führer," which meant the abolition of the previous position.[116] Goebbels's attempts to get Ribbentrop removed proved in vain. Goebbels offered to put out feelers to an "important man" from the Kremlin who was in Stockholm. But Hitler, reacting to news of the collapsing fronts with prolonged outbursts of rage, wanted nothing that could be interpreted as a sign of weakness. And once more Goebbels took refuge in self-deception: Hitler had "always had good instincts in these matters," so one could "completely trust" him.[117]

As if unwilling to see that the end was near, Goebbels threw himself into work. Along with preparations for the defense of Berlin, he devoted himself increasingly to projects for the future. He developed plans for reorganizing the broadcasting system. He drafted a new statute for direction of the press that left no provision for a Reich press chief.[118] He even worked on a new book, to be called *Das Gesetz des Krieges* (The Law of War). General Field Marshal Walter Model sent by telex a seven-hundred-word foreword that Goebbels had requested. When Goebbels finished editing it, it suggested that this book would be read later by entire generations and would "outlast the centuries as if cast in bronze."[119]

At the beginning of April Goebbels experienced "the saddest Easter" of his life. He devoted himself very little to his family during this time. They had been evacuated to Schwanenwerder at the end of March. When not burying himself in work, he studied reports from the enemy, who had begun organizing the United Nations in San Francisco. He lamented the prospect of a third world war between East and West, and talked himself into believing that what was left of Germany could still be saved.

The "troubling news bulletins" were arriving at ever closer intervals.[120] In his bunker Hitler lost sight of the situation and increasingly lost control of himself. He humiliated his troops, fired General Guderian, and when Königsberg fell, sentenced the city commandant to death in absentia. Goebbels still managed to approve of most of these actions.[121]

In Hitler's immediate circle an apocalyptic mood was taking hold, and Goebbels's uplifting examples from history were not very well received.[122]

But Goebbels continued to "struggle." He made a point of missing the farewell concert by the Berlin Philharmonic that Speer, Ley, and Dönitz organized for the afternoon of 12 April.[123] As the finale from Wagner's *Twilight of the Gods* sounded across the rubble of Potsdamer Platz, Goebbels was on his way to the Oder front, where he visited the headquarters of the Ninth Army in Küstrin. He had cigarettes and schnapps distributed, and lectured the officers on the "justice of history" that would spare the Reich from destruction.[124]

Meanwhile Goebbels's associate Semler received a telephone call from the German News Agency: that morning President Roosevelt had died in Warm Springs, Georgia. The news struck all those who had heard it as the miracle Goebbels had been promising.[125] When Goebbels returned after midnight—it was now Friday, 13 April—he, too, was overwhelmed. For the moment he believed the death of the "Jewish" archenemy Roosevelt would bring the end of the coalition between the Western plutocracies and bolshevism.[126]

The world that will come after the Führer and national socialism won't be worth living in (1945)

For a moment, the death of the American president seemed to the deluded Goebbels to offer a way out of the crisis. Hitler made no attempt to curb his most faithful vassal's self-deception. Although he himself was "without great optimism," he chimed in with Goebbels's talk of "divine Providence."[1] Goebbels counted on the enemy coalition's breaking up soon, for he expected Truman to move decisively against Stalin's designs on European territory. Goebbels was convinced that everything depended on beating back the Soviet offensive against Berlin, which might come any day now; that would gain time, during which Providence could do its work.

Goebbels therefore turned to the Germans again, to persuade them to hold out against the "bloodthirsty and vengeful enemy in east and west," for, as he wrote on 15 April in his next-to-last article in *Das Reich*, the Führer knew a way out of the dilemma. "This war will be decided at one second before midnight. But if we give up before that and lay down our weapons, the situation can only work against us."[2] In Hitler's appeal to the "fighters in the east," which Goebbels helped write, the Führer demanded urgently that they do their duty, so that "the last assault of Asia" might shatter, "just as in the end the invasion of our adversaries in the west will fail, in spite of everything." "In the moment in which fate has removed the greatest war criminal of all times from the earth, the turning point of this war will be decided."[3]

Early on the morning of 16 April the battle for Berlin began. After hours of artillery bombardment, the army groups of Soviet marshals Zhukov and Konjev, with two and a half million soldiers, 41,600 artillery pieces, 6,250 tanks, and 7,560 airplanes, left their positions along the Oder-Neisse front for a pincer attack on the capital. Despite the fierce resistance of the Wehrmacht, that same evening the Soviets broke through the defenses north of the fortress of Küstrin.

In Berlin, where the thunder of the approaching artillery announced the imminent end of the war to the three million Berliners holding out in the ruins, the remaining old men, women, and children of the Volkssturm prepared to do battle. On 17 April Goebbels had shipped the most combat-ready units to the front in Berlin city buses.[4] Near the bombed-out Propaganda Ministry members of the Wilhelmplatz Battalion threw up the last barricades. On the grounds of the Reich Chancellery, sections of wall were dismantled so that antitank guns and grenade-launchers could be set up. About eight hundred soldiers from the SS's Adolf Hitler Regiment had taken up their defensive position there.

To turn the Western powers against the Soviet Union at the last moment, Goebbels used his 19 April speech for Hitler's birthday as an occasion to paint in the darkest colors the "flood of bolshevism" that had broken over Europe and to praise Hitler as the defender of the civilized world.[5] In fact, fears did exist in Moscow that the Western powers might make a separate peace with National Socialist Germany or even enter into a military alliance against the Soviet Union. The Kremlin knew of Himmler's contacts with Bernadotte, of SS Obergruppenführer Karl Wolff's negotiations with Allen Dulles, and of Ribbentrop's feelers to the West. When Vienna was captured, the Soviets set up loudspeakers that proclaimed, "The greatest betrayal in world history is being prepared. If you don't want to continue fighting, this time in alliance with the capitalist powers against us, come over to us."[6]

Stalin saw a quick conquest of the Reich capital as critical. As the Soviet armies approached, thousands of forced laborers from the industrial areas took to their heels, trying to escape before the Russians arrived. Meanwhile endless treks of horse-drawn wagons and carts from the east clogged the city thoroughfares. At the suburban railway stations stood railcars full of wounded soldiers whom no one took care of, and those who died in the city from the incessant British and American bombing no longer got buried. The emotional numbing that had set in with the nightly bombing raids had by now become a permanent condition. People thought only of their own survival.[7]

Now the privileged members of the Nazi state began to leave the sinking ship, Berlin. On 20 April Minister of State Otto Meissner informed Goebbels by telephone from Mecklenburg that the presidial chancellery had removed itself to safety in order to keep its freedom of action. Goebbels replied in a rage that he regretted he could no longer do what he had wanted to do for twelve years—spit in Meissner's face.[8] Meanwhile other elements of the ministerial bureaucracy were also evacuated. Ministers like Goering, Ley, Himmler, and Speer waited tactfully until Hitler's birthday had passed, then "with heavy heart" obeyed their "duty" to continue the struggle elsewhere.

Since there had been no signs of a breach in the enemy coalition after Roosevelt's death, the mood during the little birthday celebration in Hitler's bunker was more than subdued. Hitler put on a show of optimism and tried to talk as though nothing were wrong, but in the course of the few hours since the Russians had broken through at the Oder his steadfastness had dwindled dramatically.[9] Upon the urging of the military leadership and his inner circle, he had already decided to withdraw to the Obersalzberg and continue the struggle in the protection of the "Alpine fortress."[10]

Goebbels knew of these plans and propped Hitler up, prompting him once again to play the role of the emissary of "Providence." In his speech for Hitler's birthday the previous evening, Goebbels had damned "international Jewry," which "wants no peace until its satanic goal of destroying the world has been achieved." He had then described Hitler as the savior appointed by God.[11] Heartened by Goebbels's words, Hitler performed for the photographers on the afternoon of 20 April, pinning the Iron Cross on the chest of a few Hitler Youths lined up in the garden of the Chancellery. Then he hurried back down into the bunker. There he issued an order that in case the Reich was split into a southern and a northern theater of war, two command structures should be formed. He also gave orders for an offensive to the north against the Soviets, who were already approaching the city limits. The fawning generals did not have the courage to inform their Führer that the situation was hopeless, so with trembling hand Hitler moved around on the map Wehrmacht divisions that had long since ceased to exist. The Führer declared his intention to offer "the Russian" the "bloodiest defeat in his history before the gates of Berlin."[12]

At the same time Goebbels was writing his last editorial for *Das Reich*. The editorial, entitled "Resistance at Any Cost," never reached the public, for this issue could not be distributed.[13] Once more he challenged the *Volk* comrades to resist. He described visions of "boys and girls" showering the enemy "with grenades and antitank mines, shooting from windows and cellars, heedless of the danger all around them."[14] This escalation of his perverted notion of total war did not remain merely a dream. In fact, girls were hauled out of party boarding schools and sent into the battle zone. On the left arm of their shirts they had embroidered the slogan "Revenge for our Brothers and Husbands." And the SS was supposed to receive reinforcements in the form of Hitler Youths trained in the last weeks of the war and thrown into the fighting on 22 April. Most of them fell shortly afterward along the Havel or in the battle for the Reich Athletics Field.[15]

During his last minister's conference, which he held by candlelight on 21 April behind boarded-up windows in his official residence, Goebbels briefly recapitulated the developments that he thought had brought Germany to this point. This was nothing less than what the German people had wanted, he said, for with the overwhelming vote in favor of withdrawing from the League of Nations, they had chosen the politics of "honor and daring" over the politics of acquiescence. Goebbels revealed his infinite misanthropy when he told his staff in conclusion that he had not forced anyone to work with him and remarked cynically, "Now your little throats are being cut."[16]

The next day Goebbels took steps to make sure his diaries were brought to safety. For some months he had had his personal stenographer Richard Otte make sure they got copied in miniature onto glass plates. On this particular afternoon Otte and Otto Jacobs, who had also taken Goebbels's dictation in the last few weeks, received instructions to pack up the originals so they could be taken to the Führer's bunker.[17]

Around 5:00 P.M. the telephone rang. On the line was the Führer, sounding utterly distraught as he lamented the treachery, baseness, and cowardice of his generals. A situation conference had just taken place in the bunker, in the course of which Hitler had realized that the offensive he had ordered and for whose success he had been waiting all afternoon had not even been launched, for lack of military personnel. He had reacted with a fit of rage, then pulled himself together and announced to those assembled around the map table that they were free to flee. He himself would stay in Berlin and fall on the steps of the Reich Chancellery.[18]

Goebbels hastened to the bunker and once more cheered Hitler up, restoring some hope, which Eva Braun, who had joined Hitler a few days earlier in the bunker, said he had lost.[19] Goebbels spoke with Hitler for a few minutes behind closed doors, then came out of the room, ignored Bormann's urging that he advise Hitler to flee, and informed Hitler's secretary, Edeltraut Junge, that Magda would come over later with the children. On the Führer's orders, they would thenceforth live in the bunker.[20]

Soon two limousines made their way through the rubble to deliver the Goebbels family and their luggage. The family were assigned five little rooms, including one that had been occupied by Hitler's physician Theodor Morell, who, along with Admiral Dönitz's liaison officer, Karl Jesko von Puttkamer, and others had just left the bunker.[21] When Hitler urged Magda Goebbels to fly to Bavaria that night on a plane leaving from nearby Gatow Airport, she refused, saying she saw it as her "duty" to remain at the side of her Führer.

On Goebbels's urging, Hitler pulled himself together and ordered various army units to rally to the defense of Berlin.[22] Meanwhile Goebbels was directing that anyone obstructing the defense of the city should be treated as a traitor and summarily shot or hanged. Hastily patched-together commandos of SS men, party leaders, or Security Service men now launched an orgy of executions that added to chaotic conditions in the city.[23]

When Speer returned to Berlin to say good-bye to Hitler, he found Goebbels raving about the "world-historical significance" of the expected rescue of the city by General Walter Wenck's Twelfth Army. But Frau Goebbels had taken to her bed, "very weak and suffering from heart attacks. . . . I could sense that she was in deep agony over the irrevocably approaching hour when her children must die."[24] The children on the other hand were behaving wonderfully, as their mother wrote to her son Harald Quandt. "Without help, they help themselves in these more than primitive conditions. Whether or not they sleep on the floor, or can wash up, or have anything to eat—never a word of complaint or any crying. Shellbursts shake the bunker. The bigger children comfort the younger ones, and their presence here must be counted a blessing if they can now and then coax a smile from the Führer." In this letter, flown out of Berlin on 28 April by the flying ace Hanna Reitsch, Magda also wrote, "Our splendid idea is being destroyed, and with it everything beautiful, admirable, noble, and good that I have known. The world that will come after the Führer and national socialism won't be worth living in, and that's why I've brought the children here. They're too good for the life that will come after us, and a merciful god will understand me when I give them salvation myself." She added that her "beloved son" should "live for Germany."[25]

On 23 April Hitler had somewhat recovered from the worst of his depression. With the constant encouragement of his propaganda minister, he resolved to "remain steadfast in an impossible situation."[26] When a radiogram arrived from Goering in Berchtesgaden in which the Reich marshal asked whether he might assume the "leadership in the entire Reich" as Hitler's deputy, Hitler flew into a rage.[27] At last Goebbels saw a wedge driven between Hitler and his old adversary, though Hitler gave orders only to have Goering arrested, not liquidated.

Goebbels continued to nourish Hitler's hopes for a breach in the enemy coalition. If Germany could prove in Berlin that it was still capable of acting, that would make the difference.[28] But instead of reports that Wenck's army was pushing successfully toward Berlin from the Elbe, on 28 April depressing news reached the bunker. British radio reported that on 24 April Himmler had met with Count Bernadotte in Lübeck and made an offer of capitulation to the Western powers. To legitimate himself, he had claimed that Hitler was ill or already dead. Again Hitler flew into a rage and issued orders for Himmler's arrest.[29]

As Hanna Reitsch took off from Berlin with a passenger, Robert von Greim, whom Hitler had named Goering's successor in charge of the

Luftwaffe, Soviet troops had reached Charlottenburg and had broken through the inner defense ring at Tempelhof Airport. The battle for the center of Berlin had begun. Only the fierce resistance of SS units made up of both German and foreign soldiers prolonged the agony.

Just a few hundred yards from the fighting, Goebbels found himself confronted with a situation that ran counter to all his notions of Hitler's mythic end. Hitler had asked him to find a justice of the peace, for he intended to marry his longtime companion Eva Braun.

At 1:00 P.M. on 29 April the wedding took place before Walter Wagner, a city councillor and licensed justice of the peace, with Goebbels standing beside Hitler as his witness. After the wedding a festive meal was served to the inhabitants of the bunker.[30] That night Hitler dictated his political last will and testament, naming Joseph Goebbels as his successor as Reich chancellor.[31]

After Hitler had gone to bed, Goebbels, who along with Bormann and two others had witnessed the testament, wrote his own appendix to it. He thanked the Führer for this final demonstration of faith in him, and explained that for the first time in his life he had to disobey an order of Hitler's: he would not leave his side to take control of the military and political situation, but would follow him in death, as would his wife and children.[32] Goebbels finished writing as dawn was breaking, and he and Bormann arranged for copies to be smuggled through the lines to the west, where they wanted the testament and Goebbels's addendum published for posterity.[33]

Late at night on 29 April, Hitler received word from Keitel that Wenck's army could not continue its movement toward Berlin. About 2:30 on the morning of 30 April, Hitler assembled those remaining in his bunker and solemnly took leave of them. But still he hesitated. The next morning, as the Soviets pounded the Chancellery with heavy artillery, Hitler issued an order that the troops defending Berlin should break out after they had exhausted their ammunition and continue the fight from the forests around the city. Then he said his farewells again. Trembling, and wearing a simple uniform with the Iron Cross on the left side of his chest, he appeared arm in arm with his wife. After about ten minutes he withdrew with Eva into his private suite. As the door closed, Magda Goebbels lost her composure. "Dissolved in tears and extremely agitated," she begged the SS men guarding the door to let her speak to Hitler again. Hitler's adjutant knocked, and when Hitler appeared at the door, angrily asking what was wrong, Magda forced her way into his room, where she begged Hitler to leave Berlin. She probably thought she could spare herself and the children the terrible end in the bunker. Hitler's "categorical 'no' put an end to the conversation. . . . After about a minute Magda Goebbels had left the living room and withdrew, weeping."[34]

Goebbels and the others present waited in the situation room. After a few minutes Hitler's adjutant Günsche came in with the words, "The Führer is dead." Goebbels, Bormann, and two others entered the suite with Günsche. Arms raised in the Nazi salute, they viewed the bodies. Goebbels, apparently undone by the sight of his dead Führer, is said to have run back into the situation room exclaiming that he wanted to go out onto Wilhelmplatz and stay there until he was hit. But he remained in the bunker, admitting that he couldn't have done it after all.[35]

After he had regained his composure, he and Bormann went up out of the bunker into the Chancellery garden. There the bodies of Hitler and Eva Braun, wrapped in blankets, had been placed in a half-dug grave a few meters from the emergency exit. Several canisters of gasoline had been poured over them. Goebbels, Bormann, Günsche, Hitler's servant Heinz Linge, his driver Erich Kempka, and Gen. Wilhelm Burgdorf watched as the gasoline was ignited, and saluted their dead Führer with a last "Heil Hitler."[36]

The new Reich chancellor, without a Reich and without any function to fulfill, hobbled through the bunker. Measures he had wanted to take for the defense of Berlin had been superseded by events. No one was interested anymore in his talk of treachery and the necessity of continuing the struggle against international Jewry. Hitler was dead, and with his death the inhabitants of the bunker had ceased to fear that they would be forced to participate in a collective suicide or other measures resulting in their death. A sense of relief spread through the group; according to some reports, there was a bit of carousing. For the new master of the bunker, whose authority was not even sufficient for him to prevent such behavior, his previous announcement that he would die at Hitler's side now became an almost insuperable hurdle. Fear seized him at the thought of his own end. He finally succumbed to this fear; in spite of his sworn promise, he decided to try to get in touch with Stalin, whose troops had already raised the hammer-and-sickle flag atop the ruins of the Reichstag.

The obstacle turned out to be Bormann, who thought the 300 to 500 soldiers garrisoned at the bunker could break through the Soviet lines and make their way to Dönitz, whom Hitler had named Reich president and supreme commander of the Wehrmacht. Only after Maj. Gen. Wilhelm Mohnke, commander of the Adolf Hitler Regiment, had given his situation report, did Bormann yield to Goebbels. Chief of Staff General Krebs offered to serve as an intermediary; he had spent time with the German military mission in Moscow and spoke Russian.

Goebbels, seconded by Bormann, now composed a letter to the "Supreme Commander of the Combat Forces of the Soviet Union." He informed Stalin, "as the first non-German" to hear the news, that Hitler had died by his own hand on 30 April and had handed power over to

Dönitz, Goebbels, and Bormann. Reich Chancellor Goebbels had commissioned Bormann to establish contact with the Soviets to work out a cease-fire, "necessary for peace negotiations between the powers that have suffered the greatest losses."[37]

The incompletely burned corpses of Hitler and his wife, along with his German shepherd Blondi, had not long been buried in a grenade crater —an SS commando had taken care of this—when Krebs arrived at the forward command post of the Soviet Eighth Guards Army near Tempelhof Airport. Krebs carried Goebbels's letter, with a list of the cabinet members and an authorization to serve as a negotiator attached.[38] He handed the letter to General Chuikov, who telephoned his superior, Marshal Zhukov, who in turn got in touch with Stalin. The answer from Moscow reached Berlin around 10:00 A.M. on 1 May. Stalin sent orders that if the Soviet demand for general capitulation or the capitulation of Berlin was not met, the Soviet forces should resume their assault on the government quarter. Krebs had to recognize that, after many hours of discussion with Chuikov and with Zhukov's emissary Sokolovski, his mission had failed. To gain time, he explained at length that he was not authorized to surrender. Shortly after 1:00 P.M. Krebs left the command post to return to the bunker. Around the same time Goebbels's old nemesis, Walter Ulbricht, along with other German Communists who had arrived the previous day from Moscow, was taking an inspection tour through the northeastern part of Berlin.

Back in the bunker Krebs reported to the group, who had been waiting there for hours. Goebbels, extremely agitated, rejected the Soviets' demand for capitulation. He immediately blamed Krebs for the failure of the mission, saying Krebs had not made it clear to Chuikov that if the provisional cease-fire were rejected, the Germans would fight to the last bullet.[39] Goebbels decided to send a second delegation to make this point more forcefully. But this delegation, too, comprised of four officers under the leadership of a colonel, failed, and two of its members were taken into custody.

After these attempts at concluding a separate peace, it no longer made sense to Goebbels to keep Dönitz in the dark about Hitler's death, as Bormann had done in two recent telexes. So he sent him a telex announcing that the Führer was dead and that Bormann would try to make his way to him. Signing that telex and the minutes of the last situation conference were the last official acts of Reich Chancellor Paul Joseph Goebbels.[40]

Goebbels then withdrew to his little study to finish his diary, the record of his life, of a huge self-deception that one might call tragic if he had not contributed so decisively to a catastrophe that engulfed first Germany, then Europe, then the world. It had been Goebbels's fateful achievement to transform Hitler into the "Führer." He had early on "proclaimed" Hitler the "savior," the "new Messiah," first to a small following, then to hundreds of thousands, and finally, with the help of a comprehensive propaganda apparatus, to an entire receptive nation. When the World War corporal had actually to a great extent overcome the dissension within Germany, revised the provisions of Versailles, and given the people new national self-respect, Goebbels's prophecies seemed to have been fulfilled. The myth of the Führer, of the "tool of Providence" had been created.

Without ever having influenced a decision on politics or warfare, Goebbels provided the psychosocial basis for Hitler's unbridled wars of conquest, for his implementation of his visions of a "Greater Germanic Reich" with *Lebensraum* in the east. When Hitler gambled with war and escaped only because of the Western appeasement policy, Goebbels celebrated his deeds as evidence of the "genius" and "mission" of the peace-loving Führer. When Hitler then led the Germans into war, Goebbels again preached his infallibility to the worried nation. And Hitler did seem infallible when he overcame France, the "hereditary enemy" in the west, in one blitzkrieg, whereas in World War I an entire generation had bled to death fighting that enemy in the trenches. The Germans followed this Führer even when he drove the country into a war on two fronts, even when defeats supplanted victories. Goebbels promised that the Führer could turn things around, and people believed him. It was Hitler they followed, only Hitler, mythically elevated, not the functionaries of the state and the party. To them Germans assigned all the blame for the terrible, cruel, vile things that happened along with the war, and that many clearly recognized. People had that formulaic saying that absolved Hitler of all responsibility: "If the Führer only knew!" This sentence epitomizes the power of the myth. It is Joseph Goebbels's historical significance to have been the originator of the myth.

Goebbels's "success" in convincing others that Hitler was a "tool of Providence" stemmed from the fact that he himself never ceased to believe in Hitler. The deeper the crisis into which the Reich plunged, the more Goebbels took refuge in irrational excesses of belief. Total war, as an aggressive conversion of that belief into action, as a fanatical war waged by a "*Volk* community" sworn to follow Hitler, was supposed to snatch victory from the jaws of defeat, to bend reality, as Goebbels's own hate-filled faith in a better future had bent his own reality in 1923. Lest he lose the basis of his own faith, Goebbels to the very end tried to convince Hitler of his greatness and his mission. In his last diary entry, which Naumann claimed to have lost while fleeing the bunker, Goebbels probably returned to his notion of the great struggle against international Jewry. For it was he who had continually pushed Hitler to confirm by deeds his rhetoric against the Jews.

But what happened in the bunker after Goebbels finished his notes around 4:00 P.M. had nothing to do with greatness. Rather it was the last expression of his hate-filled fanaticism. Apparently he hesitated for another moment after the last situation conference, at which Reich Youth Leader Artur Axmann had suggested getting his children out of Berlin. But when he went to Magda with the suggestion, she remained absolutely firm, as she had earlier on 26 April when Goebbels urged that all the women and his children be evacuated.[41] And it was Magda who then saw to the murder of her own children. She had already conferred several times with the SS doctors Ludwig Stumpfegger and Helmut Gustav Kunz of the Reich Chancellery staff about how the children could be killed quickly and painlessly.

Now, on the afternoon of 1 May, she had Kunz sent to her in the bunker. The decision had been made, she told him, and Goebbels thanked him for helping his wife "put the children to sleep." Around 8:40 P.M. Kunz gave the children morphine injections. He left the room with the three sets of bunk beds and waited with Magda Goebbels until the children were asleep. Then she asked him to give them the poison. Kunz refused, however, and was then sent by Magda Goebbels to fetch Stumpfegger. When Kunz came back with him, Magda was already in the children's room. Stumpfegger joined her there, and came back out with her after four or five minutes. In all likelihood she herself had broken the glass cyanide capsules, which she had received from Dr. Morell, in the mouths of Helga, Hilde, Helmut, Holde, Hedda, and Heide.[42]

Filled with fear of death, Goebbels was chain-smoking, his face covered with red blotches. Apparently still hoping for a miracle, he kept asking about the military situation. When time ran short, and the Soviets could be expected to storm the bunker at any moment, he made his adjutant Schwägermann promise to cremate both his and his wife's bodies. Then he took leave of those remaining in the bunker. He was clearly struggling to maintain his composure, which he tried to demonstrate with all sorts of bathetic flourishes. "Tell Dönitz," he is reported to have instructed the chief pilot of Hitler's squadron, "that we understood not only how to live and to fight but also how to die."[43]

The last details regarding the deaths of Joseph and Magda Goebbels will probably always remain unclear. It is certain that they poisoned themselves with cyanide, but it is not known whether Goebbels also shot himself in the head. Nor do we know whether they died in the bunker or outside at the emergency exit, where the Soviets found their bodies. Perhaps they went up the stairs, followed by Schwägermann and Goebbels's driver Günther Rach with canisters of gasoline, to end their lives in the garden.[44]

The next day Russian officers found the charred bodies of Joseph and Magda Goebbels. Their report read as follows: "The corpse of the man was small, the foot of the right leg was half-bent (clubfoot) in a blackened metal prosthesis. On the body lay the remains of a charred party uniform of the NSDAP and a blackened Golden Party Badge. Next to the charred body of the woman a gold cigarette case was found, and on the body the Golden Party Badge of the NSDAP and a blackened gold brooch. At the heads of the two corpses lay two Walther No. 1 pistols."[45]

The Russians had the corpses photographed, identified, and autopsied, and autopsies were also performed on the children. At some point in the summer of 1945 the mortal remains of Joseph Goebbels and his Führer were transported to Moscow.[46]

Notes

The following abbreviations are used:

BAK	Bundesarchiv Koblenz
BDC	Berlin Document Center
GC	Genoud Collection, Lausanne
GSALB	Generalstaatsanwaltschaft bei dem Landgericht Berlin/Berlin-Moabit
GSPK	Geheimes Staatsarchiv Preussischer Kulturbesitz, Berlin
Hoover	Hoover Institution, Stanford University, Calif.
IfZ	Institut für Zeitgeschichte, Munich
IMT	International Military Tribunal, German edition
JL	Jagiellonian Library, Cracow
LAB	Landesarchiv Berlin
RC	Reuth Collection
SAM	Stadtarchiv Mönchengladbach
UW	Institut für Hochschulkunde, Universität Würzburg
ZSAP	Zentrales Staatsarchiv der DDR, Potsdam

In the notes, sources are cited in abbreviated form. Complete publication data can be found in the bibliography. With some exceptions (chiefly the frequently cited works of Bramsted, Shirer, and Speer), the sources quoted are the German versions, translated by Krishna Winston. Works by Goebbels published in his lifetime are indicated by the year: 1926a, 1926b, etc.; they are listed chronologically in the bibliography. References to the published diaries use entry dates rather than page numbers, so the reader can locate the passages in various translations. "Diaries, IfZ" refers to the volumes published by the Institut für Zeitgeschichte, Munich. In the case of unpublished diaries, the archival location is indicated. For exhaustive documentation, the reader should consult the original German version (*Goebbels*, Munich and Zurich: Piper, 1990).

1. Heiber, *Joseph Goebbels*. See also the chronological listing of biographies in the bibliography.

2. Hochhuth's introduction to Goebbels, *Tagebücher 1945*; Fest, *Das Gesicht des Dritten Reiches*, 119ff.

3. Stephan, *Joseph Goebbels*.

4. Reimann, *Dr. Joseph Goebbels*.

5. Fraenkel and Manvell, *Goebbels*.

6. *Die Tagebücher von Joseph Goebbels*, ed. Elke Fröhlich. For other editions and unpublished fragments, see bibliography.

7. Communication from Frau Brachmann-Teubner to the author, 23 May 1990.

8. Boelke, ed., *Kriegspropaganda*.

9. Bramsted, *Goebbels and National Socialist Propaganda*.

10. Balfour, *Propaganda in War*.

CHAPTER ONE

1. The sources for Goebbels's origins, childhood, and youth are: copies of family birth and death records in SAM; K. Frank Korf's interviews with family members after World War II, in the Korf papers, Hoover; and especially Goebbels's diaries (see bibliography). Goebbels's autobiographical novel "Michael Voormanns Jugendjahre" (BAK) is discussed in chapter 2. See also Fraenkel and Manvell, *Goebbels*, 21ff., and Heiber, *Joseph Goebbels*, 7ff.

2. Diaries, 11 December 1929.

3. Erckens, *Juden in Mönchengladbach* 2:187.

4. Diaries, 8 and 11 December 1929.

5. Goebbels, "Michael" (1919).

6. Diaries, 8 December 1929.

7. Goebbels, "Michael" (1919).

8. Diaries, 5 July 1935.

9. Fritz Göbbels's bank statements, 1900–20, GC.

10. Diaries, IfZ 1:2.

11. Ibid.

12. In contrast to Goebbels's account in "Michael" (1919), his sister Maria reported after the war that her brother had been operated on at the age of seven. See Hunt, "Joseph Goebbels," 62.

13. See Besymenski, *Der Tod des Adolf Hitler*, 333f.

14. Information provided by Frau Hubert Hompesch in a 1987 interview with West German Radio (WDR). A cassette recording is available in SAM.

15. It is revealing of the emotional distress of young Goebbels that in his imagination his grandfather was his dearest relative, although he knew him only from his mother's stories. He was "big, broad, and muscular"— physically the exact opposite of his grandson. See Diaries, IfZ 1:1.

16. Goebbels, "Michael" (1919).

17. Diaries, IfZ 1:2.

18. Ibid., 3.

19. Fraenkel and Manvell, *Goebbels*, 24.

20. Goebbels, "Michael" (1919).

21. Oven, *Finale Furioso*, 281.

22. GC.

23. Oven, *Finale Furioso*, 281.

24. Goebbels, "Michael" (1919).

25. Ibid.

26. Ten of Goebbels's report cards from the years 1912–16 are in BAK, NL 118/113.

27. Oven, *Finale Furioso*, 283.

28. Goebbels, "Michael" (1919): ". . . and Michael became someone entirely different from who he was in reality."

29. Goebbels, "Aus meinem Tagebuch," June 1923, BAK, NL 118/126.

30. Goebbels, "Michael" (1919).

31. "Andenken an die erste hl. Kommunion der Schüler der höheren Lehranstalten," 3 April 1910, SAM, 14/2112.

32. Goebbels, "Gerhardi Bartels Manibus," BAK, NL 118/120.

33. Willy Zilles to Goebbels, 4–5 January 1915, GC.

34. Goebbels, "Michael" (1919).

35. Goebbels, "Der tote Freund," April 1919, GC. In his "Memories" Goebbels gives 1909 as the date of his first poem (diaries, IfZ 1:3).

36. Goebbels, "Der Lenz," 1914, GC.

37. Goebbels, "Michael" (1919).

38. Diaries, IfZ 1:3.

39. Goebbels, "Michael" (1919).

40. Ibid. Cf. diaries, IfZ 1:5.

41. Hitler, *Mein Kampf* (1939), 162.

42. Goebbels, "Wie kann auch der Nichtkämpfer in diesen Tagen dem Vaterland dienen?" BAK, NL 118/117.

43. Goebbels, "Aus halbvergessenen Papieren. Dem Andenken Ernst Heynens gewidmet" (22 February 1924), BAK, NL 118/113.

44. Hubert Offergeld to Goebbels, 16 November 1914, GC.

45. Zilles to Goebbels, 4–5 January 1915, GC.

46. Goebbels to Zilles, 26 July 1915, SAM. He expressed a similar idea in a letter to Ernst Heynen, as can be deduced from Heynen's reply, 12 April 1916, GC.

47. Goebbels wrote rather long essays on both writers; GC.

48. Goebbels to Zilles, 26 July 1915, SAM.

49. Goebbels, "Wilhelm Raabe" (7 March 1916), GC.

50. Goebbels, "Das Lied im Kriege" (6 February 1915). See also "Wie kann auch der Nichtkämpfer in diesen Tagen dem Vaterland dienen?" (27 November 1914). Both are in BAK, NL 118/117.

51. See letter from Hubert Hompesch to Goebbels, 6 August 1915, GC.

52. Zilles to Goebbels, 29 July 1915, GC.

53. Fritz Goebbels to Joseph Goebbels, 9 November 1919, BAK, NL 118/112.

54. Voss to Goebbels, 7 December 1915, GC.

55. Hompesch to Goebbels, 15 July 1916, GC.

56. Goebbels, "In utraque fortuna utriusque memor" (30 April 1916), BC.

57. Hompesch to Goebbels, 15 October 1916, GC.

58. Lene Krage to Goebbels, 8 December 1916, BAK, NL 118/112.

59. Goebbels, "Michael" (1919).

60. Lene Krage to Goebbels, 22 August 1916, BAK, NL 118/112.

61. Goebbels, "Michael" (1919).

62. Goebbels, valedictory address, BAK, NL 118/126.

63. Diaries, 25 April 1933; *Rheydter Zeitung*, 25 April 1933.

64. Draft of a letter from Goebbels to Voss, end of 1915, GC.

65. *Rheydter Zeitung*, 25 April 1933. The quotation is from a poem by Joseph von Eichendorff, "Frühlingsgruss."

CHAPTER TWO

1. On Goebbels's student days, see diaries, IfZ 1:5–22.

2. Goebbels, "Bin ein fahrender Schüler, ein wüster Gesell" (summer 1917), BAK, NL 118/117.

3. Goebbels, "Wilhelm Raabe," GC. This is apparently a reworked version of his 1916 school essay. See also diaries, IfZ 1:5; *Unitas* 57 (1916–17): 279; and Schrader, "Joseph Goebbels als Raabe-Redner," 112ff.

4. Klassen, "Treue um Treue" in *Sigfridia sei's Panier*, 19.

5. Fraenkel and Manvell, *Goebbels*, 34.

6. *Unitas* 57 (1916–17): 279; Goebbels to an unidentified professor, 14 September 1917; Fraenkel and Manvell, *Goebbels*, 32.

7. Goebbels, "Die die Sonne lieben" (summer 1917), BAK, NL 118/117.

8. Goebbels, "Bin ein fahrender Schüler, ein wüster Gesell" (summer 1917), BAK, NL 118/117.

9. Diaries, IfZ 1:5.

10. Goebbels to the diocesan committee of the Albertus Magnus Association, 5 and 15 September 1917, BAK, NL 118/113.

11. Comment by Father Mollen on Goebbels's letter to the Albertus Magnus Association, in Fraenkel and Manvell, *Goebbels*, 32f.

12. See the pertinent documents in BAK, NL 118/113.

13. *Unitas* 58 (1917–18): 68 and 119f.

14. Hasenberg, *125 Jahre Unitas-Verband*, 91.

15. Agnes Kölsch's mother to Goebbels, 16 November 1917, BAK, NL 118/111.

16. *Unitas* 58 (1917–18): 153.

17. Diaries, IfZ 1:6.

18. *Unitas* 58 (1917–18): 182, 215.

19. Goebbels, "Michael Voormann" (1923), GC. Goebbels gives a detailed description of the budding romance with Anke Stalherm in "Michael" (1919), part 3, BAK, NL 118/115.

20. Diaries, IfZ 1:8.

21. Agnes Kölsch to Goebbels, 15 August 1918, BAK, NL 118/112.

22. Goebbels to Anka Stalherm, 31 July 1918, BAK, NL 118/109.

23. Oven, *Finale Furioso*, 287.

24. Goebbels, "Judas Iscariot" (1918), BAK, NL 118/127. See also the correspondence between Goebbels and Anka Stalherm from this period, BAK, NL 118/109 and NL 118/127.

25. Goebbels to Stalherm, 21 August 1918, BAK, NL 118/127.

26. Goebbels, "Judas Iscariot" (1918), BAK, NL 118/127, 55 and 99.

27. Goebbels to Stalherm, 26 and 30 August 1918, BAK, NL 118/109; 11 August 1918, BAK, NL 118/127.

28. Diaries, IfZ 1:10.

29. Goebbels to Fritz Prang, 13 November 1918, in Fraenkel and Manvell, *Goebbels*, 38.

30. "Kollegienbuch des Studierenden der Germanistik, Herrn Joseph Goebbels aus Rheydt," Julius-Maximilians-Universität Würzburg, BAK, NL 118/113.

31. Goebbels to Stalherm, 29 January 1919, BAK, NL 118/109.

32. Fritz Prang to Goebbels, November 1918, BAK, NL 118/113.

33. Fritz Goebbels to Joseph Goebbels, 3 October and 14 November 1918, BAK, NL 118/113; 21 December 1918, NL 118/112; 3 January 1919, and 31 December 1918, NL 118/113.

34. Goebbels to Stalherm, 25, 26, and 30 January 1919, BAK, NL 118/109.

35. Diaries, IfZ 1:10.

36. Goebbels to Stalherm, 26, 27, and 29 January 1919, BAK, NL 118/109.

37. Diaries, IfZ 1:15.

38. Goebbels to Stalherm, 27 January 1919, BAK, NL 118/109.

39. Goebbels to Stalherm, 16 February 1919, BAK, NL 118/126.

40. Goebbels to Stalherm, 20 and 26 February 1919, BAK, NL 118/126; 24 February 1919, NL 118/109.

41. Goebbels, "Heinrich Kämpfert" (1919), BAK, NL 118/114, 39 and 56.

42. *Unitas* 59 (1918–19), "Nachtrag vom WS 18/19: Herr Goebbels ausgetreten."

43. He gave her a little story he had written, "Die Weihnachtsglocken des Eremiten," BAK, NL 118/126.

44. Diaries, IfZ 1:11.

45. Goebbels to Stalherm, 16 March 1919, BAK, NL 118/109.

46. Olgi Esenwein to Goebbels, 21 February (possibly June) 1924, BAK, NL 118/112.

47. Diaries, IfZ 1:13.

48. Fyodor Dostoyevski, *The Possessed*, trans. Constance Garnett (New York, 1936). See also Bärsch, *Erlösung und Vernichtung*.

49. The Genoud Collection contains a large number of poems, among them a collection dedicated to Anka Stalherm.

50. Contract between Goebbels and Xenien-Verlag, Leipzig, 18 June 1918, BAK, NL 118/113.

51. Goebbels to Stalherm, 20 August 1919, BAK, NL 118/109.

52. Diaries, IfZ 1:13.

53. Ibid., 14.

54. Goebbels, "Michael" (1919), parts 1 and 3.

55. Diaries, IfZ 1:17. Arco-Valley was released from custody in 1924 and in the Third Reich became the director of Lufthansa.

56. Undated notification to Goebbels from the Munich city council, GC.

57. Goebbels describes this Christmas Eve in an article published 7 March 1922 in the *Westdeutsche Landeszeitung*, "Sursum corda!"

58. Goebbels to Stalherm, 6 September 1919, BAK, NL 118/126.

59. Diaries, IfZ 1:16.

60. Fritz Goebbels to Joseph Goebbels, 9 November 1919, BAK, NL 118/112.

61. Goebbels, "Kampf der Arbeiterklasse," GC.

62. Goebbels to Stalherm, 29 and 31 January, and 6 February 1920, BAK, NL 118/109.

63. Goebbels to Stalherm, 4 March 1920, BAK, NL 118/110.

64. See Goebbels's draft of a letter to Voss, end of 1915, GC.

65. Goebbels to Stalherm, 4 March 1920, BAK, NL 118/110.

66. Goebbels to Stalherm, 13 March 1920, BAK, NL 118/110.

67. Diaries, IfZ 1:17f.

68. Goebbels, "Die Saat" (1920), BAK, NL 118/117.

69. Diaries, IfZ 1:17f.

70. Goebbels to Stalherm, 14 April 1920, BAK, NL 118/126.

71. Goebbels to Stalherm, 15 May, 6 June, 13 and 18 June, and 4 July 1920, BAK, NL 118/110.

72. Goebbels to Stalherm, 29 June 1920, BAK, NL 118/126.

73. Diaries, IfZ 1:19.

74. Goebbels to Stalherm, n.d., BAK, NL 118/118.

75. Goebbels's testament, dated 1 October 1920. There are two slightly different versions, BAK, NL 118/118.

76. Goebbels to Stalherm, 27 November 1920, BAK, NL 118/126.

77. Flisges to Goebbels, 31 October 1920, BAK, NL 118/112. See also his letters to Goebbels, 3 and 9 November 1920, BAK, NL 118/112.

78. Stalherm to Goebbels, 24 November 1920, BAK, NL 118/126.

79. Goebbels to Stalherm, 27 November 1920, BAK, NL 118/126.

80. Diaries, 30 May, 14 and 16 December 1928, and 1 April 1929.

81. Diaries, IfZ 1:21.

82. Fritz Goebbels to Joseph Goebbels, 5 December 1920, BAK, NL 118/113.

83. Diaries, IfZ 1:16.

84. Goebbels to Stalherm, 6 June 1920, BAK, NL 118/110.

85. Goebbels, "Wilhelm von Schütz als Dramatiker." See Neuhaus, "Der Germanist Dr. Goebbels," 398ff.

86. Dostoyevski, *The Possessed*, 253.

87. Goebbels, "Wilhelm von Schütz als Dramatiker," 8f.

88. Diaries, IfZ 1:21.

89. Communication from Wilhelm Kamerbeek, 21 October 1987.

90. Doctoral diploma of Joseph Goebbels, 21 April 1922, BAK, NL 118/128. The original is in GC.

91. Diaries, IfZ 1:22.

92. Ibid.

CHAPTER THREE

1. Flisges to Goebbels, 12 December 1921, BAK, NL 118/112.

2. Diaries, IfZ 1:23.

3. *Westdeutsche Landeszeitung*, 24 January 1922.

4. Goebbels, "Aus meinem Tagebuch" (June 1923), BAK, NL 118/126.

5. *Westdeutsche Landeszeitung*, 6 February 1922.

6. Ibid., 8 February 1922.

7. Müller to Goebbels, 16 October 1922, BAK, NL 118/113.

8. Diaries, IfZ 1:24.

9. Advertisement in the *Westdeutsche Landeszeitung*, 25 October 1922.

10. Goebbels, "Ausschnitte aus der deutschen Literatur der Gegenwart," GC.

11. Else Janke to Goebbels, 6 September 1922, BAK, NL 118/110.

12. Fraenkel and Manvell, *Goebbels*, 68.

13. Janke to Goebbels, 5 October 1922, BAK, NL 118/110.

14. Janke to Goebbels, 22 December 1922, BAK, NL 118/110.

15. Goebbels to Janke, Christmas 1922, in Fraenkel and Manvell, *Goebbels*, 66f.

16. Maria Goebbels to Joseph Goebbels, 16 February 1923, BAK, NL 118/113.

17. Janke to Goebbels, 11 February and 31 January 1923, BAK, NL 118/110.

18. Goebbels, "Aus meinem Tagebuch" (1923), BAK, NL 118/126.

19. Ibid.

20. Ibid.

21. Janke to Goebbels, 25 April 1923, BAK, NL 118/110.

22. Goebbels, "Aus meinem Tagebuch" (1923), BAK, NL 118/126.

23. Goebbels to Janke, 5 June 1923, in Fraenkel and Manvell, *Goebbels*, 68ff.

24. Diaries, IfZ 1:26.

25. Goebbels, "Aus meinem Tagebuch" (1923), BAK, NL 118/126.

26. Diaries, IfZ 1:27.

27. Janke to Goebbels, 11 February 1923, BAK, NL 118/110.

28. Diaries, IfZ 1:27.

29. Goebbels, "Michael Voormann" (1923), GC. This collection also contains a typewritten version and a photocopy of the manuscript (also in BAK, NL 118/127). See Singer, "Michael oder der leere Glaube"; Hunt, "Joseph Goebbels: A Study of the Formation of his National-Socialist Consciousness," 94ff; and Bärsch, *Erlösung und Vernichtung*.

30. Goebbels, "Michael Voormann" (1923), "Präludium."

31. Ibid., entry for 14 June.

32. Ibid.

33. Ibid., entry for 1 June.

34. Ibid., entry for 15 November.

35. Ibid., entry for 15 May.

36. Goebbels, "Die Führerfrage," in Goebbels 1926c.

37. Goebbels, "Schöpferische Kräfte: Richard Flisges, dem toten Freunde," *Rheydter Zeitung*, 22 December 1923, BAK, NL 118/113.

38. Olgi Esenwein to Goebbels, 3 January and 21 April 1924, BAK, NL 118/112.

39. Goebbels, *Michael* (1929).

40. Ibid., 108.

41. Ibid., 57.

42. *Die Weltbühne*, 27 January 1931.

43. Goebbels to Janke, 22 September 1923, BAK, NL 118/110.

44. Hans Goebbels to Joseph Goebbels, 18 September 1923, BAK, NL 118/110.

45. Fritz Goebbels to Joseph Goebbels, 23 September 1923, BAK, NL 118/113.

46. Fritz Goebbels to Joseph Goebbels, 27 September 1923, BAK, NL 118/113.

47. Diaries, IfZ 1:28.

48. Communication from Erich Willmes, 6 July 1988.

49. Fraenkel and Manvell, *Goebbels*, 70.

50. Job application to the Rudolf Mosse Publishing Co., n.d., BAK, NL 118/113.

51. Goebbels, "Aus meinem Tagebuch" (1923), BAK, NL 118/126.

52. Diaries, 28 July 1924.

53. Diaries, 17 July 1924.

54. Goebbels, "Aus meinem Tagebuch" (1923), BAK, NL 118/126.

55. Diaries, IfZ 1:26: "The Jews. I am giving thought to the money problem."

56. Fraenkel and Manvell, *Goebbels*, 65; diaries, IfZ 1:23.

57. Goebbels to Stalherm, 17 February 1919, BAK, NL 118/126.

58. Open letter to Propaganda Minister Goebbels from Dr. Josef Joseph, who had emigrated to the United States. Reprinted in Erckens, *Juden* 2:189f.

59. Diaries, IfZ 1:25.

60. Goebbels, "Ausschnitte aus der deutschen Literatur der Gegenwart," GC.

61. From this point on, references to the Jews become increasingly frequent. Diaries, IfZ 1:26f.

62. Janke to Goebbels, 4 November 1923, GC.

63. Diaries, IfZ 1:27; Chamberlain, *Die Grundlagen des neunzehnten Jahrhunderts.*

64. Gobineau, Joseph Arthur de, *Die Ungleichheit der Menschenrassen*, 4 vols., 1835–55.

65. Diaries, 8 May 1926.

66. In *Michael* (1929), 82, Goebbels wrote: "Christ was the first adversary of the Jews with real stature. 'Thou shalt eat all peoples!' He declared war on that. For that reason the Jews had to get rid of him. He was shaking the foundations of their future world hegemony."

67. Goebbels in *Völkische Freiheit*, 15 November 1924.

68. Goebbels 1926b, 21.

69. Goebbels, "Ausschnitte aus der deutschen Literatur der Gegenwart," GC.

70. Diaries, 4 July 1924.

71. Goebbels 1926b, 31.

CHAPTER FOUR

1. Goebbels, "Aus meinem Tagebuch," BAK, NL 118/126.

2. Goebbels, "Die Führerfrage," in Goebbels 1926c, 7.

3. Diaries, 30 June 1924.

4. Klein, "Mekka des deutschen Sozialismus" (1987), 117.

5. W. von Ameln, "Die Stadt Rheydt und die Nationalsozialistische Deutsche Arbeiterpartei," *Einwohnerbuch der Stadt Rheydt, 1936*, SAM.

6. Diaries, 30 June 1924.

7. Ibid.

8. Ibid.

9. Diaries, 15 August 1924.

10. On the meeting in Weimar, see diaries, 19 and 20 August 1924.

11. *Berliner Tageblatt*, 13 September 1930.

12. Goebbels, "Die Katastrophe des Liberalismus," *Völkische Freiheit*, 11 October 1924, Staatsarchiv Wuppertal.

13. Diaries, 22 August 1924.

14. Ameln, "Die Stadt Rheydt," SAM.

15. Diaries, 22 August 1924.

16. Fraenkel and Manvell, *Goebbels*, 71f.

17. Diaries, 27 September 1924.

18. Diaries, 3 October 1924.

19. Diaries, 27 September 1924.

20. *Völkische Freiheit*, 11 October, 1 November, 4 and 18 October 1924.

21. Ibid., 20 September 1924.

22. Ibid.

23. Ibid., 15 November 1924.

24. Ibid., 4 October 1924.

25. Ibid., 20 December 1924.

26. Hermann Fobke to Dr. Adalbert Volck, 21 September 1924, in Jochmann, *Nationalsozialismus und Revolution*, 154f.

27. *Völkische Freiheit*, 10 January 1925, Stadtarchiv Wuppertal.

28. Hitler, *Mein Kampf* (1943), 363.

29. Diaries, 15 September 1924.

30. Karl Kaufmann to Otto Strasser, 4 June 1927, BDC.

31. Heiber, *Joseph Goebbels*, 46.

32. Kaufmann to Strasser, 4 June 1927, BDC.

33. Police report, n.d., Hauptstadtarchiv Düsseldorf, Wuppertal police commissioner's file.

34. Diaries, 8 June 1925.

35. Diaries, 23 October 1925.

36. *Völkische Freiheit*, 15 November and 20 December 1924, and 10 January 1925, Stadtarchiv Wuppertal.

37. "15 Entwürfe für Schriftplakate oder Flugblätter zur Ankündigung von Vorträgen der NSDAP," issued by the office of the *Nationalsozialistische Briefe*, with an introduction by Joseph Goebbels (Elberfeld, n.d.).

38. Diaries, 26 and 28 March 1925.

39. Diaries, 16 April 1925.

40. Diaries, 28 May 1925.

41. Diaries, 22 April 1925.

42. Diaries, 18 April 1925.

43. Diaries, 27 May 1925.

44. *Völkischer Beobachter*, 8 July 1925.

45. Karl Kaufmann told Fraenkel and Manvell that the first meeting between Goebbels and Hitler took place in the fall of 1925 in Elberfeld (Fraenkel and Manvell, *Goebbels*, 95). He must have been mistaken, for in Goebbels's diaries of the time no meeting is mentioned. According to the entry for 6 November 1925, Goebbels met Hitler in Braunschweig, and from the context it is clear that this was not the first encounter. There is a gap in the diaries between 10 June and 12 August 1925; the meeting must have occurred during that time. In no source is there any mention of Hitler's having been in Elberfeld in the summer of 1925; it seems likely that they

met at the Gauleiters' conference in Weimar on 12 June 1925. Jotted in the Goebbels diary that ends in July 1925 is the entry: "25 July Hitler Weimar . . . 25 November Hitler Braunschweig."

46. Hinrich Lohse, "Der Fall Strasser," n.d., IfZ, ZS 265.

47. Diaries, 21 August 1925.

48. Diaries, 12 October 1925.

49. Diaries, 26 March 1925.

50. Klein, "Mekka des deutschen Sozialismus," 119f.

51. Bouhler to Rust, 20 April 1925, BAK, Schumacher Collection, 202/I.

52. Diaries, 18 May 1925.

53. Diaries, 12 August 1925.

54. Diaries, 4 April and 19 August 1925.

55. Klein, "Mekka des deutschen Sozialismus," 120.

56. Otto Strasser, *Mein Kampf*, 24.

57. Diaries, 21 August 1925.

58. Enclosure in a letter from Gregor Strasser to Karl Kern, 18 June 1927, BDC.

59. H. Fobke, "Aus der nationalsozialistischen Bewegung," 11 September 1925, in Jochmann, *Dokumente*, 208.

60. Ibid., 209.

61. Diaries, 11 September 1925.

62. Diaries, 28 September 1925.

63. Hitler, *Mein Kampf* (1943), 65.

64. Ibid., 107.

65. Ibid., 140.

66. *Nationalsozialistische Briefe*, 15 October 1925. See also Schüddekopf, *Nationalsozialismus in Deutschland*, 176ff.

67. Diaries, IfZ 1:27.

68. Diaries, 14 October 1925.

69. Diaries, 6 November 1925.

70. Diaries, 23 November 1925.

71. Goebbels, "Die Führerfrage," in Goebbels 1926c, 8.

72. Diaries, 23 November 1925.

73. Goebbels and Gregor Strasser, "Statuten der Arbeitsgemeinschaft der nord- und westdeutschen Gaue der NSDAP," in Jochmann, *Dokumente*, 213.

74. Diaries, 18 December 1925.

75. Goebbels, "Das kleine ABC des Nationalsozialisten," draft, BDC. See also diaries, 26 October 1925.

76. Diaries, 6 January 1926.

77. Goebbels to Gregor Strasser, 11 January 1926, BAK, NS 1-341 II-184: "It is outrageous how your draft of the program has been treated by some Gauleiters."

78. Diaries, 18 December 1925. On this important example of antidemocratic thinking in the Weimar Republic, see *Kindlers Literatur-Lexikon* (1974) 7:2874f.

79. Goebbels, "Nationalismus und Bolschewismus," *Nationalsozialistische Briefe*, 15 October 1925.

80. Diaries, 25 January 1926.

81. Ibid.

82. Ulrich Wörtz, "Programmatik und Führerprinzip," 85.

83. Otto Strasser, *Mein Kampf*, 27.

84. Diaries, 6 February and 20 January 1926.

85. Bouhler to Viereck, 9 February 1926, BAK, Schumacher Collection, 204.

86. Diaries, 11 February 1926.

87. Diaries, 12 and 15 February 1926.

88. Otto Strasser to Goebbels, 26 January 1926, in Jochmann, *Dokumente*, 222.

89. *Völkischer Beobachter*, 25 February 1926.

90. Diaries, 15 February 1926.

91. Gottfried Feder to Hitler or Heinemann, 2 or 3 May 1926, in Tyrell, *Führer befiehl*, 127.

92. Diaries, 15 February 1926.

93. *Nationalsozialistische Briefe*, 1 March 1926.

94. Diaries, 13 March 1926.

95. Diaries, 22 February 1926.

96. Feder to Hitler or Heinemann, 2 or 3 May 1926, in Tyrell, *Führer befiehl*, 125.

97. Ibid., 125f.

98. Diaries, 13 April 1926.

99. Diaries, 16 and 19 April 1926.

100. Goebbels 1926b.

101. Goebbels, "Der Generalstab," in Goebbels 1927b, 9f.

102. Feder to Hitler or Heinemann, 2 or 3 May 1926, in Tyrell, *Führer befiehl*, 124f.

103. Diaries, 8 and 10 May 1926.

104. Diaries, 16, 17, 19, and 21 June, and 6 July 1926.

105. Goebbels, "Die Revolution als Ding an sich," *Nationalsozialistische Briefe*, 15 November 1926, reprinted in Goebbels 1927b.

106. Diaries, 24 July 1926.

107. Diaries, 10 June 1926.

108. Tyrell, "Führergedanke und Gauleiterwechsel," 352.

109. Diaries, 6 July 1926.

110. Diaries, 27 August 1926.

111. Diaries, 17 September 1926.

112. Kurt Daluege in the anniversary edition of *Der Angriff* (1936), BAK, NS 26/968; diaries, 16 October 1926.

113. Erich Schmiedicke to Goebbels, 16 October 1926, in Heiber, *Das Tagebuch von Joseph Goebbels*, 112f.

114. Else Janke to Goebbels, 9 April 1924, GC.

115. Diaries, 17 August 1926.

116. Diaries, 8 June 1925.

117. Diaries, 12 October 1925.

118. Diaries, 12 February 1925.

119. Diaries, 12 June 1926.

120. Reinhold Muchow, report no. 6, in the appendix to Broszat, "Die Anfänge der Berliner NSDAP," 104.

121. Diaries, 16 June 1926.

122. Diaries, 30 October 1926.

123. Diaries, 18 October 1926.

CHAPTER FIVE

1. At this time the titles "Gauleiter" and "Ortsgruppenleiter" had not yet become established. Not until January 1930 did the Reich organization leader issue a directive stipulating that all party functionaries should thenceforth be called "Leiter," to distinguish them from the SA leaders, who were called "Führer." Until then the terms "Gauführer" and "Ortsgruppenführer" were generally used. See Tyrell, "Führergedanke," 351.

2. Brochure produced by Otto Elsner Graphics Agency for the 1929 World Advertising Congress in Berlin, in *Berlin, Berlin*, catalogue of the 1987 exhibition on the history of the city, 459.

3. Erbe, "Spandau im Zeitalter der Weltkriege," 292ff.

4. Reinhold Muchow, reports no. 5 and 6 in Broszat, "Die Anfänge der Berliner NSDAP," 101ff.

5. Summary of the charges made against Gregor Strasser at the functionaries' meeting of 10 June 1927 and his reply, BDC.

6. Diaries, IfZ 1:248.

7. Charges against Strasser, 10 June 1927, 6, BDC.

8. Otto Strasser, *Mein Kampf*, 31.

9. Charges against Strasser, 10 June 1927, 6, BDC.

10. Otto Strasser, *Mein Kampf*, 30.

11. Circular no. 1 of the administration of the Berlin-Brandenburg Gau, 9 November 1926, in Heiber, *Das Tagebuch von Joseph Goebbels*, 115f.

12. Goebbels 1934b, 24f.; Muchow, report no. 6, in Broszat, "Anfänge," 104.

13. Goebbels 1934b, 28; Muchow, reports no. 6, 7, and 8, in Broszat, "Anfänge," 104, 106, 108; diaries, 15 and 19 November 1936.

14. Diaries, 2 May 1925.

15. Goebbels 1934b, 27; *Nationalsozialistische Briefe* 31; Muchow, report no. 6, in Broszat, "Anfänge," 104.

16. Goebbels, "Erkenntnis und Propaganda," in Goebbels 1934a, 28ff.

17. Goebbels 1934b, 28.

18. Ibid., 86.

19. Circular no. 1 in Heiber, *Tagebuch*, 116.

20. *Volksblatt* and *Spandauer Nationale Zeitung*, 15 November 1926.

21. Goebbels 1934a, 44f.

22. Goebbels 1934b, 23.

23. *Havelzeitung/Spandauer Nationale Zeitung*, 9 and 14 December 1926.

24. See Oertel, *Horst Wessel*.

25. Horst Wessel, notes on politics, 1929, JL, Ms. Germ. Oct. 761.

26. Ibid.

27. Goebbels 1934b, 24f., 52.

28. Muchow, report no. 7, in Broszat, "Anfänge," 106.

29. Engelbrechten, *Eine braune Armee entsteht*, 48.

30. Muchow, report no. 8, in Broszat, "Anfänge," 108.

31. Otto Strasser, *Mein Kampf*, 31f.

32. Hitler, *Mein Kampf* (1943), 484.

33. Report of the External Service Division IA, Police Commissioner's Office, 21 March 1927, LAB, Rep. 58, Zug. 399, no. 302, vol. 4.

34. Summary of the Gauleiter's activities, Police Division IA, BDC.

35. Report of the External Service Division IA.

36. Testimony of Goebbels on 21 March 1927 in re: II P J 62/27, LAB, Rep. 58, Zug. 399, no. 302, vol. 1.

37. Indictment of Joseph Goebbels by the chief state's attorney, ibid., vol. 6.

38. Testimony of Goebbels on 21 March 1927.

39. Police report on "political brawl and inflammatory speeches," 20 March 1927, LAB, Rep. 58, Zug. 399, no. 302, vol. 1.

40. Testimony of Goebbels on 21 March 1927.

41. Report of Police Division IA, 28 March 1927, in Heiber, *Tagebuch*, 117; anonymous letter, 16 June 1927, BDC.

42. Summary of the Gauleiter's activities, Police Division IA, BDC.

43. Indictment by general state's attorney, 23 November 1927, in re: 1J372/27, LAB, Rep. 58, Zug. 399, no. 27.

44. Testimony of Fritz Stucke, 19 June 1928, report of Police Division IA, 20 June 1927, BDC.

45. *Vossische Zeitung*, 6 May 1926.

46. Ibid.

47. Summary of the Gauleiter's activities, Police Division IA, BDC.

48. *Berliner Arbeiterzeitung*, 23 April 1927.

49. Minutes of functionaries' meeting, 10 June 1927, prepared by Emil Holtz, BDC.

50. Koch to Goebbels, 26 April 1927, BDC.

51. Goebbels to Otto Strasser, 29 December 1925, and Otto Strasser to Goebbels, 30 December 1925, BAK, NS 1/341—1 fol. 56f. and fol. 47–51.

52. Mendelssohn, *Zeitungsstadt Berlin*, 306; Kessemeier, "Der Leitartikler Goebbels," 18f.

53. *Welt am Abend* and *Berliner Tageblatt*, 4 June 1927.

54. Report of the Investigation and Mediation Committee (USCHLA), 19–21 June 1927, BDC.

55. Goebbels to Hitler, 5 June 1927, in Heiber, *Tagebuch*, 121f.

56. Minutes of functionaries' meeting, 10 June 1927, prepared by Emil Holtz, BDC.

57. Holtz to Hitler, 17 June 1927, in Heiber, *Tagebuch*, 135f.

58. Wörtz, "Programmatik und Führerprinzip," 134f.

59. Report of the Munich police's political surveillance unit on the NSDAP's 20 June 1927 discussion evening, BDC.

60. Goebbels had already demanded such a declaration in a letter to Rudolf Hess, 9 June 1927, in Heiber, *Tagebuch*, 124.

61. *Völkischer Beobachter*, 25 June 1927, in Heiber, *Tagebuch*, 138.

62. Investigation and Mediation Committee to Karl Kern, 24 June 1927, BDC.

63. Gregor Strasser to Hess, 15 June 1927, in Heiber, *Tagebuch*, 124.

64. Goebbels 1934b, 188.

65. Rahm, *Der Angriff*, 214. From 1 October on, *Der Angriff* appeared every Thursday and Sunday, and from 1 November on, daily. In 1933 it became

the daily paper of Ley's German Workers' Front. Publication ceased on 24 April 1945.

66. Goebbels 1934b, 209, 202ff. In 1933 Dürr became press chief for the city of Berlin.

67. Moreau, *Nationalsozialismus von links*, 27.

68. Kessemeier, "Der Leitartikler Goebbels," 48. Schweitzer used this pseudonym for his illustrations to Goebbels's *Buch Isidor*.

69. Diaries, 15 September 1929.

70. Goebbels 1934b, 200, 202, 188.

71. Kessemeier, "Der Leitartikler Goebbels," 49.

72. Goebbels 1934b, 200.

73. Goebbels 1934a, 50.

74. Hitler, *Mein Kampf* (1943), 118.

75. *Der Angriff*, 21 January 1929.

76. Ibid., 30 July 1928.

77. Ibid. Goebbels uses the same description in 1934b, 138.

78. Goebbels 1934b, 140.

79. On Weiss, see Liang, *Die Berliner Polizei in der Weimarer Republik*, 61, 75, and 177.

80. *Völkischer Beobachter*, 8–9 May 1927.

81. *Der Angriff*, 15 August 1927.

82. For the first appearance, see *Die Rote Fahne*, 5 July 1923. The author of the article in question, Otto Steinicke, later came to work as an editor for *Der Angriff*. See Angress, *Die Kampfzeit der KPD*, 375.

83. See Bering, *Der jüdische Name als Stigma*. It is revealing that as early as 1924 Goebbels called the writer and journalist Maximilian Harden (actually Felix Ernst Witkowski) "Isidor Witkowski" (diaries, 27 June 1924).

84. See indictment by chief state's attorney, Regional Court, in re: II PJ 430/27, 2 March 1928, LAB, Rep. 58, Zug. 399, no. 24, vol. 1.

85. Diaries, 12 July 1928. By the beginning of November the first book had already gone into its second printing.

86. This passage also appears in Goebbels's article in *Der Angriff*, "Rund um den Alexanderplatz," 11 March 1929.

87. Goebbels 1924b, 217.

88. Horst Wessel, notes on politics, 1929, JL, Ms. Germ. Oct. 762.

89. Ibid.

90. *Der Angriff*, 29 August 1927.

91. BAK, NL 118/98.

92. *Der Angriff*, 10 October 1927.

93. LAB, Rep. 58, Zug. 399, no. 1708. In 1932 a police investigation of Robert Rohde was initiated in connection with an unauthorized performance in Oranienburg.

94. *Völkischer Beobachter*, 6 May 1933.

95. *Der Angriff*, 10 October 1927. See also diaries, 1 October 1928.

96. *Der Angriff*, 14 and 28 November 1927.

97. Hearing in Magistrate's Court, Schöneberg, 25 February 1928, in re: II PJ 430/27, LAB, Rep. 58, no. 24, vol. 1.

98. *Nationalsozialistische Briefe*, 1 April 1927.

99. Report of Police Division IA, 20 June 1928, on the appeal of case IJ 372/27, 19 June 1928, BDC.

100. Diaries, 20 June 1928.

101. See letter from Goebbels to the presiding judge of Regional Court I, 4 April 1928, LAB, Rep. 58, Zug. 399, no. 302, vol. 7.

102. Diaries, 14 April 1928.

103. *Vossische Zeitung*, 3 and 5 May 1928.

104. Diaries, 20 April 1928.

105. Diaries, 17 April 1928.

106. Goebbels to the Magistrate's Court, Schöneberg, 17 April 1928, LAB, Rep. 58, no. 24, vol. 1.

107. Ibid., letter from Wilke to the court.

108. Police Commissioner's Office (Division IA) to chief state's attorney, Regional Court II, Case II PJ 365/27, 18 February 1928, LAB, Rep. 58, no. 24, vol. 2.

109. Diaries, 28 and 27 April 1928.

110. Case II PJ 365/27, 20 November 1928, LAB, Rep. 58, no. 24, vol. 2.

111. Case II PJ 430/27, 2 March 1928, LAB, Rep. 58, no. 24, vol. 1.

112. Diaries, 1, 3, and 5 May 1928.

113. Diaries, 17 May 1928.

114. See Broszat, *Die Machtergreifung*, 46.

115. Diaries, 21 May 1928.

CHAPTER SIX

1. Diaries, 13 June 1928.

2. Diaries, 15 June 1928.

3. Diaries, 13 June 1928.

4. *Verhandlungen des Reichstages* 424:1389. Goebbels's speech is reprinted with an erroneous date in Goebbels 1933c, 15.

5. Diaries, 26 June 1928.

6. *Verhandlungen des Reichstages* 423:121ff.; diaries, 10 July 1928.

7. Goebbels, "IdI," *Der Angriff*, 28 May 1928. Most of his essays in *Der Angriff* are reprinted in Goebbels 1934a and 1938.

8. Diaries, 10 June 1928.

9. *Berliner Abendzeitung*, 27 May 1928.

10. Diaries, 22 June 1928.

11. Diaries, 29 June 1928.

12. Diaries, 1 July 1928.

13. Diaries, 15 July 1928.

14. Diaries, 21 June 1928.

15. *Berliner Arbeiterzeitung*, 9 September 1928.

16. Diaries, 1 September 1928.

17. Oertel, *Horst Wessel*, 57f.

18. Diaries, 3 September 1929.

19. Goebbels 1934b, 89.

20. Diaries, 8 August 1928.

21. Details on Stennes taken from an undated report from Police Division IA. Other sources on these events include a brochure by Wilhelm Hillebrand, "Herunter mit der Maske: Erlebnisse hinter den Kulissen der NSDAP," part 1, BDC.

22. Diaries, 13 August 1928.

23. Diaries, 24 August 1928.

24. Horst Wessel, notes on politics, 1928, JL, Ms. Germ. Oct. 761.

25. Diaries, 14 September 1928.

26. On Muchow, see Broszat, "Die Anfänge der Berliner NSDAP," 85ff.

27. Diaries, 11 October 1928.

28. Wessel noted: "The organization itself was based on the Communist model. Sections instead of local groups, a system of cells, advertising through the press, propaganda—all clearly revealed their influence." Wessel, notes on politics.

29. Ibid.

30. Ibid.

31. According to Broszat ("Anfänge," 87), the Gau Factory Cells Division was established on 1 May 1930.

32. Ibid.

33. Diaries, 23 September 1928.

34. *Der Angriff*, 25 June 1928. A somewhat different version had appeared in the official party publication *Die Flamme* in Bamberg, 7 October 1927. See Tyrell, *Führer befiehl*, 288.

35. Report of the External Service, Police Division IA, 2 November 1928, LAB, Rep. 58, Zug. 399, no. 697.

36. Ibid. On the basis of these remarks the police brought charges against Goebbels for violating the Statute for the Protection of the Republic, but dropped the charges when the Reichstag voted on 4 February 1929 not to lift Goebbels's immunity.

37. Diaries, 1 October 1928.

38. Diaries, 4 October 1928.

39. Diaries, 6 October 1928.

40. Diaries, 14 October 1928.

41. Diaries, 4 November 1928.

42. Diaries, 23 December 1928.

43. *Vossische Zeitung*, 18 November 1928.

44. Diaries, 17 November 1928.

45. Diaries, 18 November 1928.

46. Goebbels, "Kütemeyer," *Der Angriff*, 26 November 1928.

47. Diaries, 17 January 1929.

48. Diaries, 19 January 1929.

49. Goebbels, "Gegen die Young-Sklaverei," *Der Angriff*, 23 September 1929.

50. Fragment from Goebbels's so-called *Jahrestagebuch* (sporadic notes apparently intended for a book), RC. Portions appeared in *Der Angriff* under the heading "Political Diary," 16 February 1929. References to these notes are made in the diaries, 16 February and 1 June 1929.

51. Fragment dated 19 February 1929, RC.

52. Diaries, 17 December 1929.

53. Fragment dated 18 February 1929, RC.

54. Diaries, 5 April 1929.

55. Diaries, 6 April 1929.

56. Diaries, 12 April 1929.

57. Diaries, 13 and 16 April 1929.

58. Diaries, 28 April 1929.

59. Wörtz, "Programmatik und Führerprinzip," 134.

60. Diaries, 30 April 1929.

61. Diaries, 29 and 31 May 1929.

62. Diaries, 5 July 1929.

63. Diaries, 12 July 1929.

64. Broszat, *Die Machtergreifung*, 46.

65. *Der Angriff*, 6 May 1929.

66. *Internationale Pressekorrespondenz* 12:46 (13 June 1932): 1431; reprinted in Pirker, *Komintern und Faschismus*, 158ff.

67. Oertel, *Horst Wessel*, 60ff.

68. *Der Angriff*, 9 September 1929.

69. *Protokoll der Verhandlungen des 12. Parteitages der KPD (Sektion der Kommunistischen Internationale)*, Berlin-Wedding, 9–16 June 1929 (Berlin, n.d.), 79.

70. Buber-Neumann, *Kriegsschauplätze der Revolution*, 269ff.

71. Diaries, 30 August 1929.

72. *Der Angriff*, 24 November 1929.

73. Diaries, 23 September 1929.

74. Diaries, 24 December 1929.

75. *Der Angriff*, 29 December 1929.

76. Report of Police Division IA, 2 April 1930, LAB, Rep. 58, Zug. 399, no. 6015.

77. Diaries, 19 January 1929.

78. *Der Angriff*, 21 November 1929.

79. Reichardt, *Berlin in der Weimarer Republik*, 108.

80. Reinhold Muchow, "Die Strassenzellenorganisation des Gaues Berlin," *Völkischer Beobachter*, 11 March 1930.

81. Diaries, 11 December 1929.

82. Diaries, 19 and 23 December 1929.

83. Diaries, 29 December 1929.

84. GSALB, decision vs. Stoll et al. (500) 1polbK 13/34. (60/34). This document contains the verdict in the second Horst Wessel trial (1934). The files for the first trial (1930) were transferred to the Soviet sector of Germany in 1947 and were never returned. On the death of Horst Wessel, see Oertel, *Wessel* (1988), and Lazar, *Der Fall Horst Wessel*. On the Wessel trial, see the reports in the *Vossische Zeitung* of 23 and 24 September 1930, and Oertel, 83ff.

85. Diaries, 19 January 1930.

86. *Der Angriff*, 21 January 1930.

87. *Die Rote Fahne*, 15 January 1930.

88. Diaries, 10 February 1930.

89. Lazar, *Der Fall Horst Wessel*, 117.

90. Diaries, 1 March 1930. See also Hanfstaengl, *15 Jahre mit Hitler*, 204.

91. Diaries, 2 March 1930; *Vossische Zeitung*, 2 March 1930.

92. *Der Angriff*, 6 March 1930.

93. Goebbels, "Die Fahne hoch!" in *Der Angriff*, 27 February 1930. The "Horst Wessel Song" was the first Nazi fighting song issued as a gramophone record (15 October 1930). See *Der Angriff*, 9 October 1930.

CHAPTER SEVEN

1. Diaries, 24 January 1930.
2. 31 January, and 16, 8, 2 February 1930.
3. Diaries, 2 and 16 March 1930.
4. Diaries, 1 April 1930.
5. See *Der Angriff*, 30 March, 27 April, and 4 and 11 May 1930.
6. Diaries, 28 April 1930.
7. Ibid.
8. Otto Strasser, *Hitler und ich*, 129ff.
9. Diaries, 14 June 1930.
10. "Ein Brief des Führers," *Der Angriff*, 3 July 1930.
11. *Der Nationale Sozialist*, 1 July 1930. See also Moreau, *Nationalsozialismus von links*.
12. On this meeting, see *Der Angriff*, 3 July 1930, and diaries, 1 July 1930.
13. *Der Angriff*, 27 July 1930.
14. Ibid., 3 August 1930.
15. See the account by Goebbels's attorney, Count Rüdiger von Goltz, "Lebenserinnerungen," BAK, Kl. Erw. 653-2.
16. Diaries, 1 September 1930; Lippert, *Im Strom der Zeit*, 178f.
17. Hanfstaengl, *15 Jahre mit Hitler*, 226.
18. Diaries, 1 September 1930. Hitler removed von Pfeffer from his position as supreme commander of the SA and assumed the position himself. He appointed Captain ret. Ernst Röhm as his chief of staff.
19. Records of the Berlin Landeskriminalpolizeiamt, 16 September 1930, Staatsarchiv Bremen, 4.65, vol. 5.
20. Diaries, 1 September 1930.
21. Diaries, 11 September 1930.
22. *Völkischer Beobachter*, 10 September 1930.
23. Diaries, 11 September 1930.
24. Kolb, *Die Weimarer Republik*, 169f. Recent research on the social profile of NSDAP voters has shown that from 1930 on the middle-class element predominated (ibid., 211).
25. Diaries, 23 September 1930.
26. In the pamphlet (1927a) this phrase does not, in fact, appear.
27. *Vossische Zeitung*, 26 September 1930.

28. Ibid.

29. Diaries, 26 September 1930.

30. Scheringer, *Das grosse Los*, 236.

31. Hitler, *Mein Kampf* (1943), 345.

32. Kolb, *Die Weimarer Republik*, 127.

33. *Der Angriff*, 5 October 1930.

34. *Der Angriff*, 2 December 1930.

35. *Vossische Zeitung*, 16 October 1930.

36. Diaries, 29 October 1930.

37. Sturm 33, *Hans Maikowski, geschrieben von Kameraden des Toten*, 16.

38. Robert Kempner, *Der verpasste Nazi-Stopp*, 7ff.

39. On these events see the documents in LAB, Rep. 58, Zug. 399, no. 39, vol. 4; diaries, 29 September and 13 October 1930; *Vossische Zeitung*, 14 October 1930.

40. Diaries, 6 November 1930.

41. *Der Angriff*, 8 and 11 November 1930.

42. Diaries, 10 December 1930; *Vossische Zeitung*, 11 December 1930.

43. Diaries, 9 December 1930.

44. *Vossische Zeitung*, 10 and 7 December 1930.

45. Diaries, 10 December 1930.

46. *Berliner Tageblatt*, 2 January 1931; diaries, 3 January 1931.

47. *Die Rote Fahne* and *Der Angriff*, 23 January 1931.

48. *Die Rote Fahne*, 30 January 1931; *Berliner Tageblatt*, 2 February 1931.

49. *Die Rote Fahne*, 5 February 1931; *Verhandlungen des Reichstages* 444 (1931): 683ff., 685f.

50. Diaries, 12 February 1931.

51. *Vossische Zeitung*, 3 February 1931.

52. Diaries, 10 February 1931.

53. Diaries, 12 November 1930.

54. Diaries, 27 November 1931.

55. Diaries, 2 December 1930.

56. Diaries, 23 February 1931. See also the articles praising Stennes in *Der Angriff*, 19 and 26 February 1931.

57. Summary of the activities of the Gauleiter, prepared by Police Division IA, BDC.

58. Diaries, 6 March 1931.

59. Testimony by Eduard Weiss in re: 1 polJ 388/31, 8 May 1931, LAB, Rep. 58, Zug. 399, no. 509. Weiss had previously made a solemn declaration

to the same effect to Stennes's newspaper, *Arbeiter, Bauern, Soldaten*, 4 May 1931.

60. *Vossische Zeitung*, 17 March 1931.

61. *Der Angriff*, 14 March 1931.

62. Diaries, 14 March 1931.

63. Michaelis and Schraepler, *Ursachen und Folgen* 7:549ff.

64. Diaries, 16 March 1931.

65. Diaries, 25 March 1931; communications of the Landeskriminalpolizei Berlin, 1 May 1931, BAK, Schumacher Collection, 278.

66. Diaries, 25 March 1931.

67. Diaries, 29 March 1931.

68. Diaries, 30 March 1931.

69. Diaries, 28 March 1931.

70. Diaries, 29 March 1931.

71. *Vossische Zeitung*, 3 April 1931.

72. Diaries, 2 April 1931.

73. *Vossische Zeitung*, 3 April 1931.

74. Ibid.

75. *Völkischer Beobachter*, 5–7 April 1931.

76. Diaries, 4 April 1931.

77. Ibid.

78. Communications of the Landeskriminalpolizei Berlin, 1 May 1931, BAK, Schumacher Collection, 278.

79. Diaries, 17 April 1931.

80. Diaries, 10 April 1931.

81. *Arbeiter, Bauern, Soldaten*, 4 May 1931.

82. *Vossische Zeitung*, 15 March 1931.

83. Diaries, 6 May 1931.

84. Diaries, 4 April 1931.

85. Diaries, 7 November 1931.

86. Diaries, 3 April 1929.

87. Magda's mother, Auguste Behrend, a maid, was unmarried at the time of Magda's birth in 1901. She later married Magda's father, the wealthy engineer Oskar Ritschel. The two were divorced when Magda was three, and Auguste Behrend then married the Jewish businessman Friedländer, who adopted Magda. Apparently at Quandt's wish, Magda dropped the Jewish name on 15 July 1920 and had her father declare her legitimate; she bore his name until her marriage. Goebbels later insisted that Magda's

mother return to her "irreproachably Aryan" maiden name. See Heiber, *Joseph Goebbels*, 101.

88. The lover is supposed to have been the student Viktor Arlossoroff, a "fervent Zionist" who later emigrated to Palestine. This information comes from the publicist Curt Riess, who had attended the same Gymnasium as Arlossoroff. See Riess, *Das war mein Leben*, 326.

89. Her membership card is in BDC.

90. H.-O. Meissner, *Magda Goebbels*, 80.

91. Diaries, 1 February 1931.

92. Diaries, 15 March and 23 February 1931.

93. Diaries, 19 and 15 February 1931.

94. Diaries, 22 March 1931.

95. According to Curt Riess (*Joseph Goebbels*, 212), Auguste Behrend had a markedly bad relationship with her son-in-law and "never trusted" him. Goebbels in turn described his mother-in-law as an "awful person" (diaries, 27 May 1937) who interested him not in the slightest. By his own account, Goebbels hardly knew his father-in-law, Oskar Ritschel. His death left him completely cold (diaries, 4 April 1941).

96. Diaries, 12 April 1931.

97. Diaries, 18 April 1931.

98. Diaries, 2 May 1931.

99. Letter from Goebbels to Regional Court I, Central Berlin, 7 November 1931, LAB, Rep. 58, Zug. 399, no. 2.

100. Reply from the police commissioner's office to a query from the general state's attorney, 24 December 1931, LAB, Rep. 58, Zug. 399, no. 2.

101. See LAB, Rep. 59, Zug. 399, no. 39, vol. 12 (E 1 J 651/30). Of a fine of 1,486.77 marks he had paid a total of sixty marks by the time General Schleicher issued his Christmas 1932 amnesty.

102. Diaries, 20 April 1931.

103. Hanfstaengl, *15 Jahre mit Hitler*, 227.

104. Diaries, 7, 8, 29, and 31 May 1931.

105. Diaries, 12 May 1931. See verdict of the second court of appeals, in re: II PJ 41/28, or II PJ 430/27, LAB, Rep. 58, Zug. 399, no. 24, vol. 4.

106. Weiland, *Der Fall Mielke*, 4.

107. *Der Angriff*, 7 August 1931.

108. Ibid.

109. Diaries, 5 and 15 June, and 18 July 1931.

110. *Der Angriff*, 8 August 1931.

111. See the record of the verdict against Thunert et al. in the murder of police officers Anlauf and Lenk, 1 Pol a K 7/34, GSALB. See also Weiland, *Mielke*.

112. *Der Angriff*, 13 August 1931.

113. *Die Rote Fahne*, 23 April 1931.

114. Grzesinski, *Inside Germany*, 132.

115. See Schulthess, *Europäischer Geschichtskalender*, 1931, 243; GSPK, Rep. 219, no. 20, ser. 65; *Vorwärts*, 22 September 1931.

116. Draft of a letter from the police commissioner, Oberstaatsarchiv, Landgericht III, in re: E 1 J 1155/30, dated 5 October 1931, LAB, Rep. 58, Zug. 399, no. 20, vol. 1.

117. From the indictment of thirty-eight SA men in the Kurfürstendamm trial, E 1 J 1155/31, LAB, Rep. 58, Zug. 399, no. 20, vol. 1.

118. *Der Angriff*, 19 December 1931.

119. LAB, Rep. 58, Zug. 399, no. 20, vol. 7; ibid., vol. 3. See also diaries, 22 January 1932.

120. SA pamphlet, December 1931, LAB, Rep. 58, Zug. 399, no. 20, vol. 3.

121. Ernst Röhm to Dr. Karl Günther Heimsoth, 25 February 1929, BDC.

122. See Röhm case based on violation of Paragraph 175: 1 polJ127/31, LAB, Rep. 58, Zug. 399, no. 517, vols. 1–3.

123. Secret report to the party leadership, 21 December 1931, BAK, NS 26/87.

124. Ibid.

125. Police report, BAK, NS 26/1124.

CHAPTER EIGHT

1. H.-O. Meissner, *Magda Goebbels*, 96.

2. AP-Korrespondenz, no. 54/31, 22 December 1931, edited by Helmut Klotz, LAB, Rep. 58, Zug. 399, no. 20.

3. *Der Angriff*, 19 January 1932.

4. *Der Angriff*, 26 January 1932. The Nazi writer Arnold Littmann turned the story into a novel, *Herbert Norkus und die Hitler-Jungen vom Beusselkiez.*

5. Diaries, 22 February 1932.

6. Diaries, 19 January, 2, 9, and 12 February 1932.

7. Diaries, 22 February 1932.

8. Ibid.

9. Diaries, 23 February 1932. Two authors assume that Goebbels did act on his own in proclaiming Hitler's candidacy, but they fail to provide any evidence. See Krebs, *Tendenzen und Gestalten der NSDAP*, 167, and Wörtz, "Programmatik und Führerprinzip," 183. According to the *Vossische Zeitung*, 23 February 1932, Goebbels explained that he had been authorized to inform his friends in the party of Hitler's decision.

10. *Vossische Zeitung*, 24 February 1932; *Verhandlungen des Reichstages* 446 (1932): 2250.

11. *Verhandlungen des Reichstages* 446:2254.

12. *Vossische Zeitung*, 28 February 1932.

13. Ibid.

14. Diaries, 28 September 1932.

15. See the untitled draft by Karoly Kampmann, BAK, NS 26/968.

16. Curriculum vitae of Gauleiter Karl Hanke, dated 25 May 1943, BDC.

17. Diaries, 7 March 1932.

18. Diaries, 29 February and 6 March 1932.

19. See similar attempts at glorification of Hitler in *Der Angriff*, 1 and 4 April 1932.

20. Diaries, 13 March 1932.

21. Ibid.

22. *Vossische Zeitung*, 13 April 1932.

23. Directive from the election leadership of the NSDAP to all Gauleiters, 23 March 1932, BAK, NS 26/290. The number of laws issued by Hindenburg in the form of emergency decrees increased from five in 1930 to sixty-six in 1932, while the laws passed by the Reichstag correspondingly declined from ninety-eight in 1930 to five in 1932. The meetings of the Reichstag also declined, from ninety-four in 1930 to thirteen in 1932. See Kolb, *Die Weimarer Republik*, 128.

24. Diaries, 10 and 11 April 1932.

25. See Hillgruber, "Die Auflösung der Weimarer Republik," 189ff.

26. Diaries, 26 April 1932.

27. Diaries, 25, 23, and 26 April 1932.

28. See excerpts from D. H. von Holtzendorff, "Die Politik des Generals von Schleicher gegenüber der NSDAP 1930–33" (1946), *Vierteljahrshefte für Zeitgeschichte* 1 (1953): 268.

29. Diaries, 28 April 1932.

30. Diaries, 8 and 9 May 1932; Otto Meissner, *Staatssekretär*, 230.

31. Diaries, 4 May 1932.

32. Diaries, 10 May 1932.

33. Diaries, 11 May 1932.

34. *Verhandlungen des Reichstages* 446 (1932): 2561.

35. Ibid., 2599; *Vorwärts*, 10 May 1932.

36. *Der Angriff*, 11 May 1932.

37. Diaries, 19 May 1932.

38. *Vossische Zeitung*, 12 May 1932.

39. Diaries, 23 and 18 May 1932.

40. Diaries, 30 May 1932.

41. Ibid.

42. Diaries, 8 and 29 May 1932.

43. Diaries, 14 June 1932.

44. See Kolb, *Die Weimarer Republik*, 134. Of the nine ministers, six belonged to the aristocracy.

45. Diaries, 14 June 1932; Pohle, *Der Rundfunk als Instrument der Politik*, 165.

46. Diaries, 14 June 1932.

47. Diaries, 15 June 1932.

48. Diaries, 7, 8, and 10 July 1932.

49. The manuscript with Ministerialrat Scholz's comment is in BAK, R55/1273.

50. Diaries, 18 July 1932. See also entries for 20 June and 10 July 1932.

51. Diaries, 1 July 1932.

52. Diaries, 18 and 20 July 1932.

53. Grzesinski, notes in BAK, Kl. Erw. 144.

54. Diaries, 22 July 1932.

55. In Berlin, as well as in such cities as Hamburg, Essen, and Dortmund, the NSDAP obtained its best results in upper- and upper-middle-class neighborhoods (Kolb, *Weimarer Republik*, 210). For a detailed analysis of the vote in Berlin, see Erbe, "Spandau im Zeitalter der Weltkriege," 268ff.

56. Diaries, 1 August 1932.

57. Diaries, 2 August 1932.

58. Diaries, 5 August 1932.

59. Otto Meissner's notes on previous discussions of changes in the cabinet, in Hubatsch, *Hindenburg und der Staat*, 336. See also Wörtz, "Programmatik und Führerprinzip," 192f.

60. Diaries, 7 August 1932.

61. Diaries, 9 August 1932.

62. Ibid.

63. *Völkischer Beobachter*, 11 August 1932.

64. Diaries, 11 August 1932.

65. *Völkischer Beobachter*, 12 August 1932.

66. Quoted from Erdmann, *Die Weimarer Republik*, 297.

67. *Völkischer Beobachter*, 17 August 1932.

68. Diaries, 13 August 1932.

69. Diaries, 25 August 1932.

70. Diaries, 13 and 16 September 1932.

71. Diaries, 1 October 1932; Deist et al., *Ursachen und Voraussetzungen des Zweiten Weltkriegs*, 122f.

72. Pohle, *Der Rundfunk*, 162ff.

73. Diaries, 14 and 9 October 1932.

74. *Der Angriff*, 24 and 25 September 1932.

75. Diaries, 20 October 1932.

76. Diaries, 10 October 1932.

77. See *Verhandlungen des Reichstags* 446 (1932): 2510ff.

78. Diaries, 2 November 1932.

79. Diaries, 4 November 1932.

80. See the report prepared for the minister of the interior by an official in the police commissioner's office, dated 7 November 1932, GSPK, Rep. 219, no. 80, ser. 80–82.

81. *Deutsche Allgemeine Zeitung*, 3 and 4 November 1932.

82. Schulthess, *Europäischer Geschichtskalender* 1932, p. 194.

83. Diaries, 4 November 1932.

84. Diaries, 6 November 1932.

85. For specifics on the election results, see Erbe, "Spandau im Zeitalter der Weltkriege," 295, and Köhler, "Berlin in der Weimarer Republik," 920.

86. Diaries, 6 November 1932.

87. *Der Angriff*, 13 December 1932.

88. Diaries, 9 November 1932.

89. Diaries, 10 and 11 November 1932.

90. *Vossische Zeitung*, 10 October 1932.

91. *Völkischer Beobachter*, 8 November 1932.

92. Diaries, 11 November 1932.

93. *Schwäbischer Merkur*, 25 November 1932.

94. *Völkischer Beobachter*, 25 November 1932.

95. Diaries, 5 December 1932.

96. Otto Strasser, *30. Juni: Vorgeschichte, Verlauf, Folgen*, 36.

97. *Vossische Zeitung*, 10 December 1932.

98. Ibid., 9 December 1932.

99. *Der Angriff* and *Die Vossische Zeitung*, 9 December 1932.

100. Diaries, 9 December 1932.

101. *Der Angriff*, 12 December 1932.

102. Diaries, 24 and 25 December 1932.

103. Diaries, 1 January 1933.

104. Diaries, 10 January 1933.

105. Diaries, 8 January 1933; *Der Angriff*, 9 January 1933.

106. *Der Angriff*, 16 January 1933.

107. Diaries, 17 January 1933.

108. Diaries, 20 January 1933.

109. *Frankfurter Allgemeine Magazin* 375 (8 May 1987): 56.

110. Diaries, 25 January 1933.

111. *Der Angriff*, 23 January 1933; *Der Völkische Beobachter*, 24 January 1933.

112. *Die Rote Fahne*, 26 January 1933.

113. *Vorwärts*, 25 January 1933.

114. Diaries, 29 January 1933.

115. Erich von der Bussche-Ippenburg in *Frankfurter Allgemeine Zeitung*, 2 December 1952; Huber, *Deutsche Verfassungsgeschichte* 7 (1984): 1240; Otto Meissner, curriculum vitae, BDC.

116. Diaries, 30 January 1933.

117. Ibid.

118. Goebbels's speech, October 1938, quoted in "Der Verführer: Anmerkungen zu Goebbels," a documentary by Zweites Deutsches Fernsehen.

119. Wulf, *Presse und Funk*, 288f.

120. Diaries, 30 and 31 January 1933; *Der Angriff*, 31 January–6 February 1933.

121. Diaries, 31 January 1933.

122. Chartess, *Strategie und Technik*, 346.

123. *Vossische Zeitung*, 2 February 1933.

124. Speech by Hitler to industrialists, 20 February 1933, IMT 35:46.

125. Dorpalen, *Hindenburg*, 427f.

126. *Der Angriff*, 6 February 1933; Heiber, *Goebbels Reden* (1971), 64ff.

127. Diaries, 3 and 4 February 1933.

128. Diaries, 3 February 1933.

129. Diaries, 24 February 1933; *Frankfurter Zeitung*, 12 February 1933; diaries, 11 February 1933.

130. *Vossische Zeitung*, 2 February 1932.

131. Diaries, 6, 2, 3, 11, 10, and 13 February 1933.

132. Diaries, 14 February 1933.

133. Goering, *Reden und Aufsätze*, 27.

134. *Vossische Zeitung*, 24 and 26 February 1933.

135. See Broszat, *Der Staat Hitlers*, 96f.; diaries, 21 February 1933.

136. Hanfstaengl, *15 Jahre mit Hitler*, 294f.

137. See Hanfstaengl, *Hitler—The Missing Years*, 202: "It would not surprise me in the least . . . that Goering planned the whole thing himself as a means of wresting a piece of initiative from his hated rival, Goebbels." This sentence was omitted from the German version (*15 Jahre mit Hitler*).

138. On the continuing controversy over the Reichstag fire, see among others Tobias, *Der Reichstagsbrand*; Backes et al., *Der Reichstagsbrand*; Hofer, *Der Reichstagsbrand* and "Neue Quellen zum Reichstagsbrand." Goebbels's diaries contain a revealing comment: "On the question of the Reichstag fire he [Hitler] is betting on Torgler as the instigator. Think that out of the question; he is far too bourgeois" (9 April 1941).

139. *Der Angriff*, 28 February 1933.

140. *Der Reichstagsbrandprozess und Georgi Dimitroff*, documents 32, 24.

141. *Vossische Zeitung*, 28 February 1933.

142. Diels, *Lucifer ante portas*, 194.

143. Diaries, 27 February 1933; Picker, *Hitlers Tischgespräche*, 278.

144. *Der Angriff*, 28 February 1933.

145. Diaries, 4 March 1933.

146. Diaries, 5 March 1933.

147. Kershaw, *Der Hitler-Mythos*, 25ff.

148. Goebbels 1935a, 61.

CHAPTER NINE

1. In a diary entry dated 15 February 1933 he speaks of the "sword of our rage." Goebbels saw the *Volk* as Hitler described them in *Mein Kampf*— as "feminine in gender," in need of a "firm, sure hand" (Heiber, *Joseph Goebbels*, 268), which implied a masculine hand endowed with such positive values as strength, courage, toughness, etc. (see diaries, 19 August 1941, BAK, NL 118/21). Descriptions of human beings and human life in terms of filth can be found throughout Goebbels's diaries, e.g., 12 April 1931, 14 October 1925, 2 February 1941.

2. Decree on the establishment of the Reich Ministry for Popular Enlightenment and Propaganda, 13 March 1933, BAK, R 43 II/1150a.

3. Goebbels, "Die zukünftige Arbeit und Gestaltung des deutschen Rundfunks," speech delivered on 25 March 1933, in Heiber, *Goebbels Reden* (1971), 89; speech to the German press, 16 March 1933, in Goebbels 1933c, 137.

4. Quoted from *Presse in Fesseln* (1947), 220.

5. Goebbels 1933c, 136.

6. BAK, R 43 II/1149 Bl.5.

7. Diaries, 6 March 1933. On departments added later to the ministry, see Dieter Strothmann, *Nationalsozialistische Literaturpolitik*, 23ff.

8. Diaries, 22 January, 5 and 9 August 1932.

9. Diaries, 8 March 1932.

10. On this difference of opinion, see Werner, "Zur Geschichte des Reichsministeriums für Volksaufklärung und Propaganda," vi; Heiber, *Goebbels Reden* (1971), xix; Stephan, *Joseph Goebbels*, 31; Goebbels 1933c, 137.

11. Goebbels 1933c, 137f.; diaries, 8 August 1932. Goebbels subsequently issued directives to ensure that the word "propaganda" would be used only in a positive sense.

12. Diaries, 6 March 1933.

13. Diaries, 11 and 13 March 1933.

14. Menz, *Der Aufbau des Kulturstandes*, 13f.; Deist et al., *Ursachen und Voraussetzungen des Zweiten Weltkrieges*, 132.

15. Diaries, 18 April 1933.

16. See Bramsted, *Goebbels and National Socialist Propaganda*, 58.

17. On the growth and structure of the Propaganda Ministry, see Heiber, *Joseph Goebbels*, 138; Boelcke, *Kriegspropaganda*, 121f. and 138; and Müller, *Das Reichsministerium für Volksaufklärung und Propaganda*, 10.

18. Testimony of Hans Fritzsche at Nuremberg, IMT 17:210.

19. Testimony of Walther Funk at Nuremberg, IMT 13:106; diaries, 12 July 1933.

20. Boelcke, *Kriegspropaganda*, 139.

21. Wulf, *Presse und Funk*, 85ff.

22. Quoted from Stephan, *Joseph Goebbels*, 156f.

23. Quoted from Wulf, *Presse und Funk*, 6.

24. Boveri, *Wir lügen alle*, 547; Boelcke, *Kriegspropaganda*, 76. See also curriculum vitae of Alfred Ingemar Berndt, BDC.

25. Diaries, 15 February 1933.

26. Ibid.

27. Wulf, *Presse und Funk*, 31. Between 1932 and 1934 the number of newspapers published shrank from 4,700 to 3,100 (Heiber, *Joseph Goebbels*, 160).

28. Goebbels's diaries contain many comments like, "The *Frankfurter Zeitung* must be got rid of. That filthy rag is no good for anything" (diaries, 22 October 1936). For a thorough treatment of this topic, see Gillessen, *Auf verlorenem Posten*.

29. See the report by Fritz Sänger, longtime member of the *Frankfurter Zeitung*'s editorial staff, in Wulf, *Presse und Funk*, 81ff.

30. Ibid., 81 and 83.

31. Testimony of Moritz von Schirmeister at Nuremberg, IMT 17:263.

32. Aleff, *Das Dritte Reich*, 103; Abel, *Presselenkung im NS-Staat*, 6.

33. Stephan, *Joseph Goebbels*, 157; Goebbels 1933c, 157.

34. See Diller, *Rundfunkpolitik im Dritten Reich*.

35. Diaries, 1 March 1933; *Film-Kurier*, 8 July 1933, quoted from Wulf, *Presse und Funk*, 301.

36. Heiber, *Goebbels Reden* (1971), 87, 89, 106.

37. *Hannoverscher Anzeiger*, 17 August 1935.

38. Eugen Hadmanovsky, quoted in Pohle, *Der Rundfunk als Instrument der Politik*, 276.

39. Diaries, 17 March 1933.

40. Hanfstaengl, *15 Jahre mit Hitler*, 298.

41. Diaries, 22 March 1933.

42. Diaries, 24 March 1933.

43. *Der Angriff*, 18 May 1934.

44. Diaries, 30 August 1938.

45. Diaries, 9, 10, and 12 August 1933.

46. Diels, *Lucifer ante portas*, 304.

47. Diaries, 26 March 1933; Domarus, *Hitler: Reden und Proklamationen* 2:1030.

48. For a list of the members of the Central Committee, see IMT 29:268f.

49. Domarus, *Hitler: Reden und Proklamationen* 1:250.

50. Ibid., 251; diaries, 28 March 1933.

51. Domarus, *Hitler: Reden und Proklamationen* 1:251.

52. Goebbels 1933c, 158.

53. Report of the American consul in Leipzig, 5 April 1933, in IMT 3:586.

54. Diaries, 1 April 1933.

55. Diaries, 28 April 1933.

56. Speer, *Inside the Third Reich*, 26f.

57. Diaries, 25 April 1933.

58. *Rheydter Zeitung*, 22, 23, and 25 April 1933.

59. Ibid., 25 April 1933.

60. François-Poncet, *Botschafter in Berlin*, 129.

61. Diaries, 1 May 1933.

62. Golo Mann in Haarmann et al., "*Das war ein Vorspiel nur*." Heiber, *Goebbels Reden* (1971), 108, 109, and 111.

63. Diaries, 15 May 1933.

64. Magda Goebbels, "Die deutsche Mutter," 18f.

65. Diaries, 19 August 1941, BAK, NL 118/21; Ruhl, *Brauner Alltag*, 73; Goebbels 1934a, 118ff.

66. Diaries, 17 July and 4 June 1933.

67. Diaries, 8 July 1933.

68. *Reichsgesetzbuch 1*, 1933, 1:104.

69. See Dahm, "Anfänge und Ideologie der Reichskulturkammer," 60.

70. Diaries, 19 April 1933.

71. *Reichsgesetzbuch 1*, 1933, I, 449.

72. Abridged text in Wulf, *Die bildenden Künste* (Gütersloh, 1963), 99f.

73. Diaries, 11 May 1933.

74. Diaries, 11 April 1933.

75. Diaries, 7 August 1933. See also entries for 9 July, 23, 29, and 31 August 1933.

76. Diaries, 25 June and 23 August 1933.

77. Letter from Goering to several ministries and to several provincial governments; abridged text in Wulf, *Presse und Funk*, 292.

78. Diaries, 17 and 20 June 1933.

79. Diaries, 19 August 1933.

80. Diaries, 2 September 1933.

81. Diaries, 17 June and 19 July 1933.

82. Diaries, 29 June 1933: "The boss very good to me. I'm to get Hugenberg's official residence." Speer recalls that Goebbels "took possession of it more or less by force" (*Inside the Third Reich*, 27).

83. Draft of a letter from Darré to Hitler, BDC. The letter was apparently never sent because Darré recognized that he would get nowhere with his request.

84. Speer, *Inside the Third Reich*, 27.

85. Diaries, 1 July 1933.

86. Diaries, 27 December 1933.

87. Diaries, 16 July 1933.

88. Speer, *Inside the Third Reich*, 27.

89. Diaries, 20–23 July 1933.

90. See Dahm, "Anfänge und Ideologie," 61ff.

91. Diaries, 7 and 11 July 1933.

92. "Grundgedanken zur Errichtung einer Reichskulturkammer," July 1933, BAK, R 43 II/1241.

93. Diaries, 25 August 1933.

94. Dahm, "Anfänge und Ideologie," 66.

95. K. Werner and Biernat, *Die Köpenicker Blutwoche*.

96. Diaries, 1 September 1933.

97. Jacobsen, *1939–1945: Der Zweite Weltkrieg*, 180f.

98. Goebbels 1934a, 271.

99. Diaries, 25 September 1933.

100. Hill, *Die Weizsäcker-Papiere*, 76.

101. Diaries, 25 September 1933.

102. Schmidt, *Statist auf diplomatischer Bühne*, 283; diaries, 25 September 1933. The German diplomat Ulrich von Hassell reports in his diary on an address that Goebbels gave on 8 June 1944 before a select group of high officials, captains of industry, and the like; he says that Goebbels "adapted brilliantly to the high 'bourgeois' milieu: an elegant gray suit without the party badge, a confidential air of speaking with 'men in the know.' On most of them he definitely made an impression as a 'great intelligence' " (*Die Hassell-Tagebücher*, 431f.).

103. Hill, *Die Weizsäcker-Papiere*, 76.

104. Diaries, 28 and 27 September 1933.

105. Goebbels 1934a, 233ff. See Deist et al., *Ursachen und Voraussetzungen*, 135ff.

106. Schmidt, *Statist*, 284f., 285.

107. *The Times*, 29 September 1933; Heiber, *Joseph Goebbels*, 246.

108. Boveri, *Wir lügen alle*, 162. See also Schmidt, *Statist*, 285f.

109. Schmidt, *Statist*, 289.

110. Diaries, 27 and 21 September 1933.

111. Diaries, 27 September 1933.

112. Domarus, *Hitler: Reden und Proklamationen* 1: 306. See also Deist et al., *Ursachen und Voraussetzungen*, 136.

113. Goebbels 1934a, 270 and 269.

114. Rauschning, *Gespräche mit Hitler*, 103. For questions about the reliability of this source, see *Der Spiegel* 37 (1985): 92ff.

115. Goebbels interview in Michaelis and Schraepler, *Ursachen und Folgen* 10:52.

116. Goebbels 1934a, 323ff. and 336.

117. BAK, R 43 II/1241, Bl. 18f.

118. See Dahm, "Anfänge und Ideologie," 55ff.

119. See Brenner, *Die Kunstpolitik des Nationalsozialismus*, 54.

120. Goebbels 1934a, 332f.

121. Piper, *Nationalsozialistische Kunstpolitik*, 14.

122. Diaries, 13 April 1937.

123. *Völkischer Beobachter*, 14 November 1925; Bollmus, *Das Amt Rosenberg*, 45 and 265; diaries, 14 November 1925; *Völkischer Beobachter*, 7 July 1933.

124. Bollmus, *Das Amt Rosenberg*, 52.

125. Diaries, 2 January 1934.

CHAPTER TEN

1. Diaries, 2 March 1935.

2. Diaries, 15 August 1933.

3. Diaries, 25 and 31 March 1934.

4. Diaries, 25 January 1937, and 15 October 1935.

5. See G. Albrecht, *Nationalsozialistische Filmpolitik*, 439.

6. Diaries, 15 January 1936: "America . . . is a country without culture. But some things they can do, and pursue with great zeal: technology, for example, and film. In their hearts they have absolutely no interest in Europe. Have 12 million Negroes and 7 million Jews. That they don't understand our racial laws is obvious. No need for them to, either. Let them make films and manufacture machinery."

7. Diaries, 26 July 1933, and 30 January 1939.

8. Diaries, 12 June 1933.

9. See Wulf, *Theater und Film im Dritten Reich*, 354f.

10. Cziffra, *Es war eine rauschende Ballnacht*, 141f.

11. On the duties and organization of the Reich theater department, see Wulf, *Theater und Film*, 56f.

12. Diaries, 13 October 1935.

13. See Romani, *Die Filmdivas des Dritten Reiches*, 19.

14. G. Albrecht, *Nationalsozialistische Filmpolitik*, 439; diaries, 22 December 1937, and 15 October 1940.

15. Rauschning, *Gespräche mit Hitler*, 143f.

16. Diaries, 21 May 1934.

17. Michaelis and Schraepler, *Ursachen und Folgen* 10:157ff.

18. *Deutsche Allgemeine Zeitung*, 22 June 1934. See also *Der Angriff*, 22 June 1934, and *Völkischer Beobachter*, 23 June 1934.

19. Papen, *Der Wahrheit eine Gasse*, 349.

20. Diaries, 29 June 1934.

21. That Goebbels was truly taken by surprise can be seen from his diary entry for 29 June 1934, in which he twice speaks of the "reactionaries" as secretly "at work everywhere," and of the need to take action against them.

22. On the Röhm putsch see Longerich, *Die braunen Bataillone*, 206ff.

23. Michaelis and Schraepler, *Ursachen und Folgen* 10:166.

24. Rosenberg, *Das politische Tagebuch*, 33.

25. *Der Angriff*, 2 July 1934.

26. Ibid. See also the description by Hitler's driver, Erich Kempka, in Michaelis and Schraepler, *Ursachen und Folgen* 10:168ff. See also Domarus, *Hitler: Reden und Proklamationen* 1:395.

27. Domarus, *Hitler: Reden und Proklamationen*, plate 10.

28. Longerich, *Die braunen Bataillone*, 218.

29. This observation comes from Goebbels's adjutant, Prince Friedrich Christian zu Schaumburg-Lippe, in *Zwischen Krone und Kerker*, 173ff.

30. Goering announced proudly to the press that he had expanded his assignment. See Michaelis and Schraepler, *Ursachen und Folgen* 10:184.

31. Gregor Strasser to Rudolf Hess, 18 June 1934, BDC.

32. Frau Strasser to Wilhelm Frick, 22 October 1934; excerpt in Gruchmann, "Einleitung zum Erlebnisbericht Werner Pinders," 409f.

33. On 28 June Röhm had announced to his guests, among them General von Epp, that he wanted to use the conference in Bad Wiessee to "rip the mask from Goebbels's face." Testimony of Prince Ferdinand Karl von Isenburg, 3 January 1950, quoted in Mau, "Die Zweite Revolution," 128.

34. *Der Angriff*, 2 July 1934. Goering (in the *Völkischer Beobachter*, 3 July 1934) and Rosenberg (ibid., 4 July 1934) expressed themselves along the same lines. See Kershaw, *Der Hitler-Mythos*, 72ff.

35. Heiber, *Goebbels Reden*, 156ff.

36. *Völkischer Beobachter*, 3 July 1934.

37. Ibid., 4 July 1934.

38. This step had been anticipated since the summer of 1933. Goebbels noted on 19 July 1933 in his diary, "Question of the Hindenburg succession. Hitler must not tolerate any R.Pr. [Reich president] over him and also not become the puppet of Oskarsohn [Hindenburg's son Oskar]. Unite both offices in one person. We'll find a way to do it. Above all, have it confirmed by the people and not depend on the mercy of the R.W. [Reichswehr]." See also the entry for 5 August 1933.

39. *Berliner Lokal-Anzeiger*, 2 August 1934.

40. François-Poncet, *Botschafter in Berlin*, 242.

41. Domarus, *Hitler: Reden und Proklamationen* 1:444.

42. Rosenberg, *Das politische Tagebuch*, 39.

43. Ibid., 40.

44. Wulf, *Literatur und Dichtung im Dritten Reich*, 230.

45. Quoted from Bollmus, *Das Amt Rosenberg*, 75.

46. Diaries, 24 August 1934.

47. Goebbels to Rosenberg, 25 August 1934, BAK, NS 8/171.

48. *Die Musik*, November 1934, 138–46. See also Wulf, *Musik im Dritten Reich*, 372f.

49. *Völkischer Beobachter*, 7 December 1934.

50. Quoted from Heiber, *Joseph Goebbels*, 199.

51. Diaries, 11 September and 1 November 1939.

52. Quoted from Wulf, *Musik im Dritten Reich*, 373ff. The controversy grew out of Hindemith's *Mathis der Maler*, whose third act shows preparations for burning heretical writings, an obvious allusion to the book burnings of October 1933. Furtwäangler had conducted the symphonic version of this opera in the spring of 1934, after the opera had been banned.

53. Ibid., 376.

54. Bollmus, *Das Amt Rosenberg*, 76.

55. Ibid.

56. Diaries, 2 March 1935.

57. Wulf, *Musik im Dritten Reich*, 378.

58. Diaries, 2 March 1935.

59. Quoted from Bollmus, *Das Amt Rosenberg*, 76.

60. Ibid., 277.

61. For a revealing discussion of Furtwängler's role in the Third Reich, see Wulf, *Musik im Dritten Reich*, 85f.

62. On these tactics, see YIVO (Institute for Jewish Research), G-PA-14, "Querschnitt durch die Tätigkeit des Arbeitsgebietes Dr. Taubert (Antibolschewismus) des RNVP bis zum 31.12.1944," BAK, R55/450, 14ff.

63. Goebbels 1934a, 267.

64. Sänger, *Politik der Täuschungen*, 64.

65. Goebbels 1938, 385ff.

66. Diaries, 17 April 1935.

67. *Frankfurter Zeitung*, 21 April 1935. See Bramsted, *Goebbels and National Socialist Propaganda*, 206.

68. Rosenberg to Rust, 2 May 1935, BAK, NS 10/58.

69. Quoted from Bollmus, *Das Amt Rosenberg*, 78. See also the documents on the "Strauss case" in Wulf, *Musik im Dritten Reich*, 194ff. Among Strauss's papers are notes under the heading "Story of the *Schweigsame Frau*," in which he wrote, "But these are sad times when an artist of my rank has to ask a pipsqueak from the ministry what he can compose and have performed" (quoted from Wulf, *Musik*, 197f.).

70. Diaries, 5 July 1935.

71. *Berlin am Morgen*, 29 October 1931.

72. Diaries, 31 March 1934.

73. Diaries, 19 July 1935.

74. Diaries, 13 September 1935.

75. Goebbels 1935d, 5, 7, 4, 18, 23, and 24ff.

76. Diaries, 15 and 17 September 1935.

77. Diaries, 15 November 1935.

78. Diaries, 15 September 1935.

79. Dahm, *Das jüdische Buch im Dritten Reich*, part 1, col. 60. See also "Nicht-arier auf deutschen Bühnen," *Frankfurter Zeitung*, 6 March 1934, in Wulf, *Theater und Film im Dritten Reich*, 260.

80. "Dr. Goebbels über den geistigen und künstlerischen Umbruch im neuen Deutschland," *Börsenblatt für den deutschen Buchhandel*, 18 November 1935.

81. See Dahm, *Das jüdische Buch*, col. 114.

82. Ibid., col. 115.

83. Diaries, 21 August and 11 September 1935.

84. Bollmus, *Das Amt Rosenberg*, 80; Wulf, *Literatur und Dichtung*, 193.

85. Goebbels to Rosenberg, 7 November 1935, quoting the memorandum of 16 October 1934 from the NS Cultural Community, BAK, NS 8/171.

86. Diaries, 13 and 27 September 1935.

87. Diaries, 3 October 1935.

88. Diaries, 13 October 1935.

89. Goebbels to Rosenberg, 7 November 1935, BAK, NS 8/171; diaries, 13 and 24 October and 9 November 1935.

90. See Dahm, *Das jüdische Buch*, col. 116, and memorandum from Hinkel dated 22 January 1936, BAK, R 56 V/102.

91. Domarus, *Hitler: Reden und Proklamationen* 1:574.

92. Dahm, *Das jüdische Buch*, col. 134ff.

93. Diaries, 29 February 1936.

94. See Jacobsen, *Nationalsozialistische Aussenpolitik*, 417ff.

95. Diaries, 29 February 1936.

96. Diaries, 2 March 1936.

97. Diaries, 4 March 1936.

98. Diaries, 6 and 4 March 1936. In October 1935 fascist Italy had attacked Abyssinia from Eritrea and Italian Somaliland, and in 1936 Abyssinia was annexed, making the Italian king Victor Emmanuel III emperor of Ethiopia. These events drew London's attention away from Europe, which suited Hitler well.

99. Diaries, 8 and 4 March 1936.

100. Domarus, *Hitler: Reden und Proklamationen* 1:582.

101. Diaries, 8 March 1936. See Riess, *Joseph Goebbels*, 184f.

102. Sänger, *Politik der Täuschungen*, 79.

103. Diaries, 8 and 9 March 1936.

104. Ruhl, *Brauner Alltag*, 146.

105. Sänger, *Politik der Täuschungen*, 79.

106. *Völkischer Beobachter*, 20 April 1936.

107. Diaries, 31 March 1936.

108. On the manipulation of the outcome, see Domarus, *Hitler: Reden und Proklamationen* 1:617.

109. Ruhl, *Brauner Alltag*, 146.

110. Diaries, 22, 29, and 17 March, and 8 April 1936.

111. Max Amann, interviewed by K. Frank Korf on 4 April 1948, Korf Papers, Hoover.

112. Diaries, 15 April 1936.

113. Diaries, 22 October and 9 April 1936.

114. Diaries, 20 April 1936.

115. Diaries, 28 April 1936.

116. His diary for 3 October 1941 remarks, "Helmut is turning six. . . . Connection with other boys . . . absolutely necessary; a boy who grows up among girls does not turn out right" (BAK, NL 118/28).

117. Diaries, 13 August 1926.

118. Diaries, 9 April 1936.

119. Diaries, 27 June 1936.

120. Diaries, 9 July and 28 August 1926.

121. Diaries, 13 April 1936.

122. Dahm, *Das jüdische Buch*, 136.

123. Directive from Hinkel to the presidents of the individual chambers, 29 April 1936, BAK, R 56 V/102.

124. Krüger, *Die Olympischen Spiele*, 230.

125. Sänger, *Politik der Täuschungen*, 108.

126. Diaries, 26 June 1936.

127. Diaries, 15 August, and 29 and 30 July 1936.

128. See the plans in BAK, R 55/507.

129. François-Poncet, *Botschafter in Berlin*, 304.

130. Krüger, *Die Olympischen Spiele*, 231.

131. Ibid., 229.

132. *Völkischer Beobachter*, 1 August 1936.

133. Diaries, 18 August 1936. See Krüger, *Die Olympischen Spiele* (1972), 230, and BAK, R 55 Zg. Rep. 304/45, on the 1936 Berlin Olympics viewed through the foreign press.

134. Pohle, *Der Rundfunk als Instrument der Politik*, 414ff.

135. Bramsted, *Goebbels and National Socialist Propaganda*, 151.

136. "NSK Sonderdienst. Der deutsche Film: Neue Aufgaben der Reichspropagandaleitung," 1 February 1934, BAK, NS 26/293.

137. Diaries, 13 October 1935.

138. Diaries, 17 August and 5 October 1935.

139. Graham, *Leni Riefenstahl and Olympia*, 21f.; diaries, 21 August 1935.

140. Diaries, 17 August and 5 October 1935.

141. Diaries, 6 August 1936.

142. Diaries, 25 October 1936.

143. Diaries, 6 November 1936.

144. Diaries, 25 June, 3, 4, and 5 July, and 16 August 1936.

145. Dodd, *Ambassador Dodd's Diary*, 349. In July 1937 Goebbels gave another party on the Pfaueninsel, with equally splendid decorations (diaries, 2 July 1937).

146. Ebermeyer and Roos, *Gefährtin des Teufels*, 210. See also François-Poncet, *Botschafter in Berlin*, 305, and Riess, *Joseph Goebbels*, 186.

147. Dodd, *Ambassador Dodd's Diary*, 349.

148. On Goering's party, see the *Völkischer Beobachter*, 15 August 1936.

149. Fröhlich, *Waren das Zeiten!*, 367.

150. Ibid., 362f.

151. Diaries, 10 June 1936.

152. Lida Baarova in a discussion with the author, 3 September 1987, RC. See also diaries, 19 August and 5 September 1936.

153. Diaries, 18 June 1933.

154. Diaries, 10 May 1936.

155. Diaries, 24 October 1935.

156. Diaries, 3 August 1935.

157. Diaries, 21 and 24 September 1934.

158. Diaries, 7 August 1935.

159. In all likelihood the person in question was Kurt Lüdecke, Hitler's foreign-policy advisor in the 1920s, who later went to the United States as his special envoy to seek support and funds for the Nazi movement. See Jacobsen, *Nationalsozialistische Aussenpolitik*, 529. Diaries, 1 August 1936.

160. Diaries, 2, 4, and 7 August 1936.

161. Diaries, 6 September 1936.

162. This account is based on an unpublished manuscript of Baarova's memoirs (RC), on the tape of the conversation the author conducted with Lida Baarova on 3 September 1987, and on Goebbels's diary entries. All three sources coincide to a remarkable degree.

163. Diaries, 10 October and 11 September 1936.

164. Diaries, IfZ 2:678.

165. Diaries, 18 September 1936.

166. Diaries, 18 and 19 September 1936.

167. Diaries, 30 September 1936, and Baarova memoirs (RC).

168. Diaries, 30 October 1936.

169. Diaries, 31 October 1936.

170. Wulf, *Theater und Film*, 94.

171. BAK, NS 26/968.

172. Quoted from Heiber, *Joseph Goebbels*, 260.

173. Domarus, *Hitler: Reden und Proklamationen* 1:652f.

174. Diaries, 31 October 1936.

CHAPTER ELEVEN

1.   Diaries, 27 October 1936.

2.   Diaries, 9 September 1936.

3.   Diaries, 8 September 1936.

4.   *Völkischer Beobachter*, 11 September 1936.

5.   Guidelines were issued in March 1937. See Jacobsen, *Nationalsozialistische Aussenpolitik*, 458.

6.   Ibid., 457.

7.   Secret instructions to the German press, 17 September 1936, BAK, Sänger Collection, ZSg 102.

8.   They were joined by Italy in 1937 and by Manchuria, Hungary, and Spain in 1939.

9.   Secret instructions to the German press, 25 November 1936, BAK, Sänger Collection, ZSg 102.

10. YIVO (Institute for Jewish Research) G-PA-14, "Querschnitt durch die Tätigkeit des Arbeitsgebietes Dr. Taubert (Antibolschewismus) des RMVP bis zum 31. 12. 1944," BAK, R 55/450, 11.

11. Diaries, 31 May 1936.

12. Diaries, 19 June 1936.

13. Diaries, 18 November 1936.

14. Quoted from Münster, *Publizistik*, 149.

15. *Völkischer Beobachter*, 28 November 1936.

16. Decree on the Restructuring of German Cultural Life, 27 November 1936, quoted from Wulf, *Die bildenden Künste*, 128.

17. Diaries, 26 October 1936.

18. Decree on the Restructuring of German Cultural Life.

19. Diaries, 6 February 1937.

20. Hockerts, "Die Goebbels-Tagebücher 1932–1941," 376.

21. Diaries, 23 February 1937.

22. Quoted from D. Albrecht, "Der Vatikan und das Dritte Reich," 36f.

23. See diaries, 7 August 1933: "We want to become a church ourselves." See also 23 February and 13 September 1937, and 17 September 1935.

24. Diaries, 21 March 1937.

25. Diaries, 29 April 1941, and 24 March, and 10 and 2 April 1937.

26. Diaries, 1 May, 26 April, 30 May, 30 April, and 27 June 1937.

27. Diaries, 30 May, 30 April, and 26 May 1937.

28. See Hockerts, *Die Sittlichkeitsprozesse gegen katholische Ordensangehörige und Priester 1936/37*, 113ff.

29. *Völkischer Beobachter*, 30 May 1937.

30. Diaries, 29 May 1937.

31. Diaries, 31 December, 10 April, and 22 and 11 February 1937.

32. Diaries, 11 and 10 December, and 5 March 1937.

33. Diaries, 16 April 1937.

34. Hanfstaengl, *15 Jahre mit Hitler*, 319.

35. On these luncheons, see Speer, *Inside the Third Reich*, 117–27; Hanfstaengl, *15 Jahre mit Hitler*, 199f.; Lang and Schenk, *Portrait eines Menschheitsverbrechens*, 182. Notes the latter source: "At the Führer's table" Rosenberg never heard "a good word from Goebbels about anyone . . . but certainly always assent when criticism was expressed" (182).

36. Speer, *Inside the Third Reich*, 126f.

37. Fröhlich, *Waren das Zeiten!*, 157.

38. Diaries, 24 February and 5 September 1937.

39. Diaries, 23 March, and 13, 20, 17, and 20 January 1937.

40. Diaries, 26 January 1937.

41. Diaries, 21 April and 26 May 1937.

42. *Die Filmwoche*, 4 October 1937; *Licht-Bild-Bühne*, 4 September 1937.

43. Diaries, 13 March 1937.

44. Diaries, 5 and 12 March 1937.

45. Diaries, 11 September 1937.

46. Diaries, 6 and 7 October 1937.

47. Diaries, 8 December 1937.

48. See Wulf, *Theater und Film*, 306f.

49. Diaries, 12 and 19 November 1937.

50. Quoted from Heiber, *Joseph Goebbels*, 196.

51. In Würzburg he had attended Professor Knapp's course, "From Impressionism to Cubism: History of Modern Art" (see Goebbels's *Studienbuch*, winter semester 1918–19, BAK, NL 118/113).

52. Diaries, 2 July 1933.

53. Piper, *Nationalsozialistische Kunstpolitik*, 15.

54. Diaries, 5 June 1937.

55. Diaries, 18, 19, and 30 June, and 8 May 1937.

56. On the Geli Raubal story, see Shirer, *The Rise and Fall of the Third Reich*, 131ff.

57. Diaries, 12 June 1937.

58. Diaries, 30 June and 3 August 1937.

59. See Zweite, "Franz Hoffmann und die Städtische Galerie 1937," 283.

60. Prussian Academy of the Arts, 8 July 1937, reprinted in Piper, *Nationalsozialistische Kunstpolitik*, 188.

61. See Wulf, *Die bildenden Künste*, and Piper, *Nationalsozialistische Kunstpolitik*, 24 and 188.

62. Hitler speech in *Neueste Münchener Nachrichten*, 19 July 1937.

63. Headline, *Völkischer Beobachter*, 20 July 1937.

64. Diaries, 29 August 1924, and 17 July 1937.

65. Quoted from Schuster, *Kunststadt München*, 217.

66. Heiber, *Joseph Goebbels*, 198.

67. Diaries, 11 February and 26 November 1937.

68. Diaries, 3 December 1937.

69. Diaries, 3 March and 3 February 1937.

70. Diaries, 30 April 1937, and 20 January 1941.

71. Diaries, 9 and 15 December, and 30 November 1937.

72. *Völkischer Beobachter*, 10 September 1937.

73. Quoted from Jacobsen, *Nationalsozialistische Aussenpolitik* (1968), 460.

74. Ibid., 835.

75. Diaries, 10, 26, and 25 September 1937.

76. Diaries, 28 September 1937.

77. Diaries, 29 September 1937.

78. Diaries, 14 September 1938.

79. Diaries, 3 August 1937.

80. Diaries, 27 January 1938.

81. Ibid.

82. Diaries, 1 February 1938.

83. Diaries, 29 January 1938.

84. Diaries, 28 and 31 January 1938.

85. Diaries, 28 January and 31 August 1938.

86. Diaries, 28 and 17 January 1938.

87. Diaries, 30 January, and 6 and 1 February 1938.

88. Diaries, 12 August 1938.

89. Diaries, 1 and 6 February 1938.

90. Diaries, 5 February 1938.

91. Diaries, 6 February 1938.

92. Diaries, 6 March 1937, 1 April 1941, 27 October, and 6 March 1937, and 1 February 1938.

93. Quoted from Domarus, *Hitler: Reden und Proklamationen* 1:807.

94. Goebbels's speech for Hitler's birthday, *Völkischer Beobachter*, 21 April 1938.

95. Domarus, *Hitler: Reden und Proklamationen* 1:809.

96. *Völkischer Beobachter*, 21 April 1938.

97. Domarus, *Hitler: Reden und Proklamationen* 1:811.

98. Speer, *Inside the Third Reich*, 109, and *Völkischer Beobachter*, 21 April 1938. (Speer places the incident with Goebbels and Goering on 9 March, not on the day of the *Anschluss*.)

99. Domarus, *Hitler: Reden und Proklamationen* 1:816f.

100. Harlan, *Im Schatten meiner Filme*, 83.

101. Domarus, *Hitler: Reden und Proklamationen* 1:822f.

102. Ibid., 824f.

103. Diaries, 19 July 1938.

104. Diaries, 19 June 1938.

105. Diaries, 21 June 1938.

106. Heiber, *Goebbels Reden* (1971), 291.

107. Ruhl, *Brauner Alltag*, 149.

108. Speer, *Inside the Third Reich*, 100f.

109. Hausner, *Zeitbild*, 26. See also Kershaw, *Der Hitler-Mythos*, 118ff.

110. *Völkischer Beobachter*, 6 and 7 May 1938.

111. Diaries, 3 November and 28 December 1937; Graham, *Leni Riefenstahl*, 186ff.

112. Diaries, 31 August 1938. See Scheffler, *Judenverfolgung*, 27ff.

113. *Deutsche Allgemeine Zeitung*, 23 June 1938, BAK, Schumacher Collection, SS 115.

114. Diaries, 22 June 1938.

115. Diaries, 4 June 1938.

116. Diaries, 11 June 1938.

117. Diaries, 19 June 1938.

118. *Deutsche Allgemeine Zeitung*, 23 June 1938, BAK, Schumacher Collection, SS 115.

119. Diaries, 19 June 1938.

120. Diaries, 22 June 1938.

121. Diaries, 6 July 1938.

122. Diaries, 25 July 1938.

123. Diaries, 4 August and 25 July 1938.

124. According to the testimony of Attorney Krech, West Berlin, 11 October 1954. See also diaries, 30 and 24 March 1941.

125. Diaries, 10 August 1938.

126. Testimony of Moritz von Schirmeister in Nuremberg, 28 June 1946, IMT 17:266.

127. See statement by Hans Fritzsche, 7 January 1946, IMT 32:319.

128. Diaries, 24 August and 19 July 1938.

129. Diaries, 1 September 1938.

130. Diaries, 28 August 1938.

131. Diaries, 19 July and 28 August 1938.

132. Diaries, 22 July 1938.

133. Diaries, 2 July 1938.

134. Diaries, 5 August 1938.

135. Diaries, 6 August, 1938: "I hope that soon a new goal will be set. I need it. The last months have taken a great deal out of me."

136. Diaries, 14 August 1938.

137. Diaries, 21 August 1938.

138. Diaries, 16 August 1938.

139. Diaries, 17 August, 1938: "With the Führer. Again I talk things out with him at length. . . . I really don't see any way out anymore."

140. Diaries, 16 and 21 August 1938. See also Hassel, *Die Hassell-Tagebücher*, 57.

141. Diaries, 21 August 1938.

142. Diaries, 16 and 18 August 1938.

143. Diaries, 20, 18, and 19 August 1938.

144. Diaries, 19 August 1938: "Then I go to Mother, who is so dear and good to me. I feel really at home there. Maria supports me completely. . . . I'm happy about Mother, who is so touching. . . . Otherwise I feel so lonely I can't stand it." Diaries, 20–21 August 1938: "I visit Mother, who is very sick. I . . . go over everything with her. When all is said and done, she's the closest to me. . . . Sat with Mother and Maria for a long time. A very sad evening."

145. Diaries, 17 August 1938.

146. Diaries, 21 August 1938.

147. Diaries, 1 September 1938.

148. Diaries, 21 August 1938. See also Deist et al., *Ursachen und Voraussetzungen*, 149.

149. Diaries, 16 and 19 September 1937.

150. Diaries, 30 July 1938.

151. See Deist et al., *Ursachen und Voraussetzungen*, 149; Longerich, *Propagandisten im Kriege*, 116ff.; Boelcke, *Kriegspropaganda*; and diaries, 13 August 1938.

152. Domarus, *Hitler: Reden und Proklamationen* 1:923.

153. Hill, *Die Weizsäcker-Papiere*, 145 and 171. Reichsbank president Hjalmar Schacht told Ulrich von Hassell that Goebbels was "opposed to the irresponsible policy of war" (Hassell, *Die Hassell-Tagebücher*, 52).

154. Hill, *Die Weizsäcker-Papiere*, 171. See also Bullock, *Hitler* (1977), 453.

155. Diaries, 18 October 1938.

156. Irving, *Hitlers Weg zum Krieg*, 299f.

157. See the picture and signature in the *Völkischer Beobachter*, 25 October 1938. Supposedly the date of this meeting was marked in Bormann's diary as 23 October, with an exclamation point. See Irving, *Hitlers Weg zum Krieg*, 301. Heiber (*Joseph Goebbels*, 277) also mentions this date; on the other hand, Domarus (*Hitler: Reden und Proklamationen* 1:961) pinpoints 24 October as the date of the meeting.

158. Rosenberg, *Das politische Tagebuch*, 64f.

159. Diaries, 16 July 1938.

160. See Rudolf Likus's note to Ribbentrop on the scandal, Auswärtiges Amt (Foreign Office), Series 43, 29 042. See also Hassell, *Die Hassell-Tagebücher*, 79.

161. Cziffra, *Es war eine rauschende Ballnacht*, 149f.

162. For two years after the German Wehrmacht occupied "Rump Czechoslovakia" on 15 March 1939, Lida Baarova continued to live undisturbed in Prague. Then, in the spring of 1941, she was forbidden to appear on the stage. As the Russian troops approached at the end of the war, she fled

with friends to German territory occupied by the Americans. In the confusion of the last phase of the war, she was handed over to the Communists, who put her on trial in Prague as a collaborator. She was charged with treason. While she was being interrogated by Russian officers, her mother died of a heart attack. Her sister Zorka, also an actress, was forbidden to act and committed suicide. After sixteen months in prison, Lida Baarova received a pardon, at Christmas 1946, thanks to the intervention of a Czech cabinet minister's nephew, whom she later married.

163. Among the many accounts based on primary sources, see Graml, *Reichskristallnacht*; Lauber, *Judenpogrom*; Reitlinger, *The Final Solution*; and Adler, *Der verwaltete Mensch*.

164. Bramsted, *Goebbels and National Socialist Propaganda*, 383–87.

165. Gillessen, "Der organisierte Ausbruch des Hasses."

166. Notes of Major Engel, quoted in Lauber, *Judenpogrom*, 178.

167. Testimony of Goering at Nuremberg, IMT 9:312ff.

168. Ibid., 28:499ff.

169. Diaries, 12–13 November 1938.

170. See decree of 24 January 1939 in Adler, *Der verwaltete Mensch*, 71 and 85.

171. Gillessen, "Der organisierte Ausbruch des Hasses." See also Graml, *Reichskristallnacht*, 37.

172. See Sywottek, *Mobilmachung für den totalen Krieg*, 165f.

173. Press briefing, 9 May 1939, BAK, Sänger Collection, ZSg 102/13.

174. Letter from Hasso von Wedel, director of the press unit of the Wehrmacht High Command, quoted in Sywottek, *Mobilmachung für den totalen Krieg*, 167.

175. Ibid., 169.

176. Hassell, *Die Hassell-Tagebücher*, 82.

177. Ibid., 57.

178. Speer, *Inside the Third Reich*, 146.

179. Rosenberg, *Das politische Tagebuch*, 66.

180. Ibid., 64f.

181. Diaries, 1 November 1938.

182. Diaries, 3 November 1938, and Rosenberg, *Das politische Tagebuch*, 64.

183. Diaries, 12 November 1938.

184. Diaries, 17 November 1938.

185. Diaries, 10 and 30 December 1938.

186. Diaries, 9 December 1938.

187. Diaries, 30 December 1938. See also Hassell, *Die Hassell-Tagebücher*, 79.

188. Diaries, 3 and 1 January 1939.

189. Diaries, 3, 4, 18, 8, and 17 January 1939.

190. A conversation with Amann recorded by Rosenberg in January 1940 (*Das politische Tagebuch*, 96) alludes to the question of Goebbels's resignation: "Amann . . . reports on a conversation with Dr. G[oebbels]. A[mann] had installed publishers and managing editors in Poland. G. had come to 'inspect' afterward and threw the people out. At that A. went to G. at the ministry and gave it to him straight—for two whole hours. He asked what had come over him, what he thought he was up to with his wretched ministry. No one wanted to have anything to do with him. All the Gauleiters were fed up, etc. G. sat there looking miserable: Dear comrade, is this the way things are going to end between us? I offered the Führer my resignation a year ago, you know."

191. Diaries, 18, 19, 20, 21 [actually 22], and 24 [actually 25] January 1939.

192. Domarus, *Hitler: Reden und Proklamationen* 2:1053.

193. Ibid.: 927.

194. Lochner, *Goebbels-Tagebücher*, 62. Goebbels stresses the importance of repetition elsewhere as well, e.g., diaries, 3 January and 8 February 1940.

195. Domarus, *Hitler: Reden und Proklamationen* 2:1092.

196. Ibid.: 1093ff.

197. Reuth, *Erwin Rommel*, 24f.

198. Diaries, 19 March 1939.

199. Goebbels 1941, 70ff.

200. Diaries, 21 March 1939.

201. Rosenberg, *Das politische Tagebuch*, 66.

202. Heiber, *Joseph Goebbels*, 274.

203. Rosenberg, *Das politische Tagebuch*, 66.

204. Speer, *Inside the Third Reich*, 146f.

205. Diaries, 1 January 1939.

206. Speer, *Inside the Third Reich*, 146f.

207. Diaries, 3 April 1939.

208. Goebbels 1941, 97ff.

209. Kordt, *Wahn und Wirklichkeit*, 152f.

210. Diaries, 21 April 1939.

211. See Terveen, "Der Filmbericht über Hitlers 50. Geburtstag," 75ff.; Georg Santé, "Parade als Paradestück," excerpt in Wulf, *Theater und Film*, 382f.; Goebbels, "Der Film als Erzieher," in Goebbels 1943a, 37ff.

212. See Bramsted, *Goebbels and National Socialist Propaganda*, 217f.

213. Goebbels, "Nochmals, die Einkreiser," *Völkischer Beobachter*, 27 May 1939.

214. Ibid.

215. Ibid. See also "Klassenkampf der Völker" in Goebbels 1941, 157ff.; "Die Moral der Reichen," ibid., 84ff.; and "Aussprache unter vier Augen mit der Demokratie," ibid., 77ff.

216. See secret instructions in Wulf, *Presse und Funk*, 106.

217. Hassell, *Die Hassell-Tagebücher*, 92; Heiber, *Goebbels Reden* (1971), 333ff.

218. See Sänger, *Politik der Täuschungen*, 371ff.; Goebbels, "Wer will den Krieg?" in Goebbels 1941, 90ff.; and "Bayonette als Wegweiser," ibid., 135ff.

219. See Goebbels 1941, 90ff., 135ff.

220. Letter from Goebbels, 2 June 1937, BAK, R 55/421.

221. Diaries, 27 August 1935.

222. See notes of Dr. Karl Ott, BAK, R 55/421.

223. Ibid.

224. See Heiber, *Joseph Goebbels*, 254.

225. Listing of costs for the propaganda minister's new official residence, BAK R 55/421.

226. BAK, R 55/421 and 423.

227. BAK, R 55/1360.

228. Ibid.; Oven, *Finale Furioso*, 38.

229. Speer, *Inside the Third Reich*, 149.

230. Ibid.

CHAPTER TWELVE

1. Speer, *Inside the Third Reich*, 162f. Similar testimony came from Goebbels's press aide of many years, Moritz von Schirmeister, who said at Nuremberg that Goebbels did "not want to push toward war" (IMT 17:263).

2. Domarus, *Hitler: Reden und Proklamationen* 2:1334.

3. Speer, *Inside the Third Reich*, 162.

4. See Wulf, *Presse und Funk*, 106. Full text in BAK, Brammer Collection, ZSg 101.

5. Ribbentrop, *Zwischen London und Moskau*, 97. See also the summary of his activity as ambassador to London, "Notiz für den Führer," 2 January 1938, *Akten zur Deutschen Auswärtigen Politik*, series D, vol. 1, doc. 93, 132ff.

6. Diaries, 24 May 1941.

7. Diaries, 16 March 1940.

8. Diaries, 9 November 1939, 12 April, and 5, 9, 25, 23, and 24 August 1940.

9. Speer, *Inside the Third Reich*, 162.

10. Sänger, *Politik der Täuschungen*, 360f.

11. Ibid., 362.

12. Confidential bulletin no. 188/39, 22 August 1939, BAK, Oberheitmann Collection, ZSg 109.

13. Quoted from Sänger, *Politik*, 363.

14. Taubert, "Der antisowjetische Apparat," BAK, Kl. Erw. 617, 6.

15. Speer, *Inside the Third Reich*, 162.

16. Domarus, *Hitler: Reden und Proklamationen* 2:1238.

17. Sänger, *Politik*, 385.

18. Ibid., 364, 384.

19. Ibid., 386.

20. Ibid.

21. Ibid., 388.

22. Quoted from Fest, *Hitler: Eine Biographie*, 803. See also Sänger, *Politik*, 379ff.

23. Sänger, *Politik*, 390.

24. See Domarus, *Hitler: Reden und Proklamationen* 2:1310f.

25. Sänger, *Politik*, 391f.

26. Domarus, *Hitler: Reden und Proklamationen* 2:1314f. In fact, the attack had begun at 4:45 A.M.

27. Goebbels, express letter, 1 September 1939, files of the Reich Chancellery, BAK, R 43 II/639, 145–47. Cf. Latour, "Goebbels 'Ausserordentliche Rundfunkmassnahmen,' " 418ff.

28. Testimony of Moritz von Schirmeister at Nuremberg, IMT 17:277.

29. Karl Wahl, Gauleiter of Swabia, on his trip through Germany at that time, in Deist et al., *Ursachen und Voraussetzungen*, 25.

30. Schmidt, *Statist auf diplomatischer Bühne*, 473.

31. Ibid., 474.

32. Diaries, 11 November 1939.

33. Testimony of Alfred Jodl at Nuremberg, IMT 15:385f.

34. *Akten zur Deutschen Auswärtigen Politik*, series d, 1937–45, vol. 7: *Die Kriegsjahre* (Baden-Baden, Frankfurt am Main, 1961), doc. 331, 24.

35. Ibid., point 7, p. 24.

36. Boelcke, *Kriegspropaganda*, 125.

37. Diaries, 8 July 1938.

38. Diaries, 3 June 1938.

39. Testimony of Moritz von Schirmeister at Nuremberg, IMT 17:280; Dietrich, *Zwölf Jahre mit Hitler*, 259.

40. Diaries, 2 December 1940.

41. Diaries, 18 and 21 November 1939.

42. Longerich, *Propagandisten im Krieg*, 137.

43. Diaries, 12 January and 6 February 1940, and 5 November 1939.

44. On the relationship between Dietrich and Goebbels, see Longerich, *Propagandisten im Krieg*, 112ff.

45. See Speer, *Inside the Third Reich*, 298. See also testimony of Hans Fritzsche at Nuremberg, IMT 17:261.

46. See Longerich, *Propagandisten im Krieg*, 115.

47. Testimony of Moritz Schirmeister at Nuremberg, IMT 17:277.

48. Diaries, 28 September 1932.

49. See Boelcke, *Kriegspropaganda*, 26f. and 49.

50. Schirmeister, IMT 17:261.

51. Diaries, 9 and 12 October 1939.

52. Diaries, 12 October 1939.

53. Diaries, 3 November 1939.

54. Diaries, 13 and 12 October 1939.

55. Diaries, 14 and 13 October 1939.

56. See William Shirer, *The Rise and Fall of the Third Reich*, 636ff.

57. Diaries, 8 November 1939.

58. Diaries, 11 November 1939.

59. Diaries, 14 November and 26 October 1939.

60. Diaries, 29 October 1939.

61. Diaries, 9 September 1939.

62. Ibid. On the assassination attempt, see Shirer, *The Rise and Fall of the Third Reich*, 652ff.

63. Diaries, 10 October 1939.

64. See Boelcke, *Kriegspropaganda*, 185.

65. Diaries, 2 November 1939. Officially the Lodz ghetto did not exist until 30 April of the following year.

66. Diaries, 17 and 8 November 1939.

67. Goebbels referred to it in his diary as "my Jew film" (28 and 11 November 1939). On Hippler, see Wulf, *Die bildenden Künste*, 13.

68. Diaries, 17 October 1939.

69. Diaries, 29 October 1939; Harlan, *Im Schatten meiner Filme*, 111f.

70. Wulf, *Theater und Film*, 456 (poster).

71. These phrases come from the review in the *Deutsche Allgemeine Zeitung*, 29 November 1940, as quoted in Wulf, *Theater und Film*, 457.

72. Harlan, *Im Schatten meiner Filme*, 86; diaries, 5 December 1939.

73. Diaries, 15 December 1939.

74. Harlan, *Im Schatten meiner Filme*, 107f.

75. Diaries, 5 January 1940; Harlan, *Im Schatten meiner Filme*, 108.

76. Wulf, *Film und Theater*, 447.

77. Diaries, 12 December 1939.

78. Rosenberg, *Das politische Tagebuch*, 91. Postponing release of these films had cost the film industry millions of marks, a problem that Goebbels attributed to "a higher power" (diaries, 29 October 1939).

79. Hans Schwarz van Berk, "Von der Kunst, zur Welt zu sprechen," in Goebbels 1941, 10.

80. Rosenberg, *Das politische Tagebuch*, 91.

81. Diaries, 21 November, 15 October, and 13 December 1939.

82. See *Das politische Tagebuch*, 91.

83. Diaries, 12 December 1939.

84. Diaries, 21, 23, and 24 December 1939. See also Goebbels's Christmas speech in Goebbels 1941, 224f.

85. New Year's speech in Goebbels 1941, 238f.

86. Diaries, 1 January 1940.

87. For a more complete account, see Shirer, *The Rise and Fall of the Third Reich*, 670ff.

88. Diaries, 16 January 1940.

89. Goebbels 1941, 304, 248, 301.

90. Boelcke, *Kriegspropaganda*, 141, 92f.

91. Ibid., 93.

92. Stephan, *Joseph Goebbels*, 211; Boelcke, *Kriegspropaganda*, 304.

93. Stephan, *Joseph Goebbels*, 211.

94. Diaries, 13 February 1940.

95. Boelcke, *Kriegspropaganda*, 272.

96. Diaries, 19 February 1940.

97. Boelcke, *Kriegspropaganda*, 289.

98. For a detailed account of the preparations for the attack on Denmark and Norway, see Shirer, *The Rise and Fall of the Third Reich*, 672–712.

99. Boelcke, *Kriegspropaganda*, 314.

100. Ibid., 310.

101. Diaries, 9 April 1940.

102. Ibid.

103. Ibid.

104. Diaries, 10 April 1940.

105. Diaries, 11 April 1940.

106. Boelcke, *Kriegspropaganda*, 107.

107. Boelcke, *Wollt ihr den totalen Krieg?*, 45.

108. See Jodl diary, IMT 28:420f.

109. Goebbels 1941, 285f.

110. Diaries, 21 and 25 April 1940.

111. Diaries, 7 May 1940.

112. Boelcke, *Kriegspropaganda*, 346.

113. Domarus, *Hitler: Reden und Proklamationen* 2:1503.

114. Diaries, 10 May 1940.

115. Diaries, 16 May 1940.

116. Diaries, 26 November and 6 December 1939.

117. See Abel, *Presselenkung im NS-Staat*, 8, on Rienhardt, and the letter from Amann to Gerdy Troost in Wulf, *Presse und Funk*, 158ff.; diaries, 14 December 1939.

118. Müller, "Portrait einer deutschen Wochenzeitung," 10. See also Kessemeier, "Leitartikler Goebbels," 138.

119. See Amann to Gerdy Troost in Wulf, *Presse und Funk*, 159.

120. Müller, "Portrait einer deutschen Wochenzeitung," 10. See also diaries, 14 December and 26 November 1939. From 7 November 1941 on, Goebbels's editorial was read over the radio every Friday from 7:45 to 8:00 P.M. (Kessemeier, "Leitartikler Goebbels," 200).

121. Diaries, 19 September 1944, ZSAP; Schwarz van Berk, "Von der Kunst, zu der Welt zu sprechen," in Goebbels 1941, 9.

122. Müller, "Portrait einer deutschen Wochenzeitung," 10.

123. Rosenberg, *Letzte Aufzeichnungen*, 193.

124. Diaries, 27 and 31 May 1940.

125. Bramsted, *Goebbels and National Socialist Propaganda*, 237.

126. Diaries, 28 May 1940.

127. Diaries, 31 May 1940.

128. Bramsted, *Goebbels and National Socialist Propaganda*, 238.

129. Diaries, 6 June 1940.

130. Diaries, 4 June 1940.

131. Diaries, 15 June 1940.

132. Diaries, 18 June 1940.

133. Diaries, 22 June 1940.

134. Diaries, 25 June 1940.

135. Diaries, 23 June 1940.

136. Diaries, 13 June, 12 April, 22 August, 23 January, and 1 April 1940, and 8 May 1941.

137. Diaries, 1 July 1940.

138. Boelcke, *Kriegspropaganda*, 417.

139. *Berliner Lokal-Anzeiger*, 6 July 1940.

140. Diaries, 7 July 1940.

141. See the reports in the *Berliner Lokal-Anzeiger*, 6 and 7 July 1940.

142. Domarus, *Hitler: Reden und Proklamationen* 2:1539.

143. Goebbels 1941, 307f.

144. Boelcke, *Kriegspropaganda*, 431.

145. Domarus, *Hitler: Reden und Proklamationen* 2:1540ff.

146. Ibid., 1558.

147. Diaries, 21 July 1940.

148. Ibid. See also Ciano, *Tagebücher*, 259.

149. Diaries, 24 July 1940.

150. Ibid.

151. Diaries, 25 July 1940.

152. Diaries, 24 July 1940.

153. Boelcke, *Kriegspropaganda*, 435.

154. Ibid.

155. Bramsted, *Goebbels and National Socialist Propaganda*, 241f.

156. Diaries, 3 August 1940.

157. Diaries, 5 September 1940.

158. Diaries, 8 September 1940.

159. Diaries, 11 September 1940.

160. Walter Hagemann, *Publizistik im Dritten Reich*, 443.

161. *Berliner Lokal-Anzeiger*, 26 September 1940.

162. Diaries, 18 August 1940.

163. Boelcke, *Kriegspropaganda*, 332.

164. See Wulf, *Theater und Film*, 451. See also the Harlan file in BDC.

165. Goebbels 1941, 319.

166. Boelcke, *Kriegspropaganda*, 492.

167. Diaries, 11 October 1940.

168. Diaries, 18 and 19 September, and 12 October 1940.

169. Diaries, 16 October 1940.

170. Diaries, 7 October 1940.

171. Diaries, 14 and 18 October, and 20 November 1940.

172. Diaries, 15 October 1940.

173. Diaries, 21 August 1940. In the winter of 1939–40 Hitler had assigned chief responsibility for the propaganda operation against France to the Propaganda Ministry, thereby substantially diminishing the Foreign Office's control for the first time.

174. Diaries, 19 October 1940.

175. Diaries, 21 October 1940.

176. Diaries, 20 October 1939, 30 April 1940, 29 March and 1 April 1941.

177. Diaries, 7 November 1939.

178. Heiber, *Joseph Goebbels*, 261.

179. BAK, R 55/422.

180. Rosenberg, *Das politische Tagebuch*, 67.

181. BAK, R55/422.

182. List of the objects purchased for the Hermann-Goering-Strasse and Lanke residences, BAK, R 55/423.

183. BAK, R 55/430.

184. BAK, R 55/422.

185. Diaries, 5 November and 5 December 1940.

186. Diaries, 4 December and 20 November 1940. See also Speer, *Inside the Third Reich*, 254: "During the first, successful phase of the war, Goebbels had shown no ambition. On the contrary, as early as 1940 he expressed his intention of devoting himself to his many personal interests once the war was brought to a victorious conclusion."

187. Diaries, 12 November 1940.

188. Hillgruber, "Noch einmal: Hitlers Wendung gegen die Sowjetunion," 607. See also Jacobsen, *Karl Haushofer* 1:607.

189. Diaries, 12 April and 5 August 1940.

190. Diaries, 23 August 1940.

191. Boelcke, *Kriegspropaganda*, 476.

192. Ibid., 455.

193. Diaries, 12 and 14 November 1940.

194. *Hitlers politisches Testament*, 80. Cf. Hillgruber, "Noch einmal: Hitlers Wendung gegen die Sowjetunion," 221f.

195. Diaries, 14 November 1940.

196. Diaries, 12 December 1940.

197. Boelcke, *Kriegspropaganda*, 558.

198. Testimony of Hans Fritzsche at Nuremberg, quoted from Longerich, *Propagandisten im Krieg*, 113.

199. Letter from Dr. Hans Joachim Kausch to Joseph Wulf, in Wulf, *Presse und Funk*, 90f.

200. See Longerich, *Propagandisten im Krieg*, 139f.

201. Diaries, 22 December 1940.

202. Diaries, 7 January 1941.

203. Diaries, 6 January 1941.

204. Diaries, 10 January 1941, and 25 October 1940.

205. Goebbels 1941, 359ff., 364ff., and 375ff.

206. Diaries, 11 March 1941.

207. Goebbels, "Wenn der Frühling auf die Berge steigt," in Goebbels 1941, 417.

208. Rosenberg, *Das politische Tagebuch*, 115. See also Wulf, *Theater und Film*, 412f.

209. Diaries, 29 November 1939.

210. See Romani, *Die Filmdivas des Dritten Reiches*, 21f.

211. Goebbels to representatives of the film industry in *Völkischer Beobachter*, 2 March 1942; diaries, 3 March 1942 (BAK, NL 118/41), 26 and 27 January 1942 (NL 118/40), and 10 May 1943 (NL 118/54). See also "Der Film als Erzieher," in Goebbels 1943a, 38.

212. Goebbels 1943a, 38.

213. See Albrecht, *Nationalsozialistische Filmpolitik*, 83, and Romani, *Die Filmdivas des Dritten Reiches*, 22.

214. Romani, *Die Filmdivas des Dritten Reiches*, 23.

215. Diaries, 21 and 3 July, and 22 September 1944.

216. Diaries, 26 May 1940.

217. Diaries, 29 March 1941.

218. Diaries, 16 April and 8 March 1941.

219. Diaries, 15, 16, 6, and 14 April 1941.

220. Diaries, 24 April 1941.

221. Diaries, 13 May 1941. On Hess's flight, see W. Hess, *Mein Vater Rudolf Hess*, 90ff.

222. Domarus, *Hitler: Reden und Proklamationen* 2:1714.

223. Diaries, 13 May 1941.

224. Semler, *Goebbels: The Man next to Hitler*, 46.

225. Diaries, 16 October 1940.

226. Diaries, 14 May 1941.

227. Ibid.

228. Domarus, *Hitler: Reden und Proklamationen* 2:1715.

229. Diaries, 15 May 1941.

230. Boelcke, *Wollt ihr den totalen Krieg?*, 170.

231. Diaries, 18 May 1941.

232. Diaries, 16 May 1941.

233. Diaries, 28 May 1941.

234. Diaries, 3 June 1941.

235. Diaries, 19 August 1941, BAK, NL 118/21.

236. Semler, *Goebbels*, 38.

237. Diaries, 22 May 1941.

238. Diaries, 7 and 11–15 June 1941.

239. Diaries, 14 June 1941.

240. Ibid.

241. Boelcke, *Wollt ihr den totalen Krieg?*, 180; Semler, *Goebbels*, 39.

242. Diaries, 31 May 1941.

243. Semler, *Goebbels*, 42; diaries, 16 June 1941.

244. Diaries, 16 June 1941.

245. Semler, *Goebbels*, 36f.

246. Diaries, 16 June 1941. See introduction to diaries by Elke Fröhlich, IfZ 1:liv–lv.

247. Diaries, 16 June 1941.

248. Diaries, 22 June 1941.

249. Ibid.

250. Ibid.

CHAPTER THIRTEEN

1. *Völkischer Beobachter*, 23 June 1941.

2. Boelcke, *Wollt ihr den totalen Krieg?*, 181–83.

3. Diaries, 30 June 1941.

4. Semler, *Goebbels: The Man next to Hitler*, 46.

5. Diaries, 24 July 1941, BAK, NL 118/18.

6. Boberach, *Meldungen aus dem Reich*, 167.

7. Diaries, 7 August 1941, BAK, NL 118/19.

8. Diaries, 19 August 1941, BAK, NL 118/21.

9. Ibid.

10. Diaries, 21 and 29 August 1941, BAK, NL 118/21.

11. Diaries, 1 and 13 June 1941.

12. Longerich, *Propagandisten im Kriege*, 141f.

13. Ibid., 142.

14. Taubert, "Der antisowjetische Apparat," 7, BAK, Kl. Erw., 653-2.

15. Diaries, 21 August 1941, BAK, NL 118/21.

16. Summary of "The work of the Eastern propaganda unit of the Propaganda Ministry," attachment to a letter to Hitler, 23 May 1943, BAK, R 55/799.

17. Diaries, 14 August 1941, BAK, NL 118/20.

18. Taubert, "Die Politik in den besetzten Ostgebieten," 24 February 1943, BAK, R 55/567.

19. Taubert, "Der antisowjetische Apparat," 8.

20. Lochner, *Goebbels Tagebücher*, 123.

21. Ibid., 122f.

22. Taubert, "Der antisowjetische Apparat," 8.

23. Diaries, 24 September 1941, BAK, NL 118/24.

24. Domarus, *Hitler: Reden und Proklamationen* 2:1758ff. See also Dietrich, *Zwölf Jahre mit Hitler*, 101ff.

25. Diaries, 4 October 1941, BAK, NL 118/28.

26. Hagemann, *Publizistik im Dritten Reich*, 253; diaries, 10 October 1941, BAK, NL 118/28.

27. Semler, *Goebbels*, 56.

28. Diaries, 28 October 1941, BAK, NL 118/31.

29. *Das Reich*, 20 July 1941.

30. Diaries, 24 July 1941, BAK, NL 118/18.

31. Diaries, 20 August 1941, BAK, NL 118/21.

32. Minutes of a discussion in the Reich Propaganda Directorate, quoted from Adler, *Der verwaltete Mensch*, 152f. See also Schmidt, *Albert Speer: Das Ende eines Mythos*, 218f.

33. Diaries, 18, 20, and 19 August 1941, BAK, NL 118/21.

34. See Adler, *Der verwaltete Mensch*, 50f.

35. Diaries, 19 August 1941, BAK, NL 118/21.

36. Diaries, 24 September 1941, BAK, NL 118/24.

37. Reitlinger, *Die Endlösung*, 97f.

38. "Die Juden sind schuld!" *Das Reich*, 16 November 1941.

39. Reuth, *Erwin Rommel*, 117.

40. Diaries, 22 November 1941, BAK, NL 118/36.

41. Diaries, 13 August 1941, BAK, NL 118/20.

42. Diary fragment, 20 December 1941, RC.
43. Boelcke, *Wollt ihr den totalen Krieg?*, 196.
44. Ibid., 200.
45. See Hitler, *Der grossdeutsche Freiheitskampf*, 203.
46. Diary fragment, 20 December 1941, RC.
47. Goebbels 1943a, 134f.
48. Ibid., 178.
49. Fredborg, *The Steel Wall*, 67f.
50. *Völkischer Beobachter*, 30 January 1942.
51. Diaries, 30 and 31 January 1942, BAK, NL 118/38.
52. Heiber, *Goebbels Reden* (1972), 81; diaries, 31 January 1942, BAK, NL 118/38.
53. Diaries, 31 January 1942, BAK, NL 118/38.
54. Diaries, 24 January 1942, BAK, NL 118/38.
55. Picker, *Hitlers Tischgespräche*, 374.
56. Boelcke, *Wollt ihr den totalen Krieg?*, 210f.
57. *Das Reich*, 23 November 1941.
58. Diaries, 11 February 1942, BAK, NL 118/39.
59. Goebbels, "Schatten über dem Empire," in Goebbels 1943a, 215 and 221.
60. Diaries, 18 February 1942, BAK, NL 118/40.
61. Diaries, 20 March 1942, BAK, NL 118/42.
62. Goebbels, "Die Ostfront," in Goebbels 1943a, 322.
63. See Reitlinger, *Die Endlösung*, 175f.
64. Boelcke, *Wollt ihr den totalen Krieg?*, 243.
65. Quoted from Reitlinger, *Die Endlösung*, 111.
66. Diaries, 6 April 1942, BAK, NL 118/43.
67. Diaries, 23 May 1942, BAK, NL 118/46.
68. *Das Reich*, 31 May 1942.
69. *Völkischer Beobachter*, 23 June 1942.
70. Boelcke, *Wollt ihr den totalen Krieg?*, 249.
71. Picker, *Hitlers Tischgespräche*, 372f.
72. Boelcke, *Wollt ihr den totalen Krieg?*, 252.
73. Hitler's letter to Mussolini of 23 June 1942, in Reuth, *Entscheidung am Mittelmeer*, 200 and 250f., doc. 13.
74. Reuth, *Erwin Rommel*, 98.
75. Reitlinger, *Die Endlösung*, 176.
76. Excerpt from doc. 682-PS, IMT 5:496f.

77. Quoted from Reitlinger, *Die Endlösung*, 176.

78. Boelcke, *Wollt ihr den totalen Krieg?*, 277.

79. Ibid., 282.

80. Longerich, *Propagandisten im Kriege*, 114; Boelcke, *Wollt ihr den totalen Krieg?*, 285.

81. Goebbels, "Der steile Aufstieg," *Das Reich*, 20 September 1942.

82. Boelcke, *Wollt ihr den totalen Krieg?*, 286.

83. Quoted from Irving, *Rommel*, 295.

84. Berndt file, BDC.

85. Boelcke, *Wollt ihr den totalen Krieg?*, 229.

86. Stephan, *Joseph Goebbels*, 287.

87. Bramsted, *Goebbels and National Socialist Propaganda*, 259f.

88. Semler, *Goebbels*, 59.

89. Speer, *Inside the Third Reich*, 254ff.

90. Semler, *Goebbels*, 61.

91. See Hölsken, *Die V-Waffen*, 169.

92. Semler, *Goebbels*, 60; diaries, 19 December 1942, BAK, NL 118/48.

93. Semler, *Goebbels*, 62ff.

94. Harlan, *Im Schatten meiner Filme*, 140.

95. Boelcke, *Wollt ihr den totalen Krieg?*, 316.

96. Ibid. See also Moltmann, "Goebbels Rede zum Totalen Krieg," 234ff.

97. Boelcke, *Wollt ihr den totalen Krieg?*, 318.

98. Diaries, 18 January 1943, BAK, NL 118/50.

99. Boelcke, *Wollt ihr den totalen Krieg?*, 242.

100. Speer, *Inside the Third Reich*, 252ff.

101. Semler, *Goebbels*, 66.

102. Diaries, 21 January 1943, BAK, NL 118/50.

103. Diaries, 23 January, 1943, BAK, NL 118/50.

104. Ibid. See also Boelcke, "Goebbels und die Kundgebung im Berliner Sportpalast," 242.

105. Boelcke, *Wollt ihr den totalen Krieg?*, 326.

106. Heiber, *Goebbels Reden* (1972), 158ff.

107. Domarus, *Hitler: Reden und Proklamationen* 2:1979.

108. Heiber, *Goebbels Reden* (1972), 160, 169, 170.

109. Trevor-Roper, *Hitlers letzte Tage*, 37.

110. Diaries, 2 February 1943, BAK, NL 118/52.

111. Hinkel to Goebbels, 3 February 1943, BAK, R 55/1254.

112. *Wehrmachtsberichte 1939–1945*, 2:435.

113. Diaries, 23 January 1943, BAK, NL 118/50.

114. Boelcke, *Wollt ihr den totalen Krieg?*, 334.

115. Instructions to the press, 7 February 1943, quoted in ibid.

116. Diaries, 10 and 14 January 1943, BAK, NL 118/49.

117. Diaries, 10 January 1943, BAK, NL 118/49.

118. Diaries, 14 January 1943, BAK, NL 118/49.

119. Diaries, 31 January 1943, BAK, NL 118/50.

120. Boelcke, *Wollt ihr den totalen Krieg?*, 338.

121. Diaries, 10 and 11 February 1943, BAK, NL 118/52.

122. Diaries, 14–18 February 1943, BAK, NL 118/52 and 53. See also Moltmann, "Goebbels Rede zum Totalen Krieg," 25ff.

123. Speer, *Inside the Third Reich*, 257.

124. Heiber, *Goebbels Reden* (1972), 172ff.

125. Speer, *Inside the Third Reich*, 257.

126. Heiber, *Goebbels Reden* (1972), 208.

127. Head of the propaganda staff to Goebbels, 19 February 1943, BAK, R 55/612.

128. See Moltmann, "Goebbels Rede zum Totalen Kriege," 26.

129. For a detailed account, see Speer, *Inside the Third Reich*, 257–65.

130. Diaries, 2 March and 18 April 1943, BAK, NL 118/54.

131. Statistics from Kempner, "Die Ermordung von 35000 Berliner Juden," 180ff.

132. Diaries, 2 March and 18 April 1943, BAK, NL 118/54.

133. Reich Ministry for Popular Enlightenment and Propaganda, Listening Service, 22 December 1942, BAK, R 55/1355.

134. Cable to the Reichssicherheitshauptamt, Section IIIC, attn. SS Hauptsturmführer Dr. Hirche, 4 April 1943, BAK, R 55/115.

135. Minutes, ministerial conference, 8 April 1943, BAK, R 55/115.

136. Diaries, 16 and 17 April 1943, BAK, NL 118/54.

137. *Polish-Soviet Relations, 1918–1943*, doc. 39, 119.

138. *Soviet Foreign Policy during the Patriotic War* 1:202.

139. Diaries, 28 April 1943, BAK, NL 118/54.

140. Reuth, *Erwin Rommel*, 104.

141. Ibid., 104f.

142. Boberach, *Meldungen aus dem Reich*, 387ff.

143. Diaries, 6 March 1943, BAK, NL 118/54.

144. Diaries, 8 January 1943, BAK, NL 118/49.

145. Semler, *Goebbels*, 88.

146. Diaries, 28 May 1943, BAK, NL 118/55.

147. Stephan, *Joseph Goebbels*, 275.

148. Goebbels 1943c, 8.

149. See Hölsken, *Die V-Waffen*, 93ff. [The V in the name of the V-1 and V-2 rockets stood for *Vergeltung*, "retribution."—Tr.] According to Semler, Hans Schwarz van Berk invented the concept of the "V-weapons" (Semler, *Goebbels*, 131). See also Kessemeier, "Leitartikler Goebbels," 299f.

150. Hölsken, *Die V-Waffen*, 96.

151. Boberach, *Meldungen aus dem Reich*, 413.

152. Diaries, 21 September 1943, BAK, NL 118/56.

153. Oven, *Finale Furioso*, 115.

154. Lochner, *Goebbels Tagebücher*, 9.

155. Diaries, 10–13 September 1943, BAK, NL 118/56.

156. Goebbels, "Das Schulbeispiel," *Das Reich*, 19 September 1943.

157. Bramsted, *Goebbels and National Socialist Propaganda*, 282.

158. Diaries, 7 November 1943, BAK, NL 118/56.

159. Heiber, *Goebbels Reden* (1972), 277f.

160. Girbig, . . . *im Anflug auf die Reichshauptstadt*, 69f.

161. Springer, *Es sprach Hans Fritzsche*, 17.

162. Stephan, *Joseph Goebbels*, 268.

163. Ibid., 267.

164. Diaries, 29 November 1943, BAK, NL 118/56.

165. Stephan, *Joseph Goebbels*, 260f.

166. Schäfer, *Berlin im Zweiten Weltkrieg*, 41.

167. Semler, *Goebbels*, 111.

168. Führer's decree of 21 December 1943, BAK, R 43 II/669 d.

169. Goebbels's telegram to Hitler, Christmas 1943, and draft of a telegram to Hitler for New Year's 1944, BAK, NL 118/100.

170. Taubert, "Der antisowjetische Apparat," 9, BAK, Kl. Erw., 653-2.

171. Diaries, 17 February 1944, ZSAP. See also Domarus, *Hitler: Reden und Proklamationen* 2:1154, and Grosscurth, *Tagebücher eines Abwehroffiziers*, 179.

172. Diaries, 25 February 1944, ZSAP.

173. Diaries, 8 April 1944, and an undated entry, ZSAP.

174. Goebbels to Hitler, 20 April 1944, BAK, NL 118/100.

175. *Das Reich*, 9 April 1944. See also "Die Nemesis der Geschichte," ibid., 21 May 1944.

176. *Völkischer Beobachter*, 28–29 May 1944, reprinted in IMT 27:436ff.

177. Directive 125/44 (not for publication), "In re: people's justice for Anglo-American murderers," reprinted in IMT 25:112f.

178. From the grounds for sentencing Bormann, IMT 1:385.

179. "In re: shooting of U.S. Air Force Lieutenant Dennis by SS Brigadeführer Berndt, to Brigadeführer Dr. Klopfer (Party Chancery)," July 1944, BDC; notes, Dr. Keitel, IMT 5:20.

180. Diaries, 6 and 5 June 1944, ZSAP.

181. Diaries, 6 June 1944, ZSAP; Semler (*Goebbels*, 127), quotes Goebbels as saying, "Thank God, finally. This is the last round."

182. Diaries, 7 June 1944, ZSAP; Semler, *Goebbels*, 128.

183. Boberach, *Meldungen aus dem Reich*, 472ff. See also Hölsken, *Die V-Waffen*, 102ff.

184. Oven, *Finale Furioso*, 359.

185. Diaries, 18 June 1944, ZSAP.

186. Oven, *Finale Furioso*, 361.

187. Diaries, 18 June 1944, ZSAP.

188. Hölsken, *Die V-Waffen*, 104f., 107.

189. Diaries, 5 April 1944, ZSAP.

190. See Semler, *Goebbels*, 122.

191. Diaries, 14 June 1944, ZSAP.

192. Diaries, 16 June 1944, ZSAP.

193. See Herbst, *Der Totale Krieg und die Ordnung der Wirtschaft*, 207ff.

194. Diaries, 22 June 1944, ZSAP.

195. Ibid.

196. Diaries, 9 July 1944, ZSAP.

197. Speer, *Inside the Third Reich*, 396.

198. Diaries, 14 July 1944, ZSAP.

199. Longerich, "Joseph Goebbels und der Totale Krieg," 289ff.

CHAPTER FOURTEEN

1. Heiber, *Goebbels Reden* (1972), 342.

2. Speer, *Inside the Third Reich*, 380–89.

3. Ibid., 388.

4. Oven, *Finale Furioso*, 427ff.

5. Minutes, 22 July 1944, BAK, R 55/664a.

6. Diaries, 23 July 1944, ZSAP.

7. Minutes, 22 July 1944, BAK, R 55/664a.

8.   Ibid.

9.   Diaries, 23 July 1944, ZSAP.

10. Ibid.

11. Ibid.

12. Bramsted, *Goebbels and National Socialist Propaganda*, 346ff.

13. Report as of 24 July 1944, BAK, R 55/601.

14. Heiber, *Goebbels Reden* (1972), 400.

15. Longerich, "Goebbels und der Totale Krieg," 302.

16. Undated circular letter, "In re: style of life in total war," BAK, R 55/665.

17. Riess, *Joseph Goebbels*, 400.

18. Heiber, *Goebbels Reden* (1972), 366, 370.

19. Director of film (Hinkel) to undersecretary (Naumann), 31 August 1944, BAK, R 55/664.

20. On Goebbels's fear of Bormann, see Hans Fritzsche's testimony at Nuremberg, IMT 17:221; undated draft of cable to NSDAP Gauleiters, BAK, R 55/664.

21. Oven, *Mit Goebbels bis zum Ende* 2:118.

22. For Helldorf's account of his reasons for participating in the 20 July plot, see court proceedings in Jacobsen, *Spiegelbild einer Verschwörung* 1:104.

23. Gisevius, *To the Bitter End*, 499.

24. Diaries, 9 and 10 February 1944, ZSAP.

25. Stephan, *Joseph Goebbels*, 295.

26. Semler, *Goebbels: The Man next to Hitler*, 159.

27. Diaries, 7 June 1944, ZSAP.

28. Manfred Rommel to David Irving, 7 June 1975, IfZ, Irving Collection.

29. Ibid. See also the Berndt file, BDC.

30. For a complete listing of Goebbels's measures, see Bramsted, *Goebbels and National Socialist Propaganda*, 353–55.

31. See letters of Bormann to Goebbels, 14 and 24 August 1944, BAK, R 55/665 and 666a.

32. Oven, *Finale Furioso*, 393; diaries, 13 July 1944, ZSAP; Goebbels, "Die Überholung des Vorsprungs," *Das Reich*, 30 July 1944.

33. Steinert, *Hitlers Krieg und die Deutschen*, 497.

34. Speer, *Inside the Third Reich*, 369.

35. Diaries, 30 August 1944, ZSAP.

36. Diaries, 31 August 1944, ZSAP.

37. Diaries, probably 7 September 1944, ZSAP.

38. Diaries, 10 September 1944, ZSAP.

39. Diaries, 11–13 September 1944, ZSAP.

40. Diaries, 10 September 1944, ZSAP.

41. Lochner, *Goebbels Tagebücher*, September 1943 entries. The memorandum is cast in the form of a letter beginning "Mein Führer," BAK, NL 118/100. On the chronology, see Oven, *Finale Furioso*, 479ff.

42. Diaries, 23 September 1944, ZSAP.

43. Diaries, 25 September 1944, ZSAP.

44. Goebbels to Hitler, 25 October 1944, IfZ, ED 172.

45. Heiber, *Goebbels Reden* (1972), 405ff.

46. Report of activity as of 16 October 1944, BAK, R 55/601.

47. See Reuth, *Erwin Rommel*, 110ff., and Shirer, *The Rise and Fall of the Third Reich*, 1041f. See also diaries, probably 7 September 1944, ZSAP.

48. Reuth, *Erwin Rommel*, 132.

49. Semler, *Goebbels*, 162f.; diaries, 29 October 1944, ZSAP.

50. Domarus, *Hitler: Reden und Proklamationen* 2:2160.

51. *Wehrmachtsberichte* 3:324.

52. Diaries, 31 August, and 7 (?) and 8 September 1944, ZSAP; Speer, *Inside the Third Reich*, 410.

53. Semler, *Goebbels*, 165f.

54. See Speer's testimony at Nuremberg, quoted by Erdmann, *Der Zweite Weltkrieg*, 126f.

55. To counteract any increase in the power of the party, Hitler had made SS chief and head of police Himmler minister of the interior, which allowed him to issue directives to the Gauleiters in their capacity as defense commissars, and to operate in Bormann's domain.

56. On the swearing in, see the documents in BAK, R 55/1287.

57. Diaries, 4 December 1944, ZSAP.

58. Semler (*Goebbels*, 174), describes this event as taking place on 12 January, but in fact Hitler was at his Eagle's Nest headquarters until 16 January. There is no corroboration for the 12 January date in Goebbels's diaries. See also Riess, *Joseph Goebbels*, 44.

59. Semler, *Goebbels*, 168. See also Oven, *Finale Furioso*, 528f.

60. Semler, *Goebbels*, 170.

61. Diaries, 19 December 1944, ZSAP.

62. Riess, *Joseph Goebbels*, 410.

63. Oven, *Finale Furioso*, 533ff.

64. Goebbels to Hitler, Christmas 1944, BAK, NL 118/100; Goebbels's New Year's address, *Völkischer Beobachter*, 2 January 1945.

65. Domarus, *Hitler: Reden und Proklamationen* 2:2185.

66. Goebbels also drew on this alleged historical parallel in his speech in Cologne on 3 October 1944. See Heiber, *Goebbels Reden* (1972), 408f.

67. This passage from the *Alexanderschlacht* and Goebbels's accompanying note to Hitler, dated 10 January 1945, are in BAK, NL 118/100.

68. Diaries, 23 and 26 January 1945, ZSAP.

69. Diaries, 29 January 1945, ZSAP.

70. Ibid.

71. Domarus, *Hitler: Reden und Proklamationen* 2:2194.

72. Oven, *Finale Furioso*, 520f.

73. Ibid., 545f.

74. Domarus, *Hitler: Reden und Proklamationen* 2:2194f.

75. On the situation in Berlin, see Schäfer, *Berlin im Zweiten Weltkrieg*, 62ff.

76. Quoted from Fraenkel and Manvell, *Goebbels*, 323.

77. Oven, *Finale Furioso*, 559f.

78. Ibid., 566.

79. Ibid., 573f.

80. Goebbels, "Das politische Bürgertum vor der Entscheidung," *Das Reich*, 4 February 1945.

81. Goebbels, "Das Jahr 2000," *Das Reich*, 25 February 1945. He had already used the term "iron curtain" in a 3 December 1944 editorial in *Das Reich*. On propaganda in the last few months of the war, see Bramsted, *Goebbels and National Socialist Propaganda*, 364–73.

82. See Heiber, *Goebbels Reden* (1963), 431f.

83. Kronika, *Der Untergang Berlins*, 58.

84. Testimony of Albert Speer at Nuremberg, IMT 16:543.

85. Testimony of Adolph von Steengracht at Nuremberg, IMT 10:141.

86. Testimony of Hans Fritzsche at Nuremberg, IMT 17:283, and testimony of Albert Speer, IMT 16:542.

87. Jodl's notes for a presentation to Hitler, dated 21 February 1945, IMT 35:181ff. See also statement of Gen. August Winter of the Wehrmacht High Command, ibid., 15:660f.

88. Semler, *Goebbels*, 180f.

89. Diaries, 28 February 1945.

90. Oven, *Finale Furioso*, 576.

91. Semler, *Goebbels*, 179f.

92. Diaries, 8 March 1945.

93. Oven, *Finale Furioso*, 585ff.

94. Diaries, 28 February 1945.

95. Diaries, 5 March 1945.

96. Ibid.

97. Oven, *Finale Furioso*, 582.

98. Diaries, 9 March 1945.

99. *Völkischer Beobachter*, 11 March 1945.

100. Rupprecht Sommer, letter to the author, 16 October 1987.

101. *Völkischer Beobachter*, 11 March 1945.

102. Diaries, 4 March 1945.

103. Wagner's radio message to Hanke and comment, dated 3 March 1945, BDC.

104. Diaries, 11 March 1945; Oven, *Finale Furioso*, 606.

105. Diaries, 14 March 1945.

106. Ibid.

107. Semler, *Goebbels*, 187.

108. Ibid., 186.

109. Below, *Als Hitlers Adjutant*, 411.

110. Fraenkel and Manvell, *Goebbels*, 323f. See also Speer, *Inside the Third Reich*, 466.

111. Diaries, 5 March 1945.

112. Diaries, 18 March 1945.

113. Domarus, *Hitler: Reden und Proklamationen* 2: 2215.

114. Diaries, 30 March, and 1 and 2 April 1945.

115. Diaries, 26 March 1945.

116. Diaries, 31 March 1945.

117. Diaries, 22 March 1945.

118. Diaries, 28 March and 1 April 1945.

119. Riess, *Joseph Goebbels*, 439.

120. Diaries, 2 April 1945.

121. Manfred Rommel to David Irving, 7 June 1975, IfZ, Irving Collection; diaries, 30 March 1945.

122. Diaries, 22 March 1945.

123. Below, *Als Hitlers Adjutant*, 409. See also Speer, *Inside the Third Reich*, 463.

124. See Trevor-Roper, *Hitlers letzte Tage*, 117.

125. Semler, *Goebbels*, 190ff.; Bramsted, *Goebbels and National Socialist Propaganda*, 363f.

126. See Trevor-Roper, *Hitlers letzte Tage*, 118; Bramsted, *Goebbels and National Socialist Propaganda*, 362–64; Shirer, *The Rise and Fall of the Third Reich*, 1110; Below, *Als Hitlers Adjutant*, 408.

CHAPTER FIFTEEN

1. Below, *Als Hitlers Adjutant*, 408.

2. "Der Einsatz des eigenen Lebens," *Das Reich*, 15 April 1945. In this article Goebbels speaks in the first person, something very unusual for him.

3. Domarus, *Hitler: Reden und Proklamationen* 2:2224.

4. Oven, *Finale Furioso*, 647.

5. Heiber, *Goebbels Reden* (1972), 454ff.

6. *Frankfurter Allgemeine Zeitung*, 11 April 1985.

7. Schäfer, *Berlin im Zweiten Weltkrieg*, 69.

8. Krosigk, *Es geschah in Deutschland*, 234f.

9. Trevor-Roper, *Hitlers letzte Tage*, 122.

10. Koller, *Der letzte Monat*, 16; Trevor-Roper, *Hitlers letzte Tage*, 125f.

11. Heiber, *Goebbels Reden* (1963), 452.

12. Fest, *Hitler*, 1006.

13. Kessemeier, "Leitartikler Goebbels," 337.

14. Goebbels, "Widerstand um jeden Preis," *Das Reich*, 22 April 1945.

15. Schäfer, *Berlin in Zweiten Weltkrieg*, 70f.

16. Springer, *Es sprach Hans Fritzsche*, 30.

17. See afterword to *Tagebücher 1945*, 468, and foreword to diaries, IfZ 1:lxiif.

18. Trevor-Roper, *Hitlers letzte Tage*, 131f.; testimony of stenographer Hergesell in *Kriegstagebuch der Oberkommando der Wehrmacht* 4:2, 1696f.

19. Speer, *Inside the Third Reich*, 484f.; Fest, *Hitler*, 1007.

20. These "orders" have been mistakenly interpreted to mean that the move by the Goebbels family was initiated by Hitler. In fact it came about at Goebbels's urging. See Below, *Als Hitlers Adjutant*, 415.

21. See Oven, *Finale Furioso*, 653f., and Auguste Behrend, "Meine Tochter Magda Goebbels," *Schwäbische Illustrierte*, 23 May 1953.

22. See Gellermann, *Die Armee Wenck*, and Walter Wenck, "Berlin war nicht zu retten," *Der Stern*, 8 April 1965.

23. Goebbels's proclamation appeared in the newspaper in pamphlet form as *Der Panzerbär*, 23 April 1945. See also Schenk, *Ich sah Berlin sterben*, 102, and Kronika, *Der Untergang Berlins*, 152.

24. Speer, *Inside the Third Reich*, 481.

25. Letter to Harald Quandt, 28 April 1945, quoted in *Tagebücher 1945*, 456f.

26. Quoted from Domarus, *Hitler: Reden und Proklamationen* 2:2228.

27. Speer, *Inside the Third Reich*, 482f.

28. Gellermann, *Die Armee Wenck*, 78.

29. For one detailed description of these events, see Shirer, *The Rise and Fall of the Third Reich*, 1116f.

30. See Domarus, *Hitler: Reden und Proklamationen* 2:2233; Trevor-Roper, *Hitlers letzte Tage*, 173; Shirer, *Rise and Fall*, 1123.

31. For the exact text of the testament, see *Tagebücher 1945*, 458ff. See also Shirer, *Rise and Fall*, 1123–27.

32. For the text of Goebbels's appendix, see Shirer, *Rise and Fall*, 1128.

33. Domarus, *Hitler: Reden und Proklamationen* 2:2241.

34. See the statement by Hitler's adjutant Günsche, in Uwe Bahnsen and James O'Donnell, *Die Katakombe*, 210.

35. Ibid., 212f. See also Domarus, *Hitler: Reden und Proklamationen* 2:2248.

36. Trevor-Roper, *Hitlers letzte Tage*, 194.

37. Shukow, *Erinnerungen und Gedanken* 2:353; Lew Besymenski, *Die letzten Notizen von Martin Bormann*, 276.

38. Besymenski, *Die letzten Notizen von Martin Bormann*, 275f.

39. Bahnsen and O'Donnell, *Die Katakombe*, 229.

40. *Kriegstagebuch des Oberkommandos der Wehrmacht* 4:2, 1468f.

41. Artur Axmann interviewed by K. Frank Korf, 27 April 1948, Korf Papers, Hoover.

42. Besymenski, *Der Tod des Adolf Hitler*, 210f., 321ff.

43. Bahnsen and O'Donnell, *Die Katakombe*, 240.

44. For differing versions of the Goebbelses' deaths, see Axmann interview, Korf Papers, Hoover; Axmann in *Die Zeit*, 16 August 1968; Besymenski, *Der Tod des Adolf Hitler*, 149, 151, 313; Trevor-Roper, *Hitlers letzte Tage*, 203; Bahnsen and O'Donnell, *Die Katakombe*, 240; and Schwägermann's testimony, Trevor-Roper Papers 4:1491ff., IfZ.

45. Besymenski, *Der Tod des Adolf Hitler*, 149.

46. For details on the autopsies and the identification of the corpses, see Besymenski, *Der Tod des Adolf Hitler*, 331ff; Hans Fritzsche interview, Korf Papers, Hoover; Heiber, *Joseph Goebbels*, 419; and Trevor-Roper, *Hitlers letzte Tage*, 33.

Bibliography

A. PRIMARY SOURCES

1. Archival Collections (overview)

Berlin Document Center (BDC)
NSDAP master file (membership card, MF); party correspondence (PK); officer files for the SS (SSO); SA files (SA); Party Supreme Court (OPG, also Investigation and Mediation Committee, acronym USCHLA); Chamber of Culture (KK); Race and Settlement Central Bureau (RUSHA); documents pertaining to: Ludmilla Babkova (Lida Baarova); Alfred Ingemar Berndt; Martin Bormann; Kurt Daluege; Walter Richard Darré; Otto Dietrich; Dagobert Dürr; Franz von Epp; Hermann Esser; Roland Freisler; Wilhelm Frick; Hans Fritzsche; Walther Funk; Joseph Goebbels; Magda Goebbels; Hermann Goering; Ernst Hanfstaengl; Karl Hanke; Veit Harlan; Zara Stina Hedberg (Zarah Leander); Wolf Heinrich von Helldorf; Heinrich Himmler; Hans Hinkel; Karoly Kampmann; Erich Koch; Ingeborg von Kusserow; Julius Lippert; Otto Meissner; Georg Wilhelm Müller; Werner Naumann; Hanna Reitsch; Alfred Rosenberg; Bernhard Rüst; Marianne Simson; Walter Stennes; Gregor Strasser; Otto Strasser; Werner Studentkowski; Albert Tonak; Otto Wagner; Horst Wessel.

Bundesarchiv Koblenz (BAK) (German Federal Archives, Koblenz)
NL 118: Goebbels papers; R 43: Reich Chancellery; R 55: Reich Ministry for Popular Enlightenment and Propaganda; R 56 I: Reich Chamber of Culture (central office); R 56 II: Reich Chamber of Music; R 56 III: Reich Chamber of Theater; R 56 IV: Reich Press Chamber; R 56 V: Reich Chamber of Literature; R 56 VI: Reich Film Chamber; R 56 VII: Reich Chamber of Fine Arts; NS 8: Rosenberg Chancery; NS 10: Personal Adjutancy of the Führer and Reich Chancellor; NS 18: Reich Propaganda Director of the NSDAP; NS 22: Reich Organization Leader; NS 23: Storm Divisions of the NSDAP (SA); NS 26: Main

Where English translations or English originals exist, these have been added to the listing.—Tr.

Archives of the NSDAP; NS 42: Reich Press Chief of the NSDAP; Small Acquisitions (Kl. Erw.): Kl. Erw. 144: notes by Albert Grzesinski about his political activities, made in Paris after his emigration in December 1933; Kl. Erw. 433: Prof. Justus Hedemann's notes on the Reichstag fire trial in Leipzig; Kl. Erw. 617: Eberhard Taubert, "Der antisowjetische Apparat des deutschen Propagandaministeriums"; Kl. Erw. 653-2: memoirs of Attorney Rüdiger von der Golz (1894–1976); Brammer Collection: ZSg 101 (daily and weekly slogans from the Reich Ministry for Popular Enlightenment and Propaganda); Oberheitmann Collection: ZSg 109 ("Confidential Information" for editors in chief); Sänger Collection: ZSg 102 (secret instructions to the German press); Schumacher Collection: ZSg 115 (newspaper articles); Traub Collection: ZSg 110 ("Confidential Information" formulated according to the instructions and communications imparted at the Reich government press briefing).

Geheimes Staatsarchiv Preussischer Kulturbesitz, Berlin (GSPK) (Classified State Archives, Prussian Cultural Holdings)
I. HA Rep. 84a, no. 3157: "Die NSDAP als staats- und republikfeindliche hochverräterische Verbindung," memorandum from the Prussian minister of the interior, Berlin, October 1930; I. HA Rep. 84a, no. 4184: "Der Aufstieg der NSDAP," memorandum from the Prussian ministry of the interior, Berlin, October 1930; Rep. 219, no. 20.

Generalstaatsanwaltschaft bei dem Landgericht Berlin/Berlin-Moabit (GSALB) (State's Attorney's Office, Regional Court for Berlin and Berlin-Moabit)
Rep. 58: nos. 11, 19, 22, 29, 31, 34, 50, 52, 83, 806. Includes proceedings against Goebbels; against Höhler et al. for murder of student Horst Wessel; against Thunert et al. for shooting police captains Anlauf and Lenk (Bülowplatz, 9 August 1931).

Genoud Collection, Lausanne (GC)
About 550 originals of letters and postcards to and from Goebbels from the years 1914–24; school report cards; documents; compositions; literary writings; etc. Photocopies of most of these documents can be found in BAK, NL 118/109ff.

Hoover Institution Stanford University, Calif. (Hoover)
Joseph Goebbels Folder, miscellaneous papers; K. Frank Korf Papers; interviews with Katharina Goebbels, née Odenhausen (25 March 1948); with Konrad Goebbels (17 March 1948); with Maria Kimmich, née Goebbels (25 March 1948); with Harald Quandt (4 April 1948); with Hans Fritzsche (30 April 1948); with Max Amann (4 May 1948); with Max Winkler (1 May 1948); and with Artur Axmann (27 April 1948).

Institut für Hochschulkunde, Universität Würzburg (UW) (Institute for University Research, University of Würzburg)
Files of the Catholic Unitas Fraternity, Würzburg.

Institut für Zeitgeschichte, Munich (IfZ) (Institute for Contemporary History)
ED 172: Goebbels papers; Irving Collection: Trevor-Roper Papers; MA-596.

Jagiellonian Library, Cracow (JL)
Horst Wessel diaries, 3 vols. (Ms. Germ. Oct. 761, 762), from the former Prussian State Library, Berlin.

Landesarchiv Berlin (LAB) (Regional Archives, Berlin)
Files of the State's Attorney's Office, Regional Court for Berlin: Rep. 58, Zug. 399: nos. 2, 5, 9, 20, 23, 24, 25, 27, 30, 39, 43, 47, 302, 385, 445, 509, 694, 695, 697, 721, 742, 759, 1151, 1708, 2585, 6015 (including *Weiss vs. Goebbels; Hindenburg vs. Goebbels*, 1927–32); Rep. 244: NSDAP offices and party organizations (1932–44).

Reuth Collection (RC)
Handwritten fragments from the period January–July 1929; fragment of an early draft of "Die Saat"; drafts for *Der Angriff* essays; unpublished typescript of the reminiscences of Lida Baarova; tape recording of a conversation between Lida Baarova and the author on 3 September 1987 in Salzburg.

Stadtarchiv Mönchengladbach (SAM) (City Archives, Mönchengladbach)
Vital statistics records for the Goebbels families; honorary citizenship decree, etc.; letters and other documents.

Zentrales Staatsarchiv der DDR, Potsdam (ZSAP) (Central State Archives of the German Democratic Republic, Potsdam)
Goebbels diaries, 1944–45.

2. The Writings of Joseph Goebbels

A. DIARIES (PUBLISHED)

Die Tagebücher von Joseph Goebbels: Sämtliche Fragmente. Edited by Elke Fröhlich for the Institut für Zeitgeschichte, Munich, in collaboration with the Bundesarchiv. Part I, 1924–41. Vol. 1: "Erinnerungsblätter" ("Memories") (1897 to October 1924); diary entries from 27 June 1924 to 31 December 1930. Vol. 2: diary entries from 1 January 1931 to 31 December 1936. Vol. 3: diary entries from 1 January 1937 to 31 December 1939. Vol. 4: diary entries from 1 January 1940 to 8 July 1941. Munich, New York, 1987.

The Early Goebbels Diaries. Edited by Alan Bullock and Helmut Heiber. London, 1962.

Das Tagebuch von Joseph Goebbels 1925–1926. Edited with additional documents by Helmut Heiber. Stuttgart, 1960.

Vom Kaiserhof zur Reichskanzlei. Munich, 1934. (Selection from diaries from 1 January 1932 to 1 May 1933.)

My Part in Germany's Fight. Translated by Kurt Fiedler. London, 1935. (Translation of *Vom Kaiserhof zur Reichskanzlei*.)

The Goebbels Diaries 1939–1941. Translated and edited by Fred Taylor. London, 1982. New York, 1983.

Goebbels Tagebücher aus den Jahren 1942–1943. Edited with additional documents by Louis P. Lochner. Zurich, 1948.

The Goebbels Diaries 1942–1943. Translated and edited by Louis P. Lochner. London and Garden City, N.Y., 1948.

Tagebücher 1945. Die letzten Aufzeichnungen. With an introduction by Rolf Hochhuth. Stuttgart, 1977.

Final Entries 1945: The Diaries of Joseph Goebbels. Edited, introduced, and annotated by Hugh Trevor-Roper. Translated by Richard Barry. New York, 1978.

B. POSTHUMOUSLY COLLECTED SPEECHES

Boelcke, Willi A., ed. *Kriegspropaganda 1939–1941: Geheime Ministerkonferenzen im Reichspropagandaministerium*. Stuttgart, 1966.

————, ed. *Wollt ihr den totalen Krieg? Die geheimen Goebbels-Konferenzen 1939–1943*. Stuttgart, 1967.

————, ed. *The Secret Conferences of Goebbels*. Translated by Ewald Osers. New York, 1970. (Translation of preceding entry.)

Heiber, Helmut, ed. *Goebbels Reden 1932–1939*. Munich, 1971.

————, ed. *Goebbels Reden 1939–1945*. Munich, 1972.

C. WORKS PUBLISHED IN GOEBBELS'S LIFETIME

(in chronological order; short newspaper articles not listed separately)

1926a. *Das kleine ABC des Nationalsozialisten*. Elberfeld.

1926b. "Lenin oder Hitler?" Zwickau. (Speech delivered in the Königsberg Opera House in February 1926.)

1926c. *Die zweite Revolution: Briefe an Zeitgenossen*. Zwickau.

1927a. *Der Nazi-Sozi: Fragen und Antworten für den Nationalsozialisten*. Elberfeld.

1927b. *Wege ins dritte Reich: Briefe und Aufsätze für Zeitgenossen*. Munich.

1928. *Das Buch Isidor: Ein Zeitbild voll Lachen und Hass*. With Mjoelnir (Hans Schweitzer). Munich.

1929a. *Die verfluchten Hakenkreuzler: Etwas zum Nachdenken*. Munich.

1929b. *Michael: Ein deutsches Schicksal in Tagebuchblättern*. Munich.

1929c. *Knorke: Ein neues Buch Isidor für Zeitgenossen*. Munich.

1931. "Signal zum Aufbruch." Munich. (Speech delivered in Danzig in March 1931.)

1932a. *Vom Proletariat zum Volk.* Munich.

1932b. *Preussen muss wieder preussisch werden.* Munich.

1933a. *Wesen und Gestalt des Nationalsozialismus.* Berlin.

1933b. *Das erwachende Berlin.* Munich.

1933c. *Revolution der Deutschen: 14 Jahre Nationalsozialismus.* Oldenburg.

1934a. *Signale der neuen Zeit: 25 ausgewählte Reden von Dr. Joseph Goebbels.* Munich. (Speeches, 1927–34.)

1934b. *Kampf um Berlin.* Munich.

1934c. "Der Faschismus und seine praktischen Ergebnisse." Berlin. (Address at the Deutsche Hochschule für Politik.)

1934d. "Rassenfrage und Weltpropaganda." Langensalza. (Report at the Reich party rally, Nuremberg, 2 September 1933.)

1934e. *Student, Arbeiter, Volk.* Frankfurt am Main.

1934f. "Das Nationalsozialistische Deutschland als Faktor des europäischen Friedens." Berlin. (Speech at the Polish Cultural Association, Warsaw, in June 1934.)

1934(?)g. *Nation im Aufbau.* Munich, n.d. (Brochure for party speakers; reprinting was strictly prohibited.)

1935a. *Der Angriff: Aufsätze aus der Kampfzeit.* Munich.

1935b. *Goebbels spricht zur Welt.* Berlin.

1935c. *Richtlinien für die Gesamthaltung der Presse.* Berlin.

1935d. "Kommunismus ohne Maske." Munich. (Speech at the Reich party rally, Nuremberg, 1934.)

1935e. "Communism with the Mask Off." Berlin. (Translation of preceding entry.)

1935f. *Nationalsozialistischer Rundfunk.* Munich.

1936a. "Der Bolschewismus in Theorie und Praxis." Munich. (Speech at the Nuremberg party rally, 1936.)

1936b. "Bolshevism in Theory and Practice." Berlin. (Translation of preceding entry.)

1937. "Die Wahrheit über Spanien." Berlin. (Speech at the Nuremberg party rally, 1937.)

1939. *Wetterleuchten: Aufsätze aus der Kampfzeit.* Munich. (Second volume of essays from *Der Angriff.*)

1941. *Die Zeit ohne Beispiel: Reden und Aufsätze aus den Jahren 1939/40/41.* Munich.

1943a. *Das eherne Herz: Reden und Aufsätze aus den Jahren 1941/42.* Munich.

1943b. *Der Blick nach vorne.* Munich.

1943c. "Der geistige Arbeiter im Schicksalskampf des Reiches." Munich. (Speech at the University of Heidelberg, 9 July 1943.)

1943d. "Dreissig Kriegsartikel für das deutsche Volk." Munich, Berlin. (Goebbels's editorial in *Das Reich*, 26 September 1943.)

1944. *Der steile Aufstieg: Reden und Aufsätze aus den Jahren 1942/43.* Munich.

D.   UNPUBLISHED WRITINGS

"Lyrische Gedichte." Dem Herrn Professor Rentrop, meinem hochverehrten Lehrer, in Dankbarkeit zugeeignet. N.d., handwritten. GC.

"Wilhelm Raabe." Dated 7 March 1916, handwritten. GC.

"Der Lenz und ich und Du! Lieder von Frühling und Liebe." N.d., handwritten. BAK, NL 118/127.

"Der Postillion (von Lenau): Ein Reiseerlebnis." N.d., handwritten. GC.

"Der Mutter Gebet. Ein Idyll aus dem Kriege . . ." N.d., handwritten. GC.

"Bin ein fahrender Schüler, ein wüster Gesell . . . Novelle aus dem Studentenleben von Joseph Goebbels." Summer 1917, handwritten. BAK, NL 118/117.

"Die die Sonne lieben . . ." Summer 1917, handwritten. BAK, NL 118/117.

"Theodor Storm als Lyriker: Zu seinem 100. Geburtstag am 14. September 1917 von P. Joseph Goebbels." Handwritten. GC.

"Aus halbvergessenen Papieren. Dem Andenken Ernst Heynens gewidmet." 22 February 1924, handwritten. BAK, NL 118/113.

"Zigeunerblut." Novella. Winter 1917–18, handwritten. BAK, NL 118/117.

"Märchenballade." Novella. 1918, handwritten. BAK, NL 118/126.

"Judas Iscariot: Eine biblische Tragödie in fünf Akten von P. J. Goebbels. Anka Stahlherm in tiefer Verehrung." August 1918, handwritten. BAK, NL 118/126.

"Die Weihnachtsglocken des Eremiten: Eine Weihnachtsskizze von P. J. Goebbels. Der lieben Anka auf den Weihnachtstisch." Christmas 1918, handwritten. BAK, NL 118/127.

"Heinrich Kämpfert. Ein Drama in drei Aufzügen von P. Joseph Goebbels." February 1919, handwritten. BAK, NL 118/114.

"Goethes Anteil an den Recensionen der 'Frankfurter Gelehrten Anzeigen' aus dem Jahre 1782." (Seminar paper for Prof. Witkop, University of Freiburg.) Summer semester 1919, handwritten. GC.

"Michael Voormanns Jugendjahre." Part I, 1919, handwritten. BAK, NL 118/126. Part III, 1919, handwritten. BAK, NL 118/115.

"Gerhardi Bartel Manibus!" Contribution to the album for Goebbels's teacher, Dr. Gerhard Bartels, Rheydt, 6 December 1919. BAK, NL 118/120.

"Aus meinem Tagebuch, von Paul Joseph Goebbels. Anka Stalherm zugeeignet, München, Weihnachten 1919." Poems, handwritten. BAK, NL 118/126.

"Kampf der Arbeiterklasse. Drama von Joseph Goebbels." December 1919–January 1920, handwritten. GC.

"Die Saat: Ein Geschehen in drei Akten von P. Joseph Goebbels." March 1920, handwritten. BAK, NL 118/117.

"Wilhelm Schütz als Dramatiker: Ein Beitrag zur Geschichte des Dramas der romantischen Schule." Ph.D. diss., Heidelberg, 1921.

Doctoral dissertation. Summer 1921, handwritten draft with curriculum vitae. GC.

"Ausschnitte aus der deutschen Literatur der Gegenwart." Speech delivered in Rheydt, 30 October 1922. GC.

"Moderne Tierpoeten." Speech, n.d., handwritten. GC.

"Michael Voormann: Ein Menschenschicksal in Tagebuchblättern." 1923, handwritten and typed versions (not identical with "Michael Voormanns Jugendjahre," 1919). GC.

"Aus meinem Tagebuch." Notes for Else Janke. 1923, handwritten. BAK, NL 118/126.

"Der Wanderer: Ein Spiel in einem Prolog, elf Bildern und einem Epilog von Joseph Goebbels. Dem anderen Deutschland geschrieben." Manuscript fragment, begun 1923. BAK, NL 118/98.

3. Other Primary Sources

A. MEMOIRS

Baarova, Lida. *Útěky*. Toronto, 1983.

Baur, Hans. *Ich flog Mächtige der Erde*. Kempten, 1956.

Below, Nicolaus von. *Als Hitlers Adjutant 1937–1945*. Mainz, 1980.

Buber-Neumann, Margarete. *Kriegsschauplätze der Revolution: Ein Bericht aus der Praxis der Komintern 1919–1943*. Stuttgart, 1967.

Cziffra, Géza von. *Es war eine rauschende Ballnacht: Eine Sittengeschichte des deutschen Films*. Frankfurt am Main and Berlin, 1987.

———. *Kauf Dir einen bunten Luftballon: Erinnerungen an Götter und Halbgötter*. Munich, 1975.

Deutschkron, Inge. *Ich trug den gelben Stern*. Munich, 1985.

———. *A Jewish Girl in Wartime Berlin*. Translated by Jean Steinberg. New York, 1989.

Diels, Rudolf. *Lucifer ante Portas, . . . es spricht der erste Chef der Gestapo . . .* Stuttgart, 1950.

Dietrich, Otto. *Zwölf Jahre mit Hitler*. Munich, 1955.

———. *Hitler*. Translated by Richard and Clara Winston. Chicago, 1955.

François-Poncet, André. *The Fateful Years: Memoirs of a French Ambassador in Berlin, 1931–1938.* Translated by Jacques Le Clercq. New York, 1949.

———. *Botschafter in Berlin 1931–1938.* Berlin and Mainz, 1962.

Frank, Hans. *Im Angesicht des Galgens: Deutung Hitlers und seiner Zeit auf Grund eigener Erlebnisse und Erkenntnisse.* Munich-Gräfeling, 1953.

Fredborg, A. *The Steel Wall: A Swedish Journalist in Berlin, 1941–1943.* New York, 1944.

Fritzsche: see Springer.

Froehlich, Gustav. *Waren das Zeiten! Mein Film-Helden-Leben.* Munich, 1983.

Geissmar, Berta. *Musik im Schatten der Politik.* Freiburg im Breisgau, 1945.

Gisevius, Hans Bernd. *Bis zum bitteren Ende.* 2 vols. Darmstadt, 1946.

———*To the Bitter End.* Translated by Richard and Clara Winston. Boston, 1947.

Grzesinski, Albert C. *Inside Germany.* Translated by Alexander S. Lipschitz. New York, 1939.

Hanfstaengl, Ernst. *Hitler—The Missing Years.* London, 1957. (Also appeared as *Unheard Witness.* New York, 1957.)

———. *15 Jahre mit Hitler: Zwischen Weissem und Braunem Haus.* 2nd ed. Munich, 1980.

Harlan, Veit. *Im Schatten meiner Filme: Selbstbiographie.* Gütersloh, 1966.

Hedin, Sven. *Ohne Auftrag in Berlin.* Tübingen and Frankfurt am Main, 1950.

Hess, Wolf Rüdiger. *Mein Vater Rudolf Hess: Englandflug und Gefangenschaft.* Munich and Vienna, 1984.

Hossbach, Friedrich. *Zwischen Wehrmacht und Hitler.* Wolfenbüttel and Hamburg, 1949.

Kardorff, Ursula von. *Berliner Aufzeichungen aus den Jahren 1942 bis 1945.* Munich, 1962.

———. *Diary of a Nightmare.* Translated by Ewan Butler. New York, 1966.

Klepper, Joachim. *Unter dem Schatten deiner Flügel: Aus den Tagebüchern der Jahre 1932–1942.* Stuttgart, 1956.

Koller, Karl. *Der letzte Monat.* Mannheim, 1949.

Kordt, Erich. *Wahn und Wirklichkeit.* Stuttgart, 1948.

Lippert, Julius. *Im Strom der Zeit: Erlebnisse und Eindrücke.* Berlin, 1942.

Meissner, Otto. *Staatssekretär unter Ebert, Hindenburg, Hitler: Der Schicksalsweg des deutschen Volkes von 1918 bis 1945, wie ich ihn erlebte.* 3rd ed. Hamburg, 1950.

Niekisch, Ernst. *Gewagtes Leben: Begegnungen und Begebnisse.* Cologne and Berlin, 1958.

Oven, Wilfred von. "Der 20. Juli 1944—erlebt im Hause Goebbels." In *Verrat und Wiederstand im Dritten Reich.* Coburg, 1978.

————. *Finale Furioso: Mit Goebbels bis zum Ende.* Tübingen, 1974. (First appeared as *Mit Goebbels bis zum Ende.* 2 vols. Buenos Aires, 1949–50.)

Papen, Franz von. *Der Wahrheit eine Gasse.* Munich, 1952.

————. *Memoirs.* Translated by Brian Connell. New York and London, 1953.

Rauschning, Hermann. *Gespräche mit Hitler.* Vienna, 1973.

————. *Hitler Speaks.* London, 1939. (Also published as *The Voice of Destruction.* New York, 1940.)

Remer, Otto Ernst. *20 Juli 1944.* Hamburg, 1951.

————. *Verschwörung und Verrat um Hitler: Urteil eines Frontsoldaten.* Preussisch Oldendorf, 1981.

Ribbentrop, Joachim von. *Zwischen London und Moskau: Erinnerungen und letzte Aufzeichnungen.* Edited by Annelies von Ribbentrop. Leoni am Starnberger See, 1954.

————. *The Ribbentrop Memoirs.* Translated by Oliver Watson. London, 1954.

Rosenberg, Alfred. *Letzte Aufzeichungen: Ideale und Idole der nationalsozialistischen Revolution.* Göttingen, 1955.

————. *The Memoirs of Alfred Rosenberg.* Translated by Eric Posselt. Chicago, 1949.

Roussel, Stéphane. *Die Hügel von Berlin: Erinnerungen an Deutschland.* Hamburg, 1986.

Schaumburg-Lippe, Friedrich Christian zu. *Zwischen Krone und Kerker.* Wiesbaden, 1952.

Schenk, Ernst-Günter. *Ich sah Berlin sterben.* Herford, 1975.

Scheringer, Richard. *Das grosse Los: Unter Soldaten, Bauern und Rebellen.* Hamburg, 1959.

Schmidt, Paul. *Statist auf diplomatischer Bühne 1923–45: Erlebnisse des Chefdolmetschers im Auswärtigen Amt mit den Staatsmännern Europas.* Bonn, 1953.

————. *Hitler's Interpreter.* New York and London, 1951.

Schwerin von Krosigk, Lutz. "Der teuflische Intellekt: Joseph Goebbels." In *Es geschah in Deutschland: Menschenbilder unseres Jahrhunderts.* Tübingen and Stuttgart, 1951.

Speer, Albert. *Erinnerungen.* Frankfurt am Main, Berlin, Vienna, 1969.

————. *Inside the Third Reich.* Translated by Richard and Clara Winston. New York, 1970.

Springer, Hildegard, ed. *Es sprach Hans Fritzsche. Nach Gesprächen, Briefen und Dokumenten.* Stuttgart, 1949.

Strasser, Otto. *30. Juni: Vorgeschichte, Verlauf, Folgen.* Prague, n.d. [1934].

————. *Hitler and I.* Translated by Gwenda David and Eric Mosbacher. London, 1940.

————. *Hitler und ich.* Konstanz, 1948.

————. *Mein Kampf: Eine politische Autobiographie mit einem Nachwort von Gerhard Zwerenz*. Frankfurt am Main, 1969.

Ullrich, Luise. *Komm' auf die Schaukel Luise. Balance eines Lebens*. Parcha, 1973.

Zhukov, Georgi K. *Erinnerungen und Gedanken*. 2 vols. (East) Berlin, 1969.

————. *The Memoirs of Marshal Zhukov*. New York, 1971.

B. DIARIES, DOCUMENT COLLECTIONS, AND
    WORKS BY GOEBBELS'S CONTEMPORARIES

Akten zur Deutschen Auswärtigen Politik. Series C: 1933–37. Series D: 1937–45.

Bade, Wilfried. *Die S.A. erobert Berlin: Ein Tatsachenbericht*. Munich, 1934.

Besymenski, Lew A. *Die letzten Notizen von Martin Bormann. Ein Dokument und sein Verfasser*. Stuttgart, 1974.

Boberach, Heinz, ed. *Meldungen aus dem Reich: Auswahl aus den geheimen Lageberichten des Sicherheitsdienstes der SS 1939–1944*. Neuwied, 1965.

Ciano, Galleazzo. *Tagebücher 1939–1943*. Bern, 1947.

————. *The Ciano Diaries, 1939–1943*. Edited by Hugh Wilson. New York, 1946.

Diewerge, Wolfgang. *Der Fall Gustloff: Vorgeschichte und Hintergründe der Bluttat von Davos*. Munich, 1936.

Documents diplomatiques français, 1932–1939. 1st series (1932–35), vol. 4, 16 July–12 November 1933. Paris, 1968.

Dodd, William E. *Ambassador Dodd's Diary, 1933–1938*. London, 1941.

Domarus, Max. *Hitler: Reden und Proklamationen 1932–1945*. Vol. 1: *Triumph (1932–1938)*. Vol. 2: *Untergang (1939–1945)*. Würzburg, 1963.

————. *Hitler: Speeches and Proclamations, 1933–1945. The Chronicle of a Dictatorship*. Wauconda, Ill., 1990.

Engelbrechten, Julek Karl von. *Eine braune Armee entsteht: Die Geschichte der Berlin-Brandenburger SA*. Munich, 1937.

Goebbels, Magda. "Die deutsche Mutter: Rede zum Muttertag gehalten im Rundfunk am 14. Mai 1933." Heilbronn, 1933.

Goering, Hermann. *Reden und Aufsätze*. Munich, 1939.

Grosscurth, Hermann. *Tagebücher eines Abwehroffiziers 1938–1940*. Edited by H. Krausnick and H. C. Deutsch with H. von Kotze. Stuttgart, 1970.

Halder, Franz. *Kriegstagebuch: Tägliche Aufzeichnungen des Chefs des Generalstabes des Heeres 1939–1942*. Vol. 2: *Von der geplanten Landung in England bis zum Beginn des Ostfeldzuges (1.7.40–21.6.41)*. Edited by Hans-Adolf Jacobsen. Stuttgart, 1963. Vol. 3: *Der Russlandfeldzug bis zum Marsch auf Stalingrad (22.6.41–24.9.42)*. Edited by Hans-Adolf Jacobsen. Stuttgart, 1964.

————. *The Halder War Diary, 1939–1942*. Edited by Charles Burdick and Hans-Adolf Jacobsen. Novato, Calif., 1988.

Hassell, Ulrich von. *Die Hassell Tagebücher 1938–1944*. Edited by Friedrich Hiller von Gaertringen. Berlin, 1988.

————. *The von Hassell Diaries, 1938–1944*. New York, 1947.

Heiden, Konrad. *Geschichte des Nationalsozialismus*. Berlin, 1932.

————. *A History of National Socialism*. New York, 1935.

Hill, Leonidas, ed. *Die Weizsäcker-Papiere 1933–1950*. Frankfurt am Main, Berlin, and Vienna, 1974.

Hitler, Adolf. *Der grossdeutsche Freiheitskampf: Reden Adolf Hitlers vom 16. März bis zum 15. März 1942*. 3 vols. Munich, 1943.

————. *Mein Kampf*. Munich, 1939.

————. *Mein Kampf*. Translated by Ralph Manheim. Boston, 1943.

Hitlers politisches Testament: Die Bormann Diktate vom Februar und April 1945. Hamburg, 1981.

Hofer, Walther, ed. *Der Nationalsozialismus: Dokumente 1933–1945*. Frankfurt am Main, 1957.

Hubatsch, Walther, ed. *Hindenburg und der Staat: Aus den Papieren des Generalfeldmarschalls und Reichspräsidenten von 1878 bis 1934*. Göttingen, Berlin, Frankfurt am Main, and Zurich, 1966.

International Military Tribunal (IMT). *Der Prozess gegen die Hauptkriegsverbrecher vor dem Internationalen Militärgerichtshof. Nürnberg 14. November 1945–1. Oktober 1946*. Nuremberg, 1947. Rpt. Munich and Zurich, 1984.

————. *The Trial of the Major War Criminals before the International Military Tribunal: Nuremberg, 14 November 1945–1 October 1946*. Nuremberg, 1947–49.

————. *Der Prozess gegen die Hauptkriegsverbrecher. Urkunden und anderes Beweismaterial*. Rpt. Munich, 1989.

Iwo, Jack. *Goebbels erobert die Welt*. Paris, 1936.

Jacobsen, Hans-Adolf. *1939–1945. Der zweite Weltkrieg in Chronik und Dokumenten*. Darmstadt, 1959.

————. *World War II, Policy and Strategy: Selected Documents*. With commentary by Hans-Adolf Jacobsen and Arthur L. Smith. Santa Barbara, Calif., 1979.

————, ed. *Spiegelbild einer Verschwörung: Die Opposition gegen Hitler und der Staatsstreich vom 20. Juli 1944 in der SD-Berichterstattung. Geheime Dokumente aus dem ehemaligen Reichssicherheitshauptamt*. 2 vols. Stuttgart, 1984.

Jochmann, Werner. *Nationalsozialismus und Revolution: Ursprung und Geschichte der NSDAP in Hamburg 1922–1933. Dokumente*. Frankfurt am Main, 1963.

445

Kempner, Robert M. W., ed. *Der verpasste Nazi-Stopp: Die NSDAP als staats- und republikfeindliche hochverräterische Verbindung. Preussische Denkschrift von 1930.* Frankfurt am Main, Berlin, and Vienna, 1983.

Kriegstagebuch des Oberkommandos der Wehrmacht (Wehrmachtführungsstab) 1940–1945. Edited by Percy Schramm. 8 vols. Munich, 1982.

Littmann, Arnold. *Herbert Norkus und die Hitlerjungen vom Beusselkiez.* Berlin, 1934.

Longerich, Peter, ed. *Die Ermordung der europäischen Juden: Eine umfassende Dokumentation des Holocaust 1940–1945.* Munich, 1989.

Menz, Gerhard. *Der Aufbau des Kulturstandes.* Munich and Berlin, 1938.

Michaelis, Herbert, and Ernst Schraepler, eds. *Ursachen und Folgen: Vom deutschen Zusammenbruch 1918 und 1945 bis zur staatlichen Neuordnung Deutschlands in der Gegenwart. Eine Urkunden- und Dokumentensammlung zur Zeitgeschichte.* Vol. 10: *Das dritte Reich: Die Errichtung des Führerstaates. Die Abwendung vom System der kollektiven Sicherheit.* Berlin, 1965.

Müller, Georg Wilhelm. *Das Reichsministerium für Volksaufklärung und Propaganda.* Berlin, 1940.

Münster, Hans. *Publizistik.* Leipzig, 1939.

Picker, Henry, ed. *Hitlers Tischgespräche im Führerhauptquartier.* Stuttgart, 1976.

Pirker, Theo, ed. *Komintern und Faschismus: Dokumente zur Geschichte und Theorie des Faschismus.* Stuttgart, 1965.

Pol, Heinz. "Goebbels als Dichter." *Die Weltbühne* 27:4 (27 January 1931).

———. "Gregor der Grosse." *Die Weltbühne* 26:16 (15 April 1930).

Poliakov, Léon, and Joseph Wulf. *Das Dritte Reich und seine Denker.* Berlin, 1959.

———. *Das dritte Reich und seine Diener.* Berlin, 1956.

Polish Embassy, Washington, D.C. *Polish-Soviet Relations, 1918–1943. Official Documents.* 1945.

Rahm, Hans-Georg. *Der Angriff 1927–1930: Der nationalsozialistische Typ der Kampfzeitung.* Berlin, 1939.

Der Reichstagsbrandprozess und Georgi Dimitroff. Documents. Vol. 1: 27 February–20 September 1933. (East) Berlin, 1982.

Rosenberg, Alfred. *Das politische Tagebuch Alfred Rosenbergs aus den Jahren 1934/5 und 1939/40. Nach der photographischen Wiedergabe der Handschrift aus den Nürnberger Akten.* Edited by Hans-Günther Seraphim. Göttingen and Berlin, 1956.

Schulthess, H. *Schulthess europäischer Geschichtskalender.* For the years 1931, 1932, 1933.

Semmler [Semler], Rudolf. *Goebbels: The Man next to Hitler.* With an introduction by D. McLachlan and notes by G. S. Wagner. London, 1947.

Shirer, William. *Berlin Diary: The Journal of a Foreign Correspondent, 1934–1941*. London, 1941.

Soviet Foreign Policy during the Patriotic War: Documents and Materials. Translated by A. Rothenstein. London, 1946.

Studnitz, Hans-Georg von. *Als Berlin brannte. Diarium der Jahre 1943–1945*. 2nd ed. Stuttgart, 1963.

———. *While Berlin Burns: The Diary of Hans-Georg von Studnitz, 1943–1945*. Englewood Cliffs, N.J., 1964.

Sturm 33. *Hans Maikowski. Geschrieben von den Kameraden des Toten*. Berlin, 1933.

Turner, Henry A., Jr., ed. *Hitler aus nächster Nähe: Aufzeichnungen eines Vertrauten*. Frankfurt am Main, Berlin, and Vienna, 1978.

Tyrell, Albrecht, ed. *Führer, befiehl . . . Selbstzeugnisse aus der "Kampfzeit der NSDAP": Dokumente und Analyse*. Düsseldorf, 1969.

Verhandlungen des Reichstages, IV. Wahlperiode. Vols. 423, 424, 425, 427. Berlin, 1929–30.

Verhandlungen des Reichstages, V. Wahlperiode. Vols. 444, 446. Berlin, 1931–32.

Die Wehrmachtsberichte 1939–1945. 3 vols. Cologne, 1989.

Weizsäcker: see Hill.

Wulf, Joseph. *Die bildenden Künste im Dritten Reich: Eine Dokumentation*. 1963. Frankfurt am Main, Berlin, and Vienna, 1983.

———. *Literatur und Dichtung im Dritten Reich: Eine Dokumentation*. 1963. Frankfurt am Main, Berlin, and Vienna, 1983.

———. *Musik im Dritten Reich: Eine Dokumentation*. Frankfurt am Main, Berlin, and Vienna, 1983.

———. *Presse und Funk im Dritten Reich: Eine Dokumentation*. Frankfurt am Main, Berlin, and Vienna, 1983.

———. *Theater und Film im Dritten Reich: Eine Dokumentation*. Frankfurt am Main, Berlin, and Vienna, 1983.

C. NEWSPAPERS AND JOURNALS

Der Abend (late edition of *Vorwärts*)
Der Angriff
Arbeiter, Bauern, Soldaten
Berlin am Morgen
Berliner Arbeiterzeitung (*Der nationale Sozialist*)
Berliner Lokal-Anzeiger
Berliner Tageblatt
Deutsche Allgemeine Zeitung
Die Filmwoche

Frankfurter Zeitung
Hamburger Illustrierte
Nationalsozialistische Briefe
Der Panzerbär
Das Reich
Rheydter Zeitung
Die Rote Fahne
Schwäbische Illustrierte
Spandauer Nationale Zeitung / Das Havelland / Havelzeitung
Spandauer Tageblatt
Spandauer Volksblatt
Spandauer Zeitung
Der Spiegel
Völkische Freiheit (City Archives, Wuppertal)
Völkischer Beobachter
Volksparole: Rheydter Nachrichten
Vorwärts
Vossische Zeitung
Welt am Abend
Die Weltbühne
Westdeutsche Landeszeitung
Die Zeit

B. SECONDARY SOURCES

1. Goebbels Biographies *(listed chronologically)*

Bade, Wilfried. *Joseph Goebbels*. Lübeck, 1933.

Jungnickel, Max. *Goebbels*. Leipzig, 1933.

Krause, Willi. *Reichminister Dr. Goebbels*. Berlin, 1933.

Riess, Curt. *Joseph Goebbels*. London and Garden City, N.Y., 1948.

Borresholm, Boris von, and Karena Niehoff, eds. *Dr. Goebbels: Nach Aufzeichnungen aus seiner Umgebung*. Berlin, 1949.

Stephan, Werner. *Joseph Goebbels: Dämon einer Diktatur*. Stuttgart, 1949.

Riess, Curt. *Joseph Goebbels: Eine Biographie*. Baden-Baden, 1950. 2nd ed., Munich, 1989.

Fraenkel, Heinrich, and Roger Manvell. *Goebbels: Eine Biographie*. Cologne and Berlin, 1960.

———. *Doctor Goebbels: His Life and Death*. London, 1960.

Heiber, Helmut. *Joseph Goebbels*. Berlin, 1962.

———. *Goebbels*. Translated by John K. Dickinson. New York, 1972.

Schaumburg-Lippe, Friedrich Christian zu. *Dr. G.: Ein Portrait des Propagandaministers*. Wiesbaden, 1963.

Reimann, Viktor. *Dr. Joseph Goebbels*. Vienna, Munich, and Zurich, 1971.

——. *Goebbels*. Translated by Stephen Wendt. Garden City, New York, 1976.

Oven, Wilfred von. *Wer war Goebbels? Biographie aus der Nähe*. Munich and Berlin, 1987.

2. *Selected General Works*

Abel, Karl-Dietrich. *Presselenkung im NS-Staat: Eine Studie zur Geschichte der Publizistik in der nationalsozialistischen Zeit*. Berlin, 1968.

Adler, Hans Günther. *Der verwaltete Mensch: Studien zur Deportation der Juden aus Deutschland*. Tübingen, 1974.

Albrecht, Dieter. "Der Vatikan und das dritte Reich." In *Kirche im Nationalsozialismus*. Publication of the Geschichtsverein der Diözese Rottenburg-Stuttgart. Sigmaringen, 1984.

Albrecht, Gerd. *Nationalsozialistische Filmpolitik: Eine soziologische Untersuchung über die Spielfilme des Dritten Reiches*. Stuttgart, 1969.

Angress, Werner T. *Die Kampfzeit der K.P.D. 1921 bis 1923*. Düsseldorf, 1974.

——. *The Stillborn Revolution: The Communist Bid for Power in Germany, 1921–1923*. Princeton N.J., 1963.

Aleff, Eberhard. *Das Dritte Reich*. Hanover, 1970.

Bahnsen, Uwe, and James P. O'Donnell. *Die Katakombe: Das Ende in der Reichskanzlei*. Stuttgart, 1975.

Balfour, Michael. *Propaganda in War, 1939–1945: Organizations, Policies, and Publics in Britain and Germany*. London, 1979.

Barsch, Claus-Ekkehard. *Erlösung und Vernichtung. Dr. phil. Goebbels: Zur Psyche und Ideologie eines jungen Nationalsozialisten 1923–1927*. Munich, 1987.

Bein, Alexander. " 'Der jüdische Parasit.' Bemerkungen zur Semantik der Judenfrage." *Vierteljahrshefte für Zeitgeschichte* 13 (1965): 121ff.

Bering, Dietz. "Bernhard Weiss gegen Joseph Goebbels: Der Kampf um den Namen 'Isidor.' In *Jahrbuch 1981/82 des Wissenschaftskollegs zu Berlin*, 172ff. Berlin, 1983.

——. *Die Intellektuellen: Geschichte eines Schimpfwortes*. Frankfurt am Main, Berlin, and Vienna, 1982.

——. "Isidor—Geschichte einer Hetzjagd. Bernhard Weiss, einem preussischen Juden zum Gedächtnis." *Die Zeit*, 14 August 1987.

——. "Der jüdische Name als Stigma." *Die Zeit*, 7 August 1987.

—————. "Der Kampf um den Namen 'Isidor': Polizeivizepräsident Bernhard Weiss gegen Gauleiter Joseph Goebbels." *Beiträge zur Namenforschung*, n.s., ed. Rudolf Schützeichel, 18 (1983): 121ff.

—————. "Rittmeister der Reserve Bernhard Weiss: Zur Biographie eines preussischen Juden." In *Deutsche jüdische Soldaten 1914–1945*, issued by the Militärgeschichtliches Forschungsamt, 146ff. Freiburg im Breisgau, 1982.

—————. *The Stigma of Names: Antisemitism in German Daily Life, 1812–1933.* Translated by Neville Plaice. Cambridge, England, 1992.

—————. "Von der Notwendigkeit politischer Beleidigungsprozesse: Der Beginn der Auseinandersetzungen zwischen Polizeivizepräsident Bernhard Weiss und der NSDAP." In *Berlin in Geschichte und Gegenwart. Jahrbuch des Landesarchivs Berlin*, edited by Hans J. Reichardt, 87ff. Berlin, 1983.

Besymenski, Lew A. *Der Tod des Adolf Hitler: Der sowjetische Beitrag über das Ende des dritten Reichs und seines Diktators.* 2nd ed. Munich and Berlin, 1982.

Boelcke, Willi A. "Goebbels und die Kundgebung im Berliner Sportpalast vom 18. Februar 1943: Vorgeschichte und Verlauf." In *Jahrbuch für die Geschichte Mittel- und Ostdeutschlands*, edited by Wilhelm Berges, Hans Herzfeld, and Henryk Skrzypczak, 19:234ff. Berlin, 1970.

Bollmus, Reinhardt. *Das Amt Rosenberg und seine Gegner. Studien zum Machtkampf im nationalsozialistischen Herrschaftssystem.* Stuttgart, 1970.

Boveri, Margret. *Wir lügen alle: Eine Hauptstadtzeitung unter Hitler.* Freiburg im Breisgau, 1965.

Bracher, Karl Dietrich, Manfred Funke, and Hans-Adolf Jacobsen, eds. *Nationalsozialistische Diktatur 1933–1945: Eine Bilanz.* Bonn, 1983.

Bracher, Karl Dietrich, Wolfgang Sauer, and Gerhard Schulz. *Die nationalsozialistische Machtergreifung: Studien zur Errichtung eines totalitären Herrschaftssystems in Deutschland 1933/34.* 2nd ed. Cologne and Opladen, 1962.

Bramsted, Ernest K. *Goebbels and National Socialist Propaganda, 1925–1945.* East Lansing, Mich., 1965.

—————. *Goebbels und die nationalsozialistische Propaganda 1925–1945.* Frankfurt am Main, 1971.

—————. "What Goebbels Left Out: Some Significant Omissions in his Wartime Books." *The Wiener Library Bulletin* 9:1–2 (January–April 1955): 9f.; 3–4 (May–August 1955): 30f.

Brenner, Hildegard. "Die Kunst im politischen Machtkampf der Jahre 1933/34." *Vierteljahrshefte für Zeitgeschichte* 10 (1962): 17ff.

—————. *Die Kunstpolitik des Nationalsozialismus.* Reinbek bei Hamburg, 1963.

Broszat, Martin. "Die Anfänge der Berliner NSDAP 1926/27." *Vierteljahrshefte für Zeitgeschichte* 8 (1960): 85ff.

—————. *Die Machtergreifung: Der Aufstieg der NSDAP und die Zerstörung der Weimarer Republik.* Munich, 1984.

————. *Hitler and the Collapse of Weimar Germany*. Translated and with a foreword by V. R. Berghahn. Lemington Spa, N.Y., 1987.

————. "Soziale Motivation und Führer-Bindung des Nationalsozialismus." *Vierteljahrshefte für Zeitgeschichte* 18 (1970): 392ff.

————. *Der Staat Hitlers*. 11th ed. Munich, 1986.

————. *The Hitler State: The Foundation and Development of the Internal Structure of the Third Reich*. Translated by John W. Hiden. London and New York, 1981.

Browning, Christopher. "Zur Genesis der 'Endlösung': Eine Antwort an Martin Broszat." *Vierteljahrshefte für Zeitgeschichte* 29 (1981): 97ff.

Bullock, Alan. *Hitler: A Study in Tyranny*. New York, 1952.

————. *Hitler: Eine Studie über Tyrannei*. Kronberg im Taunus, 1977.

Chartess, Paul. *Strategie und Technik der geheimen Kriegführung*. Part 2: *Geheimpolitik und Geheimdienste als Faktoren der Zeitgeschichte*, Vol. A. Berlin, 1987.

Dahm, Volker. "Anfänge und Ideologie der Reichskulturkammer." *Vierteljahrshefte für Zeitgeschichte* 34 (1986): 53ff.

————. *Das jüdische Buch im Dritten Reich*. Part 1: *Die Ausschaltung der jüdischen Autoren, Verleger und Buchhändler*. Frankfurt am Main, 1979.

Dallin, Alexander. *German Rule in Russia, 1941–1945: A Study of Occupation Policies*. London and New York, 1957.

————. *Deutsche Herrschaft in Russland, 1941–1945*. Düsseldorf, 1958.

Deist, Wilhelm, Manfred Messerschmidt, Hans-Erich Volkmann, and Wolfram Wette. *Ursachen und Voraussetzungen des Zweiten Weltkrieges*. Stuttgart, 1989.

————. *The Build-Up of German Aggression*. Translated by P. S. Falla, Dean S. McMurry, and Oswald Osers. Oxford and New York, 1990.

Denkler, Horst, and Eberhard Lämmert, eds. *"Das war ein Vorspiel nur": Berliner Colloquium zur Literaturpolitik im "Dritten Reich."* Berlin, 1985.

Diller, Ansgar. *Rundfunkpolitik im Dritten Reich*. Munich, 1980.

Doob, Leonard W. "Goebbels' Principles of Propaganda." *The Public Opinion Quarterly* 14 (1950): 419ff.

Dorpalen, Andreas. *Hindenburg and the Weimar Republic*. Princeton, N.J., 1964.

————. *Hindenburg in der Geschichte der Weimarer Republik*. Berlin and Frankfurt am Main, 1966.

Drage, Charles. *Als Hitler nach Canossa ging*. Berlin, 1982.

Ebermeyer, Erich, and Hans Roos [Hans Otto Meissner]. *Gefährtin des Teufels. Leben und Tod der Magda Goebbels*. Hamburg, 1952.

Erbe, Michael. "Spandau im Zeitalter der Weltkriege." In *Slawenburg, Landesfestung, Industriezentrum: Untersuchungen zur Geschichte von Stadt und Bezirk Spandau*, edited by Wolfgang Ribbe, 268ff. Berlin, n.d.

Erckens, Günter. *Juden in Mönchengladbach: Jüdisches Leben in den früheren Gemeinden M. Gladbach, Rheydt, Odenkirchen, Giesenkirchen-Schelsen, Rheindahlen, Wickrath und Wanlo.* Mönchengladbach, vol. 1, 1988, and vol. 2, 1989.

Erdmann, Karl Dietrich. *Die Weimarer Republik.* Munich, 1980.

──────. *Der zweite Weltkrieg.* Munich, 1980.

Eschenburg, Theodor. "Zur Ermordung des Generals Schleicher. Dokumentation." *Vierteljahrshefte für Zeitgeschichte* 1 (1953): 71ff.

Fest, Joachim. *Hitler: Eine Biographie.* Frankfurt am Main, Berlin, and Vienna, 1973.

──────. *Hitler.* Translated by Richard and Clara Winston. New York, 1974.

──────. "Joseph Goebbels oder 'Canaille Mensch.' " In *Das Gesicht des Dritten Reiches: Profile einer totalitären Herrschaft,* 119ff. Munich, 1963.

──────. "Joseph Goebbels: 'Man the Beast.' " In *The Face of the Third Reich: Portraits of the Nazi Leadership,* translated by Michael Bullock, 83ff. New York, 1970.

Foertsch, Hermann. *Schuld und Verhängnis: Die Fritsch-Krise im Frühjahr 1938 als Wendepunkt der Geschichte der nationalsozialistischen Zeit.* Stuttgart, 1951.

Frei, Norbert, and Johannes Schmitz. *Journalismus im dritten Reich.* 2nd ed. Munich, 1989.

Fröhlich, Elke. "Hitler und Goebbels im Krisenjahr 1944: Aus den Tagebüchern des Reichspropagandaministers." *Vierteljahrshefte für Zeitgeschichte* 38 (1990): 195ff.

──────. "Die Kulturpolitik der Pressekonferenz des Reichspropagandaministers." *Vierteljahrshefte für Zeitgeschichte* 22 (1974): 347ff.

Gellermann, Günther. *Die Armee Wenck: Hitlers letzte Hoffnung.* Koblenz, 1984.

Gillessen, Günther. *Auf verlorenem Posten: Die Frankfurter Zeitung im dritten Reich.* Berlin, 1986.

──────. "Der organisierte Ausbruch des Hasses: Die 'Reichskristallnacht' vor 50 Jahren." Supplement to the *Frankfurter Allgemeine Zeitung,* 5 November 1988.

Girbig, Werner. . . . *im Anflug auf die Reichshauptstadt.* Stuttgart, 1977.

Gleiss, Horst G. W. *Breslauer Apokalypse 1945: Dokumentarchronik vom Todeskampf und Untergang einer deutschen Stadt und Festung am Ende des zweiten Weltkriegs.* Wedel, 1988.

Graham, Cooper C. *Leni Riefenstahl and Olympia.* London, 1986.

Graml, Hermann. *Reichskristallnacht: Antisemitismus und Judenverfolgung im Dritten Reich.* Munich, 1988.

Gruchmann, Lothar. "Erlebnisbericht Werner Pünders über die Ermordung Klauseners am 30. Juni 1934 und ihre Folgen: Dokumentation." *Vierteljahrshefte für Zeitgeschichte* 19 (1971): 404ff.

Haarmann, Hermann, Walter Huder, and Klaus Siebenhaar, eds. *"Das war ein Vorspiel nur": Bücherverbrennung Deutschland 1933: Voraussetzungen und Folgen.* Berlin and Vienna, 1983.

Hagemann, Walter. *Publizistik im Dritten Reich: Ein Beitrag zur Methodik der Massenführung.* Hamburg, 1948.

Hambourger, R. *Goebbels: "Chef de publicité" du IIIe Reich.* Paris, 1939.

Hasenberg, Peter Joseph. *125 Jahre Unitas-Verband: Beiträge zur Geschichte des Verbandes der Wissenschaftlichen Katholischen Studentenvereine Unitas.* Cologne, 1981.

Hausner, Hans Erik, ed. *Zeitbild: Das historische Zeitmagazin. Der Zweite Weltkrieg.* Vienna and Heidelberg, 1979.

Heiber, Helmut. "Der Fall Grünspan." *Vierteljahrshefte für Zeitgeschichte* 5 (1957): 134ff.

Henschel, Hildegard. "Aus der Arbeit der jüdischen Gemeinde Berlin während der Jahre 1941–1943. Gemeindearbeit und Evakuierung von Berlin: 16. Oktober 1941–16. Juni 1943." *Zeitschrift für die Geschichte der Juden* 9 (1972): 33ff.

Herbst, Ludolf. *Der Totale Krieg und die Ordnung der Wirtschaft: Die Kriegswirtschaft im Spannungsfeld von Politik, Ideologie und Propaganda 1939–1945.* Stuttgart, 1982.

Hildebrand, Klaus. *Deutsche Aussenpolitik 1933–1945.* 4th ed. Stuttgart, Berlin, Cologne, and Mainz, 1980.

———. *Das dritte Reich.* 2nd ed. Munich, 1987.

———. *The Third Reich.* Translated by P. S. Falla. London and Boston, 1984.

Hillgruber, Andreas. "Noch einmal: Hitlers Wendung gegen die Sowjetunion 1940. Nicht (Militär-) 'Strategie oder Ideologie' sondern 'Programm' und 'Weltkriegsstrategie.' " *Geschichte und Unterricht* 4 (1982): 214ff.

Hillgruber, Andreas, and Klaus Hildebrand. *Die Auflösung der Weimarer Republik.* 5th ed. Hanover, 1960.

———. *Kalkül zwischen Macht und Ideologie. Der Hitler-Stalin-Pakt: Parallelen bis heute?* Zurich, 1980.

Hockerts, Hans Günter. "Die Goebbels-Tagebücher 1932–1941: Eine neue Hauptquelle zur Erforschung der nationalsozialistischen Kirchenpolitik." In *Politik und Konfession: Festschrift für Konrad Repgen zum 60. Geburtstag,* ed. Dieter Albrecht et al., 359ff. Berlin, 1983.

———. *Die Sittlichkeitsprozesse gegen katholische Ordensangehörige und Priester 1936/37: Eine Studie zum nationalsozialistischen Herrschaftstechnik und zum Kirchenkampf.* Mainz, 1971.

Hofer, Walther, et al., eds. *Der Reichstagsbrand: Eine wissenschaftliche Dokumentation.* Vol. 1. Berlin, 1972. Vol. 2. Munich, 1978.

Hofer, Walther, and Christof Graf. "Neue Quellen zum Reichstagsbrand." *Geschichte in Wissenschaft und Unterricht* 27 (1976): 65ff.

Holba, Herbert, Günter Knoff, and Helmut Dan. *Erich Engel: Filme 1923–1940.* Vienna, 1977.

Hölsken, Heinz Dieter. *Die V-Waffen: Entstehung—Propaganda—Kriegseinsatz.* Stuttgart, 1984.

Huber, Ernst Rudolf. *Deutsche Verfassungsgeschichte seit 1789.* Vol. 6: *Die Weimarer Reichsverfassung.* Stuttgart, Berlin, Cologne, and Mainz, 1981. Vol. 7: *Ausbau, Schutz und Untergang der Weimarer Republik.* Stuttgart, Berlin, Cologne, and Mainz, 1984.

Hunt, Richard McMasters. "Joseph Goebbels: A Study of the Formation of his National-Socialist Consciousness (1897–1926)." Ph.D. diss., Harvard University, 1960.

Infield, Glenn B. *Leni Riefenstahl, the Fallen Film Goddess: The Intimate and Shocking Story of Adolf Hitler and Leni Riefenstahl.* New York, 1976.

Irving, David. *Goering: A Biography.* London, 1989.

———. *Göring.* Munich and Hamburg, 1987.

———. *On the Trail of the Fox.* New York, 1977.

———. *Rommel: Eine Biographie.* Hamburg, 1978.

———. *The War Path: Hitler's Germany 1933–1939.* London, 1978.

———. *Hitlers Weg zum Krieg.* Herrsching, 1978.

Jacobsen, Hans-Adolf. *Karl Haushofer: Leben und Werk.* Vol. 1: *Lebensweg 1869–1946 und ausgewählte Texte zur Geopolitik.* Boppard am Rhein, 1979.

———. *Nationalsozialistische Aussenpolitik.* Frankfurt am Main and Berlin, 1968.

Kempner, Robert M. W. "Die Ermordung von 35.000 Berliner Juden: Der Judenmordprozess in Berlin schreibt Geschichte." In *Gegenwart und Rückblick: Festgabe für die Jüdische Gemeinde zu Berlin 25 Jahre nach dem Neubeginn,* edited by Herbert A. Strauss and Kurt R. Grossmann, 180ff. Heidelberg, 1970.

———. "Der Kampf gegen die Kirche: Aus unveröffentlichten Tagebüchern Alfred Rosenbergs." *Der Monat* 1:10 (July 1949): 26ff.

Kershaw, Ian. *Der Hitler-Mythos: Volksmeinung und Propaganda im Dritten Reich.* Stuttgart, 1980.

———. *The "Hitler Myth": Image and Reality in the Third Reich.* Oxford and New York, 1987.

Kessemeier, Carin. "Der Leitartikler Goebbels in NS-Organen *Der Angriff* und *Das Reich.*" Ph.D. diss., Münster, 1967.

Klassen, Franz Joseph, ed. *"Sigfridia sei's Panier": Geschichte der Katholischen Deutschen Burschenschaft Sigfridia zu Bonn im Ring Katholischer Deutscher Burschenschaften 1910–1980.* Bonn, 1980.

Klein, Ulrich. "Mekka des deutschen Sozialismus oder 'Kloake der Bewegung': Der Aufstieg der NSDAP in Wuppertal 1920–1934." In *Über allem die Partei:*

Schule, Kunst, Musik in Wuppertal 1933–1945, edited by Klaus Goebel, 105 ff. Oberhausen, 1987.

Köhler, Henning. "Berlin in der Weimarer Republik (1918–1932)." In *Geschichte Berlins: von der März-Revolution bis zur Gegenwart*, edited by Wolfgang Ribbe, 797 ff. Munich, 1987.

Kolb, Eberhard. *Die Weimarer Republik*. 2nd ed. Munich, 1988.

————. *The Weimar Republic*. Translated by P. S. Falla. London and Boston, 1988.

Kotze, Hildegard von. "Goebbels vor Offizieren im Juli 1943." *Vierteljahrshefte für Zeitgeschichte* 19 (1971): 83 ff.

Krebs, Albert. "Dr. Joseph Goebbels." In *Tendenzen und Gestalten der NSDAP: Erinnerungen an die Frühzeit der Partei*. Stuttgart, 1959.

Kronika, Jakob. *Der Untergang Berlins*. Flensburg, 1946.

Krüger, Arnd. *Die Olympischen Spiele 1936 und die Weltmeinung: Ihre aussenpolitische Bedeutung unter besonderer Berücksichtigung der USA*. Berlin, Munich, and Frankfurt am Main, 1972.

Kühnl, Reinhard. "Das Strasser-Programm von 1925." *Vierteljahrshefte für Zeitgeschichte* 14 (1966): 317 ff.

Kunert, Günter. "Bühne der Macht, Stadt der Spiele: Berlin und sein Stadion." *Frankfurter Allgemeine Magazin*, 12 April 1990.

Lang, Jochen von. *Der Sekretär. Martin Bormann: Der Mann, der Hitler beherrschte*. Stuttgart, 1977.

————. *The Secretary: Martin Bormann, the Man Who Manipulated Hitler*. Translated by Christa Armstrong and Peter White. New York, 1979.

Lange, Serge, and Ernst von Schenck. *Portrait eines Menschheitsverbrechers, nach den hinterlassenen Memoiren des ehemaligen Reichsministers Alfred Rosenberg*. St. Gallen, 1947.

Latour, Conrad F. "Goebbels' 'Ausserordentliche Rundfunkmassnahmen' 1939–1942." *Vierteljahrshefte für Zeitgeschichte* 11 (1963): 418 ff.

Lauber, Heinz. *Judenpogrom: "Reichskristallnacht" November 1938 in Grossdeutschland: Daten, Fakten, Dokumente, Quellentexte, Thesen und Bewertungen*. Gerlingen, 1981.

Lazar, Imre. *Der Fall Horst Wessel*. Stuttgart, 1980.

Liang, Hsi-Huey. *The Berlin Police Force in the Weimar Republic*. Berkeley, Calif., 1970.

————. *Die Berliner Polizei in der Weimarer Republik*. Berlin and New York, 1977.

Longerich, Peter. *Die Braunen Bataillone: Geschichte des SA*. Munich, 1989.

————. *Propagandisten im Krieg: Die Presseabteilung des Auswärtigen Amtes unter Ribbentrop*. Munich, 1987.

Martens, Stefan. *Hermann Göring: "Erster Paladin des Führers" und "Zweiter Mann im Reich."* Paderborn, 1985.

Mau, Hermann. "Die 'Zweite Revolution'—der 30. Juni 1934." *Vierteljahrshefte für Zeitgeschichte* 1 (1953): 119ff.

Meissner, Hans-Otto. *Magda Goebbels: Ein Lebensbild.* Munich, 1978.

———. *Magda Goebbels: A Biography.* Translated by Gwendolyn Mary Keeble. London, 1980.

Meissner, Karl-Heinz. " 'München ist ein heisser Boden. Aber wir gewinnen ihn allmählich doch.' Münchner Akademien, Galerien und Museen im Ausstellungsjahr 1937." In *"Die Kunststadt" München 1937: Nationalsozialismus und "Entartete Kunst,"* edited by Peter-Klaus Schuster, 37ff. Munich, 1987.

Mendelssohn, Peter de. *Zeitungsstadt Berlin.* Berlin, 1959.

Möller, Horst. *Weimar: Die unvollendete Demokratie.* 2nd ed. Munich, 1987.

Moltmann, Günter. "Goebbels Rede zum Totalen Krieg am 18. Februar 1943." *Vierteljahrshefte für Zeitgeschichte* 12 (1964): 234ff.

Mommsen, Hans. "Der Nationalsozialistische Polizeistaat und die Judenverfolgung vor 1938." *Vierteljahrshefte für Zeitgeschichte* 10 (1962): 68ff.

Moreau, Patrick. *Nationalsozialismus von links: Die "Kampfgemeinschaft Revolutionärer Nationalsozialisten" und die "Schwarze Front" Otto Strassers 1930–1935.* Stuttgart, 1985.

Morsey, Rudolf, ed. *Das Ermächtigungsgesetz vom 24. März 1933.* Göttingen, 1976.

———. *Der Untergang des politischen Katholizismus.* Stuttgart and Zurich, 1977.

Müller, Hans Dieter. "Der junge Goebbels: Zur ideologischen Entwicklung eines politischen Propagandisten." Ph.D. diss., Freiburg im Breisgau, 1974.

———. "Portrait einer deutschen Wochenzeitung." In *Facsimile Querschnitt durch Das Reich,* edited by Hans Dieter Müller, 7ff. Bern and Munich, n.d.

Neuhaus, Helmut. "Der Germanist Dr. phil. Joseph Goebbels: Bemerkungen zur Sprache des Joseph Goebbels in seiner Dissertation aus dem Jahre 1922." *Zeitschrift für deutsche Philologie* 93 (1974): 398ff.

Neumann, Sigmund. *Die Parteien der Weimarer Republik.* 5th ed. Stuttgart and Berlin, 1986.

Oertel, Thomas. *Horst Wessel: Untersuchung einer Legende.* Cologne and Vienna, 1988.

Olympia 1936: Die XI. Olympischen Spiele in Berlin. Issued by Cigaretten-Bilderdienst Altona-Bahrenfeld, edited by Walter Richter et al. Altona-Bahrenfeld, 1936.

Piper, Ernst. *Nationalsozialistische Kunstpolitik: Ernst Barlach und die "entartete Kunst": Eine Dokumentation.* Munich, 1987.

Pohle, Heinz. *Der Rundfunk als Instrument der Politik: Zur Geschichte des deutschen Rundfunks von 1923/1938*. Hamburg, 1955.

Presse in Fesseln: Eine Schilderung des NS-Pressetrusts. Collaborative Project of Verlag Archiv und Kartei on the basis of authentic materials. Berlin, 1947.

Reichardt, Hans J. *Berlin in der Weimarer Republik: Die Stadtverwaltung unter Oberbürgermeister Gustav Böss*. Berliner Forum Series, 7. Berlin, 1979.

Der Reichstagsbrand. Die Provokation des 20. Jahrhunderts: Forschungsergebnis. Issued by the International Committee for the Scholarly Investigation of the Causes and Results of the Second World War. Luxembourg, 1978.

Reitlinger, Gerhard. *The Final Solution*. London, 1953.

————. *Die Endlösung: Hitlers Versuch der Ausrottung der Juden Europas 1933–1945*. 5th ed. Berlin, 1979.

Reuth, Ralf Georg. *Entscheidung im Mittelmeer*. Koblenz, 1985.

————. *Erwin Rommel: Des Führers General*. Munich, 1987.

Ribbe, Wolfgang, ed. *Geschichte Berlins*. Vol. 2: *Von der Märzrevolution bis zur Gegenwart*. Munich, 1987.

Romani, Cinzia. *Die Filmdivas des Dritten Reiches*. Munich, 1982.

————. *Tainted Goddesses: Female Film Stars of the Third Reich*. New York, 1992.

Rosenberg, Arthur. *Entstehung und Geschichte der Weimarer Republik*, edited by K. Ersten. Frankfurt am Main, 1983.

————. *A History of the German Republic*. Translated by Ian F. D. Morrow and L. Marie Sieveking. New York, 1965.

Ruhl, Klaus-Jörg. *Brauner Alltag, 1933–1939 in Deutschland*. Düsseldorf, 1981.

Sandvoss, Hans-Rainer. "Widerstand in einem Arbeiterbezirk." No. 1 of the series *Widerstand 1933–1945*. Issued by the Berlin Information Center, 1983.

Sänger, Fritz. *Politik der Täuschungen. Missbrauch der Presse im Dritten Reich: Weisungen, Informationen, Notizen 1933–1939*. Vienna, 1975.

Sauder, Gerhard. "Der Germanist Goebbels als Redner bei einer Berliner Bücherverbrennung." In *"Das war ein Vorspiel nur": Berliner Colloquium zur Literaturpolitik im "Dritten Reich,"* edited by Horst Denkler and Eberhard Lämmert. Berlin, 1985.

Schäfer, Hans Dieter. *Berlin im Zweiten Weltkrieg: Der Untergang der Reichshauptstadt in Augenzeugenberichten*. Munich and Zurich, 1985.

Scheffler, Wolfgang. *Judenverfolgung im Dritten Reich 1933–1945*. Frankfurt am Main, Vienna, and Zurich, 1965.

Schlamp, Hans-Joachim. *Lida Baarova*. Berlin, n.d.

Schmidt, Matthias. *Albert Speer: Das Ende eines Mythos: Speers wahre Rolle im Dritten Reich*. Bern and Munich, 1982.

————. *Albert Speer: The End of a Myth.* Translated by Joachim Neugroschel. New York, 1984.

Schneider, Hans. "Das Ermächtigungsgesetz vom 24. März 1933." In *Von Weimar bis Hitler 1930–1933,* edited by G. Jasper, 405 ff. Berlin, 1968.

Schrader, Hans-Jürgen. "Joseph Goebbels als Raabe-Redner." *Jahrbuch der Raabe-Gesellschaft* (1974): 112ff.

Schüddekopf, Otto-Ernst. *Nationalbolschewismus in Deutschland 1918–1933.* Frankfurt am Main, Berlin, and Vienna, 1972.

Schulze, Hagen. *Weimar: Deutschland 1917–1933.* 2nd ed. Berlin, 1982.

Schwarzenbeck, Eberhard. *Nationalsozialistische Pressepolitik und die Sudetenkrise.* Munich, 1979.

Shirer, William Lawrence. *The Rise and Fall of the Third Reich: A History of Nazi Germany.* New York, 1960.

————. *Aufstieg und Fall des Dritten Reiches.* Herrsching, n.d.

Singer, Hans-Jürgen. "Michael oder der leere Glaube." *1999: Zeitschrift für Sozialgeschichte des 20. und 21. Jahrhunderts* 2:4 (October 1987): 68ff.

Six, Franz Alfred. *Die politische Propaganda der NSDAP im Kampf um die Macht.* Ph.D. diss., Heidelberg, 1934. Heidelberg, 1936.

Steinert, Marlies G. *Hitlers Krieg und die Deutschen: Stimmung und Haltung der deutschen Bevölkerung im Zweiten Weltkrieg.* Düsseldorf, 1970.

Strätz, Hans-Wolfgang. "Die studentische 'Aktion wider den undeutschen Geist' im Frühjahr 1933." *Vierteljahrshefte für Zeitgeschichte* 16 (1968): 347ff.

Strothmann, Dietrich. "Die 'Neuordnung' des Buchbesprechungswesens im 3. Reich und das Verbot der Kunstkritik." *Publizistik: Zeitschrift für die Wissenschaft von Presse, Rundfunk, Film, Rhetorik, Werbung und Meinungsbildung* 5 (1960): 140ff.

Sywottek, Jutta. *Mobilmachung für den totalen Krieg: Die propagandistische Vorbereitung der deutschen Bevölkerung auf den Zweiten Weltkrieg.* Opladen, 1976.

Terveen, Fritz. "Der Filmbericht über Hitlers 50. Geburtstag: Ein Beispiel nationalsozialistischer Selbstdarstellung und Propaganda. *Vierteljahrshefte für Zeitgeschichte* 4 (1959): 75ff.

Tobias, Fritz. *Der Reichstagsbrand: Legende und Wirklichkeit.* Rastatt, 1962.

————. *The Reichstag Fire.* Translated by Arnold J. Pomerans. New York, 1963.

Tormin, Walter, ed. *Die Weimarer Republik.* Hanover, 1973.

Trevor-Roper, Hugh. *The Last Days of Hitler.* London, 1947.

Trevor-Roper, Hugh, and Hugh Redewald. *Hitlers letzte Tage.* 3rd ed. Frankfurt am Main and Berlin, 1965.

Tyrell, Albrecht. "Führergedanke und Gauleiterwechsel: Die Teilung des Gaues Rheinland der NSDAP 1931." *Vierteljahrshefte für Zeitgeschichte* 25 (1975): 341ff.

Weiland, Alfred. *Der Fall Mielke: Unternehmen Bülowplatz. Biographie unserer Zeit*. Berlin, n.d.

Werner, Andreas. "SA und NSDAP. SA: 'Wehrverband,' 'Parteitruppe' oder 'Revolutionsarmee'? Studien zur Geschichte der SA und der NSDAP 1920–1933." Ph.D. diss., Erlangen-Nuremberg, 1964.

Werner, Kurt, and Karl Heinz Biernat. *Die Köpenicker Blutwoche 1933*. (East) Berlin, 1960.

Werner, Wolfram. "Zur Geschichte des Reichsministeriums für Volksaufklärung und Propaganda," in *Reichsministerium für Volksaufklärung und Propaganda*. Koblenz, 1979.

Wheeler-Bennet, John W. *The Nemesis of Power: The German Army in Politics, 1918–1945*. London, 1953.

Wörtz, Ulrich. "Programmatik und Führerprinzip. Das Problem des Strasser-Kreises in der NSDAP: Eine historisch-politische Studie zum Verhältnis von sachlichem Programm und persönlicher Führung in einer totalitären Bewegung." Ph.D. diss., Erlangen-Nuremberg, 1966.

Wuermeling, Henric L. *August 39: 11 Tage zwischen Frieden und Krieg*. Berlin and Frankfurt am Main, 1989.

Wuppertal in der Zeit des Nationalsozialismus. Edited by Klaus Goebel. 2nd ed. Wuppertal, 1984.

Zentner, Christian. *Der Nürnberger Prozess: Dokumentation—Bilder—Zeittafel*. Munich and Zurich, 1984.

Zweite, Armin. "Franz Hoffmann und die Städtische Galerie 1937: Eine nationalsozialistische Museumskarriere, ihre Vorgeschichte und Konsequenzen." In *Die "Kunststadt" München 1937: Nationalsozialismus und "Entartete Kunst,"* edited by Peter-Klaus Schuster, 261ff. Munich, 1987.

Index

463

Hauptmann, Gerhart, 191
Haushofer, Professor, 287
Haw Haw, Lord, 276
Hearst press, 122
Heckel, Eric, 227
Heidegger, Martin, 182
Heidelberg, University of, 34, 37, 38, 52, 320
Heines, Edmund, 148, 198
Helldorf, Count Wolf-Heinrich von, 137, 138, 145, 146, 205, 234, 240, 243–44, 334–35
Henderson, Neville, 253–54, 256
Herff, Obergruppenführer Maximilian von, 335
Hess, Rudolf, 106, 112, 164, 186, 197, 199, 202, 203, 262, 287–88
Hewel, Walther, 350
Heydrich, Reinhard, 197, 223, 229, 230, 241, 255, 299, 304
Hilpert, Heinz, 226
Himmler, Heinrich, 116, 179, 197, 199, 208, 221, 229–30, 242, 261, 277–78, 307, 326, 331, 332, 335, 338, 346–47, 354, 357
Hindemith, Paul, 191, 202–4
Hindenburg, Oskar von, 162
Hindenburg, Paul von, 109, 115, 118, 129, 136, 142–45, 148, 149, 153, 158, 162–63, 166, 169, 172, 177, 196, 199–201, 349
Hindenburg Front, 144
Hinkel, Hans, 275, 278, 334
Hippler, Fritz, 261, 279
History of Rome (Mommsen), 342
Hitler, Adolf, 30, 38, 41, 44, 47, 86, 91, 96, 102, 103, 105, 106, 114–17, 122, 123, 160, 171, 196–97, 219, 225, 361; attempted assassination of, 138, 331–34; bolshevism denounced by, 155–57; and Brüning regime, 146–49; campaigns for Reich presidency, 142–45; and Catholic Church, 182, 223–24; and conservative elite, 122, 127, 137, 141, 172; and cultural policy, 203, 204, 208, 226–27; and defeat of Reich, 343–44, 346–51, 353–58; death of, 359–60, 363; and Enabling Act, 178; and establishment of NSDAP, 62–67, 69–76; expansionist policies of, 192, 204, 208–10, 220, 229–32, 237–39, 244–45; and film industry, 194, 195; and invasion of Poland, 246–50; and "Jewish question," 178–80, 221–22, 227–28, 233–35, 240–42, 260–62, 265, 275, 278, 298–99, 308, 325, 362; and League of Nations, 188–90; Magda and, 133, 162, 183, 186, 211–12, 217, 236–37, 243–44, 358; Mussolini and, 228–29, 233; November putsch of, 49–50, 54, 80, 98; and Olympic Games, 212–16; in prison, 13, 55–57, 60, 61; and Propaganda Ministry, 172–74, 176, 184, 185, 218; and Reichstag elections, 120–21; SA and, 82–85, 127–32, 135, 137, 197–200; seizure of power by,

48, 94, 151–53, 161–71, 201; spectacles staged for, 177, 181, 187; Strassers and, 79, 87–90, 99–101, 114–17, 154, 158–61; and Wessel's death, 112; during World War II, 263–83, 286–317, 319–22, 324–33, 335–42
Hitler-Stalin pact, 257, 258, 261, 296
Hitler Youth, 87, 161, 169, 355
Hoffmann, Paul, 85
Hofweber, Max, 314
Höhler, Albert, 111–12, 178
Hölderlin, Johann Christian Friedrich, 29
Holland, 258, 264, 268–70, 273, 283
Holtz, Emil, 88, 89, 100
Hompesch, Hubert, 14, 16–17
Hood (ship), 289
Hoover Moratorium, 135
Höpfners dance team, 194
"Horst Wessel Song, The," 113, 124, 125, 155, 164, 181, 231
Hossbach, Friedrich, 229
Hugenberg, Alfred, 104–5, 137, 143, 155, 162, 173, 175, 185, 226

Illustration, L' (magazine), 266
India, 40, 281, 282
Institute of Political Science, 184
Interior Ministry, 184, 328
Interministerial Committee for the Relief of Air Raid Damage, 320, 324, 335
International Red Cross, 319, 337, 345
Investigation and Mediation Committee, 80, 89, 117
Italy, 71, 73, 209, 231, 265, 272, 283, 287, 308; Allied invasion of, 325, 336; Axis Treaty with, 229; Hitler in, 233; and invasion of Poland, 254; Mussolini deposed in, 322; in North African campaign, 285, 309, 320; Pact of Steel with, 248; Tripartite Pact with Japan and, 281; in war with United States, 300–301

Jacobs, Otto, 356
Jacobsohn, Siegfried, 59
Jahncke, Kurt, 174
Janke, Else, 39, 42–46, 48–50, 52, 76–77
Jannings, Emil, 194, 284
Japan, 302; Anti-Comintern Pact with, 220, 221, 229; and Soviet Union, 286, 291, 297, 300, 337; Tripartite Pact with Italy and, 281; in war with United States, 300
Jews, 48, 51–53, 55, 58, 59, 66, 68–69, 71, 84, 86, 89, 103, 120, 137, 166, 172, 187, 227–28, 257, 362; in arts, 191, 202, 205, 208, 212, 219, 221, 226; attacked in *Der Angriff*, 91–93, 96, 102, 109, 122; Austrian, 232; bolshevism and, 205–6, 221, 289, 291; boycott of, 178–80; burning of books written by, 182–83; deportation of, 275, 278, 297–99;